RIGHT-PATTERSON AIR FORCE BASE AND ITS ANTECEDENTS

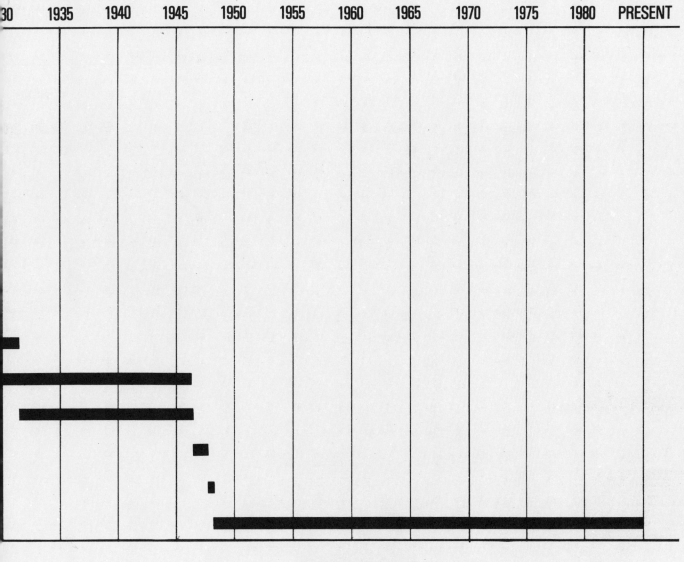

| 30 | 1935 | 1940 | 1945 | 1950 | 1955 | 1960 | 1965 | 1970 | 1975 | 1980 | PRESENT |

DATE ESTABLISHED

1904-1916)
JUNE 6, 1917
OCTOBER 13, 1917

UPPLY DEPOT   JANUARY 4, 1918
DEPOT   JANUARY 10, 1919
POT, FAIRFIELD, OHIO   NOVEMBER 3, 1919
AIR DEPOT   SEPTEMBER 20, 1920
EPOT   JANUARY 14, 1921
TION   JUNE 22, 1927

OCTOBER 12, 1927
JULY 1, 1931

BASE   DECEMBER 15, 1945
DECEMBER 9, 1947

BASE   JANUARY 13, 1948

FROM HUFFMAN PRAIRIE
TO THE MOON

The history of Wright-Patterson Air Force Base

by
Lois E. Walker
Shelby E. Wickam

Office of History
2750th Air Base Wing
Wright-Patterson Air Force Base

AIR FORCE LOGISTICS COMMAND

Headquarters, 2750th Air Base Wing
Wright-Patterson Air Force Base

FOREWORD

Today, supersonic jet fighters and giant cargo transports land on the modern runways at Wright-Patterson Air Force Base, passing within a few hundred yards of the Wright brothers' first "landing zone" on Huffman Prairie.

In May 1904, the Wrights made their first successful flights at Huffman Prairie, proving that controlled, powered flight was not only "possible to man," but was destined to change the world's future. The Wright brothers made history that month on land that would eventually become Wright-Patterson Air Force Base. The aviation pioneers that have followed in their footsteps have been making history here ever since.

Beginning with World War I, the seeds of Air Force logistics and research and development efforts were planted here. Since that time, military and civilian logisticians, scientists, and engineers have pioneered innovations that have kept this nation strong and free, highly capable of deterring any and all potential aggressors.

A glance through the pages of this book quickly illustrates that many of the Air Force's finest have passed through Wright-Patterson's gates. We are proud of that rich heritage. For nearly seven decades, the base has served as a magnet, drawing the best aviation minds from across the nation, while capitalizing on the abundant human talent of the Miami Valley. This combination of greatness has resulted in Wright-Patterson's prominent position as a key element in our national defense.

This book was written for the men and women of Wright-Patterson Air Force Base, past and present, military and civilian. To all that have served here, we acknowledge their contributions and salute their efforts. The tradition of excellence they represent has made Wright-Patterson the outstanding Air Force base that it is today.

Charles E. Fox, Jr.

CHARLES E. FOX, JR.
Colonel, USAF
Commander

DAYTON — FROM HUFFMAN PRAIRIE TO THE MOON! Mike Peters

Reprinted permission Mike Peters
Dayton Daily News

ACKNOWLEDGEMENTS

In writing a book of this scope, we have become indebted to many people. Although we have attempted here to remember everyone, some have undoubtedly been forgotten. The fact remains that this book would not be what it is without the assistance of our many colleagues and friends, and we express our appreciation to them all.

The Dayton area is home to a wealth of historical institutions and organizations, many of which provided source materials that helped shed light on hitherto forgotten chapters of Wright-Patterson's long history. We are particularly indebted to Dr. Patrick Nolan and his fine staff at the Wright State University Archives, to Mr. H. Eugene Kniess at the National Cash Register Corporation, and to Mr. Patrick Foltz and Ms Judith Wehn at the Montgomery County Historical Society.

Many hours of research assistance were provided by the Research Division of the U.S. Air Force Museum. We thank especially Mrs. Bobbie Bollinger, Ms Katherine Cassity, Mr. Wes Henry, Mr. Joseph Ventolo, Mrs. Vivian White, and Mr. Charles Worman. A note of thanks is also due to the staff of the Navy and Old Army Branch of the National Archives for assistance in locating and photocopying numerous documents related to Wright-Patterson's early history, to the staff of the Archives-Library Division of the Ohio Historical Society, to Mr. Duane Reed in the Special Collections Division of the U.S. Air Force Academy, and to the very helpful people at the Research Division of the Air Force Historical Research Center, Maxwell AFB, who graciously filled our research requests and verified innumerable details in order to satisfy our demand for accuracy.

We also extend our thanks to the Air Force Logistics Command Office of History, Mr. Bob Smith, Command Historian, and the Aeronautical Systems Division Office of History, Mr. Al Misenko, Division Historian, for permission to research and borrow extensively from their archives. Several outstanding libraries opened their facilities to us as well, among them the Dayton-Montgomery County Public Library, the AFWAL Technical Library, the WPAFB Base Library, and the Greene County District Library.

For permission to reprint proprietary information and artwork we acknowledge especially Mr. Mike Peters of the *Dayton Daily News* and the publishers of *AIR FORCE Magazine*.

Saving the most personal acknowledgements for last, we enter the close circle of people who worked most intimately with this book. To Mr. Paul E. Bierley, our technical advisor and aeronautical engineer extraordinaire, we extend our deep appreciation and the desire that we could do something more to repay him for his excellent efforts. We also thank his wife, Pauline, for her proofreading assistance. Mrs. Jean Cost is a second person that words seem inadequate to thank for many hours of work, above and beyond her duties as editorial assistant. Her professional capabilities speak for themselves, but deserve special mention nonetheless. This book, in fact, bridged the tenures of three editorial assistants. We wish to acknowledge also the very capable talents of Mr. Eugene Neal and Mrs. Jolynn Foster, who tackled the project with great enthusiasm and more than a little good humor. As historians, we stand on the shoulders of many, and are obliged to acknowledge not only the efforts of our present staff, but also those of the many men and women who have served as historians and editorial assistants for the 2750th Air Base Wing in years gone by, among them Mr. Ebert Smith, Ms Katherine Cassity, Ms Virginia Julian, and Mrs. Phyllis Moore.

To the staff of the Base Photo Lab goes a special note of thanks for their tireless efforts in reproducing literally hundreds of photographs out of the History Office archives and those borrowed from numerous other historical agencies. A special thanks is extended to those wizards of the lens Mr. William Ahern, Mr. R. Keith Cole, Mr. Rob Sprinkle, Mr. Charles Stout, and Mr. Steve Trego, and to their able assistants Ms Vicki Taylor and Ms Shelley Towe.

To the staff of the Real Estate Section of the 2750th Civil Engineering Squadron we send our special appreciation, with the reassurance that we will no longer be deluging them with calls regarding the history of nearly every building on base. We thank especially Mr. Keith McMurray (who we hope did not retire because of us), Mrs. Ann Spivey, Mrs. Verna Finn, and Mrs. Diane Green.

The staff of the Building 10 Word Processing Center is credited with entering the entire manuscript of this book into their machines (portions of it several times) and turning it into a professional product. A very personal note of thanks is extended to Mrs. Barbara Quesinberry and her staff, Mrs. Kathy Anderson, Miss Theresa Lambert, and Ms LaVerne Lawson, for their extraordinary skill, patience, and perseverance. Miss Lambert and Ms Lawson also applied their enthusiasm to additional proofreading of the typeset manuscript, which we gratefully acknowledge.

The physical layout of this book is the product of Mr. Ron Schroeder and his staff at Eastpoint Studio, Dayton, Ohio. The professionalism of his staff has made this volume what it is. We acknowledge particularly the outstanding talents of Ms Mary Callahan and Ms Debi Whistler.

Without the assistance of several people in base administrative channels this book could not have been published. Our special thanks go to Mr. Cloyd Eastham, Mr. Dave Bigl and his staff, Mr. Bob Kilcrease, and Mr. Eugene Neal. We would also like to thank three very special gentlemen, no longer with the 2750th Air Base Wing, who provided encouragement, support, and a concerted determination to see that this project reached fruition: Col. Leonard R. Peterson (USAF, ret.), former Wing Commander, Col. Jay M. Strayer (USAF, ret.), former Wing Vice Commander, and Mr. Ralph Beaver, former Executive Assistant to the Wing Commander.

The following list of persons represents yet another group of people who had a hand in producing this book. They supplied us with information, loaned us photographs, lent their expertise in artwork or publishing, and assisted in proofreading various stages of the manuscript. Our thanks to them one and all.

Dick Baughman	Capt. Jackie L. Lopez
Tom Brewer	Susan K. Lopez
Vanessa Brown	Russell S. Lyle
Bob Cavanagh	Gwen C. Marsh
Marvin Christian	Hannah J. Massie
Phyllis A. Cline	R. D. McCafferty
Frank Collins	Bill McNabb
1st Lt. Clinton Collins	Dr. Jerry Meyer
Ruth Corinne Connor	Jean Miller
Dick Cull	Norma J. Mullennex
Capt. George Cully	Rob Orlos
Lt. Col. Allan V. Cummings	Robert L. Parli, Jr.
Maj. Jan Dalby	Florence Paxton
Ted Dahlfors	Gene and Bonnie Phillips
Maj. Donald D. Decker (USAF, ret.)	Alfred J. Pikora
D. Adam Dickey	Raymond Pillion
Ronald I. Foliano	Harry S. Price, Jr.
Darlene Gerhardt	Clem Rainaldi
Robert Gettier	Lynne S. Ranney
Bob and Dottie Gheen	Don Ream
David Gold	David L. Shultz
Lance M. Grolla	Howard B. Smith
Eugene Harbrecht	Doris Suesberry
Brig. Gen. Harold R. Harris (USAF, ret.)	Bernard J. Termena
Jim Hawley	Mike Thompson
Mike Hoegler	Lt. Col. William D. Thornton, Jr.
Roberta Hoffman	Jane Trimmer
Mrs. Howell Jackson	Walter Vance
Mary Ann and Rich Johnson	Randall Wakefield
Cynthia D. King	Donald R. Wilson
William Kremer	Norma J. Wood
Frank J. Kulish	A. F. Woodall
Laura Lawson	Ed Wozniak
Clifford Lloyd	Ken Zimmerman
G. Allison Long	J. P. Zook

Lest they be forgotten, we also pay special tribute to our families, Hisako Wickam and Bill and Betsy Walker, for seeing us through this project, the magnitude of which none of us could have guessed at the beginning.

LOIS E. WALKER
Wing Historian

SHELBY E. WICKAM
Historian Emeritus

CONTENTS

STRAWBERRY SHORTCAKE AND FLYING MACHINES

Every June we heard the story.
"Mom made strawberry shortcake
for supper that night.
It was that time of year when
the sun went down late enough
that we had a bit of evening to enjoy.

Harvester's line was steam powered then.
All the tools driven by overhead pulley.
Man, we were tired!
But we had to see if it was true.

To Huffman Prairie in an
old Model T.
Only it was new then.
And we saw it . . . .
Those boys from the bicycle shop
over in Dayton, they flew!
Like one of Ben's pigeons,
they flew!

Now you go down to Florida
to see men go to the moon.
But I, I saw the beginning of it.
On Huffman Prairie
I saw Wilbur and Orville Wright fly
one June night
after Mom made strawberry shortcake."

Ruth Anne Rizer

*(Daughter of Paul L. Miller,
who witnessed the Wright flights
on Huffman Prairie, 1904)*

*To Wilbur and Orville,
who made it all possible*

*For some years I have been
afflicted with the belief that
flight is possible to man*

Wilbur Wright, 1900

*The conquest of the air is
America's gift to the progress
of the twentieth century*

Newton D. Baker

*More than anyone I have ever known
or read about, the Wright brothers
gave me the sense that nothing
is impossible. I like to think—
and during World War II—often did,
that the Air Force has rooted its
traditions in that spirit.*

Gen. Henry H. Arnold

Huffman Prairie, 1904 *(Wright State University Archives, Wright Brothers Collection)*

I. HUFFMAN PRAIRIE 1904-1916

A small group of black and white cows and two brown plow horses standing in a small lot gazed across the barbed-wire fence and regarded with mild concern the odd contraption nestled outside a small shed. The machine was too large to be a corn planter. Although steam-driven agricultural equipment often had small canvas covers to shade operators, this strange machine had two huge canvas covers on its body, at some distance from the ground. Moreover, the thing had an odd-looking beak and a ridiculous twin tail. Its claws seemed to be missing. In general profile the machine resembled a big bird—many times larger than the familiar chicken hawk.

As the animals watched, two men came from the open end of the shed where they had been awaiting the passage of a brief but heavy thundershower. The rain had lowered the temperature to 81 degrees, but the humidity remained at 66 percent. Swarms of mosquitoes and horseflies taunted and tormented their targets.

It was the early afternoon of May 26, 1904.

Despite the heat and humidity each man was dressed for business, in heavy high-top laced leather shoes, dark wool trousers, a white long-sleeved shirt with a high stiff collar, a vest, and a bow tie. One wore a derby. The other sported a cap. Turning its visor rakishly to the rear, 33-year-old Orville Wright wedged his lean body into a prone position in the V-shaped cradle on the white muslin-covered lower wing of a 700-pound biplane. He lay well forward of the leading edge of the wing, with his face about 36 inches above the ground. His shoes pushed against a footrest on the trailing edge of the left wing. He held tightly to the leading edge of the wing with his right hand while using his left to work the horizontal elevator out front. This position was awkward, uncomfortable, and potentially dangerous, but it reduced wind resistance. Within a few inches of his right ear, four cylinders of a modified automobile engine sputtered and crackled. The 18-horsepower engine turned two 8-foot counter-rotating pusher-type propellers set 10 feet apart. Sweat poured down Orville's face. Every thread of clothing was soaked. He glanced to the left wing where 37-year-old Wilbur Wright gripped a strut to help steady the biplane. Its 21-foot length was supported by wooden skids on a yoke which ran freely on two small tandem wheels along a wooden monorail.

Conditions at 2 p.m. were far from ideal; but there had been enough delays. Orville nodded to Wilbur, who dropped his hand from the strut. The fragile biplane gathered speed as it wavered along the monorail.

Orville's head and shoulders leaned forward over the edge of the wing like the bowsprit on a sleek sailing vessel. At the end of the monorail the airplane's speed was about 25

In the air over Huffman Prairie. The pilot lay prone on the lower wing.

miles per hour. The craft leaped upward to a height of 8 feet and covered a distance of 25 feet before dropping to the ground.

It skidded over the sodden pasture, spraying its pilot with black mud and brown muck. It landed with sufficient force to crack several of the 6-foot white pine spars that separated the upper and lower wings, and nearly catapulted Orville from his precarious perch.

Notwithstanding aching muscles and a sore neck, Orville smiled broadly and his blue eyes sparkled as he climbed from the wing. Wilbur grinned with delight and relief. They had flown again! They had established far better marks during their historic first flights at Kitty Hawk, but again they had prevailed. And a Huffman Prairie tradition was established.

Wilbur Wright, born April 16, 1867, died May 30, 1912 (*Wright State University Archives, Wright Brothers Collection*)

Orville Wright, born August 19, 1871, died January 30, 1948 (*Wright State University Archives, Wright Brothers Collection*)

(NCR Corporation)

KITTY HAWK, NORTH CAROLINA

Trial	Pilot	Time	Distance
1	Orville	12 seconds	120 feet
2	Wilbur	12 seconds	175 feet
3	Orville	15 seconds	200 feet
4	Wilbur	59 seconds	852 feet

Statistics of the brothers' flights at Kitty Hawk, North Carolina, on December 17, 1903, show that first Orville, then Wilbur, had made the world's first free, controlled, and sustained flights in a power-driven, heavier-than-air machine. Orville's initial flight of 120 feet matched the length of the 1982 Space Shuttle *Columbia*.

Source: Arthur G. Renstrom, *Wilbur & Orville Wright: A Chronology Commemorating the Hundredth Anniversary of the Birth of Orville Wright, August 19, 1871* (Washington, 1975), p 13.

HUFFMAN PRAIRIE: A LOGICAL CHOICE

According to Fred Kelly, the Wright brothers' close friend and biographer, the pioneers' initial incentive had been "to gain the distinction of being the first of mankind to fly." They had not envisioned any practical use for their invention. But after their success at Kitty Hawk, they had begun to think the airplane "could be developed into a machine useful for scouting in warfare; for carrying mail to isolated places; for exploration; and that it would appeal to those who could afford it for sport."[1]

But the airplane would require considerable refinement before production models could be manufactured and sold. They would also need a great deal more experience in actual flying before they could either demonstrate the machine or train pilots. "Much practice would be required . . . and that would mean more expense in proportion to income for they would have less time for building and repairing bicycles," their primary source of income.[2]

Thus financial circumstances dictated the need to locate a site for flying and experimental work close to Dayton. The brothers finally selected a 100-acre farm along the eastern shore of the Mad River (a tributary of the Great Miami River) in Greene County, about eight miles east of Dayton and two miles from the Village of Fairfield.[3] Since Mr. Torrence Huffman, a prominent Dayton banker, owned the property, it was known as "Huffman Prairie." Mostly flat land in the river bottom or flood plain, the pasture's north-

ern border was the track of the Dayton-Springfield-Urbana electric interurban rail system (known locally as the "Damned Slow and Uncertain"). Trolleys stopped every 30 minutes at the small depot known as Simms Station. Surrounding the depot lay open farm country composed of large fields, most of them grassy and bordered by fences and clusters of tall, spreading trees. Here and there, widely separated, a house or a barn lifted a gray roof amid the lush greenery.

During April and May 1904, the Wright brothers, nattily attired in business suits, commuted daily (but never on Sundays) between their workshop in Dayton and Simms Station, bringing lumber, airplane materials, and parts. When they finished the hangar that housed the Flyer II, they had, according to one writer, "erected the first airport in the world."[4]

Comparatively flat terrain and convenient, economical transportation were plus factors.* But the prairie, dotted with 50-foot high trees, bordered on the north by poles and power lines and on the west by a high bluff, was hardly an ideal test facility. In a June 21, 1904, letter to the brothers' mentor, Octave Chanute, Wilbur wrote:[5]

> We are in a large meadow of about 100 acres. It is skirted on the west and north by trees. This not only shuts off the wind somewhat but also gives a slight downtrend. However, this matter we do not consider anything serious. The greater troubles are the facts that in addition to cattle there have been a dozen or more horses in the pasture and as it is surrounded by barbwire fencing we have been at much trouble to get them safely away before making trials. Also the ground is an old swamp and is filled with grassy hummocks some six inches high so that it resembles a prairie dog town. This makes the track-laying slow work. While we are getting ready the favorable opportunities slip away, and we are usually up against a rainstorm, a dead calm, or a wind blowing at right angles to the track.

The Wright brothers' primary source of income was a bicycle manufacturing and repair business located at 1127 W. Third Street in Dayton. This seasonal business allowed them ample autumn and winter time for flight experimentation with gliders and the first Wright Flyers. *(Wright State University Archives, Wright Brothers Collection)*

---

*The major advantage to the struggling pioneers was the rent-free use of the land. Mr. Huffman's sole requirement was that the Wrights always keep the farm gates closed to prevent the horses and cattle from wandering away.

HUFFMAN PRAIRIE 1904-1905

Huffman Prairie, 1904-1905, taken from an original sketch by Orville Wright. Hangar in top photo is at lower right in map. Wright brothers' flight path (dotted line) was bounded by Yellow Springs Road, the lines of the Dayton-Springfield-Urbana interurban trolley, and tall trees. Present Wright Memorial is on high bluff beyond map range to upper left.

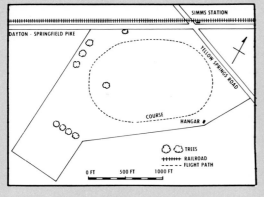

Progress was measured in seconds and in feet. On August 4, for example, Wilbur was airborne for 20 seconds (including the run down the monorail), and traveled 272 feet.[6]

In September, a new catapult launching device was used in order to increase lift at takeoff. The pyramidal tower, or "derrick" to use Wilbur's term, consisted of four 30-foot poles erected tepee-fashion at one end of the monorail. Inside the tower a heavy weight was lifted to the top and

Catapult launch. As seen in this 1905 action photo, the weight has just fallen in the starting derrick to the right and the airplane is headed leftward for takeoff. (Wright State University Archives, Wright Brothers Collection)

linked to the airplane by a series of pulleys and ropes. After considerable experimentation, a single weight of 1,600 pounds was found to be the most effective. Falling some 16 feet, the weight exerted a forward pull equal to 350 pounds, enough to get the aircraft into the air with "a run of only 50 feet even in a dead calm."[7] When the catapult was used for the first time, Wilbur flew over 2,000 feet.[8]

Thus well and truly into the air, the brothers set about mastering flight dynamics, and on September 20 made history's first controlled circle.* By December 9, 1904, their record stood at 105 launches for a total flight time of 50 minutes, and a top landing speed approaching 50 miles per hour.[9]

When the December flying season ended, the Wrights disassembled the airplane, packed it and all the tools and gear into crates and boxes, and moved them into winter quarters in the West Dayton bicycle shop. The vacated hangar on Huffman Prairie became a shelter for livestock. During the winter of 1904-1905, the aviation pioneers built the airplane that eminent aviation historian Charles H. Gibbs-Smith called the "world's first practical airplane," the Flyer III.**

In the spring of 1905, a larger hangar was built on Huffman Prairie, closer to the Simms Station depot. The flying season opened June 23, when Orville flew 272 feet in

---

EARLY WRIGHT AIRPLANES

All of the Wrights' early powered airplanes were named Flyers:

Flyer I (1903) was called the *Kitty Hawk*. After Wilbur's final flight the afternoon of December 17, 1903, a gust of wind upended the fragile aircraft. The wreckage was disassembled and the parts shipped to Dayton. In 1916, the components were reassembled, replacement parts were inserted, and the restored *Kitty Hawk* exhibited at the Massachusetts Institute of Technology. On January 31, 1928, Orville shipped the machine to the Science Museum in London on indefinite loan for exhibition. On December 17, 1948, the 1903 airplane was installed formally in the Smithsonian Institution, Washington, D.C.

Flyer II (1904) was the first airplane over Huffman Prairie. In it the brothers executed the first controlled circles. After the 1904 flying season ended, the engines, propellers, and other parts were used in the construction of the more powerful 1905 Flyer III.

Flyer III (1905) taught the Wrights "the secrets of powered flight," according to historian Charles Gibbs-Smith. Disassembled after the 1905 season, it was restored in June 1950 and placed on permanent exhibit at the Carillon Park Museum in Dayton, Ohio.

---

*Wilbur flew the first circle during a flight lasting 1 minute 35⅘ seconds on September 20. On November 9, he completed 4 circles, covering a distance of nearly 3 miles in 5 minutes, 4 seconds. Orville duplicated the record on December 1.

**British aviation historian Charles Harvard Gibbs-Smith served, in 1978, as Lindbergh Professor of Aerospace History, National Air and Space Museum, Smithsonian Institution.

HUFFMAN PRAIRIE SITE

On Pylon Road in WPAFB Area C is a large concrete marker. An adjacent sign notes this as the site of the Wrights' original 1904 hangar.* The .52-acre site was entered on the National Register of Historic Places on May 6, 1971, as a part of "Huffman Field . . . world's first flying and landing field for airplanes."

*Recent evidence suggests that this site may actually be the locale of the 1905 hangar, and therefore approximately a quarter-mile distant from the original hangar.

Katharine Wright, sister of Orville and Wilbur, was the brothers' staunchest supporter and constant companion, accompanying them on their travels in the United States and Europe. *(Wright State University Archives, Wright Brothers Collection)*

The Wright family home at 7 Hawthorn Street, Dayton, about 1900
(Wright State University Archives, Wright Brothers Collection)

9½ seconds. Then, in landing, the left wing struck the ground and cracked four corner ribs. This was hardly an auspicious start for a new campaign. But according to Gibbs-Smith, with the 1905 Flyer III the Wrights "finally learned the secrets of powered flight and solved its basic problems."[10] The pioneers learned to bank, turn, and make circles and figure eights with ease. The longest flight of the year occurred October 5, when Wilbur was airborne for 39 minutes, 23 seconds. He flew over 24 miles at an average speed of 38 mph while making 29 circuits of the pasture.[11]

For the next three years, Dayton remained home base as the brothers visited Washington and Europe and captured the attention of both. During this time the brothers' genius produced both the vehicle and the spirit that launched the U.S. Army Signal Corps into heavier-than-air flight.

THE SIGNAL CORPS MACHINE

On February 10, 1908, the newly-established Aeronautical Division of the Signal Corps accepted the Wrights' bid to provide the Army with its first heavier-than-air flying machine. The proposed machine was to weigh 1,100 to 1,250 pounds and be capable of remaining in the air for at least one hour carrying two men, with a total weight of 350 pounds. It would also achieve a speed of at least 40 miles per hour. The price was to be $25,000, and delivery was scheduled for August 28, 1908.

Milton Wright, a bishop in the United Brethren Church and a loyal supporter of his sons' activities, chronicled their successes in his personal diary. The first flight over Huffman Prairie was entered laconically, "Went at 9:00 [trolley] car to Huffman's farm. At 2:00 Orville flew about 25 feet. I came home on 3:30 [trolley] car. It rained soon after." *(Photo and diary from Wright State University Archives, Wright Brothers Collection)*

The Wrights based their bid on the capabilities of their 1908 model Flyer. Designed as a military vehicle for both training and reconnaissance functions, the new airplane contained two major improvements over earlier Flyers, one in the engine and one in the airframe. The engine had four vertical (rather than horizontal) cylinders, which raised its output to 35 horsepower, continuously.[12] The new airframe allowed for two people. And since, "manifestly, for military purposes it was essential that both pilot and passenger should sit upright," the frame was fitted with two side-by-side seats.[13] Thus, the new airplane was designed to fly faster and longer, and to carry two people, upright, either of whom could control the aircraft.[14]

Before the Army would accept it, the airplane would have to pass endurance and speed tests, set at Fort Myer, Virginia, in September 1908.

The brothers decided that Orville would fly the tests.* After extensive spring practice at Kitty Hawk, North Carolina, and summer refitting in Dayton, Orville shipped the airplane to Fort Myer in August.

According to one observer, "when the official flight trials at Fort Myer began the public journeyed there by the thousands to see the mystery of flight dissolved and the skeptics at last proved wrong."[15] Afternoon visitors from nearby Washington, D.C., included President William Howard Taft and many of the Cabinet members.

At Fort Myer the starting track and wooden tower for hoisting the catapult weight were erected on the drill ground, surrounded by buildings and tall trees. These lim-

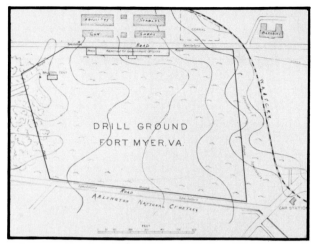

Official drawing of the drill grounds at Fort Myer, Virginia, prepared for the 1908 flight tests. The site was bounded on three sides by trees, buildings, and the rail line, and on all four sides by spectators and officials. *(Wright State University Archives, Wright Brothers Collection)*

Dignitaries inspect the Wright Flyer prior to the beginning of the trials. As noted on the photo, they included: 1) Col. Hatfield, 13 Cavalry; 2) Sec'y Newberry, Navy; 3) Maj. Fournier, French Military Attaché; 4) Lt. Sweet, USN; 5) Gen. Luke Wright, [Office of the] Sec'y of War; 6) Maj. Squier, Signal Corps; 7) Lt. Crucy, Marine Corps; 8) Mr. Fanciulli. *(Wright State University Archives, Wright Brothers Collection)*

ORVILLE WRIGHT, FT. MYER, VIRGINIA SEPTEMBER 1908

Date	Record	Statistics
Sept. 9	Flight Endurance	1 hr, 2 min, circling field 55 times at altitude of 80 ft
Sept. 11	Flight Endurance	1 hr, 10 min, circling field 57½ times
Sept. 12	2-Man Flight*	9 min, 6⅓ sec Passenger: Maj. George O. Squier, President, Signal Corps Aeronautical Board
	Flight Endurance	1 hr, 14 min, circling field 71 times at altitude of 300 ft

*First passenger in a powered airplane had been Charles W. Furnas, the Wright brothers' mechanic, on the previous May 14 at Kitty Hawk, N.C. First military passenger had been Lt. Frank P. Lahm on September 3, 1908, in acceptance trials at Ft. Myer.

---

itations constrained straight flight, without turns, to only "a few hundred yards at the most."[16]

Nevertheless, Orville treated spectators to new world's records, day after day, in flight endurance.[17]

The tests were suspended on a tragic note on September 17, when Orville and a passenger, Lt. Thomas E. Selfridge, crashed from an altitude of 125 feet "when one of the propellers split, causing it to lose pushing power, and a stay wire to the tail was then torn loose, making the tail uncontrollable." Lieutenant Selfridge sustained a fatal skull fracture when he struck one of the wooden uprights of the framework.[18] Orville suffered a fractured left leg and four cracked ribs. He remained hospitalized at Fort Myer until late October, returning to Dayton on November 1.

---

*On May 17, Wilbur departed for Europe, where he spent the next year demonstrating Wright airplanes, promoting sales, and training other pilots.

Orville Wright and Lt. Thomas E. Selfridge preparing for takeoff, Fort Myer, Virginia, September 17, 1908. Lieutenant Selfridge was a member of the trial committee. *(Wright State University Archives, Wright Brothers Collection)*

Minutes later, the flight ended in tragedy. The crash killed Lieutenant Selfridge and seriously injured Orville Wright, ending the official trials for the year. *(Wright State University Archives, Wright Brothers Collection)*

LT. THOMAS ETHOLEN SELFRIDGE

Thomas Etholen Selfridge (1882-1908) graduated from the U.S. Military Academy at West Point in 1903 and was commissioned a lieutenant in the Artillery Corps.

His interest in aviation led him to collaborate with Dr. Alexander Graham Bell and Glenn H. Curtiss in 1907. They formed the Aerial Experiment Association to design and fly motor-driven aircraft. Selfridge designed the group's first airplane, though he never flew it. He did fly their second airplane in May 1908, and thus became the first military man to pilot a heavier-than-air machine. With his fatal injury at Fort Myer in September, he also became the first military man to lose his life in one.

He was buried with full military honors in Arlington Cemetery, just a short distance from Ft. Myer, on September 19, 1908.

Shortly after his death, the Aero Club of America erected a memorial at the U.S. Military Academy. Its inscription reads:

> "In memoriam, Thomas E. Selfridge, 1st Lieutenant, 1st Field Artillery, who gave up his life in the service of his country at Ft. Myer, Va., Sept. 17, 1908, in falling with the first government aeroplane. Age 26 years. U.S.M.A. '03."

The Army, however, was impressed with the airplane's overall performance prior to the crash and granted an extension of the contract delivery date until the summer of 1909.

The interim was a productive period for the Wrights. Orville recuperated in Dayton through the holidays. In January, he and sister Katharine joined Wilbur in Europe. Wilbur had been seeking European contracts, flying in exhibitions, and training pilots in France and Italy. He flew before European heads of state, including King Edward VII of England, King Alfonso XIII of Spain, and King Victor Emmanuel III of Italy. Government and military leaders of every major power took personal note.

The Wrights were celebrated and honored wherever they appeared. Their return to the United States was marked by Presidential honors in Washington and the largest, most impressive homecoming Dayton could arrange.

The celebrations did not stop their progress, however. June was spent in Dayton, testing propellers to determine the cause of the accident at Fort Myer and to preclude similar problems in the upcoming flight tests.

The Wright family returned in force to Fort Myer on June 20, 1909, to resume flight tests. Wilbur was present, along with sister Katharine, but Orville did all of the flying. Presumably as a matter of pride, he wanted to finish what he had started the year before.

The Wrights brought with them an improved version of their "Signal Corps machine." Overall design changes included a "combination of a front movable rudder with a fixed horizontal plane in the rear of the machine in contrast to the front horizontal rudder" of the 1903-1908 models.[19]

Orville flew a series of short test flights with the new model between June 29 and July 19, then prepared for the two crucial tests of endurance and speed. To demonstrate endurance, the aircraft had to remain aloft for one hour carrying two persons. On July 27, with Lt. Frank P. Lahm aboard, Orville flew for 1 hour, 12 minutes, and 37⅘ seconds, thereby exceeding the Army standard and setting a new world record. President Taft was among the 10,000

The Wright brothers were welcomed to Dayton with a grand two-day homecoming celebration. The festivities included the formation of a giant U.S. flag by 2,500 Dayton school children, and the presentation of Congressional, Ohio, and Dayton medals to the brothers, along with the keys to the city.

(Dayton and Montgomery County Public Library)

cheering spectators as the airplane circled the drill field almost 80 times at an altitude of 150 feet.[20]

The second test was the speed test. On July 30, Orville, with Lt. Benjamin D. Foulois as passenger, flew for speed on a cross-country course between Fort Myer and Shuter's (sometimes spelled Shooter's) Hill, near Alexandria, Virginia. This first-ever cross-country flight covered a round-trip distance of ten miles.

Seven thousand witnesses, again including the President, cheered as the airplane lifted from the monorail at 6:46 a.m., then watched as it twice circled the drill field to gain altitude. Cheers dissolved into hushed murmurs as the aircraft disappeared from view in the direction of Alexandria. Even Wilbur and Katharine Wright were tight-lipped, although they had the utmost confidence in both man and machine. The airplane popped up momentarily, then disappeared again between two ridges.

When it reappeared heading straight for the drill field, the crowd waved hats, handkerchiefs, and anything else at hand. The roar of cheers and applause "was loud enough to be heard by the two air travelers despite the noise of the engine alongside them."[21] The ten-mile flight was clocked at a speed of 37.735 mph outbound, and 47.431 mph on the return, for an average speed of 42.583 mph. They had flown more than 2 miles per hour faster than their goal of 40 mph, and had done so at an altitude of 450 to 500 feet, an exceptional height.[22]

Preparing for flight at Fort Myer. The airplane is mounted on the launching rail, and is being connected to the weight in the starting derrick in the background. *(Wright State University Archives, Wright Brothers Collection)*

Poised for takeoff, June 1909. Fort Myer soldiers pull the rope raising the drop-weight to the derrick peak. *(Wright State University Archives, Wright Brothers Collection)*

Airborne with Orville Wright at the controls. Nearness of buildings surrounding the drill grounds constrained straight flight. *(Wright State University Archives, Wright Brothers Collection)*

On August 2, the Aeronautical Board formally accepted the Wright machine.* Upon payment of $25,000 for the airplane and a bonus of $5,000 for exceeding by 2 mph the specified minimum speed of 40 mph, Signal Corps Airplane Number One entered the Army inventory.

To complete the terms of their contract, the Wrights were required to instruct two men in the handling and operation of their flying machine. (No extra payment was allowed for this purpose.)[23] Since the Fort Myer Commander insisted that his drill field be returned to its primary purpose, the Army leased suitable acreage from the Maryland Agricultural College at nearby College Park, Maryland. Wilbur gave flight instruction to three Signal Corps officers: Lieutenants Lahm and Foulois, both of whom had flown with Orville during the acceptance flights, and Lieutenant Frederic E. Humphreys (on special duty from the Corps of Engineers).

When flight instruction ended on November 5, Wilbur was ready to join Orville in a bold new venture.

Officers of the Wright Company included Orville and Wilbur as chief executives. *(Wright State University Archives, Wright Brothers Collection)*

*Members of the "Board of Officers Convened by Office Memorandum No. 18, Office of the Chief Signal Officer of the Army, dated June 21, 1909, for the Purpose of Observing Trials of Aeronautical Devices, Etc.," were appointed by Brig. Gen. James Allen, Chief Signal Officer of the Army:

Major George O. Squier, Signal Corps, President
Major C. McK. Saltzman, Signal Corps, Member
Captain C. deF. Chandler, Signal Corps, Member

Lieutenant G. C. Sweet, U.S. Navy, Member
Lieutenant Frank P. Lahm, Signal Corps, Member
Lieutenant F. E. Humphreys, Corps of Engineers, Recorder

The Wright hangar at Simms Station housed both the Wright Exhibition Company and the Wright School of Aviation. *(U.S. Air Force Museum)*

THOSE DARING YOUNG MEN . . .

Aviation became an industry in Dayton with the incorporation of the Wright Company on November 22, 1909, with Wilbur Wright as President and Orville as one of two Vice Presidents. The company listed a capital stock of $1 million, a New York corporate office, and a planned Dayton manufacturing facility. It was time. Since Wilbur's European tour in 1908, Wright-designed and licensed airplanes had been sold abroad by French, British, and German companies.

Both buildings of the Wright Company factory in West Dayton were complete in 1911. The buildings are today part of the Inland Division of General Motors. *(Wright State University Archives, Wright Brothers Collection)*

Replica of the 1909 Signal Corps Machine on display at the U.S. Air Force Museum at WPAFB. It is known popularly as the Wright 1909 Military Flyer. *(U.S. Air Force Museum)*

This close-up of the Model A used at Simms Station in 1910 clearly shows the wing warp that was essential for flight stability. Clear, too, are the wheels that appeared for the first time on a Wright airplane in July 1910. *(Wright State University Archives, Wright Brothers Collection)*

By November 1910, construction was complete on the first of two factory buildings in West Dayton, and the company was turning out two airplanes a month.

A new hangar near Simms Station advertised to all that the Wrights had returned to fly over Huffman Prairie. This hangar housed two branches of the Wright corporation. One, the Wright Exhibition Company, flew airplanes at county fairs, aero shows and exhibits, speed races, and other large public gatherings that permitted the display of Wright aircraft to potential customers.

The second branch made Simms Station famous as the site of the corporation's School of Aviation, which operated from 1910 through 1916.* The School advertised "four hours of actual practice in the air and such instruction in the principles of flying machines as is necessary to prepare the pupil to become a competent and expert operator." Instruction in these necessary principles occupied students for most of their 10 days of training, with 5 to 15 minutes of each day spent in the air.

Tuition was $250 per pupil, payable at the time of enrollment, and covered any incidental "breakage to the machine." However, the airplanes used in training were equipped with duplicate controls so that the instructor could immediately assume control "should the student make any serious mistake."[24]

Close-up of the 4-cycle Wright engine in use in 1910. Note also the open-air seating. *(Wright State University Archives, Wright Brothers Collection)*

*Other Wright schools for training "operators" were instituted at Montgomery, Alabama, (location of today's Maxwell AFB) in 1910; at Augusta, Georgia, in 1911; and at Belmont Park, New York, in 1911.

The Model A skims down the monorail . . . and takes off . . . into flight over Simms Station, 1910. *(Series, Wright State University Archives, Wright Brothers Collection)*

Diverse groups of students came to Simms Station: civilians learning to fly their own new purchases, Army officers heading for instructorships at Signal Corps Aviation Schools like the one at College Park, and even officers from the Navy. (The brothers offered to train a U.S. Navy pilot if the Service would order a hydroplane from the Wright Company. The Navy agreed; the airplane was delivered July 15, 1911.) The May 1911 class included three civilian students and three military officers, Lt. John Rodgers, USN, and Lieutenants Henry H. Arnold and Thomas DeWitt Milling, both of the Army Signal Corps.

Any student at the Wright School of Aviation learned about the airplane from the inside out; how to maintain, repair, and modify his machine, as well as how to fly it. Exchanging aspiration for perspiration, Arnold, Milling, Rodgers, and their classmates took off their coats and neckties, rolled up their sleeves, and got to work, skinning their knuckles and smearing oil, grease, and dirt on their shirts, trousers, and shoes. After this indoctrination on the field and in the West Dayton factory, the students knew the function of every part of an airplane and understood the principles followed in putting wood, fabric, and a source of power together in a combination that permitted man to leave the ground and control his journey through the air.

Such familiarization was especially valuable to the military students. In his autobiography, *Global Mission,* Arnold commented, "Milling and I were soon grateful for the days spent in the factory, for in addition to learning how to fly we found we would have to master the construction and maintenance features of the Wright machine well enough to teach our own mechanics the ABC of a ground crew's job when we went to our first station. There were no crew chiefs nor aircraft mechanics in the Army in those days."[25]

The schedule for Arnold's training typified the Aviation School pattern. On May 9, 1911, Lieutenant Arnold made his first flight. The seven-minute lesson was given by chief instructor Al Welsh, who had earned his own wings just a year earlier. By the nineteenth flight, Arnold could land the airplane without assistance. After 28 flights and a cumulative flying time of 3 hours and 48 minutes, Arnold was graduated and certified as a qualified military aviator.

The Wrights taught their students more than the mechanics of flight; they imbued them with a "can-do" spirit. As Arnold wrote in his autobiography, "More than anyone I have ever known or read about, the Wright brothers gave me the sense that nothing is impossible. I like to think—and

during World War II—often did, that the Air Force has rooted its traditions in that spirit."[26]

The brothers maintained an active relationship with the Army Signal Corps aviation program, serving as consultants and teaching both pilots and instructors. These included Lieutenant Lahm and Capt. Charles deForest Chandler, Commandant of the Signal Corps School at College Park.[27]

LT. HENRY H. ARNOLD

Henry Harley Arnold was born June 25, 1886, in Pennsylvania. He graduated from the U.S. Military Academy at West Point in the Class of 1907 and was commissioned a lieutenant of infantry. He received flight instruction at the Wright School of Aviation in 1911, and while there formed a lifelong friendship with the Wrights. When Arnold returned to Dayton in 1929 as a major and Commander of the Fairfield Air Depot, Orville Wright was often a Sunday dinner guest of the family. While in Dayton, Arnold also served as Executive Officer to the Chief of the Materiel Division at Wright Field. In 1931, he was reassigned to March AFB in California.

Arnold's commitment to military aviation carried him to the five-star supergrade of General of the Army during World War II.

Although they did not know it, the brothers' career as a team was drawing to a close. On May 2, 1912, Wilbur fell gravely ill with typhoid fever during a trip to Boston, Massachusetts. He returned to Dayton two days later and his condition worsened. He died May 30, 1912, at the age of 45.

The entire nation mourned. President William Howard Taft, in his message to the Wright family, eulogized Wilbur as "deserving . . . to stand with Fulton, Stephenson, and Bell" in America's Hall of Fame for inventors.

Orville succeeded his brother as President of the Wright Company. He also carried on the tradition of invention with his development of the automatic stabilizer. Using a "special experimental machine Model E with very thick surfaces" Orville demonstrated his automatic stabilizer to three official representatives of the Aero Club of America. Seven circles of the Huffman Prairie area with "hands off controls" earned him the prestigious Aero Club of America Trophy of 1913 for this contribution to aviation.[28]

Wilbur Wright's funeral cortege, proceeding south on Ludlow Street from the First Presbyterian Church in Dayton. *(Christian Studios, William P. Mayfield Collection)*

Hawthorn Hill, the Wright home in Oakwood, Ohio, a suburb of Dayton, was meticulously planned by both Orville and Wilbur, though Wilbur did not live to see it completed. Orville and Katharine oversaw its completion in 1914. Orville resided there until his death in January 1948.

Orville Wright piloting the Wright Model E. The Model E carried the automatic stabilizer that earned Orville the Aero Club of America Trophy for 1913. It also was one of the only two Wright models with a single propeller. *(Wright State University Archives, Wright Brothers Collection)*

END OF AN ERA

Orville continued his personal flying career for only six years after his brother's death. On May 13, 1918, he flew the 1911 model Flyer one last time, alongside the first DeHavilland DH-4 manufactured by the Dayton-Wright Company at Moraine City, south of Dayton.

It was the end of an era. The aviation pioneers no longer flew at Huffman Prairie. But their names are not forgotten. There were 119 pilots who earned their wings at Simms Station between May 1910 and February 1916. Although most were civilians, there were several U.S. Army, and even U.S. Navy, officers in the cockpits. There were also three daring young women defying both gravity and convention. More than a third of the graduates were Canadians. (Eager for World War I duty, they bypassed oversubscribed Canadian flying schools to earn the wings required for acceptance into the Royal Flying Corps or the Royal Naval Air Service.)

Their names are embossed on one of the special plaques which surround the Wright Memorial at Wright-Patterson Air Force Base. The Memorial is part of a 27-acre wooded park known as Wright Brothers Hill in Area B of Wright-Patterson. It is located atop the 100-foot bluff which overlooks Huffman Prairie and Simms Station. Dedicated August 19, 1940, the Memorial was conveyed to the U.S. Air Force on September 9, 1978.

Some of the Canadians who earned their wings at the Wright School of Aviation are pictured at Simms Station in 1915. *(Wright State University Archives, Wright Brothers Collection)*

According to popular accounts, the Simms Station hangar remained standing until the early 1940s. Gen. Henry H. Arnold wrote, in 1949: "The Simms Station is gone today. . . . It would have been a fine exhibit in the midst of what is now sprawling Patterson Field, with Wright Field just over the hill—virtually in the center of the modern United States Air Force's technical proving ground."

PIONEER FLYERS TRAINED ON HUFFMAN PRAIRIE	
Henry H. Arnold	Louie Mitchell
Frank Lahm	O. G. Simmons
John Rodgers	C. L. Webster
Kenneth Whiting	Albert Elton
A. Ray Brown	Andrew Drew
Charles DeF. Chandler	A. A. Merrill
Thomas DeW. Milling	Philip W. Page
Griffith Brewer	George A. Gray
Cal P. Rodgers	C. Couturier
Robert G. Fowler	Wilfred Stevens
Walter Brookins	Arch Freeman
Ralph Johnstone	J. G. Klockler
Arch Hoxsey	Farnum T. Fish
Duval LaChappelle	F. J. Southard
A. L. Welsh	Grover C. Bergdoll
Frank T. Coffyn	Charles Wald
P. O. Parmelee	William Kabitzke
J. C. Turpin	M. R. Priest
Howard Gill	John A. Bixler
L. W. Bonney	Bernard L. Whelan
O. A. Brindley	Howard M. Rinehart
J. C. Henning	A. A. Bressman
Harold H. Brown	M. T. Schermerhorn
R. J. Armor	R. M. Wright
Harry N. Atwood	W. E. Bowersox
H. V. Hills	L. E. Brown
A. B. Gaines Jr.	K. F. Saunders
C. J. Peterson	M. B. Galbraith
L. E. Norman	W. J. Sussan
C. E. Utter	C. J. Creery
C. A. Terrell	John Galpin
Mrs. Richberg Hornsby	Basil D. Hobbs
C. LaQ. Day	James L. Gordon
Marjorie Stinson	Edward A. Stinson
C. Ando	M. C. Dubuc
Frank Kitamura	J. A. Shaw
O. A. Danielson	P. S. Kennedy
Lyle H. Scott	Lloyd S. Breadner
Ferdinand Eggena	W. H. Chisam
Robert E. Lee	Robert McC. Weir
Rose Dougan	G. A. Magor
J. M. Alexander	N. A. Magor
J. A. McRae	J. R. Bibby
Goroku Moro	G. S. Harrower
Verne Carter	George Breadner
E. P. Beckwith	C. E. Neidig
T. D. Pemberton	A. W. Briggs
B. B. Lewis	H. B. Evans
Maurice Coombs	A. C. Harland
George H. Simpson	Harley Smith
Gordon F. Ross	J. C. Watson
K. G. MacDonald	S. T. Edwards
Percy E. Beasley	Harry Swan
A. G. Woodward	L. B. Ault
A. Y. Wilks	J. C. Simpson
Paul Gadbois	C. McNicoll
W. E. Orchard	W. E. Robinson
J. A. Harman	M. S. Beal
T. C. Wilkinson	C. G. Bronson
J. G. Ireland	

The Wright Memorial at Wright-Patterson Air Force Base overlooks Huffman Prairie and Simms Station.

Six Adena Indian burial mounds adjoin the site of the Wright Memorial, within the park on Wright Brothers Hill. Because of the significance of this archeological site, the Wright Brothers Memorial Mound Group was entered on the National Register of Historic Places in February 1974.

Orville Wright and Maj. Gen. Henry H. "Hap" Arnold chat at the dedication of the Wright Memorial, August 19, 1940. *(Wright State University Archives, Wright Brothers Collection)*

IN COMMEMORATION OF THE COURAGE, PERSEVERANCE AND ACHIEVEMENTS OF WILBUR AND ORVILLE WRIGHT. THROUGH ORIGINAL RESEARCH THE WRIGHT BROTHERS ACQUIRED SCIENTIFIC KNOWLEDGE AND DEVELOPED THEORIES OF AERODYNAMICS WHICH WITH THEIR INVENTION OF AILERON CONTROL ENABLED THEM IN 1903 TO BUILD AND FLY AT KITTY HAWK THE FIRST POWER-DRIVEN, MAN-CARRYING AEROPLANE CAPABLE OF FLIGHT. THEIR FURTHER DEVELOPMENT OF THE AEROPLANE GAVE IT A CAPACITY FOR SERVICE WHICH ESTABLISHED AVIATION AS ONE OF THE GREAT FORWARD STEPS IN HUMAN PROGRESS. AS SCIENTISTS WILBUR AND ORVILLE WRIGHT DISCOVERED THE SECRET OF FLIGHT. AS INVENTORS, BUILDERS AND FLYERS, THEY BROUGHT AVIATION TO THE WORLD.

Inscription on the Wright Memorial monument

Wilbur Wright Field, winter 1918

II. WILBUR WRIGHT FIELD 1917-1925

THE EARLY YEARS OF SIGNAL CORPS AVIATION

On August 1, 1907, the Aeronautical Division was established in the Office of the Chief Signal Officer of the Army. The Division was put in charge "of all matters pertaining to military ballooning, air machines, and all kindred subjects on hand." Assigned to this new agency were Captain Charles DeForest Chandler, Corporal Edward Ward, and Private First Class Joseph E. Barrett. All three men were experienced in free balloon operations, assemblage, and maintenance.

This was especially pertinent, as the Signal Corps air fleet consisted of two free spherical hydrogen balloons. Frequent ascensions in these spherical lighter-than-air vehicles comprised aerial operations during 1907 and most of 1908, until August 12 of that year when Lieutenants Frank P. Lahm, Benjamin D. Foulois, and Thomas E. Selfridge began receiving training as pilots in the newly-acquired Signal Corps Dirigible Number One. Described as a "dirigible balloon," the aircraft required two men to operate it, and had been purchased from Thomas Scott Baldwin for $6,750.[1]

The next acquisition of the Aeronautical Division occurred August 2, 1909, when Signal Corps Airplane Number One, designed and manufactured by Wilbur and Orville Wright, was purchased for $25,000.* During October and November, Lieutenants Lahm and Foulois and Lieutenant Frederic E. Humphreys received pilot training in the heavier-than-air machine at College Park, Maryland.

Corporal Edward Ward (center) and fellow ground crewmen surround the gondola of a Signal Corps balloon. Corporal Ward was the first enlisted man assigned to the Signal Corps Aeronautical Division on August 1, 1907. He retired in 1930 with the permanent rank of first lieutenant and lived in Dayton, Ohio, until his death in 1965. (*U.S. Air Force Museum*)

*See Chapter I for specific details of this period.

Congress, however, provided no further funds to continue military aeronautics. "Economy was the watchword in Washington and vision was lacking in those who held the purse-strings."[2]

Thus, during 1910 and into the early part of the following year the Aeronautical Division's flight operations were limited to the two free balloons, one dirigible, and one airplane. Lieutenant Foulois was the Army's only active pilot, flying at Fort Sam Houston, Texas, in Signal Corps Airplane Number One. He augmented the $150 that Congress allotted him for aviation gasoline and repairs from his meager service salary. Lieutenants Lahm and Humphreys had returned to their respective branches of the service: Cavalry and Corps of Engineers. The Aeronautical Division's total personnel strength stood at 27 men (both officer and enlisted).

The situation was different in Europe. Nations there were far more visionary in recognizing the military poten-

tial of the airplane. In early 1911, France appropriated $1 million (franc equivalent) for its infant air arm. Other nations would soon follow in establishing real efforts in aviation as pressures built toward World War I.

Insulated from those pressures, the United States awakened more slowly to the potential of military aviation. In the opinion of a World War I historian, it was a "red-letter day in American aviation history" when Congress, on March 3, 1911, enacted the Appropriation Act for Fiscal Year 1912, allocating the first money ever for American military aviation.[3] Even then, the sum totalled only $125,000. Of that amount $25,000 was immediately available and it was used forthwith to purchase five new airplanes, all "pusher-type" aircraft.* A Wright Model B and a Curtiss "military model" were delivered in April to Lieutenant Foulois at Fort Sam Houston.** When flying operations moved north to College Park in the spring, both the Wright Aviation Company and the Curtiss manufacturer

(U.S. Air Force Museum)

COL. CHARLES deFOREST CHANDLER

As a captain, Charles deForest Chandler was the first Chief of the Signal Corps Aeronautical Division when it was established August 1, 1907. Chandler, a native of Cleveland, Ohio, entered the Army in 1898 as a private. He qualified as pilot of balloons in 1907, of dirigibles in 1909, and of airplanes in 1911. He was Commandant of the Signal Corps Aviation School at College Park, Maryland, 1911-1913. Captain Chandler rose in grade to the rank of colonel, and retired in 1920.

(NCR Corporation)

LT. FRANK P. LAHM

Lt. Frank P. Lahm is pictured here with a tractor-type Martin airplane, about 1915. A native of Mansfield, Ohio, Lahm graduated from the U.S. Military Academy in 1901. He was qualified by Wilbur Wright on October 26, 1909, as one of the two first American military airplane pilots. Lahm had previously qualified as a pilot of free balloons (1905) and of dirigibles (1908). He rose to the rank of brigadier general (July 1926) and appointment as Assistant Chief of the Army Air Corps. He retired from active duty on November 30, 1941.

---

*A "pusher" airplane had the propeller mounted on the rear end of the engine or propeller shaft, thus "pushing" the aircraft forward. A "tractor" airplane had the propeller mounted on the forward end of the engine or propeller shaft, thus pulling the aircraft forward.

**The second airplane purchased by the Signal Corps was manufactured by the Glenn Curtiss Company. According to Chandler and Lahm, it was designated as a Curtiss "Type IV." The weight was 400 lbs without pilot. It was powered by an 8-cylinder engine rated at 51.2 horsepower. A passenger could be carried by sitting on the lower wing immediately behind the pilot.

Wright airplane at College Park, Maryland, October 1909

LT. BENJAMIN D. FOULOIS

At Fort Sam Houston, Texas, in 1910, Lt. Benjamin D. Foulois sits in the "cockpit" of Signal Corps Airplane Number One, manufactured by the Wright brothers the previous year. The Army's third airplane pilot, Foulois was also the first Army dirigible pilot. As a brigadier general, he was Chief of the Army Air Service in France during World War I. He later served as Chief of the Materiel Division, Wright Field, in 1929. As a major general, he was appointed Chief of the Army Air Corps in 1931, and retired in that grade in 1935.

each delivered another airplane to the aviation training school. The fifth airplane purchased in the $25,000 package was a Burgess-Wright which also went to the aviation school.* By the end of 1911 the Signal Corps aviation fleet consisted of five airplanes (Signal Corps Airplane Number One had retired to the Smithsonian Institution during the year), two spherical balloons, and Dirigible Number One. The 1911 personnel strength of 23 persons included six airplane pilots. Aircraft and people were concentrated at the aviation school at College Park, Maryland, during the summer and at the school's new winter quarters in Augusta, Georgia, during that season.

Meager appropriations severely restricted the Aeronautical Division for the next two years as Congress allocated only $125,000 and $100,000 for 1912 and 1913. Austere funding notwithstanding, two significant steps forward were taken. In January 1913, the Signal Corps flying school was relocated from its College Park, Maryland, and Augusta, Georgia, locations to North Island, San Diego,

The Signal Corps flying school moved from its College Park, Maryland, and Augusta, Georgia, locations to North Island, San Diego, California, in January 1913. North Island became the Army's first permanent aviation school. *(U.S. Air Force Museum)*

---

*The manufacturer, W. S. Burgess, was a renowned designer of yachts at Marblehead, Mass. He was the first manufacturer in the United States to be licensed by the Wright Company for use of its patents.

Wright Company Model B (shown) and Model C pusher-type aircraft were used in instructing pilots at the early Signal Corps aviation schools. The last Wright Company airplane sold to the Signal Corps was delivered in late May 1915 and dropped from the active inventory June 13, 1915. The machine was a Model B, the last production model of its type. Because of "hidebound determination to stick to the biplane pusher type" the Wright Company was unable to compete to any degree in the military aviation field. *(U.S. Air Force Museum)*

California. "Year-round" flying conditions in southern California were a major, but not the sole, inducement for the transfer. The new site marked the Army's "first permanent aviation school, organized on a solid basis and providing a logical and efficient course of instruction sufficiently comprehensive in its scope to justify its graduates being rated military aviators."[4] By mid-year the West Coast school had 7 airplanes, 3 instructors (including the commandant), 14 officer students, and 48 enlisted men assigned to service and support jobs.

In addition, the military aviation program during 1913 reached the point where it was formally recognized for its potential as part of a field force. The Army prescribed a model organizational structure for a provisional aero squadron. The tables of organization, equipment, and allowances called for 20 officers, 90 enlisted men, 8 airplanes, and 6 motorcycles for each squadron.[5] Available resources were growing and by the end of the year Army aviation more than equalled the strength of one squadron, with 15 airplanes and 114 commissioned and enlisted personnel, including 11 qualified pilots* and 9 other officers in pilot training.[6]

Certainly much progress had been made since 1908, but the price had often been measured in terms of sacrifice. From 1908 through 1913 military airplane crashes cost the lives of 12 officers, including 1 non-commissioned officer. Most of these fatalities had involved pusher-type airplanes. When seven of the fatal accidents occurred in 1913, and three of these involved Wright Model C pusher airplanes, pilots' confidence in that type of aircraft was destroyed. On February 16, 1914, pushers were grounded for further investigation. In effect, this action eliminated the Wright fleet, for a board of pilots recommended student training at

North Island be limited to the tractor-type airplanes in the fleet, including one Curtiss and four Burgess airplanes.

Progress continued. According to Brig. Gen. Frank P. Lahm, the "Army's wings . . . received official sanction" on July 18, 1914, when Congress created an Aviation Section within the Signal Corps. The new Aviation Section inherited the general mission of the antecedent Aeronautical Division and in addition received the specific responsibility of "training officers and enlisted men in matters pertaining to military aviation."

Despite this recognition, American military aviation was still in its formative stages at the outbreak of the Great War in Europe on July 28, 1914. U.S. strength did not compare well to the pre-war strengths of the major European powers, in money or in resources allocated. Germany's pre-war budget reached $45 million, Russia's totalled $22.5 million, France allocated $12 million, Austria-Hungary allocated $3 million, Great Britain budgeted slightly more than $1 million, and Italy set aside $800,000. Germany had 2,600 men in uniform flying and/or supporting a fleet of 260 airplanes. France had 3,000 military personnel and 156 airplanes. Great Britain had 154 airplanes. In stark contrast, the United States Army Aviation Section's Fiscal Year 1915 appropriation was $250,000. Assigned personnel totalled 208, and aircraft inventory was 23 machines.

By March 1916 the clamor from an aroused American public stirred Congress to action. Its fervor was fueled by the embarrassing experience of the 1st Aero Squadron during the Spring of 1916 as the air element of the Punitive Expedition against Pancho Villa on the Mexican Border. Bowing to public opinion, in March 1916 Congress passed

*Among the certified pilots were two enlisted men: Sergeant (E-4) Vernon N. Burge who received his wings in August 1912, and Corporal (E-3) William A. Lamkey, who graduated in November of that year.

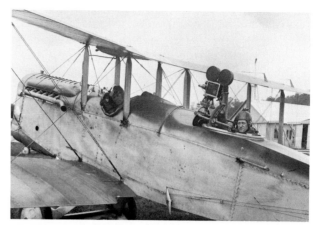

This DH-4 observation airplane, produced by the Dayton-Wright Airplane Company in 1918, was one of the first American-manufactured airplanes equipped for aerial photography. The motion picture camera was mounted on the aerial machine gun ring in the rear cockpit. *(Wright State University Archives)*

(U.S. Air Force Museum)

MAJ. GEN. GEORGE O. SQUIER

Maj. Gen. George O. Squier served as Chief Signal Officer, U.S. Army, from 1917 to 1923. A native of Michigan, Squier graduated from the U.S. Military Academy in 1887, and was commissioned as a lieutenant of Field Artillery. He later transferred to the Signal Corps. General Squier was one of the few Army officers to earn a Ph.D. after graduating from West Point, and distinguished himself in the fields of electrical science and radio. General Squier retired in 1923.

a deficiency appropriation that provided another $500,000 for military aeronautics. The National Defense Act of June 3, 1916, increased active duty officer strength in the Aviation Section to 148 and established a Signal Corps Reserve (of 297 officers and 2,000 enlisted men) for the Aviation Section.

At about the same time, a significant and beneficial action placed Lt. Col. George O. Squier as Officer in Charge of the Aviation Section.* Having just returned from four years as a military attaché to the U.S. Ambassador to Great Britain, Colonel Squier's observations concerning the "simply prodigious flying movement abroad" carried considerable weight with Congressmen.

On the strength of his testimony and that of other experts, Congress on August 29, 1916, appropriated $13,881,666 for military aviation and made a supplemental appropriation of $600,000 for the purchase of land to use as flying fields and depots. A massive search was undertaken nationwide to find suitable sites.

COMBAT-ORIENTED PILOT TRAINING

Two additional problems of major proportion confronted the Aviation Section near the eve of the United States entry into World War I: acquiring and training pilots. On February 3, 1917, when diplomatic relations with Germany were severed, none of the 132 planes on hand, nor the 293 on order, was designed for combat. No American Army pilot had ever flown a combat mission.

To compound the problem of unpreparedness, according to one historian, "the Aviation Section had no accurate knowledge of the equipment of a military airplane." No aircraft, for example, had ever been mounted with a machine gun. Aviation personnel had "practically no knowledge of radiotelegraphy and telephony, photography, bombing equipment, lights for night flying, aviators' clothing, compasses used in flying, or other aviation instruments" that were well known to European military pilots.[7]

Until 1916 the Army's flying training school at San Diego, California, had graduated a sufficient number of pilots for the small fleet. But with increased appropriations and the likelihood of the nation entering the conflict in Europe, there was an obvious need to expand the flying training program. By the end of February 1917, four additional pilot training schools had been established: at Mineola, Long Island, New York; at Ashburn Field, Chicago, Illinois; at Memphis, Tennessee; and at Essington, Pennsylvania.**

When the United States, on April 6, 1917, declared war on Germany, the Aviation Section had 132 airplanes deployed among the Signal Corps Aviation Schools (SCAS) and the 1st, 2nd, and 3rd Aero Squadrons.[8] Total strength included 131 officers, nearly all of whom were pilots or

---

*Less than a year later, Squier was promoted to brigadier general and appointed Chief Signal Officer (February 14, 1917).

**In addition, in November 1916 an ambitious program was begun to train civilian pilots in the Signal Enlisted Reserve Corps (SERC). Training began at the Curtiss Corporation School of Aviation in Newport News, Virginia, and expanded in December to another Curtiss school at Miami, Florida. By the end of the program in June 1917, Curtiss had trained 131 enlisted reservists.

student pilots, and 1,087 enlisted men. As mentioned, none of the airplanes was combat-ready and none of the pilots combat-trained. Drastic measures would certainly be needed if America were to meet French Premier Alexandre Ribot's most urgent request for 4,500 airplanes, 5,000 pilots, and 50,000 airplane mechanics to be in his country by the first part of 1918.[9]

A gigantic wave of patriotic fervor engulfed America's national defense establishment, especially the Aviation Section. Hyperbole replaced rationality. Editorials in the nation's most influential newspapers demanded an almost immediate air fleet financed by real appropriations. Maj. Gen. George O. Squier, Chief Signal Officer, in his support of a proposed $600 million appropriation bill for the Aviation Section, talked eloquently about "an army in the air, regiments and brigades of winged cavalry mounted on gas-driven flying horses."[10] Not quite as flowery, but even more of an exaggeration, was the prophecy of Dr. James S. Ames, an eminent scientist, that Germany would be defeated "within a few months of the completion of the 22,625 planes called for in the $639,000,000 programme, which it was estimated could be turned out at the rate of 3,500 [airplanes] a month."[11]

To accomplish an "aeronautical miracle," President Woodrow Wilson signed an aviation act on July 24, 1917, that provided the Signal Corps with $640 million. It was the largest single military appropriation in the nation's history. Although the end results were not as spectacular as had been envisioned, this program gave military aeronautics a permanent and major role in national defense.

Meanwhile, the Aviation Section turned to its British, Canadian, French, and Italian counterparts for direction in establishing and implementing personnel training and aircraft production programs. For example, the British-Canadian system of training flying cadets was adopted. Ground or pre-flight schools were established at six leading American universities, including The Ohio State University. The 400-hour intensified curriculum prepared 150 men every eight weeks for admission into primary flying schools. The curriculum included classroom instruction and static demonstration in the theory and principles of flight, aerial photography and reconnaissance, communications codes, meteorology, aircraft engines and airplane structures, aircraft instruments and compasses, and aerial combat tactics. These classes, according to a World War I pilot, were of "greatest value in acclimating the men in aviation and in supplying the all-important theoretical knowledge before actual flying began."[12]

After graduating from ground schools, cadets moved to Signal Corps Aviation Schools for actual flying instruction.* This primary instruction lasted a period of six to eight weeks. The actual time between the initial familiarization flight with an instructor and graduation as a Reserve Military Aviator (RMA) with the commission of second lieutenant depended on the student's progress. The curriculum covered three stages of flying and nearly 300 hours of classroom instruction in diversified subjects such as aircraft engines and structures, aerial machine guns, photographic interpretation, close-order drill, etc. The three phases of actual flying involved dual work with an instructor (4 to 9 hours), solo flying (24 flying hours total), and cross-country flying. From the very beginning "the training . . . was prescribed with the utmost care, leaving just as little to chance as humanly possible. . . . Step-by-step the cadet went on, always held back until he was doubly skilled in the

Young cadets, such as these at North Island, graduated from Signal Corps Aviation Schools as Reserve Military Aviators (RMAs) and were commissioned as second lieutenants. (U.S. Air Force Museum)

Morning calisthenics by flying cadets at the Wilbur Wright Field Signal Corps Aviation School, autumn 1917. At right are airplane hangars which housed the Curtiss Aeroplane Company JN-4D Jenny and Standard Aircraft Company SJ-1 biplane trainers used by the cadets in primary flight training. (U.S. Air Force Museum)

*Wilbur Wright Field was one of the first of these to be established.

present phase and doubly eager for the next."[13] The two-part final examination was a solo 60-mile cross-country flight and an altitude test of 10,000 feet.

After primary flying training, students transferred to one of three other installations for advanced work. At these installations the pilot specialized in pursuit, bomber, or "army-corps" flying. The last type was reconnaissance flying in which the pilot "traveled about with the aerial observers in search of information and photographs—only occasionally in battle."[14]

A final stage of training was labeled post-advanced or pre-combat. This training was done in England, France, and Italy where combat-type airplanes and battle-experienced tutors were available.

Between July 1917 and June 1918 more than 38,000 of the "finest of America's youth" volunteered for flying training with the Aviation Section. These young men were captivated by the gallant exploits of aerial knights mounting their winged steeds into cloudless skies where they would win immortal fame and glory high above the blood-drenched trenches and filthy shell-pocked no-man's land between the serpentine lines. "Constant reports of deaths of famous aviators abroad were far outbalanced by the romance of the [air] service and the opportunities for individuality."[15]

Patriotism and enthusiasm were laudable motivators, but more than a willing spirit was required. Strict physical and psychological standards eliminated 18,004 of the 38,770 candidates. Not the slightest defect was permitted in the structure and function of a candidate's cardio-respiratory system, eyes, ears, nose, throat, and other organs. Moreover, according to War Department criteria:[16]

> The candidate should be naturally athletic and have a reputation for reliability, punctuality and honesty. He should have a cool head in emergencies, good eye for distance, keen ear for familiar sounds, steady hand and solid body with plenty of reserve. He should be quick-witted, highly intelligent and tractable. Immature, high strung, overconfident, impatient candidates not desired.

Because the curriculum was exacting in technical studies, mathematics, and the sciences, the majority of flying cadets were either college graduates or undergraduates with majors in fields transferrable to aviation.

DAYTON AS A FOCUS OF AIRPLANE PRODUCTION

The Wright brothers' aeronautical achievements, the Wright Exhibition Company's aerial demonstrations, and the Wright Aviation Company's manufacturing and training operations imprinted on the community of Dayton, Ohio, a permanent interest in aviation, both civilian and military. As war clouds increased on the nation's horizon during 1914-1916, Dayton's business leaders became increasingly attuned to the economic potentialities of a greatly expanded and more powerful military aviation program. When war was declared in 1917, a group of Miami Valley industrial captains, endowed with foresight and armed with clout in political and financial circles, took action on Dayton's behalf.

Less than a week after the United States entered World War I, the Dayton-Wright Airplane Company was organized.* The impetus for the new company had been generated in a meeting between Secretary of War Newton D. Baker and Ohio Governor James M. Cox on the subject of the national need for increased airplane production.[17] Governor Cox, a Dayton newspaper mogul and financier, was well acquainted with another talented Dayton industrialist, Edward A. Deeds. Deeds had achieved national renown as an industrialist of good reputation, integrity, and more than a little patriotism. He was currently serving as a member of the U.S. Munitions Standards Board in Washington.** As such, he could have no part in the actual ownership or management of the Dayton-Wright Airplane Company. He could, however, lend his expertise in the form of advice and counsel in setting the enterprise on a sound footing.

The new company located at Moraine City, south of Dayton, and began manufacturing DeHavilland DH-4 two-place biplanes.[18] Under license from the Curtiss Company, it also produced JN-4 two-place Jenny trainers. By the end of 1918 the Dayton-Wright Airplane Company had manufactured about 3,100 of the total 4,500 DeHavilland DH-4s built in the United States, and 400 JN-4 Jennys.

The Dayton-Wright Company, Moraine City, produced nearly three-fourths of the more than 4,500 British-designed DH-4 airplanes manufactured in the United States during 1917-1918. These airplanes were equipped with American-designed and built Liberty 8-cylinder and 12-cylinder engines. *(NCR Corporation)*

---

*Board members were Harold E. Talbott, Sr. and Harold E. Talbott, Jr. (who later served as Secretary of the Air Force from February 4, 1953 to August 13, 1955), Charles F. Kettering, Thomas P. Gaddis, George Mead, Carl Sherer, and G. M. Williams. Orville Wright served as a director and as a consulting engineer.

**Deeds was subsequently commissioned as a colonel in the Signal Corps Reserve. He served as a member of the Aircraft Production Board and as Chief of the Signal Corps Equipment Division during World War I. For further details on his contributions to military aviation, see Chapter IV, McCook Field.

Headquarters and principal plant of the Dayton-Wright Airplane Company located in what is now Moraine City, south of Dayton, Ohio, as it appeared in June 1918. Organized in April 1917, the company produced about 3,100 British-designed DH-4s and 400 Curtiss JN-4D Jenny trainers during 1917 and 1918. *(Wright State University Archives, Wright Brothers Collection)*

Fuselages of DeHavilland DH-4 airplanes await their wings at the Dayton-Wright Airplane Company, August 24, 1918.

KETTERING "BUG"

While the Dayton-Wright Company manufactured airplanes, one of the company's more inventive board members, Dayton genius Charles F. Kettering, was also designing and building the world's first "guided missile," the Kettering Aerial Torpedo, nicknamed the "Bug." The tiny, 300-lb papier-mâché airplane with 12-foot cardboard wings, could carry 300 lbs of explosives at 50 mph. Total cost was about $400, including a $50, 2-cycle, 40-hp engine. The flying bombs were launched from a rail pointed precisely in the direction of the target. Distance, wind direction and speed, and engine revolutions per minute were figured into calculations that resulted in the small airplane's folding its wings and plunging to earth squarely on target. The flying bomb was first tested on October 2, 1918, but was not used in World War I.

ESTABLISHMENT OF WILBUR WRIGHT FIELD

In addition to localizing aircraft production, Edward Deeds was involved in other efforts on behalf of his Dayton community. One of the most significant of these was his role in the selection of a site on Huffman Prairie for use as a flying field and a Signal Corps Aviation School. The War Department named this installation Wilbur Wright Field.

Through personal contacts in the Aviation Section, Deeds was aware of contingency plans to establish new aviation schools when funds became available. The August 29, 1916, Congressional appropriation of $13 million for military aviation provided funds specifically to acquire land either through purchase or by lease.

The optimal situation sought was an area sufficiently large to accommodate four training squadrons. Deeds knew of such a possible site. It lay in the Mad River flood plain near the village of Fairfield in Greene County, Ohio, under the jurisdiction of the Miami Conservancy District, of which Deeds was president. The District was a political subdivision organized in 1915 and chartered by the state legislature for "building and maintaining flood control works in the Miami Valley." The District's mission was to prevent, by constructing five retarding dams, a recurrence of the conditions that led to the disastrous flood of March 1913. That catastrophe killed over 400 people in Dayton and the Miami Valley and caused over $100 million in damages.[19] The Mad River was a tributary of the Miami, and the site of one of the proposed dams. Huffman Prairie lay on its flood plain.

Mr. Deeds suggested to General Squier, Chief Signal Officer, that Huffman Prairie and vicinity might be suitable for an aviation school. The Ohioan pointed out that the Wright brothers had trained several dozen pilots at their Simms Station school in the same locale.

Consequently, Dayton was included in the Signal Corps survey of midwestern cities. On April 30, 1917, Maj. Benjamin D. Foulois of the Aviation Section and Lt. Col. C. G. Edgar, Commanding Officer of the Signal Corps Construction Department, arrived in Dayton. They were escorted by Mr. Deeds and Orville Wright on a tour of the area. Major Foulois was favorably impressed with the Huffman Prairie locale, describing it as "admirably suited for aviation purposes."[20] He had been advised that the Miami Conservancy District owned all the land, thus allowing the Signal Corps to negotiate with a sole owner for either lease or purchase of the whole parcel. In addition, Major Foulois reported, the acreage could be acquired "at a very low cost."

Cost aside, the selection of sites for new training schools was a difficult and "most delicate [political] matter, for . . . much pressure was exercised in favor of various localities, and great difficulty was experienced in making unbiased decisions."[21] Selections were therefore proposed by a board of officers for approval by the Chief Signal

On March 25, 1913, rising waters of the rampaging Miami, Mad, and Stillwater Rivers flooded 4th and Ludlow Streets and other areas of downtown Dayton, Ohio, to a depth of ten feet. The disaster claimed over 400 lives and caused more than $100 million in property damage. *(Montgomery County Historical Society)*

Five earthen dams were built by the Miami Conservancy District between 1918-1922 as part of a $35 million program designed to prevent a recurrence of the March 1913 flood in the Miami River Valley basin. Photo shows construction of Huffman Dam on the Mad River, Greene County, Ohio, March 15, 1922.

Officer and the Secretary of War. In the case of the Dayton site, General Squier recommended, on May 15, 1917, that Secretary of War Baker approve the rental with option to purchase about 2,500 acres, including Huffman Prairie and vicinity.

As a matter of fact, though, the Miami Conservancy District did not have title to the land. The District technically held options to purchase and could exercise the right of eminent domain as a last resort. It was generally easier and quicker to negotiate amicable settlements with property owners than to bring legal action against them, and in the situation at hand time was very short. Deeds sent urgent messages from his suite in the New Willard Hotel in Washington, D.C., to the austere Dayton offices of Ezra M. Kuhns, Secretary-Treasurer of the Conservancy District, to

A distinguished committee visited Wilbur Wright Field in November 1917. Convened to present Orville Wright with the Royal Arts Society Medal, the committee consisted of (left to right): Col. Harry E. Talbott; Lord Northcliffe of the Royal Arts Society; Col. Edward A. Deeds, at the time a member of the Aircraft Production Board; Lt. Col. George M. Bomford, Commanding Officer, Wilbur Wright Field; Howard E. Coffin, Chairman of the Aircraft Production Board and member of the Board of Governors of the Aero Club of America; and Capt. C. W. C. Wheatley of the Royal Flying Corps. *(Christian Studios, William P. Mayfield Collection)*

expedite the District's purchase of the farms. To do so, two concessions were offered to the farmers/owners: an inflated purchase price and an agreement to allow the dispossessed families to remain in their homes until the end of the growing season or whenever construction required their removal. Prices paid reached a maximum of $40 per acre for wheat fields, $35 per acre for corn fields, $25 for oats and alfalfa fields, and $5 per acre for pasturage.[22]

On May 22, 1917, Lt. Col. C. G. Edgar as the Signal Corps agent, signed a short-term lease with the Miami Conservancy District for 2,075 acres of land between what is now Huffman Dam and the City of Fairborn at a rental of $20,000 for the initial period ending June 30, 1917. The United States agreed to pay $73,000 to the farmers for their crops. The agreement also contained the option for renewing the lease for one year beginning July 1, 1917, to cover 2,245.20 acres (including the original 2,075 acres) at a rental of $17,600. The United States had the option of renewing the lease for three years at a cost of $20,000 per annum. Another option allowed purchase of all the acreage for $350,000.[23]

On June 6, 1917, the Office of the Chief Signal Officer issued a memorandum stating that the "recently authorized aviation school" near Dayton, Ohio, would be known as Wilbur Wright Field, Fairfield, Ohio. Moreover, it was desired that this name be used in referring to the school itself.* The same memorandum named Signal Corps Aviation Schools at Selfridge Field, Mt. Clemens, Michigan; and Chanute Field, Rantoul, Illinois.[24]

Just as it had patterned flying instruction after Canadian and British flying schools, the Signal Corps Aviation Section modeled its aviation training fields according to Canadian design. Standard specifications for all SCAS sites were drawn from Canadian blueprints by a Detroit, Michigan, civilian architectural firm during a crash 10-day program and rushed to the various Construction Department on-site supervising officers. Wilbur Wright Field was programmed to be one of the four largest U.S. aviation schools, supporting four school squadrons and 24 hangars, 1,700 personnel (including 300 flying cadets), and up to 144 airplanes.

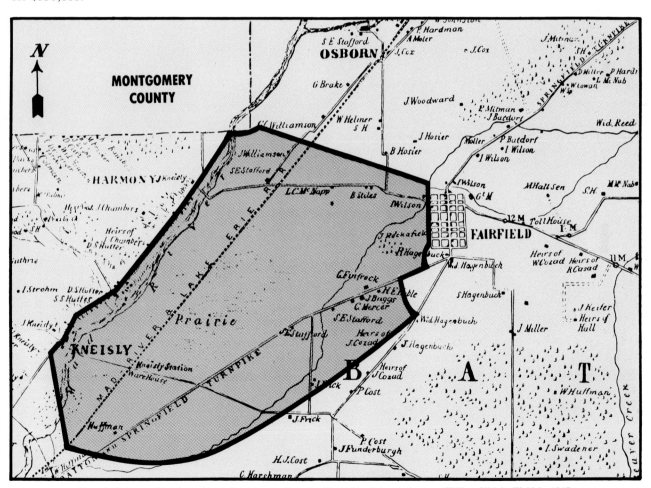

Map of Huffman Prairie and vicinity, Greene County, Ohio. Shaded area became Wilbur Wright Field in 1917.

*There has been controversy through the years as to the initial name of the installation. Although initial correspondence had referred to "Dayton Aviation Field" or the "former Wright flying field," official memorandums were clearly marked "Wilbur Wright Field." No documentary evidence has been found that officially named the Huffman Prairie-Simms Station area as "Wright Field" or "Wright Flying Field." When asked in 1982, neither Mrs. Ivonette Wright Miller nor Mr. Horace Wright, surviving niece and nephew of the Wright brothers, could recall that any such title was applied to the Huffman Prairie area prior to World War I.

FROM THE GROUND UP

On the strength of the May 22 interim lease signed by Colonel Edgar of the Construction Department, the job of converting a small civilian airfield on Huffman Prairie into a major military installation was begun. Wilbur Wright Field was intended as a two-unit, four-squadron flying field. Unit One was to be the Signal Corps Aviation School and was to be in operation by July 15, 1917. Unit Two was to function later as an Aviation Armorers' School.

Capt. Charles T. Waring arrived on May 25 from Ashburn Field, Chicago, Illinois, to assume complete charge of the project. A contractors' work force of about 3,100 laborers, together with mules, horses, wheelbarrows, steam shovels, and other machinery, awaited him. Under the press of wartime conditions, this force labored 24 hours a day, each day in the week, to have the field ready for its first contingent of flying cadets scheduled to arrive from Ohio State University ground-training classrooms on July 15.

That the airfield was ready on schedule was almost a miracle according to a detailed report published one year later by the Commander of Wilbur Wright Field, Maj. Arthur E. Wilbourn.*

Wilbur Wright Field Commander's residence, 1917. To the immediate left are the hangars of the Signal Corps Aviation School. Now known as Building 88 (Area C), this former farmhouse continues to serve as a married officer's home on Wright-Patterson Air Force Base.

MAJ. ARTHUR E. WILBOURN

Maj. Arthur E. Wilbourn graduated from the U.S. Military Academy in the class of 1908. He was commissioned in the Cavalry and placed on special duty with the Signal Corps to command various flying fields during World War I. He commanded the Signal Corps Aviation School and Wilbur Wright Field, Fairfield, Ohio, from December 30, 1917, to June 28, 1918. He retired as a colonel in 1944.

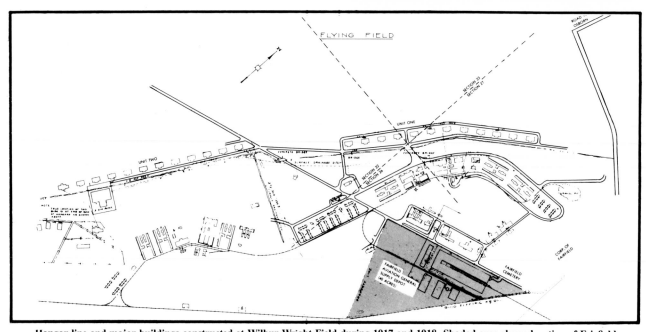

Hangar line and major buildings constructed at Wilbur Wright Field during 1917 and 1918. Shaded area shows location of Fairfield Aviation General Supply Depot, created to supply Wilbur Wright Field and other flying installations.

*Major Wilbourn was not the initial Commander. He did not assume command of the Aviation School and Wilbur Wright Field until December 30, 1917. However, he authored an extensive "annual report" covering nearly the entire first year of the installation. Unless otherwise noted, all quotes in this chapter are drawn from this primary source.

Approximately 1,600 of Wilbur Wright Field's 2,075 acres were in low-lying bottom land along the Mad River. The flat area on the floor of the valley was three-quarters of a mile wide and stretched along two miles of the river shore. Elevation above the water level in the river varied from zero to two and one-half feet. Three-quarters of a mile from the river the land sloped gently upward, with the maximum elevation about 30 feet above the river level.[25]

Most of the field's buildings were constructed on the elevated portion of the site, while flying was done from the level land near the river. Twelve wooden hangars were assigned to each Unit and were, of necessity, located on the flightline. Each hangar measured 120 ft by 66 ft and could be configured for class instruction, or for maintenance or experimentation on up to six airplanes. The hangars bordered a large open drainage ditch that crossed the installation in a northeasterly direction. Thus flying operations were bounded on the south by the main drainage ditch and on the north by the Mad River.

During the first hectic period of construction, some attempts were made to grade the land for better drainage. Major Wilbourn, in retrospect, considered these efforts "highly unsatisfactory," pointing out that some places on the flying field were still "approximately on a level with the river." He believed the drainage problem could have been resolved had all the low places been graded so as to "drain into one or two centrally located reservoirs from which water could have been pumped into the river."

Apparently time constraints did not permit such measures, and "earth was simply hauled from the high points on the field and dumped into the low places." Aggravating the situation were holes and pits made by woodchucks, chipmunks, and other animals. Consequently, the field was precariously uneven for student pilots, and during each rain the countless small depressions in the swampy turf filled with water. (As noted in Chapter I, the Wright brothers had also complained about the rough and swampy terrain.)

The drainage problem was especially severe around the Unit Two hangars (known as the South Unit). Located at a particularly low spot between the flying field and the drainage ditch, they were directly in the path of what little natural drainage there was. Water from the flying field often ran around and through them, especially during storms.

By the middle part of 1918, about $50,000 had been spent in attempts to smooth the surface of the flying field to prevent landing accidents. Drainage was also improved in the area of the South Unit hangars, though little could be done about the overall problem.

All roads within the new reservation were laid by the Construction Division. They were composed of a mixture of sand and gravel blended with tar. During the 1917-1918 winter, however, the roads proved to be "absolutely inefficient," and gravel sidewalks disappeared altogether. In his

annual report, Major Wilbourn noted his efforts to rebuild the roads and sidewalks using screened gravel with a top covering of sand, resurfaced and rolled twice.

While the Army improved roadways inside the reservation, it was powerless to do much about off-base roads, which Major Wilbourn described as being in "horrible condition." Yet for many months Wilbur Wright Field had to rely almost entirely on its own motor transport for the hauling of all food, clothing, and supplies from Dayton and Springfield.

As bad as they were, the roads were less trouble than the railroad. The nearest steam railroad depot was at Osborn, three miles away.* Between the railroad and the Post ran an electric interurban line. It was deemed "very inefficient," since the tracks, overhead wires, and pole systems had caused fires and were in "poor condition to meet any increased demands." In addition, the company refused to carry less-than-carload shipments. Major Wilbourn noted that "since these shipments were urgently needed it was necessary to use post transportation to haul them."** State and county officials were not indifferent to the problem, however, and began work in 1918 to assure that good roads would be available to the installation at all times.

After the rapid pace of the first month, building slowed but did not stop. Between July 1917 and March 1918, cost of construction of the Signal Corps Aviation School and Wilbur Wright Field rose to $2,851,694, and a continuing series of control problems became evident.

The building program had been both massive and hurried; it was not surprising that Major Wilbourn found the quality of both materials and workmanship to be inferior. He based this judgment on the "excessive amount of time, labor and materials spent in [repairing] and maintaining the buildings at this Station from July 1, 1917, to May 31, 1918." He could find no record that the Army had ever accepted the erected buildings. Indeed, he commented that "it is not believed that any board could have accepted these

High water from the nearby Mad River flows around and through the Wilbur Wright Field hangars, May 12, 1918. Local flooding was common during the early history of the field. *(U.S. Air Force Museum)*

*Major Wilbourn makes various reference to Osborn being 1½ and 3 miles distant.

**Post transport at the time consisted of a fleet of 40 trucks, 8 touring cars (including 2 Cadillacs), 4 ambulances, 1 fire truck, and 20 motorcycles with sidecars.

Wilbur Wright Field's aerodrome, awash in 1922 spring flooding. The twelve Unit One hangars stood along what is today Skeel Avenue (Area C).

Mail call on the flightline of Wilbur Wright Field, winter 1917

FIRST FLYING SEASON

Despite Wilbur Wright Field's shortcomings, the Signal Corps Aviation School (SCAS) began operations June 28, 1917, as a function of the Technical Section of the Department of Military Aeronautics. Maj. Arthur R. Christie arrived from Ashburn Field on July 6 to assume command of the new facility.*

Two days later Wilbur Wright Field came to life with the arrival of two provisional aero squadrons of enlisted mechanics from Camp Kelly, Texas (often referred to in correspondence as Kelly Field). Capt. Leo G. Heffernan, in command of the 12th Aero Squadron, led his two lieutenants and 150 enlisted men on a three-mile march down the dusty country road from the railroad depot in nearby Osborn. The trek was repeated later in the day by Capt. Maxwell Kirk, in command of the two lieutenants and 150 enlisted men of the 13th Aero Squadron.**

On July 8, 1917, Lt. William G. Merrill and three enlisted members of the Medical Reserve Corps (MRC) arrived on post. On July 31, the 19th and 20th Aero Squadrons arrived, adding 148 and 150 men, respectively, to the number of military personnel assigned to the base. The end-of-July strength stood at approximately 800.

buildings, had any inspection been made of them in December, 1917." But six months later the Signal Corps Supply Division (as the Construction Division had been renamed) still continued the policy of putting up structures "in most cases without reference to the Commanding Officer" other than to ask him where he wanted them. The fact that the civilian supervisor of the Supply Division was "carrying on construction work with civilian labor at Government expense" without any reference—or deference—to the Post Commander was a very sensitive issue.[26] This independent action, Major Wilbourn noted, "led to great confusion and duplication of effort."

---

*Since Ashburn Field in Chicago, Illinois, was being inactivated, several officers and SJ-1 biplane trainers were transferred to the new facility.

**On October 31, 1917, the 12th and the 13th Aero Squadrons were reassigned to Garden City, Long Island, New York, and subsequently moved to France. Before the year ended the 149th, 151st, 162nd, 166th, 172nd, and 211th Aero Squadrons had been assigned temporarily to Wilbur Wright Field before moving to Europe. "Permanent party" squadrons were the 42nd, 43rd, 44th, and 47th.

MAJ. ARTHUR R. CHRISTIE

Maj. Arthur R. Christie served as the first Commanding Officer of Wilbur Wright Field, Fairfield, Ohio, arriving July 6, 1917, from Ashburn Field, Chicago, Illinois. Major Christie made the first test flight from Wilbur Wright Field on July 17, 1917. He served as Commander until September 26, 1917. Christie rose to the rank of lieutenant colonel and served as Chief of Air Service, V Corps, in the St. Mihiel offensive, during World War I.

MAJ. LEO G. HEFFERNAN

Maj. Leo G. Heffernan, U.S. Military Academy Class of 1911, was commissioned as a second lieutenant in the Cavalry. He later transferred to the Air Service and completed pilot training in September 1916. In grade of captain and as Commanding Officer, he led the 152-man 12th Aero Squadron from Kelly Field, Texas, to Wilbur Wright Field on July 8, 1917, the first organization to arrive at the new installation. In the grade of major he commanded Wilbur Wright Field from December 19 to 24, 1917. He later served as an Air Service officer with the American Expeditionary Forces (AEF) in France. Heffernan retired on disability as a major in 1933.

Military strength increased dramatically in August, both in number and in capacities represented. Among those added were members of Cadet Squadron A and the three officers and 137 enlisted men of Company K, 3rd Ohio National Guard infantry, which had been called into federal service with the National Army. By the end of August, total strength of Wilbur Wright Field had risen to 38 officers and 1,579 enlisted men. (Within a year, the monthly total would exceed 3,000.)

Despite the influx of personnel, preparation for the field's main function continued apace. In early July, several Standard SJ-1 biplane trainers were shipped to the site in freight cars, reassembled, and readied for use. On July 17, facility commander Major Christie was able to make the installation's first test flight, officially launching the military aviation history which continues today at Wright-Patterson Air Force Base.

During the first six months of operations, from mid-July to mid-December, an average of 160 students per month were enrolled in the Aviation School. Eighty-two of these were graduated with the rating of Reserve Military Aviator (RMA) and received commissions as second lieutenants in the Reserve Corps. Surviving records indicate only five discharges, and almost two hundred students continued on to other stages of training at Wilbur Wright or other installations. This record stands as an eloquent testimonial to the dedication, perseverance, and professionalism of the Wilbur Wright Field population, both military and civilian. (A significant portion of the staff were civilians employed as flying instructors, aeronautical engineers, airplane mechanics, and housekeeping craftsmen.)

(U.S. Air Force Museum)

THE FAMOUS BIPLANE TRAINERS

Many pilots who served so gallantly and flew so courageously with the Air Service, American Expeditionary Forces (AEF) in France during World War I received their primary flight training at Wilbur Wright Field. The biplane trainers most frequently used were the Curtiss JN-4D Jenny and the Standard SJ-1. These single-engine airplanes featured two open cockpits in tandem, and fabric-covered fuselages and wings.

	Curtiss JN-4D	Standard SJ-1
Wingspan	43ft 7in	43ft 10in
Length	27ft 4in	26ft 4in
Engine	90-hp, 4-cylinder	100-hp, 4-cylinder
	Curtiss OX-5	Hall-Scott A-4/A-4A
Weight	1,430 lbs	1,350 lbs
Top Speed	75 mph	72 mph
Cost	$5,465	$6,000

Sources: Air Force Pamphlet 70-7, *U.S. Air Force Historical Aircraft, Background Information*, June 1970; letter, Mr. E. E. Pennewill, Vice-President and General Manager, Standard Aircraft Corp. of Elizabeth, New Jersey, to Dept. Military Aeronautics, Technical Section, Dayton, Ohio, subj: Performance of Airplanes, September 7, 1918.

(U.S. Air Force Museum)

Railroad depot at Osborn, Ohio, where soldiers bound for Wilbur Wright Field disembarked and began their dusty march to the new installation.

Signal Corps Aviation School flying cadets stand roll call behind Wilbur Wright Field hangars, spring 1918.

Taken from an airplane in flight near Simms Station, this photograph shows a train en route from Osborn to Dayton, the Yellow Springs Pike covered bridge crossing the Mad River, and the abandoned mill at Simms Station. The Simms family 20-room home is at center, partially obscured by trees. *(Bob and Dottie Gheen)*

THE VILLAGES OF FAIRFIELD AND OSBORN, OHIO

By Dottie Grey Gheen

The creation of Wilbur Wright Field and the Fairfield Aviation General Supply Depot had a significant impact on the surrounding communities in Bath Township, Greene County, Ohio. Most directly affected were the nearby villages of Fairfield and Osborn.

Although the depot and the training schools brought new activities to the area, the concept of aviation was not new to the people of Fairfield and Osborn. Both towns were within two miles of Simms Station, where the Wright brothers had conducted their flying experiments in 1904-1905 and operated an aviation school from 1910-1916.

Simms Station was a stop on the Mad River and Lake Erie Railroad, and consisted of a warehouse-depot building, probably accompanied by a water tower. It was also a well-known local landmark. The 1855 Greene County Atlas listed it as Kneisly Station. Mr. John Kneisly owned over 1,200 acres of land in the fertile valley, and both the depot and a tiny hamlet one mile to the west on the banks of the Mad River carried his name. Following local custom, when Mr. W. A. Simms later purchased the land, the small depot became known as Simms Station.

According to firsthand accounts, the Wright brothers' flights near Simms Station became spectator events for the citizens of Fairfield and Osborn. They frequently made the short ride to Simms Station, and could even rent camp stools from an enterprising area celery farmer. Local enthusiasm for aeronautics was also undoubtedly fired by the inventiveness and determination of Mr. Charles Snyder, an Osborn inventor and flyer, who designed and built seven airplanes of his own in the years between 1905 and 1917. Residents of both Fairfield and Osborn were known to be incurably air-minded from the earliest years of the century.

The village of Fairfield dated from 1816, and stood at the crossroads of four major "pikes." By 1855, Fairfield had a population of 400 and was a well-known stop on the stage coach route. Because the town refused to allow railroads to pass through it, growth stopped in the late 1800s with the disappearance of the stage coaches.

Around 1900, Fairfield gladly allowed the new Dayton-Springfield-Urbana electric interurban rail line to pass through the center of town. It was not until World War I and the construction of Wilbur Wright Field and the adjacent depot installation, however, that the town witnessed significant growth.

The village of Osborn, located two miles north of Fairfield, dated from 1851 and was named for Mr. E. F. Osborn, a local railway superintendent. By 1874, according to the Greene County Atlas, Osborn counted 700 residents, the largest town in Bath Township. By 1900, two railroads and the electric interurban serviced Osborn, and the town boasted three mills, a buggy whip factory, an egg case factory, two banks, four churches, and its own water and electric plants.

The 1913 Miami Valley flood, however, changed the course of Osborn history. The flood itself did limited damage to Osborn, but it devastated Dayton and communities to the south. Within two years, the Miami Conservancy District was formed to prevent a recurrence of the disaster, and consequently proposed that five earthen dams be built, including one across the Mad River just south of Osborn.

Intersection of Dayton Street and Xenia Pike in Fairfield, about 1900. Today, Broad Street and Xenia Drive in Fairborn intersect at this location. *(Bob and Dottie Gheen)*

Exercising the right of eminent domain, by 1919 the Conservancy District had purchased all of the land in the flood plain above the proposed dam, including the entire town of Osborn. The railroads and interurban line relocated, the three mills closed, and newspaper headlines of the day proclaimed that "THE TOWN OF OSBORN [WAS] DOOMED." These gloomy predictions failed to take into account the spirit of Osborn residents unwilling to see their town die.

Without financial help from any government agency, the people of Osborn conceived, formed, and financed The Osborn Removal Company. The Removal Company bought back all the buildings in Osborn from the Conservancy District, and purchased a new site for them in a pocket of land bounded by the relocated railroad, the interurban line, and Hebble Creek, adjacent to the village of Fairfield. Over a period of three years, Osborn citizens moved their entire town—approximately 400 buildings—to the new location. The planning, engineering, and financing involved in the project were unprecedented in the nation, and the unfolding effort was reported in national newsreels and magazines.

Meanwhile, America entered World War I, and Fairfield and Osborn soon had new military neighbors. A relationship of cooperation and mutual support developed between the military posts and the two towns. The villages supplied workers, horses, machinery, and supplies to help construct the new flying school and depot. In the years following the war, it was common for officers stationed at the installations to make their homes off base and to play active roles in community affairs. Military families of both installations sent their children to local schools and attended local churches.

On the other hand, the military bases provided employment. Throughout the 1920s and 1930s, the work forces at Wilbur Wright Field and the Fairfield depot (and later Wright and Patterson Fields) were predominantly comprised of civil service employees, furnishing hundreds of local families with weekly paychecks.

Early newspapers such as the *Bath Township Herald and Mad River Valley Journal* and the *Wilbur Wright Exhaust* documented the close relationship that existed between the military and civilian communities. A regular column in the Herald was devoted to activities at Wilbur Wright Field, and the society column covered the social doings of both on-base and community citizens. Local residents attended dances, movies, and other activities on base, and formed a wide range of organizations and clubs.

During World War II, as the base grew, so did the surrounding communities. Combined civil service employment for both Wright Field and Patterson Field soared to nearly 50,000 at the height of the war. Local communities faced the challenge of providing housing and services for the ballooning work force, and

local companies, such as the two cement plants, supplied increasing amounts of business and construction materials.

By the end of World War II, the identities of the small villages of Fairfield and Osborn had largely disappeared, and a much larger, forward-looking community stood in their stead. As a sign of the future, on January 1, 1950, the towns of Fairfield and Osborn officially merged to form the City of Fairborn, Ohio, Wright-Patterson's present-day partner in progress.

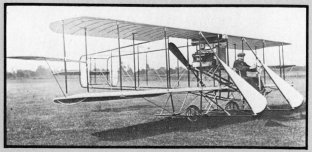

Local sources indicate that Mr. Charles Snyder of Osborn, Ohio, designed and built seven airplanes of his own invention in the years between 1905 and 1917. He incorporated the Snyder Aeroplane Company in 1911. One airplane was produced, but Mr. Snyder's inability to collect payment from the buyer caused the company to fail financially. Mr. Snyder is pictured here about 1910. Each of his airplanes incorporated a control wheel, a single direct-drive propeller, and landing wheels with brakes. *(Bob and Dottie Gheen)*

Balloon enthusiasts Fred Woodall of Dayton and Mr. McGill, an Osborn newspaperman, made double parachute drops from balloons as early as 1910. This sensational livelihood netted them as much as $500 per drop when business was good. This drop was made over downtown Osborn in 1911. *(A. F. Woodall, former Wright Field employee)*

Business district of old Osborn, about 1920 *(Bob and Dottie Gheen)*

The Osborn Removal Company was formed to move the old town of Osborn to its new location adjacent to the village of Fairfield. Approximately 200 houses and another 200 outbuildings were moved between 1922 and 1925. Here a home is being transferred onto its new foundation. *(Bob and Dottie Gheen)*

The overall effort of the "flying instruction department" was one of the few functions praised in Major Wilbourn's annual report. This sense of purpose was the real legacy of Huffman Prairie and has remained the heritage of each succeeding installation.

The flying instruction was carried out in two basic aircraft at Wilbur Wright Field and other Signal Corps Aviation Schools. These were the Curtiss Aeroplane Company's JN-4D Jenny, powered by the 90-hp Curtiss OX-5 engine, and the Standard Aircraft Corporation's SJ-1, powered by 100-hp Hall-Scott A-7 and A-7A engines. Both were single-engine biplane trainers, with two open cockpits mounted in tandem.

The Jenny evolved through the cross-breeding of an English aircraft designed by B. D. Thomas, known as Model J, with a Glenn Curtiss American design, Model N. The offspring was naturally christened "JN." The most common model of the series was the JN-4D.

The Jenny was much easier to fly than the SJ-1, and therefore saw heavier use (6,000 JN-4Ds were built by the end of 1918, as opposed to 1,601 SJ-1s). According to one historian, about 90 percent of all World War I American pilots earned their wings in this airplane. After the war ended, hundreds of these Jennys became the mainstay "barnstormer" of the 1920s. Dozens of the airplanes were still being flown in the 1930s from pastures, fairgrounds, race tracks, and other flat (but not necessarily smooth) surfaces. Many a World War II pilot got his first taste of flying as a youngster with a five-minute flight for one dollar in a Jenny that circled a local pasture at minimum altitude.

Although he praised the instructional aspects of the flying program, Major Wilbourn found that the condition of the associated records varied from haphazard to disastrous. Two weeks after the flying season ended for the year, he was unable to determine how many airplanes had been assigned on station since July or how much logistical support had been provided. The records of the Supply Department were "in a most chaotic condition" and the accounts of the Engineering Division, which he described as providing the "whole fabric of maintenance and operation of the field," were incomplete. Fortunately, enough records had been maintained to indicate the amount of flight instruction which had been given and supported during that first season. This information is summarized in the accompanying table. In total, the SCAS graduated 82 RMAs and logged 5,298 hours and 27 minutes of flight time with the loss of only 17 aircraft. At least 85 JN-4Ds and 32 SJ-1s arrived on station, and 46 Curtiss and 32 Standards were subsequently shipped to other primary bases.

Airplane gasoline consumption was 88,036 gallons; oil usage was 1,900 gallons. Operating expenses totalled $310,000 including local purchases of aviation gasoline and oil, machinery, tools, airplane spare parts, office supplies and equipment, and other items.

On December 1, the Signal Corps Aviation Section directed that flying instruction activities be transferred from Wilbur Wright Field to more "Southern stations" for the duration of the 1917-1918 winter.[27] Five of these primary training fields in the "sunshine belt" were located in Texas (Barron, Carruthers, Kelly, Love, and Taliaferro), and others were scattered through Arkansas, Tennessee, Georgia, and Alabama.[28]

By December 15, all flying activity ceased. In place of training pilots, the Wilbur Wright Field facilities were pre-

WILBUR WRIGHT FIELD SIGNAL CORPS AVIATION SCHOOL

Flying Season 1917	JUL	AUG	SEP	OCT	NOV	DEC
Total Instructors, Military and Civilian	10	20	22	26	28	27
Total Flying Cadets	19	169	165	168	148	127
Graduated RMA; Commissioned	0	9	16	28	20	9
Transferred	0	0	12	28	21	116
Discharged	0	1	0	0	2	2
Total Flying Time	58 hrs 17 min	628 hrs 22 min	1496 hrs 3 min	1386 hrs 5 min	1466 hrs 59 min	262 hrs 41 min
Total Airplanes in Commission on Average	N/A	17 JN-4D 16 SJ-1	10 JN-4D 7 SJ-1	11 JN-4D 6 SJ-1	12 JN-4D 11 SJ-1	26 JN-4D 9 SJ-1
Total Accidents	1	2	0	6	3	2
Fatalities	0	1*	0	0	0	0
Destroyed Airplanes	1	2	8	6	0	0
Period for which data is missing	2 weeks (season opened)	4 days	1 week	1 week	none missing	2 weeks (season ended)

*One enlisted man was killed when struck by a propeller.

pared for use as a temporary school for mechanics and a permanent school for armorers. This respite in flying also provided the SCAS Commandant with an opportunity to strengthen a rather shaky organizational structure.

A "MAJOR" REORGANIZATION

During the first six months of operation, Wilbur Wright Field had five Commanders:

Maj. Arthur R. Christie	Jul 6-Sep 26, 1917
Lt. Col. George M. Bomford	Sep 27-Dec 19, 1917
Maj. Leo G. Heffernan	Dec 19-24, 1917
Maj. Walter R. Weaver	Dec 24-29, 1917
Maj. Arthur E. Wilbourn	Dec 30, 1917-Jun 28, 1918

Major Wilbourn, who served as Commander for the first six months of 1918, was not perceived in a favorable light by his peers, one of whom was Major Heffernan. As a captain, Heffernan had led the first enlisted men onto the post. As a major, he had preceded Wilbourn as Commander of the post for one week in December. He had therefore spent more time at the young installation than almost any other officer, and he kept a diary of his experiences. He noted that Major Wilbourn was "a very officious type of officer and cordially disliked by all who knew him in the Air Service. He didn't last long in the game, chiefly because he could not be taken up in a plane."[29]

Though he apparently had no desire to fly—even as a passenger—Wilbourn appears to have had a good head for management and a strong hand for organization. He left an excellently-detailed annual report dated May 31, 1918, which covered operations from the installation's inception. Though highly critical of the poor state of affairs he found upon assuming command, he detailed both the situations and the remedial actions he directed. They were sometimes drastic, and therefore would have been considered unpopular, but they were effective. By May 31, 1918, the function was much improved.

Major Wilbourn gave praise sparingly, but did give it where it was due. His chief satisfactions apparently came from the "flying instruction department" and the medical corps. He praised the organization and conduct of these functions and attributed the bulk of their difficulties to outside forces. Other agencies did not fare so well at his hands, and his attention was focused sharply on internal problems.

Two departments in particular required various degrees of remedial action: Engineering and Supply. "The heart of Wilbur Wright Field," its Commanding Officer declared, was the Engineering Department. "Upon [it] depends the whole fabric of maintenance and operation of the field."[30] Yet he was clearly dismayed by the conduct of the department.

To begin with, Engineering had charge of a large span of operations in 1917-1918. To cover the same duty in the 1980s would require several separate organizations, including civil engineering, airplane field maintenance, organizational maintenance, and an aircraft engine training school.

Civil engineering functions encompassed many of the same responsibilities handled by today's civil engineers, including surveying, cartography, drafting, utilities (lighting, water, and sewage), steam and emergency electrical power, and maintenance of roads and grounds, ranging from streets to flower beds.

A major responsibility in 1917 was repair and maintenance of buildings. Major Wilbourn cited shoddy workmanship, inferior materials, and haste of the construction effort as the chief sources of the engineers' problems and declared that a large amount of unnecessary work was being done "due to the careless, if not worse, way in which work was, and is being done, on the Post." Better quality control and closer supervision during initial construction would have obviated a significant portion of the repair, replacement, and maintenance costs he was forced to assume. Compounding the problem was the "constant friction between the enlisted workmen and those furnished by the Construction Company" over the question of who was to pay for the materials and labor necessary to correct the defects.

Another principal area of responsibility of the Engineering Department was the procurement and support of the aircraft used for training by the SCAS. Major Wilbourn defined the Division's responsibilities:[31]

> It is required to secure sufficient ships; to assemble them and keep them in proper repair; supply them with fuel and lubricants; record the performance of all motors, propellers, planes etc., to care for and replace broken parts; secure and return wrecks.

Wire and metal work shop, Wilbur Wright Field, January 18, 1918. Fuselages are Curtiss JN-4D Jenny two-place biplane trainers flown by Signal Corps Aviation School instructor pilots and flying cadets.

Motor machine shop, Wilbur Wright Field, January 29, 1918. Building 252 on Allbrook Drive (Area C) now stands on the site of this shop.

Propeller repair department, Wilbur Wright Field, 1918

In order to carry out these duties, moreover, the Engineering Department had to train its own airplane engine mechanics, beginning with a "trade test" of enlisted men to determine their "trade fitness" for this new occupation.

Histories and maintenance records of individual airplanes had not been kept during the six-month flying season. Consequently, the Engineering Department could not determine the quality or quantity of work performed; even the "in-commission" rates of aircraft quoted earlier in this chapter were reconstructed after the fact by flying instruction staff from incomplete monthly records.

As far as can be determined, there were several areas that caused continuing maintenance problems. One, for example, was excessive failure of propeller blades. Shortages of propeller hubs compounded this situation and nearly forced cancellation of all flying in September until new parts arrived. When the second flying season opened on April 15, 1918, the problems remained unsolved and plagued the mechanics throughout the spring.

Serious difficulties also arose with the OX-5 engine in 12 JN-4Ds. At the time Major Wilbourn was finishing his report in May, airplane mechanics were struggling with leaking exhaust valves in the OX-5 power plant. Apparently an excessive carbon content in the valves made them too hard, or the valve seats in the motors were so soft that the valves hammered the metal away. Regardless of the primary cause, Major Wilbourn felt the problem indicated that "the assemblers of the motors [in the factory] . . . failed to seat the valves properly."

Valves and propellers were not the only parts beset by manufacturing defects. Airplanes arriving from the Curtiss Company's Canadian plants were found to be poorly assembled. The quality of dope and methods of application were "inferior to a degree" that required shipping 13 of the JN-4Ds to the Aviation Repair Depot at Indianapolis, Indiana. The Depot had to re-dope practically the entire fabric of wings, fuselages, and tails. At the end of May, the Engineering Department fully expected "upwards of 20" more airplanes to arrive from the factory in similar condition.

Major Wilbourn was also highly displeased with "the most chaotic condition" of the Supply Department. All

Military airplane mechanics balance propellers at Wilbur Wright Field, January 20, 1918. Holes punched in the wood blades were filled with solder to balance them.

1917 records were in "very bad shape," especially those pertaining to property accountability. Large numbers of vouchers were missing and dozens of invoices sent by the Supply Department were never returned. No vigorous efforts had been made by the department to prepare Reports of Survey for missing property. Moreover, attempts of the Supply Officer during the first three months of 1918 to correct the deficiencies and discrepancies proved futile. Major Wilbourn's remedy was simple. The Supply Officer was summarily relieved. A board of disinterested officers was appointed to survey all Signal Corps property on Wilbur Wright Field.

The Quartermaster Department, established in early June 1917, also had its share of problems in each of its five elements (administrative, finance, supply, transportation, and reclamation). For example, the administrative division operated for nearly a year without Quartermaster Corps-qualified administrative enlisted men. Signal Corps soldiers, unfamiliar with Quartermaster regulations, policies, and procedures, had been pressed into service as interim substitutes. It was not until March and April 1918 that 32 QMC-qualified enlisted men arrived on station.

The finance and accounting branch had been concerned solely with paying minor accounts in the local area. Officer and enlisted payrolls had been handled directly by the Office of the Department Quartermaster, Central Department, Chicago, Illinois. However, in December, the Central Department directed the local branch to pay all military personnel at both Wilbur Wright Field and at McCook Field (a Signal Corps airplane experimental testing facility established in late 1917 near downtown Dayton). It was, in addition, to pay the "expense accounts" of all Signal Corps civilian employees in Dayton. Monthly disbursements jumped from $1,146.70 in October to $168,652.48 the following May. Total disbursements during that period reached $622,024.40.

In the Quartermaster area of supplies, a limited number of records (which were not always complete even when posted) and personal interviews convinced Major Wilbourn that the Quartermaster Department had made "no attempt . . . to provide an adequate supply" of food, clothing, and incidental supplies during 1917. For example, from June through December individual squadrons had maintained their own messes (dining halls). Each organization had purchased fresh produce and meat from local area markets, and made daily runs in its own trucks.

In January 1918, a sales commissary was established. Individual purchases were consolidated into one system, thereby economizing on vehicle usage and achieving savings on bulk sales. The Wilbur Wright Field Quartermaster negotiated with local contractors for all fresh meat and vegetables. Wilbourn was satisfied that the quality of the meat furnished was excellent and the prices were good.

A further consolidation freed the installation of dependence on area bakers. Until March, all bread and pastries for the post were purchased from Dayton commercial bakeries. On March 25, "field oven number one" began operations. It had a capacity of 216 pounds of bread per run, and during the first three weeks produced 91,708 pounds of bread from 65,935 pounds of flour. In addition to filling Wilbur Wright Field's needs, sales were made to McCook Field and other Army installations in the Dayton area. This reorganization in particular helped put the commissary into the black. Between January 1 and May 31, commissary sales to all Army organizations in the Dayton area totaled $57,034.

In the area of clothing supplies, records indicate that 19,904 items of clothing were issued at Wilbur Wright Field from October through May. These included overcoats, cotton and wool coats, cotton and wool breeches, slickers (raincoats), hats, shirts, shoes, and "leggins."

A Reclamation Division was organized in March that both saved resources and earned money. Provisions were made to clean and repair or salvage clothing and shoes. The shoe repair function was well used, mending 1,207 pairs by the end of May. Other reclamation and resale efforts resulted in a positive cash flow of $608.15 in the same period.

Thus, by the end of May 1918, the Quartermaster Department was at least functional in each of its areas of responsibility.

Another essential area of Post activity was the Medical Department. Major Wilbourn gave it good marks. In fact, he was gratified that the deplorably unsanitary environment that existed at the Post had not generated an epidemic of some sort.

Wilbourn based his opinion on the ambient conditions when he assumed command, plus information gleaned from discussions with the Post Surgeon and other officers. He noted that large numbers of civilian construction employees and their families lived on the base in flimsy shacks of scrap materials. These "squatter camps," filled with men, women, and children, existed in the most primitive and squalid conditions imaginable, violating all essential laws of sanitation.

For example, open shallow-pit latrines lay within a few feet of living quarters. Food was exposed to flies and dust. Garbage was strewn on the grounds around the shacks. Military protests to employing contractors were dismissed with the excuse that any interference with the laborers' lifestyle could result in work stoppages.

The contractors themselves added to the filthy conditions by digging additional open-pit privies all over the Post for the laborers. The facilities were not screened, were seldom cleaned, and contaminated the wells that provided water for the Post, so that large amounts of chlorine had to be added before use.

Clouds of flies swarmed in all buildings throughout the field. The Post Surgeon, Maj. Alfred G. Farmer, stated that throughout his long experience in military sanitation he had never seen as many flies in a given area as those that infested Wilbur Wright Field. Adding to the lure of the piles of garbage and the open-pit toilets were huge piles of manure generated by the several hundred teams of horses and mules used in heavy construction work.

The animals were stabled in an exceedingly unsanitary corral along the field's main road. The lot was rarely policed—and never thoroughly cleaned. Major Wilbourn reported that manure was thrown on the ground in front of stalls where it accumulated to such a volume that in the 1918 spring clean-up several tons of dung were removed and burned.

Other significant contributors to the clouds of flies were, in Major Wilbourn's opinion, the "unsanitary Village of Fairfield, Ohio," which adjoined the Post, as well as several nearby farms.

As necessary steps were taken on Wilbur Wright Field to establish a healthy environment, Ohio health authorities worked to improve the general sanitary conditions in the surrounding district. By the end of May, Major Wilbourn noted that the water tests indicated chlorination was no longer necessary. He considered the Post to be in excellent sanitary condition, and the problems in the surrounding area much improved.

Despite the sanitation problems, the death rate from disease was exceptionally low. Major Wilbourn credited this to the efforts of the Medical Department, headed by Major Farmer, the Post Surgeon. On his arrival on July 16, 1917, Major Farmer had assumed command of a staff of four. The initial staff had to cope as best they could without

The Unit One hospital at Wilbur Wright Field was constructed in 1917 and expanded in 1918. Though built as a temporary structure, this and other buildings throughout the installation remained in use for a number of years.

a permanent facility; the first hospital building, one of the last on Post to be completed, was not ready until August 21.

In the meantime, on July 18, a tent was used as an isolation center when the first illness requiring hospitalization proved to be the highly-communicable scarlet fever. Since the weather was mild, the only hardship this entailed was an immediate search for a bed net to fend off flies.

Until December 21, 1917, the installation was practically free of communicable disease. On that date some squadrons arrived from Texas bases bringing ailments such as measles, mumps, and scarlet fever. The two buildings then in use as hospital facilities were soon overwhelmed, underscoring a need for additional capacity. By March an addition to the Unit One hospital building was completed and brought total beds available to 89.

In all, by May 31, 1918, the Medical Department had treated 1,873 cases. Of these, only six resulted in death: three from illness and three from accident, including the one flying mishap noted earlier. Fortunately, Wilbur Wright Field had escaped the more serious complications of measles, such as pneumonia, which resulted in high death rates at other bases. The medical staff by mid-1918 included 14 physicians and dentists, 11 commissioned nurses, and 63 enlisted men.

By mid-1918 the domestic service "utility" functions of the field were also nearing satisfactory levels of operation. As mentioned, sanitation problems connected with the large temporary work force, such as insects and impure water, had been addressed. Three driven wells were producing 340,000 gallons of pure water daily. The sewage system was nearing satisfactory function. In addition, the Dayton Power and Light Company was meeting the Post's monthly power requirement for 660 kilowatts of electricity.

A new telephone system was completed, giving Wilbur Wright Field and adjacent Fairfield Aviation General Supply

Nurses at Wilbur Wright Field, 1918.

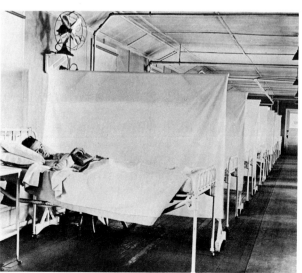

A young soldier at Wilbur Wright Field receives treatment in the post hospital.

Depot 229 instruments.* Calls averaged 5,200 a day. Fortunately for the success of the cross-country flying program, the surrounding rural districts were fairly well covered with telephone nets, according to Major Wilbourn, and thus provided quick notifications of all landings, forced or otherwise. A fairly common occurrence was a call from a chagrined pilot on his first cross-country flight who had gotten lost and run out of gas.

AVIATION MECHANICS' SCHOOL

While Major Wilbourn was addressing his internal problems, he had also to attend to his role as host for two essential Signal Corps activities that began at Wilbur Wright Field in the non-flying winter months from mid-December until April.

The first of these to be organized at the field was an Aviation Mechanics' School. According to Allied manning experience in Europe, each combat-ready airplane required the support of 47 ground-force personnel, including officers and enlisted men in engineering, supply, administration, maintenance, etc. The largest single category of these supporters was "aviation mechanicians," who carried the enlisted ranks of:

MSE (master signal electrician, which would equate roughly to the modern rank of master sergeant, or E-7, in charge of squadron airplane maintenance)

Sergeant First Class (E-6)

Sergeant (E-4)

Corporal (E-3)

Private (E-1)

Experienced aviation mechanics were in short supply after war was declared in April 1917. The few that existed outside of the military were already working for unprecedented wages in the civilian war effort. Experienced motor vehicle mechanics were generally in greater supply, but by fall most of them were also occupied by the war effort, either in the Army or in civilian support functions.

By November 1917, the Aviation Section was in critical need of both types of mechanics. As a result, on November 1 the War Department directed that 5,000 mechanics be transferred immediately from the National Army to the Aviation Section.[32] The problem then became one of transferring these mechanics' skills to the new area of aviation. This was handled through both short- and long-range program objectives.

Two programs were set to provide short-term results. One effort established short-term training schools at the five northern flying installations (Wilbur Wright Field, Chanute, Scott, Selfridge, and Hazelhurst), during the winter months when flying instruction was impossible. The other effort involved private industry. In industrial communities such as Dayton, selected airplane and engine factories and garages were asked to open their facilities to groups of 25 soldier-students for on-the-job training. Nearly a score of companies willingly inconvenienced themselves in this way, providing training for about 2,000 men.

Instructors for the five temporary schools came from both outside and inside the Army. Private companies were canvassed for experienced foremen who could add their technical competence and supervisory skills to the ranks of Signal Corps instructors. A special evaluation board selected 60 foremen for such service. Of these, 17 were commissioned as first and second lieutenants, 48 joined the enlisted ranks from corporal to MSE, and 5 accepted lower-grade duty. After three weeks of training at Selfridge Field in December, they were distributed to the new schools in January as instructors in such specialties as "woods, propellers, wing repair, fabrics, wire work, soldering, tires, alignment, fuselage, motors, and motor transport."[33]

Within the Aviation Section, the more highly skilled mechanics were tapped to serve as instructors. This was particularly necessary in the interim period between the opening of the schools and the arrival of the newly-oriented instructors from Selfridge Field.

The situation at Wilbur Wright Field was typical. The aviation mechanics' school opened December 17 in the twelve Unit One hangars which had been used for flying instruction. In command of the school was Maj. W. R. Weaver, assisted by Mr. R. E. Dunn, a civilian who also served as chief of motor transport instruction. The 42nd and 44th Aero Squadrons, permanently assigned to Wilbur Wright Field, provided base operating services to the school. Students had arrived from various midwest airfields on temporary duty from 20 aero squadrons: 42nd, 44th, 47th, 149th, 151st, 159th, 162nd, 163rd, 166th, 167th, 172nd, 211th, 255th, 256th, 257th, 258th, 259th, 260th, 265th, and the 827th.

Instructors and students at Wilbur Wright Field Aviation Mechanics' School pose behind the hangar they used as a classroom. During 1918, the school graduated 1,181 enlisted men. (*U.S. Air Force Museum*)

---

*See Chapter III for coverage of the Fairfield Aviation General Supply Depot. The depot supported aviation schools at Wilbur Wright Field and at other installations in Illinois and Michigan.

Classes were scheduled to begin on December 17 in three subject areas (airplane, airplane motor, and motor transport), but the instructors from Selfridge Field had not arrived by that date. In the interim, a faculty of 70 was drawn from the sharpest of the enlisted mechanics of the 42nd and 44th Aero Squadrons.

Early in January 1918, the faculty was augmented by the arrival of two second lieutenants and 18 recent graduates of the Instructors' School at Selfridge Field. The instruction staff continued to draw heavily for the duration of the school from the ranks of the two permanent squadrons.

The school faced continuing challenges. Besides the late arrival of Selfridge instructors, equipment had also been tardy. An epidemic of measles periodically forced entire squadrons into quarantine. Forty-eight inches of snow necessitated that all hands fall out on frequent occasion to keep roads open for essential supplies. Teaching continuity suffered; only 62 percent of the available working days were devoted to actual instruction.

Perhaps the most serious handicap faced by instructors related to the skill levels of incoming students and their potentialities (or lack thereof). In theory, all recruits were screened for trade skills at the time of induction into the Army and only those with significant mechanical aptitude were qualified for assignment in mechanical fields. However, experience showed that a significant number of draftees at the time were functionally illiterate in written English, and their oral English was limited to simple conversation. Many had arrived in this country in the arms of immigrant parents at the beginning of the new century and had used their parents' native tongue almost exclusively while growing up. Instructing them in technical matters was difficult.

Major Wilbourn also considered that the three-week courses of instruction were designed to further the knowledge of those already proficient in their trades. As it was, the staff frequently encountered students who had no former experience and no knowledge of the occupations or skills in which they were classified; they had to be instructed "from the ground up."

Nonetheless, by its April 7, 1918 closure, the mechanics' training school had 1,181 graduates: 182 in airplane motor, 386 in airplane, and 613 in motor transport courses of instruction.

The school had also produced 85 instructors. Even as the school was operating, 45 instructors were transferred to duty with other training installations. Once the Wilbur Wright school closed, 58 more were similarly reassigned. Thus a total of 103 instructors were transferred out of the school. Since only eighteen instructors had been sent to the station to begin with, this meant that "a total of eighty-five enlisted men were withdrawn from the permanent squadrons at this Station for [instructional] duty elsewhere." Major Wilbourn termed them "the very best . . . airplane and motor repair men" on post. Their loss was felt markedly in the ongoing operation of the flying school while their recently-graduated replacements gained experience and competence. By the end of May, however, Major Wilbourn

acknowledged that it was "to the very best interests of the service to cripple the flying school temporarily in order that the quality of our enlisted mechanics in general may be improved."[34]

The training school for aviation mechanics at Wilbur Wright Field contributed significantly to the overall effort of the Air Service. Its 1,181 graduates joined 1,482 more from the other four northern flying fields. Together they formed the vanguard of the 10,000 aviation mechanics trained by May 1, 1918, and provided a valuable baseline experience for the instructional heritage of the Air Service.

Instructor and students of the Mechanics' School examine a training airplane fuselage in the erection and repair shop, January 25, 1918. *(U.S. Air Force Museum)*

After a 48-hour continuous run on a test stand at Wilbur Wright Field in 1918, a 90-hp Curtiss OX-5 engine is removed for subsequent examination of all its components. This 4-cylinder engine powered the Curtiss JN-4D Jenny primary trainer.

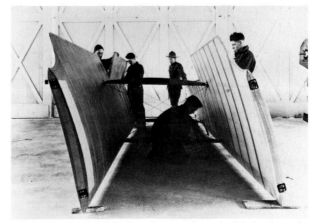

Aviation Mechanics' School students work on the fabric wings of a Curtiss JN-4D trainer.

AVIATION ARMORERS' SCHOOL

A second area of combat operations that achieved increasing importance as the war progressed in Europe was armament.

At the outbreak of the war airplanes were unarmed, although pilots occasionally traded pistol shots. The German Fokker revolutionized offensive tactics with a machine gun mounted and synchronized to fire 500 bullets a minute between the blades of the propeller. Bombs were soon added to offensive aerial strategy. These new concepts in warfare precipitated new requirements in equipment, in the training of pilots, and in support functions such as armament.

As the Allied response developed, each aero squadron needed an armament officer and a score of men to examine aerial armament before and after every flight. This involved inspecting, testing, and tuning all weapons, and ensuring that both machine guns and bombs were in working order. It was a critical responsibility, for according to a contemporary World War I source, "Scores of good aviators [were] killed by reason of guns jamming just at the critical moment."[35]

Two facets of the armament function were assigned to Wilbur Wright Field. The first was testing of all machine guns issued to the Aviation Section to ensure that they were properly adjusted and in good firing condition. The second was an armorer training school to produce new armament officers and their enlisted assistants. Both functions were scheduled to gear up for operation in March 1918, using Unit Two hangars.

In preparation, a central school for both officer and enlisted instructors opened on February 4, 1918, at Ellington Field, Houston, Texas. The curriculum concentrated on mechanism and construction rather than on actual use of bombs and machine guns. Aspects of stripping, care, cleaning, causes of stoppage, loading, and testing were emphasized as important elements of the new career field.

At the conclusion of their training at Ellington, 200 of the armorers transferred to Wilbur Wright Field as the 851st Aero Repair Squadron. On March 18, the Armorers' School opened for final indoctrination of the officers and enlisted men who formed the school's faculty and staff. The course of instruction was fixed at six weeks and covered a complete study of machine guns, their sights and synchronization mechanisms, and the storage and mounting of bombs.

Meanwhile small detachments filtered in, fresh from factory training at the Marlin-Rockwell Company, New Haven, Connecticut, and the Savage Arms Corporation, Utica, New York. Together with the 96 officers and 560 enlisted men who reported as students on April 13 and 20, respectively, they formed the 874th Aero Repair Squadron. Completing the armament network was the 231st Aero Repair Squadron, which reported on April 22 from Ellington Field.

The Armorers' School was organized under authority of the Signal Corps Air Division Gunnery Section and oper-

ated under the command of Maj. A. H. Hobley. It operated continuously from March 18 until the conversion of effort at war's end.

In April and May alone, the school hosted 95 officer and 789 enlisted students. The first class graduated June 6, with all 95 officers graduating. The enlisted program graduated 485 out of 560, reflecting the same language and trade proficiency problems that had surfaced in the Mechanics' School.

The gunnery testing function began May 1. Initially 100 Lewis and 100 Marlin machine guns were inspected and tested each day. As operations hit stride, the capacity increased to 100 Lewis and 200 Marlin guns per day.

A portion of the Aviation Armorers' School hangars at Wilbur Wright Field (*Wright State University Archives*)

Curtiss JN-4D Jenny primary trainer in flight over hangars of the Aviation Armorers' School and armament testing station, Wilbur Wright Field, 1918

Lieutenants Mathis, Keenan, Rubin, and Skinner were instructors in the Aviation Armorers' School, Wilbur Wright Field, which operated from March 1918 to February 1919.

TESTING

The gunnery program was not the first military testing function at Wilbur Wright Field. Airplane testing was inaugurated by a March 1, 1918, request from McCook Field to provide hangar space for experimental flying. McCook Field operated under the Airplane Engineering Department of the Signal Corps Equipment Division. Established October 4, 1917, it was located near downtown Dayton about 10 miles by road from Wilbur Wright Field.

McCook's mission was to research, develop, test, and evaluate U.S. military aircraft and, occasionally, to test airplanes designed or manufactured by Allied nations. Although McCook had its own flying field, space was limited. From McCook's inception, it was understood that a certain amount of both hangar space and maintenance support might be available from Wilbur Wright Field.*

The first such request was in conjunction with the brief testing of three Italian airplanes: one SVA single-place "Scout," one Pomilio two-place fighter with a Fiat engine, and one SIA two-place fighter with a Fiat engine. The airplanes' arrival on March 19, 1918, marked the debut of the facility as a test site for modern military aviation.

The initial tests were not of great moment, since both the Pomilio and the SIA had been badly damaged while enroute in crates from Italy. The SVA was in comparatively good condition, however, and underwent several weeks of flight testing by an Italian air force pilot. After the Pomilio's fuselage had been repaired, it, too, was successfully flown for several weeks of tests. Upon conclusion of testing at the beginning of May, the airplanes were disassembled and returned to Italy.

By that time, testing aspects of three other McCook programs had been moved to Wilbur Wright. The first of these began and ended on the same day. An American Morse pursuit [fighter] airplane, equipped with a small

Liberty 8-cylinder engine, was trucked from McCook and assembled for testing. On March 28, the first test flight ended abruptly when the airplane crashed from a height of about 50 feet and was destroyed.

Another short-term effort was more productive. On May 15, a French LePere pursuit equipped with a Liberty engine arrived for a series of tests that were to be conducted by three French pilots. At the time of Major Wilbourn's May 31 annual report, the airplane had flown almost daily.

This Italian Air Force SVA (Societa Verduzio Ansaldo) with U.S. Army Air Service markings was tested at Wilbur Wright Field in 1918 by McCook Field aeronautical engineers. This model was the Italian Army's outstanding fighter of World War I. (*U.S. Air Force Museum*)

Specifications of the Curtiss NBS-1 biplane, twin-engine bomber tested by the McCook Field Engineering Division at Wilbur Wright Field

*More details on McCook Field's mission may be found in the specific coverage of McCook in Chapter IV.

A longer-range program began April 20 when Wilbur Wright Field agreed to furnish McCook with accommodations and limited logistical support for eight airplanes, including British DeHavilland DH-4 reconnaissance and Bristol pursuit aircraft. The support included not only hangar and shop space, but also a force of enlisted mechanics to both assemble and maintain the airplanes, particularly the engines.

For its part, McCook Field agreed to furnish two Liberty engines and two instructors to assist in training Wilbur Wright Field mechanics. McCook also promised to provide time on the DH-4 airplanes being tested in order to upgrade Wilbur Wright Field pilots for this new type of airplane.

By April 24, one DH-4 and one Bristol fighter had arrived. The career of the Bristol fighter was brief; it crashed and was destroyed May 7. The DH-4 enjoyed more success, and was soon joined by seven more DH-4s manufactured by the Dayton-Wright Airplane Company south of Dayton. To support these aircraft, 40 to 50 enlisted mechanics received 20 days of on-the-job training on the Liberty engine. Despite the fact that McCook did not follow through in setting aside a DH-4 specifically for upgrading Wilbur Wright pilots, by the end of May at least 45 pilots had gained considerable experience in handling the new airplane. Moreover, every engineering officer on station had taken personal initiative to study the structure of both the DH-4 and its engine.

SPRING FLYING

Airplanes, cadets, and instructors migrated northward from southern "winter quarters" with the advent of spring. As the flying instruction program reorganized at Wilbur Wright Field, it was discovered that only six of the 18 Reserve Military Aviators sent to serve as instructors had flown more than 50 hours themselves. The remaining 12 needed special accelerated instructors' training before joining the staff. In the meantime, pilot training resumed on April 15, 1918, utilizing the six already-qualified instructors.

Students and instructors alike faced hazardous field conditions. In late March, a contractor had begun smoothing and seeding the turf of the flying field (there being no hard-surfaced runways), but work was not finished by the time flight training resumed. Consequently, large numbers of laborers with assorted equipment were constantly on the field, providing daily hazards for students.

To work around these conditions the cadets were divided into two groups so that while one group spent the morning in class, the other was on the flightline, with reversed schedules in the afternoon.* This kept the number of cadets on the flying field at a manageable level. At first the flying field was divided into two sectors, one for dual

control flights and one for solos. This proved impractical. A more efficient and, most likely, safer plan was adopted in which the entire field was devoted to dual instruction in the morning and solo instruction in the afternoon, with a small portion of the field permanently set aside for cross-country flying and radio airplanes.

By May 31, the faculty had increased to 25 instructors and there were 180 cadets in various stages of instruction. They flew a cumulative average of 66.6 hours per day, with an average of 22.5 airplanes in commission. One cadet had graduated as a Reserve Military Aviator, 16 were ready to graduate, two had been discharged because of flying deficiencies, and the school had suffered its first flying fatality when one cadet died in a crash.

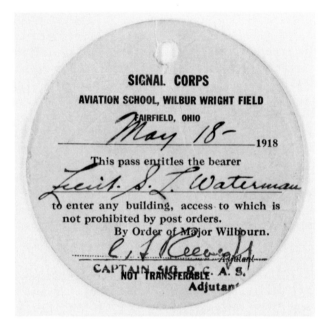

General passes such as this one permitted the bearer to enter nearly all facilities of the Signal Corps Aviation School at Wilbur Wright Field.

Life was not all work and no play at Wilbur Wright Field. Shown are members of the Wilbur Wright football team, 1917-1918.

---

*The academic curriculum included courses in military studies, gunnery, radio, photography, airplanes, engines, poison gas defense, and aerial navigation. The flying instruction proceeded from dual control to solo instruction, then to cross-country.

OVER THERE AND BACK

Records maintained between June and November 1918 indicate that both the flying instruction program and the armorers' school contributed significantly to the Air Service record in Europe. Four of the original aero squadrons at Wilbur Wright Field later earned combat credits in France. The 12th Aero Squadron was cited for its participation in aerial operations in the Lorraine, Ile-de-France, Champagne-Marne, Champagne, St. Mihiel, and Meuse-Argonne battles. The 13th and 20th Aero Squadrons flew in the Lorraine, St. Mihiel, and Meuse-Argonne engagements. The 19th Aero Squadron flew liaison missions in France between January and March 1918.[36] Wilbur Wright Field's first Commanding Officer, Maj. Arthur R. Christie, subsequently promoted to the rank of lieutenant colonel, served as Chief of Air Service, V Corps, in the St. Mihiel offensive, August 10-September 16, 1918.[37]

At 11:00 a.m., November 11, 1918, World War I fighting ceased. The Great War was over. The Magnificent Adventure ended in glory; "America's boys" had helped make the world safe for democracy.

World War I victory dance at Wilbur Wright Field, featuring Air Service amateur musicians and ladies from the nearby villages of Fairfield and Osborn, Ohio

U.S. Army soldiers march up Main Street, Dayton, Ohio, during World War I victory parade, November 1918. *(Dayton and Montgomery County Public Library)*

Priorities shifted. Just as America had clamored for instant armament in April 1917, it now demanded immediate relief from the burden of supporting nearly five million men under arms.[38] While Wilbur Wright Field's military population in November 1918 is not stated specifically in available sources, the installation was probably operating near its planned peak of 1,700 persons.

Demobilization caused drastic changes at installations across the nation. At Wilbur Wright Field, all training ceased by the end of November. Flying was limited to the experimental and test aircraft participating in McCook Field programs. Emphasis shifted abruptly from training pilots and armorers to serving as a temporary repository for war surplus materiel.

Effective January 10, 1919, Wilbur Wright Field was merged administratively with the Air Service Armorers' School and nearby Fairfield Aviation General Supply Depot.[39] The new unit was named the Wilbur Wright Air Service Depot (WWASD) and its Commander assumed control over all three organizations. The designation "Wilbur Wright Field" was continued until 1925, although functions of the field were administered by WWASD and its successors.*

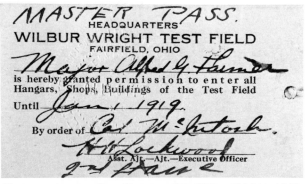

Master pass to enter all sensitive areas of the Wilbur Wright test field. In these hangars and shops were located aircraft and equipment from the Engineering Division at McCook Field in Dayton, Ohio. Because of McCook's limited runways, considerable flying of experimental aircraft was done at Wilbur Wright Field.

1100 hours, November 11, 1918
THE "WAR TO END ALL WARS" HAD ENDED.

U.S. Army Air Service strength stood at 195,023 officers and enlisted men. Airplane inventories reflected 7,800 biplane trainers (largely Curtiss JN-4 Jennys); 1,000 service airplanes (primarily DH-4s manufactured in American factories); and 5,000 combat-type airplanes (purchased abroad from English, French, and Italian companies).

Air Service strength in Europe totaled 5,707 officers and 74,237 enlisted men. Combat training had been completed by 1,647 pilots and 841 observers. Of these, 1,402 pilots and 769 observers had flown combat sorties over enemy lines.

The Air Service lost 818 brave men during the war in Europe: 164 aircrewmen were killed in action or died as a result of wounds received in action, 319 were killed in airplane accidents, and 335 died from other causes. Other Air Service casualties included 200 missing in action, 102 prisoners of war, and 133 wounded.

Sources: "An Air Force Almanac," *AIR FORCE Magazine*, May 1982, p 171; Maurer Maurer, ed., *The U.S. Air Service in World War I*, Vol. I: *The Final Report and a Tactical History* (Washington, 1978), 67.

Martin MB-2 twin-engine biplane bomber circling over Wilbur Wright Field in 1920. This all-American aircraft was produced too late for World War I service but was the Army Air Service's front-line bomber for several years into the 1920s. The heavy bomber demonstrated its capability when it sank five obsolete warships anchored in Chesapeake Bay during tests in 1921 and 1923. (*U.S. Air Force Museum*)

---

*By the time the designation "Wilbur Wright Field" was dropped in 1925, the depot function had changed name several times. These changes are explained in detail in Chapter III, Fairfield Air Depot. In brief, they are:
  Wilbur Wright Air Service Depot, January 10, 1919
  Aviation General Supply Depot, November 3, 1919
  Air Service Supply and Repair Depot, Fairfield, Ohio, September 20, 1920
  Fairfield Air Intermediate Depot, January 14, 1921.

Social gathering at Wilbur Wright Field, 1921

Military strength at WWASD was initially 70 officers and 830 enlisted men, but as demobilization continued uniformed strength declined rapidly. On February 20, the flying school, armorers' school, and Squadrons A, B, I, K, L, M, N, and O were demobilized. The continuing function of the depot was assumed by an increasing civilian population. By the end of 1918, the civilian work force peaked at 1,000 employees.[40]

As Army Air Service training fields and stations throughout the nation and overseas closed, supplies and equipment were shipped to major air depots such as WWASD for storage, inventory, and disposal. At the peak of this activity, 77 buildings under depot management, including some hangars, were used to house such items as 2,500 aeronautical engines, 700 airplanes of various series, and thousands of instruments, compasses, watches, altimeters, and gauges of all descriptions. Four of the twelve Unit Two hangars were relocated from the flightline to the interior of the installation and converted to other uses (one became a garage, one a gymnasium, and two became warehouses). Final disposition of all wartime surplus items dominated functions at the Fairfield, Ohio, depot for nearly eight years.

Meanwhile, airplane testing continued on Wilbur

Wright Field. On November 1, 1920, the field's role as a test site for programs initiated at McCook Field was formally recognized. Special Order 178 activated a "Department of Testing and Flying."[41] In 1921, the testing facilities were expanded to include a high-altitude bombing range, a two-mile electrically-timed speed course, and equipment for testing of machine gun butts. By 1924, it was clear that the site of Wilbur Wright Field would continue to be used as a center of aviation activity, maintaining the flying heritage begun there some twenty years before.

Until 1924, the site of Wilbur Wright Field was leased by the U.S. Government. In August of that year, a group of prescient Dayton citizens was responsible for the donation of more than 4,500 acres of land, including the site of Wilbur Wright Field, to the U.S. Government. On August 21, 1925, the War Department discontinued the designation "Wilbur Wright Field" in anticipation of the establishment of the new and larger reservation, to be known as "Wright Field" in honor of both illustrious brothers. In 1927, the expanded reservation was formally dedicated, and became the new home of the Air Corps Materiel Division as it relocated from McCook Field. The testing activities related to McCook programs continued in the interim from 1925 until 1927 and then became a function of the new facility.

Wilbur Wright Field, July 1923. A major addition since World War I was the balloon hangar at the extreme left on the hangar line. In the far upper portion of the photograph are the villages of Fairfield and Osborn, since merged to become Fairborn, Ohio. *(U.S. Air Force Museum)*

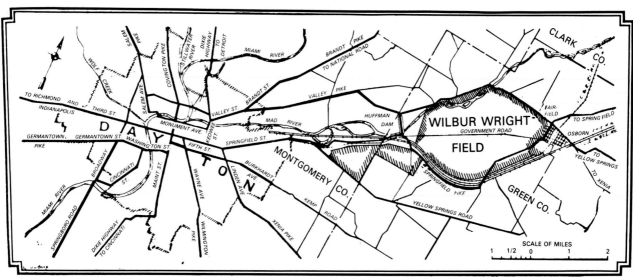

Roads to Dayton and Wilbur Wright Field

Land purchased by the Dayton Air Service Committee, Inc., and donated to the government in 1924 (outlined) was dedicated as Wright Field in 1927 in honor of both Wright brothers. This land included the site of Wilbur Wright Field plus an additional tract of land (shaded at left), part of which is currently in Area B of Wright-Patterson Air Force Base.

Fairfield Aviation General Supply Depot, 1918

III.   FAIRFIELD AIR DEPOT 1917-1931

WORLD WAR I ORIGINS

At the same time that the Signal Corps was negotiating with the Miami Conservancy District in Dayton, Ohio, to lease acreage for the establishment of Wilbur Wright Field, simultaneous discussions were underway to purchase land for a centrally-located aviation general supply depot. Such an institution was essential for logistics support of the Signal Corps Aviation Schools planned for Wilbur Wright Field, Scott and Chanute Fields in Illinois, and Selfridge Field in Michigan. The depot was to be located near Fairfield, Ohio, and would provide everything from airplane parts and engines to laces on the mechanics' shoes.

Time did not allow leisurely studies of the most favorable locations. Rapid negotiations between the Signal Corps Construction Division and the Miami Conservancy District culminated on June 10, 1917, when the Signal

Corps Equipment Division paid $8,000 for 40 acres of land, then in use as a wheat field. The triangular tract bordered Bath Township lands on the east and south, and Wilbur Wright Field on the north and west, and lay about nine and one-half miles north of Dayton. The extreme northeastern corner of the wheat field abutted the Fairfield Cemetery.* Although the depot and Wilbur Wright Field were close neighbors, they operated independently and reported to separate divisions within the Signal Corps.

In September 1917, after the grain harvest, crews that had labored during the summer months to build Wilbur Wright Field were shifted to begin construction of the depot buildings. The major brick-and-concrete building of the Fairfield Aviation General Supply Depot, Fairfield, Ohio (FAGSD), "opened its doors for business" on January 4, 1918, less than four months later.

---

*Although it has often been speculated that the cemetery located next to security Gate 1-C is a part of WPAFB, the graveyard, established in 1844, has never been a part of the military installation. A high chain-link fence delineates the periphery of Area C today and separates the base from the cemetery.

Interior view of the Building 1 trainway, Fairfield Air Depot, constructed in 1917. During World War II the trainway was used for emergency storage, as shown in this 1942 photograph.

Constructed at a cost of $981,000, this main structure was 262 feet wide, 825 feet long, and had a heated floor space of 234,300 square feet. A unique feature of the U-shaped building was a double rail spur 600 feet long between the two wings. A large roof covered both wings and the spur between them.* The spur, or "government switch" in civil engineering terms, connected the depot with the Big Four Railroad Company whose main lines had recently been relocated from the village of Osborn to the eastern side of Fairfield.

The depot building was located directly across the road from the Fairfield Cemetery. It housed the depot headquar-

Lt. Col. James A. Mars, born April 19, 1878, graduated from the U.S. Military Academy, Class of 1903, and was commissioned a lieutenant in the Cavalry. Mars later transferred from the Cavalry to the Air Service, and commanded the Fairfield Aviation General Supply Depot, Fairfield, Ohio, from January 4-December 23, 1918.

Building 1, with its covered trainway, is the oldest permanent military building at Wright-Patterson.

*So solid was the construction of the original building that it is still fully functional today. Known as Building 1 (Area C), it is considered a vital part of both the heritage and the ongoing business of Wright-Patterson AFB. Although the interior has sustained considerable modification since 1918, the rail spur still exists and is occasionally used.

Billeting area of the 246th Aero Squadron, Fairfield Aviation General Supply Depot, 1918. The pyramidal tents housed enlisted men, usually six per tent. At the end of the street are smaller, two-man tents of junior grade officers. Behind them stand the mess hall and a truck warehouse. In the far background is Building 1, the depot headquarters building. (U.S. Air Force Museum)

First Sergeant of the 246th Aero Squadron, 1918. His quarters were considered somewhat luxurious for the times. Note the wooden floor and flower garden (carefully planted and tended by privates). He also has a steel cot with springs (on the right), whereas his tentmate, a lesser-ranking NCO, sleeps on a springless canvas cot. (U.S. Air Force Museum)

ters offices and a Signal Corps weather office for the post, in addition to providing thousands of square feet of storage space for freight and supplies. Six other buildings were also constructed as part of the FAGSD depot, including three steel storage hangars and the depot garage.

The Fairfield Aviation General Supply Depot's first Commanding Officer was Lt. Col. James A. Mars. The initial station complement included 150 troops each from the 612th, 669th, and 678th Aero Squadrons that arrived from Kelly Field, Texas. Later in 1918, the first civilian employees were hired (six female clerk-stenographers and a male janitor).

FAGSD's primary mission was to provide supply support for wartime training operations. In particular, it received, stored, and issued equipment and supplies to Signal Corps Aviation Schools, Mechanics' Schools, Armorers' Schools, and other programs at Wilbur Wright, Chanute, Scott, and Selfridge Fields, and at other Army installations (such as McCook Field), as directed by higher headquarters. The depot was a direct responsibility of the Signal Corps Equipment Division in Washington, D.C., and operated independently of the various Army airfields it supported. (The airfields reported to Headquarters Central Department, Chicago, Illinois.)[1]

Early in 1918, when it became obvious that the Allies would be victorious, the Air Service surveyed its existing installations and began making plans for their use after the end of hostilities. Two factors had immediate implications for Dayton-area facilities: aviation training programs would assuredly decrease, and the job of disposing of war surplus materiel would assume great importance. Air Service headquarters decided to consolidate the installations at Fairfield, Ohio, terminating the training mission of Wilbur Wright Field and shifting control and use of vacated space to the Fairfield air depot function.

Accordingly, Wilbur Wright Air Service Depot (WWASD) was formed January 10, 1919, by consolidating

Headquarters, Wilbur Wright Air Service Depot (Building 1), 1919. This logistics center underwent a series of name changes between 1918 and 1921 but was popularly referred to as the Fairfield Air Depot. Enlisted troops occupied the tents in the right foreground. To the left were the post exchange and bachelor officers quarters. (U.S. Air Force Museum)

Wilbur Wright Field, the Air Service Armorers' School, and the Fairfield Aviation General Supply Depot.[2] Maj. Charles T. Waring, who had assumed command of the Fairfield Aviation General Supply Depot on December 24, 1918, remained as Commander of the newly-designated installation.

Demobilization began in earnest shortly after WWASD was formed. On February 20, 1919, the following organizations were demobilized: Signal Corps Aviation School; Armorers' School Squadrons D (4th Provisional Squadron), E (5th Provisional Squadron), and F (2nd Provisional Squadron); and Squadrons A (231st Aero Squadron), B (851st Aero Squadron), I (42nd Aero Squadron), K (44th Aero Squadron), L (246th Aero Squadron), M (342nd Aero Squadron); and Squadrons N and O, which were casual organizations organized at Wilbur Wright Field on October 1, 1918, to aid in the projected demobilization.[3]

Fairfield Air Depot and Wilbur Wright Field, 1923. At upper left, World War I wooden hangars border the flightline. In the center, maintenance and engineering shops mingle with warehouses and outdoor storage areas managed by the depot. Building 1 and the Fairfield Cemetery are visible at right. *(NCR Corporation)*

As military personnel at the depot were discharged from active duty their positions were filled by new civilian employees. The 50-man guard section was one of the first to become totally "civilianized." A civilian personnel office, with a staff of four, was opened on October 24, 1919, in the office of the Post Adjutant. Civilian employment zoomed to nearly 1,000 in the immediate post-war period before leveling off in March of 1920 to about half that number.

In November 1919, two significant changes occurred at the Fairfield facility. First, on the third of that month the installation was formally transferred to the Air Service's list of permanent depots and renamed the Aviation General Supply Depot, Fairfield, Ohio.[4] Second, an Air Service Stockkeepers' School, with a staff of one officer and 65 enlisted men, moved to the depot from Washington, D.C., to train the rapidly-expanding civilian work force. When the flow of surplus materiel slowed in 1921, the need for stockkeepers and the Stockkeepers' School diminished. On August 17, 1921, the school relocated to Chanute Field, Illinois.

POSTWAR DEMOBILIZATION AND REORGANIZATION

As demobilization gained momentum, buildings at Wilbur Wright Field originally used in training flying cadets, mechanics, and armorers became storage facilities. Immediately following the Armistice, an Air Service Liquidation Board was created in Paris to dispose of war materiel. The bulk of the board's work was completed in a record six months, and the steady stream of war surplus property flowing into the Fairfield supply depot from Europe, as well as from closed Air Service installations in the continental United States, became a flood. Storage and disposal of this deluge of property was a major project for depot personnel during the next eight years.[5]

Keenly mindful that austere appropriations had constrained the Air Service before World War I, and cognizant that funds might be extremely limited in the post-war years, the Air Service supply authorities at first attempted to save nearly everything for future use. Soon mountains of mate-

Members of the all-volunteer Wilbur Wright Air Service Depot band, 1919. Although assigned to other primary duties at the depot, these musicians furnished their talents and own instruments to play at ceremonies and dances. *(Frank J. Kulish)*

riel buried storage facilities. Seventy-seven buildings at the depot were crammed with more than 2,500 aircraft engines of all types, 700 airplanes of various makes, and thousands of instruments of all descriptions, as well as more prosaic items such as lumber, clothing, and personal equipment. The classification and storage systems were overwhelmed by the sheer mass of materiel involved.

Between 1919 and 1922 at the Fairfield depot alone, millions of dollars of property gradually were classified and disposed of, either by direct sale locally or through Air Service Supply Division headquarters in Washington, D.C. The latter coordinated sale of airplanes, engines, and equipment through advertisement in national magazines. A million and a half feet of hard lumber—cherry, mahogany and walnut—were sold through sealed bids, and tons of clothing were sold to merchants.

By 1922 at the aviation depot most of the non-standard and obsolete materiel had been distributed to other government agencies, sold, salvaged, scrapped, or otherwise disposed of. Serviceable airplanes and engines were inventoried and set aside at the depot for future use. Smaller remaining serviceable supplies had been cataloged into a comprehensive storage system and consolidated in Building 1 and three adjacent structures.

This monumental disposal effort was carried on in addition to the normal supply function of the depot, i.e., to furnish parts to repair shops on the post and to other Air Service organizations and installations.[6]

In January 1919, the Chief of the Air Service was Maj. Gen. Charles T. Menoher.* In conjunction with the War Department General Staff, General Menoher drew up plans for a post-war Army aviation force. They projected a force of 24,000 officers and enlisted men, with a fleet of 1,000 modern airplanes. To support such a force would require 26 flying fields, including some that had operated during World War I. In April of 1919, the Air Service further specified an active duty force of 2,000 officers and 21,850 enlisted men, using a flying inventory of 1,700 active

airplanes, and a fleet of 3,400 reserve aircraft. Active duty forces would be organized into 87 "service" squadrons, each of which would be assigned 18 airplanes. Moreover, there would be 42 balloon companies. If allowed, this total strength in personnel and equipment would put the Air Service "on a par with the infantry, cavalry and artillery divisions of the Army."[7]

Unfortunately, these grand plans ran afoul of Congressional frugality and less than one-third of the desired budget was approved. The Army Reorganization Act of 1920 provided for only 280,000 officers and enlisted men overall. The Air Service was designated a combatant arm with an authorized strength of 1,516 officers and 16,000 enlisted men, including 2,500 flying cadets. Consequently, the active duty officer corps was reduced to those men with Regular Army commissions, and reservists were relieved from active duty. Temporary commissions were terminated, so most officers remaining on active duty reverted to permanent grades. To provide needed skills and expertise in managerial positions, officers discharged through this demobilization were encouraged to accept jobs as civil service employees.[8]

Other significant parts of the Army Reorganization Act of 1920 authorized flight pay amounting to 50 percent of base pay and required that tactical units be commanded by "flyers." (The latter generally was construed to mean officers rated as airplane pilots.) The Chief of the Air Service was assigned the rank of major general, and the Assistant Chief given the rank of brigadier general. The "blueprint" of tactical organizations called for 27 squadrons in seven groups under two wings. The squadrons were further designated by function: observation squadrons (15), surveillance or reconnaissance squadrons (4), pursuit or fighter squadrons (4), and bombardment squadrons (4). The bombardment squadrons were equipped with Martin MB-2 "heavy" bombers. Balloons maintained a foothold in military aeronautics, and 32 companies were planned around them.

---

*General Menoher commanded the famous 42nd "Rainbow" Division in France between December 1917 and November 1918. He was appointed Chief of the Air Service on December 23, 1918.

THE AIR SERVICE SUPPLY AND REPAIR DEPOT

The War Department in 1919 had called for $55 million for Air Service total operations; Congress had authorized only $25 million. Not only did this lesser amount preclude, according to General Menoher, the purchase of even one new airplane, but it also forced organizational structure to an irreducible minimum. Wherever possible, organizations were merged or consolidated.

One such merger concerned the Aviation Repair Depot at Indianapolis, Indiana. One of three such aviation repair depots, the facility had functioned before and during World War I as a regional center for major repairs to airplanes and engines. On July 16, 1920, the Chief of the Air Service ordered the Aviation Repair Depot to move from its Speedway location in Indianapolis to Fairfield, Ohio, and merge with the Aviation General Supply Depot. The combined activity would be named the Air Service Supply and Repair Depot.[9]

The move was apparently not viewed as a step forward by all at the Repair Depot. A few days before the official order was published, the engineering officer at the Repair Depot, Capt. Shiras A. Blair, asserted that the rumored move could not occur "due to the fact that the flying land at Fairfield consisted of swamp land and would not make a fit flying field." Once the order was received, however, an advance crew of eight civilian workers was sent to the Fairfield depot to begin converting buildings for use as engineering shops. "Locks were broken from deserted hangars, and tractors and trucks, stored after the World War of 1918 [sic] were revamped in order that facilities might be installed for the shops."[10]

Relocating the repair facility generated the usual sparring between the losing and gaining commands. On August 9, Capt. J. H. Rudolph, Commanding Officer of the Speedway Indianapolis Repair Depot, said he had received permission from Air Service headquarters to delay the move until the Fairfield depot had completed the promised modifications to buildings allocated to house repair materials and equipment. Capt. George E. A. Reinburg, who had assumed command of the Fairfield facility on August 2, 1919, disagreed. He replied that the interior floor plans were the

responsibility of the Indianapolis depot's engineering officer because of his familiarity with his own requirements. Captain Reinburg asserted his intention to operate the aero repair function as merely a department of the Fairfield facility and not necessarily as the facility's *raison d'être*. In fact, the gaining commander stated that he could provide only three carpenters for the renovation process, implying that any additional help would have to come from Indiana.

Moreover, Reinburg advised Captain Rudolph that Fairfield's resources in other areas were critically low. Rudolph would have to provide his own pine lumber for the renovations, for example, because the Fairfield depot had no lumber of its own except "short pieces found in the Reclamation Department." Indianapolis also would have to provide its own furniture for offices, and would have to bring its own "steam radiators, piping, etc., connected with the internal heating of the departments," since the Fairfield depot was short of these items as well.

Unidentified staff officers of the Aviation Repair Depot, Speedway Park, Indianapolis, 1919. YMCA and Salvation Army buildings such as the one pictured here were not uncommon on military installations of the day, and were sometimes used for official military activities.

Members of the aero repair function, Air Service Supply and Repair Depot, 1921. Many of these employees transferred with the Indianapolis Speedway Repair Depot to Fairfield in the late summer of 1920.

Flightline of the Speedway Aviation Repair Depot, Indianapolis, Indiana, before the facility moved (in September 1920) to the Aviation General Supply Depot at Fairfield

Center of aero repair activities near the flightline, Air Service Supply and Repair Depot, Wilbur Wright Field, 1921. (Building 1 is just visible at upper center.)

Living quarters were not so much of a problem. The Fairfield installation had a large number of bachelor officer and enlisted quarters.* There were also "about 15 sets of [married] quarters for high class mechanics and civilian employees." The latter were provided by local housing policy because there were certain civilian employees "whose services [were] required at all times." These vital employees were allowed to reside in on-post government quarters. In this select category were listed the "post plumber, electrician, engineer, shop foreman and [11] department heads." It was expected that 300 other civilian employees transferring from the Speedway at Indianapolis would find adequate housing available in the nearby villages of Fairfield and Osborn where most of the depot workers lived.[11]

Mindful of the approaching winter and the consequent need to relocate the aero facility before bad weather, Air Service headquarters ended the sparring between the merging commands. The depot Commander at Fairfield was ordered to identify the exact buildings to be used by the aero

repair facility and to proceed with dispatch to renovate the structures.

Altogether, eight buildings were modified. The first aero repair building was formed in the vicinity of present-day Building 207 (Area C) by adding a wooden hangar to an existing structure. Behind this Aero Repair building lay "Drafting, Reclamation and the Gas House." Northeast of Aero Repair was "the Machine Shop and behind it were Paint and Dope, Engine Repair and the Oil House." Completing the engineering complex were a small structure southeast of Aero Repair designated for use as the "Instrument Building," and another for drafting and blueprint work.[12]

On September 20, 1920, the former Speedway Aviation Repair Depot from Indianapolis, Indiana, reopened for business as the Engineering Repair Section of the Air Service Supply and Repair Depot at Fairfield, Ohio. Organized for the "repair and maintenance of aircraft and the overhaul of engines," the section was headed by Capt. Shiras A. Blair.[13]

*As of July 1, 1920, the Aviation General Supply Depot at Fairfield had quarters, i.e., family housing, for 72 married officers and 48 married non-commissioned officers, and 4 sets of family quarters for "commanding officers." There were also quarters for 52 bachelor officers and sufficient barrack accommodations for 2,100 enlisted men. These were virtually empty following World War I, as the assigned population on base included only 16 officers, 150 enlisted men, and 504 civilian employees.

ENGINEERING REPAIR SECTION

During 1917-1918, Allied airplane manufacturers had turned out 19,600 British-designed DeHavilland DH-4 single-engine observation biplanes and about 15,600 Liberty airplane engines. After the war, thousands were stockpiled at supply depots. Repair functions drew on these "banks" of spares to support their repair and overhaul missions.

By 1921, the various Engineering Repair installations supported an active aircraft inventory of 1,108 DeHavilland DH-4 biplanes powered by Liberty engines; 721 Curtiss JN-4 and 800 Curtiss JN-6 trainers equipped with Curtiss OX-5 engines; 170 Standard SE-5 pursuit [fighter] airplanes; and 12 Martin MB-2 bombers. Additionally there were 38 free balloons, 250 observation or captive balloons, and 250 non-rigid airships.[14]

From the end of World War I until the late 1930s, the Engineering Repair Section at Fairfield (soon simplified to "Engineering Department") was a relatively compact organization. It comprised four functions: aero repair, metal manufacture and repair, engine repair, and final assembly/inspection.

Engine overhaul at Fairfield, for example, was a rather simplistic process in the Twenties. After an airplane engine had been removed from the fuselage, a mechanic and his helper disassembled the power plant, placing all components in a single specially-designed parts truck. These were then dipped into a cleansing solution. After this bath the components were closely checked by inspectors, and some were sent for reconditioning while other items were replaced outright. (Cylinders and related parts were reconditioned by "sub-assembly" and "accessories" departments.) Finally, the elements made their way back to the special truck and were reassembled by the mechanic and his helper.

Final inspections were conducted intermittently as the engine slowly resumed its identity during the rebuilding process. Using this procedure, average monthly production during the early days was 50 overhauled engines.

When first established, the Fairfield repair facility provided this service for JN-4 and JN-6 trainers from the 15th Squadron, Chanute Field, Illinois; DH-4 observation airplanes from the 1st Squadron at Chanute Field, the 5th, 11th, and 49th Squadrons at Langley Field, Virginia, and the 17th Squadron, Selfridge Field, Michigan; and MB-2 bombers from the 11th, 20th, and 49th Squadrons at Langley Field. Later in the 1920s, when more powerful, faster, and heavier airplanes had come into the inventory, maintenance standards prescribed that all pursuit [fighter] aircraft would be overhauled every 10 months "regardless of flying time." Primary trainers were overhauled every 15 months and bombers every 18 months. All other types of airplanes were overhauled every 12 months. This schedule was flexible, allowing for more frequent overhauls when particular types of airplanes were subjected to increased flying hours or above-normal stress and strain.

On November 1, 1920, the Fairfield Engineering Department added a function to test airplanes and engines which had been repaired at the depot.[15] In the spring of 1921, the separate testing facilities operated at Fairfield by the Airplane Engineering Department at McCook Field were expanded. A testing site for machine gun butts was

Liberty V-12 airplane engines in storage at the Fairfield Air Depot. Designed basically for the DeHavilland DH-4 observation airplane, these engines remained in the active Air Corps inventory until the mid-1930s.

Women employees work on Liberty V-12 airplane engines in the motor department of Plant Number 1, Dayton-Wright Airplane Company, July 1918. These power plants were installed in DeHavilland DH-4 biplanes manufactured by Dayton-Wright. *(U.S. Air Force Museum)*

operational, as well as a high-altitude bombing range. A two-mile electrically-timed speed course accurately recorded flying speeds of experimental aircraft.

In 1925, Fairfield assumed responsibility for drop-testing new parachutes and repairing and maintaining those in service. This allowed McCook Field experimental engineers to concentrate their efforts on developing new and better chutes.

Wilbur Wright Field, as part of the Fairfield depot facility, was ideal for both experimental and test programs, because of its size and the absence of flying hazards surrounding it. Consequently, until the new Wright Field opened in late 1927 (see Chapter V), practically every history-making airplane owned by the Army was tested at the same locale where the Wright brothers flew their pioneer aircraft.

Rebuilding an airplane fuselage at Fairfield Air Intermediate Depot, 1925. Employee in center is identified as the foreman, Mr. Erwin F. Boger.

THE FAIRFIELD AIR INTERMEDIATE DEPOT

The year 1921 was a period of major changes at the Fairfield depot. The first was a new name. In December 1920 the depot Commander had asked the Chief of the Air Service for a permanent designation in order to halt the confusing variety of names and titles that had identified the Fairfield installation. Since its June 16, 1917 establishment, the facility had in turn been known as the Fairfield Aviation General Supply Depot; Wilbur Wright Air Service Depot; Aviation General Supply Depot, Fairfield, Ohio; and

the Air Service Supply and Repair Depot. Since the facility had also consolidated Wilbur Wright Field, the Signal Corps Aviation School, and the Aviation Armorers' School, and served as a test function for McCook Field programs, there was lingering confusion over those names, as well.

The War Department clarified the situation by establishing "air intermediate depots" (AIDs), to serve as centers for both supply and repair. On January 14, 1921, the Ohio facility became the Fairfield Air Intermediate Depot (FAID), one of four such intermediate depots.[16] The others were located at San Antonio, Texas; Rockwell, California; and Middletown, Pennsylvania.

CHRONOLOGY OF FAIRFIELD INSTALLATION

Designation	Date Established	Commander(s)	Assumed Command
Fairfield Aviation General Supply Depot, Fairfield, Ohio	Jan. 4, 1918	Lt. Col. James A. Mars	Jan. 4, 1918
		Maj. Charles T. Waring	Dec. 24, 1918
Wilbur Wright Air Service Depot	Jan. 10, 1919	Maj. Charles T. Waring	Jan. 10, 1919
		Maj. Prince A. Oliver	May 1, 1919
		Lt. Col. George E. A. Reinburg	Aug. 2, 1919
Aviation General Supply Depot, Fairfield, Ohio	Nov. 3, 1919	Lt. Col. George E. A. Reinburg	Nov. 3, 1919
Air Service Supply and Repair Depot	Sep. 20, 1920	Lt. Col. George E. A. Reinburg	Jun. 20, 1920
Fairfield Air Intermediate Depot	Jan. 14, 1921	Lt. Col. George E. A. Reinburg	Jan. 14, 1921
		Maj. Augustine Warner Robins	Aug. 27, 1921
Fairfield Air Depot Reservation	Jun. 22, 1927	Maj. Augustine Warner Robins	Jun. 22, 1927
		Maj. J. Y. Chisum	Jul. 24, 1928
		Capt. Edward Laughlin	Mar. 5, 1929
		Maj. Henry H. Arnold	Jun. 25, 1929
		Capt. Edward Laughlin	Aug. 1, 1930
		Maj. Albert L. Sneed	Aug. 15, 1930

Vought pursuit biplane displaying the insignia of the Fairfield Air Intermediate Depot

Middletown Depot supplied units in New England, New York, Pennsylvania, and Virginia. The San Antonio AID supported organizations in Texas, Oklahoma, Colorado, New Mexico, and Arizona. The Rockwell Depot (later Sacramento Air Depot at McClellan Field, California), provided services for Air Service units in California, Washington, Oregon, Nevada, Utah, Montana, Idaho, and Wyoming. The Fairfield Air Intermediate Depot (FAID) supported 24 bases scattered across 23 states: Ohio, Kentucky, West Virginia, North Carolina, South Carolina, Tennessee, Georgia, Alabama, Florida, Louisiana, Mississippi, Arkansas, Missouri, Indiana, Illinois, Kansas, Nebraska, North Dakota, South Dakota, Minnesota, Iowa, Wisconsin, and Michigan.

All four intermediate depots at first provided supplies as well as repairs and regularly-scheduled overhauls to aircraft from all of the bases within their control areas. During the next year, however, the Fairfield facility took over the repair function of the Middletown control area and thus served the entire region east of the Mississippi River and a considerable portion of the region west and north, including regular Army Air Service bases, National Guard installations, and organized Reserve Corps sites.

At the time FAID was designated in January 1921, Capt. George Reinburg was the Commander, having continued this office through three name changes. Captain Reinburg, in turn, was succeeded by Maj. Augustine Warner Robins on August 27, 1921.[17] Fresh from the Office of the Chief of the Air Service, Robins continued in command of FAID until July 3, 1928, holding the command position longer than any preceding officer in the history of the facility. In addition, he was concurrently Commander of Wilbur Wright Field until that designation was dropped in 1925.[18] (In 1927, Robins was also detailed as Chief of the Army Air Corps Field Service Section.[19] While working in this capacity, Major Robins was instrumental in devising important policies and procedures for overall handling of Air Corps materiel.)

MAJ. HENRY H. ARNOLD

The most famous Commander of the Fairfield Air Depot was Maj. Henry H. Arnold. He commanded FAD from June 25, 1929, to the following July 30, and also headed the Field Service Section of the Materiel Division during this time. From August 1930 to February 1931, he was Executive Officer to the Chief of the Materiel Division at Wright Field.

From Wright Field, Major Arnold was reassigned to the command position at March Field, Riverside, California. In February 1935, Lieutenant Colonel Arnold was promoted to the rank of brigadier general and named Commander of the 1st Wing of General Headquarters Air Force (GHQAF). On September 22, 1938, he was promoted to major general and appointed Chief of the Army Air Corps. On June 30, 1941, General Arnold was named Chief of the Army Air Forces, which had succeeded the Army Air Corps on June 20, 1941. He was promoted to lieutenant general in December 1941. On March 19, 1943, he was promoted to the rank of full general (four stars). Under his leadership, by 1945 the AAF had grown to an awesome intercontinental force of 2,282,259 persons and 75,000 aircraft.

On December 15, 1944, he was promoted to the five-star supergrade of General of the Army, in company with Dwight D. Eisenhower, Douglas MacArthur, and George C. Marshall.

General Arnold retired in February 1946. On May 7, 1949, the President changed his title to "General of the Air Force," the only one to have held that rank to date.

Lt. Col. Augustine Warner Robins. As a major, Robins served as Commander of the Fairfield Air Intermediate Depot (August 27, 1921 to June 21, 1927) and later the Fairfield Air Depot Reservation (June 22, 1927 to July 3, 1928). He served concurrently as Commander of Wilbur Wright Field from March 26, 1923 to July 3, 1928.

THE PROPERTY, MAINTENANCE, AND COST COMPILATION SECTION

During July of 1921, just before Major Robins arrived, a new organization took up residence at FAID when the Army Air Service relocated physical control of its entire depot system from Washington, D.C., to Fairfield. The new control function, directed by Capt. Elmer E. Adler, was entitled the Property, Maintenance, and Cost Compilation Section (PMCCS) of the Air Service Supply Division. It was a "sub-office" of the Property Requirement Division of the Office of the Chief of the Air Service. Though collocated at the depot, the PMCCS was clearly not a subordinate organization and continued to report functionally to the Office of the Chief of the Air Service (OCAS). This new agency was the earliest antecedent of today's modern Air Force Logistics Command (AFLC).

As host of the Compilation Section, FAID assumed a somewhat more prominent role nationally, and was designated the central control depot for all paperwork pertaining to depot operations. All correspondence concerning requisition, issue, distribution, and storage of Air Service materiel had to be channeled through PMCCS at FAID.[20]

The PMCCS received daily reports on stock levels of materiel from the four previously-identified air intermediate depots; from the additional repair functions at Fairfield,

Ohio, Dallas, Texas, and Montgomery, Alabama; and from the smaller supply depots at Little Rock, Arkansas, and Scott Field, Illinois. Based on this information, PMCCS directed the flow of supplies nationwide between the various depots and thus indirectly controlled supplies to all Air Service bases and organizations.

The depot function at FAID operated in the same fashion as the other depots and was serviced by PMCCS in the same way. According to Lt. George V. McPike, the Fairfield depot supply officer, the supply depot at FAID distributed and coordinated supplies so that "a well balanced stock level [would] be maintained for every type of organization in the area."[21] When supplies dropped below a fixed minimum, the depot forwarded requisitions to PMCCS for restockage. The PMCCS then either directed shipment of required materiel from one of the other control depots to FAID or recommended to the OCAS that the needed materiel be purchased.

FAID, in turn, provided the same kind of service to its own "customers," exercising a control function over all supply activities within the First through Seventh Corps Areas. Air Service customers within these areas forwarded requisitions to FAID where the Supply Department balanced requests against consolidated ledger reports. This procedure determined the location of requisitioned materiel as to whether it was in stock at FAID or one of the smaller depots, or on hand at some other Air Service installation. Shipping instructions were then issued, with close attention to manifesting materiel from the source nearest the requester. For example, a requisition from Mitchel Field, Long Island, New York, would likely be filled from the Middletown, Pennsylvania, depot, and not from Fairfield or any further point.

Lieutenant McPike estimated that as of May 2, 1922, FAID had in storage $250 million of government property. He pointed out that materiel was listed on 120,000 stock record cards that were continuously updated to assure currency of inventories. This painstaking process involved identifying, describing, cataloging, and indexing entries for "hundreds of thousands of supplies of a technical nature."[22] It was a mammoth job, and had occupied about 350 civilian employees for four years.

Thus two separate functions were carried on simultaneously at FAID during the mid-1920s—a combined repair and supply function, and a central control function. The combined repair and supply function served the entire region east of the Mississippi River, plus some additional areas to the west and north, and also made extensive ship-

Commanding Officer and original staff of the Property, Maintenance, and Cost Compilation Section (PMCCS) of the Supply Division, Army Air Service, at the Fairfield Air Intermediate Depot, 1921. Left to right: Lt. R. V. Ignico (later brigadier general), Lt. Omar Niergarth (later colonel), Capt. Elmer E. Adler, Commanding Officer (later brigadier general), Lt. J. L. Stromme (later colonel), Lt. Edwin R. Page (later brigadier general), and Lt. F. P. Kenney. In 1924, the PMCCS changed its name to Field Service Section.

ments to Panama, Hawaii, and the Philippines. The central control function (PMCCS) was a national function that monitored and directed all supply and repair functions.

On January 26, 1924, at the request of the PMCCS director, the name of the Property, Maintenance, and Cost Compilation Section was changed to the Field Service Section.[23] The Section still reported to the Supply Division, OCAS, until October 15, 1926, when it became one of six major sections of the Materiel Division, a new organization operating at McCook Field. On June 21, 1927, the Section moved from FAID to newly-constructed buildings at Wright Field (now Area B) and joined the Materiel Division, which had also relocated to the new facility from McCook Field. From 1924 to 1939 the Field Service Section supervised the operations of the four intermediate depots, and in 1927 acquired formal control of the departmental depots in the Panama Canal Zone, the Hawaiian Islands, and the Philippine Islands.

In 1927, the Field Service Section offices were at the intersection of today's Pearson Road and Allbrook Drive (Area C) opposite the Base Exchange Service Station and Fire Station Number 1 (Building 163). The area occupied by these offices now forms a wide lawn adjacent to 2750th Air Base Wing Headquarters, Building 10.

THE 1924 ROUND-THE-WORLD-FLIGHT

Both the Fairfield Air Intermediate Depot and McCook Field played major, albeit largely unsung, roles in one of the Air Service's most spectacular achievements during the two decades between world wars. This was the 26,345-mile circumnavigation of the globe by four single-engine Douglas World Cruisers.

Eight young fliers, dubbed "Magellans of the Air," departed Seattle, Washington, at 8:47 a.m. on April 6, 1924.[24] When two of the four World Cruisers touched down in Seattle on September 28, they had logged about 363 hours in actual flight, suffered no fatalities, and had sustained only minor injuries on their epochal flight. This was a most remarkable record, considering their itinerary: Canada, Alaska, the Aleutian Chain, the North Pacific, Siberia, Japan, China, Southeast Asia, India, Middle East, Europe, Iceland, North Atlantic, Nova Scotia, Massachusetts, New York, Washington, D.C., Ohio, and Washington State.

Secretary of War John W. Weeks had proclaimed in November 1923 that the flight's official purpose was "to demonstrate the feasibility with which aerial communication may be established between the various continents, and to obtain much valuable information concerning the operation of present type aircraft in various climates of the world."[25] There were other less official motives for the flight. According to one source, economics and patriotism were major factors in planning the project. "The purpose . . . is to point the way for all nations to develop aviation commercially and to secure for our country the honor of being the first to encircle the globe entirely by air." This would give the United States the position of "leading power in the peace-time application of flying."[26]

Competition was keen among nations to become the first to circle the earth by air. The United States had set the pace in 1919 when, on May 17, three U.S. Navy Curtiss Flying Boats took off from Newfoundland to the Azores. One of the NC-4s, piloted by Lt. Cmdr. Albert C. Read,

continued on to Lisbon, Portugal, and Plymouth, England. The NC-4 thus became the first airplane to bridge the Atlantic, with an enroute stop.[27]

Great Britain eclipsed the U.S. achievement the very next month and scored an impressive first in aviation history. John Alcock and Arthur Whitten-Brown, both Royal Flying Corps veterans, flew non-stop from Newfoundland across the stormy North Atlantic to Ireland on June 14-15, 1919, in a Vickers-Vimy biplane.[28]

U.S. Army Air Service scientists, designers, engineers, pilots, "mechanicians," craftsmen, and support personnel maintained an unfaltering desire to expand aeronautical

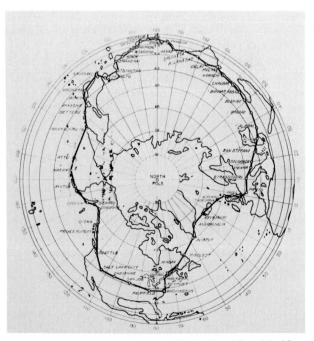

Itinerary of the 1924 Round-the-World Flight. Two of the original four Douglas World Cruisers—*New Orleans* and *Chicago*—completed the 26,345-mile global odyssey in a cumulative flying time of 15 days, 3 hours, and 7 minutes, with an average speed of 79½ mph. (*U.S. Air Force Museum*).

science and strengthen American air prowess. Between 1918 and 1923, some of the Air Service's most significant domestic and world records in aviation were set at or above McCook and Wilbur Wright Fields (including the airspace over the Fairfield Air Intermediate Depot).*

By 1923, British, French, Italian, Portuguese, and Argentine airmen, generously supported by their own governments, were challenging the United States' position in the world of aviation.[29] Not only was the external competition formidable, but there was also a keen rivalry between the air services of the U.S. Army and Navy for the biggest share of Congressional appropriations. Something exceptionally daring—near the point of impossibility—was needed to earn honor, prestige . . . and more money.

According to several writers of Air Service histories, the World Flight concept originated with Brig. Gen. William "Billy" Mitchell, Assistant Chief of the Air Service. The World Flight was perhaps the most spectacular of his "dramatic projects designed to gain public recognition—and Congressional appropriations for his hungry airmen." General Mitchell and Maj. Gen. Mason M. Patrick, Chief of the Air Service, "had promoted a series of bold aerial ventures that, they hoped, would sell military aviation to the people, the Army and the Congress."[30]

The flamboyant General Mitchell received more public adulation than any other Air Service officer; his disciples numbered hundreds of eager young pilots. General Patrick kept the Army Air Service on level flight with his conservative pragmatism. Thus the boldness and drama of their ventures was calculated, but strictly secondary to the pragmatic objectives set for each project. Based on careful planning and analysis, each was designed to test new concepts, new procedures, and new equipment; to blaze air routes; and to expand the Air Service's operational capabilities. The World Flight would advance all of these objectives in one effort.

One prominent writer who was acquainted with all of the principals involved in the historical voyage wrote, "Just who originated the idea of the World Flight will never be known. . . . General Patrick . . . General Mitchell . . . and Lieutenants Erik Nelson, Robert J. Brown, Jr., St. Clair Streett, and C. E. Crumrine were among the first to become so interested in the project that they translated enthusiasm into action. To them belongs the chief honor for its origination."[31] The ultimate success of the World Flight, however, was attributable to an extraordinary team effort. Officers and men who held no hope of glory or direct participation in the flight "worked to exhaustion preparing charts, gathering worldwide weather data, and planting fuel, oil and spare parts in remote areas around the globe."[32]

Meticulous planning for this aerial odyssey began more than a year before the four heavily-laden Douglas World Cruisers struggled off the waters of Lake Washington, near Seattle. The Air Service headquarters staff carefully selected a World Flight committee chaired by Lt. Robert J. Brown, Jr., and composed of four other members: Capt. W.

*Appendix 3 contains specific records set during this period.

Brig. Gen. William Mitchell, France, 1918 (*U.S. Air Force Museum*)

BRIG. GEN. WILLIAM B. MITCHELL

Mitchell was born in Nice, France, on December 29, 1879, of Wisconsin parents who were sojourning on the Continent. He graduated from George Washington University in 1899. Mitchell enlisted as a private, Company M, 1st Wisconsin Infantry, on May 14, 1898, was commissioned as a second lieutenant in the national army three weeks later, and integrated into the Regular Army after the Spanish-American War. Mitchell earned his pilot's wings in early 1917 at a civilian flying school, paying for his own lessons. His brilliant service with the American Expeditionary Forces, France, during World War I won him numerous U.S. Air Service and foreign decorations and wide acclaim.

Appointed Assistant Chief of Air Service in 1920 in the rank of brigadier general, Mitchell served until 1925. He was a frequent visitor to both McCook and Wilbur Wright Fields, and kept a close eye on engineering developments and experiments taking place. According to several writers of Air Service histories, it was Mitchell who originally conceived the idea of a Round-the-World Flight.

Court-martialed in 1925, Mitchell resigned his commission on February 1, 1926.

Maj. Gen. Mason M. Patrick, Air Service Chief, about 1924
(National Archives and Records Service)

MAJ. GEN. MASON M. PATRICK

Born in Lewisburg, West Virginia, on December 13, 1863, Patrick graduated from the U.S. Military Academy in June 1896, and was commissioned a second lieutenant in the Corps of Engineers. Patrick distinguished himself as Chief of Air Service, American Expeditionary Forces, France, May 1918-July 1919, and as Commandant of the Engineers School, Camp Humphreys, Virginia, July-October 1921. Patrick commanded the Army Air Service and its successor, the Army Air Corps, from 1921 to 1927, and was a strong supporter of the 1924 Round-the-World Flight. He retired in December 1927 in the rank of major general.

General Patrick earned his pilot's wings at age 60—a feat not duplicated before or since by a general officer in the Army or Air Force. According to a biographer, General Patrick "deserves the gratitude of airmen the world over for his life and work. He had the vision to foresee the future and the courage to proclaim his vision."

F. Volandt, and Lieutenants Clarence E. Crumrine, Erik Nelson, and St. Clair Streett. All were veteran pilots with hundreds of hours in the air traversing thousands of miles.

According to the flight's unofficial but renowned historian, Lowell Thomas, the Air Service staff studied three essential factors. The first consideration was to obtain several rugged aircraft so that at least one would survive the perilous voyage and thus justify the huge expenditure of manhours and money. The second task was to set up supply bases around the globe. This logistical effort would require the maximum support of all other branches of the national defense establishment, including the Coast Guard, as well as the closest cooperation of the State Department and the Bureau of Fisheries, and the assistance of generous American corporations with offices abroad. Finally, and perhaps just slightly more important than the other factors, was the imperative to select pilots and mechanics possessing the highest degrees of expertise and stamina, both physical and mental, to complete the hazardous mission.

After surveying the newspapers, magazines, and books of that period, two contemporary historians concluded that, "To the man in the street the project seemed doomed to disaster. He surmised that the fliers who engaged in it would stand little chance of returning alive." It was not until foreign governments revealed they were sponsoring pilots in similar ventures that the American public responded to these challenges to national pride. Public attitude changed to a forthright, "However slim the chances of success American fliers must lead the field."[33]

LOGISTICAL SUPPORT PLANS

Clearly, the most complex of the three requisite factors was logistical support. The venture would require the entire range of logistical support services, in a far-flung and complex network.

General planning was based on a route selected to avoid dangerous climatic conditions. By departing in early April and flying northwestward from Seattle, the aircraft would cross Alaska and the stormy North Pacific before dense fogs closed down; pass over mountainous Japan and China before the typhoon season released its furies; escape the howling monsoons across Burma and India; skirt the sandstorms of the Middle East; dodge Continental thunderstorms; and weave through North Atlantic fronts before the early Arctic winter set in. The journey was planned to last six months.[34]

For flight and logistical planning, the world was divided into six regions and a project officer selected for each division (see adjoining Flight Itinerary). About the first of July 1923, Lieutenants Clifford Nutt of McCook Field and Clarence E. Crumrine, stationed in the Philippine Islands, pioneered separate "pathfinding trips," using a variety of land and water vehicles. Lieutenant Nutt surveyed England, Greenland, Iceland, the Faroe Islands, France, Italy, and

WORLD FLIGHT ITINERARY

First Division
(1st Lt. Clayton Bissell, Advance Officer)

Statute Miles

Seattle, Washington	
Prince Rupert, BC	650
Sitka, Alaska	300
Cordova, Alaska	475
Seward, Alaska	135
Chignik, Alaska	450
Dutch Harbor, Unalaska, Alaska	400
Nazan, Island of Atka	350
Chicagoff, Island of Attu	530

Second Division
(1st Lt. Clifford E. Nutt, Advance Officer)

Kashiwabara Bay, Paramushiru, Kuriles	860
Bettobu, Yetorofu, Kuriles	510
Minato, Northeast Coast, Honshu, Japan	475
(Aomori used as supply base)	
Kasumiga Ura, Japanese Air Station	395
(Yokohama used as supply base)	
Osaka, Japan, Japanese Air Station	360
Kagoshima, Kyushu, Japan	380
(Nagasake used as supply base)	

Third Division
(1st Lt. Malcolm S. Lawton, Advance Officer)

Shanghai, China	610
Amoy, China	555
Hong Kong, China	300
Haiphong, French Indo-China	500
Tourane, French Indo-China	395
Saigon, French Indo-China	530
Bangkok, Siam	675
Rangoon, Burma	450
Akyab, Burma	445
Calcutta, India	400

Fourth Division
(1st Lt. Harry A. Halverson, Advance Officer)

Statute Miles

Allahabad, India	475
Delhi, India	380
Multan, India	425
Karachi, India	475
Charbar, Persia	330
Bandar, Abbas, Persia	330
Bushire, Persia	400
Bagdad, Irak [sic]	475
Aleppo, Syria	480
Konia, Turkey	285
San Stefano, Turkey	300

Fifth Division
(Maj. Carlyle H. Wash, Advance Officer)

Bucharest, Rumania	290
Belgrade, Serbia	290
Budapest, Hungary	220
Vienna, Austria	140
Strassbourg, France	400
Paris, France	250
London, England	225

Sixth Division
(1st Lt. Clarence E. Crumrine, Advance Officer)

Brough (Hull) England	155
Kirkwall, Orkney Islands	370
Thorshaven, Faroe Islands	275
Hofn, Hornafjord, Iceland	260
Reykjavik, Iceland	339
Angmagsalik, Greenland	500
Ivigtut, Greenland	500
Indian Harbor, Labrador	572
Cartwright Harbor, Labrador	40
Hawkes Bay, Newfoundland	290
Pictou Harbor, Nova Scotia	420
Boston, Massachusetts	520
Mitchel Field, Long Island, New York	175
Washington, DC	220

NOTE: Cities and nations are spelled according to *Aircraft Year Book for 1924*, pp 237-238; and Air Service *News Letter* VIII, Feb. 1, 1924.

Canada. Lieutenant Crumrine visited Japan, the Kurile Islands, the Aleutian Islands, and Alaska.

Via American embassies in the respective host nations, arrangements were made for the reception and accommodation of airplanes and their crews; prestockage of spare parts and equipment; maintenance facilities and tools; maps, charts, photographs, and sketches of landing fields and water areas for pontoon operations. American corporations with offices and facilities in the various countries also were influential and cooperative with foreign governments and were quite instrumental in obtaining services for the World Flight participants. This was especially true of the Standard Oil Company, which made arrangements for caching avia-

tion gasoline, oil, and lubricants, especially in remote areas.[35]

Air Service logisticians headed by Lt. Elmer E. Adler of the Field Service Section initiated the support plans for the flight. McCook Field, assisted by FAID, was named the main logistics base with subordinate supply depots in each of the six global divisions. The Field Service Section, located at FAID, was responsible for procuring, packaging, and distributing the necessary spare parts and equipment for the World Cruisers and for stocking POL supplies (petroleum/oil/lubricants) in various locations.

Part of Lowell Thomas' account, based on Air Service Records, reads:

Spare parts for planes and engines, a fairly complete outfit of tools, small quantities of standard utility parts, and material, such as tubing, shock-absorber cord, plywood and items other than spare parts, were sent to each station on the route of the Flight. The spare parts and tools were packed in specially constructed boxes designed at the Fairfield Depot and built in the repair shops. The boxes themselves were constructed of ash, spruce, and plywood so that they might be used for the furnishing of wood for emergency repairs. Carpenter tools for working up the wood were sent in the tool chests.

Tubing and other items which could not readily be bent were packed with the propellers in lengths of six feet or more. The weight, cubic contents, and dimensions of every article were carefully considered, about four hundred and eighty separate items being sent to each station, so arranged that the Fliers could find spare parts or repair material even in the dark. On the outside of each crate a diagram showed exactly where each item was located inside.

All shipments to points east of Calcutta, India, were sent from FAID to Seattle for steamship transportation, and all shipments to Karachi, India, and ports westward of that city were sent to New York for oceanic shipment.[36] Spare parts sent overseas included 15 Liberty 12-cylinder 400-hp engines, 14 extra sets of pontoons, and approximately 200 percent of airframe replacement parts.[37]

A maintenance schedule was developed for the trip. It called first for engine changes in Japan. At Calcutta new wings were to be fitted, new engines installed, and pontoons replaced with landing gear. The final engine changes would occur at Hull, England, and landing gear would be replaced with pontoons.[38] Each of the four airplanes was to carry a set of tools "deemed sufficient to maintain the aircraft along the way," plus pliers, screwdriver, hammer, wrench, and a flashlight.

Emergency/survival equipment for each airplane included two rifles and two automatic pistols, one Very pistol for flares, fish hooks and lines, concentrated food, a first aid kit, and a 60-pound ship's anchor with 150 feet of rope. Parachutes, life preservers, and rafts were not carried in the aircraft.

Personal gear for each crewmember was limited to "two changes of underwear, an 11-pound fur-lined leather flying suit, special fur-lined leather gloves, two flannel shirts, two pairs of breeches, two pairs of long, wool stockings, one pair of hunting boots, a cap, handkerchiefs, a waterproof match box, a safety razor, and a toothbrush."[39] Additional clothing was included among the pre-positioned supplies.

THE DOUGLAS WORLD CRUISER

Once the decision had been made to circumnavigate the globe, Air Service headquarters surveyed its current aircraft inventory to find a machine capable of this mission. None existed. In October 1922, the Engineering Division at McCook Field had recommended the purchase of an airplane similar to the Douglas Airplane Company's new DT-2 which was then being produced in large quantities for the

DOUGLAS WORLD CRUISER
SPECIFICATIONS

MANUFACTURER - Douglas Aircraft Company, Inc., Santa Monica, California.

TYPE - Single-engine tractor, two-place biplane (land or sea).

USED BY - U.S. Army Air Service

CONSTRUCTION - The fuselage is of steel tubing, fabric covered, built in three-sections (engine, mid, and rear) with aluminum sheet cowling. The wings are of wood box beam and built-up ribs, fabric covered. Empennage fixed surfaces are of wood; moveable are steel framed—fabric covered. Wings are externally braced. Landing gear is of steel tube with wooden fairings. The steerable tail skid is steel. The landing gear is replaceable with twin floats of 3-ply veneer and mahogany planking.

WINGSPAN - 50' (with wings folded, 10' 2")

LENGTH - 35' 6"

DIHEDRAL - Upper 0°; Lower 2°

CHORD - 7' 6"

INCIDENCE - 3°

HEIGHT - 13' 7½"

GAP - 110 inches at center section, 85 inches at outer struts

STAGGER - None

SWEEPBACK - None

ENGINE - Liberty water-cooled V-12, 400-420 hp turning a fixed-pitch wooden propeller.

FUEL - 644 gallons

OIL - 50 gallons

WEIGHT
  Empty -4,380 lbs. (landplane)
       5,180 lbs. (seaplane)
  Loaded -6,915 lbs. (landplane)
        7,715 lbs. (seaplane)

PERFORMANCE	Landplane	Seaplane
Maximum Speed	104 mph	100 mph
Cruising Speed	90 mph	85 mph
Rate of Climb	500 ft/min	500 ft/min
Ceiling	10,000 feet	7,000 feet
Range	2,200 miles	1,650 miles

Source: Manufacturer

U.S. Navy. On June 24, 1923, the War Department instructed the Air Service to obtain all available data on the Fokker F-5 transport and on the Davis-Douglas Cloudster, almost identical to the DT-2. The Douglas Company, located at Santa Monica, California, submitted specifications for a modified DT-2. The new design was named the Douglas D-WC, i.e., Douglas World Cruiser. The company promised delivery of the $23,271 prototype within 45 days after receiving a signed contract.

Lt. Erik Nelson, 35, a brilliant aeronautical engineer assigned to McCook Field and a veteran pilot, was placed on temporary duty at the Douglas factory in California. He was to work closely with Donald Douglas, assisted by John Northrop, in designing the reconfiguration of the DT-2 into a World Cruiser.

On August 1, 1923, General Patrick approved the reconfiguration plans and a contract was let for construction of the prototype D-WC. The delivery date was met and Lieutenant Nelson flew the new airplane to McCook Field for a series of tests. The Air Service Chief flew to the Engineering Division installation to inspect the prototype, and recommended a few changes to increase performance. The airplane was then flown to Langley Field, Virginia, where it was equipped with pontoons, and successfully completed additional tests.

Satisfied with the aircraft's performance, the War Department gave final approval for the World Flight on November 9, 1923. Eight days later the Douglas Airplane Company received a $192,684 contract for the manufacture of four World Cruisers and spare parts.[40]

The World Cruiser fuselage was divided into three parts: nose or engine section, mid-section, and tail section. The sections were made of steel tubing. The wings were of standard box beam and built-up rib construction. The upper wing was made in three panels and the lower constructed in two. The wings could be folded, allowing for a smaller storage space than the normal straight-wing aircraft. The Cruiser's vertical and horizontal stabilizers were of "standard I-beam and built-up rib construction." The elevator and rudder were made of steel tubing and ribs. The airplane's axles were made from alloy steel tubing which had been heat-treated after fabrication. The struts were steel tubes "streamlined with wood." The pontoons were twin floats of built-up wood construction with the top covering made of three-ply veneer, and the bottom planking made of two-ply mahogany.

The space allocated in the DT-2 to an aerial torpedo was changed in the World Cruiser to accommodate a greatly increased fuel load capability. The enlarged system was composed of a 60-gallon tank (U.S. measurement) in the center section of the upper wing; a 62-gallon cell in the root of each lower wing; a 150-gallon tank behind the engine firewall; a 160-gallon tank beneath the pilot's cockpit; and a 150-gallon cell under the observer's seat. These additional capacities increased the DT-2's original fuel load from 115 gallons to the World Cruiser's 644 gallons. The latter's range was projected to be 2,200 miles with a full fuel load.

(U.S. Air Force Museum)

LT. ERIK H. NELSON

Lt. Erik H. Nelson, of McCook Field, played an especially significant role in the Round-the-World Flight. Nelson worked closely with Donald Douglas, head of the California-based Douglas Airplane Company, during the manufacture of the prototype World Cruiser, and flew the prototype D-WC to McCook Field for initial tests. On the actual flight, Nelson piloted the *New Orleans*, one of the two airplanes to complete the entire journey.*

Born in Stockholm, Sweden, Nelson immigrated to the United States as a merchant marine in 1909. He worked at several jobs, including part-time employment for two years with the Curtiss Airplane Company at Buffalo, New York, where he acquired an expert knowledge of airplanes and airplane engines. Nelson joined the Royal Canadian Air Force in July 1917, but in October of that year was reassigned to the American Air Service, where he became a bomber pilot. He rose to the rank of brigadier general during his Air Force career.

The World Flight was not Lt. Nelson's first experience in distance flying. In late summer 1919, Nelson and a squadron of four airplanes flew a 7,000-mile circuit of 32 cities in the U.S. In 1920, Nelson was the chief engineering officer on an endurance flight headed by Capt. St. Clair Streett from Mitchel Field, Long Island, New York, to Nome, Alaska, and return, without the loss of a single airplane. Later that same year he flew from San Antonio, Texas, to Puerto Rico and return.

*Nelson's partner on the World Cruise was Lt. John Harding, also of McCook Field. Harding held a commission in the Air Service Reserve, and was returned to active duty status while participating in the World Flight. His previous active duty had been as a master sergeant with a rating of "Master Signal Electrician and Airplane Mechanician."

The World Cruiser *New Orleans*, which successfully completed the circumnavigation of the world between April 6 and September 28, 1924, is now on permanent display at the U.S. Air Force Museum. *(U.S. Air Force Museum)*

World Flight pilots hosted at Crissy Field, San Francisco, include (l to r): Lt. Leigh Wade, Lt. Lowell Smith, and Lt. Jack Harding. The ladies in the front row were Mrs. Frank P. (Grace) Lahm and Mrs. E. Emmons. *(U.S. Air Force Museum)*

To improve in-flight communications between pilot and observer, the latter's cockpit was moved forward to a position immediately behind the pilot's cockpit and "a cut-out was incorporated in the trailing edge of the center section of the upper wing to provide upward visibility for navigational purposes."[41] None of the aircraft carried radio equipment for either sending or receiving messages.

Both cockpits had identical instruments: tachometer, air-speed indicator, engine ignition switches, ampere meter, voltmeter, oil pressure gauge, gasoline pressure gauge, altimeter, "ordinary airplane compass and a new earth-inductor compass," a bank-and-turn indicator for flying in fog, an "automatic ignition cut-out switch," and six gasoline control valves. There were also altitude controls to change the proportions of gasoline and air fed to the engine at varying heights, and an engine primer for starting in cold weather.[42]

The pilot sat in the "roomy" front cockpit, with the copilot or mechanic in the aft cockpit. Behind and beneath the rear cockpit "in the tapering fuselage [was] a roomy baggage and tool compartment." Small "transparent shields" protected the crew members from the "powerful air stream" of the flying airplane.[43]

WORLD FLIGHT CREWS

As would be expected, there was an overwhelming response to the call for volunteer pilots and mechanics for the exciting, perilous world flight. The Air Service Chief, General Patrick, after "test-hopping" the prototype World Cruiser at McCook Field, is said to have remarked that he only wished he was "young enough to go on this great undertaking."[44] The only stipulations, aside from meeting General Patrick's stringent requirements of expertise, skills, character, courage, and initiative, were that the indi-

vidual volunteer be unmarried and write on the application his rationale for volunteering.

Although Air Service Headquarters never disclosed the exact criteria used in selecting the eight crew members, Lowell Thomas noted the pilots had all "clocked many hundreds of hours in either cross-country or endurance flying." Some were also exceptionally proficient in both theoretical and practical aeronautical engineering.[45]

The Air Service Chief personally selected Maj. Frederick L. Martin to command the flight, although he was married. Other airplane commanders included Lt. Lowell H. Smith, Lt. Leigh Wade, and Lt. Erik H. Nelson of McCook Field. Alternates were Lt. Leslie P. Arnold and Lt. LeClaire Schultze. These pilots arrived at Langley Field, Virginia, a few days before Christmas 1923. There they underwent concentrated courses in weather phenomena and forecasting, world geography and climatology, aerial navigation, and "enough medical and surgical knowledge to pull them out of mishaps in case of a forced landing in some region remote from civilization."

At Langley they worked closely with ten of the Air Service's best enlisted airplane mechanics who had been assigned to work on the prototype World Cruiser. By the end of the six-week indoctrination period, the aircraft commanders had chosen the mechanics they wished to accompany them on the global flight: Sgt. Alva Harvey, TSgt. Arthur Turner, SSgt. Henry Ogden, and an Engineering Division civilian engineer from McCook Field who was also a Reserve lieutenant, John Harding.[46]

At the end of February 1924 the officers and enlisted mechanics went to the Douglas factory in Santa Monica. There they watched the daily progress in manufacture of the World Cruisers in order to become familiar with every detail of the airplanes' components.

All the Cruisers were completed by March 11, 1924, and the pilots named the four aircraft. Major Martin chose

Newspapers described the Round-the-World Flight crewmen as "modern Magellans." Gathered at the Douglas Aircraft Company in Santa Monica, California, are (l to r): TSgt. Arthur Turner, SSgt. Henry H. Ogden, Lt. Leslie P. Arnold, Lt. Leigh Wade, Lt. Lowell H. Smith, Maj. Frederick L. Martin (Flight Leader), and Sgt. Alva Harvey. *(U.S. Air Force Museum)*

Seattle, Lieutenant Smith named the *Chicago,* Lieutenant Wade selected *Boston,* and Lieutenant Nelson opted for *New Orleans.*

From the Douglas factory the aircraft flew to the Sand Point flying field on Lake Washington near Seattle where wheels were exchanged for pontoons. The final selection of crews was made at this juncture:

Seattle - Maj. Frederick L. Martin and Sgt. Alva Harvey
Chicago - Lt. Lowell Smith and Lt. Leslie Arnold
Boston - Lt. Leigh Wade and SSgt. Henry Ogden
New Orleans - Lt. Erik Nelson and Lt. John Harding

SUCCESS

The quartet of Douglas World Cruisers began their historic odyssey at 8:47 a.m., April 6, 1924, lifting off from Lake Washington. Of the original four World Cruisers, only the *New Orleans* and the *Chicago* completed the circumnavigation of the world, landing at Seattle, Washington, on September 28, 1924. They had flown 26,345 miles in 363 hours' cumulative flying time over an elapsed period of 175 days.

No lives were lost or major injuries sustained when the *Seattle* crashed against a mountainside near Dutch Harbor, Alaska, on April 30, or when the *Boston,* with no oil pressure in the engine, ditched in the North Atlantic Ocean between the Orkney Islands and Iceland on August 2. However, General Patrick "felt that Wade and Ogden [crew of the *Boston*] deserved to enjoy and participate in the homecoming celebrations."[47] He directed the *Boston II,* the 1923 prototype World Cruiser, to join the *Chicago* and *New Orleans* in Nova Scotia and complete the triumphal journey with them.

President Calvin Coolidge and all his cabinet members were among thousands of spectators who greeted the six crewmen on their arrival at Bolling Field, D.C., from Nova Scotia. The final transcontinental portion of the World Flight was from the nation's capitol to Seattle, Washington, and included a stopover at McCook Field, September 14-16, 1924.

As the flight neared Columbus, Ohio, it was joined by a special escort, McCook Field test pilot Lt. Harold Harris in the huge Barling triplane, six-engined bomber. According to Lieutenant Nelson, "As we passed over Wilbur Wright airdrome we saw 'Welcome World Fliers' painted in huge letters on the ground, and between fifty thousand and a hundred thousand people cheered us a moment later as we came gliding down over McCook."

Airplane mechanics and specialists, working in shifts during the next two days, minutely examined "every bolt and wire to find out exactly how the Cruisers had mechanically withstood the strain of the flight." The aircraft were adjudged capable of flying the remaining 3,000 miles to Seattle via the southern route from Chicago. The aircrew members underwent similar thorough medical examinations by McCook Field flight surgeons. All men "were passed as very 'paragons' of physical fitness."[48]

Chicago's wheels touched down on Sand Point Field, Seattle, Washington, at 1:28 p.m. local, September 28, 1924. The World Fliers were greeted by a crowd of 50,000 people. The airplane and its sister, *New Orleans,* had flown the 26,345 miles at an average rate of speed of 79½ miles-per-hour. Flying time was the equivalent of 15 days, 3 hours, 7 minutes.[49]

Several days later other crews returned the four World Cruisers to McCook Field, ending their magnificent odyssey.*

A few months following the flight, Congress voted the Distinguished Service Medal "never before awarded except for services in war," to the six World Flight crewmen. Each received several foreign decorations (with Congressional permission), including their appointment as Chevaliers of the French Legion of Honor. All of the World Cruiser officers were advanced "five hundred files each" on the promotion rosters.[50]

The Great Adventure was over and another page of aviation history had been written in red, white, and blue ink. As a Navy admiral eloquently summed it up: "Other men will fly around the earth, but never again will anybody fly around it first."[51]

On the return leg to Seattle, Washington, the World Cruisers landed at McCook Field on September 14, 1924. The *Chicago* (number 2) led the flight, flanked by *Boston II* and *New Orleans* (number 4). *(NCR Corporation)*

Douglas World Cruiser *Chicago* outfitted with twin pontoons for water takeoffs and landings and oceanic flights *(U.S. Air Force Museum)*

Maj. J. F. Curry (left), Chief of the Engineering Division and future commander of McCook Field, greeted the World Flight pilots upon their arrival in Dayton. They were (l to r): Lt. Lowell Smith, SSgt. Henry Ogden, and Lts. Erik Nelson, Leigh Wade, John Harding, and Leslie Arnold. *(Dayton and Montgomery County Public Library)*

*The *New Orleans* was obtained on loan in April 1957 from the Natural History Museum, Los Angeles, California, rejuvenated, and placed on permanent display inside the main exhibition hall of the United States Air Force Museum at Wright-Patterson AFB. The *Chicago* is currently on display at the National Air and Space Museum, Smithsonian Institution, Washington, D.C.

1924 AIR RACES

Less than a week after the Douglas World Cruisers made their final landing near Seattle, Washington, FAID and Wilbur Wright Field were center stage in the spotlight of aviation. Two decades and twelve days after aviation pioneer Wilbur Wright flew the first complete circle in the history of powered airplanes, FAID and Wilbur Wright Field hosted the International Air Races, October 2-4, 1924.

This aviation extravaganza offered prestigious prizes such as the Pulitzer Trophy, and $80,000 in prize money (payable in U.S. Government Liberty Bonds) to the winners of 12 events. The event was sponsored by the National Aeronautic Association (NAA). NAA president that year was the President of the National Cash Register Company of Dayton, aviation enthusiast Frederick Beck Patterson.

As it turned out, the "international" aspect of the event did not materialize. The large number of expected foreign contestants cancelled out a few weeks prior to the meet. The popular explanation for the withdrawals was the known inability of the European airplanes to match the speed, maneuverability, and general performance of American civilian and military airplanes.[52]

All three Air Service installations in the Dayton area had major responsibilities in the thrilling aerial drama that attracted over 100,000 spectators during the three days of exhibits, demonstrations, and races.

Maj. Augustine Warner Robins, Wilbur Wright Field/FAID Commander, worked closely with Mr. Patterson and with Mr. Charles H. Paul, general manager of the air races organization. Major Robins' personal assistants were Lt. Elmer E. Adler and Lt. C. E. Thomas, the latter serving as

Executive Officer. Other officers in charge of air race activities at Wilbur Wright were Maj. George H. Brett, housing and entertainment; Maj. J. H. Rudolph, engineering officer in charge of flying operations; Maj. H. J. Knerr, in charge of ferrying airplanes and furnishing aircraft for aerial photography; Capt. Edward Laughlin (McCook

A special edition of the McCook Field publication *The Slipstream Monthly* highlighted events at the 1924 International Air Races held at FAID and Wilbur Wright Field.

Frederick B. Patterson (left), President of the National Aeronautic Association, chats with Maj. Gen. Mason M. Patrick, Chief of the Army Air Service. The NAA sponsored the International Air Races held October 2-4, 1924.

Panoramic view of a portion of the 100,000 spectators at the International Air Races. For safety reasons a fence and a wide road separated the crowds from the bustling flightline with its noise, dust, fumes, and whirring propellers. *(NCR Corporation)*

Commanding Officer of the Fairfield Air Intermediate Depot, Maj. Augustine Warner Robins, poses with his staff members in front of FAID headquarters during the 1924 International Air Races. Front row (l to r): Capt. W. F. Donnelly, Capt. J. B. Powers, Maj. J. H. Rudolph, Commander Robins, Maj. G. H. Brett, and Maj. H. J. Knerr. Back row (l to r): Capt. Edward Laughlin, Capt. C. O. Thrasher, Lt. L. H. Dunlap, Lt. C. E. Thomas, Lt. H. A. Bartron, Lt. L. E. Sharon, and Capt. F. F. Christine.

Field), assistant operations officer; Capt. F. F. Christine, photographic officer; Capt. J. B. Powers, surgeon; Lt. Samuel G. Eaton, Jr., communications officer; Lt. L. E. Sharon, publicity and press relations; and Lt. H. A. Bartron, in charge of the baggage and check room.[53]

The Chief of the Air Service personally selected 23 officers from among the Army's most courageous and skillful pilots to fly in the four most prestigious trophy races.

Nine principals and three alternates were picked for the Liberty Engine Builders Trophy race on October 2. Designated to fly the Standard DeHavilland DH-4 and Corps Observation airplanes were:

Maj. Clarence H. Tinker, Fort Riley, Kansas
Lt. R. J. Brown, Jr., Boston, Massachusetts
Lt. L. V. Beau, Bolling Field, D.C.
Lt. C. W. Steinmetz, Bolling Field, D.C.
Lt. E. B. Bobzien, Chanute Field, Illinois
Lt. J. B. Haddon, Brooks Field, Texas
Lt. H. D. Knapp, Maxwell Field, Alabama
Lt. C. A. Cover, FAID, Wilbur Wright Field
Lt. A. E. Simonin, Moundsville, West Virginia

Alternates were:

Lt. D. G. Duke, OCAS
Lt. Rex K. Stoner, Langley Field, Virginia
Lt. L. A. Walthall, Fort Bragg, North Carolina

Six Martin MB-2 twin-engine bombers and one Martin-Curtiss NBS-1 bomber were entered in the Dayton Chamber of Commerce Trophy race, October 3. The race featured "large capacity airplanes" (capable of carrying useful loads of 2,000 pounds and over) and offered $4,000 in Liberty Bonds as prizes. Selected to fly the largest aircraft in the regularly-assigned inventory were:

Capt. George C. Kenney, McCook Field
Lt. Carlton D. Bond, Phillips Field
Lt. D. M. Myers, Phillips Field
Lt. Hezekiah E. McClellan, Brooks Field, Texas
Lt. C. F. Woolsey, Brooks Field, Texas
Lt. H. D. Smith, Langley Field, Virginia
Lt. D. J. Canfield, Kelly Field, Texas (alternate)

For the renowned Pulitzer Trophy speed race on October 4, which offered $10,000 in prizes, General Patrick chose Capt. Burt E. Skeel, Selfridge Field, Michigan, and Lt.

Lt. James H. Doolittle (left), famed McCook Field test pilot, his wife Josephine, and Maj. Gen. Mason M. Patrick, Chief of the Army Air Service, discuss the International Air Races underway at Wilbur Wright Field. *(Mrs. Darlene Gerhardt)*

The Pulitzer Trophy

This silver trophy was donated by Ralph, Joseph, and Herbert Pulitzer, publishers of the New York *World* and St. Louis *Post-Dispatch* newspapers. The Pulitzer Trophy Race was the "speed classic" of the International Air Races, "the premier event of the meet." Gold, silver, and bronze medals were awarded to winners. The first four winning pilots shared $10,000 in prize money. *(NCR Corporation)*

Wendell H. Brookley, McCook Field, to fly Army-type Curtiss R-8 racers. Lt. Alexander Pearson, Jr., McCook Field, was picked to fly the Navy version of the Curtiss R-8. Alternate pilot was Lt. H. H. Mills, McCook Field.

The John L. Mitchell Trophy race on October 4 featured pursuit-type airplanes and offered $5,000 in Liberty bonds as prizes. Air Service candidates were chosen by Maj. Carl Spaatz, Commanding Officer of Selfridge Field. His selectees, all chosen from his command, included:[54]

Lt. George P. Tourtellot
Lt. Reuben C. Moffat
Lt. Ennis C. Whitehead
Lt. Cyrus Bettis
Lt. Leland C. Hurd
Lt. James D. Summers
Lt. Robert R. Yeager
Lt. J. T. Johnson
Lt. Thomas K. Matthews
Lt. Thomas W. Blackburn
Lt. Donald F. Stace

For several weeks before the races, FAID and Wilbur Wright Field personnel worked long hours putting final touches on the 130 racing planes and preparing the post to receive scores of distinguished guests. A huge grandstand

Race courses established for the 1924 International Air Races

over one mile in length was erected at Wilbur Wright Field, the officers' club was converted into a dining hall, and the swimming pool was drained and converted into a sunken garden. The post gymnasium was the site of a gala reception and aviation ball held the evening of October 2, attended by about 500 military and guests.

The evening's sparkling glamour was described by the Air Service Information Division, using local newspaper accounts.[55]

> Long lines of flaunting colors which bordered the room represented every nation in the world, conveying the international appeal and importance of aviation. At the farther end of the ballroom was the American crest, and in the center was erected in huge form the emblem of the major general of the United States Army.
>
> Flags of various nations were placed at intervals about the huge room to form stalls, one being allotted to each government flying field in the United States and its possessions, which sent delegates to the international classic.
>
> In direct contrast to the color scheme were placed large paintings at either end of the ballroom. Both of the works of art were executed at Wright Field [sic] and depicted a group of Curtiss pursuit planes in battle formation and the other, the epoch-making flight of Lieut. Maughan across the continent. To enhance these elaborate decorations profusion of fern and other greenery were used about the boxes and autumn flowers were banked on all tables.
>
> Despite the fact that America is a republic, the scene rivaled closely the brilliance of European court functions.
>
> Distinguished army officers, marines and representatives of foreign countries mingled with the handsomely gowned women upon the dance floor, producing a scene that will be unequalled for many years to come.

Wilbur Wright Field Officers' Club decorated for a 1924 dinner honoring Maj. Gen. Mason M. Patrick, Chief of the Army Air Service. The club stood near the present-day location of the 2750th Air Base Wing Headquarters, Building 10 in Area C.

In Dayton, enthusiasm for the races was epidemic. On Friday, October 3, all public schools were closed. Over the weekend, city and county offices were shut, and all factories, including the National Cash Register Company, Dayton Engineering Laboratories Company (Delco), and the General Motors Corporation, stopped operations to allow their workers to attend the holiday events. The annual banquet of the National Aeronautic Association was held Friday evening at the NCR dining hall with 1,000 persons attending. Notables included Mr. Patterson, who as President of the NAA presided over the dinner; Charles F. Kettering, head of the General Motors Research Corporation, who served as toastmaster; and Frederick H. Rike, President of the Rike-Kumler Company, who was honored as vice-chairman of the race officials.[56]

The first event of the weekend was an On-To-Dayton race which attracted 51 civilian entries from New York, Illinois, Texas, Kansas, Michigan, and a dozen other states, plus Canada. The brightly-painted airplanes of all makes and combinations created a wondrous spectacle.

The events held on October 2-4 encompassed twelve categories of major races, each sponsored by a different newspaper, manufacturer, labor union, civic organization, or prominent citizen. The races were interspersed with skywriting exhibitions, free balloon flights, parachute demonstrations, freak flying, aerial combat, and formation flying.

A nostalgic highlight was the display and flight of early Wright brothers aircraft. The 1903 *Kitty Hawk* itself was displayed but not flown.[57] The 1911 Model B, however, was removed from its safe storage in the FAID Supply Department and flown. McCook Field's famous test pilot, Lt. John A. Macready, thrilled Orville and Katharine Wright and throngs of spectators by circling Wilbur Wright Field at an altitude of 1,000 feet for 15 minutes at a speed of about 45 miles per hour.

Timers' stand for the International Air Races, Wilbur Wright Field. Orville Wright served as chairman of the timing committee for the prestigious Pulitzer Trophy high-speed race. In the foreground are examples of the most popular mode of transportation for the young and young-at-heart: motorcycles with sidecars. *(NCR Corporation)*

Pilots enroute to the International Air Races, including Lt. James H. Doolittle (left), publicized the race and generated public enthusiasm. *(Mrs. Darlene Gerhardt)*

Kitty Hawk, the Wright brothers' airplane that made the world's first controlled, powered flight on December 17, 1903, was reassembled and exhibited in the Wright 1910 hangar that still stood on Wilbur Wright Field. Signs announce that proceeds from this display during the Air Races would go to the non-profit National Aeronautic Association. (This was the last time the airplane was shown before shipment to England in 1928.) *(NCR Corporation)*

Another highlight was the release of the Sperry Messenger. Suspended by hooks in its upper wing, the Sperry Messenger hung from a trapeze below the TC-5, an Air Service non-rigid dirigible. At an altitude of 2,500 feet, the Messenger was released into powered flight.

The true high points were, of course, the races themselves.

Lt. D. G. Duke, assigned to the Office of the Chief of the Air Service, won the Liberty Engine Builders Trophy race in the Standard DH-4 observation biplane powered by a Liberty 12-cylinder, 400-hp engine. He averaged 128 mph over the 12-lap, 15-mile course. The John L. Mitchell Trophy competition was won at 185.45 mph. The three-lap, 200-kilometer race (124.27 miles) was taken by Lt. Cyrus Bettis of Selfridge Field in a Curtiss PW-8 biplane with a 460-hp Curtiss D-12 engine. A Martin MB-2 bomber piloted by Lt. D. M. Myers won the 150-mile Dayton Chamber of Commerce Trophy race with a speed of 109.85 mph.

Lt. H. H. Mills, McCook Field, won the Pulitzer Trophy race, flying a Verville-Sperry Racer over the 200-kilometer course at an average speed of 216.55 miles-per-hour. The race, however, was marred by two deaths.

Lt. Alexander Pearson, 29, of McCook Field, died September 2 during a practice flight for the Pulitzer Race at Wilbur Wright Field when the left wing of his Navy-type Curtiss racer failed at an altitude of about 300 feet, causing the airplane to crash. Capt. Burt E. Skeel, 30, Commanding Officer of the 27th Squadron at Selfridge Field, Michigan, died during the race on October 4 when the wings broke away from the fuselage of the Army-type Curtiss racer at 2,000 feet. He went into a dive at about 275 mph. (Skeel and Pearson Avenues in present-day Area C at Wright-Patterson AFB are named in memory of these two intrepid young pilots.)

Dayton Chamber of Commerce Trophy awarded to Lt. Devereaux Maitland Myers of the Air Service. Myers attained a speed of 109.815 mph in 10 laps over a 15-mile course. *(Wright State University Archives)*

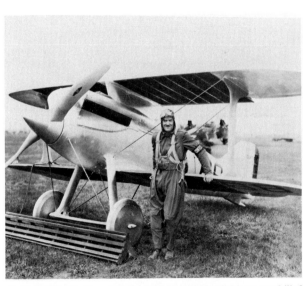

Capt. Burt E. Skeel, assigned to Selfridge Field, Michigan, was killed in the crash of his Curtiss R-6 racer during the Pulitzer Trophy race on October 4. Skeel Avenue, named in his honor, parallels the Area C flightline today.

Lt. Alexander Pearson of McCook Field died on September 2 during a practice flight for the International Air Races. Pearson Avenue in present-day Area C of Wright-Patterson AFB is named in his honor.

THE MODEL AIRWAY

In August 1925, FAID assumed administrative control of the Model Airway System. The Model Airway was an experimental Air Service airline, first in the nation to operate regularly-scheduled flights between fixed points. Established in June 1921, the Airway maintained regular service for both passengers and cargo between McCook Field, Ohio; Bolling Field, D.C.; Langley Field, Virginia; and Mitchel Field, Long Island, New York.

Increased operations and the need to expand facilities prompted the Air Service to relocate the airline headquarters from crowded McCook Field to considerably more spacious accommodations at FAID. The three coordinating functions of the Airway—administration, communications, and meteorology—operated at FAID under the direct supervision of the Commanding Officer, Maj. A. W. Robins.

In July of 1923, the Air Corps weather station moved from McCook Field and was housed in the loft of Building 1, FAID, where it began immediate operations. By December 1923, the Airway System had expanded to cover Selfridge Field, Michigan; Chanute Field, Illinois; and FAID, Fairfield, Ohio. Several other facilities were integrated into radio nets for communications and weather reporting.

FAID had become very interested in the Airway and promoted its growth by conducting a cost analysis of both cargo and passenger flights. Major Robins, Commander of both FAID and Wilbur Wright Field, reported his findings in August 1925. He noted that between June 1922 and June 1925, DH-4 aircraft in this long-term program had made 546 flights covering 1,046,610 miles. They carried 868 passengers and 46,179 pounds of cargo. Major Robins estimated that 600 of these passengers had flown on official orders. He concluded that based on an average trip of 2,000 miles, the Army had saved $600,000 in passenger travel expenses during the three-year period. Based on a figure of 1,000 miles per load, cargo savings amounted to $4,263.31.[58]

Robins was more than pleased with the progress of the Airway because it strengthened a vital link in the national defense chain. He also applauded the many benefits of the operation to the future of both military and commercial aviation, especially in the areas of instrumentation, navigation, standardization of facilities and procedures, and communications. For example:

- A special night air route was set up between McCook Field and Norton Field, Ohio, for a three-month test of night flying equipment, both on airplanes and on the ground.*

- The Airways Branch of the Engineering Department experimented with "instrument-only" flying. Cockpits were entirely enclosed to simulate fog and poor visibility and to force pilots to fly by navigation instruments alone.

- The Radio Branch at FAID developed direction-finder radio beacons. In tests, aircraft were guided by radio between McCook and Langin Field, Moundsville, West Virginia; and between McCook and Chanute Field, Rantoul, Illinois.

- A system of aviation maps was developed, showing private airfields as well as military.

- Names of small towns and villages along flight routes were marked on hangars and flat roofs of major buildings. Together with a program of installing rotating beacons, this identification system saved the lives of scores of military and civilian pilots during times of poor visibility and bad weather. During 1934, when the Air Corps assumed responsibility for flying the air mail, these markers proved invaluable.

- Standardized plans were developed for equipping emergency landing fields with hangars, radio towers, fuel tanks, etc. A "logical plan of expansion" specified dimensions of runways and standard field markers for future field development.

- Standardized procedures were developed for the filing of flight plans, invaluable for both pre-flight planning and in the event of in-flight emergency. Information that was "filed" prior to departure included airplane type and identification number, names and addresses of crew members and passengers, description and weight of cargo, volume and weight of fuel aboard, route to be flown, scheduled intermediate stops, and final destination with estimated time of arrival. Moreover, a reservation system for passengers and cargo was formulated.

- A radio net was established embracing all major stations of the airway to furnish complete mete-

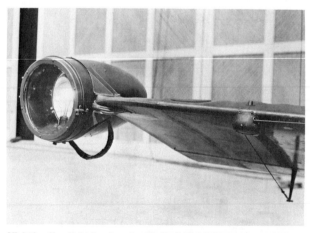

Night landing light developed at McCook Field. Mounted on a DH-4B observation airplane, the light illuminated the ground directly in front of the aircraft. The lamp was a 12-volt, 500-watt concentrated filament incandescent bulb. The entire light weighed 11 pounds. *(U.S. Air Force Museum)*

---

*Norton Field, Columbus, Ohio, was dedicated on June 30, 1923. Wilbur Wright Field and FAID sent five DH-4 observation airplanes, a photographic airplane, and two "Vought stunting planes" to the formal dedication. Norton Field, Ohio, had no connection with the present Norton Air Force Base located in California.

orological reports three times daily. This ended previous dependence on sketchy local weather reports and newspaper forecasts.

In Major Robins' judgment:[59]

> The Airway has increased the general interest in cross-country flying because of excellent maps, marked towns, emergency fields, aeronautical bulletins, radio communications, and other conveniences which have been instituted by the Model Airway over the entire country. The aeronautical bulletins, which include the latest information on all landing fields throughout the United States are published with a complete sketch and information regarding facilities at each field. These aeronautical bulletins are furnished to Air Service personnel and to all persons engaged in aeronautics.

The Airways project was discontinued in 1926, but its programs became prototypes for a growing industry.

CREATION OF THE FAIRFIELD AIR DEPOT RESERVATION

In 1924, a chain of events began which culminated in the 1927 establishment of the Fairfield Air Depot Reservation. In 1924, the citizens of Dayton donated land to the government for the establishment of a new and expanded Air Service installation (detailed in Chapter IV, McCook Field). In response, War Department General Orders No. 20, issued in August 1925, directed that the designation "Wilbur Wright Field" be discontinued. The original flying field, together with the newly-donated acreage, was designated "Wright Field" in honor of both Wright brothers.* The area occupied by the Fairfield depot (including the 40 acres that had been purchased by the government in 1917), also became part of the larger Wright Field, although the depot's mission remained unchanged.[60]

Further and more widespread changes affected the Fairfield depot in 1926. The Air Corps Act, signed on July 2, authorized the formation of the Air Corps Materiel Division, which was to have permanent facilities at the new Wright Field.[61] As mentioned earlier in this chapter, the Field Service Section at FAID performed a materiel function in its management of the Air Service depots, and thus became a major section of the new Division.

The physical removal of the Field Service Section from the Fairfield depot clarified the often-confusing distinction between the Air Corps depot command and the Fairfield depot which had been its temporary home. There were periods after the move, though, when the Field Service Section was directed by the depot Commander. This happened in 1927, from May to September, when Maj. Augustine W. Robins commanded both functions, and from September 1929 to June 1930, when Maj. Henry H. Arnold was in command.[62]

Concurrent with the removal of the Field Service Section on June 21, the depot name changed once more. War Department General Orders No. 9, dated June 22, 1927,

Gen. Henry H. "Hap" Arnold. As a Major, Arnold served as Commander of the Fairfield Air Depot from June 1929 to July 1930.

Framework of Building 13, Engineering Department, Fairfield Air Depot, 1930. The Post Hospital is visible behind the water tower at upper right.

designated the depot as the Fairfield Air Depot Reservation (FADR).[63] Again, the mission of the depot did not change, although as part of the new Wright Field, there was an increase in construction and activities.

On the new portion of Wright Field (now Area B), construction funds were appropriated early in 1930 for a complex of technical buildings to support the Air Corps expansion program. Eighteen buildings were erected between 1930 and 1933 to house research, development, and testing functions.

At the Fairfield Air Depot Reservation construction was also underway. Building 13 was built to keep pace with

*Wright Field was completed and formally dedicated in October 1927.

Thousands of spectators attend a 1930 airshow and carnival on the Fairfield Air Depot Reservation flightline. In the foreground a "modern" steel hangar (now Building 145 in Area C) carries the inscription "Fairfield Air Depot U.S. Army." FAD Headquarters (Building 1) is at center top of photo; completed Building 13 is at center left.

modern repair and overhaul functions, and was completed in June 1930. New machinery and equipment were installed in less than a month, causing no lost time in production. The hangar system of overhaul was reinstated, replacing the assembly-line method which had been in use since 1926. In November 1930, Building 54 was completed by bricking up an old hangar. This building was used to house parachute repair, the fabric department, the wood mill, and the local issue unit.[64] The depot also provided temporary space for several functions of the Materiel Division that were making the move from McCook Field, but were awaiting final completion of their facilities on the new section of the field (Area B).

On June 7, 1930, a gala Air Corps Carnival was sponsored by Wright Field and FADR. The carnival was a benefit air exhibition to raise funds for the Army Relief Association, the Enlisted Men's Fund, and the Civilian Welfare Association at Wright Field and FADR, as well as the Wilbur Wright Officers' Club. Maj. Henry "Hap" Arnold was general chairman of the event, and widespread advertising attracted a large crowd.

The 40-piece FADR band provided morning entertainment. The afternoon program offered a pursuit race, aerial combat, parachute jumping, and airplane aerobatics; visitors were welcome to take dollar airplane rides and invited to dance in the gymnasium. The evening program opened with a display of fireworks during which airplanes carried lights as they flew overhead. A display of night photography and an illuminated smoke screen closed the spectacle.[65]

THE 1931 AIR CORPS MANEUVERS

In May 1931, FADR and Wright Field hosted the 1931 Air Corps maneuvers. Much larger than previous field exercises held at the depot in 1926 and 1929, the 1931 maneuvers mobilized the entire Air Corps on an unprecedented scale and had far-reaching effects.

Brig. Gen. Benjamin D. Foulois, Assistant Chief of the Air Corps, flew his staff to FADR from Washington and personally organized the First Provisional Air Division. This temporary organization was composed of one bombardment wing, one pursuit wing, two observation wings, one attack group, and one transport group. It mustered 24 of the Air Corps' 25 tactical squadrons in the continental U.S. In addition, National Guard units from 19 states attended. In all, a total of 672 airplanes participated. Orville Wright served as honorary chairman of the Dayton committee for the maneuvers.

The maneuvers were carefully designed to test the capabilities of all facets of the Air Corps. Initial practice formations were flown over Ohio from May 15-19 to rehearse an "aerial war" to be fought on the East Coast the following week. The Division staged a full-scale review over Chicago on May 20, then headed east.

On May 22, the division landed at five different fields in New York with General Foulois setting up Division headquarters at Mitchel Field on Long Island. Operations were carried out over New York, Hartford, Springfield (Massachusetts), Boston, Atlantic City, Trenton, Jersey City, Philadelphia, and Washington, D.C. This required perfect coordination of supply lines, maintenance facilities, and staff support agencies. Orders for the maneuvers called for air transport of sufficient food, medical items, and clothing to supply 1,400 men for 15 days as they moved over a dozen states. This experience under actual field conditions gave the Air Corps command a precise picture of its ability to handle a large mobile air force, and the results were encouraging.

The maneuvers closed with an aerial review over Washington, D.C., on Memorial Day 1931, with President Herbert C. Hoover observing from the White House lawn. During the Division's mobilization, operation, and demobilization, its airplanes flew over all 48 states and accumulated four million miles without any fatalities or serious injuries.[66]

Spectators walk the main road paralleling the flightline during the 1931 Air Corps maneuvers.

MAJ. GEN. BENJAMIN D. FOULOIS

Benjamin D. Foulois enlisted in 1898 with the Army Corps of Engineers. He was commissioned in 1901 as a lieutenant of Infantry. After initial instruction at College Park, Maryland, in 1909, Lieutenant Foulois served as the Army's only pilot for most of 1910. He flew Signal Corps Number One at Fort Sam Houston, Texas, with correspondence instruction from the Wright brothers. In November 1917, in grade of temporary brigadier general, he was named Chief of Air Service for the American Expeditionary Forces (AEF) in France. In December 1927, he was promoted to permanent brigadier general and assigned as Assistant to the Chief of the Army Air Corps. In June 1929, he assumed command of the Air Corps Materiel Division at Wright Field, Ohio. Foulois was promoted to major general in December 1931 and named as Chief of the Army Air Corps. He retired in December 1935.

The First Provisional Air Division was commanded by Brig. Gen. Benjamin D. Foulois, Assistant Chief of Staff for Operations, Hq Army Air Corps. In the foreground are the aircraft of the pursuit wing. Stretching toward the horizon are a part of the total fleet of 672 airplanes that participated in the May 15-30 maneuvers.

From May 15 to 30, 1931, the largest peacetime maneuvers in Army Air Service-Air Corps history were held on the Fairfield Air Depot Reservation. This photograph shows part of the pursuit wing of the First Provisional Air Division parked beside the flightline of World War I wooden hangars. Note the balloon hangar at the far end of the flightline; in front of it is the hangar specially constructed for the Barling bomber. In the background are the growing towns of Fairfield and Osborn.

THE DESIGNATION OF PATTERSON FIELD

For the six years between August 1925 and July 1931, the area occupied by the Fairfield Air Intermediate Depot (FAID) and later the Fairfield Air Depot Reservation (FADR), was technically part of Wright Field. Wright Field was therefore composed of the land which had been purchased by the government in 1917 for depot use, and roughly 4,500 acres which had been donated to the government by the Dayton Air Service Committee in 1924.

On July 1, 1931, however, Wright Field was divided. All of the land west of Huffman Dam, including much of the area known today as Area B, WPAFB, retained the designation Wright Field. All of the land east of Huffman Dam was designated Patterson Field in honor of Daytonian Frank Stuart Patterson. Lieutenant Patterson had been killed in the

crash of his DH-4 airplane at Wilbur Wright Field in 1918. The new Patterson Field included the whole of FADR, the former site of Wilbur Wright Field, and the area known today as WPAFB Area A.

The prominent position occupied by the Patterson family in the early history of Wright-Patterson AFB is covered in Chapter IV on McCook Field. Chapter VII is devoted to the history of Patterson Field and contains information on Lieutenant Patterson.

The field name change did not affect the name or organizational structure of the Fairfield depot, but the word "Reservation" was deleted from its title, making it the Fairfield Air Depot. The depot continued to function as part of Patterson Field until 1946, when the depot was officially deactivated. The post-1931 history of the depot can be followed in Chapter VII.

McCook Field, "Cradle of Military Aviation Development," along the eastern bank of the Great Miami River in Dayton (*Mrs. Darlene Gerhardt*)

IV.   McCOOK FIELD 1917-1927

A TIME OF CRISIS

The story of McCook Field, like the story of Wilbur Wright Field, began several years prior to World War I. On March 3, 1915, eight months after the Aviation Section of the Signal Corps was created, Congress called for the establishment of a National Advisory Committee for Aeronautics (NACA). This committee was composed of representatives from the War, Navy, Treasury, Commerce, and Agriculture Departments. It was tasked to direct studies that would generate data vital to the improvement of American military aviation.

The foremost concern of the NACA was the war in Europe. Although America was not yet directly involved, leading members of the military establishment felt it would be prudent to assess American aviation capabilities. They felt that should America enter the war, an effective aerial force might well be the deciding factor in an Allied victory.

The Aviation Section, in 1916, could claim only a handful of aeronautical engineers and draftsmen. It was no secret that the U.S. lagged far behind the rapid develop-

ments taking place in Europe due to the press of wartime. U.S. engineers had little experience with military aircraft design, and aircraft production was conducted basically one airplane at a time. NACA members were determined to rectify these deficiencies.

Congress granted the Committee authority to conduct research and experimentation "in any laboratory, in whole or in part, which may be assigned to it."[1] What the NACA discovered, however, was that no such facility existed. In the summer of 1916, the Committee concluded it had no alternative but to construct its own research facility, one that would be shared jointly by NACA, the Army, and the Navy. Property was purchased near Hampton, Virginia, and in April 1917, construction began on the installation that was to become Langley Field.

Time, however, was against them; war with Germany was declared April 6, 1917. Appropriations for aviation had been increased five months earlier (to $14 million on November 16, 1916), but the engineering and aircraft manufacturing industries lacked sufficient time to gear up for the tremendous demands of wartime production. Nor could the NACA help them do so, in addition to its research and experimentation activities.

Congress appointed a second body to work specifically within the area of aircraft production. On April 12, six days after the declaration of war, the Aircraft Production Board was created to coordinate all activities of the nation's aircraft manufacturers during the massive build-up to follow. The Board was also to ensure that the resources and raw materials required by the manufacturers were available to them. The Board worked on behalf of both the War Department and the Department of the Navy, directing the completion of contracts let by both departments.

The expectations made of the Aircraft Production Board were staggering. Signal Corps records show that in the eight years prior to 1916 only 59 airplanes had been ordered and received. During 1916, 366 airplanes had been requisitioned, but only 83 had been delivered.[2] The United States Government was therefore woefully unprepared when an urgent cable was received from Premier Alexandre Ribot of France on May 26, 1917. The Premier requested 16,500 aircraft, 5,000 trained pilots, and 50,000 "mechanicians" as America's contribution to the Allied effort for the first six months of the 1918 campaign.[3] Although this goal was far greater than the U.S. ever hoped to accomplish, it did spark

Looking south onto McCook Field hangars. World War I-era airplanes had few instruments and no radios. Directional signs were often painted on flat roofs of buildings near flightlines to assist pilots. Arrows painted on hangar at upper center point in the direction of the cities named on the cross-arms: Rantoul (IL), Chicago (IL), Columbus (OH), and Toledo (OH).

Looking north on Keowee Street. Residential areas surrounding McCook Field hastened its closure and the relocation of its mission, equipment, and personnel to Wright Field in 1927. This photograph shows how civilian homes, on the right, barred expansion of the 254-acre facility.

action in the Congress. Between May 12 and July 24, 1917, President Woodrow Wilson signed a series of three bills appropriating a total of $694,250,000 for military aeronautics.[4] In a spirit of enthusiasm, a program was proposed which called for the production of 12,000 service airplanes, 4,900 primary, advanced, and fighting airplanes, and 24,000 service engines by June 30, 1918.[5]

Even these goals were out of reach. America's aeronautical engineers were not versed in mass production techniques. They knew very little about the special equipment needed to fit an airplane for military use, and even less about writing technical manufacturing specifications for mass production of that equipment. Aerial machine guns, bombing equipment, lights for night flying, aviators' clothing, compasses used in flying, and other aviation instruments had not been studied and developed to the extent they had been by the Europeans.

Moreover, the Allied nations involved in the development of military aviation were extremely secretive about their efforts. The United States, by not participating earlier in the war, had been excluded from access to these contemporary research findings. As Newton D. Baker, former Secretary of War, wrote in 1919:[6]

> Probably no military secrets were more closely guarded in Europe than developments in aircraft. As a consequence, when we entered the war, airplane construction in the United States was upon a most limited scale, and our knowledge of developments which had taken place in Europe was largely hearsay.

Attention was suddenly focused on the need for the intensive program of fundamental research and experimentation forecast earlier by the members of the National Advisory Committee for Aeronautics.

Progress at Langley, unfortunately, was painfully slow. After war was declared, the civilian contractor constructing the facilities received urgent orders to increase his work force and accelerate operations. This extra pressure only served to cause confusion and inefficiency. Construction actually slowed, and Langley was able to play only a limited role in World War I.[7]

The Navy grew impatient with these construction delays and moved its operations to experimental bases elsewhere. The Aviation Section of the Signal Corps decided to pursue a similar course.

AN ALTERNATIVE TO LANGLEY FIELD

Industrialist Edward A. Deeds was a key member of the Aircraft Production Board, and a prominent member of the Dayton business community. He was President of the Delco Company, past President of The National Cash Register Company, and a director of the Dayton Metal Products Company (which made fuses for the Russian government).[8] His interest in aviation and his understanding of the need to develop America's air power stemmed from his personal friendship with Wilbur and Orville Wright, nurtured from the early days on Huffman Prairie.

Deeds was well known in Washington circles by virtue of his service on the Munitions Standards Board. He served on the Aircraft Production Board from May 17 until August 2, 1917. On August 2, he was appointed Acting Chief of the newly-created Equipment Division of the Signal Corps. Three weeks later, on August 24, he was commissioned as a colonel in the Signal Corps Reserve and was officially promoted to the position of Chief of the Equipment Division. In order to accept a commission, Deeds relinquished his ties with private business and his financial connections, retaining only the presidency of the Board of Directors of the Miami Conservancy District (a non-partisan state-chartered public organization).[9]

The mission of the Equipment Division was to oversee the production of thousands of airplanes and engines within only a few months. The Division, under Colonel Deeds' leadership, was authorized to spend upwards of $350 million. Deeds was assigned an initial staff of 14 officers and 111 civilians, which grew, within six months, to 300 officers and 2,700 civilians.[10]

When he assumed command of the Equipment Division, Colonel Deeds found a fragmented engineering program. Pending completion of Langley Field, Signal Corps engineering projects were being conducted in a number of different locations, including Washington, Detroit, Chicago, and Buffalo.[11] Deeds was constantly frustrated by the slowness of progress in the dispersed aviation program. It was evident that production problems were exacerbated by the absence of a strong, supportive central engineering and

Col. Edward A. Deeds, Chief of the Signal Corps Equipment Division
(NCR Corporation)

experimental facility. He determined to give top priority to establishing a temporary facility, aside from Langley Field, where shops, laboratories, hangars, a flying field, offices, and other appropriate facilities could all be centralized at one location.

The area of the country most familiar to Deeds was Dayton, Ohio. He also knew a good deal about the potential for aviation development in Dayton. In 1916, Deeds had established one of the first private flying fields in the United States, South Field, at his south Dayton estate, Moraine Farm. He had equipped it with a hangar and a research laboratory, and permitted its later use as a testing ground for airplanes manufactured by the Dayton-Wright Airplane Company (which Deeds helped to establish).[12]

During 1916, Colonel Deeds had also invited Dayton inventor Charles F. Kettering and Orville Wright to inspect "a plot of 120 acres adjoining Triangle Park in the outskirts of Dayton," a tract lying between the Miami River and present-day Keowee Street, to determine its suitability for use as a public aviation field.[13] When asked if he felt the land would make a good landing field, Orville Wright allegedly replied:[14]

> This is admirably adapted for use in cross-country flights which are sure to come. The long curved stretch of land admits of landing from every direction. With coast-to-coast flying the southern route west of the Mississippi through Dayton must be taken.

Mr. Wright believed that the field, once cleared and leveled, would also be useable as a training field for light airplanes. Thus encouraged, Deeds had secured options on the land and he and Kettering purchased it in March of 1917. This site became known as North Field.

Initial leveling work at North Field was begun on March 13, 1917, but was not completed, most likely because Deeds and Kettering were almost immediately engrossed in wartime work.[15]

Thus when Colonel Deeds was asked, as Chief of the Equipment Division, to locate an appropriate site for a temporary Signal Corps experimental station, his thoughts turned first to the South Field property in Dayton. Many people, including engineers at the Equipment Division, considered Dayton to be a nearly ideal location for such a facility. It had a central location in the industrial region of the country, a centralized position with respect to the major aeronautical manufacturing agencies, and boasted a local pool of trained labor. Since time was of the essence, and since Dayton possessed facilities that were already partially developed, there seemed little need to search further.

The engineers of the Equipment Division presented a formal request to the Aircraft Production Board to locate a temporary facility in Dayton at South Field. The Aircraft Production Board appointed a committee to evaluate the site and assess its suitability. Lt. Col. Virginius E. Clark and Majors J. G. Vincent and E. J. Hull were selected to represent the Signal Corps. They were dispatched to Dayton to meet with the other committee members, Albert Kahn, an architect from Detroit, and Charles Kettering, who represented the Dayton-Wright Airplane Company.

COUNCIL OF NATIONAL DEFENSE
Aircraft Production Board
Washington

RESOLUTION passed at meeting of Board on September 27, 1917.

WHEREAS, great delays are being incurred in starting production of the army combat program because of lack of central engineering and experimental facilities, engineering now being done in Washington at the Bureau of Standards, Smithsonian Building and Old Southern Railway Building; at Mineola; New Haven; Dayton; Detroit; Chicago; and Buffalo, and

WHEREAS, a Board of Engineers, consisting of Lieutenant Colonel Clark, Major Vincent, Major Hall, and Captain Marmon, have asked that immediate steps be taken to provide for the proper facilities to meet their requirements, and

WHEREAS, after investigation they have recommended that temporary arrangements be made in Dayton where this work can be centralized, Dayton being located within a night's ride of Indianapolis, Detroit, Buffalo, Cleveland, Chicago, Pittsburgh, Washington, and the East, and

WHEREAS, a favorable location is immediately available, being in daily use by the Wright Field Company for private training and experimental work; some hangars and small repair shops already constructed, all of which can be taken over by the Government on a satisfactory basis, the field itself being particularly suitable for experimental test work, and is located within convenient distance of the Wilbur Wright Field, on which field it is possible to test out the largest and fastest machines, and

WHEREAS, this field is conveniently served by City service with water, gas, electricity, street car facilities, with an abundant supply of highly skilled labor available, and

WHEREAS, it will be perhaps considerable time before the permanent construction at Langley Field will be in effective operation, and suitable mechanics secured and housed,

NOW THEREFORE BE IT RESOLVED: that the request of the engineers be approved and the Aircraft Production Board recommend to the Chief Signal Officer that the Construction Division be instructed to provide at once such additional temporary facilities as are necessary to meet the emergency now existing.

AIRCRAFT PRODUCTION
BOARD,
By

(signed)
Executive Secretary
Capt. Signal Corps, U.S.A.

Another Dayton-Wright executive, H. E. Talbott, Sr., also joined the committee for its Dayton meeting.[16]

Although it had not yet received a report from its committee in Dayton, the Aircraft Production Board adopted a resolution on September 27, 1917, approving the request of the Equipment Division engineers. The resolution went forward to Brig. Gen. George O. Squier, Chief Signal Officer, for action.

THE ESTABLISHMENT OF McCOOK FIELD

Events in the closing days of September 1917 moved swiftly. The Aircraft Production Board resolution was adopted and forwarded on September 27. On the 28th, General Squier directed a memo to the Adjutant General of the Army recommending approval for construction of temporary buildings "on former Wright Flying Field" (South Field).* Cost was set at $350,000 plus $25,000 to pay for existing buildings.[17]

Later the same day (September 28), however, Lt. Col. C. G. Edgar of the Construction Division received a telegram from J. K. Grannis, Superintendent of Construction. Grannis was in Dayton looking over the site, and stated that per decision of the evaluation committee, the location of the experimental station was to be changed "from South Field to Triangle Park."[18] Undaunted, General Squier immediately sent a second memo to the Army Adjutant General, worded identically to the first memo, except that it recommended approval for construction of temporary buildings "in Triangle Park" (North Field). Estimated cost was still $350,000.[19]

As it turned out, events in Dayton had not unfolded as smoothly as planned. The Dayton-Wright Airplane Company objected to the Equipment Division's proposal to locate its facility at South Field. Were the Equipment Division to take over use of the flying field, it would be impossible for the Dayton-Wright Company to fulfill its defense contract obligations for engineering work on the DeHavilland DH-4 and the DeHavilland DH-9.[20]

Yet Kettering and Talbott of the Dayton-Wright Company had a genuine desire to be of assistance to the war effort. Considering the urgency of the situation, they had suggested to the committee that North Field might be an equally acceptable site for the station. They pointed out that North Field was closer to the city than the Moraine site and more easily reached by municipal transportation. Its terrain better lent itself to the construction of buildings, and it had more ready access to gas, electric, and especially sewer facilities.

The committee immediately visited the North Field location. After determining that this alternate site would fit the bill, Mr. Grannis submitted his telegram to Washington. In a confirmation letter posted the same day, Grannis quoted the plans that Colonel Clark and Major Vincent had already outlined for a main building of "two stories, Workshop below, Office and Drafting room above, 60 ft wide and 600 ft long," and for an airplane assembly building "90 ft wide and 270 ft long, having two 135 ft doors, 30 ft high on the longface."[21] Colonel Deeds gave his immediate approval to the selection of the North Field site.

By the first of October all confusion had been cleared up. A memo from Deeds to Colonel Edgar, dated October 1, stated: "Chief Signal Officer on Saturday signed the paper setting aside the appropriation for the construction work at North Field in Dayton for the experimental engineering work. Mr. Craighead, the attorney from Dayton, will be here Wednesday to close up the lease."[22]

On the same date (October 1), the Aircraft Production Board adopted a resolution to name the new temporary field:[23]

WHEREAS, the field which has been selected for temporary experimental and engineering purposes at Dayton, Ohio, has been until recently in possession of the "Fighting McCook" family for over one hundred years, and,

WHEREAS, Major Daniel McCook, the head of this family and his nine sons, were all officers in the Civil War, all but one being wounded and six being killed, one of the survivors being Major General Alexander McDowell McCook, who did such distinguished service both during and after the war,

THEREFORE BE IT RESOLVED: that this temporary experimental and engineering field be called the "McCook Field" in honor of the McCook family.

Unidentified officials of the Dayton-Wright Airplane Company pose in front of a DeHavilland DH-4 observation airplane at the Moraine facility, April 27, 1918. The company manufactured these British-designed airplanes for the U.S. Army Air Service and the Royal Flying Corps. *(NCR Corporation)*

*Not to be confused with Wilbur Wright Field, near Fairfield, Greene County, Ohio.

Maj. Daniel McCook *(National Archives and Records Service)*

Gen. Alexander McDowell McCook *(National Archives and Records Service)*

THE McCOOK FAMILY

The "Fighting McCooks" are often spoken of as one family, though in fact they were two families. The "Fighting McCooks" were the collective sons of two brothers, Major Daniel McCook and Dr. John McCook. The progeny of Major Daniel McCook included:

Surgeon-Major Latimer A. McCook
General George W. McCook
General Robert L. McCook
General Alexander McDowell McCook
General Daniel McCook, Jr.
General Edwin Stanton McCook
Private Charles Morris McCook
Colonel John J. McCook
Midshipman J. James McCook

Dr. John McCook's family engaged in the service included:

General Edward U. McCook
General Anson G. McCook
Chaplain Henry C. McCook
Commander Roderick S. McCook, USN
Lieutenant John J. McCook

A total of fifteen, every son of both families, were commissioned officers, except Charles, who declined a commission in the regular army, preferring to serve as a private of volunteers, and was killed in the first battle of Bull Run.

NOTE: Exact ranks of general officers (Brig. Gen., Maj. Gen., etc.) not given in original source.

Source: Daniel Joseph Ryan, *The Civil War Literature of Ohio, A Bibliography with Explanatory and Historical Notes* (Cleveland, 1911).

The terms of the lease agreement were worked out in Washington. Colonel Deeds first conveyed his interest in North Field to his co-owner, Mr. Charles F. Kettering. Mr. Kettering in turn conveyed the property to the Dayton Metal Products Company. An agreement was then drawn up whereby the Dayton Metal Products Company would lease the acreage to the government.* The amount of rent agreed upon for the property was $9,493.26 from October 4, 1917 to June 30, 1918, with an annual lease of $12,800 per year commencing July 1, 1918, renewable from year to year until June 30, 1921.[24]

The area occupied by McCook Field was officially measured at 254.37 acres. It was located geographically one and one-half miles from the center of the city of Dayton, bounded by Herman Avenue on the south, Keowee Street on the east, and the Miami River on the north and west. Girth of the field was 14,677 feet.[25]

On October 13, 1917, the existence of McCook Field was formalized by Signal Corps Office Memorandum No. 22. The memo announced that in order to "centralize engineering work and fix responsibility," the Engine Design Section and the Plane Design Section from Langley Field were being merged into a single organization, to be known as the Airplane Engineering Department. Its headquarters were to be located in temporary facilities at Dayton, "where its activities would be within a night's ride of Indianapolis, Detroit, Buffalo, Cleveland, Pittsburgh, Washington, and the East."[26] It was clearly stated that McCook Field was to be a temporary experimental station for engineering purposes only, and not a military post.

*Deeds had withdrawn his interest in the company at the time he went to work for the government.

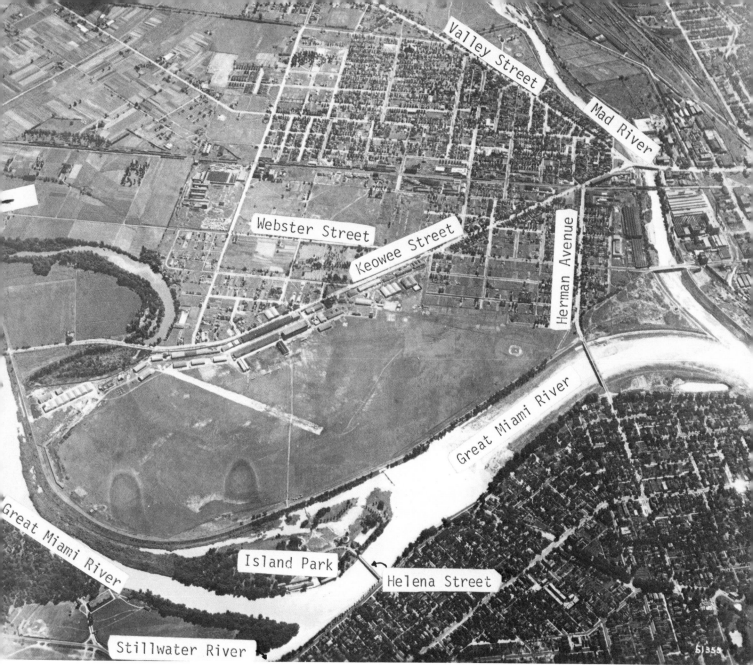

Aerial view of McCook Field showing local landmarks. Dayton's financial district, then as today, was concentrated at center right, immediately across the river.

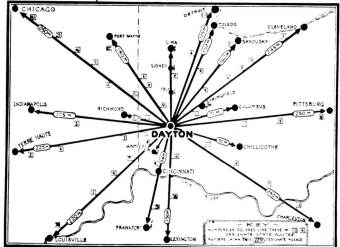

Dayton was viewed as a central location for Air Service engineering activities, being "within a night's ride of Indianapolis, Detroit, Buffalo, Cleveland, Pittsburgh, Washington, and the East."

THE CONSTRUCTION PROCESS

Although the lease for the McCook Field property was not signed until October 4, 1917, the crucial decisions had already been made and plans were underway. Mr. Albert Kahn had already finished architectural studies and drawings. Contracts for construction of the first group of buildings at McCook were awarded two days before the signing of the lease, on October 2, to the Dayton Lumber and Manufacturing Company.[27] To expedite matters, Superintendent Grannis was authorized by the Construction Division to purchase all necessary materials from local sources.

The first order of business before buildings could be erected and the runway laid was to prepare the land. Some work had already been done. When Deeds and Kettering began developing the site as a public flying field, they had ordered preliminary grading, including removal of an old

**TESTIMONIAL DINNER FOR COL.
EDWARD DEEDS**

Distinguished Dayton aviation supporters and leaders of the Army Air Service attended a testimonial dinner at the stately Miami Hotel in Dayton on February 22, 1919, honoring Col. Edward A. Deeds. As Chief of the Signal Corps Equipment Division during World War I, Deeds was instrumental in establishing Wilbur Wright Field and Mc-Cook Field. According to Deeds' biographer, no less than 500 men gathered on this auspicious occasion "in a demonstration of regard never before seen in this city."

Prominent guests at the dinner were (front row, l to r) aviation pioneer Orville Wright; Maj. Gen. George O. Squier, Chief Signal Officer; and Colonel Deeds; (back row, l to r): Charles F. Kettering, inventor of the Army's first pilotless aircraft with preset controls and master of ceremonies for the dinner; Lt. Harold H. Emmons, Chief of Liberty Engine Production, Equipment Division; Lt. Col. Leonard S. Horner, Chief of Ordnance and Instruments Production, Equipment Division; Harold E. Talbott, co-founder of the Dayton-Wright Airplane Company; Walter S. Kidder, Dayton financier; Col. Thurman H. Bane, Commanding Officer, McCook Field; Col. M. F. Davis, Hq Army Air Service; and Dr. S. W. Stratton, Director, U.S. Bureau of Standards.

river embankment. The experimental flying anticipated at McCook, however, required that the field be graded absolutely flat, rolled, and sodded.[28]

Grading problems were complicated by inadequate site drainage. The natural topography of the land constituted the primary difficulty, compounded by the fact that all of the storm sewers surrounding the field were too high for drainage. A French drain had to be constructed to handle storm drainage, and sink pumps had to be installed in the gravel stratum underlying the field to drain particularly difficult sections.[29]

According to Capt. H. H. Blee in his "History of Organization and Activities of Airplane Engineering Division," actual construction work was started on October 10, 1917, "and pushed ahead with astonishing rapidity. Large forces of workmen were employed working in shifts day and night, seven days a week."[30] Construction was carried out by two shifts of men daily, with a total of 900 men in both shifts. This pace continued for 24 working days. At that time the first building was sufficiently complete to allow the wood and metal shops to install some machinery and begin work. Subsequently, 100 men were employed for an additional 28 days in finishing the building.

Construction of the Final Assembly building was begun on October 25. It also used two shifts of men, totalling 400 in both shifts, for 35 working days. Final work was completed in 60 more days with a crew of 120 men.[31]

The initial buildings erected at McCook Field in the fall of 1917 were the engineering and shops building, the final assembly building, main hangar, garage, barracks, mess hall, cafeteria, transformer house, and engine test stands. Two existing structures at the field were used to house the dynamometer laboratory and the engine assembly building. A central heating plant was completed and provided heat to nearly all buildings on station.[32]

Because many of these buildings were designed as "temporary construction," special precautions were taken to provide fire protection to them. Modern fire equipment was provided on station, and a stand-by fire protection system was established using the Dayton water mains.[33]

The runway at McCook Field was a definite improvement over the bumpy grass strips to which most pilots of the day were accustomed. The special macadam-and-cinder runway was 1,000 feet long and 100 feet wide, to allow the best possible conditions for flight testing. The runway had to be laid across the short expanse of the field, however, in order to take advantage of the prevailing winds. This resulted in extremely short approach and take-off distances due to surrounding obstacles (trees, the river, etc.). It also led to the coining of McCook Field's motto, "This Field Is Small—Use It All," which was emblazoned on the front of one of the hangars. (As aircraft grew in size and power, this constraint became one of the major factors that forced McCook activities to relocate to Wright Field in 1927.) The macadamized runway was the principal runway used, especially under poor weather conditions or when the ground was soggy, but aircraft also made use of other portions of the flying field that were heavily rolled and sodded.

A high fence with lookout towers encircled the installation. Once research and experimentation activities commenced, military armed guards were posted 24 hours a day "in order to protect activities at McCook from the machinations of spies."[34]

OPERATIONS BEGIN

As stated earlier, McCook Field was created as the main facility of the Airplane Engineering Department, a consolidation of the Plane Design Section and the Engine Design Section from Langley Field. Lt. Col. Virginius E. Clark of the Plane Design Section was designated Officer in Charge of the new Department and thus became the first Commanding Officer of McCook Field. Maj. Jesse G. Vincent, Chief

Main Street, McCook Field, 1918

The central heating plant provided steam for buildings on McCook Field. About 5,000 tons of coal were burned annually. *(U.S. Air Force Museum)*

The motto emblazoned on McCook's main hangar cautioned all pilots to plan ahead. At 100 ft in width and 1,000 ft in length, the macadamized runway was barely adequate to accommodate the successively heavier and more powerful Air Service airplanes designed by engineers at McCook. *(Dayton and Montgomery County Public Library)*

Taxiway to the McCook Field runway (center right), spring 1918 *(AFWAL Technical Library)*

of the Engine Design Section, was named Executive Officer.

As Executive Officer, Major Vincent immediately went to Dayton to begin transfer arrangements for those activities relocating to McCook.[35] In late October, Lt. H. E. Blood (Engine Design Section) joined Major Vincent in Dayton, bringing with him the first contingent of personnel and equipment. Because construction at the field was only in its initial stages, the engineering personnel set up temporary headquarters in downtown Dayton, leasing two floors of the Lindsey Building at 25 South Main Street for department offices.[36]

On November 5, 1917, Chief Signal Officer Squier signed Office Memorandum 53 assigning functional responsibility to the Airplane Engineering Department at McCook for all technical and experimental work previously conducted at Langley.[37] On November 22, General Squier further specified the division of work between Langley and the Airplane Engineering Department. Responsibility for engine and plane development, installation of cameras on experimental airplanes, and work on the synchronization of machine guns was assigned to McCook. Work to be continued at Langley under other commands included instruction and experimentation in bombing, photography, radio, telegraphy, and all demonstrations of foreign airplanes.[38]

The first troops assigned to McCook arrived in Dayton on November 14, 1917.[39] The 246th Aero Squadron from Kelly Field, Texas, consisted of 90 men and was stationed at McCook to perform both guard duty and fire patrol. The squadron's arrival gave a certain military air to the new engineering and experimentation facility. A letter from McCook Field in 1918 indicates that a number of these troops spent their first year at the new field in tents until sufficient barracks could be constructed. The letter noted that permanent indoor living space "was badly needed on account of the sickness among the soldiers at McCook Field."[40]

By the first week in December 1917, enough buildings at McCook had been completed to allow key personnel of the Airplane Engineering Department to move from downtown Dayton to the new installation. On December 4, 1917, operations officially commenced at McCook.[41]

There was not room at the field to accommodate all of the employees from the downtown location, and some sections continued their work at the Lindsey Building in Dayton. In fact, for the duration of the war there was always more staff assigned to McCook than there was office space to house them, and the Signal Corps, as well as the Army Air Service, was forced to lease office space in several Dayton structures. The Dayton Savings Building at 25 North Main Street, the Mutual Home Building at 40 North Main Street, and the Air Service Building (later known as the Knott Building) were all utilized to make up for the lack of space at McCook.

One month after McCook opened, Signal Corps Office Memorandum 11 was issued, transferring full responsibility to McCook for the design of all airplanes and accessories.[42] This resolved a good deal of confusion that had existed since America entered the war in April 1917. At that time, responsibility for aircraft design and production was fragmented among a variety of organizations. The process of drawing diverse industries together, compounded by the haste and anxieties of wartime, had taken a full nine months. The end result, however, was an efficient operation established at McCook Field. For the remaining 10 months of the war "a rare combination of men, money, and a sense of national urgency created, almost overnight, the single most influential agency in the early years of American air power."[43] As one aviation historian has noted, "In many respects it [McCook Field] was the single most influential organization in the history of American aviation, for it not only provided a start for some of the most talented men in the industry, but it set standards which they have continued to live up to."[44]

McCook Field, from its very beginnings, was different from all other World War I Army installations in that it was essentially a business institution rather than a military post. McCook was administered in the same manner as the Signal Corps aviation general supply depots and was exempted, by Army Regulation No. 191, from control by the Secretary of War. All civilian employees at the field came under Schedule A of the Civil Service, which exempted them from competitive examinations.[45] This arrangement had a profound effect on the functioning and business-like operation of the installation, and freed it to a large extent from the complexities of military inter-agency bureaucracy.

The fact that McCook Field functioned, by and large, in a fashion similar to private industry was due not only to its independent status, but also to the nature of the employees who administered the installation and directed its principal research. The critical shortage of aeronautical engineers in the military had forced the Signal Corps to seek production and engineering expertise in the private sector. Men like Deeds with experience in industry—particularly the automotive industry—were recruited, and in some cases commissioned, to lend vital support to the aircraft development program.

Administration building which housed the offices of the Chief of the Airplane Engineering Division, the Assistant Chief, and the Adjutant, as well as the Divisional Planning Section.

Air Service officers assigned to McCook Field in 1919 included many who went on to distinguish themselves in Air Force history. Among those pictured here are: Col. Thurman Bane, Lt. Muir S. Fairchild, Lt. John Macready, Lt. Leigh Wade, Lt. Harold Harris, Lt. Albert Hegenberger, and Capt. George Kenney.

For example, Maj. Jesse G. Vincent, Executive Officer at McCook, was a former executive of the Packard Motor Car Company. E. J. Hall, who assisted in reorganization of the Engine Design Section, came to the Signal Corps from the Hall-Scott Motor Car Company, and drew with him experts from such companies as Cadillac, Dodge, Packard, Durant, and Pierce.[46] The membership of the Aircraft Production Board itself included men like Sidney D. Waldon, a former Vice President of the Packard Motor Car Company, Howard E. Coffin of the Hudson Motor Car Company, and Robert L. Montgomery of the J. F. Brill Company of Philadelphia. Other men applied their industrial experience to supervisory positions in the various shops at McCook. Mr. W. J. Rueger, in charge of the Shop Order Department in 1918, was an 11-year veteran of the Chalmers Motor Co. production department. R. J. Myers, head of the Wood Shop, brought with him extensive experience with the Curtiss Airplane Corporation and the U.S. Navy Yards. H. L. Bill of the Factory Department was employed previously at the Springfield Body Corporation, the Chalmers Motor Co., and Hayes Manufacturing, all of Detroit. C. F. Simmons, Factory Manager, held previous employment with

the American Blower Co., Detroit Gear and Machine, and the King Motor Car Co.[47] The contributions which these men made are perhaps no better exemplified than in the development of the Liberty engine, the productive genius for which was provided by Vincent and Hall.[48]

During its early years, McCook Field was a meeting ground for the foremost engineers of aviation-related industries, both from the U.S. and abroad.[49] Among other noted accomplishments, these men solved the many problems associated with adapting existing European aircraft designs to American mass production techniques.*

The McCook Field hospital provided complete medical treatment for military members and emergency treatment for injured civilian employees.

McCook Field fire department in full dress. A combined guard and fire department of about 35 civilian employees protected the installation in the years after World War I. Note the solid rubber tires and wheels with wooden spokes on the World War I-vintage trucks.

The McCook Field cafeteria served meals daily for the convenience of civilian employees.

*Chapter VI details many of the specific engineering developments of this period.

McCook Field experienced rapid growth during 1918. This further crowded conditions in the already limited space. Sketchy reports from the Factory Branch in 1918 indicate that at least one barrack, a sand test building, a mess hall, a hospital, and hangars to house foreign and exhibition airplanes were constructed that year. The lumber storage facility and cafeteria were relocated, and the macadam-and-cinder runway was extended to a total length of 1,340 feet.[50] An auxiliary heating plant was completed near the end of the field that, together with the central heating plant, supplied all buildings with steam heat.[51] In all, a total of 47 buildings occupied 371,914 square feet. By the end of the war in November 1918, the government had more than $2,352,000 invested in the buildings, machinery, and equipment located at McCook Field proper.[52]

Additional real estate was leased during and immediately after the war to support McCook operations. Leases included 212 lots from the City of Dayton for an annual rent of $3,200; 60 lots from the Dayton Savings and Trust Company for $1,461.50 per year; and 14 lots from individual citizens for approximately $561.00 per year, total.[53] (By mid-1919, nearly all operations had been reduced in size and centralized at the field.)

There were two military support units at McCook during 1918. The 246th Aero Squadron, previously mentioned, had arrived in November 1917. On January 9, 1918, it was redesignated the 807th Aero Squadron. On July 1, 1918, the 881st Aero Squadron was organized at McCook. On July 12th, the squadrons were further designated as Squadron A (807th) and Squadron B (881st). On August 1, 1918, the two squadrons were merged into "Detachment No. 10, A.S.A.P."[54]

Organizational changes within the Air Service were frequent in 1918 to conform to changing mission responsibilities. It was a tribute to the dedicated personnel at McCook Field that work continued in spite of the frequent disruptions.

In January 1918, the Signal Corps created the Department of Production Engineering to work in concert with the Airplane Engineering Department, providing the engineering information necessary for the manufacture of airplanes, engines, and accessories. The new department moved to Dayton so that the two functions would be in close proximity. There was insufficient space in the Lindsey Building, however, to accommodate the new department. On April 15, 1918, the Department of Production Engineering was transferred to Washington, although it retained its mandate to support the Airplane Engineering Department.[55]

Earlier reference was made to the monumental problems the U.S. faced in gearing up its aircraft production program in the spring of 1918. Delays in the program soon provided the impetus for a major restructuring of the aeronautical sections of the War Department. The Overman Act established authority for this reorganization on May 20, 1918. The Act gave the President full discretionary authority to redistribute functions of top government agencies for the duration of the war, plus an additional six months. President Wilson, in conjunction with ranking War Depart-

General John J. Pershing inspects McCook Field, December 16, 1919, escorted by McCook Field Commander, Col. Thurman Bane.

N O T I C E

December 15, 1919.

TO ALL EMPLOYEES:

1.   General Pershing and his staff will make an inspection of McCook Field, Tuesday, December 16, at 10:00 A.M.

2.   Upon completion of the inspection, all members of this Division will be given an opportunity to see the General. At three long blasts of the whistle, employees will assemble on Gate Street (between the flag pole and the main gate) and remain until General Pershing leaves the field, when they will return to their work without delay.

3.   All employees are requested to go about their duties as usual, and not loiter about the field or leave their work until the signal is given.

By order of Colonel Bane:

LOUIS S. CONNELLY,
1st Lt., A.S.P.,
Adjutant.

Civilian guards at the main gate of McCook Field

Brig. Gen. William Mitchell, Assistant Chief of the Air Service, confers with Col. Thurman Bane, Post Commander, during one of his frequent inspection trips to McCook Field, 1919. *(NCR Corporation)*

ment officials, created two new branches of the War Department to assume, respectively, the operations and equipment phases of the aeronautical program. A Division of Military Aeronautics was designated to assume all aeronautical functions previously assigned to the Office of the Chief Signal Officer. A Bureau of Aircraft Production was established to assume the duties previously assigned to the Equipment Division and was placed under direct supervision of the Secretary of War (thereby entirely independent of the Signal Corps). On May 24, 1918, the War Department officially recognized the Division of Military Aeronautics and the Bureau of Aircraft Production as constituting the Air Service.[56]

Within the Bureau of Aircraft Production, the Engineering Production Department and the Airplane Engineering Department were frequently at odds with each other. These two departments (the one located at McCook and the other in Washington), had been established as separate units, and had a tendency to work in isolation without properly consulting each other.[57] As a result, on June 24, 1918, a special division of the Bureau of Aircraft Production was created to centralize and coordinate their efforts. General Memorandum 23 combined the two departments with the Science and Research Department and the Technical Information Department, to form a new Engineering and Research Division within the Bureau of Aircraft Production.[58] To further stimulate cooperation, the Production Engineering Department was once more relocated to Dayton. This time, it was housed in the Air Service Building, and remained there for the duration of the war.

On August 1, 1918, the two agencies created by President Wilson, the Bureau of Aircraft Production and the Division of Military Aeronautics, which had not functioned successfully as separate entities, were also merged. The head of the new organization was designated Director of the Air Service, and Assistant Secretary of War. On August 27, the position was filled by the appointment of John D. Ryan, prominent banker, President of the Anaconda Copper Company, and former chairman of the Aircraft Board (which succeeded the Aircraft Production Board).[59]

On August 31, a further refinement was effected when the Airplane Engineering Department and the Production Engineering Department were withdrawn from control of the Bureau of Aircraft Production and merged to become a separate Airplane Engineering Division of the new Army Air Service. This action was made official with the issuance of Bureau of Aircraft Production General Memorandum No. 166, dated September 13, 1918, which laid responsibility for "complete supervision of all engineering for the Bureau of Aircraft Production" upon the new division.[60] Lt. Col. J. G. Vincent became Chief of Engineering in charge of the combined division, with headquarters in the Air Service Building in Dayton. The title "Engineering Division, Air Service," became the permanent designation for the organization at McCook Field and was retained until 1926.

On September 18, 1918, the Bureau of Aircraft Production directed that the Ordnance Department and the Armament Section of the Ordnance Department should also move to McCook in order that the ordnance engineers and draftsmen could work directly with the aircraft engineers in designing and installing bomb sights and bomb racks. The Armament Section left Washington for Dayton on October 3, under the command of Maj. Harry D. Weed. This change represented the last addition to the experimental facilities at McCook prior to the November 11, 1918 Armistice.[61]

In addition to the complications caused by these organizational changes, McCook was under the command of four

McCook Field Adjutant's Office (base administration), about 1920

different commanders during 1918. Lt. Col. Virginius E. Clark was relieved as Commander on January 24, 1918, by Maj. Frederick T. Dickman. This enabled Colonel Clark to devote his entire energies to the development of original airplane designs. Lt. Col. J. G. Vincent, Chief of Engineering, had in the meantime suggested an entirely new organization for the Airplane Engineering Department aimed at improving operations. Colonel Vincent's plan was approved by the Equipment Division on February 6, 1918, and the resulting reorganization of the Airplane Engineering Department placed Vincent in charge effective that date. He served as Commander until November 24, 1918, when Col. Thurman H. Bane, the first post-war Commander of McCook, was appointed as Chief of the Airplane Engineering Division.

Despite these many changes, the engineering work at McCook Field continued unabated. Historian Edward O. Purtee states, "Before the end of hostilities the Bureau of Aircraft Production had succeeded in accelerating airplane production to the extent of producing more than 11,700 airplanes and 32,400 engines in America."[62] The record achieved by the aeronautical engineers associated with McCook Field became known around the world as the standard of excellence.

McCOOK AFTER THE WAR

Colonel Bane actually assumed two hats when he became the first post-war Commander of McCook Field. In addition to his new position as Chief of the Airplane Engineering Division, he also continued to serve as Chief of the Technical Section of the Division of Military Aeronautics, a position he had held since August 1918. The Engineering Division at McCook Field after the war was a consolidation of the Airplane Engineering Division, the Technical Section of the Division of Military Aeronautics, and the Testing Squadron at Wilbur Wright Field.[63]

It became Colonel Bane's job to combine the work of the Bureau of Aircraft Production and the Division of Military Aeronautics on a permanent peacetime basis. He merged the facilities and personnel of the two units, consisting of 2,300 scientists, engineers, technicians, and support officers assigned to 19 sections and 75 branches, into an efficient organization. Colonel Bane's vision was instrumental in seeing McCook Field through the difficult years of the post-war period, fraught with inadequate funding and compounded by apathy toward the goals of the Engineering

Col. Thurman H. Bane, McCook Field Commanding Officer and Commandant of the Air Service Engineering School (1919-1923) (*U.S. Air Force Museum*)

"Entire personnel of the Engineering Division of the Air Service, McCook Field, Dayton, Ohio," 1920 (approximately 50 officers and 1,200 civilian employees)

Division. It was through his personal efforts that the Division was able to accomplish its mission in a relatively unfettered fashion.*

In May of 1919, the responsibilities of the Engineering Division expanded to encompass all of the aircraft experimental activities previously conducted at Langley Field in Virginia.[64] This further complicated the problem of crowded facilities which McCook already faced. With this centralization, however, McCook became the nerve center of the aircraft and engineering activities of the Air Service.

It was at McCook that virtually all significant developments took place. These major engineering developments and achievements included controllable and reversible pitch propellers, aircraft engine superchargers, bullet-proof and leak-proof gasoline tanks, the radio beam, a non-magnetic aircraft clock, an ambulance airplane, the air-cooled radial engine, mapping and night observation cameras, and the free-fall parachute. Also developed at McCook and refined at Wilbur Wright Field were night flying techniques and a model airway which was the forerunner of today's network of continental and intercontinental commercial air routes.

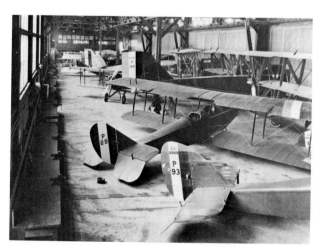

Main hangar at McCook Field, April 5, 1920. Tail number P93 belongs to a DeHavilland DH-4 observation airplane. P29 is a Curtiss JN-4H Jenny trainer. On the other side of the trainer is GAX P129, a three-winged experimental armored ground attack airplane powered by two pusher engines. (*Wright State University Archives*)

The story of these developments is told in a separate chapter dedicated to the technological advancements in aviation made at both McCook and Wright Fields, Chapter VI, Developing Air Power 1917-1951.

Manpower and funds to carry out the Engineering Division's mission after World War I were both in ever-dwindling quantity. At the end of the war, the population at McCook totalled 58 officers, 267 enlisted men, and 1,915 civilians.[65] These wartime numbers were soon scaled down, though, and from 1920 to 1926 the work of the Engineering Division was normally carried out by a personnel force of about 50 officers and from 1,100 to 1,500 civilians.[66]

Additionally, in 1919 the Air Service appropriations were severely cut to $25 million from the $55 million requested.[67] The Engineering Division's share of this budget was proportionately small, and continued to decline over the next several years, from $5 million in 1921, to $3 million in 1924, reaching low ebb in 1927.[68] As one historian has stated, however:[69]

> Ironically, the lean years . . . produced the greatest achievements at McCook Field, for during the mid-1920s the scientists and engineers of the Engineering Division had little to work with but their own genius, and it was this ingenuity alone that kept the Air Service from becoming completely obsolete.

CONTROVERSY WITH THE AIRCRAFT INDUSTRY

The greatest challenge faced by the Engineering Division was its mandate to act as a clearinghouse between the Air Service and the aircraft industry. If the Air Service had been hamstrung by lack of appropriations, the American aircraft industry had been similarly crippled by the cessation of wartime production. European nations, after the war, had adopted programs to re-channel their aviation momentum into commerce and well-organized national defense systems. No such plan operated in the United States, however, to soften the blow sustained by the American aircraft industry or to develop alternative solutions.[70]

*The mission of the Engineering Division is carried on today by the Air Force Systems Command, whose major Wright-Patterson AFB components are the Aeronautical Systems Division (including the Air Force Wright Aeronautical Laboratories and the 4950th Test Wing), and the Foreign Technology Division.

The Engineering Division at McCook acted as a middleman, so to speak, interpreting Army specifications and standards for manufacturers, testing products when they were completed, and suggesting improvements if products did not fully meet specifications. Members of the aircraft industry, in dire economic straits, complained that the operations at McCook Field infringed upon their development rights by concentrating control of all military aircraft design and testing into one organization. They feared that the Air Service was in essence forming a general "brain trust" at McCook, composed of government employees, to perform all of the work connected with design of airplanes and aeronautical equipment. They demanded that the Army transfer some of the Engineering Division's work to private enterprise.[71]

The battle that ensued between McCook and the aircraft industry, as both fought for their very existence, caused severe cutbacks in the work at McCook. Few additional airplanes were being developed for the Air Service, and there was constant pressure in the post-war period for the Air Service to "make do" with equipment and supplies left over from the war. At best, this surplus equipment was obsolete, and thus hampered experimental development; at worst, it jeopardized the safety of all who worked with it.

The accusations and complaints registered by the aircraft industry finally provoked action. An American aviation mission was dispatched to Europe in the spring of 1919 to investigate progress being made there in aircraft production. The report of this mission ultimately sparked a measure of increased government support for the U.S. aircraft industry aimed at encouraging development of civil aeronautics.[72]

IN A STATE OF READINESS

On December 1, 1921, newly-appointed Chief of the Air Service Maj. Gen. Mason M. Patrick directed basic organizational changes in the Engineering Division at McCook Field. Eight sections were established reflecting the new alignment of responsibilities: Planning, Technical, Factory, Flying, Procurement, Supply, Patents, and Military.[73]

General Patrick had assumed command of the Air Service on October 15, 1921, following Maj. Gen. Charles T. Menoher, and was a more direct advocate of engineering development than his predecessor. General Patrick had definite ideas about the job that the Engineering Division should be accomplishing. He purportedly defined the Division's duties in one sentence: "To have in readiness for immediate production and service, the most advanced types of aircraft, engines, armament and other miscellaneous equipment."[74] General Patrick initiated operation of a "Production Model Room" at McCook, which contained models of actual equipment necessary to outfit a fighting air force. Each model was complete with drawings, specifications, parts lists, and bills of materials necessary to begin production of the item in quantity, within twenty-four hours if necessary.

A captured Fokker biplane still bears its German Air Force cross insignia as it flies over McCook Field. Many foreign aircraft, both from Allied and enemy nations, were tested at McCook. *(U.S. Air Force Museum)*

The U.S. Air Force Museum had its beginnings at McCook Field in September 1923. Originally, collections consisted of World War I Allied and enemy aircraft and equipment no longer used in testing. This open storage display contains tachometers, thermometers, statoscopes, and turn indicators. The Army Aeronautical Museum, as it was then known, moved with other organizations to Wright Field in 1927. *(U.S. Air Force Museum)*

In a typical exercise, General Patrick would send a "problem" message to Colonel Bane at the Engineering Division such as, "Congress meets on the 20th for the purpose of declaring war—I will visit McCook on the 18th to review items ready for production." Materials in the Production Model Room were constantly maintained in three classifications: "Ready for Immediate Production," "Experimental," or "Obsolete." On his visits to McCook, General Patrick could thus easily review samples of fully developed products and see experimental items being tested in the field. The goal of the Air Service was to preclude, at all costs, the problems of unpreparedness that the nation had experienced in World War I, so that there would never again be the need to ask, "What shall we build? How shall we build it?"[75]

THE AIR SERVICE ENGINEERING SCHOOL

One of the most important corollaries of the work at McCook was the education of a solid corps of Air Service officers to manage new Air Service programs resulting from the tremendous growth in aeronautical engineering and aviation technology. In November 1918, Colonel Bane, as Chief of the Technical Section of the Division of Military Aeronautics, wrote to the director of the Division in Washington requesting permission to establish an Air Service School of Application at McCook. He proposed a school similar to the Ordnance School of Application at Sandy Hook Proving Ground, New York, with which he had previously been associated. The stated purpose for this school was to provide "proper technical training" to permanent officers of the Air Service. All officers in command of air stations, Bane asserted, should receive extensive technical training in order to more effectively and efficiently direct their operations—training in such fields as maintenance of airplanes and motors, machine shop installation,

shop management and cost accounting, power plant installation and operation, laboratory testing of fuels and raw materials, and principles of elementary aerodynamics.[76] The best remedy for the Air Service's lack of technical experts, to Bane's way of thinking, was for the Air Service to train its own, and the logical place to accomplish this was at McCook.

General Patrick pilots his special DH-4L airplane on an inspection trip to McCook Field. His copilot (rear) and the young lady are not identified.

Light truck used to transport aerial bombs from storage igloos to the flightline, about 1925. Spare wheels were mounted on front of the truck. Note the hand crank to start the engine.

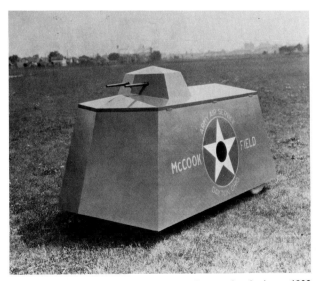

This radio-controlled "tank" was a popular novelty during a 1923 airshow and exhibition at McCook.

Although formal approval had not yet been received, Colonel Bane began drawing a teaching staff together. Among the first was Lt. Edwin E. Aldrin, who had served on the staff of the aeronautical engineering school for Army and Navy pilots at the Massachusetts Institute of Technology during World War I. In February 1919, Aldrin was transferred to McCook along with other former personnel from the school. Bane capitalized upon his experience, appointing him Chief of the School Section. As Lieutenant Aldrin put it, he "had the job of starting a school from nothing."[77]

The first unofficial classes in June 1919 were attended by approximately ten Air Service lieutenant colonels and majors under the tutelage of Lieutenant Aldrin. Under Colonel Bane's strong guidance, however, the school was carefully developed. Aldrin, as Secretary and later Assistant Commandant at McCook, shouldered most of the responsibility for getting the school underway and continued to run the school for the first few years.*

Authorization for the first official course of instruction was received from the Director of the Air Service just prior to the start of classes on November 10, 1919. Colonel Bane

Air Service Engineering School, Class of 1920, McCook Field. Front row (l to r): Lt. Edwin E. Aldrin, Assistant Commandant, Lt. Col. Benedict, Lt. Col. Rader, and Maj. Sneed, students. Back row (l to r): Mr. LaBaie, instructor, Lt. Wilcox, Lt. Col. Dargue, Maj. Frank, and Lt. Col. McIntosh, students, Pvt. Perkins, administration. Lieutenant Aldrin was in charge of the school's operations, although Col. Thurman H. Bane, McCook Field Commander, served officially as Commandant. This was the school's first group of students, who began their studies in November 1919.

During the early 1920s, the Air Service Engineering School moved its classes to more spacious quarters. Lieutenant Aldrin (standing second from right) and Mr. LaBaie, instructor (standing third from right) were still active in school affairs.

*Aldrin's son, astronaut Maj. Edwin E. "Buzz" Aldrin, Jr., was a graduate of the Air Force Institute of Technology in 1963.

Parade at McCook Field publicizing the 1924 International Air Races held at nearby Wilbur Wright Field *(AFWAL Technical Library)*

was of course appointed Commander of the new school in addition to his other duties. As described in a later history of the Air Force Institute of Technology:[78]

> The group that gathered for the first official class on 10 November 1919 was small: Aldrin, another lieutenant, two majors, and four lieutenant colonels. They assembled in a hangar. Aldrin read them an introduction to the course and gave a copy of it to each officer. In the months that followed, the course envisioned by Col Bane became a reality. The classrooms were small frame buildings and hangars clustered along McCook's small grass runway, and the main educational tools were the blackboard and practical experience. On some evenings, prominent men from colleges and commercial plants delivered lectures illustrated by lantern slides.

The students in those early years took advantage of all the resources available to them—books, civilian engineers, strategic and tactical experts, research findings, and extensive laboratory training and equipment. The first class studied hard and was graduated in September of 1920. (The school by that time had been officially named the Air Service Engineering School.)

The daily activities at McCook provided an ideal atmosphere for learning and participating first-hand in the development of aeronautics. When Colonel Bane retired at the end of 1922, the school was firmly established and its graduates were beginning to make their mark in the world.

By 1923, the Air Service Engineering School curriculum was composed of four courses of instruction, three for Air Service officers and one for employees of the Engineering Division. The most professional of these was the one-year course in General Aeronautical Engineering, primarily airplane design and aircraft engine design. This core course was supplemented by a five-month course in Maintenance

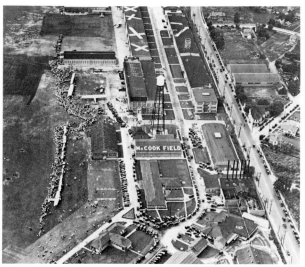

Several thousand guests attended this static exhibition and airshow at McCook Field on July 4, 1923. Proceeds were donated to the Soldiers' Emergency Relief Fund (similar to today's Air Force Aid Society).

Engineering for officers. A three-month course in Maintenance Engineering for reserve officers and a group of six evening courses in aerodynamics, metals, and other subjects for employees and officers at McCook completed the curriculum.[79]

The class of 1927 was the last to receive instruction in the crowded classrooms "clustered along McCook's small grass runway," as facilities at McCook were dismantled for the move to Wright Field. The Air Corps Engineering School, as it was then known, resumed classes at the new installation in 1928 under the auspices of the Air Corps Materiel Division. Classes were held in the Materiel Division Headquarters building, now Building 11 in Area B.[80]

CREATION OF THE AIR CORPS MATERIEL DIVISION

The most significant reorganization of activities at McCook Field took place in 1926. Under provisions of the Air Corps Act, the activities of the Air Corps were divided into three major branches, each headed by an Assistant Chief of the Air Corps. Brig. Gen. William E. Gillmore was appointed Chief of the newly-designated Materiel Division, with headquarters at McCook Field. Brig. Gen. James E. Fechet assumed command of the Operations Division, with headquarters at Washington, D.C., and Brig. Gen. Frank P. Lahm headed the Air Corps Training Center, with headquarters at Kelly Field.[81]

The logo of the McCook Field Engineering Division was retained by the Air Corps Material Division in 1926. The logo, and McCook Field, were honored by the Dayton Stamp Club in 1980.

Members of the "First Bombardment Board," July 9, 1926, meet to test and make recommendations on procurement of bombardment airplanes for the Air Corps. Included are (l to r): Lt. Harold L. George, Lt. John DeF. Barker, Maj. Louis H. Brereton (President of the Board), Lt. E. W. Dichman, Lt. Muir S. Fairchild, and Lt. Odas Moon. (U.S. Air Force Museum)

The Materiel Division was an expansion of the Engineering Division, and included not only engineering, but also supply, procurement, and maintenance of aircraft.* The mission of the Materiel Division was to furnish all aircraft and aeronautical equipment used by the Army Air Corps. This encompassed five basic responsibilities, widely expanded from the relatively specialized mission of the Engineering Division:[82]

Development, procurement, and test of aircraft and concomitant equipment

Distribution and maintenance of materiel in the field

Planning of industrial preparedness

Maintenance of an adequate engineering plant and test facility

The dissemination of technical information for the good of the service, the industry, and the general public

The Materiel Division, in fact, comprised most of the major functions of the new Air Corps, with the exception of training. Many of those functions have remained at Wright-Patterson up to the present day. Modern-day research and development, weapon systems acquisition, and supply and maintenance of current systems are carried on by "descendants" of the Engineering Division at Wright-Patterson, including the Air Force Logistics Command and the Aeronautical Systems Division of the Air Force Systems Command. The missions are the same; only the people and the technology have changed.

The organization of the Materiel Division and its component agencies were outlined in 1926 as follows: the Headquarters at McCook Field; six air depots located at Fairfield (Ohio), Little Rock (Arkansas), Middletown (Pennsylvania), Rockwell Field (California), San Antonio (Texas), and Scott Field (Illinois); three procurement districts with centers in Dayton (Central), New York City (Eastern), and Santa Monica, California (Western); and six procurement planning districts (under the Industrial War Plans Section).[83]

This massive reorganization and its consequent shifts in personnel made evident, more than ever, the inadequacy of the facilities at McCook Field. Fortunately, by 1926, definite plans for relocation of the Materiel Division had been approved and implementation was underway.

A NEW HOME IS SOUGHT

McCook Field was established originally as a temporary experimental site for wartime testing, and earned a notable reputation during World War I. As early as December 1918, however, only one month after the Armistice, rumors were afoot concerning relocation of the Engineering Division to a more permanent home.

Originally that permanent home was to have been Langley Field in Virginia, as discussed earlier. In fact, on De-

---

*More comprehensive coverage of this reorganization may be found in Chapter V, Wright Field.

cember 5, 1918, Colonel Bane received a memo from Col. Arthur Woods, Assistant Director of Military Aeronautics, stating in part that, "You will be safe in assuming that your work will stay where it is for six months and some time after that it will be moved to Langley [Field]."[84]

Thurman Bane himself was the first to admit that the set-up at McCook was far from ideal. Growth of the Engineering Division had been so rapid and extensive during the war that the initial facilities were inadequate to house its expanded functions. Bane was not entirely pleased with the prospect of moving the entire Division and its operations to Langley because moving would mean the loss of many well-trained and hard-to-replace men and significant disruption of operations, but he recognized that the problems at McCook were legion. They could not be compensated for and worked around indefinitely.

Because of the immediate press for wartime facilities, buildings at McCook had not been erected according to any master plan. As additional buildings were required and constructed, they slowly encroached upon the flying field itself. The majority of these buildings were of temporary construction, posing a great fire hazard and necessitating constant, costly maintenance.

The macadamized runway at McCook, oriented to take advantage of the prevailing winds, lay across the smallest dimension of the field—less than 2,000 feet. At the end of the runway was a dike topped with trees, which protected the field from the river.[85] Although small World War I pursuit and trainer airplanes had been able to negotiate this tight approach, it proved entirely inadequate for the larger post-war aircraft that were being developed at McCook. Those airplanes that were tested at McCook posed a very real danger to Dayton citizens living in the surrounding neighborhoods because of the field's location in the very heart of the city. A number of emergency landings during the 1920s terminated in treetops in the vicinity of McCook or in the (usually) shallow Great Miami River. Consequently, larger airplanes from McCook were flight-tested at Wilbur Wright Field near Fairfield.

In addition to these safety and space considerations, the lack of a rail line to the field posed another limitation. Supplies and equipment (284 carloads in 1923) had to be hauled two miles from the station in Dayton.[86]

One final limitation was the fact that rent on the McCook Field property increased each year. McCook Field stood in a prime location, and the original owners were anxious to convert the land to more profitable use. Annual rental of McCook Field after 1924 was quoted at $60,000 per year. In times of tight money, the Air Service felt that this was an exorbitant and unjustifiable sum to pay for facilities that were far from adequate.[87]

Although the climate of opinion in the United States during the 1920s opposed the concept of increasing the country's offensive capability and the development of air power for military purposes, it was more than evident that the science of aeronautical engineering was only beginning to show its real potential. The impetus given to development of aeronautics during the war unveiled an unlimited

Langley Field was one alternative considered for the permanent home of the Engineering Division. *(U.S. Air Force Museum)*

McCook Field's prime location in the heart of Dayton carried a hefty rental fee by 1924. Original owners were anxious to reclaim the land and put it to more profitable use.

future for the airplane, and ignited a spark in the imagination and spirit of the American ingenuity. According to one contemporary historian: "With the signing of the armistice, civilization awoke to find the infant of aviation already a growing child upon her hands. It would never again be hushed to sleep and its crib pushed out of sight."[88] The sky was literally the limit.

The fact that the Engineering Division would continue its exploration was undoubted, and clamor for a suitable facility reverberated on all sides. The unanswered question remained, "Where?" Many, including Bane, anticipated that Langley was the prime candidate. Langley did offer certain advantages, mainly its proximity to Washington (so that Congressmen and officers of the Air Service could be near to the actual work), more ample facilities for bombing and firing from the air, and a permanent physical plant. There is evidence, however, that the Virginia installation was never really strongly considered.

The National Advisory Committee for Aeronautics had been one of the only agencies to establish operations at Langley during the war. The Navy had contravened its original plans and never used Langley. Perhaps partially for status reasons, the Air Service felt, after the war, that it should also have its own independent research facilities. Colonel Bane evidently was not partial one way or the other. His only concern was that a location be selected and a decision made so that the Division could get on with its work. In the end, relocation to Langley was vetoed and Bane was forced to exercise patience with the decision to leave the Engineering Division at McCook until a more suitable location could be obtained.[89]

As mentioned previously, in May of 1919 all aircraft experimentation activities conducted at Langley during the war were transferred to McCook (providing further evidence that Langley was never seriously considered).[90] In 1920 the War Department established the Air Service Field Officers School (later the Air Corps Tactical School) at Langley. Providing facilities for this school created crowded conditions at the installation. Relocating the Engineering Division from McCook after that time would have called for major reorganization.[91]

Sites in New Jersey, Maryland, and Michigan were reportedly considered as locations for the Air Service Engineering Division, but finding a site that already possessed adequate facilities and that would require little capital expenditure was next to impossible. One site that held a degree of promise, however, was the old Dayton-Wright Airplane Company at South Field in Dayton.

At the conclusion of the war, Dayton-Wright was in the process of making final settlements with the government. It was proposed that after the final settlement of contracts with the manufacturer, the government take over the plant and relocate the Air Service Engineering Division there. The primary argument for the move was that the War Department had already invested over $634,000 in the property for additions to the plant and $366,000 in roads and other improvements, all of which would be sacrificed unless the government purchased the plant and converted it to another use. As a plus, the Dayton-Wright factory buildings were of permanent, modern industrial construction and were serviced by adequate rail and land transportation. The flying field was of a suitable shape and size, and there was a corps of the highest grade mechanics, who were familiar with operations, available for hire. Relatively little government money would need to be expended in order to render the

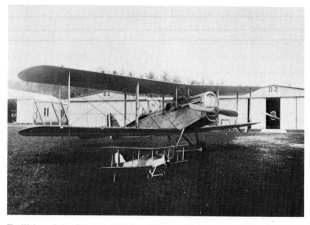

Facilities of the Dayton-Wright Airplane Company at Moraine were considered the most logical site for the relocation of the Engineering Division. (Model airplane pictured is most likely an early experiment in radio-control, a product of research by Charles F. Kettering). *(NCR Corporation)*

(NCR Corporatio

JOHN H. PATTERSON

John H. Patterson, founder of The National Cash Register Corporation, is recognized as the father of modern salesmanship and an American pioneer in industrial relations. He is also remembered by many Daytonians for his dramatic role in rescue operations during the 1913 flood, and for his subsequent work in establishing the Miami Conservancy District to protect Dayton from future disasters.

Mr. Patterson was a firm advocate of any concept which represented progress. He was a prime mover in Dayton's successful campaign to become the first major city nationwide to adopt a city manager form of government. He also foresaw a bright future for aviation.

Mr. Patterson identified strongly with Brig. Gen. Billy Mitchell's support of the engineering work at McCook Field. His opinion regarding Air Service operations, in general, was that "the remarkable progress that has been made in aviation should be continued. . . . If there is any change in the fiscal amounts the proposed appropriations should be *in*creased rather than *de*creased."

The donation of land made possible by the people of Dayton two years after Mr. Patterson's death, as a result of the work of his son, Frederick, and the Dayton Air Service Committee, solved the urgent and very thorny problem of a location for the Air Service Engineering Division. At the same time, it represented a fulfillment of John H. Patterson's ardent desire to help strengthen and expand the operations conducted at McCook so that they might make a dynamic and lasting contribution to Dayton (the birthplace of aviation), to the military, and eventually to commercial aviation.

facility suitable for the experimental work.[92] The choice was logical, but unfortunately appropriations to fund the move were not forthcoming.

The proposal to assume ownership of the Dayton-Wright facility was only one of a series of proposals to move the Engineering Division submitted to a Congress reluctant to approve any military appropriations. The Fiscal Year 1920 Report of the Air Service to the Secretary of War stated, "The Air Service has failed in its endeavors to secure from Congress an appropriation to provide a home for its Engineering Division. . . . A suitable location . . . was offered the Air Service by the Dayton-Wright Airplane Company at a price which the Air Service representatives considered very reasonable. This proposition was submitted to Congress, but permission for the consummation of the project was refused."

This report further concluded:[93]

The Air Service has been unable to date to find a suitable location for the Engineering Division on Government-owned land. The search for a location will be continued, but it is hardly believed that the Government now owns land which will be suitable for a plant of this kind. . . . At any rate, it is now clear that at its next session Congress must take the necessary legislative action for this primary and most important requirement of the Air Service.

By 1922 McCook Field's critical need for new facilities had become an irresistible force and Congress the proverbial immoveable object. It was during this crucial impasse, when federal agencies were deadlocked, that the citizens of Dayton rallied to take matters into their own hands and to provide a solution to the problem.

JOHN H. PATTERSON

John H. Patterson, founder and Chairman of the Board of The National Cash Register Company and a long-time supporter of the Air Service, was a man of insight as well as a man of action. According to Samuel Crowther, Patterson's biographer, it was during one of Brig. Gen. Billy Mitchell's visits to Dayton that Mitchell, then Assistant Chief of the Air Service, and Patterson first discussed taking more aggressive steps to keep the McCook Field operations in Dayton. Of primary importance was the pride Dayton claimed as the birthplace of aviation and as the center of aviation technology in the United States. Equally important was the economic initiative to be maintained by keeping the experimental aircraft industry and its highly-skilled work force in Dayton. In the recessionary period immediately following the war, the promise of a sizeable steady federal payroll, which was certain to expand as the field of aviation grew, was an opportunity to be seized.

Mr. Patterson was already known in Washington for his support of the Air Service. He now focused his considerable energies on two specifics: increasing Congressional appropriations to the Air Service so that essential work such as that done at McCook would continue, and negotiating with War Department officials to permanently relocate McCook activities to some other site near Dayton.

On the local level Patterson began examining various sites in the Dayton vicinity and methodically charting their advantages and disadvantages. In Washington, two NCR representatives, John F. Ahlers and Horace W. Karr, spent five weeks applying persuasive leverage in Congress on

Flying cadets from the Signal Corps Aviation School, Wilbur Wright Field, enjoy a reception on the lawn at the Far Hills estate of John H. Patterson, President of The National Cash Register Company, 1918. *(NCR Corporation)*

behalf of Air Service appropriations. They spoke to the Military Affairs Committee, the House Appropriations Committee, and the Ohio delegation to Congress. At Patterson's direction they also interviewed a total of 400 Congressmen and 96 Senators. The efforts of the two NCR representatives weighed significantly in the passage of increased Air Service appropriations for the coming year.[94]

There were no funds included in the budget, however, to relocate McCook Field. Mr. Patterson would not admit defeat or countenance delays, and resolved to stage an independent campaign to save McCook Field.

On May 5, 1922, Patterson and the Dayton Chamber of Commerce hosted a gala luncheon at the Gibbons Hotel in Dayton in honor of General Mitchell and Colonel Bane. Mr. Patterson outlined his plans for keeping McCook Field in Dayton. General Mitchell spoke on the valuable work being performed by the Engineering Division. He particularly urged Dayton citizens to take advantage of their opportunity to visit the field and become familiar with the government's activities in the development of the Air Service.[95]

Unfortunately, John H. Patterson did not live to see the fruits of his efforts. The next morning, Mitchell and Patterson met in the latter's office to discuss strategy and progress toward their mutual goal of retaining McCook Field in the Dayton area. That same afternoon Mr. Patterson departed by train for Atlantic City. Dayton was shocked and saddened two days later by the news that John H. Patterson had passed away on the train while en route from Philadelphia to Atlantic City on May 7, 1922.[96]

Patterson had laid the essential foundation, however, and formulated specific goals and objectives for the campaign to save McCook Field. His plans had only to be implemented.

THE DAYTON AIR SERVICE COMMITTEE

Patterson's only son, Frederick Beck Patterson, assumed leadership of The National Cash Register Company after his father's untimely death. Frederick had served as President of NCR under his father's tutelage since July of 1921. As such, he had been involved in the strategy meeting held in his father's office on the morning of May 6 and also had a personal interest in the McCook Field project.

During World War I, Frederick Beck Patterson was commissioned as a second lieutenant in the Army Air Service and served with the 15th Photographic Air Squadron in France. He remained active in aviation affairs after the war, eventually serving as Chairman of the National Aeronautic Association.

Shortly after John H. Patterson's death, it was rumored that a definite decision had been made by the Air Service to move the Engineering Division out of Dayton. Upon personal investigation, Frederick discovered the story to be true and acted quickly.

From May until October, Patterson conducted extensive negotiations with the Secretary of War, the Attorney General, and officers of the Air Service. He also enlisted the aid of

Frederick Beck Patterson (left) with his father, John H. Patterson *(Mrs. Howell Jackson)*

Lt. Frederick B. Patterson and his father, 1918 *(Mrs. Howell Jackson)*

numerous prominent Daytonians. The organization formed under Patterson's direction was named the Dayton Air Service Committee, and was composed of distinguished citizens who spent freely of their time and money in support of the McCook Field project:[97]

Frederick B. Patterson, President
Frederick H. Rike, Vice President
Ezra M. Kuhns, Secretary
W. M. Brock, Treasurer
W. R. Craven
Valentine Winters
H. H. Darst
I. G. Kumler
Col. Frank T. Huffman
Col. E. A. Deeds
G. W. Shroyer
F. J. Ach
J. C. Haswell
H. W. Karr
Edward Wuichet
George B. Smith
H. D. Wehrley
John F. Ahlers
C. E. Comer

In essence, what Mr. Patterson learned from Air Service officials was that if Dayton wished to retain McCook Field it would have to donate land for relocation of the Engineering Division. A number of other cities were vying for the same honor and had already made offers of land; so if Dayton was seriously interested, it would have to equal or better the incentive. This was not an unusual suggestion at the time, for during World War I Congress had passed legislation encouraging patriotic groups and individuals to make free and clear donations of land to the federal government.[98]

Frederick Patterson arranged for Air Service officials to view a site near Riverside (formerly Harshmanville), just outside of Dayton, that had been high on John H. Patterson's list of potential sites. The property involved was composed of a total of 4,988 acres, and spread across two counties. In Greene County the available property was bounded on the north by Springfield Pike and on the south by Yellow Springs Road, and included the site of former Wilbur Wright Field and land now occupied by Areas A and C of Wright-Patterson AFB. (The government already owned 40 acres adjacent to this tract, occupied by the Fairfield Air Intermediate Depot.) In Montgomery County, an additional 550 contiguous acres to the southwest were available near Riverside. A large portion of the available land (4,325 acres) was owned by the Miami Conservancy District. The remaining acreage proposed for the site was composed of seven parcels owned by the following individuals:[99]

Jannie Harshman	172.129 acres
Charles & Susan Beckel	171.260 acres
Alice Tobey	22.976 acres
William Stickle	21.000 acres
Louis Gradsky	37.023 acres
William Mathers	143.310 acres
William Mays	96.000 acres

Charts publicized by the Dayton Air Service Committee showed that a total of $325,000 would be required to purchase the eight parcels.

Frederick B. Patterson, President of The National Cash Register Company, also served as President of the Dayton Air Service Committee. *(Mrs. Howell Jackson)*

Capt. Edward Rickenbacker, World War I ace of the Air Service, and Frederick B. Patterson, President of NCR *(NCR Corporation)*

First meeting of the Dayton Air Service Committee, October 25, 1922, at the Dayton Country Club. The committee subsequently organized a campaign that yielded over $425,000 in public contributions to purchase a permanent home for McCook Field activities. Committee members, all prominent Dayton business leaders, are (from left): Irvin G. Kumler, H. W. Karr, G. W. Shroyer, Dr. D. F. Garland, Edward Wuichet, Frederick H. Rike, Frederick B. Patterson, W. R. Craven, John C. Haswell, H. D. Wehrley, Valentine Winters, and John F. Ahlers. Seated in the back row are Ezra M. Kuhns and Harold E. Talbott. *(NCR Corporation)*

The Air Service officials who viewed this vast tract of land were impressed and thrilled at the thought of obtaining enough land to comprise "the largest flying field in the world." Their response was so optimistic that the Dayton Air Service Committee proceeded immediately to secure options on all of the land. Meanwhile, Frederick Patterson continued to press the issue in Washington in order to obtain official approval of the project from the Air Service, and an iron-clad commitment from the government to accept the land when the Dayton Air Service Committee raised money to purchase it.

On October 25, 1922, Patterson announced that he had received a letter from the Air Service confirming its commitment to accept the land. With the government's approval of the proposed site also came word that the U.S. Air Service was contemplating the establishment of an air academy at the same location, a school that would eclipse both West Point and Annapolis in enrollment and importance.[100]

Patterson's response was swift and decisive. A dinner meeting of the Dayton Air Service Committee convened at the Dayton Country Club on Wednesday evening, October 25, to discuss specific strategies for raising money to purchase the land. It was decided to advertise creation of the new aviation facility as a lasting monument to the Wright brothers. The Committee believed this concept would appeal to the sentiment of the entire community. Dayton citizens at the time were sorely aware of the fact that France was the only country to erect a monument commemorating the achievements of the Wrights. They felt that the most

logical location in the United States for a similar memorial was Dayton, Ohio.

A massive public campaign was planned for the very next week, to be conducted on October 31 and November 1, 1922. The goal of the campaign was to raise $400,000. This would be enough to ensure purchase of the new lands, with a nest egg of at least $25,000 left over to erect an official memorial to the Wright brothers. It was imperative that money for the land be raised quickly, because options on the land expired January 1, 1923.

H. D. Wehrley, Executive Secretary of the Community Chest, was named campaign manager. General headquarters for the campaign were established at the Chamber of Commerce offices in the Mutual Home Building at 40 North Main Street.[101] Twenty-five team captains were appointed to head teams of five men each.

Frederick Patterson hosted a dinner at NCR for more than 200 Daytonians involved in the campaign on Friday evening, October 27, at which time the entire project was explained in detail. Maj. Gen. Mason Patrick and Col. Thurman Bane were invited. In addition, the campaigners were treated to movies of the Pulitzer aerial race in Detroit and of Lts. John Macready and Oakley Kelly making their record-breaking cross-country flight.[102]

By October 31, all of Dayton was aware of the immensity and importance of the campaign. At noon on the first day of the campaign a spectacular aerial exhibition was held over Dayton by crews from McCook Field. Factory whistles sounded simultaneously throughout the town to signal the

More than 200 team captains and workers receive campaign plans from the Dayton Air Service Committee at this dinner, October 27, 1927, hosted by Mr. Frederick B. Patterson in the NCR employee dining room. *(NCR Corporation)*

beginning of the campaign.[103] Contributions were solicited from all major businesses and intensive door-to-door canvassing resulted in many contributions from private citizens. Pledges were for a period of three years, collectable every six months commencing January 1, 1923, in order to encourage sizeable donations.

The strategy carefully planned by Frederick Patterson worked. By sundown on October 31, $278,573 had been pledged, only $50,000 short of the amount needed to purchase the land. The second day of active campaigning

The Miami Hotel, November 1, 1922. Frederick B. Patterson and his wife, Evelyn, host a post-campaign dinner for Dayton Air Service Committee workers. *(NCR Corporation)*

terminated with a victory dinner for team captains and workers at the Miami Hotel. Patterson announced that the response from the citizens of Dayton had far exceeded the committee's expectations and that the fund had already passed the goal of $400,000.[104] In fact, pledges continued to flow in until November 10. Dayton historian Charlotte Reeve Conover has written of the campaign:[105]

> For two days everybody thought and talked Wright Field. Not a man was left unapproached. All the arguments were aired; all our civic loyalty was drawn upon. When the final count of contributions to the fund was made it showed that Dayton "had gone over the top" to the tune of $425,673.

Once the final count of contributions had been tallied, Patterson wired General Patrick that the money had been raised and that steps were being made to expedite the legal transfer of land titles to the U.S. government. His telegram read, in part:[106]

> The spirit which dominated this campaign will ever mark the attitude of Dayton toward the United States Air Service. Our citizens will extend a hearty hand of fellowship to its members. We are not unmindful of the kindly interest you have taken in this great project, and desire to thank you for your many courtesies and kind consideration.

> With best wishes for the continued wonderful progress of the United States Air Service, and assurance that Dayton always may be depended upon to do its share in furthering such a splendid and necessary cause, we are,

> The Dayton Air Service Committee
> F. B. Patterson, General Chairman [sic]

The technicalities involved in purchasing land and presenting it to the government required that the Dayton Air Service Committee incorporate. Articles of incorporation for the committee were filed with the Ohio Secretary of State on November 16, 1922. The articles listed, as committee officers: President, Frederick Beck Patterson, President of NCR; Secretary, Ezra M. Kuhns, General Counsel of NCR; Treasurer, W. M. Brock, Secretary of the Gem City Building and Loan Association.

The articles of incorporation empowered the committee to acquire and hold property intended for use by the government, to receive and enforce payment of subscriptions, and to borrow money on the faith and credit of those subscriptions. A Finance Committee was formed to implement plans for financing these transactions, headed by W. R. Craven, Valentine Winters, and Harry H. Darst.[107]

Negotiations for the land took place over several ensuing months, as did debate in the Congress over the funds necessary to construct a new home for the Engineering Division and to complete the Division's transfer from McCook Field. The Air Service decided not to carry the name of McCook to the new installation. The name "Wright Field" was deemed appropriate considering the size and location of the new field, and the direct link that would thus be forged between the new installation and aviation's founding fathers.

On August 9, 1924, 428.50 acres of Montgomery County (Mad River Township) land and 4,091.97 acres of Greene County (Bath Township) land were conveyed to the government by the Dayton Air Service Committee for the consideration of one dollar ($1.00) for each tract.[108]

On August 17, 1924, Frederick B. Patterson traveled to Washington, D.C., to personally present Secretary of War John Weeks with the deeds to the acquired lands. Secretary Weeks insisted, due to the significance of the occasion, that Patterson have an audience with President Calvin Coolidge to make the presentation. Following the audience, President Coolidge addressed a very warm letter to Patterson recognizing and praising the sacrifices made by the people of Dayton.

The exact wording of the Warranty Deed presented to the government read as follows:[109]

KNOW ALL MEN BY THESE PRESENTS:

That THE DAYTON AIR SERVICE INCORPORATED COMMITTEE, a corporation organized under the laws of the State of Ohio, with principal offices at Dayton, Ohio, hereinafter referred to and styled the grantor, in consideration of One ($1.00) Dollar to it paid by the United States of America, receipt whereof is hereby acknowledged, does hereby GRANT, BARGAIN, SELL AND CONVEY to the UNITED STATES OF AMERICA, its successors and assigns forever, subject to the limitations hereinafter mentioned, the following real estate: (DESCRIPTION)

The original deeds recorded that the land was sold to the government for use as an aviation field, or for such other service of the United States as the government considered desirable. Upon abandonment or discontinuance of the use of the land, however, title to the lands, according to the deeds, would *ipso facto* revert to the grantors, with the government having the period of one year to remove or dispose of any buildings, structures, or improvements on the land, to which it would still hold title. From this original deed has undoubtedly sprung the popular misconception that the property occupied by Wright-Patterson AFB today would revert to the City of Dayton or other original owners were the government to abandon the site or cease to employ civilian workers.

On December 18, 1924, however, the Dayton Air Service Committee reversed its position on the controversial clause by means of the following resolution:[110]

RESOLUTION:

This is to certify that at a special meeting of the Board of Trustees of the Dayton Air Service Incorporated Committee, held pursuant to notice, and at which a quorum was present, the following resolution was unanimously adopted. "Resolved: that this Committee does hereby waive and release its reversionary right in and to the lands conveyed to the United States Government lying in Montgomery and Greene Counties, Ohio, as described in deeds to the United States dated February 4, 1924 and August 9, 1924 respectively, and the President and Secretary of this Committee are hereby authorized and instructed to execute, acknowledge and deliver on behalf of the Committee, Quit-Claim Deeds to the United States in and to the lands referred to, thereby releasing to the United States the Reversionary Right of this Committee to said lands, as contained in the former deeds.

IN WITNESS WHEREOF, I have hereunto set my name and the Corporation Seal of said Committeee, on this 18th day of December, 1924.

The Dayton Air Service Incorporated Committee,
Ezra M. Kuhns, Secretary

A Quit-Claim Deed was drawn up stating that the Dayton Air Service Committee did "Remiss, release, and forever quit-claim to the United States of America, its successors and assigns forever, the above mentioned reversionary rights" to the donated lands.[111] The Dayton Air Service Committee, over the next six years, continued to donate small parcels of land to the government. These were, by and large, sections of land that had been exempted in the original deeds because of existing railroad and traction line right-of-ways. As these became available for sale, the committee purchased them and donated them to the government—always for the consideration of $1.00. In all instances, following the December 1924 resolution, the property was sold to the government outright, with no reversionary rights attached.[112]

While negotiations were underway to secure the land for Wright Field, Congress held lively and sometimes heated debate over appropriations for the new field. A bill submitted to the Congress in December 1922 by Representative Roy Fitzgerald of Ohio allowed the President, through the Secretary of War, to sell and dispose of land, buildings, machinery, and equipment at air sites owned by the govern-

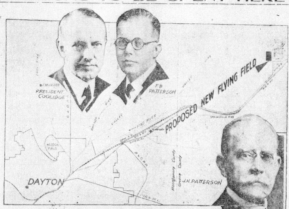

DAYTON DAILY NEWS

72 PAGES TODAY · MAIN NEWS SECTION

VOL. XXXVIII. No. 363 (SUNDAY EDITION) · DAYTON, OHIO, SUNDAY, AUGUST 17, 1924. · PRICE FIVE CENTS

U. S. ACCEPTS AIR FIELD GIFT

Military Home May Have New Hospital

DAYTON LAUDED AS PATTERSON SUBMITS DEEDS

OLD STRUCTURE FOUND UNSAFE AS PROBE ENDS

MILLIONS TO BE SPENT HERE

PROPOSED NEW FLYING FIELD

The letter reads:

THE WHITE HOUSE
WASHINGTON

August 14, 1924.

My dear Mr. Patterson:

        It was a genuine pleasure to receive this morning the call of yourself and your associates of the Dayton Air Service Committee, who were brought in by General Mitchell to tell me about the conclusion of the transactions which make the McCook Field at Dayton the property of the United States Government. In making this splendid gift to their country, the citizens of Dayton have been inspired alike by motives of high patriotism and also of pride in the fact that Dayton was the home of the Wright brothers, and that there, through their talents and tireless efforts, aviation had its birth.

        McCook Field will always be famous as the first of those training fields and terminals for aviation which now are scattered throughout the entire world. Upon it is reflected a full share of the glory won by thousands of American and other aviators who were trained there. It has been the scene of splendid services alike to the cause of science and to the national defense. The people of Dayton, in presenting this historic tract of 4500 acres to the National Government have insured that it will always be maintained for the service that has won it fame. You have enabled the creation of McCook field into a perpetual monument to the men who first realized the full possibilities of navigating the air, and to that great first generation of inventors and aviators whose services and sacrifices in the war and in the works of peace have made their list a roll of heroes. You have informed me that the transactions incident to transferring McCook field to the National Government are now completed. I am writing you because I want in this formal manner to record the Government's appreciation of this fine act, and to set down the assurance of my personal congratulations to the people of Dayton and my gratification at having had a small part in it.

Most sincerely yours,

Mr. Frederick Patterson, Chairman,
The Dayton Air Service Committee,
Dayton, Ohio.

Letter from President Calvin Coolidge to the Dayton Air Service Committee

Plaque awarded to Frederick Beck Patterson in honor of his achievements with the Dayton Air Service Committee. The occasion was the 50th Anniversary of the founding of McCook Field. *(Montgomery County Historical Society)*

AVIATION PROGRESS

Congress should provide enough money for scientific research in aviation.

Banner of the Saturday, March 11, 1922 issue of *Aviation Progress,* published by the Dayton Air Service Committee *(NCR Corporation)*

ment when such were no longer of use to the Air Service, and deposit the proceeds thereof with the Treasurer of the United States. The entire sum, not to exceed $5 million, would then be appropriated for the erection of buildings, for gas and electric systems, machinery, and equipment at the new field.[113]

A similar bill was introduced in the Senate by Senator Frank B. Willis of Ohio. Both bills were subsequently referred to the respective Military Affairs Committees of each house. Plans for the new field and architectural models had already been prepared, and the Air Service was poised to begin construction as soon as the land was officially transferred and funds were made available.

These efforts were strongly backed by the Dayton Air Service Committee. Additionally, Frederick B. Patterson reinstituted publication of a journal entitled *Aviation Progress,* first published by the Dayton Chamber of Commerce at the direction of John H. Patterson in March 1922, to educate members of the Congress about achievements taking place at McCook Field and thereby influence them to pass the critical appropriations legislation. A special notice posted on the front cover of various issues of the journal stated:

> To Every Member of Congress:
>
> Development of the United States Air Service is one of the urgent needs of our nation. Bills supporting the program for its progress will come before you during the next session. Yours is a grave responsibility, and this booklet has been prepared to help you in careful study of the subject. Aviation must have your support.

Numerous large photographs with bold, clearly worded text and impressive statistics were designed for at-a-glance reading by Congressmen. Endorsements and statements by such notables as Orville Wright and Air Service Chief Maj. Gen. Mason Patrick graced the opening and closing pages. To broaden the image of the contributions being made by the Air Service, *Aviation Progress* also elaborated on the brilliant future of aviation in general, illustrating such potential commercial applications as cropdusting, air mail service, passenger service, freight transport, medical relief, and the use of aerial photography to facilitate mapping, surveying, and city planning.

The battle to secure funding was long and controversial. The Fitzgerald bill and other efforts were blocked, and Congress adjourned without taking action. In 1925, however, and in succeeding years Congress did make appropriations both for construction of buildings and for purchase of equipment for Wright Field:[114]

FISCAL YEAR	APPROPRIATIONS BUILDINGS & GROUNDS	APPROPRIATIONS NEW EQUIPMENT
1926	$ 500,000	$297,600
1927	$1,000,000	$715,200
1928	$ 600,000	$792,300
1929	$ 300,000	$488,200

In April 1925, an initial $5,000 was transferred to the Engineering Division at McCook so that grading of the new flying field could start immediately.[115]

On August 21, 1925, the War Department discontinued the designation "Wilbur Wright Field." All of the land that had been donated to the government by the Dayton Air Service Committee in 1924, including Wilbur Wright Field, became known officially as Wright Field, honoring both Wilbur and Orville.[116]

GROUND IS BROKEN

On April 16, 1926, official groundbreaking ceremonies were held at Wright Field. More than 100 citizens of Dayton, officials from McCook and Wilbur Wright Fields, members of the Dayton Air Service Committee, and Orville and Katharine Wright, witnessed the auspicious event.

Several local dignitaries took turns operating a steam shovel provided by the construction company to symbolically break ground. They included Frederick B. Patter-

Members of the Dayton Air Service Committee, local Air Service officers, and distinguished guests attend groundbreaking ceremonies for Wright Field on April 16, 1926. Standing are (l to r): G. W. Shroyer, E. C. Berry, Howard Smith, Joseph McKenny, C. E. Comer, R. J. Hutchinson, I. G. Kumler, George B. Smith, Maj. Augustine W. Robins (Commander Fairfield Air Depot), Capt. E. M. George, Orville Wright, Frederick B. Patterson, George W. Lane, Lt. Lester Maitland (McCook Field test pilot), Maj. J. F. Curry (Chief, Engineering Division, McCook Field), W. M. Brock, Howard Egbert, John Ahlers, U. C. Thies, E. A. Johnson, and T. C. McMahon. *(NCR Corporation)*

Frederick B. Patterson (left), Secretary of War Dwight F. Davis, and Chief of the Air Service Maj. Gen. Mason M. Patrick at the Wright Field groundbreaking ceremonies *(Mrs. Howell Jackson)*

Distinguished guests at the Wright Field groundbreaking included Orville and Katharine Wright. *(Mrs. Howell Jackson)*

son, Maj. John F. Curry, Commander of McCook Field, and Maj. Augustine Warner Robins, Commander of the Fairfield Air Depot.

From that date on, progress at the new site was rapid. In less than one year, the residents of McCook Field were prepared to transfer operations to their new home and McCook Field was to become history. Many important chapters in air advancement had been written at McCook Field. Even more startling chapters of progress promised to be penned at Wright Field in the years to come.

Frederick B. Patterson, at the controls, lifts the first bucket of earth at the site of Wright Field. *(Mrs. Howell Jackson)*

Construction at Wright Field gets underway. *(Mrs. Howell Jackson)*

Wright Field, June 3, 1927

V.   WRIGHT FIELD 1927-1948

Wright Field has been described as a kaleidoscope of aerospace science, engineering, technology, and education. As home of the Materiel Division and later the Materiel Command, Wright Field was the scene of engineering development and procurement as well as the heart of Army Air Corps/Air Forces logistical support. As home of the Air Corps School of Engineering, Wright Field hosted countless young officers seeking advanced education in the developing fields of military aviation and logistics.

In the two decades between the dedication of Wright Field in 1927 and the designation of Wright-Patterson Air Force Base in 1948, the name of Wright Field was synonymous with military aeronautical development. Wright Field engineers and logisticians explored the concepts that provided the impetus for today's modern Air Force, and guided the technical development of aeronautical equipment that was at the time the most sophisticated in the world. Officers like Clinton Howard, Leslie MacDill, Franklin Carroll, Orval Cook, K. B. Wolfe, George Goddard, Grandison Gardner, Albert Stevens, and Laurence Craigie, and outstanding civilian scientists such as John B. Johnson, Ralph Ferguson, Ezra Kotcher, Adam Dickey, Opie Chenoweth, Clarence Clawson, Samuel Burka, and John Lamphier helped the Wright Field laboratories achieve international renown. Military leaders such as William E.

Gillmore, Augustine Warner Robins, Oliver P. Echols, George C. Kenney, William F. Volandt, Alfred J. Lyon, Elmer E. Adler, and Edward M. Powers made vital contributions to the logistical progress of the Air Corps.

Air-cooled radial engines, superchargers and turbosuperchargers, controllable-pitch and full-feathering propellers, high-octane fuels, pressurized cabins, blind-flying instrumentation, free-fall parachutes, helicopters, flying wings, autogiros, gliders, and jet airplanes all have their special place in Wright Field history.

The roster of Wright Field test pilots includes Air Force pioneers famous for their courage and skill: James H. Doolittle, Stanley M. Umstead, Benjamin Kelsey, Fred Bordosi, Frank G. Irvin, Ann Baumgartner, Albert Boyd, and J. S. Griffith. Some gave their lives in the path of progress at Wright Field: Hugh M. Elmendorf, Irvin A. Woodring, Ployer P. Hill, Perry Ritchie, R. K. Giovannoli, Hezekiah McClellan, and Richard Bong.

It is appropriate that Wright Field, named in honor of Dayton's most famous native sons, has been a continuous center of American aeronautical development. The achievements that unfolded at Wright Field have perpetuated the Wright brothers' legacy of aeronautical genius and their spirit of engineering excellence.

117

THE DEDICATION OF WRIGHT FIELD

The sun dawned in a grey and rainy sky on the morning of October 12, 1927. Twenty-four pilots of the 1st Pursuit Group had flown to Dayton from Selfridge Field, Michigan, to perform at the dedication ceremonies for Wright Field. All through the morning, they wandered about restlessly, eyes cast on the skies, for it seemed that the flying program would most certainly have to be cancelled.

At an early hour, distinguished guests and officials began arriving at the field. Orville Wright, the first gentleman of flight, Secretary of War Dwight F. Davis, Assistant Secretary of War F. Trubee Davison, Air Corps Chief Maj. Gen. Mason M. Patrick, and Dayton industrialist Col. Edward A. Deeds headed the list of visiting dignitaries.

At 9:30 a.m. the new and modern Wright Field laboratories were opened for public inspection. For several days the different departments, recently relocated from McCook Field, had been occupied in arranging an impressive array of their experimental equipment for display. Materiel Division engineers from the Armament, Propeller, Parachute, Photographic, Radio, and Lighter-than-Air Laboratories were kept busy throughout the day answering a battery of questions about the complicated and unusual equipment with which they worked.

Parachutes, tow targets, bombs, machine guns, airship models, aviators' clothing, and countless other items on display captured the attention of Dayton's air-minded citizens.

The earth induction compass was of particular interest to many aviation enthusiasts. A facsimile of the Hegenberger-Maitland instrument board used on the Army California-Hawaii flight in June 1927 was on display, complete with B-5 compass, vertical flight indicator, engine gauge, airspeed indicator, and special tachometer.* The non-freezing pitot-static tube developed by Materiel Division engi-

neers at the suggestion of the U.S. Air Mail Service was also available for close inspection. Thrilled groups of high school students surrounded the Ruggles Orientator to take turns simulating the maneuvers of flight.

Rain forced the official dedication ceremonies indoors to the new auditorium of the Administration Building. The band of the Tenth Infantry, Ohio, opened the ceremony at 12:30 p.m. The dedication of the new installation as Wright Field, in honor of both Wilbur and Orville Wright, established three precedents. It marked the first time that an Army installation was named for two civilians who had never been in military service; the first time an installation was named for a living individual; and, in all likelihood, it was the first time that an individual so honored by the military service was present at his own memorialization.

Symbol of the Air Corps Materiel Division, mounted above both main entrances of the Headquarters building. Modeled after the famous Rodin sculpture *The Thinker*, the symbol was originally adopted by the Engineering Division at McCook Field and was retained after the 1926 reorganization which created the Materiel Division.

Administration Building, Wright Field. Known today as Building 11, Area B, it originally served as Headquarters for the Air Corps Materiel Division when the Division moved from McCook Field in 1927.

*See Chapter VI, Developing Air Power 1917-1951, for details of this exciting flight.

Distinguished visitors at the dedication of Wright Field, October 12, 1927. Front row (l to r): Orville Wright, Secretary of War Dwight Davis, Judge Kenesaw Mountain Landis, Air Secretary F. Trubee Davison, and Maj. Gen. Mason M. Patrick, Chief, Army Air Corps. In the second row are, from the left: Brig. Gen. William E. Gillmore, Chief of the Materiel Division, Dr. Joseph Ames, and Col. Edward A. Deeds. *(Wright State University Archives)*

Principal speakers at the event were: Dwight F. Davis, Secretary of War; F. Trubee Davison, Assistant Secretary of War; Maj. Gen. Mason M. Patrick, Chief of the Air Corps; Col. Edward A. Deeds, former Chief of the Signal Corps Equipment Division;* and Brig. Gen. William E. Gillmore, Chief of the Materiel Division. Orville Wright occupied the seat of honor on the stage, although, as was his custom, he preferred not to address the audience.

The central theme of the dedicatory addresses was the vital role played by the Materiel Division and its forerunner, the Engineering Division at McCook Field, in the progress of American aviation. The very existence of Wright Field, however, was a tribute to the citizens of Dayton. It was their persistence, prescience, and philanthropy that had persuaded the War Department to keep the Materiel Division operations in Dayton, Ohio, the cradle of aviation. The official dedication program listed more than 600 individual donors who had given concrete expression to their aviation enthusiasm.

Official dedication ceremony for Wright Field, held in the auditorium of Building 11

*Chapter IV, McCook Field, details Colonel Deeds' valuable contributions to Dayton aviation.

Brig. Gen. William E. Gillmore, Chief of the Air Corps Materiel Division, Wright Field, from October 1926 to June 1929. Air Force Logistics Command (AFLC) Headquarters, Building 262 at Wright-Patterson AFB, is named in his honor.

Official Message from the Chief, Materiel Division

The establishment of a permanent home for the headquarters of the Materiel Division, and suitable laboratories for prosecuting the engineering and scientific work necessary in procuring satisfactory flying and fighting equipment for our Air Corps, is a matter that should react with general pride and satisfaction to all people of our great country, and in particular to the people of Dayton, who through their generosity and understanding cooperation have helped to make these plans possible.

It is a fortuitous circumstance that the magnificent tract of land given to the government by the citizens of Dayton, should also be the scene of the first flying experiments of Wilbur and Orville Wright.

It is particularly fitting that this historic site should for all time be devoted to further experimentation in aviation, and maintained as an active and useful monument to their great gift to mankind. The dedication of this field in honor of the Wright brothers, and of the people of Dayton who presented the site to the Government, should be splendid inspiration to the men who must carry on this important work, which in spite of the wonderful progress made in the near past, is but in its infancy.

It is pleasing to think that the name of Wright, in addition to the glory already won, will hereafter be directly associated with the future developments of aviation.

WILLIAM E. GILLMORE
Brigadier General, Air Corps
Chief, Materiel Division

Members of the 10th Infantry Band, Ohio National Guard, at the Wright Field dedication

Each of the distinguished speakers made reference to the great significance of the achievements of Dayton's famed native sons. The remarks of Secretary of War Dwight F. Davis were particularly salient:[1]

> So far as aviation is concerned, we are today on historic ground. Not very far from here stands the ramshackle structure which nearly a generation ago housed the first airplanes built by the Wright brothers—Wilbur and Orville. We are, therefore, in more than one sense, building upon the foundation laid by the Wright brothers and it is only fitting that we in this hour should recollect and honor the courage, patience and ability that made those first flying machines possible.

General Gillmore, in concluding the indoor portion of the ceremony, announced that Mr. Wright had consented to raise the first flag upon Wright Field. All adjourned to the flagpole in front of the Administration Building, where under the guiding hand of the world's first aviator, the flag of the Union was raised to the music of the national anthem, and honored with a 21-gun salute.

Although it had been announced earlier that the flying program would be cancelled, a sudden clearing of the skies led officials to reverse their decision. Crowds began to gather at the flying field near Fairfield (formerly known as Wilbur Wright Field) immediately after lunch to inspect airplanes on display and to witness the flying exhibition.

The afternoon program opened with skilled acrobatic flying by former McCook Field test pilots Lieutenants James Doolittle, James Hutchison, and Reuben Moffat. The acrobatic flying was followed by a tactical demonstration in which an unmanned observation balloon went down in flames.

The 1st Pursuit Group from Selfridge Field demonstrated 24-plane formation flying and other tactical formations. Parachute jumps were made by M. H. Clair of Wright Field and F. G. Manson, William Moore, and Owen Kindred of Fairfield, Ohio. Two of the parachutists side-slipped so that they landed impressively close to the crowd of spectators.

A free balloon, piloted by Maj. R. A. Hale and Lt. Malcolm S. Lawton, ascended from the field and landed some 45 minutes later in Clifton, Ohio. Shortly after 2:00 p.m., the Army non-rigid dirigible, Airship RS-1, appeared overhead. A photographic airplane next impressed the

Wright Field civilian police secure the halyard of the first flag flown at Wright Field after it was raised by aviation pioneer Orville Wright. Secretary of War Dwight Davis is handing Mr. Wright his hat.

Curtiss P-1 Hawk pursuits from the 1st Pursuit Group, Selfridge Field, Michigan, thrill spectators with low-level formation flying during the airshow held as part of the Wright Field dedication.

crowd as an observer took pictures over the field, developed them in flight, and dropped the finished prints to earth before landing. Spectators were delighted to hear voices from a radio airplane in flight over the field broadcasting information of all that was taking place.

The final event of the day was the John L. Mitchell Trophy Race for pilots of the 1st Pursuit Group. Fifteen Curtiss P-1 Hawk biplanes entered. When all had finished the race, it was announced that there had been just one minute and 23 seconds difference in time between the first and last airplanes. The Mitchell Trophy was awarded to the winner, Lt. I. A. Woodring, to hold for one year.* Silver trophies for the first, second, and third place winners were donated by Daytonians.

After the flying program, many of the spectators drifted over to where the visiting commercial airplanes were displayed. These included the Brock and Schlee *Pride of Detroit,* its fuselage adorned with an international collection of autographs; a Huhl Airster, in which Louis Meister had piloted a party down from Marysville, Michigan; a Stinson; a Waco; and many others. Near dusk, the three Wright Whirlwind engines on the visiting Ford Trimotor began to warm up. All passengers aboard, it headed north to reach Detroit in time for late dinner. "It would probably strike darkness before landing, but the plane was equipped for night flying, so what was the difference? Somehow, that great monoplane winging its way into the dusk, about the ordinary business of flying home, was a fitting and symbolic finale to the Wright Field Dedication Ceremonies," by far the most elaborate dedication held in the long history of Wright-Patterson Air Force Base.[2]

MOVING McCOOK FIELD

The topography of the land upon which Wright Field was located divided the field naturally into two parts. The 750 acres lying on the protected side of Huffman Dam (present-day Area B) provided a logical site for the experimental plant and the main flying field of the Materiel Division. The remainder of Wright Field, approximately 3,800 acres, lay in the flood control basin of the Mad River. This larger portion included the site of old Wilbur Wright Field and the 40-acre tract occupied by the Fairfield Air Depot (present-day Areas A and C). An old hangar in this area still stood as evidence of the flying school operated by Wilbur and Orville Wright at Simms Station from 1910 to 1916. This larger area of the field was well suited for conducting air maneuvers on a large scale.

The process of moving Materiel Division operations from McCook Field to Wright Field began in the spring of 1927, prior to the official dedication. Most of the McCook Field operations planned to relocate directly to new buildings on the smaller portion of the base. The Test Flight Section, however, planned to ship part of its equipment to the Fairfield Air Depot (FAD), closer to where its operations would be established.

In the early morning hours of March 25, 1927, the first trucks assembled at McCook Field in preparation for loading. A total of 69 buildings at McCook were to be emptied. Their contents ranged from airplanes, airplane engines, extremely sensitive instruments used in flying and precision testing, a 14-inch wind tunnel, and an 11,000-pound punch press for stamping out metal tips used on propellers, to the

---

*Lieutenant Woodring later lost his life while testing an airplane at Wright Field on January 20, 1933.

1,052 steel file cabinets, 600 desks, and other office equipment used in day-to-day operations at McCook. Also included were the McCook Field Aeronautical Reference Library and artifacts from the Army Aeronautical Museum. In all, it was estimated that more than 4,500 tons would be moved from the old field to the new.

State highway regulations prohibited moving excessive tonnage by road during the spring season when the ground was soft. Thus, only lighter equipment could be hauled in McCook Field trucks and the 28 trucks and trailers on loan from the Quartermaster Corps at Jeffersonville, Indiana. Spur tracks were laid at both McCook and Wright Fields which connected with the electric railroad and standard railroad lines. Heavier equipment was then loaded onto regular flat-bottomed freight cars and transported by rail.

At the McCook Field site, provisions of the lease required that all buildings be removed and the ground restored to useable condition. The largest portion of the demolition program involved some 35 major buildings, mostly of standard Air Service steel-hangar construction. The Chief of the Repair and Maintenance Section directed demolition operations, using Quartermaster trucks and temporary labor crews. Some of the wooden buildings at McCook were sold to a local wrecking firm for removal.

Some salvaged materials from the demolished buildings were used in construction of buildings at Wright Field, although the principal buildings at the new field had already been completed. Doors, door frames, and window sashes were salvaged, along with piping and sanitary fixtures, lighting fixtures, radiators, conduit and wire, and sheet metal work such as ventilators and cowling. The chief salvage process was aimed at the steel framework of the McCook Field buildings. They contained nearly 900 tons of steel, representing a current market value of about $81,000. The steel was dismantled and transported to Wright Field.

As mentioned, the moving process at McCook Field was initiated on March 25, 1927. By June 1, the transfer to the new field was 85 percent complete and restoration of the McCook Field property 60 percent complete. A total of 1,859 truck loads had been moved from McCook to the new field or to new quarters at the Fairfield Air Depot. An estimated 1,700 tons remained to be moved after June 1. Total cost incurred from March to June was $12,474.71.[3]

Three important activities of the Materiel Division—the dynamometer laboratory, the propeller test building and test stands, and the 5-foot wind tunnel—remained in operation at McCook Field until new quarters could be completed at Wright Field. A lease was arranged with the General Motors Company, then owner of the section of McCook Field on which these labs were situated, permitting use of the site until September 30. The lease was let in consideration of $1 and title to the buildings, thus allowing the Division virtually free use of the grounds.[4] When facilities were still not complete in the fall, General Motors allowed the lease to extend. The new dynamometer lab at Wright Field was finally completed during Fiscal Year 1929. The 5-foot wind tunnel was also relocated during that year, together with installation of sufficient equipment to begin operations. The propeller testing activity was transferred permanently to Wright Field on May 22, 1929.[5]

Wright Field facilities under construction, 1926

By June 1927, major facilities at Wright Field had progressed sufficiently to allow the Materiel Division to begin moving its mission, personnel, and equipment from McCook Field. Offices in the Administration Building (foreground) and in the laboratories behind it are already occupied.

Main entrance to Wright Field, looking north, October 1932. The flagpole and ceremonial 75-mm field artillery piece sit in front of Materiel Division Headquarters (Building 11). The cannon fired salutes during reveille and retreat ceremonies.

NEW CONSTRUCTION AT WRIGHT FIELD

1 - FOUNDRY	4 - WIND TUNNEL	7 - ARMAMENT LABORATORY	10 - OIL STORAGE BUILDING
2 - MAINTENANCE BUILDING	5 - RADIO LABORATORY	8 - PROPELLER TEST RIGS	11 - RESERVOIR, 300,000 GALLONS
3 - FIRE STATION	6 - WOOD SHOP EXTENSION	9 - GARAGE	12 - SOFTWATER BASIN, 250,000 GALLONS

Note: New construction on buildings No. 1, 2, 4, 5, 7, 9 and 10 involved the erection of permanent roofs and walls. Buildings No. 3 and 6 are new structures entirely.

Major facilities completed by the October 1927 dedication

A wood-fired steam engine roller and a Caterpillar tractor pulling a road grader level the streets at Wright Field.

Dismantling McCook for the move to Wright Field. Per terms of the McCook Field lease, buildings were razed and foundations were torn up. Materials such as steel girders were salvaged for use in construction at the new installation.

McCook Field truck loaded for the move to Wright Field. Thousands of truckloads traveled to the new field via surface streets. Heavier equipment was loaded onto flatbed cars and moved by rail.

CONDITIONS AT THE NEW WRIGHT FIELD

With passage of the Air Corps Act and creation of the Air Corps Materiel Division in 1926, Wright Field was forced to accommodate a larger number of organizations than originally anticipated. To further complicate the matter, austere funding for military aviation delayed the construction schedule at Wright Field and plans for some of the new laboratories had to be delayed indefinitely. In all, conditions at the site were far from ideal for many of the incoming organizations.

One of the larger testing laboratories, the Materials Branch, was housed in a building which had been constructed for office use (Building 16). The associated heat-treating operation and all foundry operations, however, were set up at a separate site (Building 46, now the southeast part of Building 51) across "D" street from the main laboratory.

Building 46, like many others at the time, was originally a temporary structure. At that point, it had a permanent concrete floor and steel-girder framework, but the roof and walls were covered with corrugated sheet steel, and the windows had wooden frames. Years later brick walls, metal-frame windows, and permanent roofs were added.[6] Facilities yet to be erected included the airplane hangars, the firehouse, guard house, boiler house, gymnasium, school, and a civilian cafeteria. Many other buildings were of temporary construction and lacked permanent-type walls and roofs.[7]

There were no paved streets at Wright Field in the beginning months, and no sidewalks or street lighting. Likewise, grading of the flying field and of grounds around the buildings had yet to be accomplished.[8]

Officer and enlisted housing remained on the list of projected construction. The buildings at McCook Field used for housing enlisted men had been vacated and demolished on April 1, 1927, as part of the move. In the interim, enlisted men were attached to the Fairfield Air Depot for rations and quarters, or paid a separate allowance in lieu thereof. Officers were placed on commutation status, occupying privately-owned housing in or about the city of Dayton, with the exception of officers of the Field Service Section and the Flying Branch, who occupied government quarters at FAD.[9]

Perhaps most discouraging of all, however, were the frequent curtailments of work due to lack of personnel. Government pay scales in the middle and late 1920s could not compete with salaries in the private sector. The Materiel Division experienced a high attrition rate as skilled scientists succumbed to the lure of better-paying jobs in private industry or simply tired of the heavy work loads and insufficient funding that beset military aviation. Austerity at the time prohibited filling positions left vacant, thus further increasing the work load for those who remained.

Moreover, there was no money for new equipment or lab furniture. Lab personnel had to help plan, cut, assemble, and erect such necessary items as room partitions, chemical hoods and worktables, benches, and cabinets at the new location.

Despite these many difficulties, there was much excitement surrounding the move to Wright Field and a blossoming faith in the glorious future of the new installation. Once back to working capacity, the laboratories of the Materiel Division were, in fact, the equal of other top-level research laboratories in the country.

By July 1928, practically all activities of the Materiel Division were housed in their new quarters. The only exceptions were the flight test operations at Fairfield and the propeller test facility still at McCook. Principal units added during Fiscal Year 1927 were the assembly shops building, the dynamometer laboratory, the torque stands, the generator house, foundations for the first propeller test rig, and the building for the 5-foot wind tunnel.[10] As Fiscal Year 1927 came to a close, contracts were awarded for construction of the flight hangars. Hangars 2 and 3, their headhouse (later Hangar 10), and Hangar 4 were completed and occupied in Fiscal Year 1929.[11]

The 5-foot wind tunnel was one of the last items to move to Wright Field. It was delayed until the building specially constructed for it was completed in 1929. In this tunnel, wooden airplane models with wingspans up to 20 inches could be tested at airspeeds up to 270 mph.

The McCook Field baseball team also made the move to Wright Field, and became known as the Wright Flyers. The first year that the team wore Wright Flyer jerseys, it won the Cosmopolitan League Championship with a 13-2 record.

1929 WRIGHT FLYERS
First Flying Nine

A concrete ramp, here under construction in 1931, surrounded the hangars at Wright Field. For nearly a decade, this ramp served as a "runway" for pursuit airplanes such as the Curtiss Hawk biplanes shown on flightline at left. (Permanent paved runways were laid at Wright Field in 1941.)

The hangar headhouse (Building 10, Area B), completed in 1929, joined the front ends of Hangars 2 and 3.

Civilian firefighters pose in front of the newly-completed Wright Field firehouse (today Station 3), in 1931. A plaque mounted on the front of the building dedicates it to the memory of Mr. Frank A. Smith, who lost his life during construction of the station.

The stone gatehouses guarding the Wright Field entrance were completed in late September 1931. At center left is Building 11, Materiel Division Headquarters.

THE MISSION OF THE MATERIEL DIVISION

The Materiel Division, as mentioned briefly in Chapter IV, was established at McCook Field on October 15, 1926, nearly one year prior to the dedication of Wright Field. The Division was one of three major activities of the newly-designated Army Air Corps, as established under provisions of Public Act 446 (69th Congress). This legislation, approved July 2, 1926, amended the national defense act to change the name of the Air Service to "Air Corps" and provided the chief thereof with three assistants, each with the rank of brigadier general. Brig. Gen. James E. Fechet was placed in charge of the Operations Division with headquarters at Washington, D.C., and Brig. Gen. Frank P. Lahm was assigned as head of the Air Corps Training Center with headquarters at Kelly Field, Texas. Brig. Gen. William E. Gillmore was appointed to direct the diverse and complex workings of the Materiel Division at Dayton.

The Materiel Division assumed responsibility for all functions previously performed by the Engineering Division, the Supply Division, the Industrial War Plans Division, and the Materiel Disposal Section of the Air Service, leaving only a materiel liaison office in Washington in the Office of the Chief of the Air Corps. When the Supply Division moved to Dayton in the fall of 1926, all materiel activities of the Air Corps were centralized in Dayton, with temporary headquarters at McCook Field pending completion of the permanent headquarters at Wright Field.[12]

Despite initial difficulties, this reorganization effected a more efficient and economical system of operation and placed the logistics organization of the Air Corps on a firmer footing. To accomplish the goals of the five-year Air Corps expansion program authorized in 1926, procurement, supply, and engineering functions were required to work closely together, even if relations between them were not entirely harmonious.

Under the direction of General Gillmore, six major sections conducted the operations of the Materiel Division. All six made the move to Wright Field during the spring and summer of 1927. These sections, discussed below, were:[13]

Procurement
Engineering
Administration
Field Service
Industrial War Plans
Repair and Maintenance*

In addition to materiel and engineering functions, the Chief of the Division also directed operations of the Air Corps Engineering School and the Army Aeronautical Museum at Wright Field.

Panoramic view of Wright Field, 1930. In the foreground is the boiler plant that provided steam heat for all major buildings. On the right are laboratories and administrative offices of the Materiel Division. Beyond them are hangars and the concrete ramp. To the left are shops, test facilities, and warehouses.

*Since the functions of the Repair and Maintenance Section were divided in the late 1920s, with repair operations assigned to the Engineering Section and maintenance carried out as a function of the Administration Section, that section is not discussed separately.

Maj. Gen. Benjamin D. Foulois, Chief of the Materiel Division from July 1929 to June 1930, hosts the second class of the special Navigation School at Wright Field. From left: Capt. Clyde V. Finter, Instructor, Lt. Odas Moon, Lt. Westside Larson, Lt. Lloyd Blackburn, General Foulois, Lt. Harry Halverson, Lt. Edgar Selzer, Lt. Uzal Ent, and Lt. Bradley Jones.

PROCUREMENT SECTION

Relations between the military and the civilian aircraft industry, which were somewhat strained in the early 1920s, became more amicable in the late 1920s and early 1930s. A major factor was increased public awareness of aviation, which resulted in wider interest in aeronautical development and a willingness to support it. Increased procurement activity under the five-year Air Corps development program was also instrumental in restoring health to the American aircraft industry, which had struggled under financial difficulties since the end of World War I.

The Procurement Section of the Materiel Division was responsible for purchasing practically all equipment and supplies used by the Air Corps, from new airplanes to necessary operating and maintenance supplies. In the rapidly developing field of aviation, the Materiel Division often found itself seeking parts not yet commercially available, or ones with more stringent requirements than could be met by existing products. Such needs taxed the patience and ingenuity of both the Procurement Section and cooperating manufacturers. Batteries, carburetors, spark plugs, generators, starters, radiators, radio tubes, and incandescent lamps, for example, were all commercially available for automotive purposes. Off-the-shelf auto parts did not transfer successfully to airplanes, however, because of the more severe environmental conditions to which the parts

were routinely subjected. The job of the Procurement Section was to identify the specialized aspects of thousands of items needed by the Air Corps, to locate or oversee the adaptation of suitable items, and to then establish reliable sources of supply for them. Procurement became a process of persistent, creative problem-solving.[14]

The major work of the Procurement Section was performed by its four branches. Contract Administration was responsible for securing information about individual contractors' plant facilities, resources, and finances. The Purchase Branch, with two contracting officers and approximately 60 civilians, was directly responsible for securing bids, awarding contracts, administering purchase orders, and following contracts until delivery was made. The Legal Branch delivered interpretations pertaining to the many legal questions involved in making awards and administering contracts.

Perhaps the most important and difficult work of the Procurement Section, however, was performed by the Inspection Branch. The procurement inspection program was organized into three major districts, with centers in New York City (Eastern District), Dayton (Central District), and Santa Monica (Western District). Six Air Corps officers were designated as Air Corps inspection representatives under the jurisdiction of the Materiel Division, and were assigned to airplane contractors' plants in an on-site inspection capacity. At different times, Materiel Division representatives were stationed at the following manufacturing plants:[15]

Consolidated Aircraft Company, Buffalo, New York
Curtiss Aeroplane and Motor Company, Buffalo and Garden City, New York
Keystone Aircraft Corporation, Bristol, Pennsylvania
Douglas Company, Santa Monica, California
Boeing Company, Seattle, Washington
Goodyear-Zeppelin Corporation, Akron, Ohio
Northrop Company, Inglewood, California

In addition, some 110 civilian inspection employees operated from district inspection offices located strategically throughout the country, with responsibility for inspecting contracted items wherever necessary. At Wright Field, a staff of approximately 50 civilians was responsible for controlling and coordinating requirements for inspections conducted at Division facilities or in the field. By 1937, equipment and supplies purchased by the Air Corps involved approximately $60 million in contracts, all of which required approval and acceptance by the Procurement Section.[16]

The work of the Procurement Section also supported advancements of the Materiel Division in other areas. Engineering work carried on by the Materiel Division at Wright Field, while devoted entirely to the development of military aircraft, resulted in great benefit to civil and commercial aeronautics, especially in the solution of basic problems, the development of standards, and the dissemination of technical information.

The Procurement Section served as liaison between the Materiel Division and manufacturers of airplanes and aircraft equipment. Every effort was made to impress contractors with the necessity of furnishing equipment which would continue to function reliably with only a moderate amount of maintenance. The standards maintained by the Materiel Division thus ensured the high quality of equipment for military application, and also engendered improvements in civil aeronautics.

The Procurement Section made a conscientious effort to promote standardization in several arenas. It furthered Air Corps policy to develop more than one source of supply by encouraging competing manufacturers to develop the same article. Samples of each company's product were tested for contract specifications, and several manufacturers might be listed as acceptable suppliers for the item.

The Materiel Division also worked closely with the Bureau of Aeronautics in adopting common standards, the goal being to facilitate reduction in stocks and increased use of identical processes by aircraft manufacturers. As part of this liaison, a conference devoted to developing standards was held each year, attended by representatives of the Materiel Division, the Bureau of Aeronautics, and interested manufacturers. Resulting policies were of special benefit to aircraft manufacturers doing joint work for the Army and the Navy.[17]

Standardized accounting procedures for contractors were also established by the Procurement Section in the

Attendees at a 1936 Engineering and Supply Conference sponsored by the Procurement Section of the Materiel Division. Those destined to play a future role in Wright-Patterson history include, by number: (3) Lt. Col. Junius H. Houghton; (4) Col. Frank M. Kennedy; (7) Brig. Gen. Augustine W. Robins; (18) Col. Joseph T. McNarney; (24) Capt. Joseph T. Morris; (35) Maj. Bennett E. Meyers; and (38) Lt. Edwin W. Rawlings.

early 1930s. Prior to that time, individual manufacturers had set up their accounts and determined their costs in discretionary fashion. This resulted in a diversity of methods for determining engineering costs, special tool costs, depreciation costs, and other overhead expenses. The Procurement Section made an effort to apply cost statements to each contract in order to compare the different manufacturers' costs. Comparisons could not be made on any equitable basis, however, until allowances were made for the different methods of distributing overhead expenses—a difficult process.

The Materiel Division rectified this situation by initiating a system that went a long way toward standardization of the industry. A chart of accounts was drafted, which it was felt would fit the needs of industry and still ensure uniformity in accounting and cost-finding. A conference was then convened for contractors' representatives at which the accounts were discussed and the final form of the chart was agreed upon. The provisions of these accounts went into effect on January 1, 1933, and were conscientiously applied by the contractors concerned. The new system permitted direct comparisons of the costs of different types of airplanes, considerably simplifying the process.[18]

In addition to this new way of processing cost information, Wright Field also provided direct benefit to civil aeronautics in an ambitious program of disseminating technical information to the industry. Instruction books and numerous reports were made available dealing with approaches and solutions to structural, aerodynamic, design, and maintenance problems.

ENGINEERING SECTION

The work of the Engineering Section was the most complex and the most exciting of all of the activities at Wright Field. The Engineering Section was composed of seven main engineering branches: Aircraft, Power Plant, Engineering Procurement, Equipment, Materials, Armament, and Shops. Overall, the role of the Engineering Section was to initiate experimentation, design, testing, and development of airplanes, engines, propellers, accessories, and associated ground equipment.

The responsibilities of the individual branches of the Engineering Section provide a composite view of engineering activities at Wright Field in the period from the dedication of the installation in 1927 until 1939, at which time the structure of the Materiel Division was reorganized to accommodate the rapid build-up associated with World War II.

Aircraft Branch

The Aircraft Branch was concerned with the development of new types of aircraft and with the improvement of those already accepted as standard. It included the former Airplane and Lighter-than-Air Branches which were consolidated under its jurisdiction during Fiscal Year 1932.[19] When an entirely new airplane was contemplated, the Aircraft Branch was tasked to make thorough study of the qualifications desired and draw up proper specifications. These specifications were then submitted to manufacturers across the country for their use in drafting tentative designs for the new airplane. Completed design proposals, including, in the case of procurement competitions, actual prototype airplanes, were submitted to the Division for examination.

After delivery of a prototype airplane from the manufacturer, the engineers of the Aircraft Branch submitted it to rigorous test and evaluation. Wright Field housed the most extensive and modern aircraft test facilities available, representing an equipment investment of approximately $10 million by 1938.[20] These facilities were divided into six major laboratory functions, all of which reported to the Chief of the Branch.

The *Structures Development and Test Laboratory* conducted stress analysis of all aircraft submitted to the Air Corps; tested the structural strength of aircraft after purchase; and developed new methods of assembling aircraft structures. It is to this group that the world owes the development of the all-metal monocoque airplane, and also the first sub-stratosphere airplane, complete with pressurized cabin.

The sciences of static and dynamic testing were perfected to state-of-the art levels for the late 1920s and the 1930s by this laboratory at Wright Field, building on early developmental work at McCook Field. The purpose of this testing was to calculate the maximum strength of a particular structure, both at rest and in motion. In static testing, airplane structures were kept at rest and weighted down with lead bars or shot-filled bags. In dynamic testing, the structures being tested were supported by a jib and then dropped. The height and angle of the drop were mathematically computed to give the same shock or jar to the assembly that it would actually sustain under specific land-

South side of the Wright Field Assembly Building (Building 31). Virtually every type of aircraft in the Air Corps inventory visited this hangar at one time or another during the 1930s.

ing conditions.

The structural test laboratory at Wright Field in the 1930s was one of the best equipped in existence.* The weight of the jib and its auxiliary members used in dynamic testing was 52 tons, supported on a 228-ton base of reinforced concrete and steel. Two traveling cranes of 5-ton and 15-ton capacity, respectively, made easy work of picking up a complete airplane or an entire static test set-up, steel scaffolding and all.

The *Special Research and Test Laboratory* of the Aircraft Branch prepared airplane design studies from which military characteristics were established; prepared final design specifications for new airplanes; evaluated new airplanes submitted on competition to the Air Corps; and, once an airplane was placed in service, corrected unsatisfactory design features. Many of these projects were of a strictly experimental nature.[21]

The *Propeller Research and Test Laboratory* conducted exhaustive tests to determine the characteristics of each type of propeller accepted by the Air Corps. During the 1930s, the Materiel Division possessed the largest propeller test rigs in the world. Propellers up to 45 feet in diameter could be whirl-tested for endurance at speeds up to 4,300 rpm. Electric motors were used for operating the propeller rigs, the largest being one of 6,000 hp. The demands for electric power were so terrific when the Propeller Lab and the Power Plant Lab conducted tests, that a special Dispatcher's Office at Wright Field had to coordinate testing schedules with attendants at the Dayton Power and Light Company. Personnel in the Propeller Lab performed this duty, and were also responsible for the design of the outdoor electric substation at the field.

The Propeller Research Lab also engaged in continuous research and development of new types of propellers. The introduction of controllable-speed and variable-pitch metal propellers was the result of thousands of hours of study and testing at Wright Field. The Propeller Lab also conducted all propeller tests for the Navy and the Department of Commerce.[22]

The *Aerodynamics Research and Test Laboratory* developed methods for calculating aerodynamic performance of new airplanes through predictive measurements taken in wind tunnels, as well as actual measurements of performance of the airplane in flight. This laboratory made major contributions to the science of aerodynamics, and to the establishment of design criteria for the best aerodynamic shapes for control surfaces, fairings, fillets, and the like.

Two wind tunnels, 14 inches and 60 inches in diameter, respectively, were operated at Wright Field prior to World War II. The smaller tunnel was used for the testing of small airfoils or propellers, the larger for complete airplane models. Both contained highly sensitive instruments for precise measures of performance criteria. The 5-foot wind tunnel, 90 feet in length, could test components at air speeds up to 275 mph.[23]

Superstructure of the craneway for the propeller test rigs at Wright Field, under construction in 1926. The railroad-type car which traveled along the top of the craneway housed the 20-ton crane used to carry aircraft engines to and from the test stands.

Propeller test rigs, near completion. From front to back, the three rigs were of 6,000, 3,000, and 2,500 horsepower, respectively. Propellers mounted on the rigs were tested at up to 4,300 rpm.

Inside the Wright Field 5-foot wind tunnel building, 1936

*The Structures Laboratory should not be confused with the more modern "Static Test" building (Building 65, Area B). Completed in 1944, the Static Test building at Wright Field was designed to house static structural tests on the B-36.

Wright Field airship hangar

The *Accessory Design and Test Laboratory* developed and tested wheels, brakes, tires and tubes, landing gear complete with retracting mechanism, skis, floats, hulls, and other aircraft parts. Wheels and brakes were constantly tested to produce correct drum and brake lining combinations. Oleo legs and retracting mechanisms were evaluated for each type of airplane. Hydraulic and pneumatic mechanisms were also tested and perfected, as was landing gear designed for instrument landings and take-offs.

The *Lighter-than-Air Unit* of the Aircraft Branch developed and refined Air Corps balloons, balloon accessories, and nonrigid airships. In the 1920s, for example, this unit was largely responsible for the development of the TC-13, a nonrigid airship designed for patrol and reconnaissance. (Produced by Goodyear, the TC-13 was 196 feet long, had a capacity of 200,600 cubic feet of helium or hydrogen gas, and could cruise at 47 mph for 1,650 miles, powered by two 150-hp Wright engines.)

The Aircraft Branch also concerned itself with the development of the "pressure cabin." Early experiments were conducted at McCook Field between 1919 and 1923 in an attempt to solve one of the major human problems associated with high altitude flying: in the low air pressure above 30,000 feet, pilots could not assimilate sufficient oxygen to function. The aim was to develop a pressurized compartment that could be maintained at constant air pressure regardless of the airplane's altitude. The experiments were suspended around 1923 because they involved greater complication and expense than was warranted.

By February 1935, the need was significantly greater, and a renewed effort was initiated at Wright Field. The energetic program of research and experimentation followed by Wright Field engineers resulted, in the summer of 1937, in the world's first airplane with a pressurized cabin. It proved its success over several hundred hours spent at altitudes where oxygen was usually required, and soon became a feature of both new military and commercial aircraft.[24]

Power Plant Branch

The second major component of the Engineering Section of the Materiel Division was the Power Plant Branch. Many a visitor was welcomed to Wright Field by the roar of engines under test, either on the torque stands or in the dynamometer laboratory.

The refinement of airplane engines was at the heart of aviation development. The work of the Power Plant Branch concentrated primarily on increasing the power output of engines in service, developing new types of engines, improving fuels to permit greater power output and lower fuel consumption, and extending supercharging to higher power and altitudes. The exhaust gas turbine supercharger and other types of turbine superchargers with greater capacity were successfully adapted to radial air-cooled engines.

The development of engine accessories paralleled and supported this work. The Power Plant Branch made progress during the 1930s in developing such accessories as vacuum pumps, long-reach spark plugs, magnetos and shielding, engine-driven gearboxes for accessory drives, hydraulic fuel pump drives, fuel pressure regulators, automatic oil temperature control valves, automatic supercharger regulators, automatic mixture controls, fuel injectors and controls, and hydraulic engine controls. The general trend of these improvements was to reduce the great mass of control handles and gadgets in the cockpit by replacing as many as possible with proven automatic controls.[25]

Each model of an engine submitted for evaluation to the Power Plant Branch was first subjected to a 50-hour Development Test. After any indicated modifications were incorporated, the engine was then subjected to a 150-hour Type Test. Successful completion of this test established that particular model as satisfactory for use in military aircraft, and it was assigned an Air Corps model designation. The duration and severity of the Type Test usually surfaced any major troubles of an engine, although a subsequent Service Test of the engine was the basis of its final evaluation. If, during the evaluation process, an engine was judged to possess unusual military value, it was normally a year or more before release was granted for its use on commercial airliners or export to foreign countries.[26]

Activities of the Power Plant Branch were housed in the dynamometer laboratory, the torque stands, and the fuel test laboratory.

The *Dynamometer Lab* was equipped with instruments to compute and measure performance of high-powered aircraft engines and their components. These sophisticated instruments included high-speed dynamometers for measuring output or driving torque, gauges for determining fuel consumption, scales for measuring oil consumption, revolution counters, and tachometers for measuring engine speed.

The *Torque Stand* complex was one of the more imposing structures at Wright Field. A series of 40-foot stacks, joined by enclosed passages, was built to contain seven torque stands, six for engine endurance tests and one for propeller tests. The stacks were open to the sky to take in fresh air from above and discharge air upward to be carried away by the wind. High-powered engines tested on the torque stands produced almost deafening noise, for up to 150 hours at a time. So intense was this noise that pilots flying over the stacks at altitudes up to 600 feet reported hearing it over the roar of their own engines.[27]

Each engine support pier was a huge block of concrete sunk 20 feet into the ground and completely encased in cork to absorb vibration. Observation rooms full of instruments enabled engineers to study engine performance under various tests.

The *Fuel Test Laboratory* contained six single-cylinder engines especially designed and constructed for testing fuels and lubricants. This laboratory worked to improve quality standards for fuels and lubricants used in aircraft engines, in order to effect significant increases in engine performance. An oil dilution system for cold weather starting, for example, was standardized for all types of aircraft.[28]

The Power Plant Branch made many significant contributions to overall engine development during the 1930s. Not only did it conduct extensive experimentation with high-powered air-cooled engines, for example, but it also revitalized the potential of liquid-cooled engines. The development of an anti-freeze solution (commonly called Prestone) to replace water as a coolant made it possible to reduce the size of the radiator in liquid-cooled engines by 60 percent. With Prestone cooling, supercharging, and propeller gearing, use of liquid-cooled engines was considered promising for many more years.

Wright Field torque stand complex. Each stack was 40 ft tall and joined to its neighbors by enclosed passages containing sophisticated instrumentation. Each engine support pier was a huge block of concrete sunk 20 ft into the ground and encased completely in cork to absorb the vibration generated during engine and propeller endurance tests.

Refrigeration equipment in the Power Plant Lab was used in the development of cold weather accessories and temperature controls for aircraft.

Wright Field facilities, 1934. To the right of hangars, in a line, are the Power Plant Lab torque stands, the wind tunnel building, the power house for the Propeller Lab, and the propeller test rigs and craneway.

Engineering Procurement Branch

During Fiscal Year 1933, all engineering procurement activities were transferred from the Procurement Section to the Engineering Section to simplify administration of contracts. In a further refinement, the Chief of the Engineering Section created an Engineering Procurement Branch in May 1935 to handle the engineering work pertaining to aircraft acquisition.[29]

The work of the Engineering Procurement Branch included assembling and coordinating all technical data required for the procurement of a complete aircraft. The Branch was responsible for following a complete contract, from preparing initial specifications to making necessary adjustments during the course of the contract. These adjustments might extend well beyond the delivery date of the last contracted airplane, depending on the degree of responsibility of the contractor.

As a sample of its operations, during 1936 the Engineering Procurement Branch handled the procurement work involved in the manufacture of about 1,230 airplanes, including three autogiros. These 1,230 airplanes were of thirty distinct types, which could be further broken down into forty different models. These contracts covered both production and modification. In addition, myriad other processes were carried on, such as the handling of data submitted informally, the examination of foreign and racing plane data, and the completion of the many special studies, reports, and investigations required for the information of the Chief Engineer, or for transmittal to higher authority.

The project officer for any given contract carried a heavy load of responsibilities. Typically, he maintained a file of data on corresponding foreign airplanes, as well as data on similar previously-constructed domestic aircraft. Acting as the direct representative of the Chief Engineer, the project officer visited the manufacturing plants and the tactical units operating "his" airplanes. He flew demonstration airplanes as soon as they were available, and obtained other pilots' comments on the demonstration model. Coordinating with the Air Corps representative at the manufacturer's plant, he usually ferried the first model of a contracted airplane to Wright Field. He further monitored the Wright Field tests. He was a member of the Mock-Up Board and an observer at static testing. He watched inspections and initiated any order affecting "his" airplanes that came to Wright Field for demonstration, test, acceptance, or modification. The project officer was thus required to follow the production of a given type from the inception, in the form of basic "military characteristics," through all procedures, to the delivery of the last airplane.[30]

Equipment Branch

The Equipment Branch of the Engineering Section consisted of six laboratories: Instrument and Navigation, Electrical, Parachute and Clothing, Aerial Photographic, Miscellaneous Equipment, and Physiological Research. This branch was responsible for both research and development as well as standardization of approximately 500 items of ground and air equipment. Flight indicators, turn indicators, artificial horizons, directional gyroscopes, altimeters, airspeed indicators, compasses, drift sights, and engine instruments were under constant improvement and development.

The *Instrument and Navigation Laboratory* was assigned full use of a twin-engine Douglas C-33 to conduct experimental flight tests. The airplane was utilized in testing such devices as improved gyro octants, drift sights and signals, automatic pilots, and navigation computers. In addition, the Instrument Lab tested improved versions of tachometers that also recorded engine running time and controls to synchronize engine speed in multi-engine aircraft.

The *Electrical Laboratory* specialized in aircraft and ground lighting systems. It developed advanced equipment to keep pace with the requirements of modern aircraft and newly-constructed landing field installations. Specific projects included development of portable-by-air lighting equipment for landing fields and experimentation with alternating current for aircraft application.

The *Parachute and Clothing Laboratory* developed and tested parachutes, and designed safer and more efficient flight clothing. The principal efforts at Wright Field revolved around the development of the Hoffman Triangle Parachute, designed by Col. Edward L. Hoffman, former head of the Parachute Board at McCook Field.

In 1930, Hoffman was granted two patents associated with the development of this parachute, which featured a highly stable and guidable canopy. This development represented one of the first formal attempts to apply engineering principles to canopy design.

The concept of the triangle parachute was refined throughout the 1930s. The parachute itself was expected ultimately to replace the flat-circular parachute then being used. The Hoffman Triangle Parachute canopy of 1931 resembled a flat isosceles triangle with two rounded corners and one corner cut off in a straight line. Suspension lines were attached to canopy attachment loops, formed at the end of tapes which ran over the canopy in a pattern engineered by Hoffman. The horizontal airstream captured by this unique canopy imparted a "drive" or glide of about five miles per hour. It was then possible to "steer" the parachute, by turning it through proper riser manipulation, and thus effect safer landings. The final version of the triangle parachute (about 1932) had a canopy configured basically like a clover leaf, and was called the 25.0-foot canopy.

As lives continued to be saved by individual use of parachutes, a radical idea emerged—that of lowering an entire airplane by the use of large parachutes. This would alleviate the inherent problems in equipping a large number of airplane passengers with individual parachutes. Numerous experiments were conducted in the development of this concept, including several years of work at Wright Field under Hoffman's direction.

Hoffman's early experiments with large parachutes started in the 1920s. His initial attempts in 1929 involved a 96-gore, 84-foot circular parachute which successfully carried 1,600-pound test bombs safely to the ground. With the advent of the triangle parachute design, experiments continued with a triangle parachute of the same size, intended ultimately to land a complete airplane. Although these plane-chute experiments had little impact on air safety in the years that followed, they did demonstrate that extremely large parachutes could be manufactured without fabrication problems, and that such large parachutes could be conveniently packed, deployed, and used to safely land large payloads.

Despite its many advantages as a personnel parachute, the smaller version of the triangle parachute was eventually discontinued because of its complex design and the fact that it was extremely costly to manufacture and maintain. Subsequently, the Parachute and Clothing Laboratory was concerned with the development of hemispherical canopies and rapid-opening parachutes for use in the faster military airplanes.[31]

The clothing section of the Parachute and Clothing Laboratory worked to modify and standardize flight clothing, especially winter and high-altitude clothing. Among their projects were electrically-heated clothing and rubber-soled winter shoes lined with sheep shearling. A shoulder-type safety belt, which operated in conjunction with a lap-type belt, was developed to minimize pilot injury in a crash.

Col. Edward L. Hoffman models the quick-attachable chest parachute with a triangle-type canopy known as the Hoffman Triangle Parachute, about 1931.

The *Aerial Photographic Laboratory* was able to build on the impressive reputation achieved when the Materiel Division was still at McCook Field. The first night cameras were developed at McCook and later improved at Wright Field, primarily under the impetus of aerial photography pioneer Lt. George W. Goddard (later brigadier general).

One of the most productive applications of aerial photography was in mapmaking. Air Corps officers and engineers, assisted by officers of the Corps of Engineers stationed at Wright Field, produced accurate maps of the entire United States from aerial photographs. The United States was traditionally divided by mapmakers into quadrangles according to the Geological Survey, each quadrangle covering an average area of 225 square miles. Formerly, it had taken several seasons to map each quadrangle. By airplane, this territory was covered in a few hours with great accuracy and reduced cost. In another project with the Corps of Engineers, the entire area inundated by the Ohio River in 1937 was photographed as an aid to the Corps in planning future flood control.[32]

Often, new photographic equipment had to be developed to handle the specific requirements of the project at hand. The flood-control project just mentioned utilized the Air Corps Type T-3A camera. Different types, however, were required by bombers taking pictures through haze above 10,000 feet, or by swift, low-flying reconnaissance airplanes. Both types of cameras were successfully developed at Wright Field and used sensitive films created by commercial laboratories at the instigation of the Air Corps. Processing equipment was perfected for in-flight use, making it possible to develop negatives exposed during a flight before the airplane landed. Air Corps photographers used equipment developed by experts at the Materiel Division to obtain the highest-altitude and longest-distance photographs of their day. Electrical heating systems for both the cameras and the clothing worn by aviators for high-altitude work were also developed at Wright Field.

A self-contained, mobile photographic laboratory trailer unit was designed and built during the late 1930s which featured one room equipped for printing and another for film processing and print finishing. This unit housed its own ventilation system, water supply, electric power plant, and chemical and material supply, together with all of the photographic accessories necessary to produce complete photo-mosaics wholly within the unit.[33]

The *Miscellaneous Equipment Laboratory,* the fifth laboratory of the Equipment Branch, was responsible for designing ancillary equipment to support work accomplished by the other laboratories. A steam-operated external energizer, for example, was designed especially for use in cold weather. It consisted of a small automatically-controlled steam generator weighing about 100 pounds, and a steam-driven external energizer.

Other miscellaneous equipment developed included devices for preventing ice formation on the outside of windshields and fogging on the inside; a portable, canvas-covered maintenance shelter supported by a rigid tubular framework; and lightweight, portable, collapsible wing jacks for large airplanes. The Miscellaneous Equipment Laboratory also did research and development work on transportation equipment and oxygen apparatus for use at high altitudes.[34]

The *Physiological Research Laboratory* established at Wright Field on May 18, 1935, was an antecedent of today's highly sophisticated Air Force Aerospace Medical Research Laboratory. It operated under the direction of an Army medical officer, and applied itself specifically to the medical aspects of modern military flying. The Physiology Laboratory designed experimental equipment to measure the effects that increased speeds, altitudes, and durations had on aviators, with a view to designing equipment capable of alleviating the ill effects caused by these conditions. Prominent among this equipment were three pressure chambers, the largest being 31 feet in length and 8 feet in

Night aerial photographic techniques developed by Lt. George W. Goddard produced these two photographs during the 1931 Air Corps Maneuvers. Shown are the Fairfield Air Depot (left) and Wright Field.

The Physiological Research Laboratory at Wright Field in 1937 had three altitude pressure chambers. This was the largest at 31 ft. in length and 8 ft. in diameter. It could simulate altitudes to 80,000 ft. above sea level, including temperatures to −65° F.

The centrifuge in the Physiological Research Laboratory allowed study of the effects of centrifugal force on airplane pilots. A volunteer member of the lab is positioned "head-in" at the end of the rotating arm.

diameter, designed to simulate the extraordinary pressures and temperatures of high altitudes. The chambers could simulate altitudes to 80,000 feet above sea level, and temperatures to −65° F.[35]

One of the most interesting projects of the Physiological Research Lab in the late 1930s was investigation of the effects of centrifugal force on pilots. The centrifuge used in this research consisted of a long rotating arm with a seat bolted to its outer end. Powered by a large electric motor, this arm was capable of rotating at speeds up to 80 revolutions per minute, and generated a force equal to twenty times the pull of gravity (20 Gs). Members of the laboratory acted as experimental subjects at forces up to 8 Gs, although pure research continued to much higher levels.[36] The laboratory also waged war against aeroembolism, the same painful disability which deep-sea divers call "bends," in which bubbles of nitrogen form in the bloodstream during violent climbs.

Materials Branch

The third major branch of the Engineering Section was the Materials Branch. Laboratories of this branch were devoted to the testing and further refinement of the multiplicity of materials connected with flight. Many of these materials were used directly in aircraft, such as fuels, oils, paints, varnishes, fabrics, rubber, and steel, and necessarily carried high standards. Specifications had to be developed, however, for hundreds of other specialized items commonly used in maintenance work, from paper and cleaning rags to sawdust and soaps.

Competition was keen in the field of materials science, as new and improved substances were developed with increasing frequency. Each new material posed fresh problems in terms of manufacture, and often in the study of fundamental properties as well. The work of the Materials Branch often involved extensive chemical analysis of the substances being developed.

The Materials Branch pioneered development of welded steel structures and fostered the application of chrome-molybdenum alloy steel to this type of construction. Similar experiments were conducted in connection with aluminum, magnesium, and beryllium base alloys.[37]

Although both water- and air-cooled airplane engines were used during the 1930s, primary attention was given to the development of the air-cooled type. The Materials Branch was responsible in large part for developing aluminum alloys suitable for pistons and cylinder heads in air-cooled engines. The Materials Branch foundry made hundreds of different castings of each new alloy to ensure proper design, not only from the cooling standpoint but for ease of production.[38]

Interest in magnesium alloy development was active throughout the 1930s. This material was attractive because of the substantial weight savings compared to aluminum, and because of its ready availability. In later years, development of a process to extract magnesium from sea water made it especially attractive. Magnesium castings were used on production engines for such parts as cover plates, nose pieces, housings, and practically all landing wheels in the late 1930s. Cooperative programs were carried on with the two magnesium producers of this period, the Aluminum Company of America and the Dow Chemical Company.

Materials for innumerable small airplane parts, such as tires, wing ribs, metal wing spars, cables, and propeller blades were the subjects of constant experimentation. Of critical importance was the development of a glass substitute for windows and windshields which would offer better visibility and impact resistance than non-shatterable glass. A methyl methacrylate plastic material was introduced in 1937 that successfully met these requirements.

Natural rubber was another material for which a more durable and versatile synthetic substitute was sought. Thiokol and Duprene were the principal synthetics studied. Thiokol found application in refueling hoses, balloon valve seats, and dope and lacquer hoses. Duprene was used extensively for fuel, oil, water, and ethylene glycol connector hoses, in tires and tubes, as a cement in balloon seams, and as a balloon-cloth coating to reduce gas permeability. Synthetic rubber was also used for hydraulic system components and for seals and gaskets.[39]

A zinc chromate primer was accepted, after extensive testing, for use on early aluminum-skinned airplanes. In 1933, an atmospheric exposure rack and a tidewater rack were erected at Chapman Field, near Miami, Florida, to obtain accelerated exposure performance data. Two or three months' exposure in that environment was considered equivalent to one year in Dayton. An aluminum alloy for coating exterior surfaces was introduced after exhaustive laboratory investigation of its mechanical properties at Wright Field, and corrosion tests in the bay at Chapman Field. It proved to greatly reduce the requirements for aircraft painting.[40]

A reliable technique for spot-welding of both stainless steel and aluminum alloy structures was also developed during the 1930s. The first specification covering a complete spot-welding procedure for stressed aluminum alloy parts was issued by the Materials Branch in Fiscal Year 1935. By 1938, an experimental spot-welded aluminum alloy wing for an A-17 airplane was flight-tested at Wright Field. As a result, magnesium sheet alloys were included in the spot-welding program for the following year.[41]

Another research activity conducted at Wright Field during the 1930s was development of a non-destructive inspection technique known as magnetic particle inspection. Small cracks and other surface-connected defects in steel parts were notoriously difficult to detect, posing a serious problem for inspection personnel. A trained eye and a hand-held magnifying glass were the usual tools. Since lives and expensive property were at stake, priority was given to developing reliable techniques of flaw detection. By 1935, specifications were complete for a magnetic particle inspection apparatus. It used a system of magnets and dry powder and detected minute flaws by analysis of residual magnetic particles. This equipment was procured for some repair depots and was considered suitable for inspection of all ferrous aircraft and engine parts. In 1937, the magnetic particle inspection method was also adopted in the automotive, marine, and railroad industries. The process was further developed and refined in later years.[42]

The Materials Branch expanded its fuel and lubrication activities during the 1930s. Two particularly thorny problems were resolved in collaboration with the Power Plant Branch, in the areas of gum formation in gasoline and vapor lock. The Branch also concentrated on problems associated with improving performance of lubricants under high and low temperature conditions. Paraffin, naphthalene, and vegetable oil bases were studied to determine how their coefficients of friction changed with variations in temperature. Improvements in high-viscosity engine oils resulted in engines that started easier at low temperatures without excessive oil consumption.[43]

One of the more interesting facilities of the Materials Branch was the laboratory known as the "cold room."

Workers in the Materials Lab monitor instruments in the cold chamber control room during a simulated −70° F cold weather test

Approximately 20 tons of cooling coils were used to regulate environmental conditions in this laboratory. The subfreezing temperatures experienced at high altitudes could be simulated, allowing study of their effects on fuels, engine and instrument lubricants, fluids for hydraulic control mechanisms, oil coolers, fuel systems, and engine operating parts. Starting and operating characteristics of both liquid- and air-cooled engines were tested at temperatures as low as −50° F. Such tests were absolutely necessary to ensure that the engine that operated at 85° F at ground level would operate just as efficiently at the 75° below zero of high altitudes. Tensile, impact, and fatigue properties of aircraft materials were tested by equipment installed permanently in the "cold room." Additional tests were made using portable equipment. Engineers conducting experiments in the "cold room" were furnished with electrically-heated flight clothing.[44]

Armament Branch

The Armament Branch of the Engineering Section was tasked with designing armament equipment to increase the tactical efficiency of Army bombardment, attack, and pursuit airplanes. The Branch designed systems to ensure proper mounting and efficient functioning of machine guns, bombs, and ammunition on all new and modified Army models, taking into consideration the numerous installation limitations and operational conditions involved. The Armament Branch was also responsible for preparing portions of airplane specifications that dealt with armament.

Revisions in the design of bomb racks and release control mechanisms were made at Wright Field. In bomber cockpits, an electrically-illuminated panel represented the loaded bomb rack, showing the arrangement of bombs on the different stations. A special unit in the wiring system allowed a pre-selected, timed release of bombs at successive intervals. The design process for these instruments required the careful calculation of such factors as air speed, pitch and yaw, wind speed, altitude, and bomb trajectory. The Armament Branch was also responsible for advances in pyrotechnics, including parachute flares, signal pistols, wing tip flares, smoke signals, and certain articles of equipment used on the ground, such as pyrotechnic beacons and position lights.[45]

The increased ground speed of modern attack airplanes necessitated improvements in fixed-gun installations, in order to increase fire power against ground targets. Special equipment for cooling machine guns was designed in order to extend the burst of fire. Gun sights for fixed and flexible guns and machine gun synchronizers also underwent many improvements.

Service tests were conducted at Wright Field on the equipment used to flexibly mount .30 and .50 caliber machine guns in various positions on bombardment, attack, and observation airplanes. The adoption of .50 caliber machine guns as flexible weapons gave rise to further refinements, such as the use of power-driven mechanisms to operate machine gun turrets in bombardment airplanes. The service test program at Wright Field also extended to synchronized gun equipment, pyrotechnic devices, and various items of bombing equipment, as well as practice and service bombs and other items of ammunition supplied by the Ordnance Department.[46]

Shops Branch

The Engineering Shops Branch acted as a service laboratory for the Engineering Section. Skilled mechanics assigned to this branch were responsible for the inspection, modification, and repair of both experimental airplanes and the prototype airplanes submitted to Wright Field by manufacturers. When necessary equipment was not available, the Shops Branch would create it, an example being the design and fabrication of a jack powerful enough to raise the largest of airplanes. The Shops Branch also designed, fabricated, and installed many of the parts and accessories required in the experimental work of the various other laboratories of the Section.[47] The Branch performed a major role, for example, in preparing propellers for both experimental and routine use on aircraft and in repairing them after damage by erosion or accident.

ADMINISTRATION SECTION

The Administration Section of the Materiel Division had two important functions: administration of the Materiel Division itself and operation of Wright Field as a military post. For the first ten years, from 1927 until 1937, the Chief

Central files, Wright Field, 1936

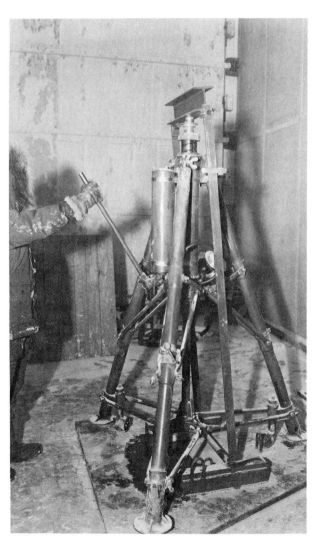

A 20-ton wing jack developed by the Shops Branch undergoes tests in the Materials Lab cold chamber.

of the Administration Section served simultaneously as the Commanding Officer of Wright Field. The Assistant Chief of the Administration Section also performed a dual function as the Wright Field Adjutant.[48] In May 1937, the Administration Section was removed from the organizational chart and its functions consolidated directly under the Materiel Division Executive office. The Executive officer thus assumed a second "hat" as the Commanding Officer, with the Assistant Executive serving as Adjutant.

The Administration Section supervised the many branches that performed actual day-to-day operations at the field. This included management of all military and civilian personnel assigned to the Materiel Division, as well as such routine affairs as mail distribution, central files, transportation, and the functions of the Quartermaster and Station Supply.

The Administration Section was also responsible for a host of additional duties that today would be considered beyond the scope of a base administrative office. The mandate of the Administration Section, as stated in the 1927 Annual Report of the Materiel Division, called for the Section to conduct official performance tests on experimental airplanes, engines, aircraft accessories, and equipment, to maintain the flying records of all aircraft operating at the Division, and to perform all maintenance of these craft. The Section was responsible for administering activities of the Office of the Flight Surgeon at Wright Field, and until 1930, was responsible for conducting the Air Corps Engineering School.* Section personnel also prepared and prosecuted all patent applications initiated by Division personnel, and supervised the compilation and dissemination of technical information generated at the field. There were 269 employees assigned to the Administration Section in Fiscal Year 1927 to perform this wide range of responsibilities.[49]

Among the more interesting activities of the Section were those of the Flying Branch and the Technical Data Branch. Of particular importance were projects conducted on base during the Depression under the various civil and public works projects.

Flying Branch

The Flying Branch conducted all authorized flight testing of experimental airplanes, engines, aircraft accessories, and miscellaneous equipment. This responsibility also included ferrying new airplanes from contractors' plants to the Division.

During August 1929, the Flying Branch moved from temporary hangars at the Fairfield Air Depot to new hangars at Wright Field. One of the most important features of the new facility was that it allowed improved calibration and storage of flight test instruments.

Once in the new location, the Flying Branch supported a variety of missions. Branch pilots flew in night missions to test development of airplane landing lights and flares. Important projects were also accomplished in support of the aerial photography work at Wright Field. During the winter of 1929, for example, Branch pilots flew a Keystone LB-5A light bomber to Fargo, North Dakota, to photograph and bomb an ice jam.

In 1929, and again in 1931, the Flying Branch provided support for the Army Air Corps Maneuvers staged at Wright Field. During the maneuvers all test and incidental flying was suspended, and all test pilots of the Branch were detailed for special duty. Mechanics and laborers assigned to Wright Field were also diverted from normal work and spent thousands of hours in support of the maneuvers.

The Flying Branch contributed many hours of public relations work for Wright Field by performing special flying exhibitions. These exhibitions stimulated great public interest in aeronautics, and in some cases raised funds to establish municipal airports and support worthy relief organizations. In Fiscal Years 1932 and 1933, for example, the exhibition itinerary included appearances at the All American Races in Miami, Florida; the christening ceremony for the U.S. Navy dirigible *Akron* at Akron, Ohio; the George

The Wright Field aircraft operations center was located in Hangar 3.

Wright Field test pilots in the early 1930s included (l to r): Capt. V. A. Strahm, Capt. Reuben C. Moffat, Lt. Ployer P. Hill, and Lt. Irvin A. Woodring.

*In 1930, the Air Corps Engineering School was transferred to the jurisdiction of the Chief of the Materiel Division.

Washington Bicentennial Military Tournament and the Progress Exposition in Chicago; the Ohio State Fair at Columbus; the National Air Races in Cleveland; and the Presidential inauguration ceremonies for Franklin D. Roosevelt in Washington, D.C.[50]

Technical Data Branch

The Technical Data Branch carried the primary responsibility for publicity, public relations, and photographic service for the Materiel Division. The major function of the Branch, however, was the collection and review of all available foreign and domestic aeronautical publications and the dissemination of the information contained in these to Division personnel. The Branch was responsible for accurate translation of applicable foreign aeronautical research, as well as detailed review of current English-language aeronautical journals, books, and reports.

In 1929, an Information Unit was created to review all aeronautical information, both foreign and domestic, published in current engineering magazines, technical reports, and the like. After technical evaluation, this information was disseminated on a daily basis to Materiel Division personnel by means of a typewritten, hectographed review entitled the *Technical News Service*. In later years, this service was provided by the *Technical Data Digest*, a semi-monthly review of aeronautical periodicals and literature received by the Technical Data Branch. The *Digest* received considerable commendation from Air Corps personnel as the best means of maintaining contact with aeronautical developments throughout the world, and it was eventually republished by special permission of the Chief of the Air Corps on a regular basis in the *Journal of the Institute of Aeronautical Sciences*. In order to further assist Wright Field military and civilian engineers in keeping abreast of current developments, a large screen was installed in the Wright Field auditorium in Building 11, and frequent showings were made of movies on aeronautical subjects.

The Branch also made efforts to update and upgrade the technical public, as well. A major publication in this effort was the *Air Corps Handbook of Instructions for Airplane Designers,* which was updated and republished regularly. Technical orders and bulletins were also generated by the staff of the Technical Data Branch, as were all manner of articles for the public press, lectures, motion pictures, and exhibits depicting the technological advances being made at Wright Field. Exhibits of Air Corps equipment were staged at various state fairs and aviation shows. Special articles on aeronautical subjects were also prepared by the Tech Data Branch for publication by the Office, Chief of the Air Corps.

In November 1938, the new Training Film Field Unit No. 2 was established to produce historical and technical films for the Air Corps. The first sound film, *Wings of Peace,* told the story of the 1938 flight of six Air Corps B-17s to South America. When sound was added to a number of early silent films, *Wings of the Army* and *Flying Cadets* were among the first projects. Three regular employees were sent to Hollywood motion picture studios to learn the latest methods and equipment for sound film production. This resulted in increased Air Corps capacity to photograph its own maneuvers, tactical concentrations, and other activities, and to produce films for release as newsreels or use in official Air Corps productions. In March 1941, the Film Unit's name was changed to Signal Corps Training Film Production Laboratory, Wright Field Branch. It continued to operate throughout World War II under the technical control of the Chief Signal Officer, but under the administrative control of the Materiel Division.[51]

Technical Data Branch film library. Film production facilities were established at Wright Field in 1938.

Public Works Projects

The Materiel Division worked in harmony with national relief programs and was able to employ a large number of personnel at Wright Field under the auspices of various public and civil works projects. Funds provided under these programs helped the Materiel Division to accomplish tasks that otherwise might have gone unfunded because of the severe budgetary restraints imposed on the Wright Field experimental and research programs.

Manpower available under the Works Progress Administration (WPA) was utilized for several projects at Wright Field during the 1930s. One of the more interesting of these involved the Materials Branch of the Engineering Section. Building 16, part of which was occupied by the Materials Branch, was originally constructed as a one-story building with no basement. Its wooden floor was supported by

Visitors view an illuminated three-dimensional model of the Materiel Division facilities at Wright Field, 1941. Constructed by workers assigned to the Army Aeronautical Museum through the Works Progress Administration, the model was enclosed in glass and displayed in the lobby of Building 12.

The Technical Data building (Building 12, Area B), constructed in 1934-1935, was funded under the Public Works Program at a total cost of $235,000. The building housed offices of the Technical Data Branch and also was home of the Army Aeronautical Museum.

concrete pillars resting on underground footers. WPA crews were assigned the arduous task of digging out a basement under the entire building. The digging was done by hand (one section at a time), and steel girders were erected. Concrete floor and wall sections were then poured. The completion of this project late in 1939 came just in time to support World War II mobilization and the attendant need for more space.[52]

In Fiscal Year 1935, over $500,000 in projects under the Public Works Program were performed at Wright Field by public contract under supervision of the Constructing Quartermaster. These projects included construction of a new static test building and the large Technical Data building which became the home of the Army Aeronautical Museum (Building 12, Area B).[53]

Annual reports of the Materiel Division showed that in Fiscal Year 1937, and again in Fiscal Year 1938, $76,000 in projects were allotted to Wright Field by the Works Progress Administration. A total of $119,579 in WPA projects was performed in Fiscal Year 1939 under supervision of the Chief of Maintenance, primarily in repairs and improvements to buildings, grounds, and public utilities. In Fiscal Year 1940, WPA funds allocated for work at Wright Field exceeded $221,000. In lesser proportion, a certain amount of work at the field was accomplished under Civil Works Administration projects, also under direct supervision of the Chief of Maintenance.

In a separate and special project area, selected professional and technical WPA workers were assigned to direct support of the Army Aeronautical Museum. Among their accomplishments were construction of an Air Corps exhibit for the 1939 New York World's Fair, including a scale model of Wright Field, a scale model of the Wright Brothers Memorial at Kitty Hawk, North Carolina, and three special glass cases for displaying $\frac{1}{16}$-scale models of Army airplanes. Other exhibits were furnished by the Army Aeronautical Museum during Fiscal Year 1939 to the Golden Gate International Exposition in San Francisco, the Aero-Medical Association of the United States in Dayton, the National Air Races in Cleveland, the Pacific International Livestock Exposition in Portland, Oregon, and the Second Annual Peninsula Charity Fair at Langley Field, Virginia.[54]

FIELD SERVICE SECTION

The Field Service Section, known formerly as the Property, Maintenance, and Cost Compilation Section, exercised control over the Air Corps depot system. Originally established in 1921, the Section was administered separately until it became part of the newly-created Materiel Division in October 1926.*

As part of the Materiel Division, the Field Service Section continued to manage all supply and maintenance operations at Air Corps depots. In 1927, there were six

*Details of this early period may be found in Chapter III, Fairfield Air Depot.

Reclamation Unit at Wright Field, 1932

depots, located at Fairfield, Ohio; Little Rock, Arkansas; Middletown, Pennsylvania; Rockwell, California; San Antonio, Texas; and Scott Field, Illinois.

Although the Field Service Section underwent several reorganizations between 1927 and 1941, when it was absorbed by the Provisional Air Corps Maintenance Command, its chief functions of supply and maintenance remained basically the same. This section supervised the issue, storage, maintenance, salvage, and disposal of all Air Corps property under the jurisdiction of the Materiel Division. It also worked to standardize Air Corps supply methods and was responsible for the annual preparation of cost estimates, programs, schedules, and reports. Annual Engineering-Supply Conferences held at Materiel Division headquarters provided a forum for discussing pertinent issues connected with the supply field.

Field Service Section personnel maintained detailed records on each item of depot materiel, including everything from airplanes and engines to goggles and cameras. Field Service records tracked the quantities of materials available, their location, condition, current performance, periods of serviceable use, and total life. Rates of consumption and replacement requirements were also tracked, as were disposal processes when Air Corps property was no longer serviceable.

In another facet of the Field Service Section mission, policies were set for the periodic repair and overhaul of Air Corps airplanes and engines. This included significant standardization of engineering methods, tools, and equipment at field and repair depots.

Technical orders, catalogs, and Air Corps circulars were published by the Field Service Section on a regular basis to keep depot personnel informed of the latest instructions on maintenance, assembly, and operation of Air Corps equipment. Manufacturers' handbooks were procured and distributed when available and suitable, so that information would get to the field as quickly as possible. In some instances, aircraft and equipment manufacturers produced instructional handbooks to accompany catalogs of parts that conformed to specifications prepared by the Materiel Division.

INDUSTRIAL WAR PLANS SECTION

Prior to World War I, military tradition called for stockpiling supplies and equipment of all kinds against future war contingencies. Logisticians realized in the aftermath of World War I that accumulating and storing war reserves was expensive. More importantly, progress was so rapid, especially in the Air Service, that much equipment placed in reserve became obsolete while sitting in storage. Air Service pilots were sorely aware of the limitations this imposed, as they had been forced to "make do" with obsolete World War I DeHavilland aircraft and Liberty engines for more than a decade, until the huge stockpiles of these were depleted.

The Industrial War Plans Section was charged with making an effective transition from the time-honored concept of stockpiling war reserves to more modern concepts of planning for the national defense. The transition involved preparation of plans for the orderly movement of supplies from factories to the front lines, computation on a month-to-month basis of the amounts that would be needed under wartime conditions, and ensuring standardization of war-essential equipment. The War Plans Section was also tasked with locating suitable sources of supply across the country and with assisting targeted factories to prepare plans for conversion from peacetime pursuits to wartime production once an emergency situation was declared. A healthy industrial complex, capable of rapid mobilization, was recognized as the best war reserve the nation could have.[55] As observed by Maj. James A. Mars, Chief of the Industrial Plans Division in 1925,* "Industry cannot win a war, but it can easily lose it."[56]

For purposes of Air Corps procurement planning, the United States was divided into six districts, with an Air Corps officer assigned to each. He was responsible for locating sources of equipment, surveying factories that were reported as suitable, and securing needed information about the industrial establishments in his district. Each district representative had a civilian advisor, a prominent businessman from the district, appointed directly by the Chief of the Air Corps to aid and support the procurement planning work.

A separate Procurement Plan was prepared for each article of Air Corps equipment. Negotiations were conducted with individual factories and schedules were proposed for production of specific equipment. Power, labor, and transportation requirements were also figured, including any expansion or special tool designs that might be needed.

A Unit Plan was prepared for each Air Corps procurement district, which in turn became part of the overall Air Corps Industrial War Plan. The Assistant Secretary of War coordinated this plan with those received from the other branches of the Army to ensure that no one district was overloaded and that distribution of the production load would be relatively equitable in an emergency situation.

*Major Mars, as detailed in Chapter III, served as the first Commander of the Fairfield Aviation General Supply Depot during World War I.

Another significant job of the Industrial War Plans Section was to develop substitutes for strategic materials not readily available within the country. Many of these projects were coordinated with the work being done by the Materials Branch of the Engineering Section in developing, for example, synthetic rubber, substitutes for tin, and American-made optical glass.

Since virtually all of the military supplies and equipment used in the Air Corps came from outside sources, the concept of war planning was closely allied with the development of commercial aviation. If the aeronautical industry did not prosper, the efficiency of industrial war plans would be severely restricted; a prospering industry guaranteed the government a larger number of potential sources of Air Corps materiel. To keep the aeronautical industry alive and healthy in the late 1920s, steady growth in commercial aviation was essential.

During the Depression of the 1930s, this cause-and-effect relationship was even more clearly defined. Government orders, in many instances, were the only means by which aircraft manufacturers were able to maintain minimum operations. Even so, new production facilities had to be secured on a regular basis to replace sources that went out of business. Had an emergency arisen, many manufacturers would have had to sustain wholesale refitting of their production organizations before proceeding with an Air Corps emergency program.

Additionally, it was judged that counting all of the aircraft manufacturers in the country, and assuming full-time operation of all plants, the facilities would still be inadequate to meet emergency requirements. Other sources of production, including facilities that did not normally supply Air Corps needs, had to be located. Efforts were directed toward placing schedules with automotive manufacturers who possessed equipment capable of conversion for the manufacture of aircraft, aircraft engines, and related equipment. It was not until the very end of the decade that industrial planners realized that it was not realistic to deal with manufacturers outside of the aircraft industry as prime contractors for wartime requirements. The aircraft industry was eventually unanimous in considering that the auto industry was not a potential source of production. The auto industry likewise concluded that airplane production was not a fertile field because of lack of trained personnel and equipment peculiar to the aircraft industry.[57]

In 1933, the 1924 War Department General Mobilization Plan was replaced with an "Industrial Mobilization Plan," a joint effort by the Army and the Navy. This necessitated recomputation of all requirements and the revision of all existing procurement plans. Since many articles required by the Air Corps in an emergency were the same as, or similar to, those required by the Bureau of Aeronautics in the Navy Department, intensive efforts were made to eliminate conflicts in the use of production facilities, and to foster cooperation between the two services for procurement of common items.[58]

In 1936, a revision of the Industrial Mobilization Plan shifted overall supervision of industrial planning from the Office, Assistant Secretary of War, to joint Army and Navy agencies. This heavily influenced the trend of Air Corps procurement planning. As Naval aviation grew, Air Corps industrial planning shifted increasingly to a joint Army-

Thousands of visitors attended the Wright Field celebration of the 30th anniversary of the Army Air Corps in August 1939. [Actually the celebration commemorated the anniversary of the purchase of the first military airplane by the Signal Corps from Wilbur and Orville Wright in 1909.]

Navy viewpoint, and finally reached a point when Navy aviation took equal share with the Army in production resources.[59]

The War Department Industrial Mobilization Plan was discontinued during Fiscal Year 1937, and was replaced by a new War Department Protective Mobilization Plan which reflected policy changes made in the mid-1930s. Substantial reorganization of the Industrial War Plans Section again took place. The name of the Section was changed from "Industrial War Plans" to "Industrial Planning" in order to "obviate deleterious effects the word 'war' at times had upon some components of the industry."[60]

In 1939, the Materiel Division consolidated procurement planning districts and inspection districts to further decentralize planning activities and reduce overhead expenses. The procurement planning offices located in Cleveland, Chicago, and Detroit were closed, and the personnel transferred to the former Central inspection district headquarters located at Wright Field. The Buffalo office was maintained as a sub-office of the consolidated Central District.[61]

Despite the valuable work performed by members of the Industrial Planning Section, the industrial war planners of the late 1930s failed to envision the scope of the war that was to come. The science of industrial war planning had progressed dramatically from concepts that prevailed prior to the First World War, but pre-World War II planners still held unrealistic ideas about the requirements that another global conflict would demand, and the ability of the American industrial complex to meet those needs.

WRIGHT FIELD AND WORLD WAR II

Hitler's Luftwaffe airplanes and panzer division tanks overran Poland in sixteen days in September 1939. Great Britain and France declared war on Germany two days after the initial assault. A second World War had begun.

Within nine months the Germans held Norway, the Netherlands, and Belgium. In June 1940, the defeat of the British on the shores of Dunkirk led to the fall of France. The overwhelming strength of the German Luftwaffe demonstrated conclusively that for the first time air power would be the deciding factor in a war.

The first step toward American rearmament occurred with passage of the Naval Expansion Act in May 1938, which called for a 3,000-airplane program. On April 3, 1939, Congress gave similar support to the Air Corps by authorizing $300 million for the creation of a force of 5,500 military airplanes. Chief of the Air Corps Maj. Gen. Henry H. Arnold was assured of open-ended appropriations and mandated to build the best air force money could buy.

On June 26, 1939, Army Chief of Staff Maj. Gen. George C. Marshall approved the First Aviation Objective, in which an Air Corps composed of 54 combat groups and 4,000 combat airplanes was to be constituted by April 1942. Even as it set about structuring this force, Arnold's staff was preparing blueprints for an even larger one. The

Second Aviation Objective was approved by the War Department in March 1941, and provided for a force of 84 combat groups, 7,800 combat airplanes, and 400,000 personnel by mid-1942.

Reorganization which became effective June 20, 1941, created the Army Air Forces (AAF). General Arnold, as Chief of the new Army Air Forces, was made responsible to the Army Chief of Staff and given responsibility for establishing policies and plans for all Army aviation activities.

In July 1941, President Franklin D. Roosevelt asked the Secretaries of War and Navy to prepare estimates of production requirements necessary "to defeat our potential enemies." The resulting report was submitted to the President in September. For a multi-theater war, the plan estimated that the AAF would need 239 combat groups and 108 separate squadrons, 63,467 airplanes of all types, and 2,164,916 men. This assessment proved to be uncannily accurate: at its peak, the Army Air Forces had 243 combat groups, nearly 80,000 airplanes, and 2,400,000 men.[62]

The logistics support for this wartime force originated at Wright and Patterson Fields. By June 1943, nearly 50,000 men and women, military and civilian, were employed at the two fields, laboring night and day to provide the materiel support for an Allied victory.[63]

Maj. Gen. Henry H. Arnold (second from left), Army Air Corps Chief, greets General Motors Corporation executives (l to r) Charles F. Kettering, William S. Knudsen, and E. V. Rippenville upon their arrival at Wright Field on August 20, 1940, to tour the Materiel Division laboratories and hangars.

EXPANSION AND REORGANIZATION
OF THE MATERIEL DIVISION

The outbreak of World War II in 1939 provided a crucial test for the Materiel Division. For the past twelve years, the Division had managed its experimental engineering and procurement functions with the limited appropriations characteristic of peacetime. It had been necessary to spend a considerable percentage of the Division's restricted budget on maintenance of the existing air force; relatively little had remained for new programs of experimentation. The crisis of 1939 demanded the immediate expansion of both activities to levels far beyond any previously considered.

The work of the Materiel Division was central to the rearmament process. Before plans for an accelerated airplane program could go forward, they had to clear the various offices and laboratories of the Division. Thus the Materiel Division was called upon to increase and expand all phases of its activities many months before the rest of the nation. By the end of 1939, the Materiel Division had already increased its activities to a pace and a degree not required of the rest of the nation until after the attack on Pearl Harbor.

The extent of this expansion may be judged by the magnitude of the increase in procurement. In July 1938, it was expected that the Division would administer less than $80 million in appropriations during the next twelve months. President Roosevelt's Message to Congress on January 12, 1939, however, outlined a vastly expanded National Defense Program. The $300 million Congressional authorization for 5,500 Air Corps airplanes was granted in April. By the end of June, the Materiel Division had awarded contracts worth more than $110 million in airplanes and equipment. During the fiscal year which began July 1, 1939, Congress appropriated more than $240 million for expenditures within the sphere of the Materiel Division.[64]

Major changes were required within the Materiel Division to accommodate the Air Corps expansion program. The organization had to be enlarged and realigned in order to sustain the procurement of airplanes in production quantities, and at the same time to provide facilities to sustain a large-scale program of testing and development.

A clear delineation was first made between the technical and administrative functions of the Division. The Office of the Executive, Materiel Division, was abolished and two new offices created in its stead—the Office of the Administrative Executive and the Office of the Technical Executive.* The former was responsible for all administrative matters of a non-technical nature, while the latter was charged with handling "all technical matters involving plans, policies, and programs for all engineering, procurement, inspection, maintenance, supply, and repair activities of the Materiel Division."[65]

The most essential changes in the technical arena included the establishment of the Production Section (later expanded into a division) to handle engineering procurement matters, and the expansion and reorganization of the Engineering Section (later the Engineering Division). The chief functions of the latter were, as the name implies, the research, testing, and development necessary to secure the safest and most effective airplanes and equipment possible.

The Procurement Section underwent additional change as it absorbed much of the field force of the Procurement Planning activity from the Industrial War Plans Section, as mentioned earlier. The three Procurement Districts (Eastern, Western, and Central) remained basically intact and

Wright and Patterson Field executives often conferred on matters of mutual concern. Shown here are (l to r): Col. Merrick G. Estabrook, Patterson Field Commander; Lt. Col. Oliver P. Echols, Technical Executive, Materiel Division; and Lt. Col. Lester T. Miller, Administrative Executive, Materiel Division.

operated under the direct supervision of the Chief of the Materiel Division.

These changes within the Materiel Division marked the beginning of much larger reorganizations throughout the Air Corps. On October 2, 1939, the Office of the Chief of the Materiel Division was relocated from Wright Field to Washington, D.C., and established in the Office, Chief of the Air Corps. Brig. Gen. George H. Brett, Chief of the Division at the time, took with him a small staff of officers and specially-trained civilian employees. His job was to advise the Chief of the Air Corps directly on materiel and supply matters and to eliminate the bottleneck within the Supply Division that resulted from the rapid pace of the Air Corps expansion program.

Although Division headquarters had moved to Washington, the mission and daily functions at Wright Field remained the same. Lt. Col. Oliver P. Echols, Assistant Chief of the Materiel Division, directed Division activities at Wright Field and in the field Procurement Districts and individual air depots.

One of the highlights of 1940 was the October visit of President Roosevelt to Wright Field. He was received with full honors and was conducted on a motorized tour of the base.[66]

In late 1940, the Air Corps proposed to separate the function of logistics from the Materiel Division and to organize it as a separate command. The proposal was approved in the spring of 1941, and the Provisional Air Corps Maintenance Command came into existence on March 15 of that year. This provisional command, however, remained under the direction of the Chief of the Materiel Division, with headquarters at Wright Field. It was composed of its Headquarters, the Field Service Section, the

*This arrangement was in effect until January 28, 1941, when the offices of the Technical and Administrative Executives were once again combined into one Executive Office.

50th Transport Wing, six major Air Corps depots (four inherited from the Field Service Section, plus two new depots at Ogden, Utah, and Mobile, Alabama), and a number of sub-depots located at various Air Corps bases. On April 29, 1941, the Provisional Maintenance Command was permanently established as the Air Corps Maintenance Command, though it remained under the guidance of the Materiel Division for some time. Col. Henry J. F. Miller (later brigadier general) was designated Commanding Officer, with assigned headquarters at Patterson Field. Maintenance Command Headquarters remained at Patterson for only two months and then returned to Wright Field on June 19.

The Maintenance Command became the nucleus of the Air Service Command (ASC), established on October 17, 1941, with headquarters in Washington, D.C. The formation of ASC marked the full separation of the logistics function from the Materiel Division. All logistics activities and installations (including the Field Service Section) were removed from the jurisdiction of the Chief of the Materiel Division and transferred to the new, independent Air Service Command. In December 1942, Hq ASC moved to newly-constructed quarters at Patterson Field (now Building 262, Gillmore Hall, Area A).

President Franklin D. Roosevelt visits Wright Field in October 1940. Also in the President's car are Orville Wright and former Ohio Governor James M. Cox.

Troops and spectators assemble to greet the President

The Materiel Division was also elevated to command status, on March 9, 1942. Materiel Command Headquarters remained in Washington, and on March 16 the Materiel organization at Wright Field was redesignated the Materiel Center.

In Washington, the Commanding General of the Materiel Command and his advisory, technical, and executive staffs determined all matters of policy, then referred them to the Materiel Center at Wright Field for execution. The Materiel Center functioned, in other words, as the operating end of the Materiel Command.

On April 1, 1943, Hq Materiel Command moved from Washington to Wright Field and absorbed the Materiel Center.[67] The Headquarters functions were housed in new buildings constructed for that purpose (Buildings 14 and 15, Area B).

The logistics and engineering procurement functions of the Army's air arm were now officially separated into two different organizations: the Materiel Command and the Air Service Command. This arrangement remained in effect until the summer of 1944, when the two commands were again merged into a single organization known as the AAF Air Technical Service Command.

PREPARING THE PHYSICAL PLANT

The reaction at Wright Field to the devastating news of Pearl Harbor was immediate and spirited. It characterized the attitude of Materiel Division personnel throughout the ensuing months of the war.

Upon receipt of the news that rocked the nation, key military and civilian personnel at Wright Field spontaneously reported to their duty posts to volunteer for any extra service they might be able to render. Military members, many of whom dressed in civilian clothes for daily work, showed up first thing Monday morning, December 8, in full military dress.

The physical protection of the field was uppermost in the minds of base officials, and plans were formulated at once to provide adequate protective measures. On December 8, 1941, a Mobile Plant Protection Force, consisting of military personnel, was established under the direct jurisdiction of the Wright Field Commander and assigned quarters in Hangar 3 at Wright Field. It was to act as a reserve force to supplement the civilian guard already on duty, and to assist in the protection of property and interests against "enemy action, mob violence, or domestic insurrection, including sabotage, espionage, incendiarism, or acts pertaining to any of these."[68]

The plans for this new unit included the assignment of a detachment commander who would receive his orders from the Chief of the Air Plant Protection Branch, and the assignment of such officer personnel from the Materiel Division as the Commanding Officer might direct. The schedule of duty was 24 hours a day, and personnel were to "be armed with side arms and machine guns mounted on vehicles."[69]

When "Mr. Big," the Douglas B-19 four-engine experimental bomber, landed at Wright Field for extensive testing in June 1942, the *Dayton Journal-Herald* gave the airplane top photographic coverage.

The flying field was already being upgraded and would soon be able to fully support wartime activities. In the spring of 1941, Materiel Division engineers had decided to lay paved runways at Wright Field in anticipation of a testing program on the experimental Douglas B-19 heavy bomber. Wright Field's grass runways could not safely accommodate the giant bomber, which had a gross weight of 140,000 lbs.

The Army Corps of Engineers agreed to take on the runway project, and Col. James B. Newman, Jr. was dispatched from the Cincinnati district office to collaborate with Wright Field civil engineers. Together, they drew up construction specifications for the new runway complex.

Bids let in April attracted contractors from across the country. Selection of the Price Brothers Company of Dayton as the chief contractor was made in May, and actual construction began in early June.

The grass flying field was relatively flat and had served the experimental flying program for light aircraft for over a decade. In the paving process, however, more than one million cubic yards of earth were moved in order to grade the field to specified elevations and to create contours to allow for proper drainage. O'Connell and Company, an earth-moving contractor from Huntington, West Virginia, accomplished the grading. Price Brothers then supplied and installed the 5,000 feet of 108-inch reinforced concrete culvert pipe needed to drain rain water from the field, across the highway, and into the Mad River at Harshmanville.

WRIGHT FIELD COMMANDERS

Maj. John F. Curry	Jul. 1927
Lt. Col. Harry Graham	Aug. 1927
Maj. Leslie MacDill	Dec. 1928
Maj. John D. Reardan	Aug. 1929
Lt. Col. Robert Goolrick	Aug. 1931
Brig. Gen. Frederick L. Martin	Jul. 1935
Col. Frank M. Kennedy	Mar. 1937
Col. Lester T. Miller	Sep. 1939
Col. George L. Usher	Dec. 1941
Col. Ralph O. Brownfield	Sep. 1942
Col. Edward L. Robins	May 1943
Col. Rudolph Fink	Nov. 1943
Col. Frank W. Wright	Sep. 1944
Col. Palmer Boyles	Jun. 1945
Brig. Gen. Joseph T. Morris	Jul. 1945

On December 15, 1945, Wright and Patterson Fields were combined for administrative purposes under an umbrella organization designated the Army Air Forces Technical Base (AAFTB). On December 9, 1947, this designation was changed to the Air Force Technical Base (AFTB). Brig. Gen. Joseph T. Morris commanded both organizations.

The mild winter of 1941 allowed the runway construction to continue throughout the fall and into the new year. The Hinton and Smalley Company of Celina, Ohio, did the actual paving, using standard Ohio highway specifications for lack of more pertinent guidelines. Areas graded and ready to receive paving, as well as runway sections completed each day, were covered with burlap, overlaid with a foot of straw, and topped with tarpaulins at night in order to take advantage of the natural heat generated by the concrete as it cured.

When complete, each of the two new runways was 150 ft in width. The E-W runway (09/27) was the longest, at 7,147.7 ft, and was laid to take advantage of the prevailing winds. The NW-SE runway (16/34) was 5,569.3 ft in length. Both runways were complete by mid-February 1942, although fine grading and seeding of the surrounding ground were not finished until June.[70]

Nearly halfway through the construction process, it was learned through captured enemy intelligence that the Germans were planning to build runways along the coast of France implementing a new technique—inclining the runways slightly to shorten take-off and landing distances. Materiel Division officials quickly decided to undertake similar construction at Wright Field to test the validity of the concept. Consequently, the Price Brothers Company con-

COMMANDERS OF THE MATERIEL DIVISION, WRIGHT FIELD

Brig. Gen. William E. Gillmore	Oct. 1926-Jun. 1929
Brig. Gen. Benjamin D. Foulois	Jul. 1929-Jun. 1930
Brig. Gen. Henry C. Pratt	Jul. 1930-Mar. 1935
Brig. Gen. Augustine W. Robins	Apr. 1935-Feb. 1939
Brig. Gen. George H. Brett*	Feb. 1939-Oct. 1939

ASSISTANT CHIEFS OF THE MATERIEL DIVISION, WRIGHT FIELD

Lt. Col. Oliver P. Echols	Oct. 1939-Nov. 1940
Brig. Gen. George C. Kenney	Feb. 1941-Mar. 1942

COMMANDING GENERAL, MATERIEL CENTER, WRIGHT FIELD

Brig. Gen. Arthur W. Vanaman	Mar. 1942-Apr. 1943

COMMANDERS, MATERIEL COMMAND, WRIGHT FIELD

Maj. Gen. Charles E. Branshaw	Apr. 1943-May 1944
Brig. Gen. Franklin O. Carroll (Acting)	May 1944-Jun. 1944
Maj. Gen. Bennett E. Meyers (Acting)	Jun. 1944-Jul. 1944
Brig. Gen. Kenneth B. Wolfe	Jul. 1944-Aug. 1944

COMMANDERS, AIR TECHNICAL SERVICE COMMAND, WRIGHT FIELD, AREA A

Lt. Gen. William S. Knudsen	Sep. 1944-Apr. 1945
Maj. Gen. Hugh J. Knerr	Jun. 1945-Dec. 1945
Lt. Gen. Nathan F. Twining	Dec. 1945-Mar. 1946

*Effective October 2, 1939, General Brett's office was transferred to Washington, D.C., Office of the Chief of the Air Corps.

Wright Field flightline, showing the first paved runway (16/34), completed during the winter of 1941. Note other major construction of hangars and the Armament Lab's 200-yard gun range (center right).

Completed Wright Field runways, 1944

A B-50 taxies up the Accelerated Runway in 1953

tract was expanded to include construction of an inclined runway just east of the new runway complex. The accelerated runway had a 10 percent grade and was completed shortly after the two main runways.*

The most critical problem for the Commanding Officer at Wright Field in the early months of America's involvement in the war was dealing with a chronic shortage of space. The emergency brought continuing increase in functions and personnel assigned to the field. The Wright Field leadership had been seeking approval for additional construction for nearly two years, to no avail. In 1940, Col. Oliver P. Echols, then Assistant Chief of the Materiel Division, sought approval for a badly needed addition to the administration building (Building 11, Area B). His report to Washington pointed out that all available space was already being utilized, and urged that further construction be undertaken immediately: "There is not a single activity at this station which is not terrifically overcrowded and becoming more so daily. Efficiency and morale is [sic] suffering because of these conditions."[71]

There was little relief during Fiscal Year 1940. Major construction during the year was confined to a substation, transformers, and a high-speed wind tunnel for the Aircraft Laboratory; a lab building and a dynamometer building for the Power Plant Laboratory; and general expansion of post utilities.[72] Construction in 1942 included several temporary and a few permanent structures which added 711,271 sq ft of floor space, but the demand for space continued to outstrip the rate of construction.[73] It was not until 1943 that the physical plant was sufficiently expanded to accommodate the functions assigned to the field.

A number of ingenious measures were taken to provide temporary relief of the overcrowded conditions. Two auto parking sheds were remodeled late in 1941 and converted into offices. A third floor of temporary frame construction (later known as the "Penthouse") was added to the administration building (Building 11) in February 1942. The

former Steele High School building in downtown Dayton was leased to accommodate the Industrial Planning Section of the Production Division.

The post garage was transformed into an office building in April 1942 and occupied by personnel of the Production Division. Desks, chairs, typewriters, file cabinets, and other office equipment were placed in corridors of all buildings to accommodate the large number of new wartime employees. Rotating eight-hour shifts were adopted so that equipment intended for the use of one person would serve three. These arrangements sometimes contributed to an impression that employees were wasting government time and occasionally gave rise to criticism in the Dayton area public press.[74]

Contributing to the general confusion and crowded conditions was a steadily increasing number of contractors' representatives and other personnel visiting the field. In August 1942, there was an average of 500 visitors per day, with a peak of 603 in one day. By December, the daily average had increased to 700.

Building 16-B, constructed in 1943 to provide wartime laboratory space, was similar in style to Building 11. (The building was destroyed by fire in 1975; Building 46, Area B, stands on the site today.)

Buildings 14 and 15, Area B, under construction in 1942 as Headquarters for the Materiel Command

*After extensive testing, it was concluded that the concept for the accelerated runway was not practical, and use of the runway was discontinued. The third major runway at Wright Field, the NE-SW which runs by the present site of the Air Force Museum, was 6,478.5 ft in length and was completed two years later.

Buildings 14 and 15, shortly after completion in 1943

Materiel Command complex at Wright Field, shortly after the end of World War II, including Buildings 14 and 15, 11 and 11-A, 16 and 16-B

Continuing space problems also led to the curtailment of a number of less essential activities for the duration of the war. Courses for the 1939-1940 term at the Air Corps Engineering School, which had been operating since 1926 under the direction of the Chief, Materiel Division, were suspended by order of the Secretary of War, and the school was later closed indefinitely.[75] The Army Aeronautical Museum was closed to all casual visitors on June 1, 1940.* Shortly after, the exhibits were removed from the museum and placed in storage, and the vacated space was occupied by the Civilian Personnel Section of Wright Field.[76]

Wright Field, 1944. The hilltop area, which was largely vacant prior to World War II, is occupied by the Headquarters building and row after row of military barracks for Wright Field personnel.

New Wright Field Administration Building (Building 125, Area B) under construction, April 1944

Once Building 125 was completed, all Wright Field Headquarters offices were transferred to the hilltop from Building 11.

*The museum remained closed until August 1954, when it reopened in new quarters at Patterson Field (Building 89, Area C).

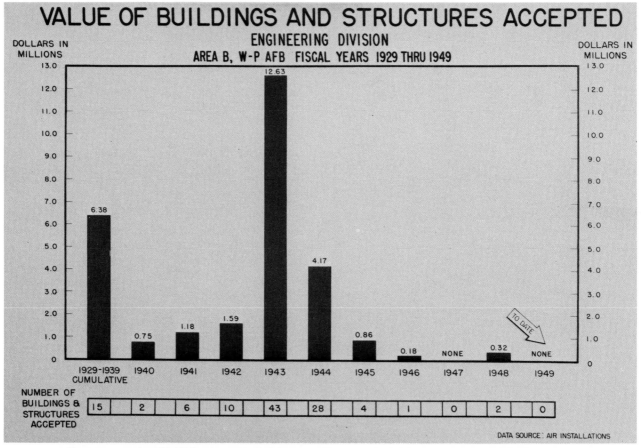

VALUE OF BUILDINGS AND STRUCTURES ACCEPTED
ENGINEERING DIVISION
AREA B, W-P AFB FISCAL YEARS 1929 THRU 1949

DATA SOURCE: AIR INSTALLATIONS

Contemporary chart highlights the tremendous investment in physical plant made at Wright Field during the war.

The rapid expansion of activities at both Wright and Patterson Fields, as well as the expansion of industrial plants in Dayton and the vicinity, put a great strain on housing facilities for base personnel. Local, state, and federal authorities negotiated for the erection of large numbers of new houses. A large percentage of the facilities built with federal funds were allocated for the use of Wright Field employees and their families. The Employees' Service Unit of the Civilian Personnel Section at Wright Field received applications for these new homes and assigned them on the basis of need. In addition, many patriotic families in the Dayton area graciously offered to open their private homes to newcomers.[77]

Overall, it was lack of funds and not of foresight on the part of Wright Field administrators that was fundamentally responsible for the delay in the construction. Requests for new buildings were routinely deferred on the basis that funds were not available currently, but would be provided by additions to future budgets.

By 1943, the national emergency was more directly under control, and the situation began to ease at Wright Field. A vast construction and improvement program was approved that included an extensive network of roads and streets, and the completion of numerous new buildings. During the year, approximately 140 buildings and major building additions were transferred to the Commanding Officer, Wright Field, by the Army Corps of Engineers. Chief among these were two large administration buildings

(Buildings 14 and 15, Area B) to house the Materiel Command, 21 civilian housing units, a jet thrust propulsion laboratory, an equipment laboratory, a post exchange, and a large number of barracks and mess halls.[78]

By 1944, Wright Field had sustained striking alterations. From an installation of only 20 buildings in 1927, the field had grown to a military establishment of approximately 40 buildings in 1941. By the spring of 1944, Wright Field had mushroomed to some 300 buildings and a vast, modern landing field, occupying some 2,064 acres in all.[79]

Early in 1944, all Wright Field Headquarters offices were moved from the lower area of the field to the newly completed Administration Building (Building 125) on the hilltop. This brought all of the Commanding Officer's staff together for the first time. It also placed the staff in closer proximity to the troops, housed in barracks along the eastern boundary of the hill, and to other activities in which they were involved.[80]

Although the initial year of the war had presented many difficulties at Wright Field, Materiel Division personnel had proved themselves equal to the task. The all-important procurement and engineering functions had managed to survive the administrative reorganizations necessary in order to stimulate and oversee the production that would eventually turn the tide of the war. The outstanding engineering and production records achieved by Wright Field personnel stood as adequate proof of the integrity and effectiveness of the organization.

WARTIME ENGINEERING ACTIVITIES
AT WRIGHT FIELD

The primary work at Wright Field during the war was conducted by two major divisions of the Materiel Command, the Engineering Division and the Production Division.

"Three years ahead of the procession," was the goal of the Engineering Division as it continuously planned newer and better airplanes and aircraft equipment for the Army Air Forces inventory. Some Wright Field engineers referred to it as the "Buck Rogers" Division because of the radically new and unorthodox designs which were frequently tested. Brig. Gen. Franklin O. Carroll was Chief of the Engineering Division, and guided this large and very important organization throughout the war years. Under his direction, neither the magnitude of production problems nor the expansion of allied military offensives deflected the scope or intensity of Engineering Division projects. In 1943, more than 800 major research and development projects were in progress under the auspices of the Engineering Division, in laboratories filled with more than $50 million in special equipment.[81]

One of the key test processes to which scale models of new airplanes were submitted was the wind tunnel. In 1941-1942 at Wright Field the largest wind tunnel in the world was completed, with a test chamber 20 feet in diameter. Among the major programs conducted in the tunnel were research in parachute stability and research on spin characteristics of model airplanes. Models with wingspreads up to 16 feet were tested at airspeeds up to 400 mph. These powerful airstreams were generated by a 40,000-hp electric motor which drove two 16-bladed fans.[82]

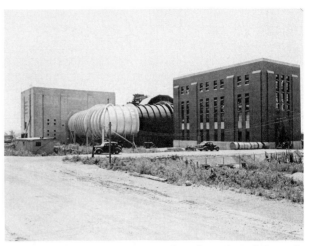

Wright Field 20-foot wind tunnel, the first of two giant wind tunnels constructed at the field during the war. This view is from the northeast, showing the power building for the tunnel, the duct structure, and the test chamber.

Interior of the 20-foot wind tunnel, showing the north run and the northeast corner vanes. Man standing at lower center is dwarfed in comparison to the huge tunnel.

Brig. Gen. Franklin O. Carroll, Chief, Engineering Division of the Materiel Command during World War II

The vertical wind tunnel (foreground) was constructed in 1942 and was designed especially for parachute testing. The 20-foot horizontal wind tunnel is visible in the background.

Civilian workers in the Materials Laboratory, August 29, 1945. Additionally, 46 officers and 73 enlisted persons were assigned to the lab.

The Materials Lab of the Engineering Division was heavily involved in the development of synthetic or substitute materials for any items of AAF equipment which might be difficult to obtain in wartime. One major achievement was in the development of nylon fabrics and other synthetic silk materials for use in such items as parachutes and corded tires. New cotton materials, in like fashion, were developed as substitutes for the linen webbing used in parachute harnesses.

The Materials Lab also developed vital camouflage paints which provided warplanes with dull, non-reflecting protective coloration. Non-glare paints and lacquers, usually dull red or black, were also developed for use on propeller blades.

Devices for rapid servicing and maintenance of airplanes were developed by Engineering Division technicians and engineers. Huge fueling trucks, crash trucks, mobile field repair outfits, maintenance stands for mechanics, jacks for hoisting bombers so that tires or landing gear could be serviced, portable field-lighting equipment, and portable steel mats to convert soggy fields into useable runways, were all developed and tested for eventual distribution by the Maintenance Command.

Inertial brake testing machine used to simulate landing conditions on the largest of new aircraft wheel, tire, and brake assemblies

Additional equipment used to test aircraft gear. This machine is a "radial and side load applicator."

Maj. Gen Kenneth B. Wolfe, Chief, Production Division of the Materiel Command, and later Chief of the B-29 Special Project Staff. From July to August 1944, he served as Commanding General of the Materiel Command.

Maj. Gen. Orval R. Cook succeeded Brig. Gen. K. B. Wolfe as Chief of the Production Division.

WARTIME PRODUCTION ACTIVITIES

The engineering developments at Wright Field were supported by the achievements of the Production Division in building America's air armada. Skilled engineers and attorneys prepared purchasing contracts at Wright Field for thousands of warplanes and vast quantities of supplementary equipment. At aircraft production facilities in the private sector, technical experts from the Production Division supervised the details of contract administration and helped speed production schedules.*

Early in the war, the Production Division was headed by Brig. Gen. Kenneth B. Wolfe, a "most vigorous and masterful chief" who later served as Chief of the B-29 Special Project Staff and as Commanding General of the Materiel Command. General Wolfe assembled a strong staff of production engineers and business executives and laid a firm foundation for the production process.[83] He was succeeded by Brig. Gen. Orval R. Cook, who assumed command of the Production Division for the latter part of the war.

Airplane production was a complex process that required detailed planning and elaborate scheduling. An airplane was not built in its entirety by one manufacturer; component parts were usually manufactured at different locations across the country. Parts such as engines, propellers, wheels, armament, radio equipment, and the like—as many as 4,000 different items—were procured by the government from any number of different sources and shipped to airframe manufacturers for final assembly. Thus, most of the famous airplane manufacturers, such as Douglas, Martin, and Boeing, produced only the airframe (i.e., the tail, wings, and fuselage). They then assembled the entire airplane, using parts furnished to them by the government for installation.

In order to ensure that production schedules were met, the Production Division coordinated and facilitated manufacturing efforts in many ways. The Production Division ensured that some 15,000 manufacturers received the necessary materials in the proper amounts at the proper time. The Division also aided manufacturers in expanding their current factories, constructing new ones, or in acquiring machines and tools to fulfill their contracts. Accomplishing all of this in a timely and efficient manner was a monumental task but was essential to sustain a smooth flow of finished airplanes to Army Air Forces units on the battlefronts.

In the overall process, the work of the Production Division was coordinated closely with the Engineering Division, which provided design work, and with the Procurement Division, which supervised the actual purchase and delivery of materials. According to a 1943 employee handbook, the Procurement Division of the Materiel Command ranked as the second largest procurement organization in the armed forces. Its authorization to spend "billions of dollars for aircraft, aircraft equipment, and supplies" reflected the combined efforts of Engineering and Production.[84]

*A detailed accounting of engineering activities at Wright Field during World War II is provided in Chapter VI, Developing Air Power.

Aerial view of the Power Plant Laboratory facilities, including the Torque Stands (upper left), in August 1944. Parked airplanes in the upper portion of the photograph range from a single-engine L-5 liaison craft to four-engine B-17, B-24, and B-29 bombers.

This close coordination was especially visible in the approach to problems with in-service battlefront equipment. As the first American airplanes joined the Allies in Europe, for example, it was discovered that they had serious problems due to inadequate fire power and the fact that they were not equipped with leak-proof fuel tanks and armor plate. These deficiencies were a natural consequence of the current philosophy in aircraft design, which emphasized superior flight performance over armament considerations.

Wright Field observers—most of them production engineers—hurried to France and England in early 1940 to study guns and armor on the airplanes being used in combat. After consultation with Engineering Division personnel and representatives of the various manufacturers involved, the Production Division recommended in-process modifications. Balance was shifted slightly from speed and range to incorporate increased fire power and provide additional defensive plating.[85]

In these problems and in the general gearing-up of production, the crucial factor was time. Prior to the war, aircraft development was a linear process. The Army bought one experimental airplane and tested it—oftentimes to destruction—before ordering a given model. It was ordered in small quantities, as needed. The whole process took anywhere from one to five years.

Building 70 was constructed to house the Fuel and Oil Branch of the Power Plant Laboratory (shown here in 1944).

As the war heightened, new models had to be produced much more quickly. The Army began making frequent exception to its linear process and ordered some new airplanes "right off the drafting boards," without requiring advance testing of a prototype. Brig. Gen. George C. Kenney, Assistant Chief of the Materiel Division, once remarked, "One of our newest bombers was ordered built after we saw it on the back of an envelope, and 18 months later the ship was flying."[86]

This abbreviated procurement procedure was often called "off the shelf procurement," since production contracts were let on the basis of drawing board plans.[87] This policy was implemented only with those manufacturers who had satisfactorily built airplanes of the same general type previously, or in cases where the new design had been thoroughly proven by wind tunnel tests and other preliminary checks. Under the new plan, Wright Field took delivery on an early production model of the new design and "put it through the wringer" to ascertain its maximum speed, range, rate of climb, ceiling, landing and take-off runs, and other vital data, while mass production on additional airplanes continued.[88]

During the latter part of the war, a huge acoustical enclosure was built over the propeller test rigs and their craneway to muffle the deafening noise produced during testing.

The Army called this routine "accelerated tests." Although the majority of these tests were conducted at Wright Field, where data was compiled by the Flight Section, a special section was also organized at Patterson Field to assist in the process. At Patterson, pilots and crews were brought from various tactical squadrons to conduct the accelerated tests. They flew each production model night and day for 150 hours, simulating actual combat conditions to see how the craft performed to Air Corps specifications. Fighters were flown at full-throttle, half-throttle—fast, slow, high, and low—through every conceivable maneuver, for the equivalent of more than a year of service for the airplane. Bombers were loaded with full crews and heavy duds to simulate the bomb loads, and flown at high altitudes for as many as 18 hours non-stop, to approximate performance under regular bombing conditions.[89]

Additional accelerated tests were also conducted at the Dayton Army Air Field at Vandalia, Ohio, under the jurisdiction of the Accelerated Service Test Branch.[90] Troop-carrying glider tests were conducted at the Clinton County Army Air Field near Wilmington, Ohio, southeast of Dayton, by the Glider Branch of the Aircraft Laboratory. Test work in electronics was conducted at the Commonwealth Airport at East Boston, Massachusetts. The military units that conducted the tests were transferred to the Materiel Command as the Electronics Experimental Detachment.[91]

In June 1943 at Wright Field, steps were taken to supplement the data being compiled by the Flight Section through its test activities. A U.S. Equipment Unit was established in the Technical Data Laboratory which not only collected information, but also arranged for conferences between Materiel Command personnel and manufacturers' representatives returning from abroad.

Completed Propeller Lab acoustical enclosure, 1944. The octagon-shaped test enclosures to the right are used for helicopter blades.

It was also during 1943 that one of the outstanding test bases of the AAF became a formal military installation. The test facility at Rogers Lake, Muroc, California, was established in March 1942. On February 17, 1943, the 477th Base Headquarters and Air Base Squadron (Reduced) was moved from Wright Field to Muroc. The Materiel Command Flight Test Base, which operated under the administrative control of the Commanding General, Materiel Command (but under the technical supervision of the Chief of the Engineering Division), was fenced off and segregated from the remainder of the Muroc Army Air Base reservation. Its establishment satisfied the demand for a satisfactory place to test aeronautical developments that required an unusual degree of physical protection and security because of their classified status, or projects that required a large flying field due to their experimental nature. In spite of the complex administrative arrangements that accompanied the base's establishment, the Flight Test Base was recognized as one of the finest test establishments of the Materiel Command, and the 1943 evaluation program carried on at Muroc more than justified the expense and labor involved in its maintenance.[92]

Testing an aircraft radio in a Freon immersion bath in the Materials Lab. The liquid protected against atmospheric change, and its cooling features eliminated danger of burn-outs or explosions.

Construction of the Static Test Building (Building 65) presented unique architectural problems. Once the outer structures were completed, giant steel trusses were installed, spanning the 180 feet between the two shells.

The completed Static Test Building, shown here in November 1944, was tall enough and wide enough to flip over a B-36 fuselage and wing assembly in order to perform a full range of static tests (see Chapter VI).

Aeromedical Research Laboratory (Building 29, Area B), shortly after completion in 1942

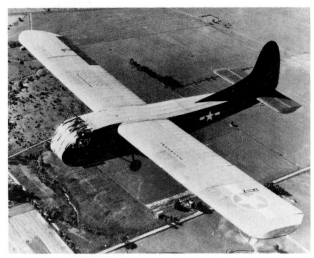

Troop-carrying gliders such as this one were tested at the Clinton County Army Air Field near Wilmington, Ohio, in connection with work at Wright Field. The Clinton County airfield later became part of the Army Air Forces Technical Base, along with Wright and Patterson Fields and the Dayton Army Air Field at Vandalia, Ohio.

Housing for Wright Field's mushrooming civilian population included several complexes near the field. These structures lined the north side of Springfield Street, just outside the main gate. Overlook Homes and Harshman Homes were privately built complexes to the west of Wright Field.

MILITARY UNITS ASSIGNED TO WRIGHT FIELD

The exact number of Army, Army Air Corps, and Army Air Forces subordinate organizations assigned to Wright Field between 1927 and 1948 has never been accurately determined. Those units which have been identified are covered briefly here.

The 10th Transport Group, activated on May 20, 1937 at Patterson Field, was reassigned to Wright Field from June 20, 1938 until January 16, 1941, at which time it returned to Patterson. The Group remained at Patterson until May 24, 1942, when it was transferred to General Billy Mitchell Field, Wisconsin. While at Wright and Patterson Fields, the Group flew C-27 and C-33 twin-engine cargo-transport type aircraft, and had five squadrons: 1st (1937-1943); 2nd (1937-1943); 3rd (1937-1940); 4th (1937-1940); and 5th (1937-1944).[93]

The 63rd Transport Group was constituted November 20, 1940, and activated at Wright Field on December 1, 1940. On February 17, 1941, it was transferred to Patterson Field, where it remained until September 9, 1941, when it was reassigned to Brookley Field, Alabama. The 63rd operated twin-engine C-33, C-34, and C-50 aircraft, and transported supplies, materiel, and personnel in the United States and around the Caribbean. While assigned to Wright and Patterson Fields, the 63rd Transport Group had three squadrons: 3rd (1940-1944); 6th (1940-1942); and 9th (1940-1943).[94]

The 50th Transport Wing was constituted January 8, 1941, and activated January 14, 1941 at Wright Field, where it remained until reassignment to Camp Williams, Wisconsin, on May 25, 1942. The 50th transported supplies and personnel in the United States, Alaska, and the Caribbean.

Barracks constructed adjacent to the Wright Memorial in Area B. According to unsubstantiated sources, this complex was used to house prisoners of war.

Wright Field theater, about 1942. Individual admission was 15 cents. The Army Motion Picture Service showed first-run Hollywood films.

Musicians of the 752nd Army Air Forces Band and Wright Field harmonizers produced a weekly program over Dayton radio station WHIO during World War II.

Consolidated bakery and butcher shop, Wright Field, about 1943. Fresh pastries and cuts of fresh meats were distributed early each day to various mess halls.

"Tea Shop" in the Wright Field Officers' Club during World War II

In January 1942, Company B of the 11th Infantry was assigned to Wright Field for guard duty.

On November 25, 1943, the Women's Army Corps Detachment, Headquarters, AAF Materiel Command was activated.[95] Also established in 1943 were: the 752nd AAF Band; the 435th, 436th, and 437th Aviation Squadrons; the 1454th Quartermaster Company, Aviation (Service); the 477th Base Headquarters and Air Base Squadron (Reduced) at Muroc, California; the Army Air Forces Detachment Number 6 at the Tucson Modification Center; and the Medical Detachment, Wright Field.[96]

Barracks headquarters of the 752nd Army Air Forces Band, Area B

Main Wright Field chapel, completed in September 1943

THE END OF THE WAR AND BEYOND

By the end of 1943, it was apparent that the wartime arrangement of separating logistics and procurement into two different organizations had its drawbacks. The Materiel Command, with headquarters at Wright Field, and the Air Service Command, with headquarters at Patterson Field, supervised functions which, although entirely different in theory, often overlapped in actuality.

The Air Service Command was concerned with maintenance and the distribution of supplies; while the Materiel Command was charged with conducting research and development, and managing the aircraft procurement program. In practice, however, it was not always easy to distinguish between their respective responsibilities. Jurisdictional entanglements over such issues as spare parts procurement, disposal of surplus property, and administration of air cargo service contracts invariably led to confusion and frustration between the two commands.

Solutions to these problems were actively pursued by both commands. Policy and coordination committees were formed to consider broad policy matters, reciprocal tours of officers of both commands were conducted, and regulations and directives were issued in an attempt to resolve conflicts and improve working relations. Time and experimentation, however, demonstrated that the most efficient method of correcting the difficulties was to eliminate the separation factor entirely.

On August 31, 1944, the Materiel Command and the Air Service Command were both discontinued and their functions merged into a single organization known as the Air Technical Service Command (ATSC). Lt. Gen. William S. Knudsen, former President of the General Motors Corporation, was designated the first Director of the new Command, with Maj. Gen. Bennett E. Meyers as Deputy Director. General Knudsen requested that his new title as head of ATSC be Director, rather than Commanding General, in order to emphasize the business aspect of the new Command's operations.[97]

Headquarters ATSC was located in Building 262 at Patterson Field. From there the Air Technical Service Command directed both the logistical and engineering operations of the Army Air Forces through the end of the war and beyond.

In order to avoid the psychologically divisive effect of having one headquarters responsible for functions on two different bases, and to give the entire headquarters a common address, Wright Field was extended to include that portion of Patterson Field occupied by Hq ATSC. To avoid confusion, the extension was designated "Wright Field, Area A" and the original Wright Field as "Area B." This trend toward combining the two bases became an increasingly practical necessity and logical eventuality which several years later culminated in the actual merger of Wright and Patterson Fields (January 1948).[98]

Building 262, Headquarters, Air Technical Service Command (ATSC). On August 31, 1944, the Materiel Command at Wright Field and the Air Service Command at Patterson Field were merged to form ATSC. To avoid confusion, the area occupied by ATSC Headquarters was designated "Wright Field, Area A." The remainder of Wright Field was designated "Area B."

V-E Day, May 8, 1945, was jubilantly hailed at Wright Field in both Areas A and B.* Maj. Gen. Bennett Meyers, acting ATSC Director, addressed Wright Field troops and employees at the Hilltop Parade Grounds in Area B. At the core of his message, however, was the reminder that the war was not yet won, and the appeal to Wright Field workers to redouble their efforts in order to bring about a speedy victory in the Pacific theater.[99]

The spirit of ultimate victory ran high in the closing months of the war. Superior officers were not the sole source of encouragement, however. During 1945, a number of big-name bands made appearances at Wright Field to bolster morale, among them Glen Gray and his Casa Loma Orchestra, Les Brown and his Band of Renown accompanied by the lovely young vocalist Doris Day, and the Stan Kenton Band. Prominent entertainers such as Bob Hope, Glenn Miller, Tommy Dorsey, Sammy Kaye, Les Elgart, and Woody Herman visited both Wright and Patterson Fields throughout the war to entertain and encourage the troops. Lawrence Welk and his orchestra played at the opening of the Area A Civilian Club (now Building 274) on December 1, 1944.[100] The CBS radio program "Cheers from the Camps" was broadcast from the old steel hangar on Patterson Field (now Building 145, Area C) and was heartily welcomed by men from both fields.[101]

Wright Field paused briefly on August 1, 1945, to celebrate the 38th anniversary of the Army Air Forces (first created as the Aeronautical Division of the Army Signal Corps in 1907). To mark the birthday occasion, and for the

Bob Hope and Frances Langford visit Wright and Patterson Fields to bolster morale and entertain the troops. *(Dick Cull)*

A CBS radio "Cheers from the Camps" broadcast, live from Patterson Field. *(Dick Cull)*

A standing-room-only crowd welcomes Bob Hope and other entertainers in the steel hangar at Patterson Field (Building 145, Area C). *(Dick Cull)*

*V-E Day (Victory-Europe), May 8, 1945, marked the unconditional surrender of the German government to the Allies. World War II in the West officially ended at midnight, May 7-8, 1945. V-J Day (Victory-Japan) came August 15, 1945, when Japanese forces laid down their arms. Official surrender to the Allies was September 2, 1945, aboard the *USS Missouri* in Tokyo Bay.

A LONG WAY TO GO!

V-E Day cartoon on the front page of *The Wright Flyer* newspaper illustrates that the war is not yet won and encourages Wright Field workers to "stick to their jobs."

benefit of some 150,000 visitors, a massive display of AAF power was exhibited on the flightline. It included not only the airplanes that had gained prominence during the war, but also the technical developments that had made them possible.

Civilian personnel were excused from duty at noon to attend the open house. The high spot of the afternoon was the review of 10,000 Wright Field troops on the Hilltop Parade Grounds by Maj. Gen. Hugh J. Knerr, who had assumed command of ATSC on July 1. At his side were Orville Wright and Edward Ward. Mr. Ward, of Dayton, was the first enlisted man in the Aeronautical Division.*

Captured enemy airplanes and equipment were placed on exhibition by the traveling "Shot From the Sky" show. Included in the displays were captured Japanese airplanes and a German Junkers that was flown from Munich in time for the birthday celebration.[102]

Beginning at 3:00 p.m., the public was treated to a spectacular airshow. The star performer of the show was the dazzling P-80 Shooting Star, the AAF's first jet-propelled fighter, revealed publicly in flight for the first time.**

When word finally was received that the Japanese had capitulated on August 15, 1945, Wright Field reacted with "bombastic glee." An account in the Wright Field enlisted newspaper, *The Post Script,* exclaimed:[103]

> Barrack after barrack rocked and trembled as shouts of pent-up emotion burst from the throats of enlisted personnel. Soldiers thumped each other on the back, shook hands, jumped about the shredded newspapers, bulletins (from bulletin boards) and bits of stationery. They poured out from the barracks, shouting the good news to each other and headed for the orderly rooms. . . . On the post the merriment hit an all-time high; the NCO Club was a mad-house of lively military personnel, the bowling alley PX rocked to all-out celebration. Headquarters Area was a scene of similar festivities.

One of the most spectacular events at Wright Field in the months following the end of the war was the staging of a huge AAF Fair. More than a million visitors from across the U.S. and from 26 foreign countries were attracted to Wright Field beginning Saturday, October 13, 1945. The Fair was originally intended as a local weekend event. Public response was overwhelming, however, and more than 500,000 people flocked to Wright Field in the opening two days. ATSC officials quickly decided to extend the Fair for an additional week.

The purpose of the Fair was to display technological advances in aviation made during the war, to show off captured German and Japanese weapons, and to present the AAF story to the American people. Over $150 million worth of equipment, much of which had been highly classified during the war, was exhibited. Cameras were welcome

---

*See details on the Aeronautical Division and photograph of Edward Ward in Chapter II, Wilbur Wright Field.

**Within 143 days of the request to build an airplane around a jet engine, a special team of Lockheed engineers and workmen, headed by Chief Research Engineer Clarence "Kelly" Johnson, had designed, built, and delivered the first model P-80 for ATSC experimental flight test.

and photographers rushed to shoot airplanes and equipment that only a week before had been strictly "hush-hush." Weapons that had been only mental pictures for many became not only visible, but touchable. "From behind locked doors and out of guarded test chambers [came] the latest in electronics, radar, jet propulsion, rockets, satellite devices and secret projects that for years [had] been mentioned only by code names."[104]

Captured German aircraft placed on display brought the enemy's most dreaded airplanes and missiles to life for the public. A Junkers 290 with "Alles Kaput" ("All is Finished") emblazoned on its side, was flown directly to the Fair from Germany by Col. Harold E. Watson. Also on display were the German V-2 rocket, the Messerschmitt 262—the world's first operational turbojet fighter-bomber, the Messerschmitt 163B Komet rocket-propelled interceptor, the Arado 234B twin-jet 500-mph reconnaissance aircraft, and a Bachem BP-20 Natter. (The Natter was a catapult-launched, rocket-propelled interceptor that would split in two and parachute to earth after completing its mission, thus enabling expensive components to be recovered and reused.)

A week-long AAF Fair in October 1945 attracted over 500,000 visitors to Wright Field.

German Junkers 290 flown directly to Wright Field by Col. Harold E. Watson

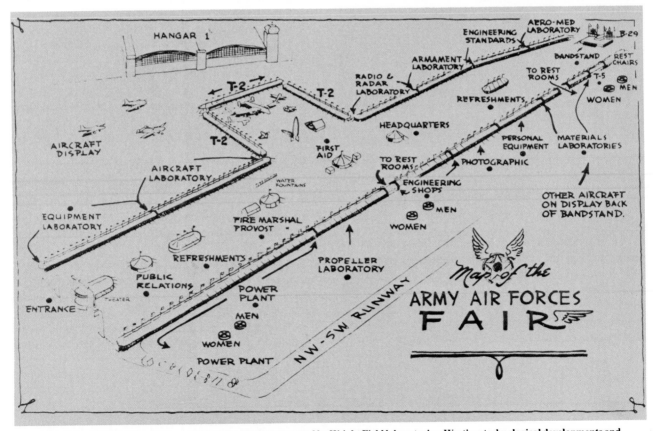

Map of the AAF Fair directing spectators to the displays prepared by Wright Field laboratories. Wartime technological developments and projects, previously top secret, were open to public view for the first time.

Col. Harold E. Watson

German ME-163B on display at the AAF Fair. Captured German and Japanese airplanes added a special aura of excitement to the fair.

German Bachem BP-20 Natter rocket-propelled interceptor

Col. Edward A. Deeds (second from left) and Orville Wright attend the 1945 Air Fair in the company of Maj. Gen. Benjamin W. Chidlaw (left) and Brig. Gen. Laurence Craigie.

Japanese spoils of war placed on display included the Mitsubishi ZEKE 52 (Zero) fighter, famed for out-maneuvering many an American fighter in the Pacific. Also on display was *Thumper,* the first B-29 to fly over Tokyo.

Virtually every type of AAF aircraft, including experimental models, was available for viewing. In the words of General Knerr, ATSC had, in effect, turned its laboratories "inside out to show our visitors the wonders of modern science that went into the creation of the world's greatest air force."[105]

Distinguished visitors to the Air Fair included top-ranking officers of the War Department and the AAF, members of Congress, state and municipal officials, leading industrialists, and of course, with the Fair being held in Dayton, aviation pioneer Orville Wright. On Sunday, October 21, the Fair honored Gen. George C. Kenney, Commander of the Far East Air Forces at the time of the Japanese surrender.

So enthusiastic was public response to the Fair that a selection of the exhibits was later developed by ATSC into a traveling show. The 4140th Army Air Forces Base Unit (Research and Development Exhibition) was formed to organize and handle the road show.[106] The traveling display proved a popular concept and was continued; the 4140th became the predecessor of today's modern Orientation Group, United States Air Force (AFOG), headquartered for many years at Wright-Patterson AFB.*

Another modern-day WPAFB organization that traces its roots to the World War II period is the Foreign Technology Division (FTD). During World War II, the Technical Data Laboratory at Wright Field (successor to the Technical Data Branch of the Administration Section) was responsible for evaluating foreign documents, aircraft, and related equipment. At one time, the mass of captured German and Japanese items was so large that it occupied six buildings at

GEN. GEORGE C. KENNEY

George Churchill Kenney enlisted as a flying cadet in the Aviation Section of the Signal Corps Reserve in June 1917. He was commissioned as a lieutenant in the Aviation Section in November 1917 and served with the 14th Foreign Detachment and the 91st Aero Squadron during World War I.

Captain Kenney graduated from the Air Corps Engineering School at McCook Field in 1921. He next returned to Wright Field in 1939, in the rank of major, as Chief of the Production Engineering Section of the Materiel Division. From 1940 to 1941, Lieutenant Colonel Kenney served as the Technical Executive at Wright Field, and in January 1941 became Assistant Chief of the Materiel Division, Wright Field, in the rank of brigadier general, a post he held until February 1942.

In March 1942, Major General Kenney assumed command of the Fourth Air Force. In July of that year he assumed command of Allied Air Forces in the Southwest Pacific, and also the Fifth Air Force. In June 1944, he was given command of the Far East Air Forces, which combined the Fifth and Thirteenth Air Forces. Kenney was promoted to the rank of general in March 1945.

In the years following World War II, Kenney served as Commanding General of the Strategic Air Command from 1946 to 1948, and as Commanding General of Air University from October 1948 until his retirement in August 1951.

Thumper, the first B-29 to fly over Tokyo

*AFOG, since 1981, has been headquartered at Gentile Air Force Station, Dayton, Ohio.

Wright Field, a large outdoor lot on the hilltop area (Area B), and part of a flightline hangar.

The Technical Data Laboratory also prepared performance characteristics reports on various German and Japanese aircraft and weapons, distributed them to the combat forces of all services, and introduced the assignment of nicknames for Japanese aircraft. This latter procedure standardized aircraft identification: feminine names such as BETTY and NELL were used for bombers, and masculine names such as FRANK, ZEKE, and NATE were used for fighters and observation airplanes.

With the formation of the Air Technical Service Command (ATSC), the Technical Data Laboratory changed its name. Under the new T-system organizational concept, the name became simply T-2 Intelligence. T-2 Intelligence continued to play a major role in the organization and exploitation of captured materiel, manpower, and documents.[107]

One such documentation effort began in the waning days of the war and burgeoned into a major program operated out of T-2 at Wright Field. Prior to the Allied victory, the Army Air Forces assumed prime responsibility for seeking out and impounding Luftwaffe documents, for locating German scientists and technicians, and for securing the records of German engineering developments. As Allied armies pushed the Germans from their strongholds, Army Air Forces intelligence teams and similar U.S. Navy and British organizations followed close behind, "liberating" ton upon ton of German aeronautical research materials.

Under Project LUSTY, all of these documents were flown to an Air Documents Research Center organized in London for processing. Initial sorting and classification of 1,500 tons of this material was accomplished at a rate of some 10 tons per day, until the bulk had been reduced to 250 tons.

In September of 1945, an Air Documents Research Office was established at Wright Field under the Commanding General of ATSC. In November 1945, operations of the Air Documents Research Center in London were moved intact to Wright Field, with all personnel and selected equipment, and placed under T-2 Intelligence.[108]

Work started in December 1945 on some 55,000 documents, representing the cream of German aeronautical research and development. Nearly 400 civil service employees, and over 100 officers and enlisted personnel of the Army Air Forces and the Navy Bureau of Aeronautics, were involved in cataloging the documents, drawing abstracts and indexes, and scheduling the documents for translation. The goal was to organize the German documents in such a manner that they would form the nucleus of a huge catalog, embracing the entire science of aeronautics. It was hoped the project would save hundreds of millions of dollars over a period of time, and hundreds of thousands of valuable man hours, by avoiding duplication and wasted efforts.

A cartoon depicting Wright Field's role as a test base for captured German aircraft appeared four decades later in *AIR FORCE Magazine*. (Reprinted by permission)

Project LUSTY also included the collection of foreign equipment as well as documents. Late model German aircraft and engines were flown to Wright Field for study.* T-2 personnel also participated in a Technical Air Intelligence unit which was formed in October 1944 and attached to the Far East Air Forces. Its mission was to take possession of all captured Japanese aircraft and equipment in the Pacific Theater.

When the Air Technical Service Command became the Air Materiel Command in 1946, the Air Documents Division (ADD), as the Air Documents Research Office was then called, proceeded uninterrupted with its work. The Wright Field Technical Library was a section of this division. (Organized originally at McCook Field in 1919, the library moved to Wright Field in 1927 as a component of the Technical Data Branch. For many years it was housed in the Army Aeronautical Museum, Building 12, Area B.)

The German documents program, originally scheduled for completion by the end of 1948, was finished 14 months ahead of schedule in November 1947. When completed, this effort represented one of the outstanding events in the history of documentation, as an entire nation's aeronautical research and development literature was indexed, abstracted, and microfilmed. A master card index of the cataloged materials was maintained at Wright Field, while smaller indexes were maintained by qualified government, scientific, and industrial organizations throughout the United States. By August 1947, over 10 million cards and hundreds of thousands of copies of documents had been distributed to the holders of these indexes and to more than 2,500 government agencies and contractors. One useful result of this exploitation of German documents was the publication of a dictionary containing over 110,000 German aeronautical terms related to new technological areas.[109]

---

*Details of this project may be found in the FTD portion of Chapter XII.

Another significant achievement of the Air Documents Division was the initiation of a Standard Aeronautical Index. Accomplished under joint contract to the Air Force and the Navy by the Institute of Aeronautical Sciences, this index was considered at the time to be the most radical innovation in the history of classification, and was accepted as an authoritative source by major organizations concerned with the indexing and dissemination of aeronautical literature.

Paving the way for the future, that portion of the German documents program involved in pure intelligence work was broken out in August 1947 to form a separate department of AMC known as the Technical Intelligence Department. This organization, a direct antecedent of today's Foreign Technology Division (FTD) of the Air Force Systems Command, concerned itself with the larger task of collecting, processing, and evaluating data pertaining to foreign military and industrial capabilities, and matters relating to foreign military technological advancement.*

As Wright Field settled into a post-war routine, many activities which had been curtailed for the duration of the war were reestablished. Chief among these was the Army Air Forces Engineering School. With a mission expanded to include "Maintenance Engineering" and "Air Logistics," the Army Air Forces Institute of Technology (AAFIT) was

Headlines of the FATSC newspaper *Postings* announce the formation of the Army Air Forces Technical Base. The merger became official on December 15, 1945.

Components of the AAF Technical Base were Wright Field and Patterson Field, the Dayton Army Air Field, Vandalia, Ohio (above), and the Clinton County Army Air Field, Wilmington, Ohio (below).

Lt. Gen. Nathan F. Twining, Commanding General of the Air Technical Service Command. Twining was later the first Air Force general to serve as Chairman of the Joint Chiefs of Staff.

*In May 1951, the functions performed by the Technical Intelligence Department were transferred directly under Hq USAF, and redesignated the Aerospace Technical Intelligence Center (ATIC). ATIC was transferred to the Air Force Systems Command in 1961, and assigned its current designation as the Foreign Technology Division.

Panorama of Wright Field at zenith of its growth, July 1945

authorized at Wright Field on December 15, 1945. The Institute of Technology was to operate under the jurisdiction of the Air Technical Service Command. Lt. Gen. Nathan F. Twining, Commanding General of ATSC, appointed a resident committee of ATSC officers to prepare an operating plan for the proposed Institute. The Institute was formally dedicated by General Twining on September 3, 1946.[110] The first classes were opened that same month.*

On December 15, 1945, Wright Field (home of the Air Technical Service Command) and Patterson Field (home of the Fairfield Air Technical Service Command) were consolidated along with two smaller installations, for administrative purposes, into an umbrella organization entitled the Army Air Forces Technical Base. The other installations affected by this merger were the Dayton Army Air Field at Vandalia, Ohio and the Clinton County Army Air Field at Wilmington, Ohio.

Brig. Gen. Joseph T. Morris, Wright Field Commanding General, was appointed Commanding General of the new Technical Base and charged with providing operational support for the primary elements of the Technical Base, Wright and Patterson Fields, as well as the Clinton County and Vandalia airfields. (The latter two organizations were subsequently separated from the Technical Base in 1946.)

On December 9, 1947, consequent to the establishment of the U.S. Air Force as a separate service, the AAF Technical Base, Dayton, Ohio, was redesignated the Air Force Technical Base. One month later, on January 13, 1948, the name was finalized to its present form when the installation was redesignated Wright-Patterson Air Force Base.

LOGISTICS AND RESEARCH IN THE POST-WAR PERIOD

The Air Materiel Command (AMC) was tasked with two major functions in the post-war period: demobilization and on-going research and development. Directing these efforts was Lt. Gen. Nathan F. Twining, Commander of AMC from March 1946 to October 1947.

First on AMC's agenda was the overwhelming task of post-war demobilization. The highly effective wartime machinery that had provided the logistical support for victory had to be shifted into reverse. Gorged supply pipelines connecting the U.S. to points around the world had to be cleared. Stations had to be deactivated and vast quantities of materials withdrawn from distant battle areas.

*The AAF Institute of Technology, antecedent of today's prestigious Air Force Institute of Technology (AFIT), became part of Air University, Maxwell AFB, Alabama, on April 1, 1950, although the school's principal operations remained at Wright-Patterson. Details on the AFIT story may be found in Chapter XI.

Domestically, wartime industries had to be reoriented without major dislocations to the economy. With the sudden surrender of Japan, work had stopped on some 31,000 military aircraft. At AMC Headquarters and throughout the various procurement districts, procurement, supply, and adjustment personnel worked at top speed to shut off contracts, curtail all forms of Air Force manufacture, and facilitate the conversion to civilian production.[111]

Meanwhile, millions of dollars of surplus supplies had to be disposed of or identified and warehoused. Materiel and physical property had to be readied for turnover to the War Assets Administration. Airplanes and equipment had to be "cocooned" or otherwise prepared for storage as war reserve. From a wartime peak of 80,000 aircraft, for example, by mid-1947 the active inventory was reduced to only 12,000 airplanes.[112]

Simultaneous reductions in manpower were occurring at all echelons. From a wartime peak of almost 2.5 million uniformed personnel, the AAF diminished to little more than 300,000 military members by mid-1947. This drastic reduction also challenged AMC as it struggled to adjust to the needs of the peacetime Air Force.

The second major responsibility given the Air Materiel Command was aeronautical research and development. Throughout most of World War II, this responsibility had belonged to the Materiel Command. With the creation of the Air Technical Service Command in 1944, however, research and development had become an adjunct of the logistics function.

Under ATSC, the Engineering Division was essentially a collection of laboratories. During 1945 there were fourteen in total—nine aeronautical laboratories and five electronics laboratories. The aeronautical laboratories were all located at Wright Field and were concerned with the development of airplane components and special categories of aeronautical equipment, including armament. Four of the five electronics labs were also at Wright Field, while the fifth, the Watson Laboratories, was located at Eatontown,

New Jersey. The electronics labs at Wright Field worked with airborne electronic equipment, while Watson Labs was responsible for the development of ground electronic equipment, both communication and radar.

Other installations and liaison offices operated by ATSC, and later AMC, were closely linked to the research work conducted at Wright Field. Ladd Field, Fairbanks, Alaska, housed a testing detachment concerned with the winterization testing of all items of equipment, from ground equipment to complete aircraft. The Muroc Flight Test Base in California was used for flight testing of experimental airplanes. A pilotless aircraft and guided missile testing range was located at Wendover, Utah. A testing station at Dover, Delaware, worked under the Armament Laboratory in testing rockets and rocket installation on airplanes. Eglin Field, Florida, also provided excellent range facilities for the testing of armament equipment. At Boca Raton Army Air Field in Florida, a Watson Laboratories substation worked to develop and test radar bombing equipment.[113]

An additional association was maintained with the Cambridge Field Station in Massachusetts, established as an AAF installation in June 1946. It absorbed personnel and facilities of the former Radiation Laboratory of the Massachusetts Institute of Technology and the Radio Research Laboratory of Harvard University.[114]

Special tower constructed to test aircraft ejection seats. Sgt. Lawrence Lambert of Wright Field became the first person in the United States to exit an airplane in flight by means of an ejection seat on August 17, 1946.

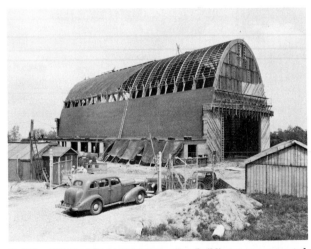

Building 821, the Wright Field Radar Test Building, was constructed in 1947. Nicknamed "The Cathedral," the building is often misidentified as a dirigible hangar. When originally constructed, the building was made entirely of wood, including the use of wooden pegs rather than metal nails.

During the summer of 1946, three major events highlighted activities at Wright Field. On June 3, 1946, Lt. Henry A. Johnson set a world speed record of 426.97 mph in a Lockheed jet-engine P-80 over a 1,000-km course (without payload). On the same day, Wright Field Capt. James M. Little established another world record by flying a B-29 over a 2,000-km course between Dayton and St. Louis at an average speed of 361 mph. Captain Little's skill narrowly averted a crash ending to his flight as he was forced to land on one engine.[115] On August 17, 1946, Sgt. Lawrence Lambert of Wright Field became the first person in the United States to exit an airplane in flight by means of an ejection seat. While his P-61 airplane was traveling 302 mph at an altitude of 7,800 ft, Sgt. Lambert activated a pilot ejector seat developed at Wright Field.[116]

In December 1946, AMC utilized Kirtland Army Air Field, Albuquerque, New Mexico, to provide flight services for the Manhattan District at Sandia and Los Alamos in atomic bomb testing.[117]

In addition to its own facilities, AAF research and development drew on the facilities of outside agencies, especially the principal organization for basic aeronautical research at the time, the National Advisory Committee for Aeronautics. Close liaison and coordination was also maintained with agencies of the Navy and the Army Technical Services. AMC also made a strong effort to utilize the knowledge and facilities of non-profit scientific institutions, universities, and colleges, and the aircraft industry itself. Among the most important of these outside agencies involved in AAF research were the Jet Propulsion Laboratory at the California Institute of Technology in Pasadena, California, the Applied Physics Laboratory at Johns Hopkins University, the Aberdeen Proving Ground in Aberdeen, Maryland, the Bureau of Aeronautics of the Naval Research Laboratory, and the Office of Naval Research.[118]

Research and development programs during World War II had been in the hands of the National Defense Research Council (NDRC) and private industry. In the years following the war, however, with the NDRC disbanded and contracts with private industry cancelled, the Air Materiel Command initiated more and more of its own research

programs and slowly assumed responsibility for a greater proportion of research and development efforts, until research became a major part of the logistics mission. By 1947, AMC was actively engaged in more than 2,000 research projects.

Important changes were made in the focus of research after the war, as AMC developed new channels of technological advancement. During the war, for example, the Engineering Division had concentrated on aeronautical weapons of war, with emphasis on perfecting and producing those items which had been in an advanced state of development prior to 1942. In the months following V-J Day, the Engineering Division turned its attention from the airplanes and weapons of World War II to the development of concepts for the future such as jet-propelled aircraft and guided missiles. Emphasis also shifted from development of individual items to a coordinated systems approach. Modification and improvement of existing models therefore assumed a lesser role, as the overall focus turned to the development of entire new systems and models.[119]

Under Project OVERCAST, and later Project PAPERCLIP, prominent German scientists were released and brought to work at Wright Field. By the end of World War II, the Germans had spent nearly a decade in developing

Technicians perform adjustments following the cold weather test of a J-34 turbo jet engine. The bell mouth at the right of the picture is the air intake for the engine.

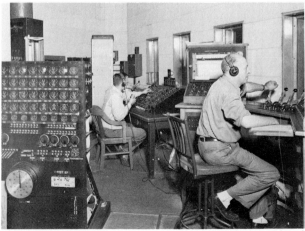

Wright Field engineers operate test chamber controls during testing of an early jet engine.

missiles such as the V-1 and V-2. They contributed valuable experience at Wright Field to such modern-day projects as the perfection of rockets and gliders, ramjets, heavy presses, and ribbon parachutes, as well as the farsighted design of rocket refueling bases which would serve as orbiting space stations some 4,000 miles from the earth. By December 1946, the War Department estimated that the background and experience contributed by German scientists to U.S. efforts had already saved more than $750 million in basic research.[120]

Wright Field personnel were involved in a variety of special accomplishments during 1947. Important strides were made in developing gyro-computing sights for the guns, bombs, and rockets mounted on fighter aircraft. On February 10, 1947, Maj. E. M. Cassell set an unofficial world helicopter altitude record of 19,167 ft in a Sikorsky R-5A. On August 8, 1947, Adolf L. Berger received the

Thurman H. Bane award for his work in developing new high-temperature ceramic coatings for use in aircraft engines. On September 22, a Wright Field C-54 landed in London after completing the first robot-controlled flight across the Atlantic Ocean. On October 14, Capt. Charles Yeager flew faster than the speed of sound in the Bell XS-1, a feat based on a plan originated at Wright Field, where much of the theory and testing had been accomplished.[121] The stage was set for even greater discoveries and developments as Wright Field boldly entered the Aerospace Age.

When Wright Field merged with Patterson Field to become Wright-Patterson AFB on January 13, 1948, the new installation inherited a long and proud heritage. In retrospect, the kaleidoscope of activities at Wright Field had achieved a spectrum and brilliance that even the most optimistic of its early promoters found marvelous to behold.

The crew of President Harry S. Truman's airplane *The Independence* poses at Wright Field during a visit to the field in September 1947.

McCook Field, 1918

VI.   DEVELOPING AIR POWER 1917-1951

Dayton witnessed the refinement of controlled, powered flight through the dedicated efforts of the Wright brothers in 1904-1905 on Huffman Prairie. From 1917 to 1926, Dayton enthusiastically supported Air Service efforts at McCook Field to develop the muscles and sinews of military aviation. With the establishment of Wright Field in 1927, Dayton and the nation witnessed the opening of an even greater era in the development of American air power. Military and civilian Air Corps scientists, aeronautical engineers, craftsmen, and pilots assigned to Wright Field during the 1930s and 1940s expanded the science of aeronautics beyond all earlier horizons. Their contributions helped carry America to victory in World War II and guided the country to the threshold of the Aerospace Age.

This chapter sketches some of the major achievements and developments that occurred at McCook and Wright Fields from 1917 to 1951. The discussion is divided into five sections: McCook Field 1917-1918; McCook Field 1919-1926; Wright Field 1927-1934; Wright Field Contributions to World War II 1935-1945; and Post-War Contributions to Aviation 1946-1951.

McCOOK FIELD 1917-1918

During 1917-1918, the experimental facility at McCook Field developed "almost overnight [into] the single most influential agency in the early years of American air power."[1] During its remaining eight years, McCook served as the bellwether of American aviation. In ten short years, the visionary engineers, scientists, artisans, and pilots of McCook Field established traditions of excellence that stand to this day.

On November 22, 1917, the Chief Signal Officer in Washington, D.C., described McCook's wartime mission: technical and experimental work would concentrate on the correlated areas of airplane and airplane engine development, on aerial cameras installed on experimental aircraft, and on "work pertaining to the synchronization of machine guns." McCook's companion in aircraft experimentation, testing, and development, Langley Field, Virginia, was given responsibility for "all matters pertaining to instruction and experimentation in bombing, photography, radio and telegraphy." Langley was also identified as the center of

Drafting Room, McCook Field, where the engineering drawings for most of America's early military airplanes were produced

Fokker D-7, one of many foreign aircraft brought to McCook Field for test and evaluation

foreign aircraft demonstration, although several types of foreign aircraft were later assembled and flown at McCook Field as well.[2]

McCook Field opened officially on December 4, 1917, as the arena of the Airplane Engineering Department, a major element of the Signal Corps Equipment Division. The Airplane Engineering Department concentrated on advance design and engineering. Its responsibilities included exhaustive tests on experimental aircraft and those standard production types which were being modified into advanced

*Details of these aircraft are discussed later.

models, and on related accessories. Once aircraft and accessories were developed, designs, models, and engineering information were passed to the Production Engineering Department, which released the information to manufacturers. The Production Engineering Department also conducted stringent tests on the airplanes and accessories as they neared and entered production.[3]

The focal point of airplane engineering was the McCook Field Experimental Factory, an amalgamation of the former Plane Design and Engine Design Sections. The Factory's components were the wood, metal, assembly, and dope shops. All of the work performed in these shops was of experimental nature and included nearly all phases of airplane and engine manufacture and modification. Prominent products of the Experimental Factory were the USAC-1 combat aircraft, the USD-9A bomber, the USXB-1 and USXB-2 bombers, and the USAC-11.*

The McCook Field Machine Shop produced experimental engines ranging in size and horsepower from small single-cylinder test machines to the 24-cylinder Liberty engine. The famous Nelson machine gun control system was also developed in the Machine Shop.

The Aeronautical Research Department, organized in November 1917, was the service center for other McCook Field functions. The Department's original mission was stress-testing. A few weeks after operations began, the Department formed a close partnership with the Massachusetts Institute of Technology (MIT) aerodynamical laboratory in its stress-testing research. Together they designed the methods and procedures which became standard in the field. An airplane (less engine and accessories) was subjected to stress analysis of its various components by placing sandbags of different sizes, configurations, and weights on the surfaces of wings, tails, and various sections of fuselages. These procedures determined the ultimate strengths of materials and structural design.

The Aeronautical Research Department also conducted flight tests and materials tests. A special experimental airplane (never numbered or identified) was configured as a flying aerodynamic laboratory. Another section of the Aeronautical Research Department was dedicated to materials testing, including studies of fittings, struts, spares, and similar parts. An area of special interest was the testing of various types and designs of ribs.

The Mechanical Research Department at McCook received special note for its development of the Loomis cooling system. This significant improvement over previous systems "fulfilled all the rigid requirements for service planes used over the battlefront," and was named after Mr. Allen Loomis, head of the Mechanical Research Department and an "experimental engineer of wide experience in the automotive industry."[4] The new system featured an expansion tank that surrounded the honeycomb cooling element and formed an integral part of the nose radiator, thus replacing the usual shell. A second improvement was

Early static testing performed by the Aeronautical Research Department. Stress-testing of airplane components was conducted by loading sandbags of different sizes, configurations, and weights onto the surfaces of the wings, tail, and various sections of the fuselage.

The McCook Field Machine Shop produced experimental engines and all other metal accessories for airplanes.

Development of flight instrumentation went hand in hand with aircraft development. These McCook Field engineers and members of the Flight Test Branch worked closely together to develop some of the world's earliest altimeters, tachometers, airspeed indicators, flight compasses, and navigational aids.

The Wood Shop fabricated fuselage and wing structures.

an injector in the water connection between the radiator and the circulating pump. The latter drew water from the bottom of the expansion tank and injected it into the circulation system, thereby keeping a constant volume of water in motion.

The Chemical and Physical Material Laboratories conducted ongoing tests and experiments on various engine fuels, lubricating oils, metals, and metal alloys. Special examinations and studies were also conducted on a multitude of materials associated with work in the other laboratories at McCook.

Laboratories of the Engine Assembly and Testing Department performed tests of all types on aviation engines and accessories, including radiators, gasoline assemblies, and heating and lighting systems. The Department tested experimental engines and accessories; standard production engines sent to McCook either for calibration or for installation in experimental model airplanes; and routine overhauling and testing of machines at McCook. In particular, the Engine Testing Department contributed significantly to the increased power and general efficiency of the powerful Liberty engine.

THE McCOOK FIELD 14-INCH WIND TUNNEL

The first wind tunnel constructed for testing purposes at McCook Field was patterned after one designed by Orville Wright, though it was much larger. It was composed of 2,100 pieces of propeller-quality walnut, taken from the trimmings of propeller laminations, as well as quantities of mahogany and birch woods. Each three-quarter-inch length consisted of six segments which were glued and nailed in circular shape before being turned on a lathe. The tunnel's interior surface was highly polished enamel. It had a diameter of 14 inches at the choke and 60 inches near the exit. The tunnel was slightly less than 22 feet long and was mounted on a massive wooden base.

A 24-blade fan with a diameter of 60 inches drew air through the tunnel. Driven through a jack-shaft, the fan was mounted on ball bearings and flexibly connected to a Sprague electric dynamometer, rated at 200 to 300 hp. The dynamometer drove the fan at a maximum speed of 2,000 rpm, producing an airspeed of 453 mph at the choke of the tunnel.

The tunnel was used to test or calibrate airspeed instruments and to study the aerodynamic properties of different shapes. Objects to be tested were mounted in the choke of the tunnel through a plate glass observation door at the side. Smoke pictures could be taken to help study how air flowed around a body of a given shape at different speeds.

This wind tunnel, a vital part of McCook Field research, is now on permanent display at the U.S. Air Force Museum.

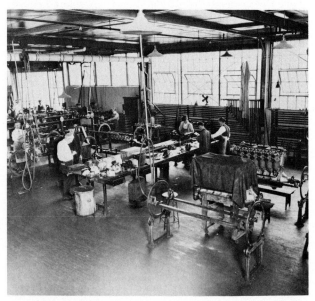

Engine Assembly Shop in 1918, equipped with twelve engine stands for overhauls and repairs

Wooden propellers constructed in the Propeller Shop were formed from wood laminations glued to the desired thickness, then shaped, carved, and finished to exact specifications. Experiments were also made on propellers manufactured from duralumin and Bakelite Micarta.

Main Assembly hangar, where final assembling of fuselages, wings, and accessories took place. Airplane in the foreground is a Vought VE-7 advanced trainer.

The Propeller Department developed propellers for various experimental, standard, and training aircraft. This included all Air Service and numerous Navy machines. The Department also researched a wide range of propeller problems by means of full-flight and destructive whirl tests. Some of the most notable experiments involved tipping propeller blades with copper, brass, pigskin, linen, and other materials as protection against abrasion. Other work was done on propeller thrust and torque meters used in full-flight testing and propeller construction. A variable-pitch propeller which showed "interesting possibilities" was tested thoroughly in 1918 but was not widely used.

A crucial problem confronting the Armament Department, headed by Mr. A. L. Nelson, was how to control/synchronize the fire of a fixed machine gun through the propeller disc of an airplane without shattering the blades. Under Nelson's leadership, a "single shot" trigger mechanism was developed for the Marlin, Vickers, and Browning .30 caliber fixed (mounted) guns. The previous system, called the Constantinesco, operated on "a pressure-wave principle, transmitting the timing impulses from the engine to the gun through a tube containing a column of oil under high pressure." The Nelson control system sent the timing impulses "by means of a positive mechanical connection between the engine and the gun, thus eliminating the lag inherent in a system that operated on the pressure-wave principle."[5]

Thoroughly tested at McCook and Wilbur Wright Fields, the Nelson gun control system proved its superiority over earlier devices. The Nelson was more accurate and could be used with both twin-bladed and four-bladed propellers over a wide speed range. The new system confined the shots within a narrow arc, and when used with the single shot trigger mechanism eliminated stray shots entirely.

AIRPLANE ENGINE DEVELOPMENTS

Even before McCook was built, many of the military and civilian mechanical and electrical engineers who would become the nucleus of the McCook Field staff—especially those with considerable experience in the automotive industry—were in the vanguard of the nation's military aviation effort. They provided outstanding service in designing one of America's most significant contributions to Allied air power—the Liberty engine—and in preparing it and another stalwart, the British DeHavilland DH-4 biplane, for mass production in American factories.

A few weeks after the United States entered World War I, the Aircraft Production Board decided that one of America's most expedient contributions to victory would be the large-scale production of a high-powered airplane engine. No other country was producing any single engine in large quantities; in late 1916 and early 1917, Great Britain was experimenting with 37 different service engines while France was testing 46 types. No country was better suited to the mass production of airplanes and engines than the United States, with its well-developed automotive industry. It remained only to develop a single suitable design.

By June 4, 1917, an American engine design was approved and given the appropriate name of Liberty. The first Liberty engine was completed late that month and tested, appropriately, on July 4. It was an 8-cylinder, 200-hp model, and was shortly joined in production by more powerful 12-cylinder, 300-hp versions. Further refinement eventually increased the horsepower of the 12-cylinder Liberty to 440 hp. By the end of the war, six American automobile manufacturers had produced about 15,600 Liberty engines and another 60,000 were on order by the United States and its Allies for use on a wide range of aircraft.[6]

The Liberty 12-cylinder engine was America's greatest engineering contribution to World War I. (*U.S. Air Force Museum*)

Curtiss JN-4D Jennys (foreground) in the main hangar at McCook, March 1918

Liberty 12-cylinder engine mounted on a torque stand (*U.S. Air Force Museum*)

Throughout the war, McCook Field was heavily involved in testing and improving airplane engines and accessories. In an October 21, 1918, status report, Col. Jesse G. Vincent, Chief Engineer at McCook, listed "no less than 46 current experimental projects" which concentrated heavily on aircraft engines. These included the improved Liberty 8-cylinder and design of the single-cylinder and 2-cylinder Liberty test engines for laboratory experimentation.

THE LIBERTY AIRPLANE

Much of the success of Allied air power in the latter months of World War I stemmed from the marriage of the Liberty engine with the British DeHavilland DH-4 two-place biplane. This aircraft was the only foreign machine to be produced in quantity in the United States. In fact, only one American airplane was built on a similar scale—the Curtiss Corporation's JN-4D Jenny primary trainer.

The DH-4 was an all-wood machine, designed originally for the dual functions of observation work and light bombing. The airplane's original power plant was a British Rolls-Royce engine. The DeHavilland's basic specifications were: wingspan 42 ft, 6 in; length 30 ft, 6 in; gross weight 3,557 lbs; speed 128 mph; range 400 miles.[7] Its operational combat armament when serving with American Air Service squadrons in France consisted of twin .303 caliber British Lewis aerial machine guns mounted on the rim of the rear cockpit, and two more mounted on the

Completed DH-4 fuselages await final assembly of the wings and tails at the Dayton-Wright Airplane Company.

The 1,000th DH-4 rolled off the assembly line at Dayton-Wright in July 1918.

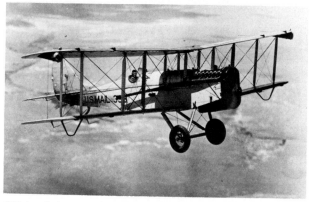

DH-4 variations remained in the Air Corps active inventory through 1931. This model was reconfigured to fly mail.

fuselage in front of the pilot which fired through the propeller arc. The airplane could carry up to 200 lbs of bombs. The 50- or 100-lb bombs were placed in racks beneath the lower wing.

A sample DH-4 airframe arrived in the United States on August 15, 1917. It was rushed in the original shipping crates by rail to McCook Field. Over the next two months the machine underwent "extensive detail redesign" to accommodate American production methods, and was fitted with the new 12-cylinder 400-hp Liberty engine which was specifically designed for it. It was a good marriage, and the modified English bride was renamed the "Liberty Airplane."[8] On October 18, 1917, the Dayton-Wright Airplane

Company received an initial order for 250 redesigned DH-4s equipped with Liberty engines. The first production model was test flown at McCook Field on October 29.

The first American model DH-4 reached France in May 1918. In the course of testing and using the airplane, serious questions arose concerning its combat reliability and performance. American Air Service pilots both in the United States and in France were uneasy drivers of the machine.

After considerable—and often heated—discussions in Washington, a board of veteran military and civilian aeronautical engineers and pilots convened at McCook Field from April 24 to May 2, 1918, to examine and evaluate the American version of the DH-4. Many significant mechanical problems were found in both the engine and the fuselage. (On May 2, an assembly-line model used as a test aircraft spun into the ground at Wilbur Wright Field from 300 ft, killing Lt. Col. Henry J. Damm and Maj. Oscar Brindley. Brindley, with 2,000 flying hours, was considered one of the most highly skilled pilots in the Air Service.) After tests and modifications, the major mechanical and structural shortcomings were corrected before large numbers of DH-4s reached American squadrons in France.

By the end of November 1918, more than 4,500 Liberty airplanes (DH-4s) had been produced by American manufacturers; Dayton-Wright had constructed 3,106 of them.[9] War's end in Europe, however, did not mean the end of the ubiquitous DH-4. Through a long list of changes from the DH-4A to the DH-4M, the airplane remained in the Air Corps active inventory through 1931.[10]

NEW AIRPLANE DESIGNS

Although the DH-4 was America's major direct contribution to the war effort in Europe, other significant projects were also underway at McCook Field. Modification and production of the most combat-effective British, French, and Italian warplanes was an immediate priority. As the war progressed, however, increased military needs and a keen sense of national pride led McCook Field engineers to also apply their efforts toward developing original American designs.

Immediately following the amalgamation of the Plane Design and Engine Design Sections at McCook on October 13, 1917, design work began on the USAC-1 (U.S. Army, Combat-1) two-seat biplane.

The model for the USAC-1 was the British Bristol Fighter. The American version had a plywood fuselage and a "rather fancy empennage" (defined as "the rear part of an airplane, comprising the stabilizer, elevator, vertical fin, and rudder").[11] The USAC-1 weighed about 3,500 lbs and was powered by a high compression, straight spur-geared Liberty-12 engine. The airplane was equipped with five .30 caliber machine guns. Two of the three flexible weapons were mounted on the gunner's (rear) cockpit. The third flexible gun was positioned to fire through the bottom of the fuselage (thus antedating by several generations of airplanes the ball turret of the B-17 Flying Fortress bomber).

Artist's inboard profile of the USD-9A, a reconnaissance version of the DH-9 redesigned and standardized at McCook in 1918 *(U.S. Air Force Museum)*

Overhead view of the USD-9A *(U.S. Air Force Museum)*

Two fixed machine guns were mounted on the nose of the fuselage in front of the pilot's cockpit for firing through the propeller disc. About 2,400 separate engineering drawings were made before the prototype was built. Preliminary drawings were also begun for the USAC-2, an experimental model of similar design but with a streamlined veneer fuselage.

The prototype USAC-1's performance was adequate but only a little better than either the British DH-4 observation-bomber or the Bristol Fighter; production was not approved. Nevertheless, the USAC-1 left a valuable legacy in that it firmly established an engineering discipline at Mc-Cook which permitted the rapid development of other aircraft.

In March 1918, work commenced on redesigning and standardizing the DeHavilland DH-9 (a later model of the DH-4) for production. The McCook Field version, named the USD-9, was equipped with the high compression Liberty 12-A engine. As design work progressed, some significant variances were made from the original body. These changes included omitting the bomb-carrying compartment in the fuselage and increasing the fuel capacity. Incorporated into the modified aircraft were the latest mechanical improvements such as the Nelson gun control system, the Loomis cooling system, and the McCook gasoline system.

Flexibility of design permitted the airplane to be flown as a day bomber, night bomber, or as a reconnaissance aircraft. In the reconnaissance version, the follow-on

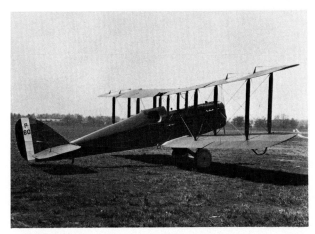

Modified USD-9A in which Lt. Harold R. Harris made the world's first pressurized high-altitude flight in 1921

Antioch College and University of Cincinnati students work on a Vought VE-7 advanced trainer under the tutelage of their McCook Field instructor.

model, USD-9A, had a gross weight of 4,520 lbs and a top speed of 124 mph.[12] It carried two parallel flexible turret .30 caliber Lewis aerial machine guns on the rim of the rear cockpit. A fixed .30 caliber Browning gun was mounted on the right side of the fuselage and fired through the propeller disc. The weapon had two sights. One was a ring on the gun, per se. The second was an Aldis sight on the left side of the pilot's windshield. A control mounted directly on the "camshaft driving member" of the Liberty engine timed the gun's firing through the propeller disc. According to one authority, this was not the "ultimate synchronizer," but it was reliable and adaptable to all aircraft.[13]

After the wing structure was modified, the USD-9A was scheduled for mass production. This was the first aircraft for which a complete set of construction drawings was created. Approximately 3,000 were published for the parts and assemblies, exclusive of the engine and standard appurtenances such as machine guns and mountings.[14]

Plans called for the Curtiss Aeroplane and Motor Corporation of Buffalo, New York, to manufacture 4,000 USD-9As. The order was cancelled, however, when Allied victories in France during the summer of 1918 forecast Germany's ultimate defeat. Fragmentary records indicate that at least four USD-9A airplanes were manufactured at McCook, but none were built by a contractor.

Meanwhile, in April 1918 work commenced on re-designing the British Bristol single-place biplane fighter to accommodate the 8-cylinder 300-hp Hispano-Suiza engine. This aircraft, renamed the USB-1, was intended for contract manufacture, and thus about 2,500 production drawings were made of parts and assemblies.

A short time later, work started on two experimental models of the USB-1; these were designated the USXB-1 and USXB-2 (X denoting experimental). The first model incorporated a "carefully stream-lined [sic] three-ply veneer fuselage and steel landing gear" but made use of all USB-1 "flying surfaces." The USXB-1 carried two flexible .30 caliber machine guns on the rear cockpit, and two .30 caliber fixed guns mounted forward and fired through the propeller arc. The USXB-2 was very similar, except that it was powered by the Liberty 8-cylinder engine.[15]

By late summer, with the approaching end of hostilities, all plans for mass production of the USB-1 were halted. In early November, however, firm orders were placed for the manufacture of three airplanes of this type.[16]

In the Experimental Non-Production category, McCook Field engineers worked on two American airplanes and one Italian aircraft. In mid-June 1918, the Airplane Engineering Department, in coordination with a contractor, initiated redesign and standardization of the Vought VE-7 two-place biplane advanced trainer. This Lewis and Vought Corporation product was an experimental airplane equipped with a 180-hp Hispano-Suiza engine.[17] It was followed by the VE-8 model, four of which were ordered by the Air Service for testing at McCook Field. The VE-8 was basically wood, and in the final analysis was not a satisfactory performer. Pilots claimed that it was "sluggish on controls and handled like a heavy DeHavilland 4 two-seater." Ground crews complained of "excessively difficult maintenance problems." Of the four VE-8s ordered, only two were delivered to McCook. One was static-tested and the other was flight-tested. No further orders were placed for the aircraft.[18]

Another airplane whose future terminated with the end of the war was the Pomilio FVL-8. (The F designated fighter, and the VL-8 identified the small V-8, 290-hp

Italian Pomilio FVL-8 with four-bladed propeller (*U.S. Air Force Museum*)

Liberty engine designed for fighters.) The aircraft bore the name of Octavio Pomilio, a noted aircraft designer and manufacturer on loan to McCook by the Italian government. The airplane had a length of 21 ft, 8 in, a wingspan of 26 ft, 8 in, and a wing area of 264 sq ft. The airplane's gross weight was 2,284 lbs. It used a four-bladed propeller and had a maximum speed of 135 mph. The fuselage was built of plywood over oval formers, and the wood-frame wings were covered with clear doped fabric. Six prototypes were to be built in McCook Field shops, but only one was constructed.

Perhaps the most important native American airplane to emerge from World War I was the Glenn Martin bomber, the GMB-1. This big twin-engine biplane, designed for both day and night bombardment, has been credited with establishing "an aviation dynasty . . . [which] shaped U.S. bomber strategy, tradition and history." The GMB-1 "sired a long line of follow-on aircraft . . . influential on world aerial and naval policy. It was the right plane at the right time, built by the right company."[19]

The GMB-1 made its maiden flight at Cleveland, Ohio, on August 17, 1918. On September 2, the aircraft flew to McCook Field. The next day, McCook Field pilots and engineers began a series of thorough acceptance tests on the GMB-1 at Wilbur Wright Field. On October 22, the Glenn L. Martin Airplane Company of Cleveland received a War Department order for 50 bombers.[20]

Given the urgency of wartime testing, probably little if any thought was given to the fact that America's largest airplane was flying over the birthplace of military aviation. The bomber's almost 72-ft wingspan was nearly three times the length of Orville Wright's initial flight of 25 ft at Huffman Prairie (which during World War I was incorporated into Wilbur Wright Field). Each of the two powerful Liberty 12-cylinder engines on the GMB-1 generated nearly 25 times the horsepower of the tiny 18-hp engine that pushed the Wright's fragile biplane eight feet into the air on the initial launch over Huffman Prairie in 1904.

The GMB-1 had an impressive profile and strength: wingspan 71 ft, 5 in; wing area 1,070 sq ft; length 46 ft, 10 in; height 14 ft, 7 in. The aircraft was powered by two 12-cylinder 420-hp Liberty engines to a top speed of 99.8 mph at an optimum altitude of 6,500 ft. The bomber carried a crew of four: pilot, observer, and two gunners. Armament consisted of five Lewis .30 caliber machine guns. Maximum bomb load was one ton, with ordnance carried both within and beneath the fuselage.[21]

The Martin bomber was manufactured too late for combat service in Europe. (The Allies' successful bombers were the French Breguet and British DH-4 biplanes and the heavier twin-engine British Handley-Page and Italian Caproni bombers.[22]) After the war ended, the order for GMB-1s was reduced from 50 to 4. The airplane's immediate successor was the GMB-2—more specifically identified as the MB-2—which played a major role in the development of the Air Service immediately after World War I.

The only "native" two-place biplane fighter to go overseas in late 1918 (although it never flew against enemy

GMB-1 Glenn Martin bomber *(U.S. Air Force Museum)*

Martin M12P 12-passenger transport (second adaptation of the MB-1)

Italian Caproni Ca42 triplane bomber *(U.S. Air Force Museum)*

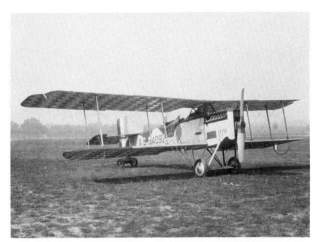

French Breguet 14 with distinctive experimental wing camouflaging *(U.S. Air Force Museum)*

Packard-LePere LUSAC-11 *(Dr. Jerry Meyer)*

LUSAC-11 over McCook Field. This airplane (tail number P53) was used as a test bed for the Hart controllable-pitch propeller (not shown) and the supercharged Liberty 12 V-1650 engine (shown). It was also flown by Lt. Rudolph "Shorty" Schroeder in setting new solo and two-man world altitude records in 1919 and 1920.

forces) was the Packard-LePere LUSAC-11. Manufactured by the Packard Motor Car Company, the LUSAC-11 was designed by French Army Capt. G. LePere, who was on loan by his government to the Army Air Service at McCook Field. The first model was manufactured in the mid-summer of 1918, and trial flights occurred August 13-16. The airplane was a "strikingly handsome" machine somewhat similar in appearance to the British Bristol Fighter. The LUSAC-11 had an overall wingspan of 41 ft, 7 in; a length of 25 ft, 3 in; and a height of 9 ft, 6 in. The power plant was a Liberty 12-cylinder engine generating 425 hp; top speed was 136 mph. Armament consisted of two forward-firing .30 caliber Marlin machine guns and two Lewis .30 caliber guns fired by the observer from the rear cockpit.

Twenty-seven of this model airplane were built. According to one aviation writer, the LUSAC-11 program put the Army "firmly into aeronautical research and development" and constituted "a major step forward in the development of American flight test methods and research."[23]

McCOOK FIELD 1919-1926

At the end of World War I, the impact of military demobilization and curtailed operating budgets slowed the tempo of activities at McCook Field, but did not diminish the mission itself. Much of the momentum of late 1918 carried over into the earlier part of the new year. On November 11, 1918, McCook had a work force of 58 officers, 267 enlisted men, and 1,915 civilian employees. By January 1, 1920, the number had shrunk to 286 military and 1,061 civilians. Between that date and 1926, the work force averaged about 50 officers and from 1,100 to 1,500 civilians.[24]

Jewelers in the McCook Field Instrument Laboratory perform intricate adjustments and repairs on airplane instrumentation.

187

The torque stands housed in this building were used to test engines under conditions resembling those encountered in actual flight. Three double observation rooms separated the three torque stands and enabled engineers to monitor and measure engine performance.

The reduction in personnel resulted from sharply reduced appropriations. For Fiscal Year 1920 (which began July 1, 1919), the Engineering Division at McCook operated with less than $6 million of the total Air Service allocation of $25 million. This was a pittance compared to 1917-1918, when McCook's "patriotic, involved, intelligent young men . . . had more damn money than they knew what to do with."[25]

The fiscal drought continued, with appropriations evaporating from $5 million in 1921 to $3 million in 1924. The active inventory followed suit, decreasing from 1,970 airplanes in 1923 to 289 machines in 1926.[26]

For years, a large percentage of the inventory consisted of World War I aircraft. At the end of hostilities the Air Service had more than 3,400 DeHavilland DH-4s and nearly 12,000 Liberty engines on hand, as well as several Handley-Page and Caproni heavy bombers. At first nearly all replacement airplanes and equipment were drawn from these stocks, and the Engineering Division was forced to modify existing models rather than develop new aircraft and engines. Of far greater concern was the operational danger of the wartime stocks. During 1920 alone, 150 warweary airplanes crashed, causing a high rate of casualties.[27]

When the Engineering Division asked for 50 Martin MB-1 bombers for experimental purposes, Chief of the Air Service Maj. Gen. Charles T. Menoher denied the request. He pointed out that the Air Service had British Handley-Page bombers in the active inventory which could be used for experimentation. An exasperated Col. Thurman H. Bane, Engineering Division and McCook Field Commander, was not pleased. He described the British bomber

as "an antiquated old bus," a "flying barge" that did not handle like an airplane, and claimed that "the best thing which could happen for us would be for a fire to occur and burn them all." He clearly preferred the Martin bomber, proclaiming it as "probably the greatest development of the war."[28]

Despite the unsettled ambience and restrictive funding of the immediate post-war period, McCook's engineers and pilots did make significant progress in many areas. As one author has commented, "Ironically, the lean years . . . produced the greatest achievements at McCook Field, for during the mid-1920s the scientists and engineers of the Engineering Division had little to work with but their own genius."[29]

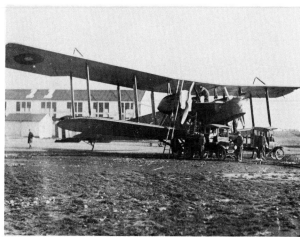

British Handley-Page O/400 twin-engine bomber (U.S. Air Force Museum)

The Cycleplane and its inventor, Dr. W. Frederick Gerhardt

THE GERHARDT CYCLEPLANE

McCook Field engineers pursued a variety of interesting personal projects in their off-duty hours. One such project was a human-propelled multi-winged vehicle called the Cycleplane. The aircraft was designed and built by Dr. W. Frederick Gerhardt, with the assistance of fellow workers in the Flight Test Section at McCook, and financed by private funds. Preliminary construction was completed in secrecy in a barn loft. Engineering Division officials then permitted Dr. Gerhardt to use the McCook helicopter hangar for final assembly of the unusual vehicle and to house it during tests.

The Cycleplane had seven vertically-mounted wings. Inside, the operator powered the aircraft by pedalling a bicycle gear attached to the propeller. An automobile towed the Cycleplane into the air, glider-fashion, after which Dr. Gerhardt was able to maintain steady, level flight for brief periods. This was considered by aeronautical engineers to be the first instance in which a man accomplished the feat of free flight by his own power. *(Photographs courtesy of Mrs. Darlene Gerhardt)*

The multi-winged Cycleplane stayed aloft "solely by the pro-pulsive power of the pilot," as evidenced by this July 1923 action photo.

During 1919, the Engineering Division devoted its efforts to the design, development, and test of airplanes, engines, and associated equipment:[30]

The Airplane Section of the Engineering Organization worked on various types of pursuit and bombardment aircraft, for both day and night operations and powered by both liquid and air-cooled engines. The Power Plant Section devoted its efforts to developments for Liberty, Hispano-Suiza, and new liquid-cooled and air-cooled engines, superchargers, testing rigs, cooling systems, and fuel systems. The Equipment Section concentrated on such aspects as parachutes, leakproof tanks, flotation gear, modification of DH-4's for photography, a gyro compass, a portable field engine cranker, a pressure fire extinguisher, and a central electric power plant. Approximately 48 different types of tests were run on aircraft, engine, and equipment materials by the Material Section, while the Armament Section worked on developments for various types of machine guns, flexible mounts, armament installations, synchronizing devices, aircraft cannon, and bombs and bombing equipment.

Air Service Engineering School classroom at McCook Field in the early 1920s. Engineering students worked side-by-side with McCook scientists to gain hands-on experience in such areas as the early design of superchargers for aircraft engines (on blackboard and below).

189

In fact, until McCook Field closed in 1927, these were the dominant areas of development in the field of aviation engineering.

Flight tests of all aircraft and equipment were conducted by the Flight Test Section at McCook. Among the most exciting tests conducted during 1919 were those performed on a LePere fighter with a Moss supercharger. Altogether, 1,276 test flights and 3,550 incidental flights were conducted by McCook Field test pilots during 1919 alone.

TEST FLYING AT McCOOK FIELD, 1919

HEADQUARTERS TECHNICAL DIVISION
BUREAU OF AIRCRAFT PRODUCTION

Dayton, Ohio, February 5, 1919

SPECIAL MEMORANDUM
NO. 27.

1. Test flights have priority over all other flying. All test flights will be under the direction of Major Schroeder. He will designate the pilot to fly the test, the time at which the test will be flown, and he will give all instructions covering the flying of the test. The Planes & Engines Maintenance Department will furnish the machine and the crew.

2. Pilot will inspect machine before taking it up.

3. Pilots will make sure that they thoroughly understand the operation of all controls, especially the motor controls, before taking off.

4. Be certain that the air pressure, the oil pressure, and the temperature are right before leaving the ground.

5. Taxy machines slowly, well away from the hangars before taking off in order not to blow a cloud of dust and dirt into the hangars.

6. Take full advantage of the wind and the size of the field in getting away.

7. Never leave the ground with a missing motor or if anything else is wrong.

8. Pilots will remain within gliding distance of McCook Field at all times. There is no excuse for forced landings outside the field.

9. Whenever possible land into the wind.

10. No stunting will be done below 2,000 feet.

11. Report any trouble that may develop during flight, or anything else that is wrong with motor or machine, no matter how slight, to the crew chief immediately upon landing.

12. Owing to the small number of machines available and the large number of Officers desiring flights, no machines will be flown to Wilbur Wright Field or to other outside fields, except on important official business that can not be handled otherwise. This rule will be strictly observed.

13. Certain parts of the field have recently been graded and seeded. These spots are soft in wet weather. In order not to cut up the field, avoid these spots when field is in a muddy condition.

14. Whenever the field is muddy and the wind is from the right direction, take off and land on the runway.

15. All flying, except important tests that cannot be delayed will stop at 4:00 P.M. from Monday to Friday, and at 11:00 A.M. on Saturday, and all machines will be at the hangars by that time.

16. Except on test flights, flying will be limited to one hour per day per man.

T. H. BANE
Col., A.S.A.
Chief of Division

By

DELOS C. EMMONS
Lt. Col., A.S.A.
Business & Military
Executive

HEAVIER-THAN-AIR DEVELOPMENTS

In the immediate post-war period, the Air Service classified all aircraft—both domestic and foreign—into five main categories: pursuit, attack, bombardment, observation, and training. These five main categories were further divided into 15 types. There was also a "miscellaneous" grouping which encompassed such machines as racers, rotary wing, etc.[31] Engineering activities at McCook Field were involved with nearly all of these types, as well as with lighter-than-air developments, in the years from 1919 to 1926.

Type	Description	Type Symbol
I.	Single-seat Pursuit—Water-cooled engine	PW
II.	Single-seat Pursuit—Night attack	PN
III.	Single-seat Pursuit—Air-cooled engine	PA
IV.	Single-seat Pursuit—Ground attack	PG
V.	Two-seat Pursuit	TP
VI.	Two or multi-seat Ground Attack	GA
VII.	Two-seat Infantry Liaison	IL
VIII.	Two-seat Night Observation	NO
IX.	Two or multi-seat Army and Coast Artillery Observation and surveillance	AO
X.	Two-seat Corps Observation	CO
XI.	Two or multi-seat Day Bombardment	DB
XII.	Two or multi-seat Night Bombardment—Short distance	NBS
XIII.	Multi-seat Night Bombardment—Long distance	NBL
XIV.	Training—Air-cooled engine	TA
XV.	Training—Water-cooled engine	TW
XVI.	Miscellaneous	
XIV.	Training—Air-cooled engine	TA
XV.	Training—Water-cooled engine	TW
XVI.	Miscellaneous	

Airplanes of *Type I (PW)* were designed to destroy enemy aircraft within a specified region and/or to protect friendly airplanes such as bombers, ground attack, and reconnaissance-observation. These single-seat pursuits had water-cooled engines and were "high speed, quickly maneuverable [airplanes] . . . carrying machine guns [either .30 or .50 caliber] synchronized to fire through the rotating propeller." The two models of this type which the Engineering Division accepted were the Orenco D-1 and the Thomas-Morse MB-3.

Type II (PN) single-seat aircraft were intended for night operations, but no airplanes produced during World War I were placed in this classification. Day pursuit aircraft were used in the limited amount of after-sundown operations. In 1920, at Engineering Division request, Curtiss built a single-place, externally-braced biplane for this purpose. Three models were delivered to the Engineering Division for testing and evaluation.

Type III (PA) airplanes featured air-cooled engines, but otherwise shared the purpose and nearly the same characteristics as the Type I (PW) pursuits. One example of this type was the PA-1, designed by the Loening Aeronautical Company. The PA-1 was a "thick-wing" externally-braced biplane with a Wright 350-hp radial engine.

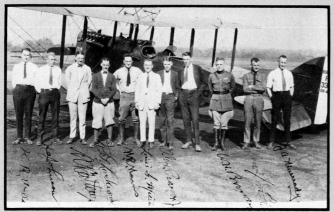

Flight Test Section, McCook Field, 1924. The only man who did not autograph the photograph is Lt. Eugene "Hoy" Barksdale, who died in the line of duty on August 11, 1926. *(U.S. Air Force Museum, Eugene Barksdale Collection)*

Flight Test Section, McCook Field, 1925. The Section's mascots, the Flying Jackass and the Quacking Duck, were placed on the desks of braggarts and those who pulled boners. *(U.S. Air Force Museum, Eugene Barksdale Collection)*

FLIGHT TEST SECTION

The most exciting and glamorous unit of the Engineering Division was the Flight Test Section. Test pilots pushed, pulled, and in all other ways punished and pounded airplanes, especially experimental models, to demonstrate their strengths and uncover their weaknesses. This activity was the literal "proof of the pudding." (Most of the records and accomplishments were attributed to McCook Field since the pilots were members of the Engineering Division at McCook. The actual scene, however, was often Wilbur Wright Field. As a case in point, the XNBL-1 Barling bomber's size prohibited it from using McCook; it lived and died at Wilbur Wright Field.)

Two of the most distinguished Chiefs of the Engineering Division's Flight Test Section were Maj. Rudolph "Shorty" Schroeder* and Lt. Harold R. Harris. Another McCook Field test pilot who achieved international fame was Lt. James H. "Jimmy" Doolittle.

One of Major Schroeder's most daring exploits was an altitude record of 33,113 ft, set February 27, 1920, over McCook in an open cockpit LePere biplane. (At that altitude the temperature was 67 degrees below zero.) Schroeder nearly lost his life on the record flight due to an oxygen shortage and carbon monoxide poisoning from the exhaust gases.

Lieutenant Harris, who became a brigadier general in World War II, set 10 world and 15 American records for speed, distance, altitude, and endurance. Lieutenant Doolittle, who rose to the rank of lieutenant general in 1944, established many outstanding records during his career. These included the September 4, 1922, first transcontinental crossing of the United States, east-west, in a single day. This exploit earned him the Distinguished Flying Cross. He won both the Schneider Trophy speed race and the Mackay Trophy in 1925 while assigned to McCook.

Major records and accomplishments established between 1919 and 1923 at McCook Field are listed in Appendix 3.

Often the price of progress was paid in blood, pain, and death. From January 22, 1919, through May 25, 1936, 17 military and civilian pilots and crew members of the Engineering Division died in airplane crashes. The "Roll of Honor" included:

Lt. Frank Banks	Jan. 22, 1919	Lt. F. W. Neidermeyer	Mar. 13, 1922
Capt. W. F. Jones and George Buzane	Jul. 14, 1919	Lt. L. P. Moriarty and William P. Stonebraker	Aug. 14, 1922
Sgt. Strong B. Madan	Oct. 4, 1920	Lt. Theodore S. VanVechten	Apr. 8, 1924
W. W. Stryker, Thomas H. Harriman, Allan B. MacFarland, Robert H. Hanson, Charles N. Schulenberg, William O'Laughlin	Feb. 21, 1922**	Robert Anderson	May 13, 1924
		Lt. Alexander Pearson, Jr.	Sep. 2, 1924
		Lt. Eugene H. Barksdale	Aug. 11, 1926

*Major Schroeder was nicknamed "Shorty" because of his stature: 6 ft 4 in and 155 lbs.
**Killed in the crash of the airship *Roma* near Norfolk, VA.

McCook Field personnel, 1919. Maj. Rudolph "Shorty" Schroeder is the tallest man in the photograph. *(U.S. Air Force Museum)*

Lt. Wendell H. "Brook" Brookley displays the Test Section's Oilcan and Dumbbell Trophies. *(Mrs. Darlene Gerhardt)*

The *Type IV (PG)* airplane was designed as a "high-speed, armored, single-seater biplane" primarily for attacking enemy ground forces and enemy airplanes. The Aero-marine Plane and Motor Corporation built such a machine for the Engineering Division for testing and evaluation purposes. It was an externally-braced biplane powered by a 300-hp Wright K engine.

Within the *Type V (TP)* two-seat biplane pursuit category the best known example was the British-designed Bristol Fighter. Although the Engineering Division evaluated the respective merits of the Curtiss Wasp biplane and triplane, the LePere two-place biplane, the Loening two-place monoplane, and the Thomas-Morse two-seat monoplane MB-1 and biplane MB-2, none were ever mass produced.

Type VI (GA) was a heavily armored ground attack airplane designed to provide sustained aerial support of ground forces under enemy fire. The first pilot model GA was the LePere triplane. Using that model's general specifications and characteristics, the Engineering Division designed and manufactured the GAX-1, the Air Service's only twin-engine triplane. It was impressive, with an overall wingspan of 65 ft, 6 in, a length of 35 ft, 6 in, and a height of about 14 ft. The GAX-1 used two 400-hp Liberty engines and was specifically equipped for on-the-deck strafing. One ton of quarter-inch armor shielded the crew and engines. In lieu of bullet-proof glass, "revolving slotted armor-plate discs" gave the gunners protection against enemy fighter action. The airplane carried eight .30 caliber Lewis machine guns and a 37-mm Baldwin cannon. The weapons fired from the armor-plated nose which protruded beyond the wings.[32]

Type VII (IL) was a two-seat infantry liaison biplane. The best-known machine in this category was the armored German Junkers biplane. The Air Service counterpart was the Orenco IL-1, a two-place externally-braced biplane with a 400-hp Liberty 12-cylinder engine.

Type VIII (NO) aircraft were two-seat biplanes used for night observation. The Engineering Division did not develop a specific airplane for this purpose since most two-seat Corps Observation (CO) biplanes could be modified for night work as required.

Type IX (AO) machines were two- or three-place biplanes used for Coast Artillery observation and reconnaissance. The Air Service did not employ this type of airplane although "this field [had] some very interesting possibilities" and was considered worth studying.[33]

Type X (CO) was the Corps Observation airplane. This category included several familiar names, i.e., the De-Havilland DH-4, British Salmson, and French Breguet. McCook's XB-1A, which was similar to the Bristol and equipped with a 300-hp Wright engine, was manufactured by the Dayton-Wright Airplane Company under contract with the Air Service. Several of these airplanes were delivered to pursuit squadrons in the field. Later developments in the area of Corps Observation aviation included the Engineering Division's CO-1, CO-2 (only one model was built, for static testing), and CO-5; the Fokker CO-4 and the Gallaudet CO-1. McCook's CO-1, CO-2, and the Gallaudet

Boeing MB-3A pursuit with water-cooled engine assigned to the 94th Pursuit Squadron

1924 Curtiss model PW-8 Hawk pursuit assigned to the 17th Pursuit Squadron

British Bristol Fighter (*U.S. Air Force Museum*)

Engineering Division TP-1 pursuit (*U.S. Air Force Museum*)

The Engineering Division armor-plated GAX-1, designed and manufactured at McCook, was the Air Service's only twin-engine triplane. *(U.S. Air Force Museum)*

CO-1 were high-wing metal monoplanes with enclosed cabins. The other aircraft were two-place, open cockpit biplanes. The monoplanes were internally braced; structural members were steel and the covering was made entirely of duralumin.[34]

Type XI (DB) aircraft were two- or multi-seat day bombardment machines. The best known of this series was the Engineering Division's first product, the USD-9A (discussed earlier). In late 1923, the Gallaudet DB-1 was tested. It was a two-place open cockpit low-wing monoplane. Its 700-hp engine was an Engineering Division-developed W-1-A.*

Type XII (NBS) two- or multi-seat night bombardment, short-distance machines included the famous World War I British Handley-Page and Italian Caproni bombers. These airplanes formed the nucleus of the Allied heavy bombardment squadrons in Europe. Also in this category was the American Glenn Martin bomber (GMB-1) completed in August 1918 but never sent overseas.

Type XIII (NBL) multi-seat night bombardment, long distance. The two best known foreign aircraft in this category were the British Super-Handley-Page and the German Zeppelin Giant bombers which were operational during World War I. The most famous American machine of this type—and one of the milestones in WPAFB history—was the six-engine triplane designed in 1920 by Walter Barling, the NBL-1.

Fokker CO-4 Corps Observation *(U.S. Air Force Museum)*

Curtiss NBS-1

*The "W" engine, designed and developed entirely in-house, consisted of 18 cylinders mounted in a "W" formation, 6 cylinders in a row. It developed 700 hp at 1,700 rpm and weighed 1,720 lbs.

Prototype Model "A" parachute, modeled by Floyd Smith. This parachute was successfully drop-tested 11 times and then used in the first live free-fall jump by Leslie Irvin on April 28, 1919.

Maj. E. L. Hoffman, head of the special parachute development team at McCook Field.

Guy Ball demonstrates the original seat-pack parachute, developed because existing airplanes would not accommodate back-packs. This type of parachute was used by Lt. Harold R. Harris in the first emergency jump from a disabled airplane in 1922.

PARACHUTE DEVELOPMENT AT McCOOK FIELD

One of the most important achievements in the long history of aviation was the design of a reliable manually-operated parachute for airplane pilots. Invention of the first practical free-fall parachute is credited to J. Floyd Smith, a civilian employee of the Engineering Division Equipment Section.

A special parachute development team was established at McCook in 1918. This team was headed by Maj. E. L. Hoffman, and was composed of a dedicated group of men including Floyd Smith, Guy M. Ball, James M. Russell, and James J. Higgins. Their ultimate goal was to develop a parachute which would allow an aviator to leave an airplane under any condition, that would open promptly upon operator demand and withstand the shock of opening at high speed, that would be steerable to a reasonable degree, and which would be as simple as possible to minimize the labor involved in repacking and servicing.

Drop tests were conducted on a wide variety of designs. The prototype Model "A" parachute designed by Smith was the only one that met the required specifications. The first live free-fall jump with the Model "A" was made on April 28, 1919. Leslie L. Irvin, a recent addition to the McCook Field team, jumped from a USD-9 airplane piloted by Floyd Smith, at an altitude of 1,500 ft. Aside from the broken ankle which Irvin sustained on landing, the experiment was a total success.

Irvin's jump was soon followed by leaps made by other members of the parachute group, including Major Hoffman. They firmly established the worth of the free-fall, manually-operated parachute and spurred an entirely new era in its development.

Source: David Gold, "Early Development of the Manually Operated, Personnel Parachute, 1900-1919," Paper presented to AIAA 2nd Aerodynamic Deceleration Systems Conference, El Centro, California, September 23-25, 1968.

Parachute Branch at McCook Field, responsible for the design, development, and improvement of all Air Service parachutes

Live jump from a Martin bomber over McCook (*Mrs. Darlene Gerhardt*)

British Avro 504K trainer (*U.S. Air Force Museum*)

Cox-Klemin TW-2 trainer with water-cooled engine (*U.S. Air Force Museum*)

Type XIV (TA) trainer, air-cooled engine. The best known foreign aircraft of this type were the British Avro, the Thomas-Morse S-4C, and the French Nieuport 23. Four trainers (all two-place biplanes) in this category were evaluated at McCook.

Type XV (TW) trainer, water-cooled engine. TWs were close kin to their counterparts with air-cooled engines, i.e., the TA classification. The best known of the TWs was the famous Curtiss JN-4D Jenny biplane which saw considerable service at Wilbur Wright Field and at other Signal Corps Aviation Schools. The Airplane Engineering Division at McCook Field tested and evaluated four TWs during the early Twenties: the Engineering Division TW-1 biplane, the Cox-Klemin TW-2 biplane, the Dayton-Wright TW-3 biplane, and the Fokker TW-4 high-wing monoplane.

Type XVI was a miscellaneous category. Though the airplanes had no particular letter designation, this classification held some of the most famous airplanes to be associated with the Engineering Division and/or McCook Field (including the smallest, the largest, and several "first-evers"). In 1922, among the four aircraft in this classification was the Dayton-Wright PS-1 (Pursuit Special), a rigidly-braced high-wing monoplane constructed around the 200-hp Lawrance J-1 radial air-cooled engine.

By the middle of the 1920s, the categories of airplanes had been reduced from sixteen to five: P for pursuit, B for bomber (with variations such as LB for light bomber and HB for heavy bomber), C for cargo, O for observation, and T for trainer. The symbol "-1" (dash one) indicated the first model in the category. The prefix "X" indicated the experi-

McCook Field Library
Airplane Engineering Department
McCook Field, Dayton, Ohio.

Bookplate used by the McCook Field Aeronautical Reference Library, antecedent of today's Air Force Wright Aeronautical Laboratories (AFWAL) Technical Library

TECHNICAL PUBLICATIONS AND LIBRARY DEPARTMENT

An achievement of inestimable value was the accumulation, organization, and publication of aircraft engineering knowledge gained at McCook and other early experimental facilities. In the spring of 1918, a Technical Publications and Library Department was organized at McCook Field as a service agency for collecting and disseminating technical information. Originally the Department was charged with obtaining and maintaining technical data and information for use by engineers working at McCook. By the end of 1918, however, the Department was reorganized to form the McCook Field Aeronautical Reference Library, one of the most impressive collections in the country. In November 1918, the Library reported holdings of 700 technical reference books, 200 pamphlets, and 42 aeronautical and technical magazine subscriptions.

Particular emphasis was placed on publishing the experimental findings of engineers at McCook. The first publication of the Reference Library was a monthly entitled "Bulletin of the Experimental Department, Airplane Engineering Division," which gained national recognition for its valuable contribution to aeronautical literature.

Similarly impressive was the series of Technical Orders published by the Technical Data Branch of the Technical Section, located in the Air Service Building in Dayton, beginning in September 1918. These tech orders dealt directly with defects in aviation materiel, proper correction of defects, and other technical information of general interest to engineers working in the field. Also published at a later date was an Information Circular dealing with aviation equipment, and a series of Aircraft Technical Notes giving instructions in processes and techniques used by mechanics, as well as information for specific experiments and tests.

The McCook Field Reference Library is regarded as the earliest antecedent of today's prestigious Air Force Wright Aeronautical Laboratories Technical Library, located in Area B.

Sources: Capt. H. H. Blee, *History of Organization and Activities of Airplane Engineering Division, Bureau of Aircraft Production,* August 15, 1919, p 84; Walter D. House, "Warbird Tech Data," AAHS *Journal* 26 (Fall 1981), 206, 208.

mental status of a design. In 1929, the prefix "Y" was added to designate service test status.

By 1924, the Engineering Division at McCook had ceased all aircraft construction and was concerned solely with monitoring airplane design and aircraft produced by private manufacturers. Although the Air Service devoted almost one quarter of its 1924 appropriations to research and development, the total budget amounted to only $3 million. According to one source, "this period of post-war retrenchment [continued] until the budget for research reached its lowest ebb in 1927."[35]

Of the many aircraft associated with McCook Field in the early 1920s, several models drew considerable attention to the work being accomplished by McCook Field engineers. Four in particular stand out as all-time favorites in the history of aviation.

The Sperry Messenger

Rightfully known as the smallest airplane at McCook Field, the Sperry Messenger was a single-seat externally-braced biplane designed by Alfred Verville, a civilian employee of the Division. The airplane was designed specifically for liaison operations and was manufactured by the Lawrence Sperry Aircraft Company. The machine was less than 18 ft in length and 7 ft in height, with an overall wingspan of 20 ft. Its motor was a 60-hp, 3-cylinder Lawrance radial engine. The 862-lb Messenger could carry a useful load of 239 lbs at a top speed of 96.7 mph. It could climb to 6,500 ft in 21 minutes. Service ceiling was 13,400 ft and absolute ceiling was 15,600 ft.[36]

One of the intended uses of this versatile airplane was that of a "dispatch rider of the sky." To play this role, a "trapeze hook-up arrangement" was mounted on the upper wing. In several demonstrations the tiny bird made both hook-ups and drop-offs from beneath the cabin of the Air Service TC-5 airship. Such a complete maneuver was one of the highlights of the October 1924 International Air Races at Wilbur Wright Field.*

The Air Service ordered 42 Messengers. Some were fitted with "skids and special jettisonable landing gear for specialized missions." Others were used to test various air foil sections.

The Sperry Messenger single-place biplane was the smallest airplane ever designed at McCook. The airplane, built to Engineering Division specifications by the Lawrence Sperry Aircraft Corporation, was designed to carry written messages and orders between front lines and higher headquarters. Using the "trapeze hook-up arrangement" on the upper wing, the Messenger hung suspended from the gondola of the Air Service TC-5 airship.

*See Chapter III, Fairfield Air Depot, for an account of the 1924 International Air Races.

The Barling Bomber

Dramatically overshadowing the tiny 862-lb Sperry Messenger was the largest airplane associated with Mc-Cook, the 42,000-lb XNBL-1 Barling bomber. About the only thing the two aircraft had in common was maximum flying speed: with its single 3-cylinder engine, the Messenger biplane flitted at 96.7 mph; the six-engine triplane lumbered along at a top speed of 95.5 mph.

Historians have attributed the bomber to Brig. Gen. William B. Mitchell, colorful, farsighted Assistant Chief of the Air Service. He recruited Walter J. Barling, Jr. of England as an aircraft designer for the Engineering Division. Shortly after Barling arrived in the United States in late 1919, he was asked by General Mitchell to design and build an airplane of sufficient size to carry enough bombs to sink a battleship during a sustained attack. On May 15, 1920, the Engineering Division sought bids on the construction of a triplane bomber based on statistics and modified sketches made by Barling.

Several weeks later the Witteman-Lewis Company of Hasbrouck Heights, New Jersey, received a contract to build two of the six-engine triplanes at a total cost of $375,000. At General Mitchell's insistence, the Air Service named Barling as the chief engineer in complete charge of the project—with salary and expenses paid by the aircraft manufacturer. Plans called for the airplane's components to be shipped by rail to Wilbur Wright Field for assembly and testing.* By the time the project was completed in 1923, the costs had risen from the original $375,000 for two bombers to over $525,000 for just one prototype. The manufacturer had to absorb the costly overrun. (This cost was never recovered, the second triplane was never built, and a few months after delivery of the Barling the aircraft company closed its doors.) Ninety-four days after work began on assembling the bomber at Wilbur Wright Field the aerial leviathan was ready for its initial flight on August 22, 1923.

The XNBL-1 was not, technically, a triplane. More correctly it was a two-and-one-half wing aircraft, since the middle wing was shorter and narrower than the other two and had no control surfaces (the upper and lower wings had ailerons). The tail structure which looked "more like a box kite than an airplane" had vertical fins.

According to one description:[37]

> The top and bottom wings had a chord of 13 ft. 6 in. and each had an area of approximately 2,000 sq. ft. There were 575 sq. ft. in the stabilizer and elevator surfaces, which had an 8-ft. chord, and 250 sq. ft. in the fins and rudders.

XNBL-1 Barling bomber, designed at McCook Field by Walter J. Barling, Jr., and assembled at Wilbur Wright Field

A TRIO OF HEAVIES

	Barling Bomber	B-36	B-52D
Wingspan	120 ft	230 ft	185 ft
Length	65 ft	162 ft, 1 in	157 ft, 7 in
Wing area	4,017 sq ft	4,772 sq ft	4,000 sq ft
Empty wt.	27,132 lb	145,000 lb	175,000 lb
Gross wt.	42,569 lb	358,000 lb	400,000 lb
Top speed	95.5 mph	435 mph	600 mph

Construction of the Barling bomber was of great interest to Army Air Service personnel assigned to McCook and Wilbur Wright Fields, as well as civilian employees and local residents.

*Only six fields were large enough to accommodate the huge aircraft: Hasbrouck Heights, N.J. (near the manufacturer); Mitchel Field, Long Island, New York; Langley Field, Virginia; Ellington and Kelly Fields, Texas; and Wilbur Wright Field. Wilbur Wright Field was selected because of its proximity to McCook Field.

The wingspan was 120 ft, fuselage length was 65 ft, and height 28 ft. Power came from six 420-hp 12-cylinder Liberty water-cooled engines. Two tractor engines and one pusher engine were situated on each side of the fuselage. The Engineering Division had no choice but to use engines from wartime stocks though they were greatly underpowered for the job. They barely produced the power required to lift and propel the heavy aircraft, leaving the bomber only a one-engine reserve. One authority pointed out, "if two engines had to shut down, the plane had to land—as quickly as possible."[38] That factor restricted the machine's practical operational range to the Midwest, between the Mississippi River and the Appalachian mountains.

The Barling carried seven .30 caliber Lewis machine guns which were operated from five positions, thereby covering "practically the whole field" of incoming hostile fire. Bomb racks beneath the gasoline tanks were designed to carry any of the bombs in the Air Service inventory, including the giant 2,000 and 4,000-lb bombs developed for use against battleships. "Trap doors" in the bottom of the fuselage permitted bomb drops.

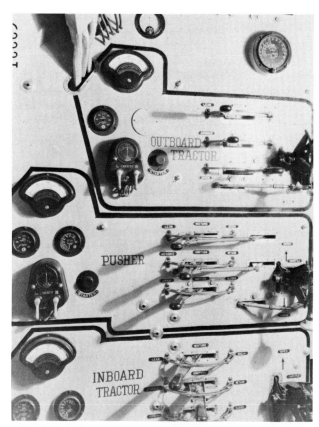

A portion of the complex instrument panel of the Barling bomber

Barling bomber in flight over Wilbur Wright Field

The Barling bomber sits inside the hangar being constructed specifically to house it.

Postcard issued to commemorate the maiden flight of the Barling bomber on August 22, 1923, signed by pilots Lts. Harold R. Harris and Muir S. Fairchild (*Bob and Dottie Gheen*)

**BARLING BOMBER WORLD RECORDS
OCTOBER 25 AND 27, 1923**

Record with a Useful Load of 2,000 kg (4,409.24 lbs):
October 25, 1923: Altitude of 2,049 meters (6,722.4 ft)

Record with a Useful Load of 3,000 kg (6,613.86 lbs):
October 27, 1923: Altitude of 1,629 meters (5,344 ft)
Duration of 1 hr, 19 min, 11.8 sec

Source: "New World's Records," *Aviation* 16 (Feb. 11, 1924), 147.

With Lt. Harold R. Harris (later brigadier general), Chief of the McCook Field Flight Test Branch, and Lt. Muir S. Fairchild (later general) in the cockpit, the XNBL-1 made its maiden flight of 28 minutes in the afternoon of August 22, 1923, at Wilbur Wright Field. Also aboard were the bomber's "father," Walter J. Barling, and McCook Field civilian employees Douglas Culver as flight engineer and Daniel Comansea as crew chief. After a takeoff roll of 320 yards in 13 seconds (thereby astounding the spectators), the huge bomber was aloft. During its initial flight the airplane climbed to 2,000 ft.

In October 1923, the giant bomber set four very significant world records, thereby firmly establishing the concept of the heavy bomber. The Barling bomber also made a number of exhibition flights during its career. Perhaps the most spectacular occurred on September 14, 1924, when it accompanied the Douglas World Flight Cruisers on their inbound flight from Columbus, Ohio, to McCook Field. The bomber's last flight of record was made May 7, 1925.

Despite criticism that the bomber failed to reach its popular expectations, the airplane was not a total waste of money and effort. In retrospect, according to Gen. Henry H. Arnold in his autobiography, *Global Mission*, the Barling resolved many technical problems. "Records from wind-tunnel tests, theoretical analyses of details of assemblies and newly devised parts on paper are all right, but there are times when the full-scale article must be built to get the pattern for the future." He pointed out that "if we look at it without bias certainly [the Barling] had influence on the development of B-17s . . . and B-29s."[39]

The Barling's inability to cross the Appalachian mountains with any degree of safety, plus costly overruns and the unforeseen expense of $700,000 to construct a special hangar, curtailed any additional funding for the project. In 1927, the machine was dismantled and stored at Fairfield Air Depot. Shortly after Maj. Henry H. Arnold became Depot Commander in 1929, he submitted a Report of Survey to the Office of the Chief of the Air Corps, seeking permission to salvage parts of the bomber and to burn the rest. Because of residual Congressional interest in the airplane, permission was denied. Undaunted, Major Arnold then submitted a similar Report of Survey on the "XNBL-1"—carefully omitting a reference to the Barling bomber by name. Higher headquarters approved this request, and the machine was destroyed in 1930.[40]

The Fokker T-2

A significant milestone for both military and civil air transportation was the construction, at Engineering Division direction, of an internally-braced high-wing monoplane powered by a 420-hp Liberty 12-cylinder engine. This aircraft, the Air Service Transport Fokker T-2, was a product of the Netherlands Aircraft Company. The T-2 had a wingspan of 79 ft, 8 in, a length of 49 ft, 1 in, and a height of 11 ft, 10 in. The eight-passenger airplane had a gross weight of 10,750 lbs and a top speed of 95 mph. A slightly smaller version of the T-2 transport had an overall wingspan of 62 ft, was 42 ft long, and had a height of 9 ft. It was powered by a 400-hp Liberty 12-cylinder engine.

Fokker T-2 transport (center), flanked by a Boeing MB-3A pursuit (left) and a Verville-Sperry monoplane racer

Lts. John A. Macready (left) and Oakley G. Kelly and the Fokker T-2 in which they made the first continental nonstop flight, May 2-3, 1923

The Coast-to-Coast T-2 over McCook Field *(Mrs. Darlene Gerhardt)*

Lieutenants Macready and Kelly relax beside their airplane *(U.S. Air Force Museum)*

The airplane was designed by Anthony Herman Gerard Fokker (1890-1939), a native of the Netherlands who was one of the chief designers of German pursuits in World War I. He was noted for his triplanes and biplanes. One of the most famous was the Fokker D-7 which was called the "best single-seater" of the war by both friendly and enemy airmen. (As part of post-war reparations, a Fokker D-7 was brought to McCook Field for evaluation.)

It was in a T-2 that McCook Field test pilots Lts. John A. Macready and Oakley G. Kelly made the first continental nonstop flight, from Roosevelt Field, New York, to Rockwell Field, San Diego, California, on May 2, 1923. They flew a T-2 modified at McCook to carry 790 gallons of gasoline in special fuel tanks in the cabin. They made the 2,520-mile odyssey in 26 hours and 50 minutes at an average speed of 94 mph. For this spectacular achievement the pilots shared in the prestigious Mackay Trophy awarded annually for aerial achievement, and each man received the Distinguished Flying Cross.[41]

This same type aircraft, redesignated the A-2, was modified for use as an aerial ambulance. It accommodated four litters and as many vertical seats for passengers or medical attendants. This role was soon abandoned as better types of aircraft were designed for this purpose. (The first-ever aerial ambulance was designed in 1919 by McCook Field aeronautical engineer and designer A. V. Verville. The airplane was a modified DH-4A and carried two litters.)[42]

The de Bothezat Helicopter

McCook Field designers and engineers not only improved the proficiency and effectiveness of reciprocating, fixed-wing airplanes of one, two, and three-wing construction, but they also experimented with rotorcraft that later became known as helicopters. The first rotorcraft constructed at McCook for the Engineering Division in 1921 was designed by the distinguished Russian émigré, inventor and mathematician Dr. George de Bothezat. The aircraft weighed 3,550 lbs and cost about $200,000 to build. It was described as having:[43]

> Four six-bladed rotors mounted at the ends of beams 65 feet, 7⅜ inches (20 metres) in length, forming a cross and intersecting in all directions. The rotor axes were not parallel but slightly inclined inwards so that if prolonged they would have met at a point directly above the centre of gravity. Besides the rotors with variable-pitch blades, the helicopter had two horizontal propellers called "steering airscrews" as well as two small airscrews placed above the gearbox and acting as regulators for the 220 h.p. engine. The power plant was a LeRhone engine.

The initial flight was made December 18, 1922, with Col. Thurman Bane, McCook Field Commander, at the controls. The machine reached an altitude of six feet and hovered for one minute and forty-two seconds, then "drifted along with the wind for three hundred feet or more." On the following January 23, the aircraft lifted two persons to a height of four feet, and on April 17, 1923, lifted five people off the ground. Although the helicopter demonstrated a high degree of inherent stability and completed a successful series of sustained flights, "the Air Service rapidly lost interest in it."[44]

The de Bothezat helicopter, designed and manufactured at McCook Field *(Bob and Dottie Gheen)*

The de Bothezat helicopter in flight, with pilot and three "passengers" *(Bob and Dottie Gheen)*

Inventor Dr. George de Bothezat and McCook Field Commander Col. Thurman H. Bane, the first man to fly the machine

An Air Service nonrigid dirigible lands at McCook Field after flying from its home base at Scott Field. These "blimps" were used for observation/reconnaissance missions. As late as 1923, the Army Air Service tactical force included two airship and two balloon squadrons.

LIGHTER-THAN-AIR DEVELOPMENTS

Brig. Gen. William B. Mitchell, Assistant Chief of the Air Service, was a staunch champion of the Army's airship operations. He envisioned huge airships as transports for carrying troops and supplies long distances, as gun platforms for destroying enemy airplanes, and as air bases in the clouds "on to which heavier-than-air pursuit planes could hook, refuel, then disengage for heavier-than-air operations" such as controlling air superiority and close support of ground troops.

In 1919, a Joint Army-Navy Board decision virtually ended the Air Service lighter-than-air fleet by giving the Navy exclusive operation of rigid airships. The Air Service was relegated to flying the smaller, less effective (and far

less dramatic) semirigids, nonrigids, and blimps.* The Air Service lighter-than-air inventory also included free and captive balloons of World War I heritage.

In March 1922, the Balloon and Airship Section from Omaha, Nebraska, was transferred and attached to the Engineering Division and acted in an advisory capacity on balloon and airship matters. The aeronauts advised Mc-Cook designers and engineers on such matters as improved inflation equipment, better equipment for mooring and handling balloon envelopes, development of motorized observation balloons, use of helium gas in balloons, and airship mechanical devices.[45] Testing activities of the Balloon and Airship Section, especially those involving flying, took place mainly at Wilbur Wright Field where considerably more space was available and where there was less

---

*A rigid airship consisted of "a weather-resistant fabric envelope stretched tautly around a giant metal framework containing gas-filled cells to impart lift." The nonrigid airship, or blimp, relied almost entirely on internal gas pressure to maintain the vehicle's shape. "A rubberized, gas-tight streamlined envelope which was stressed internally with cross cables and fabric curtains" was inflated with either hydrogen or helium. Beneath the envelope was a control car, similar to an airplane fuselage, that housed the crew. It also carried the engines and control surfaces for the airship.

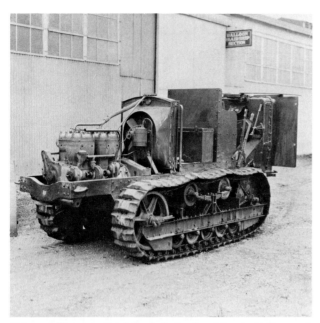

B-1 caterpillar-type dirigible winch developed by the Balloon and Airship Section at McCook. It replaced about 150 crewmen previously needed to handle a semirigid airship.

Although much of the work at McCook centered on heavier-than-air machines, considerable attention was devoted to improving lighter-than-air nonrigid dirigibles and spherical balloons. This 35,000-cu ft balloon is one-fifth inflated in a test of its fabric.

interference with airplane flying. A 72-ft high Terry mast was installed at Wilbur Wright Field especially to accommodate the TC-5 training airship.

Special emphasis was placed on devising equipment for balloons, such as portable gas plants, generators, and compressor units for use on motor trucks and railroad equipment. Blimps required special engines, propellers, fabrics, gases, and valves. The Balloon and Airship Section researched improved methods of inflating and deflating envelopes and of reclaiming gas. One of the more significant improvements in ground-handling equipment was the "grab winch" similar in design to a Caterpillar tractor. The machine replaced about 150 crewmen previously needed to handle a semirigid airship.

The Section built a free balloon that could ascend to 50,000 ft to obtain meteorological data. In place of the usual open wicker basket beneath the gondola, there was a dural cylinder of air-tight construction with weather instruments mounted on the outside. This allowed the balloon pilot within the cylinder to observe weather phenomena without suffering the effects of high altitude.[46]

Air Service airships averaged top speeds of 65 mph and service ceilings of about 11,000 ft. The largest airship purchased was the semirigid *Roma*, an Italian-made vehicle of 1,200,000 cu ft gas capacity, powered by six 400-hp Ansalno engines. The aircraft was 410 ft in length and 82 ft in diameter. It had a cruising speed of 68 mph and a 5,300-mile cruising range. It ordinarily carried a crew of twelve, although there were 45 men aboard when it crashed and burned near Norfolk, Virginia, on February 21, 1922. Among the 34 killed were six McCook Field employees.

Disaster was brought closer to home on June 6, 1923, when the TC-1 training airship burned at Wilbur Wright Field. The three-man crew managed to escape without injury.

A 72-ft high Terry mast similar to this one was installed at Wilbur Wright Field to moor dirigibles so that they could be worked on and boarded outside the hangar. (*U.S. Air Force Museum*)

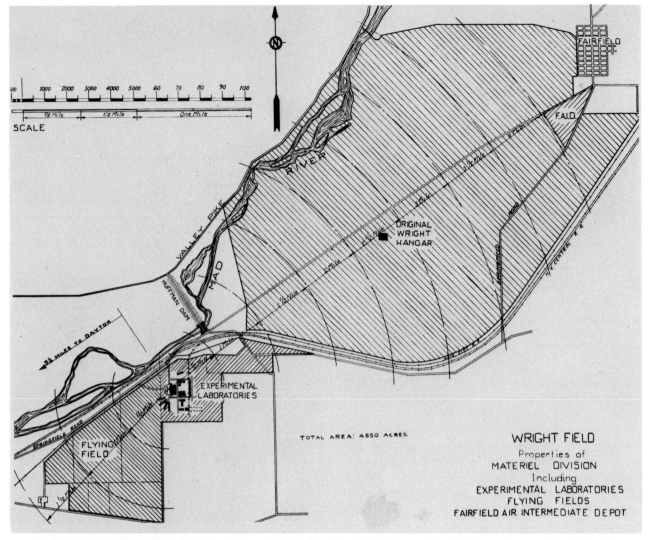

Outline of Wright Field facilities, 1927. The 4,550 acres included the Materiel Division experimental laboratories, two flying fields, and the maintenance and supply facilities of the Fairfield Air Depot Reservation.

WRIGHT FIELD 1927-1934

STATE-OF-THE ART 1927

For many who attended the formal dedication of Wright Field on October 12, 1927, the main attraction was the aerial extravaganza at the adjacent Fairfield Air Depot Reservation (FADR).* In the spotlight were 22 military airplanes aligned wing tip to wing tip on static display in front of the Depot's wooden hangars.

Representing the Air Corps' finest that day were:[47]

DH-4M-2P Atlantic—Special Photographic
DH-4M-2S Atlantic—Special Supercharger
P-1A Curtiss—Pursuit
AT-4 Curtiss—Advanced Training, Pursuit
AT-5 Curtiss—Advanced Training, Pursuit
PW-7 Fokker—Pursuit
PW-9 Boeing—Pursuit
O-1 Curtiss—Observation
O-2A Douglas—Observation

*Formerly the Fairfield Air Intermediate Depot (FAID).

O-2H Douglas—Observation
XO-6 Thomas-Morse—Observation (Experimental)
CO-4A Fokker—Corps Observation
XCO-5 Engineering Division—Special Altitude, Corps Observation (Experimental)
XCO-6 Engineering Division—Corps Observation (Experimental)
XCO-8 Atlantic—Corps Observation (Experimental)
XA-3 Douglas—Attack (Experimental)
XHB-1 Keystone—Bomber (Experimental)
XB-2 Curtiss—Bomber (Experimental)
C-2 Atlantic—Transport
PT-1 Consolidated—Primary Training, Steam Cooled
XPT-3 Consolidated—Primary Training (Experimental)
VE-9 Vought—Training, Adjustable Propeller

Among the airplanes displayed for visitors were a number of models of World War I acclaim. Others were post-war models destined to earn banner headlines in military and civilian aviation in the coming years. All were outstanding examples of their respective categories of service.

The DeHavilland DH-4M-2P Special Photographic airplane and the DH-4M-2S Special Supercharger exemplified the progression from World War I to modern aviation. These were modernized versions of the venerable British-designed DH-4 single-engine biplane which had been used during World War I as a bomber, as a reconnaissance-observation machine, and as a "battle plane" for close support of ground troops. The post-war version was constructed around a skeleton of welded steel tubing, a method developed by Anthony Fokker and made standard in the mid-Twenties for all Air Corps airplanes.

Although the DeHavilland was a bit trimmer in its new togs, it remained somewhat dowdy when compared to the three fast, sleek-lined pursuits displayed at FADR. The most attractive—aesthetically, aerodynamically, and operationally—was the Curtiss P-1A Hawk pursuit. This was the first standard model in the family of Hawk aircraft which, in the view of a distinguished early pilot, Brig. Gen. Ross C. Hoyt, dominated the Air Corps pursuit field from 1925 to 1930.[48]

The P-1A displayed at FADR was a single-place tractor biplane. Its power plant was the 440-hp Curtiss D-12 water-cooled engine. Its maximum speed at sea level was 170 mph. The machine could climb to 15,000 ft in 14 minutes, and had an absolute ceiling of 22,150 ft. Armament was two .30 caliber Browning fixed machine guns firing through the propeller disc. Small bombs could be carried under the bottom wing.[49]

Sharing the spotlight on the FADR flightline were handmaidens to the P-1 pursuit, the AT-4 and AT-5 advanced trainers used in pursuit pilot training. The AT-4, a single-seat biplane, was the first Air Corps production trainer for pursuit pilots. Initially manufactured in 1927, the AT-4 used a water-cooled 180-hp engine and had a top speed of 126 mph. It carried two .30 caliber machine guns. The companion AT-5, also produced in 1927, was equipped with a 220-hp engine.[50]

Two other biplane pursuits equipped with water-cooled engines were the Fokker PW-7 and the Boeing PW-9. The Fokker had been imported to Wright Field on a trial basis from the company's plant in the Netherlands. It was equipped with a 440-hp Curtiss D-12 engine and had a top speed of 150 mph. The Boeing—last of the water-cooled engine type—also had a 440-hp Curtiss D-12 engine. Top speed was 155 mph. Armament on both airplanes consisted of twin .30 caliber machine guns.

Of the three pursuit airplanes exhibited on the FADR tarmac, only the Curtiss was long-lived. In 1927, two P-1 Hawks took first and second place in the Spokane, Washington, air races with respective top speeds of 201 and 189 mph. Impressed with these performances the Materiel Division ordered eight more airplanes for further service testing at Wright Field. Continued experimentation with engines and improved streamlining during the subsequent five years produced more powerful and faster airplanes and resulted in the P-6E Hawk pursuit.[51] In the opinion of many pursuit pilots the P-6E was one of the most beautiful fighters ever built. In July 1931, an order for 46 of these airplanes was

Curtiss P-1 Hawk pursuit *(U.S. Air Force Museum)*

Curtiss AT-4 Hawk advanced trainer *(U.S. Air Force Museum)*

Unusual composite photograph of the AT-4 fuselage *(U.S. Air Force Museum)*

placed with the Curtiss Airplane Division of Curtiss-Wright. The P-6E series remained in active service until 1934 when it was succeeded by the Boeing P-26A, the Air Corps' first all-metal monoplane.[52]

The two categories of combat airplanes with the largest number of representatives at the Wright Field dedication were the Observation (O) and its twin, the Corps Observation (CO). The eight airplanes in these categories displayed at FADR were: the Curtiss O-1, the Douglas O-2A and O-2H, the Fokker CO-4A, the Engineering Division XCO-5 and XCO-6, the Thomas-Morse XO-6, and the Atlantic XCO-8.

Within the observation category the Curtiss and Douglas Airplane Companies were the principal suppliers. A development of the Curtiss O-1 was especially satisfactory

Curtiss Condors of the 11th Bombardment Squadron in formation *(Bob and Dottie Gheen)*

for observation missions where speed and maneuverability were prime conditions. The Curtiss O-1B and the improved version, the O-11B, mounted Curtiss D-12 and Liberty 12-A engines respectively. Both models had a 38-ft wingspan, a length of 28 ft, 4 in, and a top speed of 135 mph.[53]

The Curtiss XA-3 attack aircraft on display was developed in response to the needs of tactical organizations within the Air Corps. In the mid-Twenties, emphasis was placed on developing specific attack and bombardment airplanes as temporary expedients until an "ideal service type" could be identified. The Curtiss XA-3 and Douglas XA-2 were modified from standard observation to attack airplanes by adding machine guns in the wings and light bombs in the fuselage. The A-3 became the Air Corps' first production attack airplane. It was a two-seat open cockpit biplane with a 435-hp Curtiss V-1150 engine. The vehicle carried six .30 caliber machine guns and 300 lbs of bombs and had a top speed of 140 mph. The Douglas XA-2 was a variation of the O-2 family of Douglas observation biplanes. The XA-2 was equipped with a 420-hp Liberty V-1410 engine and had a top speed of 130 mph with a range of 500 miles.[54]

The three largest airplanes on display at FADR were two bombers and a transport. In addition to size, their power and load capacity reflected a significant progression in those categories of airplanes since World War I.

The Huff-Daland (Keystone) XHB-1 Cyclops bomber was a single-engine biplane.* Its wingspan was 84 ft, 7 in, and length was 59 ft, 7 in. It carried a four-man crew, six .30 caliber machine guns, and 4,000 lbs of bombs. Built in 1926, this machine was the Air Corps' only single-engine heavy bomber experiment.

Just a few weeks prior to the Wright Field dedication, the newest Air Corps bomber arrived for testing and evaluation. This was the Curtiss XB-2 Condor biplane, equipped with two 600-hp Curtiss engines. Wingspan was 90 ft and length was 47 ft, 5 in. The airplane carried a five-man crew, six .30 caliber machine guns, and 4,000 lbs of bombs. Maximum speed was 128 mph and service ceiling was 15,000 ft.[55] A unique feature of the aircraft was that gunners were placed in a turret in the rear of each engine nacelle.

The most popular airplane at the October 1927 exhibit was the Fokker C-2 trimotor transport built by the Atlantic

*Huff-Daland Airplanes, Inc. was reorganized as the Keystone Aircraft Corporation in 1927.

Aircraft Corporation.* First manufactured in 1925, the airplane was already making headlines in the world's newspapers. In its original configuration, the high-wing cabin-plane had a wingspan of 63 ft, 4 in, a length of 49 ft, 2 in, and a height of 12 ft, 9 in. (Later, special types of missions led to altered specifications and measurements.) The original power plants were three 220-hp Wright Whirlwind 9-cylinder radial air-cooled engines. Top and cruising speeds were 122 mph and 100 mph respectively.[56] The Fokker fuselage and wings were constructed from plywood, in contrast to the equally famous and much safer all-metal Ford trimotor transport.

A Fokker transport made the first flight over the North Pole on May 2, 1926, with Lt. Cmdr. Richard E. Byrd, USN, as navigator and Floyd Bennett as pilot. Thirteen months later, two airplanes of the same type flew across the Pacific and Atlantic Oceans respectively—on the same day! Wright Field and the Dayton area had a special interest in the Pacific adventure, for that airplane (*Bird of Paradise*) was modified locally and one member of the two-man crew was assigned to the Materiel Division.

The *Bird of Paradise*

In September 1926 the Materiel Division purchased a Fokker C-2 to fulfill a special mission, the testing of experimental radio directional beacons as navigational aids. Plans called for one such beacon to be installed near San Francisco and another on the island of Maui in the Hawaiian archipelago. An airplane was to fly between Oakland, California, and Wheeler Field, Hawaii, guided solely by the beacons. If such navigational aids proved to be effective, both military and civilian aviation would take a collective giant stride forward. There was also an unpublished reason for the experiment—to generate favorable publicity for the Air Corps in its struggle to secure more funds and better airplanes in order to expand its mission beyond the coastlines.

Shortly after the C-2 was accepted, it flew to FADR where Wright Field technicians installed additional fuel tanks and made other modifications to prepare it for the perilous Pacific flight. Among the experts engaged in this effort were the Assistant Chief of the Materials Laboratory, L. B. Hendricks; aeronautical engineer Fred Herman; navigation engineers Bradley Jones and Victor E. Showalter; radio engineers Clayton C. Shangeraw and Ford Studebaker; and airplane mechanic James Rivers.

Pilot for the historic flight was Lt. Lester J. Maitland, Assistant Executive Officer to the Assistant Secretary of War for Aeronautics, Washington, D.C., and former McCook Field test pilot. Navigator was Lt. Albert F. Hegenberger of McCook Field. A former Chief of the Instrument and Navigation Branch, Hegenberger was a pioneer in the development of aerial navigation.[57]

Charles Lindbergh visits Wright Field, June 22, 1927. Left to right: Orville Wright, Maj. John F. Curry, former McCook Field Commander, Lindbergh, and Brig. Gen. William E. Gillmore, Chief, Air Corps Materiel Division.

TRANSOCEANIC PIONEERS

In no later year did the aviation world thrill to as many spectacular achievements as were flown in 1927. All involved extremely hazardous nonstop transoceanic flights which tested to the maximum degree the courage and professionalism of the aviators and the mettle of their machines.

Perhaps the most famous flight, logged forever in the hearts of aviation buffs, was the May 20-21 nonstop 3,610-mile mission of Charles A. Lindbergh from Mineola, Long Island, New York, to Paris, France, in 33 hours, 29 minutes, 30 seconds. His Ryan airplane, the *Spirit of St. Louis*, was a high-wing monoplane equipped with a single Wright J-5C engine.

On June 4-5, 1927, Clarence D. Chamberlain and Charles Levine flew the high-wing Bellanca single-engine monoplane *Columbia* from Roosevelt Field, New York, to the outskirts of Berlin, Germany. The nonstop 3,911-mile flight was made in 43 hours, 49 minutes.

Yet a third Atlantic crossing was made June 29-July 1, 1927, when Lt. Cmdr. Richard E. Byrd, USN, and a three-man crew flew the Fokker T-2 high-wing cabinplane *America* from Roosevelt Field, New York, to Ver-Sur-Mer, France. The 3,477-mile flight was completed in 46 hours, 6 minutes, and established a new record for a four-man transoceanic flight.

These flights, and the signal mission of the *Bird of Paradise*, were more than transitory banner headline achievements. These exploits made the general public permanently "air-minded," in the words of Brig. Gen. William E. Gillmore, Chief of the Air Corps Materiel Division at Wright Field. They were also, General Gillmore observed, a "most convincing demonstration of the improved reliability of aircraft," which had been obtained only through "constant experimentation and service use" of Air Corps equipment before it was released for quantity production.

Sources: Air Force Pamphlet 190-2-2, p 25; Brig. Gen. W. E. Gillmore, "Review of Air Corps Developments in 1927," press release prepared by Hq Materiel Division, Wright Field, January 31, 1928.

*The Atlantic Aircraft Corporation went into business in 1924. Anthony Fokker was the company's first President. Atlantic-Fokker, as it was sometimes known, became General Aviation Corporation, an affiliate of General Motors, in May 1930. Fokker-designed products of Atlantic and General Aviation were commonly known as Fokker airplanes.

Fokker C-2 *Bird of Paradise*

The intrepid airmen picked up the modified Fokker C-2, named the *Bird of Paradise*, at FADR on June 15, 1927, and headed toward California. On this "shakedown" flight, a select crew of Wright Field civilian experts closely monitored the performance of both airplane and equipment in preparation for the transoceanic flight. At Rockwell Field, San Diego, a 70-gallon auxiliary fuel tank was installed in the Fokker's already cramped fuselage.

The radio directional beacon system to be tested on the flight to Hawaii was described by Lieutenant Maitland in a contemporary article:[58]

> An electric current [is] sent through the air at a set wave length and forms an airway along which the plane travels to its destination. The airway has three parallel zones—the T, N, and A zones. The T zone is the center of the road. It is about two miles wide at its maximum. While his ship stays in the center zone the pilot gets the [Morse] code letter T through his receiving set. If he veers to the right the T changes to an A; if he swings to the left the T gives way to N. All the pilot has to do when he hears N or A is to correct his course.

The beacon also operated three lights on the aircraft instrument panel. A white light indicated the airplane was on the correct or true course; a red light indicated the airplane had strayed to the left, and a green light warned when it wandered too far to the right.

By June 28, the airplane and crew were prepared, and at 7:15 a.m. the *Bird of Paradise*, with Lieutenants Maitland and Hegenberger aboard, took off from the Oakland Municipal Airport. Shortly after departure the new earth induction compass failed, and Lieutenant Hegenberger was forced to navigate by other means. The crew's radio receiver also failed and could be used only intermittently throughout the long flight. Lieutenant Hegenberger resorted primarily to celestial navigation, making sextant observations through a port located in the top of the aircraft's fuselage. He also took drift readings and utilized basic dead reckoning techniques throughout the flight. His navigation was so accurate that the flight ended directly on target.[59]

Lts. Lester J. Maitland (right) and Albert F. Hegenberger, crew of the historic 1927 C-2 Hawaiian Flight

The *Bird of Paradise* circles Wheeler Field before landing. The first-ever aerial crossing from the mainland to Hawaii was completed in 25 hours, 50 minutes on June 28-29, 1927.

Lts. Maitland and Hegenberger decorated with traditional Hawaiian leis *(U.S. Air Force Museum)*

By optimistic estimate, the *Bird of Paradise* should have touched down at Wheeler Field on Oahu about 3:00 a.m. Hawaiian Standard Time, June 29. Island residents and military people turned out by the thousands, bringing picnic baskets under their arms to welcome the fliers. After waiting for two hours, much of the crowd sadly concluded that the airplane and its crew had probably been lost at sea.

Not so. Lieutenant Hegenberger had sighted the Kauai lighthouse on schedule, but then had to circle offshore for about three hours waiting for first light and clear visibility of the Wheeler runway. The airplane landed at 6:29 a.m., Hawaiian time, thus completing a 2,407-mile journey in 25 hours and 50 minutes.

The courageous aviators were feted by the military and civilian communities. "Feather capes of the Hawaiian Alii—the royalty—were presented amid appropriate ceremony at a banquet at Waikiki's plush New Royal Hawaiian Hotel."[60] The officers returned to California several days later aboard the Army transport *Maui*. Both received the Distinguished Flying Cross and were awarded the Mackay Trophy for 1927.

EARLY WRIGHT FIELD DEVELOPMENTS

Development of 500- and 600-hp engines to the point where they could be mounted in existing airplanes was a major milestone in 1928. These improved power plants included the Curtiss H-1640 hexagon air-cooled radial engine; the Curtiss V-1570 vee-type water-cooled engine; the

Wright Field, 1929. This small nucleus of laboratories and shops grew to a powerful industrial complex during World War II.

Pratt & Whitney R-1960 Hornet air-cooled radial engine; and the Wright R-1570 Cyclone and V-1640 air-cooled radial engines.

Over the next several years, progress continued to focus on improvements in power plants and in the "aerodynamical, flying, and structural characteristics of service airplanes."[61] Three significant achievements, for example, were realized in the area of improved engines. One was the development of ring-type cowling for cooling air-cooled radial engines. This innovation increased a typical pursuit airplane's speed by 17 mph. Another gain was the first successful application of high-temperature liquid cooling to water-cooled engines, which reduced the size of the radiator by 70 percent. The third area of significant research was continued development of anti-knock aviation gasoline.

Many improvements were made in aerodynamic and structural characteristics. Drag was reduced through improved airfoil design, retractable landing gear, faired chassis, and better streamlining of cockpit enclosures, windshields, and other external portions of the airplane. Streamlining was also improved by "varying the aspect ratio of the fuselage and by adding ring cowling." Other efforts at improving the overall structure explored using wings of various sections as "high, low, and mid-wing monoplanes with single and twin-engined installations and in some cases by using slots, flaps, and floating ailerons."[62] Development of the all-metal airplane continued "with a decided tendency toward monoplane monocoque con-struction because of its more efficient structural and aerodynamic qualities."[63]

The active airplane inventory in the late 1920s and early 1930s contained eight general types of vehicles:

Class	Designation
Attack	A
Bombardment	B
Transport (cargo, ambulance, workshop)	C
Observation	O
Pursuit	P
Photographic	F*
Primary Training	PT
Basic Training	BT

Their specific status was defined by the use of prefixes:

Experimental Status	X
Service Test Status	Y, Y1
Obsolete Status	Z

Attack Airplanes

In the attack category, the Curtiss Falcon A-3 biplane was the standard attack vehicle in the late 1920s. The Curtiss A-3A served as "limited standard," while the A-3B served as a "substitute standard" attack aircraft. Improvements in the A-3B model included Frise ailerons, oleo-type landing gear, and simplified wing gun installations. By

EVOLUTION OF USAF AIRCRAFT INSIGNIA

AIRPLANE COLORS

From 1917 through 1926 Army Air Service airplanes were painted olive drab (OD) color. In 1927, airplanes were brightened with wings and tail surfaces painted chrome yellow; fuselages, wheels, and struts continued to be OD. In 1934, Air Corps blue was substituted for the OD color on the fuselage, cowling, struts, and wheel pants. Wings and tails remained yellow. In 1938, aluminum (silver) finish was adopted for all Air Corps tactical aircraft. Trainers and amphibians retained their blue and yellow scheme into World War II.

The color of tails was changed. The original 1917 scheme had vertical red, white, and blue with blue at the rudder post. During 1918, the pattern was changed briefly, putting red at the rudder post, but returned to the original form after the end of World War I. In 1927, the pattern became "thirteen alternating horizontal red and white stripes added to the vertical blue."

Sources: Peter Bowers, "Forgotten Fighters," *Air Progress* (Fall 1962), 41; Memo, Office Chief of Air Service to Engineering Division, no subj., February 12, 1925.

---

*During Fiscal Year 1934, the designation Photographic (F) was discontinued since all photographic work was henceforth to be accomplished from observation airplanes. In a related move, the Observation category divided to include a separate classification for Observation Amphibian (OA).

1930, the A-3B had become the standard attack type.

During Fiscal Year 1930, the Materiel Division purchased two additional airplanes for evaluation purposes, a Fokker XA-7 and a Curtiss XA-8. Both were single engine two-place low-wing monoplanes of all-metal monocoque construction.*

The Fokker XA-7 was equipped with a 600-hp Curtiss G1V-1570 Prestone-cooled engine and a cantilever-type wing, carried 400 lbs of bombs, and was armed with four fixed M-2 .30 caliber machine guns (two in each lower wing firing outside the propeller disc) and one flexible machine gun mounted on the rear cockpit.** The Curtiss XA-8 had a direct drive V-1570 Prestone-cooled engine and a multiple-spar cantilever wing with external bracing, slots, and flaps. Armament was identical to the XA-7.

By the beginning of Fiscal Year 1932, the XA-8 had progressed to the point where a service test contract was let for 13 aircraft of this type. (The XA-7 was not produced in quantity.) Three A-8 Shrikes were delivered by the end of the year. The Shrike had a wingspan of 44 ft and a length of 32 ft, 6 in. It was powered with a 600-hp Curtiss V-1570 Conqueror engine. Top speed was 196 mph. The Shrike featured two enclosed cockpits "fully convertible for the pilot and semi-convertible for the gunner."[64]

Subsequent improvements in the Curtiss A-8 design led to the development of the Curtiss A-10, with a Pratt & Whitney R-1690 engine, and the Curtiss A-12, powered by an R-1820-21 air-cooled engine. Forty-six Model A-12 Shrikes were purchased by the Air Corps during Fiscal Year 1933.

Materiel Division engineers also monitored developments in attack/pursuit aircraft made by the Consolidated Aircraft Corporation, such as the four A-11 airplanes produced for the Air Corps during the early 1930s. The A-11, which also carried P-30 and PB-2 designations, was an all-metal low-wing monoplane with an unbraced cantilever wing, enclosed cockpit, and retractable landing gear. The power plant was a liquid-cooled 675-hp V-1570 engine; top speed was 225 mph. The airplane was a two-seater and carried five guns and 300 lbs of bombs.[65]

Curtiss A-3 Falcon

A-3 Falcon with Curtiss D-12D engine, 1927 *(U.S. Air Force Museum)*

Curtiss XA-8 all-metal monoplane *(U.S. Air Force Museum)*

Consolidated A-11 attack with retractable landing gear (33rd Pursuit Squadron) *(U.S. Air Force Museum)*

Flexible machine gun mounted on the rear cockpit of the XA-8 *(U.S. Air Force Museum)*

*Monocoque is defined as a fuselage structure in which "the stressed outer skin (of metal or plywood) carries all or a major portion of the torsional and bending stresses."
**Prestone was a commercial name for ethylene glycol.

Bombardment Airplanes

Steady progress was made in the development of bombardment airplanes during the 1930s. The procurement of the Boeing B-9 and the Martin B-10 in the early years of the decade represented important steps in the design of true bombardment aircraft and presaged the development of the bombers that would play a deciding role in World War II.

During 1928, six prototype bombers were tested at Wright Field. Two proved to warrant limited production, the Curtiss B-2 Condor and the Keystone XLB-6. Both were twin-engine biplanes; the B-2 had two 600-hp Curtiss V-1570 engines and the Keystone featured two 525-hp Wright R-1750 power plants.

By Fiscal Year 1930, the Keystone B-3A biplane, powered with twin 525-hp direct-drive Pratt & Whitney R-1690-A engines, had become the standard Air Corps bomber. It had a single rudder, unlike the prototype LB-6 series which had dual rudders. The B-3A had a span of 74 ft, 9 in and a length of 48 ft, 10 in. It carried a four-man crew, three guns, and 2,500 lbs of bombs. Its top speed was 114 mph.

During Fiscal Year 1930, the Air Corps began pushing for development of a twin-engine monoplane bomber "suitable for fast day-and-night missions." Materiel Division specifications called for a machine equipped with Prestone-cooled V-1570 engines, capable of carrying 1,250 lbs of bombs, with a service ceiling of 18,000 ft and a top speed of 170 mph.

Boeing B-9 bomber and Boeing P-26 pursuit. Note the Wright Field "spearhead" insignia painted on the fuselage of each airplane. *(U.S. Air Force Museum)*

Dynamic test of the Keystone B-3A landing gear. The airplane structure is in position for a six-inch drop. *(U.S. Air Force Museum)*

Keystone B-3A bomber *(U.S. Air Force Museum)*

Douglas XB-7 experimental light bomber *(U.S. Air Force Museum)*

Five manufacturers submitted either prototypes or designs for the new bomber. Ford submitted the XB-906, similar in design to the company's C-4A transport. The XB-906 was powered with three SR-1340-D supercharged engines and carried a ton of bombs on a rack within the fuselage.

Boeing submitted the XB-901, an all-metal low-wing monoplane powered with two 600-hp Pratt & Whitney R-1860 engines, featuring retractable landing gear and external bomb racks beneath the fuselage. The aircraft had a four-man crew and could carry 2,000 lbs of bombs.

The Fokker XB-8 bomber candidate was similar to the Fokker XO-27, a model previously submitted as an observation airplane. The XB-8 had two 600-hp Prestone-cooled V-1570 engines and could carry 1,100 lbs of bombs on a rack installed in the fuselage.

Keystone Aircraft designed the XB-908, a low-wing all-metal monoplane with two G1V-1570 geared engines and retractable landing gear. The bomber could carry a five-man crew and a ton of bombs.

Douglas submitted the XB-7 (originally designated XO-36) which had two 600-hp Curtiss Prestone-cooled V-1570 geared engines and externally-mounted bomb racks below the fuselage.[66]

Boeing's XB-901 survived the rigorous competition to become the B-9 bomber. When it reached the production and acquisition stages in 1932, it represented a new concept in aerodynamic design. The mid-wing, all-metal monoplane had a span of 76 ft, 10 in, a length of 52 ft, and a height of 12 ft. Its twin Pratt & Whitney R-1860-11 engines gave the aircraft a top speed of 188 mph. Ceiling was 20,750 ft and range was 540 miles. Despite a 14,320-lb gross weight, the bomber was comparable in speed to contemporary pursuit airplanes. Although the B-9 had open cockpits in tandem for the four crew members, it had the "big bomber" look and raised the hopes of airmen who believed in strategic bombardment.[67]

The Douglas XB-7 later found acceptance as an experimental light bomber, and seven were ordered for service testing. It became the first twin-engine monoplane bomber in Air Corps history, with a wingspan of 65 ft, 3 in, a length of 46 ft, 7 in, and a top speed of 182 mph. The vehicle had retractable landing gear and carried a four-man crew, two guns, and 1,200 lbs of bombs.[68]

During Fiscal Year 1933, the Martin Company produced the B-907, a mid-wing light bomber featuring a full skin-stressed, box cantilever wing developed originally by the Materiel Division. After initial flight tests, during which the airplane achieved a top speed of 196 mph, the B-907 returned to the manufacturer for modifications. Significant changes included a slight increase in wing area, the use of wing fillets, reworking of the rudder, alteration of the engine nacelles, and the installation of new twin 775-hp Wright 1820 engines. A front gun turret was also installed, and the airplane's bomb racks were relocated inside the fuselage.*

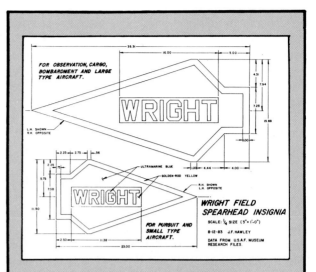

WRIGHT FIELD
SPEARHEAD INSIGNIA

SCALE: 1/4 SIZE (3"=1'-0")

8-12-83   J.F.HAWLEY

DATA FROM U.S.A.F. MUSEUM
RESEARCH FILES.

WRIGHT FIELD INSIGNIA

The Wright Field "Spearhead" insignia is believed to have been designed by Maj. (later general) Hugh Knerr, and authorized for use on Wright Field aircraft no later than January 1931. The apparent significance of the spearhead emblem was that it "pointed the way forward."

The emblem became the model for a standard Materiel Division aircraft insignia for Air Corps air depots. Each depot utilized the standard spearhead outline, with its own initials inside, i.e., FAD (Fairfield Air Depot), SAD (Sacramento Air Depot), SAAD (San Antonio Air Depot), and so forth. Two sizes of spearheads were apparently authorized, one for large aircraft such as cargo and bombardment types, and another for smaller aircraft such as pursuit and attack airplanes.

In 1942, Technical Order 01-1-21 directed that the spearhead insignia be replaced by the emblem of the Air Service Command, an internal gear wheel overlaid with a four-bladed propeller. Despite the Tech Order, the spearhead emblem continued in use at several locations—notably Middletown and San Antonio—as late as December 1953.

Source: Air Force Museum Foundation *Friends Bulletin* 6 (Fall 1983), 17-20.

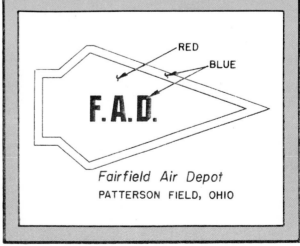

Fairfield Air Depot
PATTERSON FIELD, OHIO

---

*One authority indirectly attributes much of the success of the Martin machine to the advanced wing designed by Maj. Carl F. Greene, an expert on structural design assigned to the Materiel Division at Wright Field.

Upon return to Wright Field the airplane was redesignated the XB-907A (XB-10) and tested as a heavy bomber. According to the official report, "the modifications produced the desired results and the airplane attained a high speed of 207 miles per hour at 4,000 ft altitude and a service ceiling of 21,000 ft."[69] According to a second account, when the airplane returned for testing in October 1932 it was nicknamed the "Flying Whale." Its top speed of 207 mph made "all other bombers then in the Army obsolete," including the Boeing B-9 and the Keystone series.[70]

After reviewing the bomber's performance and evaluation reports, the Headquarters Air Corps Bombardment Group (Office, Chief of Air Corps) recommended the purchase of "additional airplanes of this type to be designated the YB-10 and the YB-12." Both established historical "firsts" although the B-10 gained wider and lasting fame. Their respective specifications were:

	B-10	B-12
Wingspan	70 ft 6 in	70 ft 6 in
Length	44 ft 9 in	45 ft 3 in
Engines	Two 775-hp	Two 775-hp
	Wright Cyclone	Pratt & Whitney
	R-1820-33	R-1690-11

The B-10 had a gross weight of 16,400 lbs and a maximum speed of 212 mph, with a ceiling of 24,200 ft and range of 1,240 miles. The bomber carried a four-man crew, three guns, and 2,260 lbs of bombs. It was the first twin-engine,

all-metal, mid-wing monoplane bomber produced in quantity. Salient features included an enclosed cockpit, a power-operated turret, retractable landing gear, newly-designed engine cowling, and the famous Norden bombsight.[71]

The B-12 varied only slightly from the B-10. It had the distinction of being the Air Corps' first coastal defense "float-fitted" long-range bomber. Like the B-10, it had retractable landing gear and carried a four-man crew, three guns, and 2,260 lbs of bombs. Top speed was 215 mph.[72]

B-12 in flight (*U.S. Air Force Museum*)

Martin B-12 bomber

Alaskan Flight personnel at Bolling Field, July 19, 1934. Their 8,290-mile round-trip odyssey to Fairbanks, Alaska, and return lasted 33 days and involved extensive mapping of airways in and out of Alaska from Siberia and across the Arctic Circle. *(U.S. Air Force Museum)*

Martin B-10 bomber fully restored with markings of the 1934 Alaskan Flight for display in the U.S. Air Force Museum. This particular airplane was an export of the B-10 sold to Argentina in 1938. It was donated to the Air Force Museum in 1971 by the government of Argentina and was restored by the 96th Maintenance Squadron at Kelly AFB. *(U.S. Air Force Museum)*

The Air Corps ordered a total of 119 B-10s and 32 B-12s during the 1933-1936 period, at an individual cost of $55,000, the largest procurement of bomber aircraft since World War I. The Martin B-10 remained in the Air Corps active inventory until the Douglas B-18 and Boeing B-17 arrived in the late 1930s. China and the Netherlands flew export models of the B-10 against Japanese targets prior to and during the early months of World War II.

After the first months of operation the Air Corps became so confident of the reliability and durability of the B-10 that Lt. Col. Henry H. Arnold led a flight of 10 bombers on an 8,290-mile round trip between Bolling Field, D.C., and Fairbanks, Alaska. The purpose of the flight was to test the concept of reinforcing outlying possessions by air. An unprecedented survey was conducted during the month-long flight, mapping airways in and out of Alaska from Siberia and across the Arctic Circle. This historic Alaskan journey occurred between July 19 and August 20, 1934. The northbound flight required 25 hours and 30 minutes; the return took 26 hours. For this spectacular flight Colonel Arnold received the Mackay Trophy on behalf of the crews, and the Distinguished Flying Cross.[73]

Transport Airplanes

In the early years at Wright Field, the "standard" airplane in the cargo or transport category was the Atlantic C-2 (*Bird of Paradise* model). It was later joined by the C-2A, an improved version featuring an increased wing area, an additional 90-gallon fuel tank, and "a more ideal ambulance arrangement."[74]

In the early 1930s, transport developments aimed generally toward a new ideal: a single-engine monoplane that could operate more economically than the multi-engine models. A host of new transport aircraft were evaluated by Materiel Division engineers and test pilots in the early part of the decade, as a number of manufacturers vied for acceptance. Among the early airplanes evaluated and tested were the Ford C-3A, C-4 and C-4A; the Atlantic C-5; the Sikorsky C-6 and C-6A (the Air Corps' first amphibian cargo transport); the Atlantic C-7 and C-7A; and the Ford C-9. These were all twin-engine or trimotor models. The Atlantic-Fokker trimotor F-10A cargo monoplane was specially modified, redesignated as the C-5, and assigned to the Assistant Secretary of War for Aeronautics, F. Trubee Davison. Only one model was manufactured.[75]

One of the first single-engine transports tested was the Fairchild XC-8. It was modified so that in addition to its transport/passenger capacity, it could be used as a special photographic airplane (F-1, UC-96). It was equipped with a 140-hp Pratt & Whitney Wasp R-1340 engine. The airplane accommodated a three-man crew and seven passengers at a top speed of 140 mph.

During Fiscal Year 1931, General Aviation Corporation (formerly Atlantic-Fokker) sold 20 Y1C-14 single-engine airplanes to the Air Corps for service tests. The Y1C-14 was a parasol-type monoplane with a conventional fabric-covered steel tube fuselage and a plywood-covered cantilever wing. The high-wing cabinplane accommodated a pilot, six passengers, and 215 lbs of baggage.[76]

One Y1C-14 was converted into an ambulance and redesignated the YC-15. The remainder were designated C-14 and performed credibly in the transport service organized by the Materiel Division during Fiscal Year 1932. The new service flew both freight and passengers throughout the Division's air depot control area (including Fairfield Air Depot on Patterson Field).[77]

During Fiscal Year 1932, the American Airplane and Engine Corporation (Fairchild) provided four models of its Y1C-24 Pilgrim for service tests. The Pilgrim was a single-engine high-wing monoplane that accommodated a pilot, eight passengers, and 131 lbs of baggage. Without seats the airplane could transport airplane engines or two standard litters for medical evacuation.[78]

An additional entry in the transport airplane competition was the Bellanca Company's Y1C-27 Airbus. It was a high-wing monoplane of somewhat unusual construction in that the external wing bracing, the landing gear, and the fuselage were utilized as an additional lifting surface. Another unusual feature was its "fancy pants," or housing for its nonretractable landing gear struts. The airplane mounted

Atlantic C-2 transport (*U.S. Air Force Museum*)

Ford C-4A transport (*U.S. Air Force Museum*)

This Sikorsky C-6A with Wasp engines was the first Air Corps amphibian transport. (*U.S. Air Force Museum*)

Bellanca Y1C-27 Airbus (*U.S. Air Force Museum*)

This Fokker C-14 made the world's first entirely automatic landing at Patterson Field, August 1937.

Curtiss YC-30 Condor transport *(U.S. Air Force Museum)*

Douglas Y1C-21 Dolphin amphibian transport *(U.S. Air Force Museum)*

a single Pratt & Whitney geared Hornet engine and normally accommodated a two-man crew, ten passengers, and 142 lbs of baggage.[79] During 1933, ten C-27s were delivered to various Materiel Division depots for service tests.

Within the special high-speed transport category, eight airplanes were placed in service testing in the early 1930s. Consolidated provided one C-11A and three Y1C-22 Fleetster high-wing monoplanes with monocoque fuselages and wood cantilever wings. Lockheed submitted two entries, the Y1C-12 Vega and the Y1C-17 Speed Vega powered by single Pratt & Whitney R-1340 engines. Northrop manufactured three YC-19 Alphas, low-wing monoplanes equipped with 450-hp Pratt & Whitney R-1340 engines.[80]

In Fiscal Year 1933, the major development in high-speed transport was the purchase of two Curtiss-Wright Condors which were designated C-30. The C-30 was a twin-engine biplane with a twin-finned tail section, powered by two Wright R-1820 engines. The C-30 could carry 15 passengers and 4,000 lbs of cargo at a top speed of 130 mph. (This same type of airplane was used by Rear Admiral Richard E. Byrd, USN, on his second Antarctic expedition in October 1933.)

In the amphibian transport field, in-service aircraft in the early Thirties included the Sikorsky C-6A with twin R-1340 engines, the Douglas Y1C-21 Dolphin, and the Douglas Y1C-26A, also called Dolphin. The Y1C-21 was a twin-engined high-wing monoplane with a 60-ft wingspan and a length of 43 ft, 10 in. It carried seven persons, including the pilot, and had a top speed of 140 mph. The aircraft were dispersed among Army bases in the Panama Canal Zone, Hawaii, and Philippine Islands. The Douglas Y1C-26A was built on similar lines, but had a longer flying range and could carry one more passenger. It was purchased for newly-organized coastal patrol and frontier defense. Two other Dolphins procured in 1933 were designated C-29 and were equipped with Pratt & Whitney R-1340 engines.

217

Observation Airplanes

In the closing years of the 1920s, the Air Corps observation airplane category included observation, corps observation, and amphibian type aircraft. The observation type inventory was dominated by the Curtiss O-1 Falcon family (especially the O-1B and O-1G models) and the Douglas O-2 family (particularly the O-2C, O-2H, and O-2K models). The standard amphibian aircraft in the observation class was the Loening OA-2.

The Thomas-Morse O-19 series, developed in 1928 and 1929, was the first successful all-metal observation biplane. A total of 175 O-19s were produced for the Air Corps.[81]

The Douglas O-25 series was introduced in 1929. It was followed in 1930 by development of the Douglas O-38 series. Models of both families became standard Air Corps types in the early 1930s, particularly the O-25A, the O-25C, the O-38, the O-38B, and the O-38E.[82]

To meet the need for long-range missions with maximum reliability, development of the Fokker YO-27 was encouraged. The YO-27 and the Y1O-27 became the first monoplane observation airplanes in the Air Corps. Both were twin-engine, high-wing aircraft with retractable landing gear. The wing featured veneer-covered, wood con-

Douglas O-25A, bearing the Wright Field "spearhead" insignia (*U.S. Air Force Museum*)

Douglas O-31 observation monoplane (*U.S. Air Force Museum*)

Curtiss O-1 Falcon observation fitted with wing ballast tanks (*U.S. Air Force Museum*)

Curtiss O-39 Falcon assigned to the 94th Observation Group (*U.S. Air Force Museum*)

Thomas-Morse O-19B (*U.S. Air Force Museum*)

218

Douglas O-38 observation biplanes *(U.S. Air Force Museum)*

struction with water-tight bulkheads for flotation. The fuselage was of conventional steel tube construction, fabric
covered, with an efficient convertible enclosure for the
pilot's cockpit. Six YO-27s and six Y1O-27s were delivered
to the Materiel Division during 1931 and 1932 for service
tests.

Scheduled for service testing in 1933 were five Douglas
YO-35 high-wing monoplanes. This aircraft had an externally-braced gull wing, part-metal monocoque fuselage,
and twin 600-hp G1V-1570-E engines.[83]

On order in 1933 were two single-engine type observation aircraft, the Douglas O-31 and the Curtiss YO-40A.
The O-31 was an all-metal butterfly-wing monoplane, with
a wingspan of 45 ft, 8 in, and a length of 33 ft, 10 in. It was a
two-seater with enclosed cockpits, a 600-hp Curtiss V-1570
engine, two guns, a sliding canopy, and a top speed of 190
mph. The Curtiss YO-40A was of "sesquiplane" construction, and used the Wright Cyclone SR-1820-E supercharged radial engine.*

At the end of Fiscal Year 1933 the standard Corps
Observation airplanes were the Curtiss O-39 Falcon; Douglas O-25C and O-38E/F, and the Thomas-Morse O-19E.
Seventeen earlier models produced by these three manufacturers were classified as limited standard types.

**The rear cockpit enclosure for this O-39 observation biplane was made
and installed at the Fairfield Air Depot on Patterson Field in 1937.**
(U.S. Air Force Museum)

*A sesquiplane was a biplane having one wing of less than half the area of the other.

Pursuit Airplanes

In 1929, the Curtiss P-1C Hawk and the Boeing PW-9D were the standard pursuit biplanes. Both used the Curtiss D-12E engine, though future plans were to replace it with faster Curtiss V-1570 and H-1640 power plants. Also being standardized was the Boeing P-12B, a quite versatile airplane used by the air mail service of the U.S. Post Office and also by the Navy (as the F4B-1). In pursuit configuration, this single-engine biplane was equipped with a 525-hp engine, mounted two guns, carried 232 lbs of bombs, and had a top speed of 166 mph.

In search of a pursuit airplane capable of reaching 225 mph at 15,000 ft of altitude, the Materiel Division contracted with the Boeing Airplane Company to produce the XP-9, and with the Curtiss Aeroplane and Motor Corporation to produce the XP-10. The Boeing XP-9 was a monoplane equipped with a single 600-hp Curtiss V-1570 engine. The Curtiss XP-10 was a biplane with the same engine.

To answer the need for a two-seat pursuit, the Berliner-Joyce Aircraft Corporation received a contract for the XP-16, a biplane equipped with a 600-hp Curtiss V-1570 supercharged engine. The first production model of the P-16 rolled out in 1932, the first two-seat biplane pursuit since 1924.

By 1930-1931 the Boeing P-12C/E models had joined the Curtiss P-1C Hawk family as standard service pursuit airplanes. Many aircraft historians consider the P-12 single-place biplane one of the most successful fighters in the long line of Air Corps fighter aircraft. It was the first production-built pursuit with an all-metal monocoque fuselage. It had a wingspan of 30 ft, a length of 20 ft, 5 in, and a gross weight of 2,536 lbs. Its engine was a 450-hp Pratt & Whitney R-1340-7 air-cooled radial. Top speed was 171 mph.[84]

The P-12 series had a long life, serving with front line squadrons from 1929 to 1936. Boeing manufactured 366 of this series, of which 110 were "E" models. According to the Secretary of the Air Force Office of Information:[85]

> During the 1930's this plane was flown by more young officers who were to become renowned and successful generals than any other aircraft. Lessons learned flying this aircraft were applied in combat during World War II. The prewar era of biplanes, helmets, and goggles was probably most typified by this fine little pursuit.

During Fiscal Year 1932, a new airplane in the light pursuit category, the Boeing Y1P-26, was considered most promising. It was a semi-low wing, wire-braced monoplane of all-metal construction, built around the SR-1340-G supercharged engine. The Y1P-26 had a high speed of 227

Close-up of a Curtiss P-1C pursuit (*U.S. Air Force Museum*)

Synchronized gun installation on the Curtiss P-1 (*U.S. Air Force Museum*)

Curtiss XP-10 experimental pursuit

Boeing P-12C, the first production-built pursuit with an all-metal monocoque fuselage

P-12E during and after restoration at the U.S. Air Force Museum. Markings are those of the 6th Pursuit Squadron. *(U.S. Air Force Museum)*

Boeing P-26 Peashooter *(U.S. Air Force Museum)*

Restored Boeing P-26C in markings of the 34th Bombardment Squadron

mph at 6,000 to 10,000-ft altitudes.[86] After extensive tests, a contract was placed with Boeing for 136 of the airplanes, designated the P-26A.

The P-26A was popularly known as the "Peashooter." Once in production, it had the distinction of being "for the first time in several years the only standard pursuit airplane in the Air Corps." (The P-6, P-12, and P-16 had been reclassified as limited standard.) The "A" model included many improvements over the experimental aircraft, such as a tapered wing, internal aileron control, flush rivets on all exterior surfaces, a redesigned landing gear with single fork strut, improved cowling, air-oil oleo gear, and friction dampers on the wing brace wires in place of the anti-vibration "birds" originally installed.[87] One spokesman described the P-26A as representing the "first major attempt by the Air Corps to modernize its fighter force, departing from designs based on outdated fabric-covered biplanes." The durable fighter became the oldest pursuit in World War II when it operated valiantly against the technically superior Japanese Zero fighter in the Philippine Islands during the early days of World War II.

During Fiscal Year 1933, the Materiel Division tested two Y1P-25 experimental pursuits manufactured by Consolidated. The Y1P-25 was a two-place monoplane with an internally-braced low wing. It was equipped with a 600-hp

Curtiss geared V-1570 engine; one model was supercharged. During tests each model displayed remarkable performance at its appropriate altitude, i.e., high performance at low altitude for the unsupercharged model and high performance at high altitude for the supercharged model. Unfortunately, both airplanes crashed and burned at Wright Field before the testing cycle was completed. As a follow-on, the Materiel Division ordered from Consolidated four airplanes of improved design that were designated P-30 when completed.[88]

Consolidated P-30 monoplane pursuit *(U.S. Air Force Museum)*

Photographic Airplanes

In February 1930, a board of Materiel Division officers recommended the development of a high-wing single-engine cabin monoplane for photographic work. It would have to display "good stability directionally, longitudinally, and laterally" and operate at 16,000 ft. Other requirements were "controllability at all speeds, good visibility, and ample cabin space for camera installation and operation."[89]

A long series of comprehensive tests and careful evaluations were made of the 12 competitors. The Fairchild 71 monoplane was selected and was procured as the F-1, becoming the first officially designated Air Corps photographic airplane. The high-wing monoplane had a wingspan of 50 ft and a length of 33 ft. Powered by a 410-hp engine, the airplane had a three-man crew and flew at a top speed of 131 mph.[90] For the following 10 years it was the Air Corps' sole photographic type.

The Fairchild YF-1 high-wing monoplane was the Air Corps' sole photographic type during the 1930s. *(U.S. Air Force Museum)*

Training Airplanes

The two classifications within the training category during the late 1920s and early 1930s were PT, for Primary Trainer, and BT, for Basic Trainer.

The Consolidated PT-3 Trusty, a modification of the PT-1, became the standard primary trainer in 1928. (In use since 1924, the PT-1 had been the first trainer ordered in quantity since the Curtiss JN-4 Jenny.) The PT-3, and later the PT-3A, were standard biplanes with tandem open seats and single 225-hp Wright J-5 engines. The PT-1 and the PT-3 were the mainstays of the Air Corps fleet of primary trainers until introduction of the Stearman PT-13 in 1936.[91]

Consolidated PT-3A Trusty primary trainer *(U.S. Air Force Museum)*

Douglas BT-2B basic trainer on the Wright Field compass rose *(U.S. Air Force Museum)*

Consolidated Y1PT-11 primary trainer (*U.S. Air Force Museum*)

In the basic trainer category, the Douglas BT-2C biplane was the "standard service" basic trainer. The BT-2C was powered by a 450-hp Pratt & Whitney R-1340 engine and had a top speed of 135 mph. Earlier models (BT-1 through BT-2B) were classified as "limited standard." The BT-1 was the last aircraft in the Air Corps active inventory to be equipped with a World War I 420-hp Liberty engine and had a top speed of 132 mph.

Early in 1929, the Materiel Division considered buying a light commercial airplane for use as a military primary trainer. By the close of the fiscal year, 28 commercial trainers had been inspected. A contract was awarded to Consolidated Fleet for 15 airplanes (10 YPT-6 and 5 YPT-6A) for further service tests.

To satisfy the needs of the Pilot Training Center at Brooks Field, Texas, specifications for an intermediate type of airplane were issued to the industry in January 1930. Six manufacturers submitted airplanes. These were the Consolidated XPT-933, the Inland XPT-930, the New Standard XPT-931, the Spartan XPT-913, the Stearman XPT-912, and the Verville XPT-914.

The Materiel Division officers appointed to evaluate these airplanes found the Stearman, Verville, and Consolidated entries satisfactory for service test; four of each model were then purchased. Redesignated, the Stearman YPT-9s and the Verville YPT-10As were delivered to the Training Center at Brooks Field in March 1931, and the Consolidated Y1PT-11s in May. The popular Stearman PT-9 Cloudboy, when equipped with a 200-hp engine, served as a primary trainer; with a 300-hp engine it was a basic trainer.

The Materiel Division also sought a biplane that could serve as both a primary and as a basic trainer, affording considerable economies both in initial and operating costs, and simplifying the training process. The Stearman XBT-915, similar to the YPT-9, came close to satisfying both needs and was brought to Wright Field for initial testing during Fiscal Year 1931. The XBT-915 was fitted with a 300-hp Wasp Junior engine and additional fuel capacity, and sent to the Pilot Training Center at Brooks Field for further evaluation.

During Fiscal Year 1932, Consolidated joined the competition for the combined-function trainer. The Consolidated XBT-937 biplane, equipped with a 300-hp Pratt & Whitney R-985 engine, was accepted. The XBT-937 also served as the prototype for the Y1PT-12 primary trainer.[92]

WRIGHT FIELD CONTRIBUTIONS TO WORLD WAR II 1935-1945

By Fiscal Year 1935, the Materiel Division had begun working on plans and designs which would, less than a decade later, drastically change world history and introduce a new age of air power. According to Air Force historians Wesley Craven and James Cate, the Army Air Forces fought World War II with aircraft that were all either in the production stage or under development before December 7, 1941.[93] The time lag between approved design and the acceptance of production models usually ranged from three to five years. This meant that the AAF's first-line tactical and non-tactical fleets between 1941 and early 1944 had their origins in the mid-Thirties—1935 in the case of the Boeing B-17 Flying Fortress.

These, and the considerably more sophisticated and destructive airplanes of the latter years of the war were the products of the dynamic development triad of pilot, engineer-scientist, and manufacturer, represented nowhere better in America than at Wright Field. Together, they met the ultimate challenge to produce machines capable of forcing the enemy into surrender.

Specific developments in military aviation from 1935 forward continued the trend toward diversification, expansion, and modernization of aircraft design begun in the early Thirties. In 1935, the Air Corps increased its aircraft classifications from eight to twelve:[94]

Attack	A
Autogiro	G
Bombardment	B
Bombardment, Long Range	BLR
Observation, Corps and Army	O
Observation, Long Range	OLR
Observation, Amphibian	OA
Pursuit, Monoplace	P
Pursuit, Biplace	PB
Transport, Cargo	C
Training, Primary	PT
Training, Basic	BT

The work at Wright Field contributed to the war effort in each of these categories. One historian summarized this effort:[95]

> They don't build airplanes at Wright Field. They don't teach men to fly them. But they dictate the size and shape and number of every plane we use for military purposes. They buy it, follow it into production. They test it to see if it meets with required standards. And they do the same thing with every piece of equipment that pertains to military aviation.

It was air power that ultimately determined the course of World War II, in both the European and Pacific theaters. All eyes were upon Wright Field, the "nerve center of air power," as the airplanes responsible for Allied victories were conceived and put into production.

PRINCIPAL DEVELOPMENTS

Attack Airplanes

The foremost attack airplane developed at Wright Field for use in World War II was the Douglas A-20 Havoc. Developed from the Douglas DB-7B bomber, the A-20 was the first Air Corps combat airplane to have a tricycle landing gear. The high-wing monoplane was powered by twin, 1,600-hp Wright R-2600 engines, carried a three-man crew, and was equipped with seven .50 caliber machine guns. The airplane carried 2,600 lbs of bombs internally and another 1,400 lbs under the wings. Maximum and cruising speeds were 350 mph and 230 mph respectively. Range was 675 miles and service ceiling was 28,175 ft. When A-20 production stopped in 1944, more than 7,000 Havocs (models A through K) had been manufactured for the United States and its allies.

The A-20 was normally used as a low-level attack bomber. It fought in the Pacific, Middle East, Russian, and European theaters, as well as in North Africa, where it was instrumental in defeating the German Afrika Korps during the desert campaign. On July 4, 1942, six A-20s of the 15th Bombardment Squadron made the first U.S. daylight bombing raid over Europe. The targets were four German airfields in the Netherlands. Final statistics from the European theater indicated that A-20 Havocs flew 39,500 sorties, dropped 57 million pounds of bombs, and shot down 12 enemy aircraft.[96] Later in the war, A-20s equipped with radar and additional nose guns were redesignated P-70s and used as night fighters until the Northrop P-61 Black Widow became operational in 1944.*

Autogiros and Helicopters

According to Materiel Division reports, the Air Corps had recognized "a definite military requirement for autogiros" by Fiscal Year 1935.** These versatile machines were intended particularly for missions involving observation, reconnaissance, and photography. Once requirements were established, the Air Corps contracted for one autogiro from the Kellett Aircraft Corporation and a similar machine from the Pitcairn Autogiro Company for testing at Wright Field.[97] These early rotary aircraft were precursors of the AAF helicopters used so effectively during World War II.

The Kellett Gyroplane was designated YG-1. It had a span of 40 ft and a length of 28 ft; the fuselage contained two open-tandem seats. The machine had a top speed of 125 mph. It was powered by a single 225-hp engine but had no tail rotor. The commercial (and original) version was designated the KD-1 ("K" for Kellett, "D" for direct control). The pylon containing the aircraft's rotor was in front of the

The Douglas A-20 Havoc, developed at Wright Field, became the foremost attack airplane of World War II.

forward seat so that there was free access to both front and rear cockpits. The YG-1 version at Wright Field "was tested for all types of missions [and] also given comparative tests against balloons for artillery fire control, night missions with flares to illuminate moving targets, etc."[98]

The Pitcairn autogiro was designated the YG-2, had two open seats in tandem, and was powered by a single 400-hp Wright R-975 engine.

Pitcairn YG-2 autogiro with a Wright Whirlwind engine (*U.S. Air Force Museum*)

Kellett YG-1B autogiro

*A model of the A-20 (A-20G) was placed on exhibit at the U.S. Air Force Museum in 1961.
**An autogiro is defined as an aircraft having a conventional propeller for forward motion and a horizontal rotor, rotated by airflow, for lift.

Orville Wright with helicopter pioneer Igor Sikorsky at Wright Field

Boeing XB-15 long-range heavy bomber, initiated as "Project A" at Wright Field in 1933

In 1941, the "G" designation for Gyroplane was replaced by the "R" for Rotating Wing. Two surviving Kellett YG-1 Gyroplanes were redesignated the XR-2 and XR-3. In 1942, seven XR-25s were delivered as YO-60 Observation aircraft, the first autogiros to carry an "O" designation.[99]

The Vought-Sikorsky R-4, developed in 1942, was the first full-production helicopter for the American military forces. The R-4 and its successors, the R-5 and R-6, were used very successfully in World War II by the Air Rescue Service.

Bombardment Airplanes

The big bomber program at Wright Field is an epic in the annals of military aircraft procurement. In the years preceding World War II, the Air Corps struggle to produce effective medium and long-range bombers significantly shaped activities at Wright Field and brought both victory and tragedy to the facility.

In July 1933, following several months of detailed study, the Materiel Division theorized it possible to build an airplane capable of carrying 2,000 lbs of bombs a distance of 5,000 miles at a speed of 200 mph. Six months later, the Air Corps submitted to the War Department a detailed proposal ("Project A") to manufacture such an airplane. On

December 19, 1933, the War Department General Staff gave tentative approval to the concept, and on February 12, 1934, a $609,300 Air Corps budget was approved "in principle" for long-range bomber development.

On May 12, 1934, the Army Chief of Staff authorized negotiation of contracts for preliminary design work with the Boeing and Martin corporations. Preliminary contracts were completed in late June 1934.[100] This program culminated in the 1937 production of the gigantic four-engine Boeing XB-15. Although the airplane proved too large for the power plants then available, the engineering knowledge gained from the XB-15 provided great benefit in the design of the B-17, and later the B-29.

During 1934, the Materiel Division began efforts to develop a medium-range bomber. Army Circular Proposal 35-356, containing design specifications for such a bomber, was distributed to the industry. General requirements called for a multi-engine machine capable of carrying 2,000 lbs of bombs for 2,000 miles at over 200 mph. Three manufacturers submitted designs: Bellanca, Douglas, and Boeing. The first two firms planned twin-engine airplanes. Boeing, however, taking advantage of the ambiguous term "multi-engine," submitted a design for a four-engine bomber—and won the competition. The contract called for Boeing to deliver a prototype airplane for testing within one year of receiving the contract.

Boeing's speculation was not a shot in the dark, but was based on the company's signed contract of June 28, 1934, with the Army Air Corps for design of the experimental XB-15. In addition, Boeing had a design in process for a four-engine civilian transport (Model 300) which matched the general specifications contained in the Army circular.

On July 28, 1935, the Boeing four-engine mid-wing monoplane, designated company Model 299, made its maiden flight at Boeing Field near Seattle. According to a contemporary account:[101]

> It was a beautifully designed, streamlined, gleaming giant of a plane. The wings spread to more than a hundred and three feet; the cylindrical fuselage stretched almost sixty-nine feet from turret to tail. Immediately striking was the array of four giant Pratt & Whitney engines [750-hp R-1690] protruding from the wing, each with a three-bladed, eleven and a half foot in diameter, propeller. In the nose, a complex of plastic and steel stripping, was a gun position—another bulged from the rear of the cabin, yet another underneath the fuselage and two more on either side of the fuselage. These five gun emplacements won the 299 the name of Flying Fortress. So did the size, as has been suggested.*

After a month-long series of test flights at the factory, Model 299 took off on August 20 for even more strenuous competitive tests by Materiel Division experts at Wright Field.** On its maiden cross-country flight the sleek bomb-

Four-engine Model 299 bomber at the Boeing plant near Seattle, Washington (*U.S. Air Force Museum*)

The Model 299 arrives at Wright Field to undergo competitive tests, August 20, 1935. (*U.S. Air Force Museum*)

*According to one account, legend has it that one Seattle newspaperman, on seeing the Model 299 for the first time, exclaimed, "Why, it's a Flying Fortress."

**The 299 vied for acceptance with the Douglas Aircraft DB-1 (similar to the DC-2) and the Martin Company 146 (an updated version of the B-12). Areas of competition included speed, endurance, time-to-climb, service ceiling, structure and design, power plant, armament and equipment installation, maintenance, landing characteristics, and utility as a type. Boeing Model 299 far surpassed all of the Army specifications for speed, range, and load-carrying.

Military and civilian experts present for official flight test of the Boeing 299 at Wright Field. Left to right: Mr. C. B. Benton of Boeing, Mr. Mark Koogler, Capt. Stanley M. Umstead, Mr. Roy Grooms, Maj. Y. D. Corkille, Mr. E. K. Lasswell, and Lt. Leonard F. Harman. Mr. Benton was on board the 299 when it crashed; Lt. Harman was badly burned in heroic rescue efforts. *(U.S. Air Force Museum)*

er set records, covering the 2,100 miles from Boeing Field to Wright Field nonstop in 9 hours at an average speed of 232 mph, flying at an average altitude of 12,000 ft.

It was at Wright Field that disaster struck. On the morning of October 30, 1935, the Boeing bomber was to undergo a flight test in view of Air Corps military and civilian experts and representatives of the three competing airplane manufacturers. Maj. Ployer P. "Pete" Hill, Chief of the Wright Field Flight Testing Section, was the pilot. In the copilot's seat was Lt. Donald Putt, the project test pilot. Behind them stood Boeing's chief test pilot, Leslie Tower, the first man to fly the 299 when it rolled from the hangar in July 1935. Also aboard were the Pratt & Whitney representative, Henry Igo, and C. B. Benton of Boeing.

The 299 warmed up and taxied down the field. The four engines roared as the airplane began the takeoff run, smoothly lifted from the ground and began to climb. Then the great airplane stalled, turned on one wing, plunged to the ground, and burst into flames.

Lieutenant Putt and company representatives Igo and Benton staggered from the burning fuselage. Spectators sped to the crash. Lt. Robert K. Giovannoli jumped onto the burning wing and "in spite of the fierce heat, reached the

The crash of the Model 299 on October 30, 1935, killed Wright Field Chief Test Pilot Maj. Ployer P. Hill and resulted in the death of Boeing Chief Test Pilot Leslie Tower. *(U.S. Air Force Museum)*

copilot's window . . . forced it open, thrust head and shoulders into the smoke-filled cockpit . . . and struggled to work [Leslie] Tower's body through the window."[102]

Major Hill was trapped, however, his foot caught under the rudder. Lieutenants Leonard F. "Jake" Harman and Giovannoli struggled with a penknife to cut the shoe off his foot and ease him through the window of the cockpit. Then, badly burned, they made their own exit.[103]

Major Hill never regained consciousness and died the same day in the base hospital. Tower, according to one historian, "blamed himself for the disaster and [although not seriously injured] died a few days later because he no longer wished to live."[104] (On December 1, 1939, the Army Air Depot at Ogden, Utah, was named Hill Field in honor of Major Hill.)

A thorough investigation of the wreckage and a review of actions prior to the fatal plunge of the 299 disclosed that neither Major Hill nor Lieutenant Putt "nor any of the others remembered to disengage the mechanism that locked the elevators and rudder while the plane was parked, a simple matter of pulling a short lever."[105] Ironically, it was this locking of elevators when the airplane was on the ground that was considered to be one of the best innovations of the Model 299. In fact, the horizontal tail surfaces of the 299 were so large that "if the elevators were not secured while the plane was on the ground a strong wind could damage them."[106] Prior to taxiing the airplane, the pilot was supposed to unlock the tail surfaces by releasing a spring lock in the cockpit.

While such a tragedy hardly could be described as having a silver lining, it was instrumental in establishing a standard operating procedure which is used today for all airplanes, i.e., a preflight checklist. The checklist for the B-17 (successor to the 299) was developed by the 2nd Bombardment Group, Langley Field, Virginia. Indirect proof of the value of the procedure was the fact that the Group's fleet of B-17s flew more than 9,000 hours totalling 1,800,000 miles during a two-year period without serious mishap.[107]

The loss of Model 299 almost—but not entirely—eliminated Boeing from further contention. The initial Air Corps contract went to Douglas, for 82 B-18 low-wing twin-engine medium bombers; this order was shortly increased to 133 airplanes with deliveries to start in October 1936.[108] (The Air Corps ultimately purchased 350 of these bombers.)

The Douglas B-18 Bolo was an outgrowth of the renowned Douglas DC-3. The all-metal bomber had a wingspan of 90 ft, a length of 56 ft, 9 in, and a height of 15 ft, 1 in. It was powered by two 1,000-hp Wright R-1820-53 engines. It carried a six-man crew, three machine guns, and 6,500 lbs of bombs on racks within the fuselage. A radar-equipped version of the B-18 was used in the early months of World War II for antisubmarine patrol off the eastern coast of the United States and around the Caribbean Sea. Other models of the aircraft were used for bombardier training.[109]

Despite the acceptable performance of the B-18, the decided superiority in all aspects of the Model 299 could not be ignored. Because of the "exceedingly interesting possibilities" of the Boeing bomber, the Air Corps contracted for the delivery of 13 airplanes under the designation YB-17 for service tests within a year. Later a fourteenth bomber was ordered specifically for static testing. The YB-17 differed from the Model 299 in only one respect: it had 850-hp Wright 1820 engines, while the 299 had mounted 750-hp Pratt & Whitney power plants.[110]

Douglas B-18 Bolo (U.S. Air Force Museum)

B-18s of the 42nd Bombardment Group (U.S. Air Force Museum)

Ten Boeing Y1B-17 four-engine Flying Fortress bombers were delivered to the Air Corps in early 1937 and began a year-long period of service-testing. At the conclusion of the year, the Materiel Division analysis stated that "the exceedingly interesting military possibilities of this type reported last year have been well demonstrated."[111] The Materiel Division Chief in his Fiscal Year 1938 report to the Chief of the Air Corps observed that "the success of the B-17 airplane in service indicated clearly the soundness of the basic principles underlying current procurement procedure." In the opinion of Maj. Gen. Henry H. "Hap" Arnold, Air Corps Chief, the B-17 Flying Fortress proved to have "only one predecessor of equal importance in air history . . . [the] Wright brothers' first 'military aircraft' in which Lt. Thomas Selfridge was killed."[112]

Another truly significant date in military aviation history was October 15, 1937, when "Project A" reached fruition with the launching of Boeing's long-range bomber, the huge four-engine XB-15. Designed in 1934 as mentioned earlier, this progenitor of the B-17 and forerunner of the B-29 had a wingspan of 149 ft (45 ft more than the B-17), and a length of 87 ft, 11 in (13 ft longer than the B-17). The XB-15 weighed 37,609 lbs empty. It carried a ten-man crew, six guns, and 12,000 lbs of bombs. Fully loaded, however, the aircraft strained its four 1,000-hp Pratt & Whitney radial engines to capacity, limiting it to a top speed of only 197 mph (in contrast to a top speed of 310 mph for the B-17G).[113]

The Flying Fortress and the XB-15 became shining stars in the Air Corps firmament during the late 1930s. One of the most spectacular achievements was the goodwill flight of six B-17s assigned to the 2nd Bombardment Group, Langley Field, to South America and return in 1938. The flight departed Miami, Florida, on February 17 and landed at Buenos Aires, Argentina, the following day. The bombers returned to Langley on February 29. The southbound flight required 33 hours and 30 minutes total flying time; the return flight was made in 33 hours and 35 minutes. This flight, acclaimed as "the most important one since . . . Arnold led a mission of Martin B-10 bombers from Washington to Alaska and return in the summer of 1934," clearly demonstrated the Flying Fortress' range and dependability.[114]

The XB-15's best known flight was an emergency airlift from Langley Field to Chile in February 1939, carrying 3,250 lbs of medical supplies for earthquake victims. Total flying time for the 10,000-mile round trip was 29 hours, 53 minutes, with refueling stops in Panama and Peru. Generating smaller headlines in newspapers, but of far greater significance to heavy airplane research and development, were two world's records for altitude and payload set by the XB-15 at Wright Field. On July 30, 1939, the giant bomber lifted 22,046 lbs to 8,228 ft and 31,164 lbs to 6,561.6 ft.[115]

B-17 Flying Fortresses are assembled at the Boeing Aircraft factory. (U.S. Air Force Museum)

B-18 Bolo specially modified for photographic work. Standing with their standard and experimental aerial photographic gear are (l to r): Ed Woodford, Robert Feicht, Maj. George W. Goddard, father of modern military reconnaissance, and Roy Whitacre. (U.S. Air Force Museum)

B-17 *My Oklahoma Gal* at Patterson Field for reconditioning by Fairfield Air Service Command repair crews. Decorations on the fuselage translate to: 203 missions, six Japanese aircraft downed, eight Japanese ships sunk, and five Purple Hearts awarded to crew members. (U.S. Air Force Museum)

B-17 in flight over Wright Field

Crew of an XB-15 assigned to the 2nd Bombardment Group, Langley Field, during the February 1938 emergency airlift of medical supplies to earthquake victims *(U.S. Air Force Museum)*

During World War II, the B-17 became known as "the plane that carried the war to the enemy's homeland." Following attacks on Pearl Harbor and the Philippines in 1941, B-17s flying from Del Monte Field became the first U.S. aircraft in offensive action as they attacked Japanese shipping off the coast of Luzon. They showed that Japan had, indeed, "awakened a sleeping Giant." In the summer of 1942, B-17s flew softening-up raids in the Solomons prior to the American invasion of Guadacanal that marked the beginning of the Allied offensive in the Southwest Pacific. In Europe, Forts assigned to the 12th Air Force participated in the defeat of Germany's crack Afrika Korps in October 1942. B-17s flew the first raids over occupied France and made the first raid on Germany in early 1943. By the end of the war in Europe, B-17s had shot down 6,660 enemy aircraft and devastated the German industrial complex by dropping 640,000 tons of bombs on enemy targets.

Although overshadowed by the accomplishments of the Flying Fortress and other four-engine bombers, the XB-15—called "Old Grandpappy" by Boeing engineers—did see limited "stateside" service during World War II, carrying passengers and oversize cargo between air bases within the continental United States.

Even as the B-15, the B-17, and the B-18 entered the inventory, the Materiel Division continued to seek better machines. During Fiscal Year 1939, for example, North American delivered one XB-21 twin-engine bomber. More importantly, Consolidated Aircraft was awarded a contract to produce seven B-24 four-engine Liberator bombers, to be delivered in 1940.

The B-24 represented one of the earliest products of President Roosevelt's intervention in behalf of air power. In January 1939, Air Corps Chief Maj. Gen. Henry H. Arnold asked Consolidated to manufacture a four-engine bomber with a 3,000-mile range and a top speed above 300 mph, capable of a ceiling of 35,000 ft. "Drawing heavily upon experience with the B-15 and B-17," Consolidated produced the prototype by December 1939.[116]

The Liberator had a wingspan of 110 ft, a length of 66 ft, 4 in, and a height of 17 ft, 11 in. It used four 1,200-hp Pratt & Whitney R-1830 engines. The bomber carried a ten-man crew. Early models had three .50 caliber and four .30 caliber machine guns and carried 8,800 lbs of bombs.

The bomber went into mass production in 1941 and experienced many modifications before production stopped near the end of World War II. More than 18,188 B-24s were manufactured, more than any other World War II combat airplane. The three models most widely used in combat operations were the D, H, and J series. Major additions to the early vehicles included turbosuperchargers, more protective armor, power-operated gun turrets, ten .50 caliber machine guns, and an increased bomb load of 12,800 lbs.

The B-24 Liberator operated in every combat theater, especially in the Mediterranean and the Pacific. Insufficient armor and armament limited B-24 operations in the European theater, since the aircraft was more vulnerable to German fighters than was the "rugged and steady" B-17. In 1959, a Liberator which flew combat missions from North

B-24 of the 465th Bombardment Group, 15th Air Force, over Italy
(U.S. Air Force Museum)

Africa with the 512th Bomb Squadron during 1943-1944 was put on permanent display at the U.S. Air Force Museum.[117]

Two airplanes ordered in FY 1940 which gained battlefield fame were the North American B-25 Mitchell and the Martin B-26 Marauder medium bombers. Both were twin-engine all-metal mid-wing monoplanes. Each carried a six-man crew. Other similarities were:[118]

	B-25B Mitchell	B-26G Marauder
Wingspan	67'7"	71'0"
Length	52'11"	58'3"
Height	15'9"	19'10"
Gross wt.	28,460 lbs	38,200 lbs
Engines	Two 1,700-hp Wright R-2600-9	Two 2,000-hp Pratt & Whitney R-2800-43
Top speed	300 mph	283 mph
Range	1,350 mi	1,000 mi

The B-25 roared into history on April 18, 1942, as Lt. Col. James H. Doolittle led a flight of 16 bombers on a low-level attack of Tokyo, Japan. The B-25s were launched from the deck of the U.S. Navy aircraft carrier *Hornet*. The Mitchell was flown in every combat arena of World War II by American, Australian, British, Chinese, Dutch, and Russian crews.

North American B-25 Mitchell bomber

Lt. Col. James H. Doolittle, Rear Admiral Marc A. Mitscher, and the Tokyo "Doolittle Raiders" crews aboard the *USS Hornet,* April 1942

Douglas XB-19 (*U.S. Air Force Museum*)

WORLD WAR II HEAVY BOMBERS, WRIGHT FIELD

	XB-15	B-17E	B-18	XB-19	B-29
Wingspan	149 ft	103 ft, 9 in	89 ft, 6 in	212 ft	141 ft, 3 in
Length	87 ft, 11 in	73 ft, 10 in	56 ft, 8 in	132 ft, 2 in	99 ft
Gross wt.	70,700 lbs	54,000 lbs	25,130 lbs	160,332 lbs	133,500 lbs
Engines	Four 1,000-hp Pratt & Whitney R-1830	Four 1,200-hp Wright R-1820	Two 930-hp Wright R-1820	Four 2,200-hp Wright R-3350	Four 2,200-hp Wright R-3350
Top Speed	197 mph	317 mph	217 mph	204 mph	330+ mph

Source: James C. Fahey, *U.S. Army Aircraft 1908-1946* (New York, 1946), pp 22-23.

Martin B-26 Marauder bomber at Wright Field

The B-26 Marauder entered combat in the Southwest Pacific theater during the spring of 1942, but saw more extensive use in Europe and the Mediterranean. Aside from the United States, six nations flew the Marauder. Single models of both the B-25 and the B-26 are on display at the U.S. Air Force Museum.[119]

On June 21, 1941, the maiden flight of the Douglas XB-19 Hemisphere Defender culminated "seven years of engineering challenges." The low-wing four-engine bomber had originated in October 1935 as "Project D," the "ultra-long range bomber" intended to succeed the Boeing XB-17. Air Corps intent to develop a long-range bomber, however, dated from "Project A" in 1934, which led to the XB-15.

The XB-19 was enormous, with a wingspan of 212 ft, a length of 132 ft, 2 in, an empty weight of 84,431 lbs, and a gross weight of more than 140,000 lbs. The bomber had an eleven-man crew and carried twelve guns (two 37-mm cannon, six .30 caliber machine guns, and four .50 caliber machine guns). It carried 16,000 lbs of bombs internally and an additional 20,000 lbs on exterior racks.

The behemoth was originally equipped with four 2,200-hp Wright R-3350-5 18-cylinder Cyclones. These power plants were insufficient for the demand and could pull the bomber through the air at a top speed of only 204 mph. In 1943, these engines were replaced with four 2,600-hp Allison V-3420-11 liquid-cooled engines, but even these increased top speed to only 265 mph (XB-19A). The bomber was still too slow to escape most enemy fighters. In the final analysis, the B-19, "like the B-15, served only to test, and thus to advance, the engineering knowledge that went into the construction of other and more successful planes," such as the four-engine B-29 and B-50, and the ten-engine B-36.[120] During 1942 and 1943, the XB-19A was a frequent visitor to Wright Field, where its various components were tested.

On June 15, 1944, the first bombs fell on the Imperial Iron and Steel Works at Yawata, the "Pittsburgh of Japan" located on Kyushu Island. The airplanes that carried out the mission were the culmination of a Wright Field program that began September 6, 1940. On that date contracts were let to Boeing Aircraft and Consolidated Aircraft for one experimental model each of a "super bomber." Boeing developed the XB-29; Consolidated designed the XB-32. Both airplanes were flown two years later, but only the B-29 Superfortress went into mass production.

The project officer for the "very heavy bomber" program was Capt. Donald L. Putt, Materiel Command aeronautical engineer and test pilot who had survived the fiery crash of Boeing Model 299 at Wright Field in 1935. Perhaps few military airplanes and sustained programs ever received as much Wright Field attention and effort as did the B-29. It became one of the largest wartime projects at the field, involving scores of Wright Field scientists, engineers, and pilots. (These dedicated individuals later became the nucleus of the organization that evolved into today's Aero-

Boeing B-29 Superfortress (*U.S. Air Force Museum*)

B-29s on the Boeing assembly line *(U.S. Air Force Museum)*

AIRPLANES ON HAND IN THE AAF BY MAJOR TYPE:
JULY 1939-AUGUST 1945

Year—As of June 30

AIRPLANE TYPE	1940	1941	1942	1943	1944	1945 (Aug. 31)
Very Heavy Bombers	—	—	—	2	445	2,865
Heavy Bombers	54	120	846	4,421	11,720	11,065
Medium Bombers	478	611	1,047	4,242	5,427	5,384
Light Bombers	166	292	696	1,689	2,914	3,079
Fighters	477	1,018	2,950	8,010	15,644	16,799
Reconnaissance	414	415	468	486	1,056	1,971
Transports	127	144	824	4,268	9,433	9,561
Trainers	1,243	4,124	12,610	22,849	27,907	9,558
Communications	7	53	1,732	3,051	4,211	3,433
Total	2,966	6,777	21,173	49,018	78,757	63,715

Source: ATC Pamphlet 190-1, *History of the United States Air Force* (Randolph AFB, Tx., 1961), p 7-4.

Consolidated-Vultee B-32 Dominator

War correspondents witness a press preview of the first B-32s to reach the overseas war zone at Clark Field, Philippines. (*U.S. Air Force Museum*)

nautical Systems Division of the Air Force Systems Command.*)

The aircraft's specifications and its stellar performance in combat justified the B-29's classification as a Very Heavy Bomber (VHB) or Very Long Range (VLR) bomber. The B-29 Superfortress had several unique features: it was the AAF's first pressurized cabin bomber, it had a central fire control system, and it was equipped with a complex radar system for both offensive and defensive use. The bomber's maximum fuel load of 9,548 gallons gave it a range exceeding 5,000 miles. By the end of World War II, three manufacturers (Boeing, Bell, and Glenn L. Martin) had produced 3,960 Superfortresses. Most were configured as bombers, but eighteen were converted to F-13 photographic-reconnaissance vehicles.

The huge bomber hastened the end of World War II by dropping the first two atomic weapons used in warfare. The first uranium device exploded over Hiroshima, Japan, at 9:15 a.m. on August 6, 1945. The second weapon, a plutonium bomb, was dropped over Nagasaki on August 9.** In summary, "the technological breakthroughs of this plane [B-29], coupled with the simultaneous development of the atom bomb, ushered in a new era in warfare and strategic air power."[121]

Unlike the B-29, the Consolidated-Vultee B-32 Dominator bomber program was crippled by lengthy technical difficulties. The first production airplane was not service-

tested until August 1944, and only 13 were accepted by the end of that year. The B-32 had a wingspan of 135 ft and was 83 ft in length. The four 2,200-hp engines were Wright R-3350 power plants. The airplane carried 8,000 lbs of bombs and 5,460 gallons of fuel. Cruising and top speeds were 290 mph and 357 mph. Maximum range was 4,200 miles and ceiling was 30,000 ft.

Total production by the end of August 1945 was 118 bombers, but only 15 saw combat in the Pacific theater during the closing days of World War II. The production contract was cancelled in October 1945 and the existing airplanes were declared surplus.[122]

COSTS OF REPRESENTATIVE AIRCRAFT, WORLD WAR II

AIRPLANE	COST
Very Heavy Bombers	
B-29	$509,465
Heavy Bombers	
B-17	187,742
B-24	215,516
Medium Bombers	
B-25	116,752
B-26	192,427
Light Bombers	
A-20	100,800
A-26	175,892
Fighters	
P-38	97,147
P-39	50,666
P-40	44,892
P-47	83,001
P-51	50,985
Reconnaissance	
OA-10	207,541
Transports	
C-43	27,332
C-45	48,830
C-46	221,550
C-47	85,035
C-54	259,816
Trainers	
PT-13, PT-17, PT-27	9,896
PT-19, PT-23, PT-26	15,052
BT-13, BT-15	23,068
AT-6	22,952
AT-7, AT-11	68,441
Communications	
L-4	2,701
L-5	8,323

Source: ATC Pamphlet 190-1, *History of the United States Air Force* (Randolph AFB, Tx., 1961), p 7-4.

*See Chapter X of this history.
**"Bockscar," the B-29 which bombed Nagasaki, was flown to the U.S. Air Force Museum for permanent display on September 26, 1961.

Transport Airplanes

Air Corps active inventory in the transport category in 1935 totalled only 61 airplanes. By the end of the fiscal year, however, the Materiel Division was evaluating bids from four airplane manufacturers who had responded to a new Air Corps circular proposal. Among those airplanes proposed were the first members of the famous Douglas DC family which later dominated the transport field in the World War II years and beyond.*

The Douglas C-32 was the first Air Corps cargo transport from the DC series. Produced in 1936, the C-32 was a redesignated DC-2, a twin-engine low-wing personnel transport. It had a crew of two and carried accommodations for fourteen passengers or a cargo load of 4,000 lbs.[123]

Included on the same contract with the C-32 was the C-33. At a top speed of 205 mph, the C-33 was the first Air Corps transport to exceed 200 mph. The C-33 was also a DC-2, but with more powerful engines and the addition of a large door in the fuselage for handling bulky freight. The C-33 became a familiar airplane at Patterson Field in the years prior to World War II. Local organizations equipped with the C-33 were the 1st Transport Squadron (1936-1939), the 5th Transport Squadron (1939-1942), and the 9th Transport Squadron (1940-1941).[124]

In 1937, the Lockheed XC-35 became the world's first cargo transport to have a pressurized cabin. For its development, Lockheed was awarded the 1937 Collier Trophy for aircraft achievement. The follow-on model to the XC-35 was the twin-engine low-wing Y1C-36 Lockheed Electra. The airplane had a wingspan of 55 ft and a length of 38 ft, 7 in. It carried a two-man crew and eight passengers at a top speed of 205 mph. Three Electras were purchased for use by command and staff personnel during Fiscal Year 1937.

The acquisition of the Y1C-36 indicated a Materiel Division tendency toward procuring transport airplanes off-the-shelf from contemporary commercial aircraft sources, thus avoiding the significant costs involved in modifying civilian aircraft to meet military requirements.[125] Twenty-six twin-finned C-36s (later designated UC-36, Utility Cargo) were delivered to the Air Corps in 1942.

A procurement order was placed during Fiscal Year 1939 for three single-engine Beechcraft Traveler YC-43 light transport biplanes. This model was referred to as the "Staggerwing" because of the negative or backward stagger of the top wing from the lower wing. The airplane was later redesignated as the UC-43, and orders for an additional 207 production models were submitted in 1942.

Of more prominence during Fiscal Year 1939 was the acquisition of 11 Beechcraft Expediter C-45 twin-engine cabinplanes. Affectionately dubbed the "Bugsmasher" by pilots, the C-45 was a low-wing monoplane with a twin-fin tail section and conventional three-wheeled retractable landing gear. Engines were two 450-hp Pratt & Whitney R-985s. Maximum and cruising speeds were 215 mph and 150 mph respectively. The airplane accommodated two

Douglas C-32 cargo transport *(U.S. Air Force Museum)*

Instrument board of the Douglas C-33. Included on the same contract as the C-32, the C-33 was also a DC-2, but had different engines and a large cargo door. *(U.S. Air Force Museum)*

Lockheed Y1C-36 Electra *(U.S. Air Force Museum).*

Curtiss C-46 Commando. Pursuit in the background is a Curtiss P-40. *(U.S. Air Force Museum)*

---

*DC stood for Douglas Commercial. Famous models of the DC family included the DC-2, DC-3, and DC-4.

crewmen and six passengers. In 1943, the C-45 was re-designated the UC-45 and became, according to many, the most popular light cargo transport of World War II.

Another twin-engine transport that earned a permanent niche in military aviation history was the Curtiss C-46 Commando which came into the active inventory in July 1942. The twin-engine low-wing monoplane had a wing-span of 108 ft and a length of 76 ft, 4 in. Maximum weight was 50,675 lbs. Power plants were two 2,000-hp Pratt & Whitney R-2800s. Maximum and cruising speeds respec-tively were 245 mph and 175 mph. The airplane could carry 50 troops, 33 litters, or 16,000 lbs of freight. The C-46 Commando gained its greatest fame by flying war materials to American, British, and Chinese forces over the Himalaya Mountain Range, i.e., "the Hump," between India and China during 1943-1944 after Japanese forces interdicted the Burma Road. In addition to transporting cargo, the

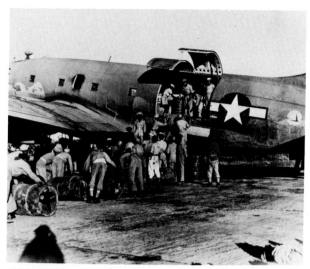

C-46 being loaded for a flight "over the Hump" from India to China (*U.S. Air Force Museum*)

Curtiss C-46s in production. Note that the wartime censor has carefully masked out the tail numbers of airplanes in the foreground. (*U.S. Air Force Museum*)

C-46 Commandos were also used to tow gliders filled with paratroopers. In this 1950 photograph, a C-46E is towing a Waco CG-4A glider. *(U.S. Air Force Museum)*

airplane also towed gliders filled with paratroopers. Altogether, the AAF accepted 3,144 C-46s during the war. In 1972, a C-46D was placed on permanent display at the U.S. Air Force Museum.

One of the most legendary airplanes of either civilian or military aviation was the militarized Douglas DC-3 low-wing monoplane, the C-47 Skytrain. When the DC-3 first rolled off the production line in 1936 it was a luxurious airplane designed to carry passengers (the claim was 14 berths or 21 seats). The vehicle had a wingspan of 95 ft, 6 in, a length of 63 ft, 9 in, and used two 750-hp Pratt & Whitney power plants. The passenger liner weighed 24,000 lbs and cruised between 165 and 180 mph. Within a few months after it was introduced commercially the airplane was carrying about 95 percent of all passenger traffic.[126]

In Fiscal Year 1940, the Materiel Division ordered the DC-3 modified to austere military needs. Designated the C-47, the airplane entered the active inventory in 1942. Thousands of Americans in uniform during World War II came to know the airplane as the "Gooney Bird," the epitome of reliability. The AAF purchased 10,000 DC-3 type airplanes.* This amount was nearly half of all transport aircraft procured between 1940 and 1945.[127]

In the early part of World War II the C-47 was flown by the 5th, 9th, 11th, and 13th Transport Squadrons at Patterson Field. Gooney Birds continued to fly actively at WPAFB as late as December 1968. According to one author, the DC-3/C-47 series was "the most famous transport family ever built." Serving in over 40 countries, these

Douglas C-47 Skytrain *(U.S. Air Force Museum)*

C-47 cabin with seats installed for transporting troops *(U.S. Air Force Museum)*

*The DC-3, with slightly different modifications, was also designated C-48, C-49, C-50, C-51, C-52, and C-53.

airplanes have flown more miles, hauled more freight, and carried more passengers to date than any other aircraft in history.[128]

Another transport that came off the 1942 production lines to gain a reputation for sterling performance and reliability was the Douglas C-54 Skymaster, the first four-engine cargo transport in USAAF history. This was the military variation of the DC-4, and had a wingspan of 117 ft, 6 in and a length of 93 ft, 11 in. The Skymaster could accommodate 50 passengers, 26 stretchers, or 14,000 lbs of cargo. Top speed was 285 mph. More than 1,000 of these airplanes entered the AAF inventory before the end of World War II. The C-54 served on long hauls such as the "Hump" route between India and China. The airplane also made over 100,000 transoceanic flights.[129]

The AAF's primary long-range heavy cargo transport during the war, however, was the C-87, a modified version of the B-24 Liberator four-engine bomber. Introduced in 1942, the heavy transport had a five-man crew, accommodations for 25 seats or 10 berths, and a capacity for 12,000 lbs of cargo. The airplane's top speed was 305 mph, and its range was 2,900 miles. Much of the C-87's work was hauling large quantities of aviation fuel "over the Hump" into China.

Observation Airplanes

In 1935, the Materiel Division awarded Douglas a contract for the delivery of 71 (later increased to 90) O-46A single-engine monoplanes. This observation aircraft had a wingspan of 45 ft, 9 in, a length of 34 ft, 10 in, and was powered by a 725-hp Pratt & Whitney R-1535 engine. The airplane carried two crew members in an enclosed cockpit with a sliding canopy. Its armament was two .30 caliber Browning machine guns (one mounted in the wing and another that was flexible). Maximum and cruising speeds were 200 mph and 171 mph respectively; range was 635 miles and ceiling was 24,500 ft.

The O-46A was the last of a long line of distinguished Douglas observation airplanes. It was designed to operate from established bases behind "fairly static battlelines" as existed in World War I. In 1939, at the outbreak of World War II, the Air Corps decided that this newest observation airplane was too slow and too heavy to outrun and out-maneuver enemy pursuits. It was also too heavy to operate from small, wet, unprepared landing strips and too large to conceal beneath trees. Although at least 11 O-46As were sent overseas, the remainder of the inventory were used primarily in training and in utility roles such as photogra-

C-47 assigned to the Aero Medical Laboratory at Wright-Patterson AFB, 1950 (*U.S. Air Force Museum*)

Douglas O-46 observation aircraft designed to carry sophisticated photographic equipment (*U.S. Air Force Museum*)

Douglas C-54 Skymaster assigned to the Air Materiel Command ice research group at Ypsilanti, Michigan (*U.S. Air Force Museum*)

North American O-47 observation (*U.S. Air Force Museum*)

Curtiss O-52 Owl *(U.S. Air Force Museum)*

phy. The only remaining O-46A was restored by the Department of Aviation Technology, Purdue University, and placed on display at the U.S. Air Force Museum in 1975.[130]

In Fiscal Year 1937, the Materiel Division placed an order with North American Aviation for 109 O-47A three-place, single-engine monoplanes. The first machine was delivered in April 1938 and the remainder were scheduled for Fiscal Year 1939.

The O-47A represented a marked advance in corps and division observation aircraft. In addition to the high speed characteristics required for observation, the airplane was well suited for photographic missions and was "an outstanding weapon for direct support of ground forces."[131] It had a wingspan of 46 ft, 4 in, and a length of 33 ft, 3 in. It was powered by a 975-hp engine, and carried a three-man crew and two machine guns. Top speed was 223 mph.[132]

In Fiscal Year 1939, the Materiel Division ordered 74 North American O-47B airplanes. The O-47B was similar to the O-47A but was fitted with a 1,060-hp engine and an extra 50-gallon tank. The O-47B also had a single-lens aerial camera.[133]

In contrast to the armed, high-powered O-47 series, the Air Corps ordered 74 Stinson O-49 (later the Vultee L-1) high-wing cabinplanes, equipped with a single 295-hp Lycoming R-680 engine, for observation and liaison work. Maximum and cruising speeds respectively on the O-49 were 129 mph and 109 mph. Range was 280 miles. Maximum altitude was 18,000 ft. The 3,325-lb airplane had a two-man crew and carried no armament.

The O-49 featured full-span automatic slots on the leading edge of the wing and pilot-operated slotted flaps on the trailing edge. This configuration resulted in low takeoff and landing speeds, allowing the airplane to use short fields or landing strips. The versatile O-49 was used both in the continental U.S. and overseas in diverse roles such as towing training gliders, artillery spotting, liaison missions, emergency rescue and ambulance airlift, transporting sup-

Observation work is performed from a Curtiss Owl assigned to the 119th Observation Squadron (formerly New Jersey National Guard) *(U.S. Air Force Museum)*

Stinson O-49 observation (later the Vultee L-1 Vigilant) *(U.S. Air Force Museum)*

plies, and special espionage flights deep in enemy territory. On occasion, the aircraft was used to drop light bombs.

Other observation aircraft procured during World War II included the Curtiss O-52 Owl and the Taylorcraft O-57 Grasshopper. The Owl was an all-metal high-wing monoplane powered by a 600-hp Pratt & Whitney R-1340 engine. The O-52 was never used in combat, but helped to fill the need for trainers in the early years of the war. The O-57 Grasshopper was a light, unarmed cabinplane designed for liaison duty in support of front line ground troops. In 1942, all O-57s were redesignated L-2 (Liaison) Grasshoppers.[134]

Throat of the 20-foot wind tunnel at Wright Field, constructed in 1941-1942. Models with wingspans up to 16 ft were tested at airspeeds up to 400 mph in this tunnel during the war years.

Interior of the power building for the Wright Field 20-foot wind tunnel. The giant 40,000-hp motor for the tunnel (into which this rotor and stator are being installed) drove two carefully-synchronized 16-bladed fans.

Pursuit Airplanes

Just as bombers underwent rapid development in the Thirties, pursuit airplanes also changed significantly. In the mid-1930s the Air Corps began to establish requirements for single-place pursuits that could double as interceptors and "multi-place fighter types." The P-series airplanes developed into the dynamic and effective fighters of World War II renown.*

During Fiscal Year 1936, the Seversky Aircraft Corporation was chosen over Northrop and Curtiss to produce a single-place all-metal pursuit. A procurement contract was signed for 77 P-35 airplanes with deliveries starting in 1936.** The low-wing cantilever all-metal monoplane was the Air Corps' first pursuit with an enclosed cockpit and retractable landing gear. The P-35 had a wingspan of 36 ft, a length of 25 ft, 2 in, and a height of 9 ft, 9 in. A machine gun was mounted on each side of the fuselage (.50 caliber and .30 caliber, respectively). Its power plant was a 950-hp Pratt & Whitney R-1830; respective maximum and cruising speeds were 281 mph and 260 mph. The P-35 had a service ceiling of 31,400 ft and a range of 950 miles.[135]

The Japanese Navy ordered 20 of a two-seater version of the P-35 in 1938. This was the only American-built airplane used by the Japanese during World War II. Sweden also placed an order for 60 improved P-35s, but the order was preempted by the Air Corps in 1940. This improved model, designated the P-35A, had a 1,200-hp engine, carried four guns, 350 lbs of bombs, and had a maximum speed of 320 mph. The "A" models were assigned to the 17th and 20th Pursuit Squadrons in the Philippine Islands and all were lost in action during the early weeks of World War II. The only surviving P-35 was later restored and placed on display at the U.S. Air Force Museum.

Seversky P-35 pursuit (U.S. Air Force Museum)

---

*After May 1942, airplanes previously identified as pursuit, interceptor, or fighter were officially designated "fighter"; however, the "P" prefix continued throughout World War II.

**The P-35 was the last Seversky airplane accepted by the Air Corps before the company became Republic Aircraft in 1939. The latter, in turn, merged with Fairchild in 1965.

P-35s of the 27th Fighter Squadron (*U.S. Air Force Museum*)

The Curtiss Aeroplane Division of the Curtiss-Wright Corporation won the 1937-1938 competition to produce a single-seat fighter, the P-36 Hawk all-metal low-wing monoplane. The P-36 evolved from the Hawk Model 75, originally a French design. It was distinguished as a pioneer in wing-mounted machine guns (two .30 caliber) and had a top speed of just over 300 mph. Range was 825 miles and service ceiling was 33,000 ft. Eventually the Air Corps/ Army Air Forces (AAF) acquired a total of 210 P-36A pursuits. English and French air forces flew the Hawk 75A against German fighters in 1939 and 1940. In 1941, the AAF transferred 39 P-36As to Wheeler Field, Hawaii. During the Japanese attack on Pearl Harbor, December 7, 1941, two P-36As from the 46th Pursuit Squadron at Wheeler Field shot down two enemy aircraft. The first P-36A delivered to the Air Corps in 1938 is on permanent display at the U.S. Air Force Museum.

Another famous pursuit aircraft to emerge from Wright Field on the eve of World War II was the Curtiss-Wright single-engine, low-wing P-40 Warhawk (also dubbed the Hawk, Tomahawk, and Kittyhawk by other nations). The airplane had a semi-monocoque fuselage and hydraulically-operated retractable landing gear. The prototype carried two

fixed, sychronized .30 caliber machine guns in each wing, plus six bombs. (Subsequent models increased armament to six .50 caliber guns and 700 lbs of bombs.) The P-40 wingspan measured 37 ft, 4 in; length was 31 ft, 9 in. The single engine was a 1,040-hp Allison V-1710-33; maximum and cruising speeds were 362 mph and 235 mph respectively. Range was 950 miles and service ceiling was 32,750 ft. The manufacturer received an order for 524

Curtiss P-36 Hawk pursuit (*U.S. Air Force Museum*)

242

Curtiss P-40 Warhawks (on right) in production *(U.S. Air Force Museum)*

Curtiss P-40 pursuits on the Patterson Field flightline, about 1940. The officers' brick quarters are visible at top left.

P-40s to be delivered during Fiscal Year 1940. By the time production stopped in 1944, a total of 13,738 of these pursuits had come off the production lines.

The P-40, with its nose painted to resemble a shark's snout, gained fame with the Flying Tigers of the U.S. 14th Air Force in China in 1942-1943. During an eight-month period, American pilots in P-40s shot down 286 Japanese airplanes while suffering only 8 losses. The Warhawk flew on nearly every fighting front in World War II. Dozens of P-40s were shipped to Russia and 27 other Allied nations. A P-40E Warhawk is on display at the U.S. Air Force Museum.[136]

Bell XP-39 Airacobra *(U.S. Air Force Museum)*

Making its initial flight at Wright Field in April 1939 was another pursuit destined for combat fame in practically every arena in World War II, the Bell P-39 Airacobra. A single-engine low-wing monoplane, the P-39 had a wingspan of 34 ft and a length of 30 ft, 2 in. Its power plant was a 1,200-hp Allison V-1710 mounted behind the cockpit; the propeller shaft passed between the pilot's feet. Top speed was 385 mph. The airplane had a 37-mm gun mounted in the nose and four .50 caliber machine guns in the wings.

The Airacobra was especially prominent in the Southwest Pacific and Mediterranean theaters. Not equipped with a turbosupercharger, the airplane achieved its best performance below 17,000 ft of altitude, making it an effective ground support weapon. Because of this characteristic, the Soviet Union ordered 4,773 of this type airplane under the lend-lease policy. This figure represented nearly half of the 9,558 P-39s manufactured by the time production ceased in August 1944.[137]

Lockheed P-38 Lightning *(U.S. Air Force Museum)*

Another pursuit airplane evaluated at Wright Field about the same time as the P-39 was Lockheed's P-38 Lightning, described in contemporary reports as a "high-flying twin-engine fighter of outstanding qualities." It was a strikingly beautiful airplane with a distinctive short center fuselage and twin booms which housed the two 1,425-hp engines, superchargers, radiators, and landing gear. One of the Lightning's outstanding characteristics derived from its opposite rotating propellers, which eliminated torque and gave it superior maneuverability. The airplane's wingspan was 52 ft; length was 37 ft, 10 in. The Lightning's gross weight was 15,340 lbs; maximum speed was 390 mph. Armament consisted of one 20-mm cannon and four .50 caliber machine guns. It could also carry ten 5-inch rockets or 4,000 lbs of bombs. Without bombs and with a maximum fuel load, the airplane was an outstanding long-range fighter escort vehicle, with an operational range of 1,500 miles.

The P-38 Lightning was credited with shooting down more Japanese airplanes than any other fighter in the Pacific theater. *(U.S. Air Force Museum)*

Analysis of the January 1939 tests on the P-38 coincided with the Presidential thrust to expand airplane production, and the Materiel Division ordered 13 service test models from Lockheed for delivery in Fiscal Year 1940. In September 1939, Lockheed received a firm order for 607 Lightnings. Between that date and the cessation of production in August 1945, 9,923 P-38s were built. Confidence in the P-38 proved to be completely justified—the Lightning set an enviable combat record that few other fighters could match and none could surpass. It was credited with shooting

Republic P-47 Thunderbolt *(U.S. Air Force Museum)*

North American XP-51 Mustang *(U.S. Air Force Museum)*

P-51D fighter assigned to the 375th Fighter Squadron of the 361st Fighter Group, 8th Air Force, flies bomber escort during the Normandy invasion, 1944. Note wing tank for extended range. *(U.S. Air Force Museum)*

down more Japanese airplanes than any other fighter in the Pacific. The P-38's "rapid roll, ability to dive at extremely high speeds, and concentrated firepower made it a formidable adversary." The airplane flew a variety of missions with ease: bomber escort, level bombing, dive bombing, ground strafing, and photographic. German Luftwaffe pilots in North Africa called the P-38 "the forked-tail devil." A P-38L bearing realistic combat markings was placed on display at the Air Force Museum in 1961.[138]

In 1942, Republic Aviation's production line began turning out another of America's leading fighter airplanes. The P-47 Thunderbolt earned a reputation for being "the roughest, toughest fighter of the war, with the ability to take a tremendous amount of punishment." The airplane was affectionately and more commonly called the "Jug" (for "Juggernaut"). A direct descendant of the tiny Seversky P-35 manufactured in 1935, the P-47 had a wingspan of 40 ft, 9 in. Its length was 36 ft, 1 in, and height was 14 ft, 2 in. The single 2,000-hp Pratt & Whitney R-2800 engine "put the P-47 ahead in this category of all single-engine fighters of the AAF and gave it rank with any other contemporary single-engine fighter in the world." Armament varied from six to eight .50 caliber machine guns and six 5-inch rockets with a 2,000-lb bomb load, or ten rockets without bombs. Gross weight was 14,500 lbs.

The Thunderbolt started out with a top speed of 425 mph, but subsequent improvements to the engine increased the top and cruising speeds respectively to 460 mph and 260 mph. In 1943, the airplane had a range of 500 miles as a fighter-bomber and 1,000 miles as an escort fighter for heavy bombers. Additional fuel capability with external tanks increased the respective ranges to 800 and 2,000 miles—deep into Germany. Equipped with a turbosupercharger, the P-47's service ceiling was 42,000 ft.

On April 8, 1943, the Thunderbolt made its initial sweep over western Europe. By the end of World War II this powerful fighter had flown 546,000 sorties (mainly in the European and Mediterranean theaters), had destroyed 11,874 enemy airplanes, 9,000 locomotives, and 160,000 railroad cars and equipment. A P-47D, one of 15,600 Thunderbolts manufactured, was donated in 1964 by Republic Aviation Corporation to the U.S. Air Force Museum for permanent display.[139]

An airplane described as the best all-around American-built fighter of World War II was the North American Aviation P-51 Mustang, developed from a British request in 1940 for a machine similar to the P-40 Kittyhawk pursuit. The machine was a single-engine, low-wing monoplane. The Royal Air Force (RAF) used the airplane for close ground support missions and quickly labeled it "the best American fighter" of its day.

The P-51 rolled off the North American production line in 1943. It had a wingspan of 37 ft, a length of 32 ft, 3 in, and a height of 13 ft, 8 in. Maximum weight was 8,400 lbs. The aircraft's power plant was a 1,380-hp British Rolls-Royce Merlin V-1650 (built by American Packard). Armament consisted of six .50 caliber machine guns and ten 5-inch rockets, or 2,000 lbs of bombs (without rockets). The Mustang's maximum and cruising speeds were 437 mph and 275 mph respectively, and its service ceiling was 31,350 ft. Drop fuel tanks gave the airplane a range of 1,000 miles and permitted its use as an escort for heavy bombers from England to Germany, and for B-29s from Iwo Jima to Japan in 1945.

The first AAF P-51 entered combat in Europe in December 1943. By the end of the war Mustangs had destroyed 4,950 German airplanes in the air. Between 1942 and 1945 the AAF ordered 14,855 Mustangs (including A-36A dive bomber and F-6 photo-reconnaissance variations). Of total procurement, 7,956 were P-51D models. In 1957 a P-51, the last propeller-driven USAF fighter assigned to a tactical unit, was transferred from the West Virginia Air National Guard to the U.S. Air Force Museum for permanent display.[140]

In late 1943, Northrop Aircraft Corporation began manufacturing the first AAF airplane specifically designed for service as a night fighter. The P-61 Black Widow was a coal-black twin-engine monoplane with a twin fuselage and a twin tail. The P-61 resembled the P-38, but was larger and considerably more powerful with its two 2,000-hp Pratt & Whitney R-2800 engines. In size and weight the Black Widow was nearer to a medium bomber than a fighter.

The P-61 wingspan measured 66 ft; its length was 49 ft, 7 in; and its maximum weight was 38,000 lbs. The airplane

carried a pilot, radar operator, and gunner, and was crammed with radar and electronic equipment, much of it stored in its elongated nose.* The P-61 located enemy aircraft in total darkness, using sophisticated equipment to guide it into proper attack position. Armament consisted of four .50 caliber machine guns in the upper turret, four 20-mm cannon in the belly, and 6,400 lbs of bombs.

An internal fuel capacity of 640 gallons supplemented by two or four wing tanks holding either 165 or 310 gallons of gasoline gave the airplane an ultimate combat range of 1,200 miles and a ferrying range of nearly double that figure. Maximum speed was 360 mph and service ceiling was 33,100 ft.

About 700 P-61s were manufactured during 1944-1945 and were used in both the European and Pacific theaters. Thirty-six others were produced in 1946 as F-15A unarmed photo-reconnaissance airplanes. Although the P-61 was twice the weight of the P-47 and three times the weight of the P-51, the Black Widow "proved to be highly maneuverable—more so than any other AAF fighter." A P-61 was donated in 1958 to the U.S. Air Force Museum for permanent display.[141]

Northrop P-61 Black Widow night fighter, with twin fuselage and twin tail (*U.S. Air Force Museum*)

*The airplane used both airborne and ground radar in locating and tracking targets.

Training Airplanes

Following the progress of bombers and pursuits, the Air Corps made major improvements in training-type airplanes. Three classes of airplanes composed this category: primary trainers (PT), basic trainers (BT), and advanced trainers (AT).

A circular proposal for primary trainers during Fiscal Year 1935 elicited bids from the Stearman Aircraft, Consolidated Aircraft, and St. Louis Aircraft companies. Stearman (later Stearman-Boeing) received a contract for 25 PT-13 Kaydet primary trainers, with delivery starting in March 1936. This popular biplane had two open cockpits, a wingspan of 32 ft, 2 in, and a length of 24 ft, 8 in. Gross weight was 2,571 lbs. The original model was powered by a 220-hp Lycoming R-680 engine. Maximum and cruising speeds were 125 mph and 104 mph respectively. The same airplane was designated the PT-17 when equipped with a Continental engine, and the PT-18 with a Jacobs engine. A later version, the Boeing PT-27, had a cockpit canopy and was built entirely for export to the Allies.

The favorite monoplane primary trainer of the war period was the Fairchild Cornell series, the PT-19, the PT-23, and the PT-26. These had 175 to 220-hp engines and top speeds to 130 mph.

Yet another popular monoplane trainer was the Ryan series of Recruits, the PT-20, PT-21, and PT-22. These were low-wing all-metal airplanes with tandem open seats, 125 to 160-hp engines, and top speeds of 130 to 140 mph.[142]

A new concept proposed for the basic trainer category was that of a low-wing monoplane to serve as a transition between the low-speed primary training type and the high-speed advanced trainer. It would carry "as many [of the] special instruments, controls, and devices found on modern high performance service aircraft as practical."[143] These would include "complete instrument flying-and-landing equipment, complete radio installation, flaps or other high lift devices, controllable pitch propellers, and a retractable alighting [sic] gear." Accordingly, Circular Proposal 35-15 published these requirements to airplane manufacturers during Fiscal Year 1935. Bids were received from Seversky, Douglas, Consolidated, Chance-Vought, and General Aviation. Seversky won the competition with its model SEV-3XAR, designated the BT-8, and received a contract for 35 trainers. The BT-8 was the first low-wing monoplane basic trainer with enclosed cockpit, and had a wingspan of 36 ft, a length of 24 ft, 4 in, and a height of 9 ft, 9 in. It had a 400-hp Pratt & Whitney R-985 engine and a top speed of 175 mph.[144]

In Fiscal Year 1936, North American Aviation was awarded a contract for 82 BT-9 basic trainers. This low-wing monoplane was the Air Corps' first combat trainer. The machine had a wingspan of 42 ft and a length of 27 ft, 7 in. It was powered by a 400-hp Wright R-975 engine. The airplane had an enclosed cockpit, carried two .30 caliber machine guns and a camera. Top speed was 172 mph.

In Fiscal Year 1937, North American received a contract for 117 BT-9Bs. Later procurement included 33 ma-

Stearman PT-13A Kaydet primary trainer *(U.S. Air Force Museum)*

Fairchild PT-19 Cornell *(U.S. Air Force Museum)*

Ryan PT-20 Recruit

North American BT-9D basic trainer *(U.S. Air Force Museum)*

chines for the Organized Reserve Corps and 40 for the Naval Bureau of Aeronautics (which the Navy designated NJ-1). During World War II, basic training for both the AAF and the Navy was largely dominated by the Vultee BT-13 and BT-15 Valiant trainers. These were single-engine monoplanes with 450-hp engines, retractable landing gear, and a top speed of 185 mph.[145]

In the advanced trainer category, North American received a sizeable procurement order in Fiscal Year 1939 for 92 BC-1A trainers. This single-engine low-wing monoplane subsequently became famous as the AT-6 Texan advanced trainer. Nearly all AAF advanced single-engine training was conducted in the AT-6, as was a considerable amount of Navy advanced training.

The AT-6 had a wingspan of 42 ft, a length of 29 ft, and a height of 11 ft, 1 in. The power plant was a 600-hp Pratt & Whitney R-1340 engine. The airplane's respective maximum and cruising speeds were 210 mph and 145 mph, with a range of 870 miles and service ceiling of 24,750 ft. Between late 1938 and 1945, North American produced 15,495 Texans. Of these, 10,057 were sold to the Army as AT-6s. Others went to the Navy as SNJs, and still others were sold to 30 Allied nations. A later model Texan T-6G was put on display in 1957 at the U.S. Air Force Museum.[146]

Several outstanding multi-engine advanced trainers were developed during this period for training bomber pilots and aircrews. One of these was the Beechcraft AT-10 Wichita, an all-wood four-seat low-wing monoplane with two 295-hp Lycoming R-680 engines and a top speed of 190 mph. Another multi-engine advanced trainer was the Cessna AT-17 Bobcat, a four-seater with twin 245-hp Jacobs R-775 engines and a top speed of 195 mph. A third was the Curtiss AT-9 Jeep, a four-seater with 295-hp engines and a top speed of 197 mph. Later in the war, the North American AT-24 Mitchell, converted from the versatile B-25 bomber, became the most popular transition and aircrew trainer.[147]

Rounding out the advanced trainer category were the aircraft used for training navigators and bombardiers, the Beechcraft AT-7 Navigator and the AT-11 Kansas. Nearly all of the 45,000 bombardiers and 50,000 navigators trained during the war were taught in these aircraft. The AT-11 was configured with a transparent nose, a bomb bay, internal bomb racks, and two .30 caliber machine guns. The AT-11A was retrofitted with astrodomes placed in the ceiling of the fuselage. An AT-11 is on permanent display at the U.S. Air Force Museum.[148]

North American AT-6C Texan advanced trainer

Beechcraft AT-7 Navigator (*U.S. Air Force Museum*)

POST-WAR CONTRIBUTIONS TO AVIATION 1946-1951

In 1944, the Materiel Command at Wright Field merged with the Air Service Command at Patterson Field to form the Air Technical Service Command (ATSC). This wartime merger of research, procurement, and logistics was perpetuated when ATSC was redesignated the Air Materiel Command (AMC) in March 1946. In the post-war period from 1946 to 1950, AMC supervised research, development, and procurement efforts at Wright Field and, after January 1948, at the consolidated Wright-Patterson AFB. With the creation of the Air Research and Development Command (ARDC) in 1950, USAF airplane research and development again became a separate command, and thus entered a new era, as detailed in other chapters of this book.* Throughout these organizational changes, the Dayton installation continued to make significant contributions to military aviation through the development of specific aircraft.

As the curtain descended on World War II, on stage were such AAF veterans as the B-17, P-38, P-39, P-47, P-51, C-46, and C-47. Three new stars were in the center spotlight: the P-61 Black Widow, the C-54 Skymaster, and the B-29 Superfortress. These actors would continue to play prominent roles in the next act—the birth of the USAF. They would share the stage with newcomers like the P-82, the C-82, the C-118, and the B-50. And in the wings awaited even newer aircraft, such as the B-35 and B-36, that would bridge the transition between the reciprocating engine generation and the Jet Age.

The North American P-82 Twin Mustang was the last AAF propeller-driven fighter acquired in quantity, and was also the last aircraft to carry the designation "P" for pursuit. (Starting in 1948, all such airplanes carried the new designation of "F" for fighter, including many of the existing World War II pursuits.) The P-82 was a twin P-51 Mustang, i.e., two P-51 airframes wedded at the wing to form a twin-engine, twin-tail, twin-cockpit airplane. The wingspan was 51 ft, 3 in; length was 38 ft, 1 in. Maximum weight was 24,600 lbs. Armament consisted of six .50 caliber machine guns, twenty-five 5-inch rockets, and 4,000 lbs of bombs. The two engines, one in each airframe, were 1,380-hp Packard V-1650s. Maximum speed was 482 mph. Range was 2,200 miles and service ceiling was 39,000 ft.

The P-82 was developed to carry a pilot and copilot/navigator on long-range bombing missions. Although the first production airplane arrived in late 1945, it was not until the following year that these radar-equipped airplanes were produced in quantity.

The Fairchild C-82 Packet, a twin-engine, twin-boom, twin-fin, high-wing monoplane, was designed as a troop carrier and cargo transport. It came off the production line in late 1945 after hostilities ended. Wingspan of the C-82 was 106 ft; length was 75 ft, 10 in. The airplane had 42

North American XP-82 Twin Mustang *(U.S. Air Force Museum)*

Fairchild C-82 Packet with experimental belt landing gear at Patterson Field *(U.S. Air Force Museum)*

seats, a top speed of 223 mph, and carried 11,500 lbs of cargo.[149] In 1947, a C-82 modification appeared with a longer wingspan (109 ft, 4 in), an extended fuselage (85 ft), and an increased top speed (280 mph). It was designated the Fairchild C-119 Flying Boxcar. The C-119 retained the "twin" configuration of the C-82, and had a five-man crew, 62 seats, and a cargo capacity of 20,000 lbs.

Another cargo airplane designed in late World War II and procured by the Air Materiel Command in 1947 was the Douglas C-118 Liftmaster. A stretched version of the C-54 Skymaster, the Liftmaster had the same wingspan (117 ft, 6 in) but was about 12 ft longer (105 ft, 7 in). Assigned to the Military Air Transport Service (MATS) as a transoceanic personnel and cargo carrier, the C-118 had accommodations for 76 seats or 60 litters and 27,000 lbs of cargo. It had a 4,910-mile range and a top speed of 370 mph, nearly 100 mph faster than the C-54.[150]

Fairchild C-119A Packet

---

*See Chapter VIII for details of this time period. Chapter X is devoted to the history of the Aeronautical Systems Division and includes details on the early history of ARDC.

The versatility of the B-29 Superfortress had not been fully realized when World War II ended. This magnificent machine had already undergone a slight change when it was modified for use as the F-13 photographic-reconnaissance vehicle, but two far more significant modifications were already programmed.

The first—and perhaps most significant—was the 75 percent modification which resulted in the B-50 Superfortress (initially designated the B-29D). This follow-on had more powerful engines, a taller rudder, a new wing structure and hydraulic nosewheel steering. Respective specifications of the two versions of the Superfortress were:

	B-29	B-50
Wingspan	141'3″	141'3″
Length	99 ft	99 ft
Gross wt.	124,000 lbs	168,408 lbs
Engines	Four 2,000-hp Wright R-3350-23	Four 3,500-hp Pratt & Whitney R-4360-35
Top Speed	385 mph	385 mph
Range	3,250 mi	4,650 mi
Ceiling	31,850 ft	37,000 ft

Boeing B-50 Superfortress *(U.S. Air Force Museum)*

The B-50A Superfortress *Lucky Lady II* **was the first airplane to complete a nonstop circumnavigation of the world, departing February 26, 1949.** *(U.S. Air Force Museum)*

The B-50 Superfortress had at least two claims to fame. It was the last propeller-driven bomber delivered to the Air Force. It was also the first airplane to fly nonstop around the world. The B-50A *Lucky Lady II* departed Carswell AFB, Texas, on February 26, 1949, and completed a 23,452-mile nonstop circumnavigation of the world in 94 hours, 1 minute. The bomber was air-refueled four times: over the Azores in the mid-Atlantic, Saudi Arabia in the Middle East, the Philippine Islands in Southeast Asia, and Hawaii in the central Pacific.[151]

KB-29 tankers provided air-to-air refueling of the *Lucky Lady II*. The KB-29 was the second major modification of the B-29, basically a stretched version. The KB-29 entered the active inventory in 1948 with the same wingspan as the bomber (141 ft, 3 in), but was about 21 ft longer (120 ft, 1 in). In the tanker, ordnance and weapons gave way to huge fuel cells. The KB-29 initially used a gravity-flow system of fuel transfer. Two years later Boeing developed the more versatile flying boom in the tail of the tanker, a "telescoping aluminum tube that could be used up, down, or to either side," a precursor of modern refueling systems.[152]

AMC's aeronautical and logistical experts at Wright Field also played prominent roles in the development of the B-36 Peacemaker intercontinental bomber, the largest combat airplane to reach full production status without ever flying a combat mission, and in the concurrent development of the YB-35 Flying Wing.

The concept of the intercontinental bomber germinated with the XB-15 and B-19 programs in the 1930s. On April 11, 1941, the Air Corps returned to the concept and invited manufacturers to submit preliminary designs for a very heavy, long-range bomber. On May 3, Consolidated responded with a proposal for "a high-wing, single-tail, pressure-cabin bomber with a range of 10,000 miles carrying a 10,000 pound bomb load." Northrop submitted a daring design for an all-wing bomber "without the drag-producing fuselage and tail assembly of conventional craft."

Fuselage and wing of the XB-36 in the Wright Field Static Test facility (Building 65, Area B), being turned upside down in order to conduct positive angle of attack structural tests (*Bob Cavanagh*)

In October 1941, the AAF awarded a contract to Consolidated for two of its experimental six-engine bomber, designated the XB-36, for delivery within 36 months. In November 1941, Northrop received a contract to produce an experimental model of its airplane, designated the XB-35.

In June 1943, Gen. Henry H. Arnold, AAF Commanding General, requested procurement of 100 B-36s. In August 1944, the Secretary of War approved the contract, at an estimated cost of $154,250,000. Wartime conditions, however, hampered development of both the XB-36 and the XB-35 and neither aircraft was completed before the end of the war.

Northrop's XB-35 became the first of the "very, very heavy bombers" (VVHB) to fly, taking off from the company's plant in Hawthorne, California, in June 1946. The aircraft had a wingspan of 172 ft and a length of 53 ft. Four Pratt & Whitney R-4360 engines propelled the airplane to a top speed of 391 mph. With an 18,000-gallon fuel capacity, the XB-35 had a range of 10,000 miles, sufficient to fly

Northrop YB-35 four-engine Flying Wing (*U.S. Air Force Museum*)

Northrop YB-49 jet-powered Flying Wing

nonstop across the Atlantic and return. Bomb load was 41,200 lbs, and armament consisted of twenty .50-caliber machine guns.

After limited production of XB-35, YB-35, and YB-35A aircraft, the project was abandoned because of serious problems with reduction gear arrangements and propeller governors. On June 1, 1945, Northrop received a contract to modify two YB-35s into jet-powered YB-49 Flying Wing aircraft. These delta-designed airplanes were equipped with eight Allison J35-A-5 turbojet engines with 4,000 lbs of thrust each. Within two months after they took the air in October 1947, both YB-49s were destroyed and plans for a reconnaissance version were abandoned shortly thereafter.[153]

Meanwhile, the first XB-36 Peacemaker (manufactured by Consolidated-Vultee) made its maiden flight August 8, 1946, at Fort Worth, Texas; the first production model B-36 flew a year later. The XB-36 featured "a graceful tubular fuselage" that was 163 ft long. At the rudder it stood 46 ft,

10 in tall. The wing had a span of 230 ft and a total area of 4,772 sq ft. The high-wing monoplane was powered with six Pratt & Whitney R-4360-25 Wasp Major engines that delivered 3,000 hp to each of the 19-ft pusher propellers. The bomber's gross weight was 260,000 lbs. Integral fuel tanks in the wing spar held 19,197 gallons. Top speed was 346 mph and range was 10,000 miles.

An improved "B" model flew July 8, 1948. The model "D," which came out in 1949, was even further improved by adding four General Electric J-47-GE-19 jet engines, each having a thrust of 5,200 lbs.

The "J" model, last of the B-36 line, was the most powerful of all, with six 3,800-hp Pratt & Whitney R-4360s and four General Electric J-47s with 5,200 lbs of thrust each. Maximum speed on the "J" model was given as 435 mph, with a range of 10,000 miles and a service ceiling of 45,700 ft.* By the time production ended in August 1954, more than 380 B-36s had been manufactured.

---

*The last B-36 flight of record was on April 30, 1959, when a B-36J was flown from Davis-Monthan AFB, Arizona, to WPAFB for permanent display in the U.S. Air Force Museum.

Consolidated-Vultee XB-36 Peacemaker on its maiden flight, August 8, 1946, Fort Worth, Texas *(U.S. Air Force Museum)*

The giant XB-36 was so large that a special tunnel, two feet in diameter and 85 feet long (shown here), was designed to allow crew members to move from the front of the airplane to the aft cabin while in flight. This crew member is lying on a four-wheeled scooter and moves by pulling on an overhead cable. *(U.S. Air Force Museum)*

The last ten-engine B-36J rolls off the Convair production line at Fort Worth, 1954.

The AAF had entered the age of jet-engine aircraft in October 1942, with the maiden flight of the Bell Aircraft Company XP-59A Airacomet at Rogers Dry Lake, California (now a part of Edwards AFB). Four Wright Field engineers played key roles in the project. Maj. Donald J. Keirn of the Power Plant Laboratory had studied jet airplane engines and airframes in England prior to America's involvement in the war. Maj. Ralph P. Swofford of the Fighter Project Office was given responsibility for developing the airframe of the XP-59. Choosing the location of the flight test site was the responsibility of Maj. Gen. Benjamin J. Chidlaw, Chief of the Materiel Command Engineering Branch. He and Colonel Swofford selected Rogers Dry Lake for two key reasons: it permitted the long takeoff roll required by jet aircraft (based on RAF experience) and it met the requirement for absolute secrecy. Lt. Col. Laurence C. Craigie, Chief of the Aircraft Projects Branch at Wright Field, became the first AAF jet pilot when he flew the Airacomet on October 2, 1942. (Bell's chief test pilot Bob Stanley had made the first jet flight in American history in the XP-59A the day before.)

The XP-59A was a "shoulder-wing single-seat monoplane." It had a wingspan of 45 ft, 6 in, and a length of 38 ft, 2 in. Its power plants were twin General Electric I-A jet engines, giving the airplane a top speed of 415 mph at 30,000 ft. Combat range with 1,000 lbs of weapons was 525 miles.

The first production models of the P-59A Airacomet were delivered to the 412th Fighter Group, 4th Air Force, at March Field, California, in August 1944. The 412th became America's first all-jet unit.[154] Bell manufactured a total of 66 P-59A and P-59B Airacomets.

At Wright Field in October 1944, WASP* pilot Ann Baumgartner became the first American woman to operate a jet airplane when she flew the XP-59A for thirty minutes. (She was not, however, the first woman pilot in the world to fly a jet. Hannah Reitsch of Germany flew the rocket-powered Messerschmitt Me 262 in 1943.)[155]

The P-59 Airacomet never flew in combat, but it served a valuable role as the precursor of more advanced jet aircraft, such as the P-80. In May 1943, the Materiel Command asked Lockheed to manufacture an experimental airframe to be powered by a British jet engine. Lockheed began work prior to actual signing of the contract for the XP-80 in October 1943, and the airplane made its first test flight January 8, 1944, at Rogers Dry Lake.

By that time, a modified version of the XP-80 was already in development (the XP-80A), using a considerably

MAJ. GEN. LAURENCE C. CRAIGIE

Laurence Cradee Craigie was born in Concord, New Hampshire, in January 1902. He graduated from the U.S. Military Academy in June 1923 and was commissioned in the Air Service. In 1935, he graduated from the Air Corps Engineering School at Wright Field.

In the course of his distinguished military career, Craigie served four tours of duty at Wright Field. He was assigned to the Materiel Division from 1935 to 1937, and again from 1939 to 1942. During 1941 he held the important position of Chief of the Aircraft Projects Branch. In 1944, Craigie returned to Wright Field as Deputy Chief of the Engineering Division of the newly-created Air Technical Service Command. During his final tour at Wright Field/Wright-Patterson AFB, from 1948 to 1950, he served as Commandant of the U.S. Air Force Institute of Technology.

Robert M. Stanley, Bell test pilot, in the Bell XP-59A Airacomet at Rogers Dry Lake, California (*U.S. Air Force Museum*)

*Women Airforce Service Pilots.

THE WASPs

The Women Airforce Service Pilots (WASPs) were a special category of civil service employees, experienced female pilots who performed auxiliary flying services for the Army Air Forces. Altogether, a total of 1,074 women served as WASPs between September 1942 and December 1944; a small number of them were assigned to Wright and Patterson Fields during this time.

The WASPs flew nearly every type of aircraft in the active inventory ranging from single-engine light liaison airplanes to heavy and very heavy four-engine bombers and transports. Ferrying airplanes and towing anti-aircraft targets and aerial gunnery sleeves constituted much of the work performed, but flight duties also included engineering flight testing, tracking and searchlight missions, radio control (drone) flying, simulated strafing, smoke laying and chemical missions, and administrative/support flying. WASPs also served as flight instructors, safety pilots, check pilots, and demonstration pilots. They flew 60 million miles of operational flights, ferried 77 types of airplanes, and flew over 9 million miles of ferrying operations. Thirty-seven were killed in the line of duty.

In 1977, Congress authorized WASP wartime service to be considered active military service for calculation of veterans benefits. The U.S. Air Force Museum has a permanent display dedicated to all WASP members.

WASP display at the U.S. Air Force Museum (*U.S. Air Force Museum*)

more powerful American engine, the General Electric I-40 (later named the J-33). The first XP-80A Shooting Star with the improved power plant made its maiden flight in June 1944. The P-80A had a wingspan of 39 ft and a length of 34 ft, 10 in. Gross weight was 13,780 lbs.

The first Shooting Star to carry the "F" designation was the F-80C. Its single engine was an Allison J-33 with water-cooled injection that developed 5,400 lbs of thrust. Armament consisted of six .50 caliber machine guns and eight 5-inch rockets or 2,000 lbs of bombs. Maximum and cruising speeds were 580 mph and 437 mph respectively. Of 1,731 Shooting Stars produced, 798 were "C" models.

The Shooting Star was used extensively as a fighter-bomber during the Korean War, especially for low-level rocket, bomb, and napalm strikes against ground targets. On November 8, 1950, an F-80C shot down a Russian-built MiG fighter in the world's first all-jet fighter air battle. In 1970, a restored F-80C Shooting Star became a permanent exhibit at the U.S. Air Force Museum.[156]

A series of post-war changes in command structure gave fresh impetus to engineering research at Wright Field. Culminating these realignments was the establishment of the Wright Air Development Center (WADC) on April 2, 1951, in the Wright Field portion (Area B) of Wright-Patterson Air Force Base.* WADC was one of the ten research and development centers organized under the Air Research and Development Command.** The Center comprised four elements broken out from the Air Materiel Command: the Engineering Division, the Flight Test Division, the All-Weather Flying Division, and the Office of Air Research.

Wright Field's "golden era," however, was drawing to a close. Since the time of McCook Field, every Air Force airplane designed and constructed, tested and evaluated, could call Wright Field its "home." By 1951, Wright Field's testing program had largely been assumed by the Proving Ground at Eglin AFB, Florida, and the new facilities at Edwards AFB, California. Design and procurement systems were entering a new, more sophisticated age. Under WADC, the procurement process underwent continuous development and refinement in an effort to meet the demands of an ever-advancing technology.

The continuing story of the Wright Air Development Center and its successor organizations, including today's modern Aeronautical Systems Division, is contained in Chapter X of this volume.

The important activities that took place at Patterson Field in the years between 1931 and 1948 and which paralleled the technical developments discussed in this chapter are covered in Chapter VII of this volume. The story of Wright-Patterson AFB and its many activities since 1948 continues in Chapter VIII.

*Wright and Patterson Fields, which had been administratively merged in 1945, were redesignated Wright-Patterson Air Force Base on January 13, 1948.

**ARDC Headquarters was also located in the Wright Field area of WPAFB until June 1951, when the function moved to Baltimore, Maryland.

Patterson Field, 1942

VII.   PATTERSON FIELD 1931-1948

On July 1, 1931, that portion of Wright Field east of Huffman Dam was redesignated Patterson Field in honor of Lieutenant Frank Stuart Patterson. War Department General Orders No. 5, over the signature of General Douglas MacArthur, Chief of Staff, U.S. Army, established the designation. In general terms, Patterson Field consisted of the area now known as Area A, Wright-Patterson AFB, and the whole of the Fairfield Air Depot Reservation (Area C).* Although located on Patterson Field, the Fairfield Air Depot retained its title and continued as a major function of the new installation.

Insofar as can be determined, there was no formal memorialization or dedication ceremony for Patterson Field. Local news on July 1 focused on the dedication of the Edwin F. Brown Hospital at the National Military Home in West Dayton. Headlines in the Dayton newspapers for the entire first two weeks of July 1931, in fact, were dominated by details of the epic world flight of Wiley Post and Harold Gatty.

Though Patterson Field was established with little fanfare, it soon made its mark in the field of aviation. It was the scene of many exciting events during the 1930s and throughout the war years of the 1940s. Patterson Field became especially noted for its achievements in the field of logistics during the war.

Patterson Field, with its logistics mission, and Wright Field, dedicated to engineering advancement, continued from 1931 until the end of World War II as separate installations. By 1945, Wright and Patterson Fields had increasingly merged functions and identities until it was generally considered that the two bases were joined, although their official merger was not effected until January 13, 1948. The story of Patterson Field, as presented in this chapter, is the story of the continuing logistics heritage of Wright-Patterson Air Force Base.

*The Reservation, in turn, included Huffman Prairie and the World War I sites of the Fairfield Aviation General Supply Depot and Wilbur Wright Field.

THE PATTERSON NAME

Frank Stuart Patterson was born in Dayton, Ohio, on November 6, 1897, son of Frank Jefferson Patterson and Julia Shaw Patterson. The elder Patterson and his brother, John H. Patterson, founded The National Cash Register Company and figured prominently in local Dayton history.

Young Frank Stuart descended from a long line of military officers. His great-grandfather, Col. Robert Patterson, was a veteran of the Revolutionary War, the War of 1812, and skirmishes with Indians in Ohio, Indiana, and Illinois. Three uncles were Union Army Civil War captains.

Frank Stuart carried on the family military tradition. After initial schooling at the Florida-Adirondack preparatory school, he enrolled at Yale University, from which he received his Bachelor of Arts degree in the spring of 1918.* On May 21, 1917, he enlisted as a private in the Aviation Section of the Enlisted Reserve Corps, U.S. Army.[1]

He received ground training at the Massachusetts Institute of Technology, Cambridge, Massachusetts. After completing primary training at Buffalo, New York, and advanced flying training at Mineola, Long Island, New York, he was assigned to Post Field, Fort Sill, Oklahoma, for training in aerial observation.

Upon completing observation training, Private First Class Patterson was honorably discharged from the Enlisted Reserve Corps on September 14, 1917, at Fort Sill, and commissioned the following day as a first lieutenant in the Officers Reserve Corps, U.S. Army, with the aeronautical rating of pilot.

On May 10, 1918, Lieutenant Patterson was assigned to the 137th Aero Squadron at Wilbur Wright Field, near his hometown of Dayton.[2] Orders issued on May 9 at the new station assigned him to a board of officers "for the purpose of conducting tests of the DeHavilland Four and Bristol Fighter airplanes."[3]

Test pilot Lt. Frank Stuart Patterson was killed in the crash of his DH-4 biplane while testing a machine gun synchronizer over Wilbur Wright Field, June 19, 1918.

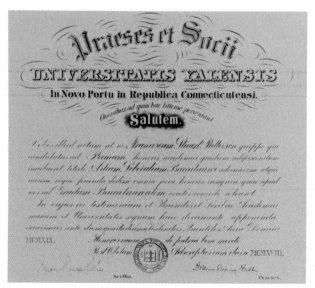

Lieutenant Patterson graduated from Yale University (in absentia) in the class of 1918.

Lt. Frank S. Patterson (standing sixth from left), with fellow test pilots, May 1918

*He received his degree "in absentia," as did many of his fellow classmates who had joined the Signal Corps.

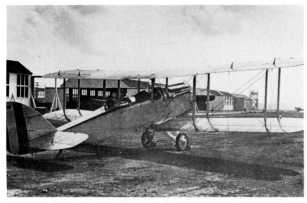

Army Air Service DH-4 #32098, assigned to Lt. Frank Stuart Patterson and his aerial observer, Lt. LeRoy Swan, for conducting machine gun tests at Wilbur Wright Field. Contrary to popular belief, their fatal accident was not caused by gunfire shattering the propeller blades, but by the shearing of a tie rod, which allowed the wings of the aircraft to fold back and separate from the fuselage.

Following a military funeral on June 21, 1918, Frank Stuart Patterson was buried next to his father in Woodland Cemetery, Dayton.

On June 19, 1918, little more than a month after his arrival at Wilbur Wright, Lt. Patterson and his aerial observer, Lt. LeRoy Amos Swan, went aloft in their DH-4, Army Air Service Serial #32098, to test newly installed machine guns synchronized by Nelson interrupter gear equipment. Their instructions were to fire about one hundred rounds into the field from 6,000 feet, 10,000 feet, and 15,000 feet. They completed the first two trials successfully, firing the guns through the propeller as they dived. Lt. Patterson then climbed to 15,000 feet and pointed the airplane downward in a steep dive. Just as reports of the guns reached the earth, the wings of the airplane were seen to collapse and separate completely from the fuselage, leaving it to travel nearly across the field at full power during its fall. The machine was completely wrecked and the crew crushed beyond recognition.[4]

The initial report of the accident wired to Washington indicated that it was not clear whether the wings folded up or were swept back. It was subsequently determined by the aircraft accident investigation board that:[5]

> Patterson's accident believed to be due to shearing of tie rod that passes through fuselage near radiator and connects the two fittings to which are attached nose drift wires. Accident occurred while diving hence considerable strain put on those two fittings. Tie rod sheared but fittings show very little elongation showing that weakness lay in tie rod. There being nothing else to take backward strain on wings, wings probably folded back and separated from fuselage.

This report clarified the popular, but erroneous assumption that bullets from the machine gun shattered the propeller blades, which flew back and tore the wings from the airplane.

Lieutenant Patterson was buried next to his father in Woodland Cemetery, Dayton, on June 21, 1918, following a military funeral. He was survived by his mother, Julia Shaw Patterson Carnell; by a brother, Jefferson, who was a lieutenant in the field artillery serving with the 83rd Divi-

sion in France; by a sister, Mary, who was active in wartime Red Cross work; and by other members of the illustrious Patterson family.*

LeRoy Amos Swan was born June 5, 1894, in Norwich, Connecticut. After attending public schools and the Norwich Free Academy, he graduated in 1917 with a bachelor of science degree in mechanical engineering from the Massachusetts Institute of Technology.

Swan enlisted in the Air Service on July 14, 1917, and was commissioned in the Officers Reserve Corps the following September. He was assigned to the Air Service and attended the aerial observers school at Post Field, Oklahoma, as had Lieutenant Patterson. He was assigned to Wilbur Wright Field in April 1918, and participated in a number of flights involving machine gun testing.

Lieutenant Swan was buried with military honors in his hometown. According to the local newspapers, he was the first military man from Norwich to die during the war.[6]

The Patterson-Swan accident was not the first involving a DH-4 aircraft in the local area. The earliest recorded crash in a DH-4 occurred May 2, 1917, and killed Lt. Col. Henry J. Damm and Maj. Oscar Brindley.[7] Perhaps the earliest fatality altogether at the site occurred before it became Wilbur Wright Field. On May 21, 1912, it is reported that "Fred Southard stole an airplane . . . and went aloft for his solo flight," falling 100 feet to his death when the engine failed.[8]

A LOGISTICS HERITAGE

Patterson Field's principal functions from July 1, 1931 through 1945 were those of logistics. Patterson Field was assigned to the Air Corps Materiel Division from its designation until October 17, 1941, when the Air Service Command assumed the logistics functions of the Materiel Division.

---

*It was Frank Stuart's first cousin, Frederick Beck Patterson, who later headed the Dayton Air Service Committee in its drive to acquire and donate more than 4,500 acres of land, including the site of Wilbur Wright Field, to the government in 1924 for the creation of Wright Field.

Fairfield Air Depot (FAD), Patterson Field. A major portion of Patterson Field was occupied by FAD until the depot closed in 1946. The large building at lower right is Building 1, the original depot headquarters.

The major portion of Patterson Field was occupied by the Fairfield Air Depot (FAD).* By the early 1930s, the control area of the Fairfield Air Depot had expanded to 23 states, serving 28 of the approximately 50 Air Corps stations in the United States.[9] Fairfield was linked to other depots in the system by an air transport supply service, a descendant of the earlier Model Airway. The transport service was staffed at FAD by the 1st Provisional Air Transport Squadron, constituted March 1, 1935 and redesignated the 1st Transport Squadron on June 25, 1935. The 2nd, 3rd, and 4th Transport Squadrons were stationed

C-33 cargo transport, able to carry 5,000 lbs of cargo at a top speed of over 200 mph. Along with C-27 and C-39 transports, C-33s were flown by the 1st Provisional Air Transport Squadron assigned to FAD. *(U.S. Air Force Museum)*

FAD AREA OF CONTROL IN 1931

State	Installations
Alabama	Maxwell Field; Roberts Field
Arkansas	Little Rock
Florida	Chapman Field
Georgia	Candler Field; Lawson Field (Ft. Benning)
Illinois	Chanute Field; Scott Field; Municipal Airport (Chicago)
Indiana	Schoen Field; Stout Field
Iowa	None
Kansas	Ft. Leavenworth; Marshal Field (Ft. Riley)
Kentucky	Bowman Field
Louisiana	Barksdale
Michigan	Selfridge Field; Wayne County Airport
Minnesota	St. Paul Municipal Airport; Minneapolis
Mississippi	None
Missouri	Lambert Field; Richards Field
Ohio	Cleveland Airport; Lunken Airport; Norton Field; Patterson Field; Wright Field
Nebraska	Offutt Field
North Carolina	Pope Field (Ft. Bragg)
North Dakota	None
South Carolina	None
South Dakota	None
Tennessee	Sky Harbor
West Virginia	None
Wisconsin	None

*FAD succeeded the Fairfield Aviation General Supply Depot, founded in 1917, and its several successor organizations. See Chapter III for the story of the depot to 1931.

Building 13, constructed in 1930, was FAD's primary engine overhaul and aero repair facility.

Aero Repair, Building 13, during World War II

Aerial view of FAD, 1930s. Building 13 is at center. Building 1, just above it, served as FAD Headquarters from 1918 until 1933, when a new administration building (Building 11) was completed.

Building 11, Area C, served as Patterson Field Headquarters from 1933 to 1948.

at San Antonio, Middletown, and Rockwell, respectively. These squadrons comprised the transport system within the Air Corps, an idea proposed by Lt. Col. Augustine Warner Robins while he was Executive Officer to the Chief of the Materiel Division.

Statistics from 1931 show that, at the time of the name change (to Patterson Field), personnel strength at the field ranged between 12 and 15 officers and 500-550 civilian employees. The monthly civilian payroll was approximately $67,000. The level of activity at the base was moderate. During June 1931, depot supply received 784 shipments totalling 875,815 pounds and dispatched 1,379 orders totalling 1,099,277 pounds. The repair shops received 44 airplanes and 67 engines for overhaul. Airplane overhauls completed that month totalled 36, while engine overhauls numbered 85.[10]

In 1931 there were 437 airplanes of all types assigned in the FAD control area: attack, bomber, observation, photographic, pursuit, basic training, primary training, and cargo craft. FAD was responsible for maintaining these airplanes in flying condition. The overhaul schedule in force at that time called for bombers to be overhauled every 18 months, primary trainers every 15 months, pursuits every 10 months, National Guard airplanes every 2 years, and all other types once each year. All of this work was accomplished by the FAD Engineering Department in Building 13 and two small adjacent buildings, 52 and 54.

Administrative personnel were originally housed in Building 1 at the depot. In March 1933, however, a new headquarters building, Building 11, was completed and accepted.[11] A government radio station, WYD, was first located at the depot and served both the depot and Wright Field. In September 1933, the radio station and telegraph office were consolidated with the message center at Wright Field and subsequently moved their operations there.

THE DEPRESSION YEARS

As Fairfield Air Depot entered the 1930s, the Air Corps was in the midst of the five-year expansion program outlined by the 1926 Air Corps Act. This program, which got off to a late start, extended until 1932. Numerical goals of the program included 1,800 serviceable airplanes, 1,650 officers, and 15,000 enlisted men. In terms of quality, the goal was continual improvement of aircraft systems. World records for altitude, speed, and distance flying were routinely broken and reset as the Air Corps struggled to come of age.

Notwithstanding progress made under this five-year expansion program, the economic conditions of the Great Depression were reflected in operations at the Fairfield Air Depot. Non-critical departments were reorganized to enable employment of personnel in mission essential departments. In some cases, positions held by male employees were reassigned to women, who were hired at lower salaries. In February 1930, the station supply department was consolidated with depot supply to eliminate duplicate receiving, shipping, and inspecting departments. In April 1930, the finance and personnel departments were combined in the interest of efficiency.[12] By July of 1933, funds to meet the civilian payroll were restricted to the point where it became necessary to declare an occasional administrative furlough of personnel without pay.

Beginning in 1934, the work force at the depot was augmented by the addition of temporary laborers employed under Depression-era programs. This provided an interesting chapter in Wright-Patterson's history.

In May 1934, the depot set aside several acres of land for use as a camp for men forced to live as transients by the economic conditions of the Depression. By 1935, 527 men were living in this camp, according to one account. Many of

Members of the Fairfield Air Depot baseball team, 1933

Located at the south end of Patterson Field, the Transient Camp stood approximately where Buildings 262 and 266, Area A, stand today.

these men possessed skills of use to the depot. Thus arrangements were made for them to receive lodging and meals at the camp in exchange for twenty hours of work per week on the reservation. They also received a subsistence pay of approximately $1.50 per week in cash.[13]

One valuable service performed by the transient workers was renovation of buildings on the base. A number of frame structures had been hastily built during the First World War. Buildings 2, 3, and 4, for example, had been quickly erected south of Building 1, and were essentially "shells" of corrugated metal with cinder floors. They were still in use as storage buildings, but had deteriorated greatly through the years. Building 2 was renovated by a commercial contractor and Building 3 by the Civilian Work Administration, a federal agency created to help relieve the nation's unemployment situation. Building 4, however, was renovated by the men living at the "Transient Camp."*

The same group of men performed most of the landscaping associated with construction of the brick officers' quarters in 1934. The brick quarters complex, composed of 92 units of officers' quarters and the Wilbur Wright Officers' Club (today the Officers Open Mess), were completed by July 1, 1935.

Officers' brick quarters under construction on Patterson Field, October 24, 1934. The Officers' Open Mess is already complete at center left.

THE BRICK QUARTERS

The officers' brick quarters on Patterson Field were constructed between 1933 and 1935. At the time of their completion, the new homes housed all officers stationed at both Patterson and Wright Fields. To minimize effects of the perpetual rivalry between officers of the two fields, north-south streets were assigned numbers and east-west streets were given letter designations rather than names. On July 22, 1977, ten of these streets were dedicated in honor of selected Army Air Corps and Air Force officers.

The first house completed on "B" Street (now Brett Drive), early 1935

*These three buildings were later linked together to form what is today Building 2, Area C.

The Officers' Club (Building 800) was completed October 13, 1934, and was open to all officers stationed at both Wright and Patterson Fields.

Building 700 (today the AFLC Commander's residence), shortly after completion. First resident of the home was Brig. Gen. Augustine Warner Robins, Commander of the Air Corps Materiel Division at Wright Field from 1935 to 1939.

In 1935, the Civilian Conservation Corps also maintained a camp on Patterson Field. The young men in this organization had no official relationship with the depot, but they did assist in sodding lawns, landscaping, and other tasks during 1935 and 1936.

In January of 1936, with the federal Works Progress Administration absorbing large numbers of unemployed laborers, the Transient Camp was discontinued, although the site of the camp retained the unofficial name "Transient Camp" for many years.[14]

FAD ACTIVITIES DURING THE 1930s

In April and May of 1933, FAD supported the Air Corps Anti-Aircraft Exercises based at Patterson Field. The exercises were designed primarily to perfect new techniques and tactics which were being developed in bombardment aviation. FAD personnel were responsible for installing special equipment on the airplanes as they arrived from their bases in Virginia, Texas, California, and New York. This was a considerable task, and the new equipment also required constant maintenance.

A period of one month was devoted to intensive training and equipment conditioning. Squadrons whose normal peacetime stations were widely separated and which were made up of many different types of airplanes learned to function as a composite group. The bombardment section itself was composed of squadrons of twin-engine Curtiss B-2 biplane bombers, Douglas monoplane B-7 bombers, and Boeing all-metal monoplane B-9 bombers.

Final exercises were held May 15-24. The entire proceedings received the commendation of Air Corps Chief Brig. Gen. Benjamin D. Foulois, who was in attendance.[15]

In 1934, FAD tackled a new project as the Air Corps assumed responsibility for flying the U.S. mail. During the winter of 1933, the federal government decided to cancel its air mail contracts with commercial airlines and to delegate the job to the Army Air Corps. In February 1934, FAD activities were sharply accelerated to furnish supplies for

Keystone B-6A, 1931. Keystone B-4A and B-6A bombers were modified at Fairfield Air Depot for use by the Air Corps in flying the U.S. air mail in 1934. *(U.S. Air Force Museum)*

42696

Keystone B-6A cockpit *(U.S. Air Force Museum)*

the aircraft required to support the mission. Although the Air Corps was poorly equipped and critically unprepared to take over responsibility for the air mail on such short notice, the Engineering Department at Fairfield did its best to meet the challenge. In eleven days the Engineering Department performed modifications on sufficient airplanes to support operations. Rear controls in the cockpits of "stick and wire" Keystone biplanes were removed to make room for the baggage compartments, and the airplane structure was reworked. The airplanes were equipped with instruments to enable blind flying so that air mail schedules could be met day and night.

Supply personnel at Fairfield took turns sleeping in the depot in order to meet emergency requests for stock that might be received during the night. Depot supervisors worked diligently with commercial businesses to ensure that supplies, including oil and gasoline, would be available. In addition, supply personnel were sent to various Air Corps and commercial installations throughout the country, where they acted as liaison men for FAD to facilitate operations.

Despite these Herculean efforts, the mission was doomed to failure, the victim of insurmountable difficulties. By June 1934, in the face of numerous fatalities and tragic accidents, the project was abandoned and contracts for flying the mail returned to commercial airlines. Although Air Corps facilities were proven inadequate and inappropriate for such service at the time, valuable experience was gained and lessons learned.[16] Perhaps most importantly, the Air Corps' inadequate funding support was dramatically brought to public attention, and the argument for increased Air Corps appropriations strengthened.

Public awareness was also increased by the popular long-distance 1934 Alaskan flight initiated by Lt. Col. Henry H. "Hap" Arnold and Maj. Ralph Royce. Ten new Martin YB-10 twin-engine bombers were specially equipped for the journey to Fairbanks, Alaska, and return. In June and July of 1934, FAD personnel provided support for the project, preparing the airplanes for the flight. Trial flights were conducted from Patterson Field to March Field in California, and to Dallas, Texas, although the Alaskan trip itself was launched from Bolling Field in Washington, D.C. The complete flight occupied one month and included a brief stop on the return trip at Patterson Field on August 19.[17]

A number of developments in military meteorology can be traced to activities at Patterson Field in the 1930s. On March 26, 1935, the Adjutant General of the Army explained a new War Department policy designed to improve the meteorological service furnished to the Air Corps. It involved closer technical supervision of the Army service, more contact and closer cooperation with the larger services of the U.S. Weather Bureau and the Department of Commerce, and the introduction of air mass analysis weather forecasting, and was expected to yield great benefits to military pilots. A Signal Corps officer was assigned to each Army Corps area in which there was considerable military air activity to implement the new policy.

A radio transmitter was installed at Patterson Field on January 8, 1936, to broadcast local weather conditions at hourly intervals. Pilots and operations officers received this weather data on a frequency of 379 kilocycles under the call letters WXA.[18]

On July 1, 1937, the Meteorological School at Fort Monmouth, New Jersey, was transferred to Patterson Field by order of the Chief of the Air Corps. Its name was changed to the Air Corps Weather School, and the Fairfield Air Depot Commander was designated as the school commandant. The first class of 20 students graduated from the six-month course at Patterson Field on January 28, 1938. The school operated until June 1, 1940, when it was transferred to the Air Corps Technical School at Chanute Field.[19]

Another significant event in Patterson Field history was the opening of the first military Autogiro School in the United States on April 20, 1938. The purpose of the school was to train officers as pilots, and enlisted men as maintenance crews, for the service testing of autogiros. The school started with three new YG-1B direct control autogiros, and augmented its small training fleet until seven were on hand,

Kellett YG-1 autogiro. The Autogiro School established at Patterson Field in April 1938 was the first military school in the U.S. to train pilots and mechanics with rotary wing aircraft.

A cachet issued by the Dayton Stamp Club in 1982 commemorated the 45th anniversary of the world's first entirely automatic landing.

the largest assembly of such machines ever before gathered in one location. Hangar 5, erected during World War I, served as classroom and workshop for the four-week course.

During the first and second course sessions, 12 officer pilots and 15 enlisted mechanics were trained. These graduates were then sent to Fort Monroe, Fort Sill, and Fort Bragg to conduct further tests with the ground services. Lt. H. F. Gregory, one of three faculty members for the pilots course, subsequently went to Wright Field to become project officer for all of the Army's rotary wing aircraft.[20]

Among other significant achievements realized at Patterson Field was the world's first entirely automatic landing, on August 23, 1937. Capt. George V. Holloman piloted the Fokker C-14B transport airplane used in the test. Capt. Carl J. Crane, the inventor of the system, and Raymond K. Stout, the Project Engineer, were also present. (All three were assigned to the Materiel Division at Wright Field.) The landing was successfully completed without any assistance from the human pilot or from the ground. Captains Crane and Holloman were awarded the Mackay Trophy and Distinguished Flying Crosses for their achievements.[21]

The foregoing special activities provided occasional breaks in the normally routine work of the Fairfield Air Depot. As the 1930s came to a close, however, the days of such routine activity were numbered. Fairfield was soon to become one of scores of depots in the United States charged with maintaining and distributing the largest stockpile of wartime materiel in history.

WORLD WAR II

Prior to World War II, the depot supply operation at Patterson Field was modest in size, even though it provided service to Air Corps stations nationwide. In 1939, the depot Supply Department of FAD occupied approximately 7,500 square feet of office space and 306,000 square feet of warehouse floor space, and employed less than 200 workers. Operations were housed almost entirely in Building 1, which had been constructed during the First World War. Additional workers employed by the Engineering Department, the Signal Corps radio section, the fuels and lubricants unit, the lumber yard, the air freight terminal, and other related units brought total employment at the depot to nearly 500 persons. A standard 40-hour work week was in effect, with six or eight civilians remaining on duty over weekends to handle emergency shipments. Railroad service consisted of two tracks, which entered Building 1 from the east, and a single track which ran from Patterson Field to Osborn.[22]

Patterson Field NCO Club, 1939

Buildings 2, 3, and 4 at Patterson Field were originally constructed as separate buildings. During 1940, they were joined together with annexes to form one large structure, known today as Building 2, Area C.

In light of engineering advancements made during the 1920s and 1930s, both in the United States and abroad, it was widely recognized that a rapid expansion of the Air Corps and its tactical capabilities would be central to the nation's rearmament program. Prodded by President Franklin D. Roosevelt, in April 1939, Congress authorized $300 million for Air Corps development. This allowed the Air Corps to schedule the production of unheard-of quantities of warplanes. At the Air Corps depots, the need for supply and repair materials and associated equipment to keep the new airplanes in flying condition increased geometrically. These drastic changes brought a new way of life to the depot at Fairfield, Ohio.

In May 1935, Col. Fred H. Coleman, Commanding Officer of Fairfield Air Depot, had prepared for the Chief of the Materiel Division a detailed, 45-page outline of construction needed at Patterson Field, as well as a revised station plan showing proposed locations. For five years the program was studied, proposed, bypassed, and reconsidered by the Materiel Division, the Field Service Section, the Quartermaster Corps, and the War Department. In 1940, funds amounting to $1,970,000 were finally earmarked for these projects, as part of the Air Corps Expansion Program. Major construction to be accomplished included:[23]

Repair Dock	$640,000
Expansion of Engineering Shops	572,000
Engine Test Building	260,000
Equipment Repair Building	158,400
Telephone System	18,000
Changes in Electric Service	70,000
Enlargement of power plant	300,000
Rebuilding steam distribution system	53,000
Rebuilding water distribution system	6,000

This nearly $2 million allocation fell short of Colonel Coleman's original estimate of funds required by more than $270,000. It was, however, the beginning of a tremendous wartime build-up at the depot. From 1938 to 1945, the face of Patterson Field was altered drastically as shops, warehouses, and military and civilian housing complexes began to dominate the landscape.

Supplies arrived at the Fairfield depot in ever-increasing quantities—by rail, by mail, by truck, and by airplane. The Receiving Department in Building 1 soon proved inadequate and was greatly expanded.[24] Plans were hastily made to construct additional buildings and to relocate some of the various Supply Department sections. During a special visit to the depot in late 1940, Brig. Gen. Henry H. Arnold addressed employees. He outlined in graphic terms the scope of physical growth and increased depot activities that could be expected, and which in fact soon became reality.[25]

Buildings 2, 3, and 4, south of Building 1, were joined together with annexes during 1940 to form one large structure. Barracks, mess halls, and other buildings were rapidly constructed to house mushrooming numbers of newly-recruited and transferred military personnel. Large barracks complexes were located on Wright Avenue across from Building 1, on Wright Avenue west of Pearson Road, in the area across Route 4 which became known as "Wood City" (so named because all of its structures were of wooden construction), and on Skeel Avenue at the far north end of Patterson Field. Hebble Homes, a wartime housing development constructed near the base in Fairfield, housed primarily civilian employees.

The Wood City complex at Patterson Field, located east of Route 4, was occupied largely by military housing and recreation facilities. Wood City was renamed Kittyhawk Center in 1972.

Chapel 1, shown here after the war, was constructed in 1942.

Barracks at the north end of Patterson Field, across the street from today's 2750th Civil Engineering Squadron complex.

Building 206 was constructed in 1940-1941. The center section of the airplane repair facility was completed in the spring of 1941, providing offices for Patterson Field Operations and a convenient hotel for transient pilots. The hotel became known as the FADO Hotel (Fairfield Air Depot—Operations), a break in the Air Corps tradition of referring to all airfield hotels as "DeGink."[26] A new air terminal, Building 146, was constructed adjacent to Building 206 in 1943 (on the site of the old Barling bomber hangar).

A repair warehouse was set up in Building 6 in the fall of 1942 to accommodate the huge mass of reparable materiel arriving from overseas. In June 1943, Building 80 was completed to further augment storage space and relieve the already crowded conditions in Building 6. It was constructed by combining eight demountable steel hangars, thus placing 32,000 square feet under roof in a single structure.[27]

A complex of warehouses was constructed in the vicinity of Buildings 1 and 2 during 1941-1943 to accommodate the steady deluge of supply materiel at the depot. New structures included Buildings 70, 71, 72, 114, 174, 252, 253, 254, 255, 257, and 258. In addition, warehouse space was leased in some 14 buildings in the Springfield, Ohio, area, totalling more than 561,000 square feet, as auxiliary storage for the depot. A packing and shipping department was eventually established in Springfield to facilitate operations and save time and expense.

The Patterson Field NCO Club moved to these more spacious quarters in the early 1940s.

Patterson Field Post Exchange. During World War II, the PX sat across the street from Post Headquarters (Building 11), adjacent to present-day Building 10.

Base Operations (Building 206), completed in December 1941 on the Patterson Field flightline. The FADO (Fairfield Air Depot—Operations) Hotel for transient pilots was located in the center portion of the building.

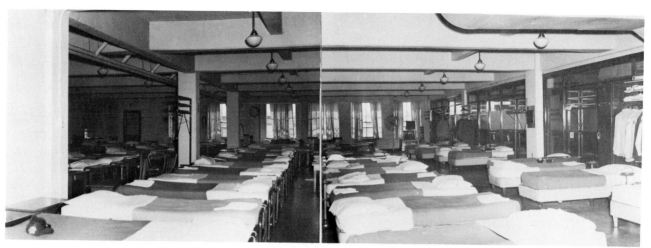

The FADO Hotel provided comfortable though crowded quarters for visiting pilots.

Patterson Field control tower, 1940

The Patterson Field Air Transport Terminal served the field's needs during the 1930s and early 1940s. In 1943, a new terminal, Building 146, was constructed on the site of the old Barling bomber hangar.

Patterson Field, 1943, showing the build-up that occurred in the early years of World War II. In the foreground are numerous depot maintenance and storage buildings essential to wartime depot operations.

FAD leased storage space in some 14 buildings in the Springfield area to augment warehouse space available at Patterson Field.

Building 89, Patterson Field. Constructed in 1943 as an engine overhaul and repair facility, Building 89 later served as home of the U.S. Air Force Museum (1954-1971).

Building 13, used for engine overhaul and repair, was expanded by consolidating and connecting several existing buildings during this same period. Building 89, also used for overhaul and repair, was completed in 1943. Building 95 was erected during 1943 to house the salvage and disposal branch.

As operations at Patterson Field expanded, so did administrative and support needs. The Patterson Field power plant was expanded in 1942 to service the increased energy needs of the field. The Patterson Field post hospital, Building 219, was completed and was activated June 17, 1942. It was staffed initially by 15 medical officers, 550 enlisted personnel, and 6 civilians. By December 1942, even this new facility was inadequate to minister to the ills of all personnel at both Wright and Patterson Fields. A cantonment-type hospital was activated December 21 in Wood City, and soon became the main base hospital.[28]

In 1943, Building 10 was constructed as headquarters for the Fairfield Air Service Command.* Building 11 continued to serve as Patterson Field Headquarters. Extension wings were added to both ends of Building 11 in 1942 to house additional offices and personnel.

Permanent runway construction took place on Patterson Field during 1942 and 1943. Concrete runway "A" (now Taxiway No. 8) was completed in December 1942. New concrete taxiways and an extension to Runway "B" (no longer in use) were built the following summer and accepted on September 3, 1943. An extension to Runway "C" (now Taxiway No. 12) was accepted on October 11, 1943.

Land acquisition during World War II became an important factor in Patterson Field's later development. Of particular importance was the purchase during 1943 and 1944 of some 851 acres of Greene County land from the Miami Conservancy District and private landowners. This acreage

*Building 10 today serves as Headquarters for the 2750th Air Base Wing.

Final Assembly Section of Engine Repair, Building 89

Building 219, completed in 1942, one of two hospitals serving Wright and Patterson Fields during the war years. The second hospital was a cantonment-type temporary facility in Wood City.

Building 10 shortly after completion. Located across the street from Patterson Field Headquarters (Building 11), it housed Headquarters for the Fairfield Air Service Command (FASC).

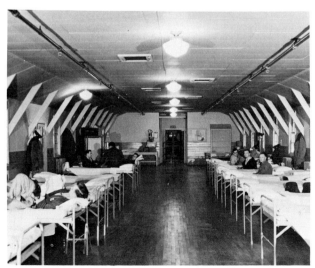
Interior of the cantonment-type hospital in Wood City

Completed Patterson Field runway complex, 1945

expanded Patterson Field to the northeast, and allowed the 1947 construction of the Very Heavy Bomber (VHB) runway, as detailed later in this chapter.

A major construction project at the south end of Patterson Field in 1942 and 1943 was the headquarters complex for the Air Service Command. The central structures, Building 262 and its annex, 262A, were completed and occupied in 1942. Surrounding the headquarters building were numerous warehouses, as well as barracks for ASC personnel. Area A, as the ASC area came to be known, was connected to the existing complexes on Patterson Field by an extension of Skeel Avenue, but was, in effect, a separate area. From 1944 until 1948, in fact, Area A was administratively considered part of Wright Field.

The housing area known as Skyway Park, at the intersection of present-day Kauffman Avenue and Colonel Glenn Highway, was constructed under provisions of the Lanham Act during the summer of 1944 and provided housing for ASC civilian personnel. Skyway Park consisted of 546 family housing units and Skyway Lodge, a dormitory complex that housed another 640 individuals and had its own cafeteria and clinic. On October 25, 1947, Skyway Park was transferred from the National Housing Agency to the Army Air Forces and was designated as "Area D" of the base.*

The extensive physical growth of Patterson Field was accompanied by significant increases in the military and civilian work forces. By July 1940, civilian employment at FAD had risen to 1,013, double the average of the preceding decade. By January 1942, employment had soared to 9,041; in March of 1943 it peaked at 19,433.[29]

Building 262, Area A, under construction in 1942. Air Service Command Headquarters moved from Washington, D.C., to Building 262, Patterson Field, in December 1942. The Air Service Command (ASC) emblem, as shown on the Command flag, was displayed above the main entrance of Building 262.

A large ASC complex was constructed at the south end of Patterson Field between 1941 and 1943. The complex initially consisted of the Headquarters buildings (262 and 262-A), several large warehouses, and officer and enlisted housing for all ASC troops. The Civilian Club (Building 274) was completed nearby in 1944.

Buildings 262 and 262-A, at center, are flanked by row after row of warehouses and barracks. Large buildings at center right are Buildings 287 and 288.

*In 1963, the Skyway Park property (190.115 acres) was officially transferred to the State of Ohio, via the General Services Administration. It now comprises a portion of the Wright State University campus.

Skyway Park (left) was constructed as housing for ASC civilian employees. Located at the intersection of present-day Kauffman Avenue and Col. Glenn Highway, this property is now part of the Wright State University campus.

The complexion of the work force also changed significantly. Prior to 1939, less than 10 percent of the employees at the depot were women. They were concentrated in office positions since women were prohibited from working in storerooms and industrial areas. The critical need for workers in the early months of the war, however, altered this situation rapidly. By 1942, women worked alongside men in warehouses as storekeepers, and later as tug and truck drivers. By 1944, more than 50 percent of the work force at the depot was female.[30] Many of them had been actively recruited by the Air Service Command in its effort to fill essential swing and graveyard shifts. ASC hired not only in the Dayton area but also literally went into the hills and hamlets of Appalachia to recruit women employees.

By March 1941, to serve the increasing number of employees at the depot, a system of payroll checks was instituted to replace cash disbursements. By 1945, the total military and civilian payroll at both Patterson and Wright Fields reached $131.5 million, equivalent to 35 percent of Dayton's total industrial payroll.[31]

When wartime operations at Patterson Field shifted to a 24-hour, 7-day-a-week basis, the nature of civil service appointments was altered. Under the former standard probation system, new employees achieved permanent civil service status after a six-month to one-year period. Under war service appointments, workers were not hired permanently, but were placed on the civil service payroll "for the duration and six months."[32]

Women employees were recruited by ASC to fill many critical jobs at the Fairfield depot. Here, women work side by side with men overhauling engines in Buildings 13 and 89 on Patterson Field.

During World War II, women filled jobs in storage and maintenance previously reserved for men.

FAD women employees perform intricate repairs and maintenance on aircraft instruments.

To acknowledge the very real contribution that civilian employees were making to the war effort, the War Department directed that a special recognition ceremony be held at each military establishment in the nation. At Patterson Field the ceremony took place on December 8, 1943. Civilian employees with at least six consecutive months of satisfactory government service were recognized with a special ribbon. Locally 11,400 employees qualified for and received this recognition from the Patterson Field Commander, Brig. Gen. Merrick G. Estabrook, Jr. The attractive service ribbon awarded was of dark blue fabric, with horizontal silver stripes on which was centered the Army Air Forces insignia.[33]

The work of depot personnel was complicated by prewar systems and procedures not designed to handle the massive increases in materiel activities which resulted from the war effort. Existing forms and procedures needed to be analyzed, simplified, and streamlined. A more efficient stock control system needed to be devised and implemented. Methods had to be perfected for receiving and screening tremendous quantities of materiel from overseas, and there was the perpetual problem of insufficient warehouse and storage space.

Many new concepts were devised by Fairfield Air Depot personnel and tested at the facility. In fact, because of its past history and experience, FAD was often used by the Army Air Forces as a proving ground for new ideas before they were adopted for use throughout the supply system. Thus, in a very real sense, FAD pioneered advances that presaged many of today's modern logistics systems.

The emergency in the supply field was echoed in maintenance and repair. The war provided a skyrocketing volume of maintenance and repair work linked to the warplane production program. The Engineering Section at Fairfield met this challenge with a like amount of innovation. More

Chief Warrant Officer Charles M. "Smitty" Smith

BRIG. GEN. MERRICK G. ESTABROOK

Brig. Gen. Merrick G. Estabrook, Jr. oversaw many of the dramatic changes that occurred at Patterson Field immediately prior to World War II and during the early years of the war, serving as Commander of both Patterson Field and the Fairfield Air Depot from 1939 to 1943.

According to many who served under him, General Estabrook spent long days and nights, at the expense of his own health, overseeing the massive construction projects at Patterson Field and supervising a staff of steadily-increasing proportions. His right-hand men were Chief Warrant Officer Charles M. "Smitty" Smith and the Post Adjutant, Maj. Eugene M. Becher, veterans of the operations at Fairfield Air Depot. The relatively quiet and closely-knit Patterson Field community of the 1930s disappeared almost overnight as depot operations geared up and the post became a center of wartime activity.

General Estabrook first served at Wright-Patterson from September 1927 to January 1928, when he was assigned as Assistant to the Chief of the Supply Branch, Materiel Division, at Wright Field. He graduated from the Air Corps Engineering School at Wright Field in June 1932, and from the Army Industrial College in Washington in 1936. In 1936, he returned to Wright Field as Chief, Engineering and Shops Branch, Materiel Division, and subsequently became Assistant Chief of the Contract Section at Wright Field.

On September 8, 1939, Colonel Estabrook assumed command of Patterson Field, and of the Fairfield Air Depot. In 1943, he served as Commander of the nine-state Fairfield Air Depot Control Area Command, supervising all Air Service Command units contained therein. On May 21, 1943, he became the first Commander of the newly-created Fairfield Air Service Command, one of the eleven ASC "Keep 'Em Flying" organizations in the U.S. In September 1943, Estabrook was promoted to the temporary rank of brigadier general in this position.

On February 16, 1944, General Estabrook was transferred to ASC Headquarters at Patterson Field. He retired from active service due to disability on August 31, 1944, and died December 19, 1947.

Brig. Gen. Merrick Estabrook, Patterson Field Commander, receives a congratulatory scroll from (l to r): Col. Edwin R. Page, Brig. Gen. Elmer E. Adler, Brig. Gen. K. B. Wolfe, and Col. Frank Wolf.

Employees of the FAD Supply Department in front of Building 1, 1941

Open-air storage at FAD, July 1942

During overhaul, engines were carried by means of an overhead system of electric hoists.

Stored on heavy metal racks at FAD, these engines await packaging for shipment to other AAF depots and overseas.

complete and detailed work order records were kept on airplane and engine operations. Work order and airplane parts-handling procedures were standardized and published. Cost accounting was discontinued and replaced with job control, which recorded man-hour expenditures for the various operations. Even these streamlined procedures required a dramatic increase in personnel to handle the load. By December 1942, the civilian work force in the engineering shops had increased to 600 workers.[34]

Transportation of supplies and equipment presented another major problem. Railroads and trucklines became so overburdened that supply missions were jeopardized. Rail and motor transportation, formerly under the Quartermaster's control, were assigned to a specialized Transportation Corps under the jurisdiction of the Post Commander. A tug pool was established to move materiel and equipment between the various storerooms and the shipping department at the depot. A truck pool was then organized to move supplies between the various depots. Finally, a post Traffic Section was established to facilitate more efficient rail service and to supervise the receipt of all commercial rail shipments to Patterson Field.[35]

A summary of the monthly activity report submitted September 30, 1944, by the Supply Division of the Fairfield Air Technical Service Command to Air Technical Service Command headquarters illustrated the scope of the work the depot had very capably organized and accomplished. During the month of September, the Supply Division received 28,791 individual requests involving 96,511 different items of stock. These requests resulted in the preparation of 41,060 individual shipping tickets. The materiel involved filled 460 freight cars with 6,165 tons of domestic and 2,350 tons of overseas shipments. During the same period, warehouse personnel received 630 incoming freight cars loaded with 17,622 tons of supplies and equipment, of which 3,187 tons were gasoline and oil shipments.[36]

Thus Patterson Field and the Fairfield Air Depot exemplified the drive and enthusiasm that existed throughout the Army Air Forces during the war, in the national effort to "Keep 'Em Flying."

These engines are carefully wrapped in Pliofilm and crated to survive shipment to all parts of the world.

MAJOR ORGANIZATIONS

Since Patterson Field was primarily a logistics hub, its subordinate tactical organizations were mostly transport units. The 10th Transport Group, activated May 20, 1937 at Patterson Field, was a consolidation of the 1st Transport Group and the 10th Observation Group. The 10th Transport Group subsequently was reassigned to Wright Field on June 20, 1938, but returned to Patterson on January 16, 1941. The Group transferred to General Billy Mitchell Field, Wisconsin, on May 25, 1942.

The 10th Transport Group trained at Patterson and Wright Fields with C-27 and C-33 aircraft, and consisted of five subordinate squadrons: the 1st (1937-1943), 2nd (1937-1943), 3rd (1937-1940), 4th (1937-1940), and 5th (1937-1944).[37]

The 1st Provisional Transport Squadron, as mentioned previously, was activated July 15, 1935 at Fairfield Air Depot and assigned to the 10th Transport Group on May 20, 1937. While at Patterson, the squadron flew C-27, C-33, and C-39 aircraft, as well as various civilian and military modifications of the DC-3.[38] The 5th Transport Squadron was activated at Patterson Field on October 14, 1933, and operated C-33 and C-39 aircraft.

Douglas C-39 cargo transport, looking toward the cockpit. The C-39, along with the Bellanca C-27 Airbus and the Douglas C-33, were standard aircraft flown by Patterson Field Transport Squadrons. (U.S. Air Force Museum)

Douglas C-33 transports fog-bound at Selfridge Field, Michigan

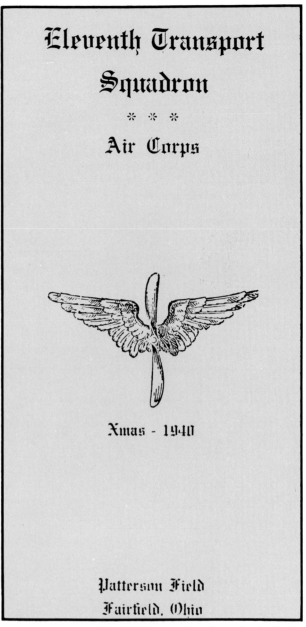

Christmas program of the 11th Transport Squadron, shortly after its December 1, 1940, activation at Patterson Field

Enlisted personnel and civilian workers assigned to Patterson Field enjoy an evening of entertainment.

Members of the Second Airways Communications Squadron

A second tactical organization to be located at Patterson was the 63rd Transport Group. It was constituted November 20, 1940, activated December 1 of the same year at Wright Field, and transferred to Patterson February 17, 1941. While at Patterson, the 63rd operated C-33, C-34, and C-50 aircraft. Its fleet transported supplies, materiel, and personnel in the continental United States and in the Caribbean area.[39] On September 9, 1941, the group moved to Brookley Field, Alabama.

For a short period of time a third transport group was located at Patterson Field. The 316th Transport Group was constituted February 2, 1942 and activated February 14 at Patterson, where it was equipped with C-47 aircraft. On June 17 the organization, with its subordinate transport squadrons (the 36th, 37th, 38th, 44th, and 45th), was reassigned to Bowman Field, Kentucky.[40]

Four other squadrons were assigned briefly to Patterson Field as the Air Corps began expanding for World War II. The 11th Transport Squadron, assigned to the 60th Transport Group, was activated December 1, 1940 at Patterson Field; the 13th Transport Squadron, assigned to the 61st Transport Group, was activated December 1, 1941 at Patterson; the 19th Bombardment Squadron (Medium), assigned to the 2nd Bombardment Group (Medium) at Mitchel Field, New York, was activated February 1, 1940 at Patterson; and the 33rd Bombardment Squadron (Medium), assigned to the 22nd Bombardment Group (Medium), was also activated February 1, 1940 at Patterson.[41] The 19th and the 33rd Bombardment Squadrons both flew Douglas B-18 medium bombers.

MILITARY TRAINING PROGRAMS

One of the most vital functions at Patterson Field during World War II was the amazing array of training programs conducted by the Fairfield Air Depot. One of the most impressive military training efforts involved teams of military specialists known as air depot groups, formed and trained at Patterson Field to perform all of the functions of a miniature mobile depot at remote field locations. Other military programs included training for service groups and squadrons, and depot repair squadrons. During 1942 and early 1943, military personnel were recruited from the Fairfield Air Depot Control Area Command (FADCAC) and trained for duty with these combat support functions in maximum numbers, frequently approximating 10,000 men.[42]

One of several Patterson Field mess halls for enlisted personnel

An unidentified Service Group band performs at the Field, 1944.

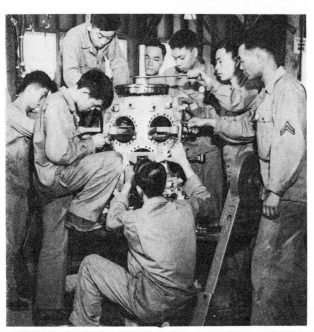

Members of the 407th Service Squadron, Chinese-Americans from across the country. They received their technical training from Fairfield Air Depot personnel at Patterson Field in 1943-1944.

Fairfield Air Depot was responsible for Phase I (activation and unit training) and Phase II (group training). Final or Phase III training was normally conducted at specific field training stations, although a certain amount of Phase III training did take place at Fairfield.

In February 1943, FADCAC assumed training responsibility for the service groups at Lockbourne Army Air Base, Ohio, Kellogg Field, Michigan, and Baer Field, Indiana. The instruction of other arms and services units was also supervised by the special staff at Fairfield.

Two special efforts of the Fairfield training program resulted in the preparation of the 96th Service Group, consisting of Black officers and enlisted personnel, and the training of three Chinese-American service squadrons. The 96th was the only such Service Group trained at Fairfield.[43] In another special effort at Patterson Field, AAF Nurses Training Detachment No. 6 was activated on November 10, 1943, to train nurse recruits.[44]

Special training facilities for officers at FAD included the U.S. Army Materiel Division Supply School, established in October 1940 at the direction of the Chief, Materiel Division, and the Engineering Maintenance Officers'

Women's Army Corps officers assigned to the WAC Supply School at Patterson Field, 1943

ORGANIZATIONS AND UNITS TRAINED BY FAD PERSONNEL

The available list of organizations and units trained by Fairfield Air Depot personnel during World War II include:

Hq 2054th Ordnance Company (Aviation)	Patterson Field
1157th Signal Depot Company (Aviation) (Chinese)	Springfield, Illinois
912th Engineer Headquarters Company	Patterson Field
Detachment 905th Quartermaster (Aviation)	Patterson Field
Detachment 859th Signal Service Company (Aviation)	Patterson Field
838th AAF Specialized Depot Detachment	Marion, Ohio
555th Service Squadron (Chinese)	Springfield, Illinois
315th Depot Repair Squadron	Patterson Field
97th Depot Supply Squadron	Patterson Field
96th Service Group (Black)	Oscoda, Michigan
88th Depot Repair Squadron	Patterson Field
85th Depot Repair Squadron	Patterson Field
55th Air Depot Group	Patterson Field
18th Medical Supply Platoon	Patterson Field
1st Mobile Rubber Repair Detachment	Patterson Field
18th Air Depot Group	Patterson Field
407th Service Squadron (Chinese)	Patterson Field
345th Aviation Squadron (Black)	Patterson Field
1916th Quartermaster Truck Company (Aviation) (Black)	Patterson Field
2007th Quartermaster Truck Company (Aviation) (Black)	Patterson Field

Source: Hist., FADCAC and FASC, 1943-1944, p 125.

Training School, established July 1942 at the request of the Air Service Command.[45] The Supply School also conducted training of enlisted personnel from various supply squadrons and service groups.

CIVILIAN TRAINING PROGRAMS

Equally important at Fairfield was the training of civilian depot workers to support "Keep 'Em Flying" operations. Prior to 1939 there had been little need for training programs for new workers, because skilled employees were readily available in the Dayton area and could be hired as needed. When job training was necessary, it was handled on an individual basis. Wartime expansion demanded that an ever-increasing number of workers be trained for jobs requiring a multitude of technical and mechanical skills. By February of 1943 the civilian employment office at Patterson Field was hiring 300 new employees a day.[46] FAD was responsible for creating training programs for not only its own employees, but also for thousands of employees scheduled to work in many sub-depot supply and engineering departments activated across the country.

A shops training school was activated in June 1941 (replacing the older aircraft training unit) to provide instruction in all phases of aero repair, engine overhaul, machine shop operations, sheet metal manufacturing, and welding.[47] Instructors at the school were often challenged to create innovative programs to compensate for the lack of current textbooks. Engines, starters, and generators built from rejected parts were used for demonstration purposes. A visual aids unit provided a variety of technical films for instructional purposes.[48]

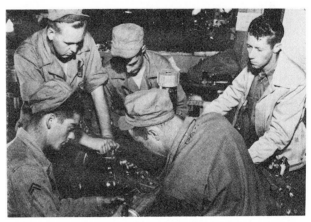

Enlisted mechanics in training at Patterson Field for subsequent transfer to other AAF depots in the U.S. and abroad

In the Supply Division, civilian workers received job-related training beginning in March 1941.[49] Classroom instruction was given in such supply procedures as warehousing, stock records, inspection, and shipping and receiving.

Although originally separate, all training activities conducted by the Engineering and Supply Departments were eventually consolidated under a separate post training department, and later the Personnel and Training Division. A special curriculum unit was assigned responsibility for issuing study guides, manuals, worksheets, and other instructional materials for use in the Fairfield training programs. Within a short time, the group of curriculum writers was augmented by artists, photographic illustrators, draftsmen, veritypists, and other professionals, who together

Patterson Field officers' wives prepare personal items for shipment overseas.

The wartime newspaper was the *Patterson Field Postings*. *(Dick Cull)*

First Lady Mrs. Eleanor Roosevelt addresses officers' wives involved in Red Cross work at Patterson Field.

Patterson Field main gate, adjacent to Building 1, 1940

produced a number of quality training publications. Many of these manuals received wide distribution in other air depots in the U.S., and served as the basis for national standardization of ASC manuals.[50]

As classes grew larger, the makeshift classrooms used on base became inadequate. For a short time, education of civilian supply personnel was conducted at Osborn High School during after-school hours and during the summer of 1943. In September 1943, the supply school classes were moved to the new depot training school buildings in Wood City, Buildings 50, 1044, 1045, and 1046.[51] The move ensured that more space and permanent fixed equipment were available to accommodate larger supply and maintenance classes. Engineering Division courses were held in a special building erected as a theater and auditorium in Area C. This building remained in use until 1943, when the engineering training school also moved to new quarters in Wood City.[52]

Recruiting for the depot training programs at Fairfield was a continual challenge. In order to ensure a high number of qualified trainees at Fairfield and other ASC depots, the

Civilian workers in the Supply Division at FASC

Air Service Command initiated pre-induction or pre-service training programs at various high schools and junior colleges.

Patterson Field cooperated with the Ohio State Board of Vocational Education and local boards of education in Ohio to establish this pre-service instruction. The first course was set up at Springfield High School on March 1, 1943, with a class of 22 senior boys in a program of aircraft engine repair. Other centers offering pre-service training in engine repair were set up at Norwood, Portsmouth, Zanesville, Washington Court House, Cambridge, Franklin, Ironton, and Hamilton. In addition, Portsmouth and Zanesville offered a course in aircraft repair. During the spring of 1944 there were 12 classes with a total enrollment of 190 students, and by June 20 the graduates were ready to enter the armed services or accept employment at Patterson Field.[53]

Additional off-reservation schools were instituted by the Fairfield Air Service Command in October of 1943, as the local employment situation became acute. In cooperation with the State Board of Vocational Education, training centers were established at nine selected schools in Ohio and four in Kentucky. Machine shop and sheet metal courses were offered in four-week sessions. A two-week engine course was also offered.

The off-reservation schools were soon supplying trainees to the civilian training branch at the rate of approximately 75 new workers per week. The Maintenance Division at Fairfield came to depend almost wholly upon this source for personnel replacements.[54]

A 1944 report to the FASC commanding officer revealed that from May 1, 1943 to May 1, 1944 alone, a total of $676,065.94 had been invested by the government in the civilian training program at Patterson Field, including the off-reservation training mentioned above and a radio mechanics training program conducted in part under contract at the University of Wisconsin.[55]

ASSISTING WITH THE CREATION OF NEW DEPOTS

As the American air fleet grew, decentralization of repair and maintenance facilities became imperative. FAD, as one of the oldest permanent repair depots in the country, was called upon to apply lessons learned from its many years of experience to support this program. It became one of FAD's most important missions during the war to provide expertise in the establishment, layout, and manning of new depots and sub-depots.

Organization of new depots was coordinated by the Provisional Air Corps Maintenance Command, which was organized with headquarters at Patterson Field in the spring of 1941. Service and training at depots in the eastern part of the country were the responsibility of the Fairfield Provisional Maintenance Group. Key personnel for new sub-depots were recruited from among the engineering and supply employees at FAD. A total of 41 sub-depots were established by FAD by September 1942, of which 21 remained under FAD control.[56]

Once new depots were established, the crucial need for trained, experienced personnel had to be met immediately. Training for these personnel was provided by FAD instructors both at Fairfield and on-site. Trained personnel from FAD often remained at these depots as key supervisors:[57]

Enlisted mechanics at Patterson receive hands-on training in critical armament repair work.

> Everything was rush, both at Fairfield and at the sub-depots as each was established. Thousands of new employees were being hired and all departments of the Fairfield Air Depot were being rapidly expanded. The relative handful of trained and qualified employees were urgently needed in each department to train and supervise hundreds of new workers. . . . Gradually however the training program at Fairfield produced sufficient trained personnel to ease the situation.

SUB-DEPOTS UNDER FAIRFIELD AIR DEPOT CONTROL, 1942

OFFICIAL NAME	OFFICIAL ADDRESS	DATE ACTIVATED
Alliance Sub-Depot	Alliance, Nebraska	Sep. 2, 1942
Baer Sub-Depot	Fort Wayne, Indiana	Mar. 21, 1942
Berry Sub-Depot	Nashville, Tennessee	Jan. 10, 1942
Bowman Sub-Depot	Louisville, Kentucky	Mar. 21, 1942
Chanute Sub-Depot	Rantoul, Illinois	Sep. 16, 1942
Coffeyville Sub-Depot	Coffeyville, Kansas	Aug. 2, 1942
George Sub-Depot	Lawrenceville, Illinois	Jun. 16, 1942
Kellogg Sub-Depot	Battle Creek, Michigan	Sep. 1, 1942
Lockbourne Sub-Depot	Lockbourne, Ohio	Jul. 2, 1942
Madison Sub-Depot	Madison, Wisconsin	Jun. 19, 1942
Rapid City Sub-Depot	Rapid City, South Dakota	Jul. 20, 1942
Salina Sub-Depot	Salina, Kansas	Sep. 7, 1942
Scott Sub-Depot	Belleville, Illinois	Aug. 15, 1941
Sedalia Sub-Depot	Sedalia, Missouri	Sep. 2, 1942
Selfridge Sub-Depot	Mt. Clemens, Michigan	Mar. 12, 1942
Shaw Sub-Depot	Sumter, South Carolina	Oct. 1, 1941
Sioux City Sub-Depot	Sioux City, Iowa	Aug. 1, 1942
Sioux Falls Sub-Depot	Sioux Falls, South Dakota	Jun. 19, 1942
Smyrna Sub-Depot	Smyrna, Tennessee	May 15, 1942
Topeka Sub-Depot	Topeka, Kansas	Aug. 1, 1942
Wayne County Sub-Depot	Romulus, Michigan	Jan. 10, 1942

Source: Hist., FAD, 1917-1943, Exhibit 64.

Air depot repair squadrons were trained at Patterson Field to perform all of the functions of a mobile miniature depot at remote field locations.

During 1942 and 1943, emphasis was given to the concept of specialized depots with each depot assigned one or more classes of spare parts, equipment, and supplies for specified aircraft. By the end of 1943, specialized depots had become the backbone of the Air Corps supply system, with 68 of the Air Corps depots classified as such.[58]

COMMAND ASSIGNMENTS

The story of the Fairfield Air Depot's command assignments from 1941 until the depot's deactivation in 1946 is a complex but interesting one. Changes in command occurred both prior to and during the war with some frequency, to reflect organizational changes pursued at the national level. They were necessitated by changing wartime needs and continuous efforts to improve materiel management in support of AAF programs.

As part of the Air Corps depot system, Fairfield was under the jurisdiction of the Field Service Section of the Materiel Division from 1926 until 1941. As supply and maintenance requirements intensified, the Materiel Division was divided, and its logistics functions separated from those of engineering and procurement. Effective March 15, 1941, logistics became the responsibility of the Provisional Air Corps Maintenance Command, established as a "service test" of the maintenance command system under the direction of the Materiel Division. The Provisional Maintenance Command consisted of its Headquarters, the Field Service Section, the 50th Transport Wing, and the six major depots, including Fairfield. Subordinate to this Command, two Provisional Maintenance Group Areas (PMGAs) were established, the Fairfield PMGA and the San Antonio PMGA. The Fairfield PMGA encompassed the Fairfield Air Depot and sub-depots at Selma, Montgomery, and Maxwell Fields in Alabama, and Eglin Field in Florida.

On April 29, 1941, the designation "Provisional" was dropped and the Air Corps Maintenance Command was officially established by the War Department, although it

remained under the guidance of the Materiel Division for some time. The new command was headquartered at Patterson Field. The Field Service Section, however, retained its quarters at Wright Field. The awkwardness of this arrangement soon became apparent, and on June 19 the Maintenance Command offices moved to Wright Field. On August 28, 1941, the Maintenance Command was instructed to establish sub-depots at all stations under the direct control of the Chief of the Air Corps. As previously mentioned, FAD played a large role in this program.

The Air Corps Maintenance Command, however, had been established to perform a specific, limited job—that of supplying the Air Corps and maintaining its equipment. By the summer of 1941, the nature of the Air Corps had changed, with the establishment of the combined Army Air Forces and the rapid expansion of the Air Force Combat Command (formerly GHQ Air Force). It was clearly evident that an expanded maintenance organization was needed, one that would assume supply and maintenance functions for both branches of the Army Air Forces.

In October 1941, the Maintenance Command was reorganized as the Air Service Command to meet this need. Air Service Command Areas were established with boundaries that at first coincided with Air Force boundaries, and later followed depot control area boundaries. On December 11, 1941, the Air Service Command was separated from the Materiel Division entirely and became directly responsible to the Chief of the Army Air Forces, with headquarters in

---

PATTERSON FIELD COMMANDERS

Maj. Albert L. Sneed	Jul. 1931
Lt. Col. Fred H. Coleman	Nov. 1933
Lt. Col. Junius H. Houghton	Jul. 1936
Col. Merrick G. Estabrook, Jr.	Sep. 1939
Col. James A. Woodruff	Feb. 1943
Col. Raymond E. Culbertson	Dec. 1943
Col. Elmer E. Jose	Jul. 1944

Colonel Jose was the last Commander of Patterson Field as a separate facility. From December 9, 1944, until Wright and Patterson Fields were redesignated Wright-Patterson AFB on January 13, 1948, care of the facility shifted increasingly toward the merger.

From December 9, 1944, to November 5, 1945, the Patterson Field commander, per se, was Brig. Gen. H. A. Bartron, Commander of the Fairfield Air Technical Service Command. On November 6, 1945, a combined staff was appointed for the concurrent operations of Wright and Patterson Fields under Brig. Gen. Joseph T. Morris, current Commander of Wright Field and the 4000th Army Air Forces Base Unit. General Morris continued in command on December 15, 1945, when Wright and Patterson Fields were combined for administrative purposes under an umbrella organization designated the Army Air Forces Technical Base (AAFTB), and on December 9, 1947, when the AAFTB was redesignated the Air Force Technical Base (AFTB).

Intersection of Wright Avenue and Pearson Road. Patterson Field Headquarters (Building 11) is at right. Fairfield Air Service Command Hq (Building 10) is at left, along with Patterson Field Officers' Dining Room. Patterson Field Base Operations (Building 206) is visible in the background.

Washington. The Field Service Section remained at Wright Field until the new ASC headquarters building (Building 262) was completed at Patterson Field. In September 1942, Field Service Section headquarters moved to the new Patterson Field location. Meanwhile, in March 1942, the Materiel Division was elevated to command status. The Materiel Command retained responsibility for the engineering and procurement work of the Army Air Forces and was headquartered temporarily in Washington. On April 1, 1943, Materiel Command headquarters returned to Wright Field.

As the war progressed, further changes were made in the Air Service Command. In December 1942, ASC headquarters moved from Washington to Patterson Field, Building 262. Coinciding with the move, the Field Service Section was officially discontinued. On December 19, the Air Service Command was authorized to disband the Air Service Area Commands and to activate Air Depot Control Areas. On February 1, 1943, the Air Service Command outlined a new organization of eleven Air Depot Control Areas. At that time, the depot at Fairfield was redesignated the Fairfield Air Depot Control Area Command (FADCAC), with responsibility for a nine-state area (Ohio, Iowa, Michigan, Wisconsin, Minnesota, Illinois, Indiana, Missouri, and Kentucky). Installations contained in this nine-state area included 21 storage depots, 16 sub-depots, 3 servicing detachments, 4 air depot detachments, 2 air cargo depot detachments, and 2 overhaul detachments.

FADCAC officer strength on February 22, 1943 stood at 1,013, with 41 assigned to area headquarters, 197 to the Fairfield Air Depot, 81 to sub-depots, 90 to storage depots, 348 to tactical units, and the remainder to smaller organizations.

ASC Headquarters, Building 262. The Fairfield Air Depot came under the jurisdiction of the Air Corps Maintenance Command in the spring of 1941. In October 1941, the Maintenance Command was reorganized as the Air Service Command (ASC). In December 1942, Hq ASC moved from Washington, D.C., to newly-completed Building 262 on Patterson Field.

Offices for the FADCAC organization were established in the Patterson Field post headquarters, Building 11, side by side with base offices. To an extent, functions of the FADCAC offices and the base administrative offices were intermingled, with area and base officers performing duties of either headquarters. This situation resulted from a shortage of available officers to staff both offices and the familiarity of most personnel with base operations. A clear and distinct separation of the two offices was not achieved until March 8, 1944, at which time Building 10 was completed as a separate headquarters for the control area command.[59]

Meanwhile, a conference of all control area commanding officers was held at Air Service Command headquarters on March 1-2, 1943, to explain the new ASC organizational structure, how the various ASC divisions were to operate within it, and how the system extended down through the depots and into the sub-depots. In all, the internal reorganization of the Air Service Command was completed in slightly more than four months. It had been ably implemented under the direction of Maj. Gen. Walter H. Frank and his staff at Patterson Field, with special guidance

provided by Brig. Gen. Robert E. Wood (Retired). Wood, then President of Sears Roebuck Corporation, assisted General Frank in applying modern industrial organizational concepts to the military supply and maintenance system.

As the system of depot control areas was further refined, General Frank recommended that each control area be identified as "Air Service Command," preceded by the name of the town in which the respective headquarters were located. Thus, effective May 17, 1943, the Fairfield depot command was redesignated the Fairfield Air Service Command (FASC).[60] Responsibilities of the command remained the same.

On August 31, 1944, the Materiel Command at Wright Field and the Air Service Command at Patterson Field were combined and redesignated the Army Air Forces Technical Service Command, once again centralizing control of all logistics and engineering operations. New command headquarters were set up at the former ASC headquarters building (Building 262).[61]

The name of FASC was changed to the Fairfield Air Technical Service Command (FATSC) on December 6, 1944, reflecting the organizational change.* Just prior to this name change, on November 27, 1944, FASC headquarters and the Patterson Field base command were again merged, so that the Commanding General of FATSC also commanded the Patterson Field Army Air Base and the

Close-up of Building 206, hub of World War II air traffic operations at Patterson Field

Brig. Gen. H. A. Bartron and staff in front of FATSC Headquarters (Building 10), 1945

*Other depot control areas also changed from "Air Service Commands" to "Air Technical Service Commands."

4100th Army Air Force Base Unit. The designation Fairfield Air Technical Service Command remained in effect until the depot's deactivation in January 1946.

On March 9, 1946, the Air Technical Service Command was renamed Air Materiel Command (AMC). Headquarters for the command remained in Building 262. The Air Materiel Command (predecessor of today's Air Force Logistics Command) remained the parent command for both Wright and Patterson Fields until their merger in January 1948, and subsequently assumed command authority over Wright-Patterson AFB.

The 361st AAF Band was organized at Patterson Field in 1942. It was redesignated the 661st Army Band in 1944, and finally the 661st Air Force Band in 1947.

The Civilian Club on Patterson Field (Building 274, Area A) opened on December 1, 1944, to the strains of Lawrence Welk and his orchestra. Weekend dances attracted large numbers of the young and young-at-heart from nearby on-base civilian housing in Skyway Park as well as other areas of the base community. Nationally-known dance orchestras often provided the entertainment. The Civilian Club continued as a recreation facility until 1979, when it was converted for use as a Wright-Patterson AFB Conference Center.

PATTERSON FIELD AND THE END OF THE WAR

The small air depot at Fairfield, Ohio, had opened in 1918 as the Fairfield Aviation General Supply Depot to serve World War I Signal Corps aviation schools. By 1945, it had greatly expanded, ably serving the needs of the World War II Army Air Forces around the world. Its host, Patterson Field, had expanded from a small, closely-knit 1930s installation to a major logistics center and midwest hub of World War II activities.

In the months following the war, Patterson Field was an active separation center for military personnel. In September 1945, the 4265th AAF Base Unit Separation Center was activated under the command of Col. Richard Gimbel. The Center was located in Wood City at Patterson Field, in buildings formerly used for civilian training. In the early weeks, up to 150 men were separated daily, with the pro-

World War I

World War II

289

cessing period per man averaging nearly 36 hours. By the end of December the Center had accelerated the separation process to nearly 1,000 men per day. As of November 13, 1945, records indicate that 14,675 enlisted men and 3,508 officers had been processed. In total, more than 35,000 men were separated through the Center.

The Separation Center was established primarily to discharge officers and enlisted men arriving from Army Air Forces posts elsewhere, but did everything possible to expedite the discharge of men stationed at Patterson Field. Initially, members of the Women's Army Corps (WACs) were not processed at Patterson but were sent to the nearest service and groundforce point of separation. Base newspapers indicate, however, that WACS were eventually allowed to separate at Patterson as well.[62]

Depot functions at Patterson Field underwent substantial reduction, and were eventually discontinued entirely in the months following V-J Day (August 15, 1945). Post-war reorganization called for supply-maintenance depot functions to be concentrated in selected Air Materiel Areas (the successors to the Air Technical Service Command control areas). Fairfield was one of the depots selected for deactivation, and the long history of the air depot at Fairfield thus came to an end. On the first of January 1946, the Fairfield Air Technical Service Command was officially deactivated and its functions reassigned to other Air Materiel Areas. Most ATSC personnel were assigned to other agencies on Wright and Patterson Fields or transferred to other Air Materiel Areas.

The physical appearance of Patterson Field also changed as the base settled into its post-war mission. Experience gained during the war had emphasized the importance of coordinated planning. From 1943 on, construction at Wright and Patterson Fields, as well as land acquisition, had been handled through the action of coordinated planning boards. Master plans were drawn up by city planners of national reputation, approved by the Commanding General of the Army Air Forces, and executed under the direction of local installation planning boards. In 1945, the master plans for both Wright and Patterson Fields were integrated into a single master plan for the Wright-Patterson complex, presaging the eventual integration of both fields into one installation.[63]

One of the major projects of the new master plan was the construction of the VHB runway at Patterson Field in 1946-1947. Designed to service the very heavy bombers and jet-powered aircraft anticipated in the post-war period, the new runway was 8,000 feet long and 300 feet wide, with an additional overrun of 1,000 feet at each end, and a load capacity of 300,000 lbs/ft^2.* Patterson Field was chosen as the site of the VHB runway rather than Wright Field because of the more flexible limits on its military reservation boundaries, and because the existing topography was more adaptable to the physical proportions of a VHB runway.[64]

By late 1945, Wright and Patterson Fields had begun to merge functions and services. As detailed in Chapter V, Wright and Patterson Fields, along with two satellite organizations, were consolidated under an umbrella organization

Construction of the VHB runway at Patterson Field, 1947

*Initially the runway was popularized as "the B-36 runway."

known as the Army Air Forces Technical Base, Dayton, Ohio. On December 15, 1945, Brig. Gen. Joseph T. Morris, previously the Wright Field Commanding General, took command of the new administrative organization.

On December 9, 1947, the AAF Technical Base, Dayton, Ohio, was redesignated the Air Force Technical Base, reflecting the independent status of the U.S. Air Force. One month later, on January 13, 1948, the installation's designation was finalized as Wright-Patterson Air Force Base, culminating more than thirty years of development.

Trainway entrance to Building 1 in 1948, entering its 30th year of active service to the facility

Col. Joseph T. Morris (seated), Commander of the Air Force Technical Base and former Wright Field Commander

Patterson Field, 1947, just prior to its merger with Wright Field to form Wright-Patterson AFB. Another merger was also eminent—the adjacent towns of Fairfield and Osborn merged to become the City of Fairborn in 1950.

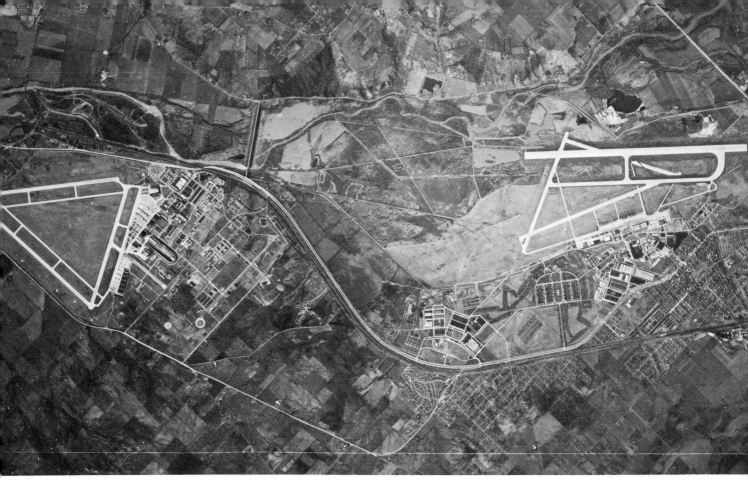

Wright-Patterson AFB, 1950

VIII.   WRIGHT-PATTERSON AFB 1948-1982

On January 13, 1948, Wright Field and Patterson Field were merged into a single installation and designated Wright-Patterson Air Force Base.[1] The name change coincided with the renaming of numerous Air Force fields as bases, and ended a long succession of designations applied to the Dayton installations. Wright-Patterson was assigned to Hq Air Materiel Command (AMC), and received operating support from the 4000th Air Force Base Unit.

By September 1948, Wright-Patterson AFB was ready to display both its pride and its success. A gala Air Force Day celebration was held on September 18 in commemoration of the first birthday of the autonomous U.S. Air Force. Technological advances in Air Force weapons and equipment were highlighted during the day-long open house on the Area B flightline.* Some 150,000 spectators attended the celebration.

On central display was the Strategic Air Command's new Consolidated-Vultee B-36 Peacemaker six-engine bomber. Attendees also enjoyed flight demonstrations by the AMC Flight Test Division and the 162nd Fighter Squadron of the Ohio National Guard. A huge six-foot birthday cake was cut and served in celebration of the Air Force's first anniversary.[2]

The message conveyed by the Air Force Day open house was that the Air Materiel Command, through its Wright-Patterson AFB offices and laboratories and personnel stationed around the world, would play a key role in making the new Air Force a valuable instrument for international peace.

Operation VITTLES, more popularly known as the Berlin Airlift, was the first event of global import to affect the newly-designated base and a significant challenge to the effectiveness of the Air Materiel Command. Wright-Patterson employees, both military and civilian, played an important role in the success of this operation.

On June 22, 1948, a Soviet-imposed rail and highway blockade of West Berlin isolated the American, British, and French occupied zones of the city, including more than two

---

*As part of the consolidated base, Wright Field became known as Area B, Wright-Patterson. The south end of Patterson Field, including Hq Air Materiel Command and the officers' brick quarters became known as Area A. The north end of Patterson Field, including the former Fairfield Air Depot, became known as Area C.

Crowds line the apron on the Area B flightline during the gala Air Force Day celebration held September 18, 1948.

Star of the 1948 open house was the Consolidated-Vultee B-36 Peacemaker, the largest combat airplane to reach full production status without ever flying a combat mission.

A huge six-foot birthday cake was baked in honor of the first anniversary of the USAF.

Four-engine C-54 transports (shown) and twin-engine C-47s maintained the round-the-clock aerial supply line into Berlin.

Hq Air Materiel Command (AMC) at Wright-Patterson AFB provided aircraft parts and supplies for airplanes involved in Operation VITTLES (popularly known as the Berlin Airlift), during 1948-1949. Here sacks of flour are unloaded from a C-47 at Templehof Airdrome, West Berlin. *(U.S. Air Force Museum)*

million German citizens. U.S. response to the Berlin crisis demonstrated to the world the ingenuity and flexibility of the U.S. Air Force and called attention to the intense logistics planning necessary to maintain a long-term aerial supply line. Over a fifteen-month period, from June 26, 1948 to September 30, 1949, Operation VITTLES airlifted more than two million tons of food, fuel, and supplies into West Berlin.

Hq AMC at Wright-Patterson was responsible for providing the parts and supplies necessary to maintain the Air Force fleet involved in the airlift. The only transport airplanes available at the beginning of Operation VITTLES were twin-engine C-47s. AMC's first priority was to supervise the transfer of the Air Force's larger and faster four-engine C-54 transports to Germany. The second priority became to ship sufficient spare parts to Europe to keep the C-54s in operation.

As the blockade continued, a priority requisition system was established between AMC Headquarters and the airlift nerve center at Rhein-Main Air Base in West Germany. Daily cables were received at Wright-Patterson, many as long as 20 teletyped pages with 20 items to the page, listing the parts needed to keep the cargo transports airworthy. Orders were disseminated to the various AMC depots, given highest priority, and filled immediately for air shipment to Germany. With the support of Hq AMC personnel, the airlift's round-the-clock schedule was sustained, uninterrupted by maintenance or parts delays.[3]

Although the Soviet surface blockade was finally lifted in May 1949, the airlift continued an additional four months to allow reserve stocks in Berlin to reach satisfactory levels and assure that the international political situation was clarified. By the time the final flight was completed in September 1949, Wright-Patterson AFB had laid a firm foundation for its enduring role in the history of the modern United States Air Force.

THE 2750TH AIR BASE WING

Base operating support for Wright-Patterson AFB was initially furnished by the 4000th Air Force Base Unit, which had provided support for Patterson Field prior to the merger. On August 28, 1948, the 4000th and its subordinate units were redesignated as Hq and Hq Sq 2750th Air Force Base.[4] The following year, on October 4, 1949, the 2750th Air Force Base was redesignated as Hq and Hq Sq 2750th Air Base Wing. The "Hq" and "Hq Sq" were subsequently deleted, leading to the modern designation for Wright-Patterson's base operating unit, the 2750th Air Base Wing.

In addition to directing the Wing's support operations, the Wing Commander also served as the Base Commander. This dual position of Commanding Officer of the 2750th Air Base Wing and WPAFB was filled by Brig. Gen. Joseph T. Morris, former Commander of Wright Field and subsequently of the Air Force Technical Base. General Morris was a master planner, with an impressive breadth of vision. He served Wright-Patterson and its antecedents in a leadership capacity from July 1945 until August 1952. A contemporary of General Morris described him as the "architect" of Wright-Patterson AFB, having skillfully guided the installation from a wartime to a peacetime configuration and from the age of propeller aircraft into the era of jet aircraft and missiles.

For his meritorious services, General Morris was popularly recognized as the "Father of Wright-Patterson Air Force Base." The 2750th Air Base Wing Headquarters building (Building 10, Area C) was named in honor of General Morris during formal memorialization ceremonies on August 28, 1981.

HEADQUARTERS
WRIGHT-PATTERSON AIR FORCE BASE
DAYTON, OHIO

GENERAL ORDERS   TSWAJ2/eb
NUMBER   32   27 Aug 1948

        SECTION   I - REDESIGNATION OF UNITS AND DESIGNATION OF TABLE OF
                      DISTRIBUTION UNITS
        SECTION II - TRANSFER OF PERSONNEL
        SECTION III - GENERAL PROVISIONS

        SECTION I - Redesignation of Units and Designation of Table of Distribution
Units. Pursuant to authority contained in letter Headquarters, United States
Air Force, 18 June 1948, subject: "Numbering and Designation of Air Force Table
of Distribution Units", Air Force Regulation 20-52 dated 17 June 1948, General
Order No. 53 Headquarters Air Materiel Command dated 20 August 1948 and General
Order No. 57 Headquarters Air Materiel Command dated 26 August 1948, the 4000th
Air Force Base Unit and units comprising the 4000th Air Force Base Unit are
redesignated, and the following Table of Distribution Units are designated
effective as indicated:

OLD DESIGNATION	NEW DESIGNATION	LOCATION	EFFECTIVE DATE
4000th Air Force Base Unit	Hq & Hq Sq 2750th Air Force Base	Wright-Patterson Air Force Base, Dayton, Ohio	28 August 1948
Sq R 4000th AFBU	Hq & Hq Sq 2750th Air Force Base	Wright-Patterson Air Force Base, Dayton, Ohio	28 August 1948
Sq W 4000th AFBU	Hq & Hq Sq 2750th Air Force Base	Wright-Patterson Air Force Base, Dayton, Ohio	28 August 1948
Sq A 4000th AFBU	3060 AVC Hq Support Sq	Wright-Patterson Air Force Base, Dayton, Ohio	28 August 1948
Sq E 4000th AFBU	2790 Station Medical Sq	Wright-Patterson Air Force Base, Dayton, Ohio	28 August 1948
Sq E 4000th AFBU	3051 Air Base Support	Wright-Patterson Air Force Base, Dayton, Ohio	28 August 1948
Sq D 4000th AFBU	3000 WAF Sq	Wright-Patterson Air Force Base, Dayton, Ohio	27 August 1948
4140th Air Force Base Unit	United States Air Force Exhibit Unit	Wright-Patterson Air Force Base, Dayton, Ohio	28 August 1948
None	Hq & Hq Sq 2925 Base Supply	Wright-Patterson Air Force Base, Dayton, Ohio	28 August 1948
None	Hq & Hq Sq 2926 Base Maintenance	Wright-Patterson Air Force Base, Dayton, Ohio	28 August 1948

        2. Newly designated units listed in Paragraph 1 are assigned to the Wright-
Patterson Air Force Base and remain under the jurisdiction of the Commanding
Officer, Wright-Patterson Air Force Base.

General Orders Number 32, Hq WPAFB, redesignated the 4000th Air Force Base Unit as Hq and Hq Sq 2750th Air Force Base (later the 2750th Air Base Wing), effective August 28, 1948.

Brig. Gen. Joseph T. Morris (right) is popularly recognized as the "Father of Wright-Patterson AFB." Col. C. Pratt Brown (left) succeeded General Morris as WPAFB Commander in March 1952.

BRIG. GEN. JOSEPH T. MORRIS

Joseph Theodore Morris was born in Punxsutawney, Pennsylvania, April 17, 1894. He graduated from Pennsylvania State College with a Bachelor of Science degree in 1917.

Enlisting in February 1918, Morris was commissioned June 13, 1918, as a second lieutenant of Air Service in the National Army and became a radio officer with the First Provisional Wing at Mineola, Long Island, New York.

In 1931, he entered the Air Corps Engineering School at Wright Field, Ohio, and graduated the following June. He returned to Dayton next in 1941, as Assistant Chief of the Maintenance Division of the Air Service Command at Patterson Field, Ohio.

In July 1943, Morris was appointed Commander of the 8th Air Force Service Command in England. The following January he became Chief of Maintenance for the U.S. Strategic Air Forces in the European theater. In February 1945, he assumed command of the 12th Air Force Service Command in Italy. After the war ended in Europe, he returned to Ohio once more, this time as Commander of Wright Field. He served subsequently as Commanding Officer of the AAF Technical Base, Dayton, Ohio, from December 1945 to December 1947, of the Air Force Technical Base from December 1947 to January 1948, and of Wright-Patterson Air Force Base from January 13, 1948 to March 28, 1952.

Brigadier General Morris retired from the Air Force on July 31, 1953. Upon retirement he returned to Dayton from Spokane Air Force Depot, his last assignment. He served as Vice President of United Aircraft Products, Inc., until 1959. General Morris resided in Fairborn from 1959 until his death, on May 21, 1980, in the USAF Medical Center, Wright-Patterson. He was buried at Arlington National Cemetery on May 27, 1980.

Building 10, headquarters for the 2750th Air Base Wing, about 1960.

2750TH AIR BASE WING EMBLEM

The official emblem of today's 2750th Air Base Wing was adopted in April 1969 and bears the Wing's motto, "Strength Through Support." The emblem is symbolic of the Wing and bears the Air Force colors, golden yellow and ultramarine blue. Ultramarine blue denotes the sky, the primary theater of Air Force operations. Yellow denotes the sun and the excellence of personnel in assigned duties. The vintage airplane, a Wright Flyer, is indicative of the heritage of aviation at Wright-Patterson AFB, which the Wing has supported since 1948. Wright-Patterson is known as the birthplace of military aviation and the 2750th has been assigned to no other air base. The stylized aircraft on the shield represent modern-day weapon systems. The center portion—mach cone or shock wave—denotes the aerospace mission of the unit. The Lamp of Knowledge represents the research imparted by personnel of the Wing.

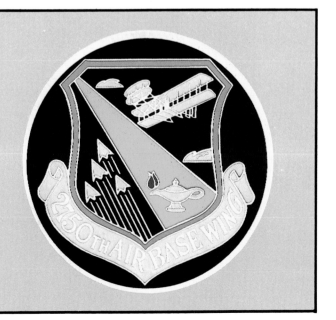

WRIGHT-PATTERSON IN THE 1950s

A TIME OF TRANSITION

Air Force blue uniforms were on order as the Air Force entered the 1950s, but olive drab and fatigue green were to continue as the predominant uniforms for another three years. On June 27, 1950, the Air Force was back in combat, this time in South Korea.

The Air Force was better prepared for this conflict than it had been for World War II, though not by much. Most of its 20,000 aircraft were of World War II vintage, and a significant percentage of these, especially combat aircraft, were in storage. Congressional emphasis over the previous three years had been on reducing military expenses, and accordingly, acquisition of new airplanes came very low on the list of priorities. Although the Far East Air Forces (FEAF) in South Korea and Japan had a variety of fighters and bombers in its combat fleet, only one model, the F-80, was a jet.

Support aspects of the conflict in Korea rested heavily on the Air Materiel Command at Wright-Patterson. To meet immediate demands, aircraft in storage were overhauled, modified, and sent into action. By November 1950, just a few months after the start of the war, AMC depots had modified and reconditioned more than 400 aircraft for use in the Far East. But what the Air Force really needed was thousands of aircraft that incorporated the latest develop-

ments in technology, delivered to the front as fast as possible. Congress appropriated $10 billion to buy new airplanes, and AMC was tasked with setting goals for the industrial effort, scheduling industrial output, and evaluating the impact of aircraft programs on basic national resources. As the result of significant efforts at Wright-Patterson, new airplanes at the front by the end of the Korean conflict on July 27, 1953, included the F-84 Thunderjet and the F-86 Sabre, both capable of engaging and defeating Communist MiG aircraft in aerial combat.

The flow of supplies to Korea was ably managed by AMC, a difficult assignment under the best of circum-

The North American F-86 Sabre was the first successful American swept-wing military jet fighter. Sabres like this F-86E earned renown during the Korean War in combat against Russian MiG-15 fighters.

Area C flightline, about 1950

298

stances. The long pipeline to the Far East called for extraordinary efforts in maintaining an effective and reliable logistical support system.

As the Korean War was prolonged, Air Force activities expanded on a global basis. Activities at Wright-Patterson reflected this expansion. Problems confronting the Base Commander pyramided as the pace of base functions escalated to nearly wartime levels. A significant increase in the military and civilian work force took place as new organizations were added to the base and greater work loads were levied on all departments. The addition of personnel in turn compounded the chronic family housing shortage that the base had faced throughout the 1940s.

To meet an expanded mission, the Ground Controlled Approach (GCA) on the Area C flightline accelerated to 24-hour operations due to the increased amount of flying. The Air Base Chaplain's office monitored a clothing drive for the aid of Korean war victims. Korean War wounded arrived at the Wright-Patterson hospital for treatment. A special blood donor center was operated at WPAFB during the crisis to meet the demand for blood. The Air Reserve Training Branch, established to continue the military training of reserve officers in civilian life, was deactivated; its activities had ceased almost entirely as reserve officers were recalled to active service.[5]

In December 1950, the Air Materiel Command was designated the sole procuring activity within the Department of the Air Force. Under the impetus of wartime support and rearmament, its role became mammoth. Its work force grew from 93,600 in 1948 to 137,000 in 1951, and reached 224,000 by the late 1950s. Fiscal year expenditures during the Korean conflict further reflected the extent of the overall logistics mission: $1.7 billion in 1950; $3.6 billion in 1951; $8.1 billion in 1952; and $10.5 billion in 1953.[6]

AMC began to decentralize its many functions in the early 1950s. Gen. Edwin W. Rawlings, AMC Commander, initiated the decentralization process in early 1952. Under his direction, Hq AMC's primary mission shifted from operations to program management and field commanders of the various Air Materiel Areas became responsible for selected aspects of supply, maintenance, and procurement. The respective depots were also specialized to handle specific commodities and given exclusive responsibility for computing requirements, purchasing, receiving, storing, shipping, and maintaining the particular items assigned to them. Once relieved of the voluminous load of paperwork these processes involved, Hq AMC was able to concentrate on the most important phase of procurement—purchasing complex and expensive aerial weapon systems and the required supporting subsystems.

The 2750th Air Base Wing, as the base support organization at WPAFB, assisted in moving many of the AMC divisions to outlying areas. The work load of each component of the 2750th Air Base Wing was affected in some

Hq AMC underwent significant decentralization during the 1950s under the leadership of Gen. Edwin W. Rawlings, AMC Commander.

manner by this major effort. The civilian personnel branch carried the heaviest load. It was responsible for processing all paperwork involved in the transfer of employees and their positions to fifteen AMC installations throughout the United States. An Employee Utilization Section dealt with special problems in connection with the decentralization program. An Out-Service Placement sub-unit assisted people who were unable to transfer with their positions and could not be reassigned at WPAFB. A Transportation sub-unit arranged travel of employees and their dependents to the new locations and transportation of household goods.[7] By 1957, the decentralization process was complete and the new arrangement was working well.

In July 1954, AMC acquired its first computer, a Remington Rand UNIVAC, signaling a new age in the field of logistics. The complex work of computing logistics requirements was soon automated, allowing supply, maintenance, and procurement information to be integrated quickly and accurately, in ways previously unimaginable.

Although decentralization and automation of AMC were dominant themes during the early 1950s, perhaps the most significant change in the command structure was the separation of the research and development function of AMC into a distinct R & D command.

Research and development was one of three pillars of AMC's World War II antecedent organization, the Materiel Division, and dated from the early experimental work at McCook Field.* In the closing stages of World War II, it

---

*Besides research and development, major Materiel Division activities were procurement-acquisition and maintenance-logistical support.

had become increasingly apparent that science and technology would determine America's future air supremacy and consequently the nation's security.

The research program of the Air Materiel Command was, by nature, largely oriented toward development of new and improved equipment, and hence toward service and production engineering. This meant that more often than not, basic research took second place to applied research. The inherent danger was that, over a period of time, the technological base so crucial to future military superiority would suffer.

Mindful of this dangerous tendency, Air Force Chief of Staff Gen. Hoyt S. Vandenberg appointed a special committee of the USAF Scientific Advisory Board in 1949. Its mission was to conduct a series of studies into the current capability and future requirements of the Air Force research and development program. This committee, under the chairmanship of Dr. Louis N. Ridenour, recommended that research and development be divorced from production engineering and placed in a separate command.

Wright Air Development Center (WADC) Headquarters were established in Building 14, Area B, in 1951.

Plans for the final organization of the Air Research and Development Command (ARDC) were made at Wright-Patterson in early 1951. Reviewing the organizational structure of the new command are (l to r): Dr. M. J. Kelly; Brig. Gen. Ralph P. Swofford, Jr., Deputy Commanding General for Operations, ARDC; Maj. Gen. David M. Schlatter, Commanding General, ARDC; and Mr. Donald A. Quarles. Kelly and Quarles were civilian scientists and Vice Presidents of Bell Telephone Laboratories, serving as advisors to General Schlatter. (Quarles later served as Secretary of the Air Force from 1955 to 1957.)

The Air Force agreed, and proceeded to establish such a command, drawn from elements of AMC. The Air Research and Development Command (ARDC), created in 1950 and activated in April 1951, became responsible for all research and development engineering on aircraft and aeronautical equipment. ARDC was thus the direct antecedent of today's Air Force Systems Command (AFSC).

The laboratories in Area B were reorganized on April 2, 1951, to form the Wright Air Development Center (WADC), the largest of ten research and development centers under ARDC. WADC was composed of four elements drawn from the Air Materiel Command: the Engineering, Flight Test, and All-Weather Flying Divisions, and the Office of Air Research. The twelve laboratories under their jurisdiction were responsible for supervising the development of most weapon systems, airborne components, ground equipment, and materials.[8]

In June 1951, ARDC relocated its headquarters from Wright-Patterson to Baltimore, Maryland. The Wright Air Development Center functions in Area B, however, remained essentially the same.

A major accomplishment of ARDC during the 1950s was the introduction of the concept of weapon systems—as opposed to individual development efforts—to the aeronautical industry, and the application of the broader "systems" concept to the production process. An important corollary of the systems concept was coordinating the efforts of the various Air Force commands involved in planning and using a given system. Selected agencies within AMC, especially, had to be represented in the planning and production stages.

The answer to this challenge was the creation of joint project offices (JPOs), each concentrating on the development and production of a specific weapon system. An individual JPO drew highly qualified people from ARDC, AMC, and the command which would ultimately use the weapon being developed (e.g., Strategic Air Command, Tactical Air Command). The task of the joint project office was to manage the development and production phases of a weapon system, integrating all aspects of the project and dealing with problems that arose. Joint project offices thus bridged the technological gap between ARDC engineering and AMC procurement.

In September 1953, AMC was assigned responsibility for developing support plans for all Air Force weapon systems. These plans were vital to the continuing support and maintenance of weapon systems once they were operational. Accordingly, joint project offices were superseded by what were known as weapon systems project offices (WSPOs).[9]

In January 1958, ARDC moved from Baltimore to its present headquarters at Andrews Air Force Base, D.C., and in 1961 was redesignated as the Air Force Systems Command. The continuing story of research and development and weapon systems acquisition conducted at Wright-Patterson by AFSC and its predecessors is contained in Chapter X, The Aeronautical Systems Division.

Airplane model undergoing test in the vertical wind tunnel at WADC

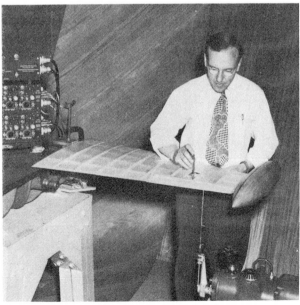

WADC engineer calibrates the wing aileron on a flutter model of the F-89 Scorpion

THE 2750TH ABW SUPPORT MISSION

The mission of the 2750th Air Base Wing in the 1950s and succeeding decades was to provide services and support to the many associate/tenant organizations located at Wright-Patterson AFB, and to provide limited services to other governmental agencies and components of the Department of Defense located off-base. This support encompassed the operation and maintenance of the base's airfields, aircraft, buildings and grounds, communications systems, automotive equipment, supply facilities and medical facilities, and the housing, messing, and training of military personnel. The Directorate of Base Air Installations (forerunner of today's 2750th Civil Engineering Squadron) was an essential part of this support system, responsible for the care and maintenance of the base's many buildings, surfaced areas, railroads, and utility plants, comprising a multi-million-dollar housekeeping operation. It monitored the work of numerous private contractors, as well as personnel attached to a resident office of the Army Corps of Engineers.

In addition to these day-to-day responsibilities, the Wing maintained a national Air Force records staging area on base during the early 1950s. Known as the Air Force Records Center, WPAFB, this center was responsible for the accession, temporary storage, service, and disposition of noncurrent and infrequently-referenced records for the base and certain tenant and command headquarters organizations.*

Later in the decade, the 2750th ABW also assumed responsibility for managing the worldwide distribution of USAF publications and forms, as well as continental U.S. commodity management of administrative publications and blank forms. Responsibility for these mission objectives was transferred to Wright-Patterson on June 8, 1958, from Shelby Air Force Depot at Wilkins Air Force Station, Ohio. Storage and distribution of these publications and forms was contracted out to a firm in the Washington, D.C. area.

The Flight Training Branch of the 2750th ABW was responsible for assuring a high degree of flying proficiency among pilots assigned to Wright-Patterson. To fulfill its mission, the Branch conducted extensive training programs in instrument flight, jet transition flight, and conventional transition flight.

The Area B (Wright) and Area C (Patterson) flightlines were busy places during the 1950s. Area C, especially, became very active with the advent of more advanced jet aircraft. Annual takeoff and landing operations on the two landing fields by 1959 rivaled in number the commercial movements of New York's International Airport at Idlewild.

The Area C flightline was an active center of operations in the early 1950s, especially with the advent of more advanced jet aircraft like these B-47s.

The WPAFB Air Terminal (Building 146, Area C) increased functions dramatically in 1954 with the introduction of LOGAIR.

*The center was discontinued at WPAFB on February 10, 1953.

The Area C flightline logged 139,276 takeoffs and landings that year, and Area B 44,699. (Area B was closed to jet aircraft operations on February 27, 1958.)

To ensure mail delivery during the 1951 national rail strike, the 2750th Air Base Wing initiated administrative flights linking Wright-Patterson (Hq AMC) and Washington, D.C. (Hq USAF). This shuttle service proved so satisfactory that it was continued and became known as the "Kittyhawk" flight. In November 1952, the shuttle's schedule was extended to six days a week, with ten dedicated crews.[10]

In July 1951, all base flying activities, with the exception of the Base Instrument School, were consolidated in Area B. In turn, WADC's Flight Test Division was transferred to Area C. The longer and heavier Patterson runways were better suited for the types of aircraft used by the Flight Test Division. Using the Area C facilities also eliminated the inherent danger of mishaps occurring in the housing areas adjacent to the Area B flightline.

In connection with the move, all aircraft operations activities were moved from Building 206, Area C, to Building 8, Area B. Certain rooms of the FADO Hotel were also occupied by WADC offices.* The only Base aircraft left on the Patterson side of the base were two B-17s, twelve C-47s, and one C-54 used for administrative flights and instrument training.

Two AMC courier flights, known as the Dixieland and the Alamo, were inaugurated at Wright-Patterson on October 6, 1952, to provide military air courier service for AMC personnel on official business. The flights were also used to expedite mail service between Hq AMC and outlying Air Materiel Areas. The Dixieland departed on Monday, Wednesday, and Friday for points east and south, and the Alamo departed on the same days for points west and south. Beginning in 1954, weekly passenger-cargo flights were also made between Wright-Patterson and Brookley AFB, Alabama.

In July 1953, the Area C control tower was shut down temporarily for rehabilitation. A modern FRC-19 console was installed in the tower and the approach control was moved from the tower to the new radar traffic control room in Building 206. Normal control of air traffic was resumed on August 16. Transmitters for the tower were located in Building 199, with receivers off Sand Hill Road, east of the flightline.[11] The installation of UHF equipment broadened the facilities available in the tower, and the new equipment proved easier to operate.

During 1954, Wright-Patterson joined other Air Force bases in establishing a special jet transition program for its pilots, using F-80 and T-33 type aircraft to carry out the program. Ground school instructors from the WPAFB Flight Training Branch completed the jet indoctrination course at Craig AFB, Alabama, and opened the ground school phase of the WPAFB jet program on July 27. The Pilot Transition Branch was eventually transferred from the main Training Branch located in Area C to Wright Field

Operations in Building 8, Area B, and the remainder of this vital program continued from that locale.

A new era opened at Wright-Patterson in 1954 with the creation of the Logistics Airlift (LOGAIR) system. AMC had long been convinced of the need for an efficient air transportation network to support its logistics distribution operations. Airlift capability was recognized as a key factor in constructing a modern system of logistics management capable of global mobilization.

Mercury Service, as the AMC airlift system was first known, was approved in February 1954 as a scheduled airlift within the continental United States (CONUS). Its purpose was two-fold: to move materiel quickly to CONUS-based operational units, and to shuttle materiel between the AMC air depots. Aircraft and services to support this system were contracted from civilian airlines, much as they had been in emergency situations during World War II, Korea, and the Berlin Airlift.

Wright-Patterson became a major warehousing and shipping center for Air Force tires during the 1950s.

WPAFB Supply Division personnel, 1959

*The FADO Hotel served as transient pilot quarters. See Chapter III, Fairfield Air Depot, for details.

Mercury Service was composed of eastern and western trunks, operated by Capital Airlines of Nashville, Tennessee, and the American Export and Import Company of Miami, Florida, respectively. Wright-Patterson AFB was included in the Eastern Zone, which consisted of five-day-a-week round-trip service from Kelly AFB, Texas, to Tinker AFB, Oklahoma; Wright-Patterson AFB; Olmsted AFB, Pennsylvania; Westover AFB, Massachusetts; Robins AFB, Georgia; and Brookley AFB, Alabama. The Western Zone provided flights from Kelly to Tinker; Hill AFB, Utah; Travis AFB, California; Norton AFB, California (flag stop only); and McChord AFB, Washington.[12]

Initial contracts under LOGAIR, as it became known in August 1954, expired on October 31, 1954.* A second phase began in November and included a new transcontinental operation. Daily service was established from the principal Air Materiel Areas to aerial ports of embarkation for transport to overseas destinations.[13] The transcontinental operation was conducted by Resort Airlines, while the eastern and western trunks were retained by the original contractors. Twin-engine C-46 and four-engine C-54 aircraft were used throughout the system.

Priority within the LOGAIR system was placed on transporting items that were urgently needed or which would represent significant savings, such as aircraft engines and spare parts. LOGAIR also provided a means of moving some sensitive items, such as hazardous materials, that civilian airlines were not allowed to carry.

During the last few months of 1954 and the first half of 1955, the young airlift system grew impressively. One year after the beginning of LOGAIR, the number of route miles flown and amount of tonnage transported had doubled, and a year later had doubled again. Operations had increased to round-the-clock, seven days a week at key locations.

As service expanded, other Air Force commands also negotiated for use of LOGAIR service, including the Strategic Air Command, the Air Defense Command, and the Air Research and Development Command. LOGAIR's capacity for rapid response and flexibility soon established the system as an essential element in America's combat readiness.**

On September 9, 1957, the Air Traffic Control Division of the Civil Aeronautics Administration (CAA) accepted operational responsibility for controlling air traffic within a six-airport area, including WPAFB. This organization, designated Dayton RAPCON (radar approach control), handled civilian and military air traffic for Wright-Patterson

Mail service between Hq AMC and outlying Air Materiel Areas during the 1950s was speeded by two AMC courier flights known as the Dixieland and the Alamo, and by ground express deliveries.

---

*Since American Airlines also used the Mercury designation for part of its fleet, the AMC Council changed the name of its system to LOGAIR.

**Today, Wright-Patterson AFB and the five AFLC Air Logistics Centers (at Hill AFB, Utah; Kelly AFB, Texas; McClellan AFB, California; Robins AFB, Georgia; and Tinker AFB, Oklahoma) serve as hubs for the LOGAIR system. Contracted by Military Airlift Command and operated by AFLC, LOGAIR in a typical year flies more than 12 million miles and transports more than 121,000 tons of materiel.

AFB, Clinton County AFB, and the Dayton, Springfield, and Richmond (Indiana) municipal airports.

Also during 1957, Wright-Patterson, with WADC assistance, furnished materiel support and services to the Strategic Air Command for 11 Boeing B-52 Stratofortress combat-mission airplanes. As RED SCRAMBLE heavy bombers committed to initial-phase missions, these aircraft had to be maintained in combat-ready status. In November 1957, WPAFB provided support and services to five Strategic Air Command Boeing KC-135 Stratotanker airplanes during Operation SUN RUN, a transcontinental speed and effectiveness test.[14]

ASSOCIATE ORGANIZATIONS

As the host organization at WPAFB, the 2750th Air Base Wing provided support services for a wide range of associate, or tenant, organizations during the 1950s.

Then as today, the largest organizations on base were Hq Air Materiel Command (predecessor of the Air Force Logistics Command), located in Building 262, Area A; and the Wright Air Development Center (predecessor of the Aeronautical Systems Division), located in Building 14, Area B.*

The Air Force Institute of Technology, the Air Technical Intelligence Center (antecedent of today's Foreign Technology Division), and the USAF Orientation Group were also located at Wright-Patterson. The Air Force Technical Museum, which had been closed since World War II, reopened its doors to the public in Building 89, Area C, in 1954. In 1956, it officially became the Air Force Museum.

Lockheed F-104 Starfighters were flown by the 56th Fighter-Interceptor Squadron, assigned to Wright-Patterson from 1955 to 1960.

Other major associate organizations on Wright-Patterson during the post-war 1940s and into the 1950s were:

1914th Airways and Air Communications Service Squadron
2046th Airways and Air Communications Service Squadron
6th Weather Group (formerly Hq lst Air Weather Squadron)
661st Air Force Band
2750th USAF Hospital
2702nd Explosive Ordnance Disposal Squadron (formerly 1st EODS)
1350th Photo Squadron (MATS)
4602nd Air Intelligence Services Squadron
3079th Aviation Depot Wing
5th District Office of Special Investigations
7th Group, Ohio Wing, Civil Air Patrol
779th Aircraft Control and Warning Squadron
Armed Forces Technical Information Agency

In addition to providing support services, the Wing exercised administrative control over the USAF Orientation Group and command jurisdiction over the 661st Air Force Band and the 2750th USAF Hospital.

Four major associate organizations joined the Wright-Patterson family between 1951 and 1959:

97th Fighter-Interceptor Squadron (Air Defense Command)
3500th USAF Recruiting Wing (Air Training Command)
58th Air Division (Air Defense Command)
4043rd Strategic Wing (Strategic Air Command)

The 97th Fighter-Interceptor Squadron (FIS) was a component of the Eastern Air Defense Force. It arrived at Wright-Patterson on January 8, 1951, as part of the Air Defense Command's program to provide aerial defense for all industrial areas of the United States. The squadron was equipped with F-86D Sabre all-weather interceptor jet aircraft, and was placed under the operational control of the 56th Fighter Wing at Selfridge AFB, Michigan. This marked the first time in the long history of Wright-Patterson that an Air Force fighter squadron had been based here.

The 97th moved its aircraft into new operations facilities constructed for them at the north end of Area C in December 1952 (location of the WPAFB Aero Club and Bldgs. 151 and 152.) The squadron maintained a 24-hour state of alert readiness. Four aircraft loaded with live ammunition, and their crews, were stationed near the end of the Patterson flightline, ready to scramble within five minutes.

The squadron also occupied Buildings 1445-1451 in the Sherwood Area as well as portions of Building 206 (base operations) and Building 146 (the air cargo terminal).

In August 1955, the 97th FIS was redesignated the 56th Fighter-Interceptor Squadron. The squadron's specific mission was to provide air defense for the heavily populated and industrial areas of the greater Miami Valley, which included Ohio, Indiana, Kentucky, and Tennessee. From mid-summer of 1958, the squadron flew F-104 Starfighter airplanes. On March 1, 1960, the 56th FIS, with a strength of 300 assigned

*In late 1959, WADC underwent reorganization and from 1959 until 1961 was known as the Wright Air Development Division (WADD).

individuals and 25 F-104s, was inactivated at Wright-Patterson, one of four such squadrons inactivated by the Air Defense Command.

On March 6, 1954, the Secretary of Defense ordered the Air Force to take over the job of recruiting its own military personnel.* Consequently, the 3500th USAF Recruiting Wing (Air Training Command) was designated on April 10, 1954. In late April, representatives of the new Recruiting Wing arrived at WPAFB to arrange for the establishment and location of their headquarters at this installation. The headquarters was established on May 31, 1954, and the Wing began full operations in Buildings 287 and 288 (Area A) on July 1, 1954.

With an authorized strength of 422 officers, 2,723 airmen, and 53 civilians, the Wing consisted of its headquarters and six recruiting groups located in or near principal population centers in six areas of the United States. The mission of the 3500th USAF Recruiting Wing was to select from civilian sources a sufficient number of qualified men and women to meet the requirements of the USAF. The Wing also monitored the important career retention program. (In 1965, after 11 years at WPAFB, the 3500th moved to Randolph AFB, Texas.)

Wright-Patterson, which had received the 97th Fighter-Interceptor Squadron in 1951, became further involved in air defense with the establishment in September 1955 of the 58th Air Division (Air Defense Command). Air defense was composed of four functions: detect, identify, intercept, and destroy. The 58th Air Division, upon receipt of ground observation and radar information, was responsible for transmitting "scramble" messages to appropriate fighter-interceptor squadrons, Air National Guard components, and Navy units; and target information to Army anti-aircraft artillery organizations. The 58th was designated as the control center for the air defense forces in 11 states of the Eastern Air Defense Region.**

An arm of the Eastern Air Defense Force, headquartered at Stewart AFB, New York, the 58th Air Division was activated at WPAFB on September 8, 1955, with an authorized personnel strength of 75 officers, 24 airmen, and 14 civilians. It was one of four such divisions activated. Buildings 1419, 1420, and 1421 in the Sherwood Area of WPAFB were modified for use as headquarters for the new division.

The 58th remained at Wright-Patterson for three years. On August 11, 1958, both the 58th Air Division and the associated 4717th Ground Observer Squadron were inactivated here.

USAF directives issued in early 1958 led to the signing of a joint tenancy agreement between the Air Materiel Command and the Strategic Air Command (SAC) for the support of SAC units at WPAFB. The location of a SAC B-52 strategic wing at Wright-Patterson was part of the SAC dispersal program initiated in 1958 to decentralize large concentrations of bomber aircraft and thus make SAC bases less attractive targets for enemy missiles. Under this USAF-mandated program, not more than 15 aircraft were to be stationed at each of 33 locations. A $549 million construction bill was passed by the House of Representatives authorizing construction at 29 locations, including $22.6 million for facilities at Wright-Patterson.

Because of tight security requirements for strategic air operations and the existing layout of Wright-Patterson, it was decided that facilities for the new strategic wing would be constructed as a separate complex in Area C. The project started in August 1958 and was completed by mid-1960.

The 4043rd Strategic Wing was activated at Wright-Patterson on April 1, 1959. Major components were the 42nd Bombardment Squadron and the 922nd Air Refueling Squadron (assigned effective December 1959).[15] On September 15, 1959, the 66th Aviation Depot Squadron was also assigned to the 4043rd. Effective October 1, 1959, four additional units were designated and organized at WPAFB and assigned to the 4043rd Strategic Wing:

4043rd Armament and Electronics Maintenance
 Squadron
4043rd Organizational Maintenance Squadron
4043rd Field Maintenance Squadron
4043rd Support Squadron

The first KC-135 refueling aircraft was delivered on February 29, 1960. On June 15, 1960, the 42nd Bombardment Squadron moved its B-52Es in combat-ready status to Wright-Patterson from the 11th Bomb Wing, Altus AFB, Oklahoma and the SAC B-52 strategic wing became fully operational.

Hq 4043rd Strategic Wing (SAC), Building 4010, Area C. The 4043rd was the largest tactical associate organization to join WPAFB during the 1950s. Its major components were the 42nd Bombardment Squadron and the 922nd Air Refueling Squadron.

---

*Prior to that time, recruiting for the Air Force had been a joint responsibility of the Air Force and the Army.
**The Eastern Air Defense Region encompassed the states of Alabama, Georgia, Illinois, Indiana, Kentucky, Mississippi, North Carolina, Ohio, Tennessee, Virginia, and West Virginia.

Facilities constructed for the 4043rd Strategic Wing at the north end of Area C (known as the West Ramp). The first KC-135 aerial tankers assigned to the 4043rd arrived in February 1960, followed by the Wing's B-52s in June.

A DECADE OF GROWTH

The face of Wright-Patterson was altered significantly during the decade of the 1950s, as new facilities were constructed and wartime structures were modified to meet current needs.

A major facet of the new construction program was additional housing and community facilities for base personnel. Providing adequate quarters for military and civilian workers at the base had been a persistent problem throughout World War II and during the early post-war years. With the swift upturn in defense requirements during Korea, the housing shortage became critical.

Housing on base could accommodate only a small percentage of the military families assigned to Wright-Patterson. Hundreds of officers and enlisted personnel legally entitled to government-furnished quarters were forced to commute from areas around the base, some from as far away as Cincinnati. Many were still living in temporary wartime barracks and in hastily-built substandard housing in local communities adjacent to the base.

These conditions precipitated an in-depth study of the problem, which in turn led to a coordinated military/civilian housing drive. Conferences initiated by the Base Commander between civil, governmental, and military officials explored several proposed programs designed to provide more housing for the Wright-Patterson area. Extensive publicity campaigns were carried out, urging home and apartment owners to make their units available to base personnel, and builders were urged to begin construction programs to alleviate the critical housing shortage. Colleges in the area were requested to provide additional space for unmarried personnel.[16]

Real relief in the area of family housing did not come, however, until 1953, with completion of the 2,000-unit Page Manor Housing Development (named in honor of Brig. Gen. Edwin Randolph Page). Plans for the construction of Page Manor were drawn up in 1949 and 1950 under authorization of the Wherry-Spence Amendment to the National Housing Act (August 1949), which permitted the Federal Housing Administration to insure privately-financed housing on or near military installations.

Groundbreaking ceremonies for the new complex, located on the south side of Airway Road in Mad River Township adjacent to Area B, were held July 12, 1951. On October 29, 1952, Brig. Gen. C. Pratt Brown, WPAFB Commander, cut the ribbon during opening ceremonies for the first 1,000 units of Page Manor. The second 1,000 units were completed and occupied in 1953. The Page Manor development represented a major step forward in the effort to retain critically needed specialists and highly skilled technicians at Wright-Patterson.*

---

*Page Manor was privately owned from its completion in 1953 until August 15, 1960, when the entire complex, consisting of 103.17 acres, was purchased by the Air Force at a cost of $18,876,154.33. The 2750th Air Base Wing acquired jurisdictional and operational responsibility effective October 1, 1960.

Construction of the first 1,000 units of the Page Manor housing development began in July 1951. A second 1,000 units were constructed during 1953. (Page Manor is named in honor of Brig. Gen. Edwin Randolph Page.)

Aerial view of Page Manor, south of Airway Road, adjacent to Area B runway 09/27

The influx of Wright-Patterson families into the new housing project, however, precipitated yet another concern for base planners—providing education for the children of the post-war "baby boom." In October 1953, base officials forwarded a request to the U.S. Department of Health, Education and Welfare, through the Ohio Department of Education, for permission to construct an elementary school on Wright-Patterson to accommodate the Page Manor children. Simultaneously, the superintendent of the Mad River Township School District, which adjoined the base, applied for federal assistance to construct additional school facilities in the event that the base request was denied. In the meantime, the school district was provided space in Buildings 1445 and 1448 on base for emergency school rooms to accommodate students from the Page Manor area. In 1954, the Mad River Township School District received a federal grant to construct a new elementary school on Spinning Road in lieu of a base school for WPAFB.[17]

Meanwhile, additional on-base quarters for bachelor military personnel were being constructed elsewhere on the base. Building 825, Area A, was erected as bachelor officers' quarters (BOQ). When it opened for occupancy on July 13, 1954, 223 officers were assigned to rooms. The Wood City troop housing area in Area C, which dated from World War II, was scheduled to be replaced with permanent buildings. When the Korean conflict developed, however, the vintage wooden barracks were covered with siding and thus quickly upgraded to "permanent" status. In 1956, funds were made available to construct three new dormitories and a dining hall for airmen (Buildings 1212, 1213, 1214, and 1215). All four buildings were accepted for occupancy on February 12, 1957. In 1959, 194 units of visiting officers' quarters (VOQ) were opened in Building 826, providing hotel-type units for both men and women officers.

As new housing went up, some of the old came down. In Skyway Park (constructed under the Lanham Act during World War II), 536 family units were removed by December 31, 1957.*

Construction of facilities other than housing continued throughout the decade. Twenty-five new buildings, for example, were under construction during 1955 and 1956. Among these were several devoted to community services, including a new NCO Club and a new hospital. The original NCO Club, built in 1943 and enlarged and modified in 1952, was destroyed by fire November 8, 1953. In June 1956, a new NCO Club was completed in Wood City and opened to serve the Wright-Patterson community.

Serving the community's medical needs was the new 348-patient USAF Hospital in Area A. Administrative and professional staffs at the hospital had begun reviewing plans for the new facility during 1952. In November 1952, the location for the new hospital was decided upon and construction began the following October. Effective Oc-

Building 825, Area A, constructed originally as bachelor officers' quarters (BOQ)

*Skyway Park was located at the intersection of Col. Glenn Highway and Kauffman Avenue. This land is now part of the Wright State University campus.

Building 1212, one of three new airmen's dormitories constructed in Wood City in 1956

Building 826, Area A, opened as visiting officers' quarters (VOQ) in 1959

Newly-completed NCO Club in Wood City, 1956. The original Wood City NCO Club, opened in 1943, was destroyed by fire in 1953.

Wood City provided a wide range of recreational facilities and was open to all base personnel.

Wooden barracks constructed during World War II in Wood City were upgraded in the 1950s to provide many more years of productive use.

The 348-bed 2750th United States Air Force Hospital was completed in June 1956. It is known today as the USAF Medical Center Wright-Patterson.

Warehouse 209 in Area C served as the Base Exchange from 1957 to 1980.

The Nuclear Engineering Test Facility, completed in Area B in 1960, was the seventh largest of its kind in the United States.

tober 15, 1953, the Hq 2750th Base Medical Group, as it was then known, was redesignated the 2750th United States Air Force Hospital. Construction of the hospital was completed in June 1956, at a cost of just over $5 million.

In 1957, Warehouse 209 in Area C was remodeled to provide a new Base Exchange store. A new chapel in Wood City was completed and occupied during late 1959.

A significant amount of non-housing construction occurred during the 1950s to accommodate operational needs of the base. On the Patterson flightline, Runway 5L23R was extended in 1957. In Area B, major additions were made to facilities of the Armament Lab and the Materials Lab. A Propeller Control and Fatigue Research Building, the Fuel Systems Components Test Building, a Rocket Test Laboratory, the Compass Testing Building, and the Microwave Building were constructed. The Gas Dynamics Research Building was accepted in 1959. Also near the end of the decade, the Universal Dynamic Sight and Computer Test Facility was completed and planning was begun for several new buildings to house the Air Force Institute of Technology.

One project that drew considerable attention during this time was construction of the Nuclear Engineering Test

Facility in Area B. This facility, which originally was to be a small Materials Laboratory nuclear reactor, grew far beyond expectations. The initial concept envisioned a 100-kilowatt capacity materials test reactor. When the requirements of other WADC organizations besides the Materials Lab were interjected, however, the facility was scaled up to 10 megawatts. In 1956, the project was removed from the Materials Lab and placed under the Directorate of Research for ARDC. Construction of the final facility, with a capacity of 20 megawatts and the capability to accommodate a full-scale jet engine, was begun in 1958. The building was the seventh largest of its kind in the United States, and was

Hadden Park, second location, 1960s

HADDEN PARK

Hadden Park was dedicated on September 19, 1953, as tribute to the services of Mr. William Hadden. Mr. Hadden began his career as a non-commissioned officer in charge of utilities at Wilbur Wright Field in 1917. In later years Hadden served as Chief of Maintenance in the Directorate of Base Air Installations. Prior to his retirement in 1952, Mr. Hadden was instrumental in developing this park area.

In 1958, the decision to build an operational complex on the north side of Area C to house the 4043rd Strategic Wing (SAC) required the abandonment of Hadden Park. Dissatisfied that the park should be lost permanently, Brig. Gen. John D. Howe, Base Commander, established a Joint Welfare Long-Range Recreational Council to develop another, larger site for the park. A tract of land located on 46 acres of forest and grassland between National and Zink Roads was selected as a site. The relocated Hadden Park was dedicated on June 3, 1960.

In the early 1970s, time and change again caught up with the park when the land was appropriated for the construction of the 300-unit Woodland Hills housing area. Again, an even larger, more permanent site was set aside. Sixty-five acres of land adjacent to Woodland Hills was developed into a modern park facility featuring hiking trails, picnic areas, sport and other facilities. Work began on the site in August 1972, and was conducted almost entirely on a self-help basis.

Official dedication ceremonies for new Hadden Park were held in August 1976, with Base Commander Col. Rano E. Lueker presiding. Hadden Park continues today as a source of relaxation and recreation for all Wright-Patterson AFB families.

completed and accepted in 1960.[18] (Internal facilities were not completed in full until late 1965.)

Construction of facilities to house new associate or tenant organizations assigned to Wright-Patterson was another major facet of the overall construction program during the 1950s. During 1951 and 1952, buildings were erected at the north end of the Area C flightline (on the present site of the WPAFB Aero Club) in anticipation of the arrival of the 97th Fighter-Interceptor Squadron. Personnel of the 97th moved into their new facilities in December 1952.

On October 13, 1954, the base acquired 465 acres of land on its northeastern boundary. This property was valued at $74,300, and lay along the Mad River adjacent to the Area C Very Heavy Bomber runway, near the site of the former village of Osborn. This area was admirably suited for strategic air operations and soon became the home of the 4043rd Strategic Wing (SAC).

Between August 1958 and the mid-1960s, an entirely separate complex was created for the 4043rd, at a cost of more than $25 million. The construction required that the land be leveled and subgraded, and that the Mad River be widened at that point. The decision to build on the north side of Area C also required the relocation of the Fairborn, Ohio, sewage and waste treatment plant and a base recreational area known as Hadden Park.

When complete, this area became known as the West Ramp. It is home today of the 4950th Test Wing (AFSC).

ACTIVITIES

A wide variety of events and activities occurred at Wright-Patterson AFB during the 1950s, only a few of which can be mentioned here.

In February 1951, new work schedules were implemented to help ease traffic congestion surrounding the base during peak rush hours. Under this plan, the first contingent of employees arrived for work beginning at 7:30 a.m., followed by second and third shifts at 8:00 and 8:30 a.m., respectively.

Traffic congestion surrounding the base in the early 1950s was eased by the introduction of staggered work schedules for base personnel.

On April 16, 1952, an official change of address was registered for the base, from Wright-Patterson Air Force Base, Dayton, Ohio, to Wright-Patterson Air Force Base, Ohio.

On August 13, 1953, aircraft from Dover, Delaware, and from Andrews AFB, D.C., were evacuated to Wright-Patterson to escape hurricane damage. In September, the base again provided haven for aircraft from Moody and Tyndall AFB during Hurricane Florence.

On July 1, 1954, a Class "B" printing plant was chartered on base, with fixed capital assets of $168,174 and working capital of $200,000. The WPAFB Printing Plant, formerly in the WPAFB budget, commenced operation as a component of the Air Force Printing Service.

The Wright-Patterson Non-Commissioned Officers (NCO) Academy was established in 1955, and provided a concentrated four-week course in leadership, management principles, problem solving, oral and written communications, military justice, world conditions, drill, and command. Each month, 25 non-commissioned officers were selected from the 2750th Air Base Wing and base tenant organizations to attend the academy. The academy received official accreditation on December 11, 1957.[19]

The 661st Air Force Band was an active part of base life in the 1950s. Organized on Patterson Field in 1942 as the 361st Army Air Forces Band, it was redesignated two years later as the 661st Army Band. It became the 661st Air Force Band in 1947. In addition to its normal on-base duties (participating in and providing music for military formations and other appropriate ceremonies), the band also presented concerts each week at schools and other locations throughout the Dayton and southern Ohio area.*

Chief Warrant Officer Carl J. Hehmsoth, Director of the 661st Air Force Band (formerly the 361st AAF Band), from 1942 to 1948. The band presented concerts throughout the southern Ohio area in the 1950s.

*Today the band, a component of Hq AFLC, makes more than 600 appearances and travels more than 50,000 miles each year in accomplishing its mission. It is popularly known as the "Band of Flight."

On July 1, 1958, the 2750th USAF Hospital was re-designated the United States Air Force Hospital, Wright-Patterson Air Force Base. The hospital remained under the jurisdiction of the 2750th Air Base Wing.

The 2750th Air Base Wing also maintained responsibility for the base news publications. During the 1950s these house organs were *The Post Script* newspaper and *Wingspread* magazine. *Wingspread* began publication in September 1956. A commercial publication, it was supported by commercial advertising, and was planned to meet the publicity needs of not only the 2750th Air Base Wing, but all tenant organizations on base, and civilian as well as military employees. One of the many special events that received coverage in the 1950s was the 50th anniversary of powered flight, observed in December 1953.

The Annual American Radio Relay League "Field Day" exercises were held on the Hilltop Area of Area B at Wright-Patterson on June 19-20, 1954. Military Amateur Radio System (MARS) members and radio amateurs of Hq AMC, WPAFB, and WADC participated in the event. The exercises were designed to test the capabilities of MARS radio stations operating in the field under conditions approximating those encountered during an actual emergency. During the two-day event, the group made radio contact with other amateur radio stations in all 48 states and in the Canadian Amateur Radio District, some of which were beyond the Arctic Circle. They also worked stations in Alaska, Puerto Rico, and North Africa. The success of the exercises led to the formation of an official WPAFB MARS and Amateur Radio Club. The goals of the club included participating in subsequent contests and field exercises and providing back-up communications during actual emergencies in the Dayton area.*

A number of traditions in community service were initiated at Wright-Patterson during the 1950s. Many of these projects became annual events, and provided a firm foundation for Wright-Patterson's continuing commitment to community service and involvement.

Annual observance of Air Force Day was initiated in 1948. During the 1950s, the event was celebrated as part of a combined Armed Forces Day held each May. The celebration was traditionally an open house in Area B, featuring static displays of aircraft and including participation by the Army, the Navy, Civil Air Patrol, the Ohio National Guard, the Civil Defense Organization, and the Air National Guard.

Base participation in Annual Fire Shows and later Fire Expos dates from 1952, when the base first became involved in National Fire Prevention Week.

Wright-Patterson began its active involvement in the National Aircraft Show at Cox Municipal Airport in 1953. For many years, WPAFB served as the staging base for aircraft in the show. The base also provided logistical support for participating armed services organizations, providing housing and messing facilities for personnel, procuring, storing, and dispensing fuels, lubricants, and other items required in support of the airshow, and placing its maintenance facilities and services "on call" for emergency duty.

Armed Forces Day celebration, Area B. This annual May event became a tradition during the 1950s.

*The MARS designation today stands for Military Affiliate Radio System and is a component of the 2046th Communications Group at WPAFB. The primary mission of MARS is to supplement normal Air Force communications channels and provide a back-up for telephone services in the event of failure. MARS also provides a primary on-scene communications network at air crash disasters and in the event of civil emergencies.

Wright-Patterson has become a traditional location for summer encampments for Air Force Reserve Officer Training Corps (AFROTC), Civil Air Patrol (CAP), U.S. Military Academy (West Point), and U.S. Air Force Academy cadets, as well as Explorer and other scout groups. During the 1950s, thousands of AFROTC cadets from midwestern colleges and universities received special preflight briefings and other instruction in preparation for flight experience in C-45, C-47, and T-33 aircraft at WPAFB.

Wright-Patterson employees have always been enthusiastic supporters of area-wide charity drives and service projects. March of Dimes campaigns on base during the 1950s included a Wright-Patterson March of Dimes Revue broadcast over radio station WING. Campaigns against polio also received the wholehearted support of the Wright-Patterson community in the mid-1950s.

American Red Cross blood campaigns have been part of base community life for nearly forty years. During the Korean conflict, a blood center was established for base personnel to give blood every third Thursday. Although this center was discontinued after the war, a permanent blood donor center was established several years later.

DISASTERS

Natural disasters and fires have not been uncommon in the Miami Valley/ WPAFB area over the last century. The 1950s were no exception to the norm.

An unusually heavy snowstorm blanketed nearly the entire state of Ohio over Thanksgiving weekend, 1950. A snowfall of 10 inches was recorded overnight on Saturday, with two more inches the following morning. The storm resulted in drifts up to five feet high and halted all city, county, and state traffic. It was the deepest 24-hour snowfall recorded by the Dayton weather bureau until that time. WPAFB employees were unable to report to work until the following Wednesday.

In the early morning hours of Sunday, November 8, 1953, fire gutted the NCO Open Mess in Wood City. Only the club office and boiler room remained standing among the charred ruins. Estimated damage from the blaze was $87,000. Temporary quarters for the club were set up in the recently-vacated Stockade dining hall across the street from the club. A new NCO Club was completed in June 1956.

Between January 20 and 25, 1959, flood waters from the Mad River, impounded by Huffman Dam, closed the Patterson airfield to jet aircraft operations. All except 6,000 feet of runway were inundated. Night aircraft operations were suspended, and transient air traffic was diverted from Area C to Area B.

Flooded conditions at the base resulted in the loss of 441.45 flight hours, with the cancellation of numerous jet and conventional navigation and instrument training flights. Low temperatures and ice following in the wake of the flood impaired efforts to clean up the airfield with bulldozers and graders and resulted in $16,250 damage to the field night lighting system. Damage to construction

Remains of the famous 1950 Thanksgiving weekend snowfall. WPAFB employees were unable to report to work for three days.

projects, property, and equipment on base was estimated at $219,950.

On January 21, 1959, base personnel participated in rescue missions to evacuate people marooned by the flood along the shores of the Miami River and in the west Springfield area. A total of nine missions were flown. A Bell H-13 and two Army helicopters, one local and one transient, made up the rescue fleet.

WRIGHT-PATTERSON IN THE 1960s

On April 1, 1961, shortly after the inauguration of John F. Kennedy as President, a major realignment of Air Force commands occurred, resulting in new names for the major organizations at Wright-Patterson AFB. The Air Research and Development Command (ARDC), with headquarters at Andrews AFB, D.C., assumed the Air Materiel Command's functions of procurement and production for new systems and was redesignated the Air Force Systems Command (AFSC). AMC was redesignated the Air Force Logistics Command (AFLC) effective the same date.

This restructuring of commands was the result of years of search for the most efficient method of weapon systems acquisition and maintenance. It was also the result of advancing technology, in that as Air Force weapon systems grew more complex, fewer were produced. The new organizational structure meant that one single command (AFSC) was responsible for the entire acquisition process and another (AFLC) for supply and maintenance of all systems.

The most dramatic organizational changes at Wright-Patterson occurred on the Wright Field (Area B) side of the base. As part of the realignment of commands, the procurement and production duties of what was known as the Aeronautical Systems Center were added to the research and development functions of the Wright Air Development Division (WADD). The resulting organization was named the Aeronautical Systems Division (ASD). Accompanying the realignment was a revised organizational nomenclature for the Area B complex. The former directorates became deputies. Thus, the three principal directorates emerged as

Air Materiel Command (AMC) was redesignated the Air Force Logistics Command (AFLC) on April 1, 1961. Headquarters remained in Building 262, Area A.

Hq Aeronautical Systems Division (ASD), Building 14, Area B. The Wright Air Development Division also changed its name in 1961. The Division assumed the procurement and production functions of the Aeronautical Systems Center and was redesignated the Aeronautical Systems Division of the Air Force Systems Command.

the Deputy for Systems Management, the Deputy for Engineering, and the Deputy for Technology. This system remained in effect until April 1962, when AFSC announced a further realignment aimed at emphasizing research and technology. A Research and Technology Division (RTD) was established at Bolling AFB in the District of Columbia, and two ASD functions, technology and engineering, transferred to its control.

The 2750th Air Base Wing remained the host organization for Wright-Patterson AFB and its many associate/tenant organizations during the 1960s. At the beginning of the decade, approximately 100 tenant support agreements, representing over 150 diverse organizational units, were in force, making the Wing mission a very complex one.

Headquarters AFLC, in keeping with command management and organization policies, exempted the 2750th Air Base Wing from air materiel area command jurisdiction. Under a mission and organization regulation, the 2750th reported directly to the parent headquarters in Buildings 262-262A. WPAFB's real property was geographically located within the ten-state Mobile (Alabama) Air Materiel Area of responsibility. Fixed capital assets of Wright-Patterson AFB at the end of Fiscal Year 1961 amounted to more than $208 million on base, and nearly $6 million off base.

To keep pace in its management of resources, the 2750th ABW established an electronic data processing system in Supply early in the 1960s and implemented a micro-mechanized Engineering Data Automated Logistics Program.

A Consolidated Military Personnel Center was established at WPAFB on July 1, 1962, using mechanized payroll and record services. Civilian and military gross payrolls handled by the 2750th Wing Comptroller in FY 1961 totalled nearly $135 million, reflecting Wright-Patterson's impact as a major employer in the southwest Ohio area.

On November 3, 1960, Hq USAF directed the 2750th Air Base Wing to provide mission support airlift for organizations assigned or attached to WPAFB. Sixteen aircraft

were transferred to the Wing from 10 tenant units on base for purposes of scheduling, operation, and maintenance. Responsibility for operation of staff aircraft from Hq AFLC was transferred to the base Transport Flight office effective October 11, 1960.[20]

WPAFB received the USAF Flying Safety Award for the first time in its history on September 27, 1961. In the period from January to June 1961, base pilots flew more than 25,000 hours in a wide variety of aircraft without a single accident or incident. The Wing subsequently received the AFLC Command Flying Safety Award for the period from January 1 to December 31, 1961, in recognition of more than 54,000 hours of accident-free flying.[21]

To ensure survival and mission continuity, a Wright-Patterson AFB Central Command Post was established in Building 11, Area C, effective August 1, 1960. As an element of the Plans and Programs office, this post provided a controlling point for emergency operations and test exercises.

A new unofficial base newspaper, *The Skywrighter*, was first distributed on February 5, 1960. The Winkler Company, a civilian printing firm, published the newspaper with the full cooperation and permission of the Department of Defense. Starting circulation was 16,000 copies. In February 1962, The *Skywrighter* won third place in the AFLC Base-Newspaper-of-the-Year competition, the first in a long series of awards the newspaper has won over the years. *Skywrighter* continues today as the unofficial base newspaper of WPAFB, with a weekly circulation of 31,000.

In 1962, sixteen new T-39 aircraft were received by the 2750th ABW. These airplanes provided advanced facilities for jet pilot checkout on base and supplanted the older C-47 aircraft in carrying passengers. The air terminal at WPAFB handled an average of 472 flights and 1,310 tons of cargo per month in 1962. Takeoffs and landings averaged 192,000 per year.

During the autumn of 1964, the mission of the 2750th ABW gradually changed to reflect Wing support of AFLC requirements in Southeast Asia (SEA). The AFLC mission

WPAFB pilots earned both the USAF Flying Safety Award and the AFLC Command Flying Safety Award in 1961, flying more than 54,000 accident-free hours during the year in a variety of aircraft.

Skywrighter, the unofficial Wright-Patterson AFB newspaper, has been published by the Winkler Company of Oakwood, Ohio, since 1960, and has earned several prestigious awards.

during the Vietnam conflict involved providing materiel support to the major Air Force commands engaged in combat zones. The bulk of this support was provided through the Sacramento Air Materiel Area. In addition to the massive airlift of airplane parts, supplies, munitions, and other materiel, highly skilled teams of depot maintenance technicians, known as Rapid Area Maintenance (RAM) teams, were deployed to Southeast Asia to repair weapon systems that had sustained crash or battle damage. Teams often worked to salvage valuable airplanes and equipment at the crash site, under highly dangerous conditions.

The level of 2750th ABW support to Southeast Asia operations was limited in comparison to other AFLC Air Materiel Areas, but the Wing did provide certain essential services and a limited number of personnel in support of the AFLC mission. Wing support of USAF operations in SEA began in September 1964, when the Wing shipped flying and hangar equipment to the 2851st Air Base Group at Kelly AFB, Texas. The 2750th ABW became a prime procurer of loaders, revetments, and shelters used in the protection of resources in Southeast Asia. The first prototype revetments were erected and tested at Wright-Patter-

*Base Engineering Emergency Force.

son in May 1965. Subsequently, contracts for more than $18 million were let by the 2750th ABW Procurement Division for manufacture of revetments. Standard revetments consisted of rectangular steel bins, 10 ft by 7.7 ft and 16 ft high, made of 16-gauge steel. At their destination, the bins were filled with dirt, sand, or gravel to provide maximum protection to aircraft from enemy mortar fire and accidental explosions on the ground between air missions.

2750th ABW agencies were involved in processing civilian and military personnel bound for Vietnam. For example, in November 1965, Wright-Patterson's first 15-man team of maintenance specialists left for four months temporary duty in Southeast Asia. These airmen, all from the 2750th ABW, were AFLC's first contribution to the Air Force Prime BEEF concept of a mobile military civil engineering force.*

Flight training, small-arms weapon training, and vehicle operator training were conducted on base in support of SEA operations, as were courses in laundry management. The 2750th also handled shipments from the Lexington Blue Grass Army Depot, Kentucky; the Ravenna Ordnance Plant, Ohio; the USS Enterprise; and the National Cash Register Corporation. The Wing supplied vehicles and weapons in accordance with levies, and provided for off-loading, temporary storage, and reloading of SEA-bound materiel. A limited maintenance mission was also supported by the Wing. Stock number user directory reconciliations were handled on base, and the Wing furnished supplies, in-flight lunches, quarters, and rations as tasked. Support operations continued for the remainder of the decade.[22]

In 1967, Wright-Patterson Air Force Base celebrated its Golden Anniversary. A half century of dedication and progress separated the establishment of Wilbur Wright Field as a Signal Corps training school for World War I pilots and the sophisticated research and flight operations that characterized Wright-Patterson Air Force Base on the horizon of the aerospace age. Celebrations on base were accompanied by publication of a pictorial history of Wright-Patterson's 50 years of accomplishments.

ASSOCIATE ORGANIZATIONS

During the 1960s, the 2750th Air Base Wing performed services and provided resources to support an increasing number of associate/tenant organizations located on base. Largest in terms of size and scope were Hq Air Force Logistics Command, the Aeronautical Systems Division, the 6570th Aerospace Medical Research Lab, the Air Force Aero Propulsion, Avionics, Flight Dynamics, and Materials Labs, the 17th Bomb Wing of the Strategic Air Command, the Air Force Museum, the Air Force Orientation Group, and the 661st Air Force Band. In addition to these, by 1969 the Wing provided support services to 155 other organizations, on and off base, under 112 host-tenant and interservice agreements.

Cover of the pictorial history published in 1967 to commemorate the 50th anniversary of WPAFB

Headquarters
2750th Air Base Wing (AFLC)
United States Air Force
Wright-Patterson Air Force Base, Ohio 45433

Office of the Commander   15 May 1967
All Personnel
Wright-Patterson Air Force Base, Ohio

Dear Friend

This marks the 50th anniversary of military aviation at Wright-Patterson Air Force Base. During this span of fifty years, our contribution to the growth of aviation and to our nation's air power has been enormous.

Only at Wright-Patterson can one trace all aspects of an aircraft system literally from the cradle to the grave. That is, from the original concept of research and development, through the entire operational life phase supported by the Air Force Logistics Command, to its final resting place, the Air Force Museum. As a consequence, Wright-Patterson is today one of the greatest and best known air bases in the world.

The contribution this base has made to air power and the significant role we have played in Air Force history was made possible only through the individual efforts of the many thousands of military and civilian personnel who were and are stationed and employed here.

You, as a member of this great team, should be justly proud of the role you have played; for the true history of any organization is really written in the combined efforts of its people.

• • •

JOWELL C. WISE
Brigadier General, USAF
Commander

To support these organizations, WPAFB managed real property resources in June 1969 amounting to nearly $281 million. These fixed capital assets consisted of real estate, supply and other facilities, and utilities and ground improvements at 20 locations in Ohio, Indiana, Kentucky, Maryland, and West Virginia.[23]

Many notable changes occurred in associate organizations during the decade, including the activation of Detachment 15, 15th Weather Squadron, which today provides weather forecasting services to Wright-Patterson AFB. Det. 15 was established on base effective July 8, 1961.

The USAF Hospital, WPAFB, was reassigned from 2750th ABW jurisdiction to Hq Air Materiel Command (later AFLC) effective January 1, 1961. The hospital was assigned its current designation as the USAF Medical Center Wright-Patterson, on July 1, 1969.

On January 1, 1962, Hq AFLC transferred its fully operational Dayton Air Force Depot at Gentile Air Force Station, Dayton, Ohio, to the Department of Defense Supply Agency for the establishment of the Defense Electronics Supply Center (DESC). Certain elements, supported by the 2750th ABW, continued to be managed by the Air Force, and one major component, the Heath calibration and internal guidance complex at Newark, Ohio, was reassigned to the Middletown Air Materiel Area (Pennsylvania) of AFLC.*

The 8318th Air Force Reserve Base Support Group was called to extended active duty at WPAFB effective February 1962. The Hq 2750th ABW Reserve (Mobilization Assignment Reserve Section) was discontinued April 1, 1962.

The Dayton Air Force Depot at Gentile Air Force Station was transferred from Hq AFLC to the Department of Defense Supply Agency in January 1962 for the establishment of the Defense Electronics Supply Center (DESC).

*This installation is known today as the Aerospace Guidance and Metrology Center (AGMC) and is a component of the Air Force Logistics Command.

Emblem of the 17th Bomb Wing, formerly the 4043rd Strategic Wing. Known as the Black Knights, the Wing was redesignated in order to continue the tradition of the 17th Bomb Group, the "Doolittle Raiders" of World War II fame.

Hq AFLC's 3079th Aviation Depot Wing and its five aviation depot groups were also inactivated at WPAFB effective July 1, 1962.

On July 1, 1963, the 4043rd Strategic Wing (SAC) was reorganized as the 17th Bombardment Wing (Heavy). The 4043rd's redesignation was part of an Air Force-wide program to retain units with rich historical traditions. The 17th Bomb Group of World War II fame distinguished itself in 1942, when 80 of its men flew with Lt. Col. James "Jimmie" Doolittle on his historic Tokyo raid. The Group also earned two Distinguished Unit Citations for exceptional service in Europe during World War II and a third for interdiction and close support missions during Korea. Nicknamed the Black Knights, the unit had been inactivated on June 25, 1958.

Also effective July 1, 1963, one of the 17th Bomb Wing's components, the 42nd Bombardment Squadron (Heavy), was inactivated. It was replaced by the 34th Bombardment Squadron (Heavy), a unit which had been prominently connected with the old 17th Bomb Group. The 42nd had been assigned to the 4043rd Bomb Wing on June 1, 1960.*

The reconstituted 17th Bomb Wing was awarded the Air Force Outstanding Unit Award in 1963. On July 1, 1968, the Wing converted to B-52H model aircraft, which came to Wright-Patterson from Homestead AFB, Florida. Between 1968 and 1973, the 17th Bomb Wing deployed 70 B-52 strategic bomber crews to Southeast Asia in support of the ARC LIGHT program. Over 125 KC-135 aerial tankers and crews also participated in YOUNG TIGER or COMBAT LIGHTNING operations in Southeast Asia.

The 661st Air Force Band was reorganized effective July 1, 1964, with an authorized strength of 1 officer and 44 airmen.

The 2046th Communications Squadron, composed of the former 1914th and 2046th Airways and Air Communications Service Squadrons, was redesignated the 2046th Communications Group on January 1, 1965.

The U.S. Air Force Museum, WPAFB, was reassigned from Air University, Maxwell AFB, Alabama, to Hq AFLC on October 1, 1965. Effective September 15, 1968, this directive was modified to read that the Air Force Museum was attached to the 2750th ABW for administrative and logistical support.

The Air Force Packaging Evaluation Agency (AFPEA) was officially transferred to Wright-Patterson from Brookley AFB, Alabama, in July 1967, in connection with the scale-down of the Mobile Air Materiel Area. The mission of the AFPEA was to investigate, develop, test, and evaluate packaging materials, containers, methods, and technologies. It provided packaging engineering services to all Air Force commands.

The 2863rd Ground Electronics Engineering Installation Agency Squadron (GEEIA) moved from Brookley AFB, Alabama, to WPAFB on October 1, 1968.

The Air Force Contract Maintenance Center, constituted and assigned to Hq AFLC, was activated at WPAFB effective April 8, 1969. The mission of this center was to provide contract management direction and control over contract management functions at contractor plants assigned to AFLC by the Department of Defense.

On February 8, 1969, the following activities which had been assigned to the 2750th ABW were inactivated and their unit designators reverted to Department of the Air Force control: the USAF Radiological Health Laboratory, WPAFB; the Regional Environmental Health Laboratory, Kelly AFB; and the Regional Environmental Health Laboratory, McClellan AFB. These units were subsequently constituted, activated, and assigned to Hq AFLC.

*The 42nd's 1960-1963 tour marked the second time it had been assigned locally. The organization's earliest antecedent, the 42nd Aero Squadron, was transferred from Camp Kelly, Texas, to Wilbur Wright Field on August 25, 1917. The 42nd Aero Squadron was redesignated as Squadron I (Eye) on October 1, 1918, and demobilized at Wilbur Wright Field on February 21, 1919.

GROWTH

In 1960, new ground test facilities were constructed by the Wright Air Development Division for simulation of aerospace operations for the X-20 Dyna-Soar and the B-70 bomber programs. The $7.7 million addition to the structural test complex at WADD made it the largest and most versatile facility of its kind in the country.

The base gained an additional nine-hole golf course during the summer of 1961. Construction of the 3,439-yard Twin Base course was completed by fall, and the course opened to both military and civilian personnel. A second nine holes were added to the course in 1963.

The free world's largest aerospace and missile sonic test chamber was constructed at WADD during 1961. The sonic test chamber was used to measure the effects of sonic fatigue—the weakening and malfunction of flight vehicles and components from sound wave pressures.

Ground was broken December 18, 1962, for the Air Force Institute of Technology School of Engineering building. Gen. Curtis E. LeMay, Air Force Chief of Staff, was guest of honor at the ceremonies. Dedication of the completed building was held August 28, 1964. The Honorable Eugene Zuckert, Secretary of the Air Force, presided at the ceremonies.

One of the most significant projects in Area C in the early years of the decade was construction of the new Patterson airfield control tower. The old tower, although modified and upgraded several times since the 1940s to improve air and ground traffic control, was no longer cost-effective to maintain and was obsolete in regard to modern safety standards. In FY 1962, Congress approved $237,000 for construction of a new tower. The new Wright-Patterson control tower was officially opened on June 17, 1963. Nine stories tall, the new tower was constructed on the West Ramp near the 17th Bomb Wing (SAC) area.

Construction of facilities and extension of utilities continued on the West Ramp in the early 1960s in support of the 17th Bomb Wing mission. Hot water transmission mains, a liquid oxygen generating plant, missile fuel storage, a missile research test shop, and a propulsion research test facility were all constructed. The purchase of 1.32 acres of land along State Route 235 in September 1959 prevented private ownership adjacent to this sensitive area and provided right-of-way for highway acceleration and deceleration lanes.

Easements for 269 acres in Clark and Greene Counties, valued at $60,000, extended the Area C airfield approach area in 1961. The clearance easement deeds granted the United States the right to remove all aerial obstructions from the land. The Universal Atlas Cement Division of the United States Steel Corporation retained ownership of the properties and continued quarry operations.

Plans to relocate the Air Force Museum to a new multi-million dollar facility were revealed in 1962 by the Air Force Museum Foundation, a private, non-profit organization. Eugene W. Kettering, son of the Dayton inventor and President of the Charles F. Kettering Foundation, was named Chairman of the Museum Foundation board. Frank G. Anger, President of the Winters National Bank and Trust Company, was named as President of the Foundation. As proposed, the new facility was to have about 500,000 square feet under roof, seven times more space than the current structure (Building 89, Area C).

On November 19, 1964, Secretary of the Air Force Eugene Zuckert presented the deed to 225 acres of Air Force land along the west edge of Springfield Pike to the Air Force Museum Foundation. Public-spirited citizens in Dayton and across the nation contributed more than $6

Twin Base golf course, opened in 1961

The present-day WPAFB control tower, located on the West Ramp, was completed and became operational in June 1963.

318

The U.S. Air Force Museum at Wright-Patterson AFB was constructed with funds donated to the Air Force Museum Foundation by citizens across the nation.

Gathered at dedication ceremonies for the new museum are (l to r): Harold and Ivonette Wright Miller (niece and nephew-in-law of the Wright brothers), Mr. Mark Sloan (Curator), and Col. Bernard Bass (Director of the Museum).

million to the Foundation over the next several years, allowing construction of the new museum to begin in June 1970. Formal dedication ceremonies were held September 3, 1971, with President Richard M. Nixon and members of the Wright family in attendance.

The WPAFB NCO Club in Wood City underwent a $110,000 renovation during the summer of 1963. A new two-story brick Airmen's Service Club was also opened in Wood City, on May 1, 1965. The original Service Club had been destroyed by fire on January 28, 1963. Groundbreaking for a modern 1,000-seat motion picture theater in Wood City took place in February 1966.

Construction of a chapel in the Page Manor housing area began in April 1967. The new facility was dedicated February 25, 1968. Guest speaker at the event was Maj. Gen. Edwin R. Chess, Chief of Air Force Chaplains.

The world's largest optical collimator was completed at Wright-Patterson in 1967. It was housed in a new $5 million Optics Laboratory that enabled Air Force scientists to test all sizes of precision photographic lenses for accuracy and clarity. The lens of the gigantic collimator was a fused silica mirror 100 inches in diameter and 12 inches thick. Weighing 9,000 lbs, the lens was installed at the bottom of a 155-foot vertical vacuum chamber that extended 85 ft above and 70 ft below the ground. The new facility was part of the Air Force Avionics Laboratory, Reconnaissance Division.[24]

Gen. John P. McConnell, Air Force Chief of Staff, presided at the June 8, 1967 opening of the $2 million Electronic Warfare Research Facility in Area B. The reinforced concrete, double-towered building was the first in a three-phase construction program for the Air Force Avionics Laboratory. Prior to completion of the structure, the Electromagnetic Warfare Branch and the Electromagnetic Warfare Applications Branch conducted their research in Building 22, Area B.[25]

The Airmen's Service Club in Wood City was a popular gathering place for nearly 20 years before it was destroyed by fire January 28, 1963. A new Airmen's Service Club was constructed on the same site and opened in 1965.

In 1969, the Aerospace Medical Research Laboratory completed a six-year program aimed at doubling its capacity to conduct research in toxicology. The improved Toxic Hazards Research Facility contained eight long-term exposure chambers called Thomas Domes, four ambient pressure laboratory exposure chambers, several laboratories, and animal pre-conditioning facilities.[26]

The Electronic Warfare Research Facility in Area B, dedicated in June 1967, was the first building completed in a three-phase construction program for the Air Force Avionics Laboratory.

Hq Air Force Aerospace Medical Research Laboratory, Building 29, Area B. Aerospace Med will celebrate its 50th anniversary in 1985.

ACTIVITIES

A landmark in aviation history was commemorated at WPAFB on June 15, 1960. Brig. Gen. Frank P. Lahm, the first military man to fly with one of the Wright brothers, was recognized as the "Father of Air Force Flight Training" during official ceremonies at the base.* General Lahm traveled from his home in Mansfield, Ohio, for the occasion. Six hundred Air Force Academy cadets were on hand for the celebration, which included an aerial demonstration by pilots of the Wright Air Development Division. The inscription on the plaque presented to General Lahm read in part:[27]

> Presented to Brig. Gen. Frank P. Lahm . . . in recognition of his lifelong devotion to aviation and aeronautical science. Taught to fly by Wilbur Wright in the first military aeroplane, Signal Corps No. 1, at College Park, Md., in 1909. Awarded by "The Early Birds," an organization of those who flew solo before December 17, 1916.

Air Force chiefs of staff of 15 South American countries made a brief visit to Wright-Patterson on April 18, 1961, to inspect Strategic Air Command facilities and operations. The visit, at the invitation of Gen. Thomas D. White, U.S. Air Force Chief of Staff, was part of the Inter-American Air Forces commanders' conference and tour of United States Air Force facilities. The agenda of discussions included technical training, airport and air traffic control, personnel procedures and logistics, and the role of Latin American military in internal security and civic advancement.

Two huge moving vans parked in front of Hq AFLC the week of April 17, 1961, spelled the end of an era at Wright-Patterson. The vans were chartered to carry off the huge UNIVAC computer, dismantled to make room for more up-to-date equipment. The machine being torn down was a 1951 model, first installed at AFLC headquarters in the spring of 1954. The machine was the first of its size to go into operation in the Dayton area. Many employees at the headquarters remembered the dedication ceremony when the machine was first installed. Festivities that day in 1954 had been attended by General of the Army Douglas MacArthur (USA-Ret.) in his capacity as a Sperry-Rand official, and by Air Force dignitaries.

Seven Wright-Patterson scientists received recognition for their scientific knowledge and achievements during a 12-day International Air Show in Paris, France, in June 1961. Forty-four American scientists in all were selected as representatives of American industry and the Department of Defense. A photograph of each and a biographical sketch of accomplishments were featured in a segment of the U.S. exhibit entitled "Salute to Scientists." Designed, constructed and directed by the Wright-Patterson-based Air Force Orientation Group, the "Salute" included seven WPAFB scientists of international renown: Harrell V. Noble, Dr. Alan M. Lovelace, and Dr. Henning Edgar von Gierke from the Aeronautical Systems Division; and Dr.

*Lieutenant Lahm was the passenger when Orville Wright flew the first official test flight of a military airplane on July 27, 1909, at Fort Myer, Virginia.

1962 Armed Forces Day celebration in Area C

Hans von Ohain, Radames K. H. Gebel, Dr. Goottfried Guderley, and Dr. Demetrious G. Samaras from the Aeronautical Research Laboratory, an element of the Office of Aerospace Research.[28]

The first official reunion of World War I flyers was held at the Air Force Museum June 24-27, 1961. The reunion, the first in 43 years, was attended by over 400 World War I aviators, including Capt. Eddie Rickenbacker, the country's "Ace of Aces"; Douglas Campbell, the first U.S. ace; and George Vaughn, the second ranking living ace. Also in attendance were such dignitaries as Gen. Carl Spaatz, and Brigadier Generals Frank P. Lahm and Benjamin D. Foulois, two of the first three military pilots taught to fly by the Wright brothers.[29]

Large Armed Forces Day celebrations, begun in the 1950s, were continued at Wright-Patterson during the 1960s. In May 1962, the airshow was particularly im-

pressive. Both days of the event began with a fly-by of jet aircraft led by the ASD Commander, Maj. Gen. W. A. Davis, piloting a T-39 Sabreliner. Aerial demonstrations by fighters, bombers, and cargo airplanes followed, including midair refueling of a B-52 bomber by a KC-135 tanker. On the ground, numerous USAF and U.S. Navy aircraft and missiles were on static display, together with a variety of exhibits by industrial and military concerns. Air Force Museum indoor and outdoor displays were also open to the public.

On May 17, 1962, civil authorities renamed the Greene County portion of Airway Road, which terminated at the main AFLC gate to the base. It became Colonel Glenn Highway, in honor of Ohio native and astronaut, Lt. Col. John H. Glenn, USMC. Colonel Glenn completed three orbits of the earth in the space capsule Friendship 7 on February 20, 1962.

Wright-Patterson AFB officials were closely involved in the creation of Wright State University (WSU) in 1963. The WSU campus encompasses 190 acres of former Air Force property, including the site of Skyway Park at the intersection of Col. Glenn Highway and Kauffman Avenue.

Beginning in 1963, officials at Wright-Patterson were closely involved in the development of a new state university. Dayton leaders had long sought a solution to the need for expanded higher education opportunities in the Dayton area. The new institution would be known as Wright State University, in honor of both Wilbur and Orville, and would be located on land adjacent to the base. The university was to open as a joint branch of The Ohio State University (Columbus) and Miami University (Oxford).

AFLC Commander Gen. Mark E. Bradley, Jr. acted on behalf of the Air Force in the formal transfer of 190 acres of vacant Wright-Patterson property to the new branch campus in April 1963. The Air Force gift was a significant portion of the 613 acres eventually acquired by the university. The donation involved two tracts along Kauffman Avenue, including the old Skyway Park housing area and a former section of the Miami Conservancy District, both of which had been declared excess by the base. Title to the lands was presented to Dr. John W. Millett, President of Miami University, and Dr. Novice G. Fawcett, President of The Ohio State University, by General Bradley at a luncheon at the Wright-Patterson AFB Officers' Club.

Throughout the planning stages, officials from the Dayton campus worked closely with Wright-Patterson officials. Because the new university was to be a commuter campus, traffic control and the master land-use plan for the university required close coordination between the two institutions.

Construction of the first building at Wright State, Allyn Hall, was completed during the summer of 1964. Classes for the fall quarter began on September 8. Formal dedication ceremonies for Wright State University were held in Allyn Hall on September 18, 1964, with representatives from Wright-Patterson and the local community in attendance.

The sixth annual Dayton Soap Box Derby was held July 11-12, 1964, on the inclined Accelerated Runway in Area B. This was the second year in a row that the base helped sponsor this event. Seventy-five boys in the Dayton area competed. The derbies, initiated originally in 1933, continued as a base and community tradition into the 1980s.

Soap box derbies have been a part of Dayton life since the 1930s. On occasion they are held on the abandoned Accelerated Runway in Area B.

On April 9, 1964, Brig. Gen. Arthur J. Pierce, Commander of the Foreign Technology Division (AFSC), directed groundbreaking ceremonies for a new laboratory facility adjacent to the Hq FTD building in Area A. Construction on the new L-shaped, single story laboratory building (Building 829) was completed the following year.

On April 22-24, 1965, the "Doolittle Raiders" held their 23rd annual reunion in Dayton and were warmly received at Wright-Patterson. Dayton was an especially significant site for the annual gathering because the Raiders' World War II unit, the 17th Bomb Group, had been reconstituted by the Strategic Air Command as the 17th Bombardment Wing (Heavy), and stationed at Wright-Patterson AFB effective July 1, 1963.

The Supply Division of the 2750th ABW marked the beginning of a new logistics era in February 1966, with the programming of a new UNIVAC 1050 II computer system. The new system was designed to hold data on more than 100,000 supply items and 30,000 equipment items, and was one of only 12 such systems Air Force-wide. This specialized computer system was developed by the Air Force Systems Command for universal use throughout the Air Force. It provided the capability for standardization of requisitioning, purchasing, receipting, storage, stock control, issue, shipment, reporting, disposition, identification, and accounting functions.

A ten-year timber management program was adopted by WPAFB in 1966, in cooperation with the Ohio Division of Forestry and Reclamation. The goal of the program was to reforest a total of 420 acres of base land over the following decade. Tens of thousands of trees were planted by volunteers from various base organizations, most notably by members of the Twin Base Rod and Gun Club. The overall scheme provided for adequate road and firebreak development, erosion control, insect and disease control, and wildlife habitat conservation. Simultaneously, a survey was made of existing base timberland to identify saleable saw timber and timber products. As a result of this inspection, 75,000 board feet of sawlogs and 200 tons of pulpwood were harvested in the fall of 1966.

Base records, in fact, reflect a long history of cooperation and association with state forestry officials. From 1928 through 1954, more than 7,500 trees were planted, primarily for ornamental purposes. In 1960, 10,000 multiflora rose trees were planted in conjunction with the state fish and wildlife conservation program. Some 51,000 trees were planted on base in the spring of 1964 as part of a base beautification project entitled Operation GREEN RUSH.

Wright-Patterson AFB was awarded the General Thomas D. White Fish and Wildlife Conservation Award by Hq USAF four times during the 1960s. This prestigious award is given annually to the two Air Force installations showing the most improvement in their conservation programs. Wright-Patterson took the Class B award, given to bases with less than 2,000 acres under active conservation management.

DISASTERS

Several disastrous fires at Wright-Patterson in the first three years of the 1960s destroyed a number of World War II-vintage buildings and damaged others.

On September 2, 1960, a fire in the 2750th Air Base Wing headquarters building (Building 10, Area C) resulted in $6,500 in damages. Four months later, in January 1961, over $15,000 in damages was sustained to a base cold storage facility adjacent to the base commissary store (Building 94, Area C). The base had earlier sought replacement of this building. Soon after the fire, Congress approved $80,000 for construction of a new facility.

On November 21, 1961, Wednesday evening before the Thanksgiving holiday, the annex of the AFLC headquarters building (Building 262-A, Area A) and its contents were totally destroyed by fire. Two base firemen, Station Chief Dale V. Kelchner and William J. Collins, lost their lives fighting the blaze. Fire damage was set at nearly $1.5 million.

Losses included destruction of approximately 3,200 official personnel records housed in the Central Civilian Personnel Office. Row after row of files, heavy office equipment, and safes crashed to the basement of the two-story wooden building as the first and second floors collapsed. The only documents spared were those stored in

Building 262-A blaze, Thanksgiving eve, 1961. Two WPAFB firemen, Station Chief Dale V. Kelchner and William J. Collins, lost their lives fighting the fire.

Approximately 3,200 official personnel files and countless other records smoulder in the ruins of Building 262-A. Building 266, built on the same site, was dedicated in July 1964.

Less than one week after the Building 262-A fire, this blaze in Wood City destroyed three buildings and damaged four others.

classified safes, but identification of the individual safes was difficult because dials, numbers, and other markings were burned off. Reconstruction of personnel 201 files required more than one year but was completed by April 1, 1963.

Building 262-A was replaced during 1963 and 1964 with a new $2.7 million building (Building 266), built on the same site. Gen. Mark E. Bradley, Jr., AFLC Commander, cut the ribbon at opening ceremonies on July 6, 1964.

Less than one week after the Building 262-A fire, on November 25, 1961, fire claimed three buildings in the Wood City area (now Kittyhawk Center) and damaged four others. The three buildings were one-story structures occupied by the USAF Orientation Group. Except for a small amount of equipment which was evacuated, the buildings and their contents were completely destroyed. Total loss was set at $693,920.

The Airmen's Service Club in Wood City was completely destroyed January 28, 1963, by the third major fire on base in 14 months. The spectacular blaze caused an estimated $66,000 damage, and was particularly difficult to control in the sub-zero January weather. Fourteen persons were treated for frostbite at the USAF Hospital, as firemen fought the blaze.

In February 1962, it was ice rather than fire that brought disaster to Wright-Patterson. Freezing rain and sleet turned the base into an icy wonderland, coating the entire out-of-doors with a thick and hazardous layer of ice. Base maintenance crews labored long hours to cut down broken tree limbs and branches, clear away fallen debris, salt roads and walks, and make emergency repairs.

February 1962 ice storm which coated Wright-Patterson trees, roads, and walks

WRIGHT-PATTERSON IN THE 1970s

The 1970s was a decade for celebrating anniversaries, welcoming home heroes, responding to emergency situations, and bidding farewell to familiar friends.

WPAFB joined the nation in celebrating the country's 200th birthday in 1976, and in marking the 75th anniversary of powered flight in 1978. In 1973, thirty USAF officers were received at Wright-Patterson following their release from North Vietnamese prison camps as part of Operation HOMECOMING. A 1974 tornado in Xenia, Ohio, and a blizzard during the winter of 1978 tested Wright-Patterson's disaster response capabilities, and a world-wide energy crisis called for new approaches to the management of vital resources. Also in the 1970s, the 2750th Air Base Wing witnessed the departure of one of the base's finest associate organizations, the 17th Bomb Wing (SAC), and lost its own fleet of administrative support aircraft.

One of the most touching scenes in Wright-Patterson history unfolded between February 15 and April 1, 1973,

during the base's support of Operation HOMECOMING. The return to U.S. control of former Southeast Asia prisoners of war culminated a series of plans that had begun in June 1968. In July 1969, these plans were called SENTINEL ECHO, and in September 1972 were renamed EGRESS RECAP. On the eve of the POW release, Secretary of Defense Melvin R. Laird changed the project's title to HOMECOMING.

Based upon World War II and Korean War experiences, it was expected that the returnees might require significant medical and psychological assistance. Therefore, the prisoners were placed under military medical auspices as soon as possible after their release and remained in medical channels for transportation to the continental U.S. After initial examination, treatment, and processing at the overseas point of return to U.S. control, the men were to be evacuated by air to CONUS medical facilities of the respective services. The USAF Medical Center Wright-Patterson was one of ten Air Force medical facilities named to receive and process returnees, many of whom had been incarcerated for more than five years, some for as long as eight years.

The 2750th Air Base Wing's principal role in the programmed repatriation was to provide logistical support for the operation. Wing agencies were responsible for providing family quarters for next of kin, as well as operational facilities for the USAF debriefing team, the WPAFB pro-

A tearful reunion marks the welcome of a repatriated prisoner of war on the WPAFB flightline.

Lt. Col. William J. Breckner, one of 30 former prisoners of war received at Wright-Patterson as part of Operation HOMECOMING, expresses his sentiments to a hushed audience.

Colorful posters drawn by area school children welcome the heroes home.

cessing team, and the HOMECOMING Press Center. Dependents were housed in Visiting Officers' Quarters (Buildings 832 and 833), which were reconfigured temporarily as family-type accommodations. The reception room for visitors was located in Building 833. The debriefing team used rooms in the north wing of the USAF Medical Center for administration and consultation. The Dodge Gymnasium (Building 849) ballroom and lobby housed the HOME-COMING News Center. All returnees were quartered in the north wing of the Medical Center.

Actual repatriation began February 12, 1973, when 143 American servicemen landed at Clark Air Base, Republic of the Philippines, in the first of 12 increments of release. Immediately following their arrival at Clark, invitational orders were issued, authorizing dependents to travel at government expense to the CONUS hospitals receiving the repatriates. The initial phase of Operation HOMECOM-

ING ended on April 4, 1973, at Clark Air Base, by which time 597 former captives of Asian Communists had been returned to freedom.

Thirty of the repatriated prisoners were flown to Wright-Patterson between February 15 and April 1. Upon disembarking, the returnees were warmly greeted by Gen. Jack J. Catton, AFLC Commander, or by Lt. Gen. Richard M. Hoban, AFLC Vice Commander, and by Brig. Gen. Irby B. Jarvis, 2750 ABW Commander. The returnees walked down a red carpet extending from the aircraft and smartly saluted the American flag held by a four-man Color Guard. Most returnees were then greeted by their families on the flightline, in view of media representatives and spectators, before being transported to the Medical Center.

Processing of the former POWs involved intelligence debriefing, medical examination and evaluation, personnel records updating and counseling, fiscal affairs, chaplain's visitation, family assistance, and public affairs activities. Five news conferences were held by families in the News Center.

Once processing was completed, the returnees were granted 90 days of convalescent leave. All repatriates, along with their wives or mothers, were invited by President and Mrs. Richard M. Nixon to a White House reception and formal dinner on May 24, 1973.

Conservation policies and efforts, which were a matter of continual concern at WPAFB, were suddenly intensified in November 1973 as Arab oil-producing nations cut off shipments to the United States in retaliation for the U.S. support of Israel during the Yom Kippur war. This embargo on crude oil and petroleum products precipitated the AFLC PACER ENERGY fuel conservation program which continued through the end of Fiscal Year 1974.

On November 1, 1973, the 2750th Air Base Wing established a PACER ENERGY Task Force to plan, implement, and administer a comprehensive energy conservation program at WPAFB. The Task Force outlined three general target areas for fuel savings in Fiscal Year 1974: 14 percent reduction in aviation fuels, 15 percent reduction in motor fuels, and 15 percent reduction in utilities, especially heating fuels and electricity.

USAF, AFLC, SAC, and AFSC guidance directed the aviation fuel conservation practices of the three flying wings at Wright-Patterson: the 2750th ABW, the 17th Bomb Wing, and the 4950th Test Wing. Programmed flying hour reductions for each of the three wings were in effect by January 1974. Through reduced flying hours and greater economies in ground and air operations, the 2750th ABW during the first eight months of FY 1974 used 12.3 percent less GP-4/5 jet fuel and 22.7 percent less aviation gasoline than the previous year. Monetary savings were $743,000 and $114,600 respectively.

Similar reductions were achieved in consumption of motor fuels and utilities. Overall, significant energy savings were achieved during Fiscal Year 1974 due to the vigilance and cooperation of Wright-Patterson military and civilian workers and by on-base residents. In dollar terms, between July 1, 1973 and March 31, 1974, WPAFB saved

A three-phase, $37 million coal-fired heating plant modification program resulted in significant energy savings during the 1970s and brought base coal-fired operations into line with federal and state environmental standards.

Aviation and motor fuels became primary targets for conservation measures at Wright-Patterson during the 1970s Arab oil embargo.

$1,347,018 in energy consumption compared to a similar period during the previous fiscal year.

Nor did energy conservation efforts end with the project's termination. Plans were formulated to cover future contingencies, aimed at achieving up to 75 percent curtailment of specific energy sources. By September 1976, the Wing had achieved a 6.8 percent reduction in energy consumption (i.e., electricity, natural gas, coal, motor vehicle fuels, and fuel oil for heating purposes) over Fiscal Year 1974. The decrease was greater than had been anticipated when the campaign began. Throughout the remainder of the 1970s, especially during the severe winters of 1976-1977 and 1977-1978, emphasis was placed on continuing and enlarging the base's energy conservation program. The Base Conservation Committee, chaired by the Wing Vice Commander, spearheaded these efforts.

Considerable progress was also made during the 1970s in the area of environmental protection. The single largest project conducted during the decade was a three-phase, $37 million coal-fired heating plant modification program. Six new large-capacity boilers were installed to replace 17 antiquated units that dated from the 1930s. High-efficiency electrostatic precipitators removed nearly all particulate matter exhausted from the heating plants. Overall, the new system provided Wright-Patterson with the most modern solid fuel boiler plants and fuel handling facilities in the Air Force, and enabled the base's coal-fired operations to com-

ply with both federal and state environmental standards in regard to particulate and sulfur dioxide emissions.

On July 31, 1974, the 2750th ABW received the Air Force Outstanding Unit Award for "exceptionally meritorious service in support of military operations" for the period February 1, 1972 through January 31, 1974. Wing Commander Brig. Gen. Irby B. Jarvis, Jr. received the honor on behalf of the Wing from AFLC Vice Commander Lt. Gen. Edmund F. O'Connor during an impressive ceremony held October 23, 1974, in the base theater. The award was referred to by General O'Connor as the "highest peacetime unit award."

In early November 1974, the AFLC Deputy Chief of Staff for Procurement and Production announced that the 2750th ABW had been selected as the command's "lead base" for implementing the Customer Integrated Automated Procurement System (CIAPS). CIAPS was an automated system designed by the Air Force Data Systems Design Center for all USAF base procurement activities. The system provided computer-produced delivery orders for the Federal Supply Schedule. CIAPS used the Burroughs B-3500 computer as an automated link with the Base Supply Univac 1050-II computer system and the Medical Supply B-3500 computer system. The WPAFB implementation was completed in April 1976.[30]

In 1975, the 2750th ABW received the USAF Flight Safety Certificate in recognition of three years of accident-free flying. This was the last such award for the Wing. By June 1975, the 2750th had transferred all of its support aircraft to other Air Force units, in compliance with Air Force directive.

In November 1974, Hq USAF decided, for financial reasons, to drop nearly 400 aging administrative support aircraft from the active inventory. A tentative disposition schedule was released affecting 343 aircraft, including both reciprocating-engine aircraft and jet-engine T-33s. Among the 36 AFLC airplanes involved were six T-33s from Wright-Patterson AFB scheduled for transfer to AFLC's Military Aircraft Storage and Disposition Center (MASDC) at Davis-Monthan AFB, Arizona. In early December 1974, AFLC published a more comprehensive phase-out schedule covering the remainder of the 2750th ABW support fleet. It called for the transfer of all remaining aircraft to MASDC, except for five T-39s, by the end of the fiscal year.

Meanwhile, the Military Airlift Command (MAC) was selected as the single manager for "pooled T-39 aircraft located in the CONUS." Wright-Patterson was chosen as one of 15 host bases. MAC subsequently announced that WPAFB would bed down nine T-39s, including the five transferred to MAC from the 2750th ABW.

The Wing began dispersing its aircraft in February 1975 with the reassignment of the T-33s to MASDC. On April 21, 1975, MAC began central scheduling for a portion of its new T-39 fleet. Central scheduling for WPAFB began on June 20.

By June 1975, the 2750th had transferred all of its 24 support aircraft. The five T-39s were reassigned to the Military Airlift Command and operated by the newly-established Det. 2, 1401st Military Airlift Squadron (MAS). The initial personnel for this detachment came from the 2750th ABW's Flight Operations Branch.

For the first time since 1948, the 2750th ABW did not possess its own aircraft. The Wing did, however, continue to operate the airfield and to support the 4950th Test Wing (AFSC), Det. 2, 1401st MAS, and transient aircraft in terms of aircraft supplies, petroleum, oil, and lubricants. Base-level maintenance was assumed by the 4950th Test Wing effective July 1, 1975. This included the transient alert function and such responsibilities as chief of maintenance, quality control, maintenance control, organizational maintenance, field maintenance, survival equipment maintenance, avionics maintenance, and the Precision Measurement Equipment Laboratory (PMEL).

The transfer of support aircraft also affected the mission of the 2750th ABW Simulator Training Branch. As of July 1, 1975, the Branch ceased all operations with the exception of the T-40 Trainer. The Branch's equipment was transferred to the 4950th Test Wing effective September 15. Instructor and maintenance personnel were reassigned to the 4950th on October 26.

Insofar as real property was concerned, the 2750th transferred facility responsibility for a number of Area C buildings to the 4950th Test Wing, including Buildings 13, 105, 148, 152, 169, 206-North, 256, and 884. Building 188 in Area B was also assigned to the 4950th.

Following closely on the reassignment of the 2750th ABW aircraft, another era in Wright-Patterson's long history ended in September 1975, with the planned transfer of the 17th Bombardment Wing (Heavy). On September 30, the Bomb Wing was transferred in name only, without personnel or equipment, to Beale AFB, California. The Wing's 14 B-52 bombers and 15 KC-135 tankers were dispersed to other SAC bases and to the Ohio Air National Guard. Wing personnel were assigned to other installations or organizations.

As the 17th Bomb Wing vacated its facilities on the West Ramp in Area C, the buildings were reassigned one by one to the 4950th Test Wing. Reassignment of facilities began July 23 and was complete by September 15.

In June 1976, yet another era ended at Wright-Patterson. Effective June 1, the aerodrome in Area B (Wright Field) was officially closed, ending nearly 50 years of service to the Air Force and its antecedent organizations. All air traffic operations at Wright-Patterson today are handled on the Area C (Patterson) runways.

Although the 2750th Air Base Wing dispersed all of its administrative support aircraft during 1974 and 1975, the Wing Operations and Training Division retained management of the WPAFB aerodrome.

The 4950th Test Wing (AFSC) assumed occupancy of West Ramp facilities vacated by the 17th Bomb Wing in 1975.

In 1975, WPAFB was selected as one of 15 bases to host Military Airlift Command (MAC) T-39 aircraft. The MAC fleet at WPAFB is assigned to Det. 2, 1401st Military Airlift Squadron.

A milestone in air traffic history occurred at Wright-Patterson on September 20, 1978, when the precision approach radar AN/FPN-16 in Area C was decommissioned after 26 years of continuous operations. A new solid-state dual instrument landing system was installed to assist pilots using Runway 5L23R. With the new equipment, a pilot received control tower permission to land, then automatically received the required instrument data to make an instrument landing without further assistance.

On June 6, 1978, the Federal Aviation Administration (FAA) relocated the Dayton approach control facility (activated in 1957) from WPAFB to the Dayton International Airport, Vandalia, Ohio. Predicated by the relocation of equipment and personnel from Wright-Patterson, the memorandum of understanding between the 2750th Air Base Wing, the 2046th Communications Group, Det. 15, 15th Weather Squadron, and the FAA terminated October 1, 1978. Space that the FAA had occupied in Buildings 206 and 841 in Area C of WPAFB was released effective January 15, 1979. The 2750th ABW Operations and Training Division maintained its management of the WPAFB aerodrome in coordination with other USAF and federal government agencies.

A significant project begun in the 1970s but with far-reaching implications for the future, was the Air Installation Compatible Use Zone (AICUZ) program. AICUZ is a community interface program designed to coordinate the needs of the Air Force with the development of surrounding communities, in order to assure continuance of Wright-Patterson AFB as a center of flying operations.

The conceptual goal of AICUZ is to achieve compatible land uses around military installations. The development of lands near Air Force bases is a continuing concern to Air Force officials. On the one hand, the Air Force recognizes the responsibility to protect public areas surrounding airfields from noise, pollution, and flight hazards. On the other hand is the undeniable fact that lands near air bases are intrinsically attractive areas for development.

Due to the growth of the air base and surrounding communities, 2750th Air Base Wing commanders have for many years been aware of the potential adverse impact of business and residential encroachment on Wright-Patterson flying operations. As early as 1962, Base Commander Brig. Gen. Glen J. McClernon held meetings with community leaders concerning land use and development in areas adjacent to the base. In October 1966, a WPAFB Airport Zoning Regulation became law. Although subsequently challenged and rescinded, this basic document provided a firm foundation for the AICUZ concept. The key element was an atmosphere of mutual trust and helpfulness between the base and the surrounding communities.

In May 1975, after years of careful planning, the final AICUZ study developed by the base was released to the public. Invitations from the Base Commander were extended to state and local officials and Ohio's U.S. Congressional representatives to attend a special briefing on the study. In July 1975, a revised WPAFB Airport Zoning Regulation was finally enacted by the four-county Joint

Wright-Patterson Air Force Base, Ohio

AICUZ

AIR INSTALLATION COMPATABLE USE ZONE REPORT

The Air Installation Compatible Use Zone (AICUZ) program at WPAFB is designed to coordinate the needs of the Air Force with the development of surrounding communities to assure the continuance of Wright-Patterson as an active center of flying operations.

WPAFB Airport Zoning Commission (counties involved were Montgomery, Greene, Clark, and Miami). The regulation defined noise and accident zones about the air base and suggested compatible land use for these zones. Some areas were recommended to remain in open space, while other more densely settled areas could limit construction and design noise reduction features into buildings along with other planning measures.

ASSOCIATE ORGANIZATIONS

By 1973, the 2750th Air Base Wing had logged 25 years of service to its associate organizations, including Hq AFLC, ASD, FTD, the 17th Bomb Wing (SAC), the Air Force Museum, the USAF Medical Center Wright-Patterson, AFOG, and the 2046th Communications Group. During the remainder of the 1970s, a number of new organizations were assigned to WPAFB, and several departed.

The 3025th Management Engineering Squadron was organized and designated at WPAFB effective October 1, 1973. The squadron was assigned to AFLC headquarters under the operational control of the Directorate of Manpower and Organization. To support this reorganization, Detachment 7, 3030th Support Squadron, was inactivated and succeeded by Detachment 1, 3025th MES.

These changes were part of an effort to upgrade the manpower function. The manpower program at WPAFB as it is known today was established in 1966, when the Manpower Validation Program and the manpower and organization functions were consolidated under the Management Engineering Team concept. In the early 1970s, USAF conducted a two-year study to further identify headquarters and headquarters squadron manpower costs. As a result, all major USAF commands were directed to withdraw management engineering and manpower and organization resources from previously designated headquarters support squadrons like the 3030th, and to consolidate these functions into major command management engineering squadrons/detachments. Det. 1, 3025th MES was thus established at AFLC. Det. 1 continues today to provide manpower management services to the 2750th ABW. Its major responsibilities are management of manpower resources, development of wartime and peacetime manpower requirements, and the preparation of cost studies to assess the feasibility of contracting out Air Force services. In addition, Det. 1 provides management consulting services to the Wing Commander.

Wright-Patterson continued to set a fast pace in aerospace exploration and development during the 1970s. On July 1, 1975, the four AFSC laboratories in Area B were realigned into the Air Force Wright Aeronautical Laboratories (AFWAL). Retaining their organizational titles, identities, and functions were the Aero Propulsion, Flight Dynamics, Materials, and Avionics Laboratories. The Aerospace Research Laboratory was disestablished and its programs distributed elsewhere.[31]

Also effective July 1, 1975, the 4950th Test Wing underwent a major realignment as it absorbed the Precision Measurement Equipment Laboratory (PMEL) and the base aircraft maintenance and allied support functions which had previously been the responsibility of the 2750th Air Base Wing.

The 17th Bombardment Wing (SAC) moved, in name only, without personnel and equipment, from Wright-Patterson AFB to Beale AFB, California, effective September 30, 1975, as mentioned earlier in this chapter. The SAC aircraft from Wright-Patterson were transferred to other Strategic Air Command bases and the Air National Guard. The Wing's B-52H bombers were dispersed to other "H" model bases in Michigan and North Dakota, while KC-135 tanker aircraft were transferred throughout SAC and to the Ohio Air National Guard at Rickenbacker AFB near Columbus, Ohio. Although many bomb wing personnel were reassigned to bases throughout the U.S. and overseas, a large segment were stationed together with the bombers at SAC bases in the upper Midwest. Approximately one-third of the Wing's 1,200 military members remained at Wright-Patterson and were assigned to other base units such as AFLC, ASD, and the 2750th ABW.

The official "Buckeye Farewell" was extended to the departing 17th Bomb Wing on July 7, 1975, as its two remaining KC-135s and one B-52H left Wright-Patterson's VHB runway for the last time. Facilities vacated by the 17th Bomb Wing were reassigned to the 4950th Test Wing.

The Air Force Museum, a named activity at WPAFB, was inactivated effective August 8, 1975, and the unit designation reverted to the Department of the Air Force. The Museum was then activated as a named unit and assigned to the Air Force Logistics Command at Wright-Patterson, effective the same day. The Air Force Museum subsequently was assigned to the 2750th Air Base Wing for logistical support.

A significant event within AFLC was the July 1, 1976 activation of the Air Force Acquisition Logistics Division (AFALD). The new division was formed from existing AFLC sources, primarily the Deputy Chief of Staff for Acquisition Logistics and the 2732nd Acquisition Logistics Operations Squadron. AFALD's mission was to expand and strengthen the interface between AFLC and the Air Force Systems Command (AFSC), thus improving operational utility, field availability, and supportability of new systems, while reducing their operating and support costs. The Air

Air Force Wright Aeronautical Laboratories (AFWAL), Area B. AFWAL is comprised of four major Air Force research laboratories: Propulsion, Avionics, Flight Dynamics, and Materials. Formed July 1, 1975, AFWAL reported to Hq AFSC until November 1982, when it joined the Aeronautical Systems Division (ASD) at WPAFB.

Hq Air Force Acquisition Logistics Division (AFALD), Building 15, Area B. Activated in July 1976, AFALD was formed to expand and strengthen the interface between the Air Force Logistics Command and the Air Force Systems Command.

Force Acquisition Logistics Division was designed to act as a catalyst to stimulate and improve the AFLC/AFSC interchange of knowledge, particularly the flow of feedback information from users in the combat commands.[32]

A second major AFLC organization was created at WPAFB in 1978. The AFLC International Logistics Center (ILC), identified as a "major field organization," was activated effective May 1, 1978. The new center merged elements of the Hq AFLC Office of the Assistant for International Logistics and most of the international logistics functions of AFALD. The ILC had three principal offices: plans and procedures, programs and resources, and operations. Its charter was to establish and implement an AFLC International Logistics Program for the development, negotiation, and management of AFLC Security Assistance programs. This included foreign military sales, grant aid, and international military education and training.

On October 1, 1976, the Air Force Institute of Technology asked for 7,390 sq ft of space in Building 288, Area A, to accommodate the newly-established Defense Institute of Security Assistance Management (DISAM). DISAM was an element of the Defense Security Assistant Management Education (DSAME) program which was scheduled to become fully operational at Wright-Patterson in June 1977. (DSAME was programmed originally to operate as a department of the AFIT School of Systems and Logistics.) The DSAME program was subsequently elevated to the status of a "separate school with an expanded mission within AFIT." DISAM held its first classes in Building 288 on January 18, 1977, and later relocated to the second floor of the west center section of Building 125 in Area B.

The 15th Weather Squadron (MAC) moved without personnel and equipment from Scott AFB, Illinois, to WPAFB effective January 1, 1976, where it was reassigned from the 5th Weather Wing to the 7th Weather Wing. The 15th was assigned the following detachments: Det. 1, Tinker AFB, Oklahoma; Det. 6, Hill AFB, Utah; Det. 7, Kelly AFB, Texas; Det. 8, McClellan AFB, California; Det. 13,

The AFLC International Logistics Center (ILC) was established in May 1978 to develop, negotiate, and manage AFLC Security Assistance programs.

Robins AFB, Georgia; and Det. 15, WPAFB, Ohio. On June 1, 1980, the 15th Weather Squadron moved, again without personnel or equipment, from WPAFB to McGuire AFB, NJ. Det. 15, 15th Weather Squadron remained at WPAFB and continues today as the weather support organization for the base.

A new tenant organization at Wright-Patterson effective December 1, 1976, was the 87th Port Squadron (Air Force Reserve). Located in Building 146, Area C, the squadron moved to WPAFB without personnel and equipment from McClellan AFB, California.

On December 12, 1977, the 3552nd USAF Recruiting Service Squadron (ATC) completed its relocation to Building 1, Area C, from the Defense Construction Supply Center (DCSC) in Columbus, Ohio. The squadron supported 25 Air Force recruiting offices in the Southern Ohio area.

On April 5, 1979, Hq USAF approved a plan to relocate all of the facilities of the Air Force Orientation Group (AFOG) from Area B, WPAFB to the Defense Electronics Supply Center (DESC) at Gentile Air Force Station, Dayton. The move was initiated in April 1981 and the Group was settled in its new quarters by August of that year. AFOG currently occupies Buildings 4 and 74 at DESC.

GROWTH

Two major construction programs during the early 1970s greatly improved military family housing at WPAFB. Traditionally, the demand for on-base housing had been high, particularly among enlisted personnel. In 1970, it was noted that there were approximately 4,900 families assigned to Wright-Patterson, while there were on-base accommodations for only 1,900. Contracts were subsequently awarded by the Base Procurement Branch on April 5 and June 14, 1971, for the design and construction of two new projects of 300 and 500 family housing units, respectively.

The Defense Institute of Security Assistance Management (DISAM), now located in Building 125, Area B, held its first classes at Wright-Patterson in the winter of 1977.

GENTILE AIR FORCE STATION

Gentile Air Force Station, a 165-acre site on Wilmington Pike in Kettering, is the home of the Defense Electronics Supply Center (DESC). The facility was first opened in 1944 to serve as a centralized storage facility for the Army Signal Corps and was known as Dayton Air Force Depot. Prior to that time, it had served as a commercial flying field for the Johnson Flying Service. On August 14, 1943, approval was granted by the Chief Signal Officer for the construction of a $3 million depot on Wilmington Pike. Ground was broken October 5, 1943, and the project completed in less than a year. Formal dedication ceremonies were held in October 1944.

In 1945, Signal Corps functions were integrated into the Army Air Forces and the installation became known as the 862nd Army Air Forces Specialized Depot. In 1951, it was renamed Gentile Air Force Depot in honor of World War II flying ace Maj. Don S. Gentile of nearby Piqua, Ohio. In 1955, under the jurisdiction of the Air Force Logistics Command, separate titles were given the organization and the installation, the organization being designated Dayton Air Force Depot and the installation Gentile Air Force Station. The site still retains the title Gentile Air Force Station, owned by the Air Force and leased to DESC. The 2750th Air Base Wing is the real property manager for the station.

Maj. Don S. Gentile

Work began May 21, 1971, on the $7.5 million Woodland Hills 300-unit project in Area B. This package, awarded to the National Homes Construction Corporation, Inc. of Lafayette, Indiana, was the first military family housing built on base since the brick quarters were erected in Area A during the mid-1930s. Ground was broken July 9, 1973, for the construction of 500 military family housing units—430 located in Area A, adjacent to the USAF Medical Center and 70 sited in Area B, off Zink Road, near Woodland Hills. The $12.1 million contract was also awarded to National Homes, Inc. In addition to these new construction projects, $8.7 million plans were underway at the end of June 1974 to convert 904 apartments in the Page Manor housing area into 640 larger, more modern quarters.

Wood City underwent dynamic changes during the 1970s, including a name change. That portion of the base, traditionally used for housing and recreation, became known as Kittyhawk Center. Kittyhawk quickly changed from a quiet, residential neighborhood into a bustling community. It was designed to be "people oriented," providing the products, services, and accommodations needed by and for Wright-Patterson's military population and their dependents.

During 1971, nearly $350,000 in combined appropriated and non-appropriated funds were expended to upgrade dormitories, the dining hall, and recreational facilities in Kittyhawk Center. In October 1978, the Noncommissioned Officers' Open Mess completed a $363,000 modernization program. Nearby, a $463,909 child care center opened in August 1979 (Building 1235), replacing three wood-frame single story buildings erected during World War II.

Outdoor sports benefited from a program completed in October 1979. To replace sites lost during construction of other facilities, $396,700 was spent to construct new recreation facilities including softball diamonds and a football/soccer field.

The crown jewel of the new Kittyhawk Center, however, was the four-acre, $7 million Community Shopping Center Complex. Housed within the new complex were the main

Woodland Hills housing project under construction in 1971

sales store of the Base Exchange, as well as concession shops, a commercial bank branch, and the Base Commissary store. The center resulted from a coordinated effort by the Army-Air Force Exchange Service, the Air Force Commissary Service, the 2750th Air Base Wing, and the Winters National Bank and Trust Company, Dayton, Ohio. The center was opened for business following gala ceremonies on August 26, 1980.

Employees of the Foreign Technology Division moved into Building 856, the newest addition to the FTD complex in Area A, on August 24, 1976. More than 600 dignitaries attended dedication ceremonies on September 16, including Secretary of the Air Force James W. Plummer and U.S. Representative Clarence J. Brown of Ohio's 7th Congressional District.

On July 5, 1977, the Air Force Institute of Technology also moved into new quarters. AFIT's School of Systems and Logistics was relocated from Building 288 in Area A to the new $3.5 million Building 641 in Area B. The Honorable Hans M. Mark, Under Secretary of the Air Force, was the principal speaker at dedication ceremonies on October 4.

Progress on base during the 1970s was sometimes tinged with bittersweet as old landmarks changed. Many current and former employees had cause to reminisce when it was announced in 1979 that Buildings 2, 3, and 10 in Area B, the first hangars constructed at Wright Field (1928) were to be razed. In their place, ASD planned to construct an $11 million Fuels and Lubricants Laboratory. Groundbreaking ceremonies for the new facility were held on July 30, 1980.

Conversion of the Civilian Club, Building 274 in Area A, also evoked memories for many people associated with the base. Constructed during World War II and opened on December 1, 1944, the Civilian Club was open to all WPAFB civilian employees, military members, their families and friends. The club was noted for hosting nationally famous dance orchestras and square dance groups, and was the scene of countless dances, wedding receptions, and other popular events.* In 1979, the Club was closed, and remodeling began to convert it for use as the Wright-Patterson AFB Conference Center.

Ribbon cutting ceremonies for the new Base Exchange and Base Commissary complex, August 26, 1980

The Foreign Technology Division complex in Area A consists of Buildings 856, 828, and 829.

The Air Force Institute of Technology (AFIT) School of Systems and Logistics, Building 641, Area B

The modern $7 million Community Shopping Center Complex in Kittyhawk Center

The AFIT School of Engineering, Building 640, Area B

*Chapter VII, Patterson Field, contains further details of this time period.

ACTIVITIES

Among the most exciting activities at Wright-Patterson AFB during the 1970s were those associated with celebration of the nation's bicentennial. Throughout the nation, the Bicentennial observance was divided into three themes: Heritage '76, Festival USA, and Horizons '76. At Wright-Patterson, separate parallel committees were established to carry out programs based on all three themes. Overall direction of the base-wide program for the Bicentennial celebration was coordinated by the WPAFB Planning and Coordinating Committee, chaired by the Base Commander. Wright-Patterson also supported the civilian Bicentennial efforts of cities, towns, and villages located in the base's immediate vicinity.

A Community Day observance opened the base schedule of events on May 24, 1975, one week after Armed Forces Day. The highlight of the local six-hour program was an aerobatic demonstration by the USAF Thunderbirds team flying six T-38 Talon aircraft. The Ninth Virginia Regiment, attired in Revolutionary War uniforms and regalia, gave two demonstration drills with muskets. (The original regiment was organized November 19, 1776, and fought in many major campaigns, including incursions into the Ohio River Valley during the Revolutionary War.)

On August 19, 1975, the American Revolution Bicentennial Commission officially recognized Wright-Patterson AFB as a "Bicentennial United States Air Force installation." During the autumn and winter months of 1975-1976, the various Bicentennial committees coordinated with each other and with their counterparts in civilian communities to assure the best possible local and area observance of the nation's 200th anniversary. The thoroughness with which they planned was reflected in the diversity of programs that took place during the Bicentennial year.

The Air Force Museum was the scene of the first activities during July 1976. From July 11-13, an Ohio Region Bicentennial Boy Scout Jamboree held on the Museum grounds attracted nearly 10,000 scouts and their troop leaders. On July 23, the Museum dedicated its new $1 million Visitors Reception Center, a gift of the Air Force Museum Foundation. Principal speaker at the dedicatory ceremonies was Senator Barry M. Goldwater. Also present was Secretary of the Air Force Thomas C. Reed, who snipped a symbolic ribbon to open the Center. The scissors used during the ceremony had belonged to Orville Wright and were loaned for the occasion by Mr. Wright's niece, Mrs. Ivonette Wright Miller.

Nearly 10,000 scouts enjoy the Ohio Region Bicentennial Boy Scout Jamboree on the grounds of the Air Force Museum in July 1976.

A simple Indian teepee contrasts with the modern architecture of the Avionics Lab Electronic Warfare Research Facility during the 1976 Boy Scout Jamboree.

AMERICAN REVOLUTION BICENTENNIAL
1776-1976

Certificate of Official Recognition

Accorded to

Wright-Patterson Air Force Base
Dayton, Ohio

as a Bicentennial United States Air Force Installation
By the
American Revolution
Bicentennial Administration

Administrator

Wright-Patterson was recognized as an official Bicentennial United States Air Force Installation in 1975. The base hosted a wide range of activities in connection with the nation's 200th birthday.

The dedication of the Visitors Center coincided with the annual enshrinement ceremonies of the Aviation Hall of Fame and with the Dayton Air Fair '76. The Fair, which attracted over 100,000 spectators, featured both military and civilian aircraft and performers, and was supported, as in past and future years, by a wide range of WPAFB organizations, including the 2750th ABW.

Activities on base during August and September included the National Meet of the American Model Aircraft Association, the reopening of Hadden Recreation Park, and the staging of the 2750th Air Base Wing's Festival '76.

The highlight of the base Bicentennial celebration, however, was the grand People-for-People Festival held September 20, which attracted nearly 16,000 visitors. The purpose of the Festival was to "promote human relations through awareness, communication, and understanding," and to provide a suitable program to represent the heritage of America "through arts, crafts, drama, display, dance, cuisine, fashion, music, and song."

Honoring Air Force members of past decades was also an important part of Wright-Patterson's Bicentennial observance. An initiative that grew out of the Bicentennial in this regard was the formation of a Base Memorialization Committee. Established as part of the USAF memorialization program, this committee was tasked with naming appropriate streets, buildings, recreational areas, and medical facilities in honor of distinguished deceased Air Force military members.

The first such action on Wright-Patterson was the October 27, 1976, dedication of Building 262, Area A, in honor of Brig. Gen. William E. Gillmore, first Chief of the Air Corps Materiel Division, McCook Field. The Materiel Division was an antecedent of today's Air Force Logistics Command, whose Headquarters occupy Building 262.

The final observance in Wright-Patterson's year-long celebration of the Bicentennial was the dedication of an "Employees' Monument," to honor all military members and civilian employees who have ever worked at Wright-Patterson AFB, from its World War I origins to the present. Designed by Wright State University art student Ray Williams, the monument was a sculpture in stainless steel, mounted on a reinforced concrete pedestal. The design was described as an abstract of upswept wings, symbolizing man's reach toward outer space which started from the first day that work began at WPAFB. Six feet high and approximately 20 feet wing tip to wing tip, the monument was erected in the spring of 1977 at the corner of Skeel Avenue and Novick Road in Area A, overlooking the site of the Wright brothers' original 1904 hangar on Huffman Prairie.

In the four years following the Bicentennial, three additional memorializations of facilities on Wright-Patterson took place. Following the dedication of Gillmore Hall, the Memorialization Committee recommended redesignation of the lettered and numbered streets in the senior officer brick quarters in Area A. Ten officers, all Ohio natives,

were selected for this honor. Five of them had spent a portion of their Air Force career at Wright-Patterson. The collective span of service represented by these men spread from August 1, 1907, when the U.S. Army Signal Corps Aeronautical Division was established, to July 31, 1957, when the last individual among them retired. The honorees represented the following Ohio hometowns:

Gen. Benjamin W. Chidlaw	Cleves
Lt. Gen. George H. Brett	Cleveland
Lt. Gen. David M. Schlatter	Fostoria
Lt. Gen. Barton K. Yount	Troy
Maj. Gen. Robert G. Breene	Dayton
Brig. Gen. Frank P. Lahm	Mansfield
Brig. Gen. Nelson S. Talbott	Dayton
Col. Charles deF. Chandler	Cleveland
Col. Gerald R. Johnson	Akron
2nd Lt. William E. Metzger*	Lima

Dedication ceremonies were held on July 22, 1977. Gen. F. Michael Rogers, AFLC Commander, presented the dedicatory address to the assembled guests and next of kin of the men being honored.

AFLC Headquarters (Building 262, Area A) is named in honor of Brig. Gen. William E. Gillmore, first Chief of the Air Corps Materiel Division at McCook Field.

Mrs. Michael J. Lally, granddaughter of the late General Gillmore, views the dedicatory bronze plaque for Building 262 with Gen. F. Michael Rogers, AFLC Commander, during ceremonies October 27, 1976.

*Lieutenant Metzger received the Medal of Honor posthumously in 1945, for valor above and beyond the call of duty as a B-17 copilot over Germany.

The "Employees' Monument," located at the corner of Skeel Avenue and Novick Road, was dedicated during the Bicentennial to honor all military members and civilian employees who have ever worked at Wright-Patterson.

Memorialization ceremony for the Area A brick quarters streets, July 22, 1977. Ten lettered and numbered streets in the senior officer brick quarters housing area were redesignated in honor of outstanding officers who were native sons of Ohio.

Frank G. Barnes Memorial Park was dedicated in September 1977 in honor of Maj. Gen. Frank Barnes, former Deputy Chief of Staff for Engineering and Services, Hq AFLC.

Prater Hall, named for TSgt. Roy D. Prater, is one of six buildings in the Kittyhawk Center dedicated in honor of Ohio airmen who died from enemy action in South Vietnam.

On September 23, 1977, a beautiful living memorial was dedicated to the memory of Maj. Gen. Frank G. Barnes. General Barnes served as Deputy Chief of Staff, Engineering and Services, Hq AFLC, from February 1973 until his death in 1976. The Frank G. Barnes Memorial Park is located adjacent to Building 266 in Area A. The park features twenty-one varieties of deciduous, flowering, and conifer trees, flowering bushes and shrubs, and eleven species of perennial flowers.

Following the renovation of five dormitories and the dining hall in Kittyhawk Center, these buildings were dedicated in honor of six Ohio airmen who died from enemy action in South Vietnam. This marked the first time in the current series of formal dedications that deceased enlisted men were honored. General Bryce Poe II, AFLC Commander, and Col. James Rigney, 2750th ABW Commander,

presided at the ceremonies held June 22, 1979, and unveiled six bronze plaques bearing the names of the honorees:

    TSgt. Roy D. Prater
    SSgt. James R. Lute
    SSgt. Frederick Wilhelm
    AlC William H. Pitsenbarger
    AlC James E. Pleiman
    Sgt. James D. Locker

Walnut plaques with sketches and biographies of the airmen were placed on permanent display in the dayrooms of the respective dormitories and in the dining hall.*

*Three more memorializations occurred in the first years of the 1980s. On June 19, 1981, streets in the vicinity of the U.S. Air Force Museum were named in honor of Gen. Carl A. Spaatz, Maj. Richard I. Bong, and 1st Lt. Edward Ward. On August 28, 1981, the 2750th Air Base Wing Headquarters, Building 10, Area C, was named in honor of Brig. Gen. Joseph T. Morris, first Commander of the 2750th ABW. On November 18, 1982, the Air Force Institute of Technology dedicated its School of Engineering (Building 640, Area B) in honor of Col. Thurman H. Bane, the first post-World War I Commander of McCook Field and founder of the Air School of Application, forerunner of AFIT.

The year 1978 was celebrated as the 75th Anniversary of Powered Flight. A special steering committee of the Greater Dayton Area Chamber of Commerce coordinated the various local observances of the anniversary. Chairing the group was Lt. Gen. James T. Stewart, USAF-Retired, who had commanded the Aeronautical Systems Division from June 1970 to August 1976. At Wright-Patterson a special "75th Anniversary of Powered Flight" logo was adopted and proudly displayed on all letters posted from the base during the year.

On September 9, 1978, three parcels of land that had been intimately associated with the Wrights were transferred to the Air Force and the 2750th Air Base Wing by the Miami Conservancy District. The first was a 0.52 acre plot of land on Pylon Road in Area A commemorating the site of the Wright's first hangar on Huffman Prairie. The concrete monument that marks the spot was completed in June 1941 by the Wilbur and Orville Wright Commission in cooperation with the Miami Conservancy District. The other two parcels of land comprised a 27-acre park and memorial site dedicated to the memory of the Wright brothers. Known as Wright Brothers Hill, this property is in Area B near the intersection of State Route 444 and Kauffman Avenue.

About 150 guests and visitors attended the formal ceremony marking the transfer of properties. Mr. Robert S. Oelman, President of the Miami Conservancy District Board of Directors, conveyed the original copy of the special warranty deed to General Bryce Poe II, AFLC Commander. In his remarks, General Poe stated that it was fitting that the memorial, "which for 38 years has rested on Miami Conservancy District land is now a part of Wright-Patterson—just as Huffman Prairie—also once Conservancy land, is now part of the Base."

Among the distinguished attendees were two U.S. Congressmen, Clarence J. Brown of Urbana, and Charles W. Whalen of Dayton, as well as Mrs. Ivonette Wright Miller of Dayton, and Mr. Horace A. Wright of Xenia, niece and nephew of Wilbur and Orville Wright.

An unusual honor was accorded Wright-Patterson later in the month. On September 23, the Dayton Stamp Club and the 75th Anniversary of Powered Flight Committee, supported by the U.S. Air Force Museum, hosted the first day sale of two commemorative stamps honoring the Wright brothers. U.S. Postmaster General William F. Bolger spoke at the ceremony preceding the initial sale of the two differently designed 31-cent airmail stamps.

On December 16, the eve of the official anniversary, about 700 persons attended a "First Flight Banquet Honoring the 75th Anniversary of Powered Flight" held at the Dayton Convention and Exhibition Center. Participating dignitaries included Lowell Thomas, famous newscaster and author; Lt. Gen. James Doolittle, USAF-Retired; former Astronaut Neil Armstrong, the first man to walk on the moon; and Milton Caniff, nationally-known cartoonist (creator of the Steve Canyon series).

The morning of December 17th marked the actual anniversary of the first flight. Visitors began arriving early on Wright Brothers Hill, base employees and local citizens alike. The formal ceremonies began with appropriate remarks by Gen. Bryce Poe and Lt. Gen. James Stewart. Mrs. Ivonette Miller and Mr. Horace Wright laid large wreaths at the base of the granite Wright Brothers Memorial monument. At 10:35 a.m. a bugler sounded taps and two T-39 aircraft flew overhead in trail. This precise hour and minute coincided with Orville Wright's historic first lift-off at Kitty Hawk, North Carolina, on December 17, 1903. The ceremony served as fitting tribute to the spirit and accomplishments of the Wright brothers and to the thousands who followed them in the intervening 75 years.

The 0.52 acre plot of land on Pylon Road in Area A commemorating the site of the Wright Brothers' first hangar was one of three parcels transferred from the Miami Conservancy District to Wright-Patterson AFB in September 1978.

All letters posted from Wright-Patterson during 1978 carried this "75th Anniversary of Powered Flight" commemorative postmark.

Ceremonial wreaths are placed on the Wright Memorial each December 17th in honor of the Wrights' achievements.

The 27-acre Wright Brothers Hill park and memorial site were also transferred to the Air Force during ceremonies on September 9, 1978.

DISASTERS

Once data from the national disaster control center were tallied, April 3, 1974, entered United States history as the "Day of the 100 Tornadoes." Slightly more than 10 percent of the deaths resulting from these natural disasters occurred in and around the city of Xenia, Ohio, a quiet but progressive community twelve miles southeast of Wright-Patterson AFB. Residents of the city included 1,297 WPAFB employees (1,064 civilian and 233 military).

The killer tornado struck Xenia at 4:40 p.m., carving a swath of destruction four miles long and one-half mile wide. In its wake, 34 persons lay dead and 500 injured. More than a thousand homes were destroyed (including those of 293 base employees), 660 were heavily damaged, and another 904 slightly damaged. Insurance adjusters placed losses at $500 million.

At 5:00 p.m., Brig. Gen. Irby B. Jarvis, Jr., 2750th ABW Commander, activated the base Disaster Preparedness Control Center and the entire base moved into action. The USAF Medical Center and the 2750th ABW responded quickly to two of Xenia's most pressing needs: medical aid for the scores of injured victims and assistance in sorting through tons of debris to recover other casualties. At 6:30 p.m., a medical team was dispatched to Xenia, as were three on-scene commanders from the Wing to direct WPAFB's assistance. From that time forward, until 1:00 p.m. April 4, roads between WPAFB and Xenia were filled

with a steady stream of traffic from the base to the disaster scene. Thirty-seven of the most seriously injured were admitted to the USAF Medical Center. Drugs, medicine, and equipment from St. Elizabeth Hospital in Dayton were airlifted to Greene Memorial Hospital in Xenia. A 4950th Test Wing CH-3 helicopter flew eight sorties to fulfill this mission. Five hundred volunteers at the base contributed blood at the Medical Center for use in the emergency.

Meanwhile, base civil engineers had dispatched heavy equipment convoys to Xenia to assist in search and recovery operations and to open traffic arteries. As the first long night following the tornado waned, other supplies and assistance arrived, including generators for emergency lighting, floodlights, gasoline, 7,000 gallons of water, box lunches, and 30 gallons of coffee for volunteer rescue workers.

Wright-Patterson's support continued throughout the entire next week. Volunteers were recruited from nearly all WPAFB organizations. Among the more significant contributors was the 2046th Communications Group, which moved its Military Affiliate Radio System (MARS) van to downtown Xenia. VHF, UHF, and radio-telephone communications were established, linking on-scene civil defense, the WPAFB Fire Department, and base Security Police with the Disaster Preparedness Control Center. The 2046th also opened the Springfield (Ohio) Municipal Airport tower to assist Ohio National Guard helicopters ferrying emergency supplies.

337

Aftermath of the Xenia tornado. The violent tornado struck the neighboring city of Xenia, Ohio, on April 3, 1974, killing 34 people and causing more than $500 million in damages. The USAF Medical Center at Wright-Patterson and the 2750th ABW immediately dispatched medical teams and convoys of heavy equipment to the scene. The Wright-Patterson Disaster Preparedness Control Center coordinated the assistance offered by virtually every organization on base to help sort through the debris and return order to Xenia.

President Richard M. Nixon and Congressman Clarence J. Brown (right) arrive at Wright-Patterson on April 9 to make a helicopter survey of the tornado damage. Base Commander Brig. Gen. Irby Jarvis and AFLC Commander Gen. Jack J. Catton (left) briefed the Presidential party.

Aerial photography was provided by the 4950th Test Wing and the 155th Tactical Reconnaissance Group, Nebraska Air National Guard at Lincoln, with assistance from the 2750th ABW Operations and Training Division.

On April 6, a Federal Disaster Assistance Team (FDAT) established temporary offices in Building 89, Area C, and assembled a staff of 30 people. A 5th Army liaison officer to the FDAT arrived at WPAFB from Fort Knox, Kentucky, to coordinate all military assistance efforts. In coordination with these agencies, WPAFB's major support of disaster operations was terminated on April 8.

On April 9, President Richard M. Nixon arrived on base via Air Force One to survey the disaster area. Included in the Presidential party were James T. Lynn, Secretary of Housing and Urban Development; Thomas J. Donne, Chief of the Federal Disaster Assistance Administration; and Presidential Press Secretary Ronald Ziegler. After viewing the disaster area from the air, the President's helicopter landed at an elementary school on the outskirts of Xenia and the party drove into town, where the President conferred with Greene County and other officials. That afternoon the President returned to Wright-Patterson where he was greeted by about 500 spectators.

On April 11, the Wing's Disaster Preparedness Control Center was inactivated. In all, Xenia disaster relief assistance from April 3-8, 1974, amounted to $61,701 for the 2750th ABW ($13,000 of which was reimbursable). An additional $31,410 in expenses was incurred by the USAF Medical Center Wright-Patterson (of which $6,370 was reimbursable).

The winter of 1976-1977 entered Ohio history as one of the worst on record. "The most unforgiving weather this region has ever seen," was how General F. Michael Rogers, AFLC Commander, described the winter which blasted WPAFB and the surrounding vicinity. January 1977 set a record with an average temperature of 11.6 degrees Fahren-

heit. During the month there were 13 days with temperatures at zero or below. A total of 20.2 inches of snowfall in January was second only to the record of 34.4 inches recorded in January 1918. Temperatures in February registered 2.9 degrees below normal. As temperatures descended, energy usage ascended, causing a state-wide crisis in supplies of natural gas.

Paced by the 2750th Civil Engineering Squadron and the 2750th Logistics Squadron, the Air Base Wing exerted extra efforts to keep WPAFB fully operational and to simultaneously help distressed local communities struggling with blocked roads and frozen water lines. Assistance to local communities included delivery of 1,500 gallons of fresh water to Trotwood, Ohio, where many homes had frozen pipelines, and the dispatching of snow blowers to Clark, Greene, Preble, Clinton, and Fayette Counties. Water-thawing equipment was loaned to the cities of Fairborn, New Carlisle, and Xenia. Water containers were supplied to Miamisburg, West Milton, and the American Red Cross. The quality of the Civil Engineering Squadron's assistance to local communities helped the organization earn the Air Force Outstanding Unit Award for the period April 1, 1976 to March 31, 1977.

As the winter of 1977-1978 approached, early indicators pointed toward a repetition of the 1976-1977 season, and the 2750th ABW made preparations accordingly. Forecasts proved to be accurate. The 1977-1978 season was almost as harsh—and decidedly more dramatic. A severe blizzard with 75 mph gusts and 7-12 inches of snow whipped the Miami Valley, reducing activities on base to minimum essential operations from January 26 to January 29. Wright-Patterson was closed to all aircraft traffic from 4:33 a.m. January 26 until 4:00 p.m. January 27. The 2750th Civil Engineering Squadron assisted beleaguered communities within a seven-county area through the loan of snow removal equipment and military operators.

The winter of 1976-77 exposed Ohio to extraordinarily severe weather. The month of January recorded 13 days with temperatures at or below zero.

Emergency measures notwithstanding, snow removal on base was hampered by insufficient equipment in the active inventory, especially front-end loaders and dump trucks. The services of commercial contractors were needed into mid-February to supplement base efforts to clear and haul snow from WPAFB streets and parking lots.

According to a local newspaper, Dayton's 1977-1978 snowfall totalled 62.7 inches, bettering the 1976-1977 winter total of 38.8 inches. Both years set new records for the Dayton area.

The 2750th Logistics Squadron earned the Air Force Outstanding Unit Award for "exceptionally meritorious service" for the period from April 1, 1977 to March 31, 1978. The squadron was honored specifically for sustaining vital base functions during the January 26, 1978 blizzard.

The 2750th Logistics Squadron was cited specifically for its efforts to sustain vital base functions during the 1978 blizzard. The squadron was awarded the Air Force Outstanding Unit Award for the period April 1977 to March 1978.

THE 1980s AND BEYOND

Today Wright-Patterson is one of the nation's most important military installations. It is the headquarters for a vast, worldwide logistics system and is a major research and development center for the United States Air Force. More than 85 organizations, representing several different Air Force commands and a host of Department of Defense organizations, are located at Wright-Patterson.

By many measures, Wright-Patterson is the largest, most diverse, and organizationally complex base in the Air Force. Civilian visitors compare the base to a large industrial park with city-like characteristics. And the base is steeped in tradition. It has been a leader in military aviation development from the open cockpit era of the Wright brothers to today's aerospace age.

From any perspective, Wright-Patterson's vital statistics are impressive. It encompasses 8,176 acres of land in Montgomery and Greene Counties, Ohio, with approximately 1,600 buildings on base plus more than 2,300 family housing units. The fixed capital assets of WPAFB in March 1982 totalled $463,583,872, consisting of real estate, utilities and ground improvements, and facilities at eight locations within Kentucky and Ohio.

More than 30,000 people are employed at Wright-Patterson, making the base the fifth largest employer in Ohio and the largest employer at a single location. Included in that figure are about 16,000 Department of the Air Force civilian employees, 8,000 military, and an additional 6,000 service and contractor employees. Nearly one of every eleven people employed in the greater Dayton area works at Wright-Patterson. The fiscal year 1982 payroll to Wright-Patterson employees amounted to $636 million—equivalent to more than $1.7 million in salaries per day.

The work force payroll is only one indicator of the base's impact on the Dayton-area economy. The importance of the area defense industry to southwest Ohio is also reflected in dollars spent by the base on local purchases in the community and in the large flow of government contracts to local business. In the greater-Dayton area, $53 million was spent on construction, supplies, equipment, and services in support of Wright-Patterson's mission in 1982. Another $60 million in military contracts—mostly for research and development of sophisticated military hardware—was divided among 30 Dayton-area contractors by various divisions and laboratories at Wright-Patterson.

Clearly, Wright-Patterson is "big business" for local communities. The base has traditionally played a significant role in the Dayton-area economy. It has acted as a stabilizing force during years of recession in the auto and housing industries, and provided stimulation to the local economy during periods of increased government spending for military hardware and research.

Wright-Patterson stands out among U.S. Air Force bases in many ways. It is the home of the United States Air Force Museum, recognized as the largest and most complete military aviation museum in the world. It is also the home of the Air Force Institute of Technology and the Defense Institute of Security Assistance Management, which provide professional education for Air Force and Department of Defense personnel and for military and civilian representatives of foreign nations. Wright-Patterson has the third largest medical center in the Air Force, one of six regional centers serving more than 40,000 family members of Department of Defense active duty and military retirees throughout the northeastern and north central United States.

The host organization for Wright-Patterson AFB is the 2750th Air Base Wing. In addition to providing base support, the 2750th also operates the largest aircraft tire storage and distribution depot in the Air Force. About 50 percent of the tires and tubes distributed DOD-wide are shipped annually from WPAFB. The 2750th ABW also offers Wright-Patterson military members and civilian employees one of the largest Morale, Welfare, and Recreation (MWR) programs in the Air Force. Annual revenue from the program's 12 branches and clubs grossed $13.1 million in FY 1982. The Wright-Patterson AFB Aero Club, which operates as a function of the MWR program, is the largest and one of the most successful in the Air Force.

Wright-Patterson Air Force Base today encompasses 8,176 acres of land, with approximately 1,600 buildings on base and an additional 2,300 family housing units.

Tree-lined streets of the officers' brick quarters in Area A

The Turtle Pond reflecting pool has been enjoyed by generations of Wright-Patterson families.

341

Wright-Patterson's impact on the economy of the greater-Dayton area is measured in hundreds of millions of dollars.

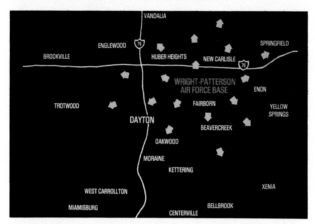

Wright-Patterson's partners in progress include numerous communities in surrounding Montgomery and Greene Counties.

Wright-Patterson's greatest resource is its people, who possess a wide range of highly capable skills. Wright-Patterson employees likewise constitute a significant resource for surrounding local communities. When not working at their jobs on base, many serve as elected non-partisan officials in the communities where they reside, serve on school boards and other committees, teach as adjunct professors at area universities, serve as technical advisors to local governmental bodies and industry, and contribute generously of their time, expertise, and financial resources to numerous charitable and community service programs. In addition to their personal commitments and activities, WPAFB employees collectively donate more than $1 mil-

The Fam-Camp on Marl Road in Area C is a popular summer spot for sport and relaxation, and an important feature of the Morale, Welfare, and Recreation (MWR) program at WPAFB. The Wing MWR program is one of the largest in the Air Force.

WRIGHT-PATTERSON AFB AERO CLUB

The Wright-Patterson AFB Aero Club is one of the oldest aero clubs in the Air Force, having been an active organization on base since the late 1940s. The club can also boast that it is one of the largest, the most modern, and the safest in the Air Force. With over 400 members and 19 aircraft, the club flew a total of 10,240 accident-free hours in 1982.

The primary purpose of the Aero Club is to make general aviation flying available to Air Force military and civilian personnel and their families. Many club members, however, also use Aero Club aircraft during temporary duty (TDY) assignments rather than travel by commercial airlines. In addition to saving money for the government, such flights offer convenience for the traveler and a way to log additional flying hours.

The "largest" and "most modern" aspects of the organization date from the 1980 Aero Club campaign to increase membership and expand its fleet. The club accomplished both aims with tremendous success. Membership increased by nearly 70 percent, and the club inventory was expanded with the purchase of 12 new aircraft from the Piper Aircraft Corporation. This sale represented not only the largest new aircraft acquisition in Air Force aero club history, but also the largest block sale ever made by Piper to a government-affiliated club.

Orville Lambert and Tom Moorman perform a 100-hour maintenance inspection on one airplane of the Aero Club fleet.

342

Observance of Black History Month, Hispanic Heritage Week, Asian-Pacific American Heritage Week, and other cultural events underlines Wright-Patterson's commitment to equal opportunity and strength through diversity.

WELCOME TO THE ASIAN PACIFIC AMERICAN HERITAGE LUAU

Youth participants of the 1982 Domestic Action summer encampment

lion to the Combined Federal Campaign each year, which helps to support some 147 private and community agencies locally and nationally.

As an Air Force installation, Wright-Patterson itself is also closely involved in community affairs. Annually, the base supports the Dayton International Airshow and Trade Exposition at Cox International Airport, a Fire Expo on WPAFB which attracts exhibitors of fire-fighting apparatus and safety equipment, and AFROTC summer Field Training Encampments for students representing colleges and universities throughout the nation. The base maintains close relations with a wide range of educational institutions. The University of Dayton, Sinclair Community College, Central Michigan University, and Park College (main campus in Parkville, Missouri) offer degree programs on base from the associate to the masters degree level. Representatives from many other colleges associated with the Dayton-Miami Valley Consortium of Colleges and Universities, including Wright State University, the University of Dayton, Wittenberg University, Central State University, Wilberforce University, and Sinclair Community College, provide registration services and courses on base for military and civilian personnel. Youth employment programs for local high school and college students are coordinated by the base Equal Employment Opportunity Office. Additionally, the base participates in cooperative education programs with about 30 colleges and universities nationwide. Locally, co-op programs are conducted with many of the universities mentioned above.

Wright-Patterson provides camping facilities for area Boy Scout and Girl Scout councils and from time to time hosts regional scouting "jamborees." Other community activities supported periodically by the base include the Greater-Dayton Soapbox Derby, civilian fly-ins, visits by civic officials from other Air Force base communities, and various sports tournaments. The base also promotes and supports the Junior ROTC and Civil Air Patrol programs in local high schools. The Air Force Museum is especially noted for hosting a wide variety of special programs throughout the year, including symposiums, band concerts, film festivals, guest lectures, and hot air balloon rallies.

Wright-Patterson military and civilian employees contribute more than $1 million annually to the Combined Federal Campaign.

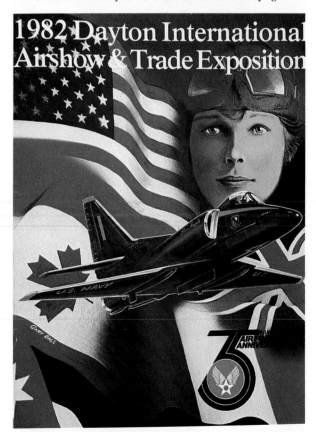

Many of the organizations assigned to Wright-Patterson support and participate in the annual Dayton International Airshow and Trade Exposition at Cox International Airport.

Fire Expo at WPAFB, 1982

The 661st Air Force Band, popularly known as the "Band of Flight," supports Air Force recruiting efforts and community relations activities.

Band leader Ray McKinley directs the Glenn Miller band during a tribute show at the U.S. Air Force Museum, August 1982.

Hot Air balloon rally on the grounds of the U.S. Air Force Museum

A $113 million addition to the USAF Medical Center, Wright-Patterson, is scheduled for completion in 1987.

The most important community associations the base holds are with government and civic leaders in the surrounding communities. Base representatives meet regularly with local officials to exchange ideas on such issues as airport zoning, proposed highway systems, citizen concerns, and other subjects of mutual interest. To carry out its mission effectively, Wright-Patterson Air Force Base must depend upon healthy relations and efficient communications among the base and its immediate neighbors.

For the remainder of the 1980s, Wright-Patterson faces many challenges. New facilities must be constructed to accommodate modern Air Force programs. Current base facilities must be maintained and actively upgraded to meet the changing needs of a modern Air Force installation with many specialized associate organizations.

By June 1982, construction was underway on a $115.3 million addition to the USAF Medical Center Wright-Patterson (scheduled for completion in 1987). Also under

Under the Air Force Civic Leaders Tour Program, Miami Valley community leaders exchange visits with their counterparts in other Air Force communities.

construction were a major addition to the Biotechnology Laboratory of the Air Force Aerospace Medical Research Laboratory, and two new dormitories and a modern gymnasium for the Kittyhawk Center.

Other new facilities under consideration for the remainder of the decade include a Logistics Air Freight Processing Facility to replace the existing air freight terminal, the third and final phase of the ASD Materials Laboratory complex, a Base Conference Center, a Base Heritage Center, additional dormitories in the Kittyhawk Center, and a major addition to the U.S. Air Force Museum.

Base officials also face many familiar challenges in the 1980s. Their overall goal remains the same today as it has been in the past: to provide the support necessary to maintain Air Force readiness. The challenges are also essentially the same: rising costs, aging facilities, and the mandate to spend public monies wisely and effectively.

Wright-Patterson Air Force Base looks to the future with optimism. Wright-Patterson represents a tremendous investment, not only in terms of physical plant, but also in terms of technical skills and knowledge. It is these skills and a dedication to excellence that have earned Wright-Patterson its reputation as a significant force in America's national defense for over 65 years. The legacy of the Wright brothers is part of day-to-day life at Wright-Patterson. It is a legacy which the employees of the base consider a proud part of their heritage. It is also an enduring foundation for the role that Wright-Patterson will continue to play in the future of the U.S. Air Force and in the life of the Miami Valley.

Wright-Patterson Air Force Base—65 years of progress

IX. AIR FORCE LOGISTICS COMMAND

THE EARLY YEARS

THE BEGINNINGS

One of the antecedents of what is now called the Air Force Logistics Command (AFLC) was a small supply depot at Fairfield, Ohio, operated by the Army Air Service in the closing days of World War I. At that time the Fairfield depot was only one of many such activities carried on by the Army Air Service. Not far away, at McCook Field, Dayton, Ohio, was the other antecedent of AFLC—an experimental laboratory also belonging to the Army Air Service. This laboratory was known as the Airplane Engineering Division and later, simply the Engineering Division. Together, these two small organizations helped carry out several of the basic functions of military support— procurement, supply, and technological research—and in doing so, they represented the beginnings of what would grow into a vast, complex acquisition and support apparatus that would change its form many times in the following decades.

In 1926 the Army Air Service changed its name to the Army Air Corps, and the Engineering Division and Fairfield Air Depot were combined under one command, the Materiel Division, which moved its headquarters in the following year from McCook Field to Wright Field. This new organization was responsible for maintenance and repair, supply and procurement, and experimental engineering. The first chief of the Materiel Division was Brig. Gen. William E. Gillmore. He was followed by six other chiefs, including Brig. Gen. Benjamin D. Foulois, who led the Division from July 1929 to June 1930. Among the officers who served with the Division in later years were the illustrious names of Carl Spaatz and George C. Kenney.

SUPPLY BETWEEN THE WARS

After World War I, the Air Service had large quantities of excess airplanes, engines, and other aeronautical equipment. Trainloads of unsorted supplies, both serviceable and obsolete, were shipped to the depots from all of the inactivated airfields in the United States. In addition, vast quantities of miscellaneous materiel were shipped to the depots from overseas. All of this materiel had to be sorted, classified, and placed in storage, which was especially difficult because the depots had very little storage capacity. The vast amounts of excess supplies also created serious record-keeping problems. In 1922, the supply officer at Fairfield reported that he had needed more than 120,000 stock record cards just to list all of the materiel stored at the depot and that the "tremendous labor of sorting, classifying, and storing this materiel consumed approximately two and one-half years, and it was not until the middle of 1921 that this depot could be said to be arranged according to any system or order."

The establishment of a property classification system was undoubtedly one of the most important steps taken by the Air Service after World War I. The system adopted by the Air Service was first worked out by Lt. Edwin R. Page during the winter of 1919-1920 when he was assigned to the Supply Division in the Office of the Chief of the Air Service. This system divided all equipment and supplies into 29 classes for the purpose of identification, storage, and issue. For example, Class 01 was used to identify airplanes and airplane parts; Class 02, engines and engine parts; and Class 03, airplane accessories. Later, the major property classes were broken down into subclasses. Thus, Class 01-A designated a complete airplane; Class 01-B, parts for airplanes manufactured by Consolidated; and Class 01-D, parts for airplanes manufactured by Douglas. The same type of system was used for engines.

The Fairfield Air Depot in the late 1920s

Aerial view of the Air Corps Carnival at Fairfield Air Depot, 1930

Stockroom for the Engine Department at Kelly Field in the early 1920s

Aircraft wings in storage at Rockwell Field in the late 1920s

This system had to be modified in 1929 because tabulating machines for recording stock balance and consumption data were installed at Materiel Division headquarters, and later, at all of the depots. Since the new machines could only record figures on the tabulating cards, two digit code numbers were substituted for the letter symbols. As new items came into the inventory, two additional digits were added to the original two. For example, the class code for all kinds of pumps was 48, while the number 4801 referred to a certain kind of pump produced by a specific manufacturer. In 1930, the Air Corps also began to use part numbers as an element of the stock number. Normally, the part numbers were assigned to a part by the manufacturer. In some cases, however, the depots manufactured a part in their shops and gave the part an Air Corps number.

Another major problem encountered by the Army Air Service and Air Corps in the 1920s and 1930s was the replenishment of parts. The aircraft received from the Allies in fulfillment of war contracts and from Germany as war booty were useful until they had to be repaired; at that point they were permanently grounded because no spare parts were available. The result was that in the 1920s both the Air Service and the Air Corps had to rely almost entirely on the aircraft and engines produced during World War I. In 1924, Maj. Augustine W. Robins, Commanding Officer of the Fairfield Air Depot, reported that "the Air Service would have ceased to exist as far as flying is concerned had it not been or the existence of material manufactured during the World War."

After the creation of the Air Corps in 1926, some supply officers began to complain that the depots were placing more emphasis on their maintenance functions than on supply responsibilities. In the words of one contemporary, "at all conferences the general trend of the conversation in always toward Engineering. . . . Supply is standing still." Although it was not actually standing still, the supply function had to operate under extreme difficulties in the 1920s and 1930s. Funds were always low in the 1920s because of Presidential, Congressional, and Army policy. All of these factors, along with the economic depression, kept funds low in the 1930s. As the World War I stocks began to deteriorate during the 1920s and only limited amounts of new equipment entered the inventory, maintenance became more and more important. As a result, the supply function at the depots received only a small share of the depot dollar, about 16 percent compared to 50 percent for maintenance.

MAINTENANCE IN THE 1920s AND 1930s

Throughout most of the 1920s, the Air Service and Air Corps were primarily concerned with the repair of wood and fabric aircraft. During this period, aircraft were sent to the depots when routine inspections showed that they were in need of overhaul, or when they were badly damaged. After the overhaul system became more regulated in 1930, aircraft were sent to the depots for scheduled maintenance every 12 or 24 months, depending on the type. Because they generally were not provided with extensive shop facilities or highly skilled personnel, the service squadrons and service companies at the air stations were specifically prohibited from performing such maintenance tasks as overhauling aircraft, repairing and replacing large assemblies, and remodeling aircraft into special types. The stations were authorized to patch fabric, install surfaces, and assemble "knocked-down" aircraft.

Airplanes with metal rather than wooden frames began to appear at the depots for overhaul in late 1925; thereafter they gradually became more numerous than the old stick and wire type. The wings and fuselage of the new aircraft were constructed of a welded steel frame, usually tubular, which was covered with fabric. The process for overhauling a metal and fabric airplane was not much different from the one used for the wood and fabric type. Whenever the fuselage was found to be sprung because of a crash or bad landing, the distorted metal pieces were sawed out of the frame and replaced with new pieces.

The first all-metal aircraft began to arrive at the depots in the early 1930s, and by 1935 all air depots had gained experience in repairing these new aircraft. From the outset, the Materiel Division recognized that the all-metal aircraft would require new maintenance procedures. For example, it found that these aircraft could remain in service for longer periods than the older types, but that overhaul, when required, would be a more difficult process because of the need to shape and replace sections of the metal skin. Although overhauling the all-metal airplane involved only five steps—cleaning, dismantling, inspection, repair, and final assembly—these five steps entailed more than 160 separate operations.

Another complicated task for the depot maintenance crews was the overhaul of engines, specifically the 12-cylinder Liberty engine that was produced in vast quantities in 1917 and 1918 and was the standard engine for

LIBERTY ENGINE

HISPANO-SUIZA ENGINE

The engine repair shop at the Fairfield Air Intermediate Depot in about 1926

Engine test stands at the Fairfield Air Intermediate Depot in about 1926

Army aircraft in the 1920s. Throughout that decade, this engine was required to undergo a complete overhaul after 50 hours of service. In 1930 the Air Corps lengthened the period between overhauls to 125 hours and stipulated that only four major overhauls needed to be performed on the engine during its service life.

In the process of overhauling the Liberty engine, the most tedious operation was the cleaning of the engine, which involved scraping off grease, carbon, and rust by hand, with wire brushes and gasoline or kerosene. In 1926, however, the job became easier when the Fairfield depot developed a new cleaning spray containing dissolved cleaning powders. While it was customary at this time for one group of mechanics to perform all of the steps in the overhaul process, cleaning was usually assigned to the apprentices.

By the early 1930s, the use of liquid-cooled engines such as the Liberty had declined sharply, for manufacturers were now making the more powerful and technologically advanced air-cooled static radial engine, such as the Wright R1820 Cyclone. The period between overhauls for this engine ran from 300 to 375 hours, and the most complex phase of that process was the inspection and repair of subassemblies. For example, the repair of cylinders and valves involved such steps as testing for leaks, deep valve seats, cracks, flaws, and wear; replacing worn valve guides; refacing valves and valve seats; grinding cylinders; lapping valves to seats; connecting the valves and springs to the cylinders; assembling the camshafts and adjusting the clearances; and installing the cylinder covers.

During the 1930s, each of the major depots of the Materiel Division overhauled an average of more than 150 aircraft and 500 engines annually. The cost of overhauling an aircraft was $2,182 in 1931, $2,496 in 1935, and $4,289 in 1939. The cost for overhauling an engine was $493 in 1931, $589 in 1935, and $753 in 1939. In part, the increase in costs could be attributed to the development of more complex and larger aircraft and engines. At the same time, however, the newer aircraft were being flown from 20 to 130 percent longer than the older models, and the time between overhauls was approximately 100 percent greater. The time between overhauls for engines also increased significantly. For example, the average number of hours between overhauls for the R1820 engine increased from 162 in 1933 to 260 in 1939.

EXPERIMENTAL ENGINEERING

Out of McCook and Wright Fields in the 1920s and 1930s came the engineers and pilots who paved the way for many of the later accomplishments of the Army Air Forces. Although they rarely received any public acclaim, these men worked tirelessly on the very edge of the state of the art to improve both the performance and safety of aircraft.

Long before the emergence of the Materiel Division, the engineers of McCook Field were conducting a number of important aeronautical experiments. On April 28, 1919, for example, Leslie Irvin made the first jump from an airplane with a free-fall type backpack parachute. The airplane from which he jumped was flown by Floyd Smith, the designer of the parachute. On February 27, 1920, Maj. Rudolph W. Schroeder set a new official world altitude record of 33,114 feet in a Lepere-Liberty 400 airplane at McCook Field, and in September of the following year, Lt. John A. Macready pushed the world altitude record higher when he reached 34,509 feet in a Lepere biplane over Dayton, Ohio. Shortly thereafter, on December 18, 1922, the Air Service's first helicopter, the de Bothezat, was successfully test flown at McCook Field for almost two minutes by Maj. Thurman H. Bane.

This proud start was continued by the Materiel Division engineers at Wright Field. On February 3, 1928, Lt. H. A. Sutton began a series of tests to study the spinning characteristics of aircraft. Four months later, the Wright Field engineers made a number of successful tests on superchargers that were designed to provide sea level pressure of 30,000 feet. In early May 1932, Capt. Albert F. Hegenberger made the first blind solo flight, and in the summer of 1934, Capt. Donald L. Bruner, the inventor of landing lights, continued his experiments in night flying. During this period, the engineers at Wright Field also began to investigate aerodynamic flutter and vibration. Their work was basic to the development of flaps, trim tabs, and power operated control surfaces.

Among their many other accomplishments, the Wright Field pilots and engineers accomplished pioneering work in their investigations of human reactions to flight stress, performed the first completely automatic landing, and set a new Air Corps speed record of 350 miles per hour. In July 1939, furthermore, a B-17B piloted by Maj. Stanley M. Umstead, the Chief of the Materiel Division's Flying Branch, set a new world's record of 9 hours, 14 minutes, 30 seconds for a flight with passengers and crew from Los Angeles to New York City. A few days later, Maj. Carl Greene, a former chief of the Materiel Division's Aircraft Branch, and Capt. A. H. Johnson were decorated for their work in developing the first pressurized cabin airplane, the XC-35.

THE WAR YEARS

A FRAMEWORK FOR SUPPORT

In the spring of 1941, the Air Corps separated logistics from the Materiel Division and organized that function under a new command, the Maintenance Command, which was established on March 15 of that year. But in the following months, the Air Corps itself gave way to a new organization, the Army Air Forces (AAF), and before the end of the year the Maintenance Command was replaced by another logistical organization, the Air Service Command (ASC), whose headquarters was at first in Washington, D.C. In addition to the Fairfield depot, the Air

Service Command controlled five other major air depots in the United States, as well as many smaller depots. Over the next few years, the number of major depots increased to 11. The responsibilities of the command included storage and distribution; depot maintenance, repair, and overhaul; issuing technical orders and instructions; and procurement of supplies and equipment.

When the United States entered World War II, the task of the Air Service Command was nothing less than to build a complete air logistics system almost from scratch. With only a small inheritance from its predecessors, the overriding concern of this command was to expand its physical holdings and its work force as rapidly as possible. This it did in an amazingly short time, and by the fall of 1942, its physical assets and work force were already larger than those of General Motors. There was still a long way to go, however, for seven of the command's depots were still under construction, and the remainder were not yet operating at full capacity. Furthermore, the enormous and rapid expansion had left behind a huge agenda for construction, recruitment, training, and organizational refinements.

It was the last of these matters which weighed most heavily on the mind of Maj. Gen. Walter H. Frank when he took command of ASC in November 1942. The basic problem, as General Frank saw it, was a confusion of authority between the command elements in Washington and those in Dayton. Furthermore, at every echelon the command suffered from an overlapping and duplication of functions. The result of these defects was to inhibit the initiative of the field commanders and to delay the execution of the command's mission.

Armed with the full backing of the Army Air Forces, General Frank lost no time in instituting a series of corrective measures. His first act was to transfer the headquarters back to Dayton, not to Wright Field but to a new site on the adjacent Patterson Field. The next act followed immediately and was more significant. What General Frank really wanted was to revise the basic structure of the command so that it reflected its quasi-industrial nature. The most suitable organization, General Frank believed, was one divided according to the command's three principal functions: training technicians, maintaining equipment, and providing supplies. Each of these functions would constitute one of the main divisions of the command, in effect a semi-autonomous component, with its own commander, operating within a large military federation. Ultimate control of the command would continue to reside, of course, with the commander of ASC.

One other major organizational problem remained, and this was the most complicated of all. The problem originated with the reorganization of the Army's air arm at the beginning of the war, when the logistics and procurement functions were separated from each other and placed into two different organizations, the Air Service Command at Patterson Field and the Materiel Command at Wright Field. In theory the missions of the two commands were entirely different: ASC was concerned with maintenance and the distribution of supplies, while the Materiel Command was responsible for research and development and the procurement of aircraft and accessories. In practice, however, the activities of the two commands often

Aerial view of Wright Field in August 1929

overlapped and it was not always easy to distinguish between their respective responsibilities. This led to any number of jurisdictional disputes, not to mention duplication of effort and confusion. The problem was not solved until well into the war, when in the summer of 1944 the two commands were disestablished and their functions merged under a new organization, the Air Technical Service Command (ATSC).

THE MACHINERY OF SUPPLY

At the outset of World War II and for more than a year thereafter, the greatest single problem confronting the Air Service Command was the lack of spare parts for the tactical units of the Army Air Forces. In a word, there were simply not enough spare parts to go around. This situation had been bad enough before the war, when as late as 1941 the Air Corps had grown accustomed to "cannibalizing" almost 20 percent of its new aircraft to provide needed parts for the rest of the fleet. But in the months following Pearl Harbor, supply shortages had worsened to the point that 40 to 45 percent of the combat aircraft in the United States were grounded for lack of parts, and it was not at all uncommon to remove engines from U.S.-based aircraft for shipment overseas.

Essentially, there were two reasons for the alarming shortages. In the first place, the construction of complete aircraft was more profitable than the production of spare parts, and in the prewar years government agencies had found it difficult to obtain the concurrent delivery of aircraft and spares. Once we entered the war, however, the Joint Aircraft Committee in Washington acted swiftly to correct this fault, stipulating that no aircraft could be delivered from the manufacturer without its full complement of spares. This action brought about a decided improvement, but it was not enough to solve the problem. All the supplies in the world would not help the AAF until the Air

Service Command could obtain the right types and numbers of items and have them shipped to the tactical units. This meant that the logistics command had to learn to determine as precisely as possible what and how much was needed by the forces in the field. Throughout the war, the greatest single challenge for those in charge of supply was to determine requirements, sometimes by as much as two years in advance. The command not only had to determine purchasing needs, but also calculate the requirements for the salvage and disposal of thousands of items. This too was a complex task, and until ASC improved its inventory system, the command more than once found itself in the embarrassing position of procuring items with the one hand while it was disposing of them with the other.

What ASC needed was a methodology for gathering and organizing information that would show what and how much to stock, and in August 1942 the command took a big step towards that goal with the creation of a new staff organization, the 15th Statistical Control Unit. After setting up field reporting units at the depots and an analysis branch at the command headquarters, the statisticians went to work, and soon enough more accurate, more detailed, and more timely information began to flow in.

Although the determination of requirements was the most complex challenge for the supply function, it was by no means the only problem. Two other problems quickly emerged from the start and for a time hampered the supply mission. The first of these was the lack of experienced personnel; the second was the lack of storage space.

As the depots and subdepots proliferated across the country, ASC soon discovered that it did not have enough experienced personnel. Whenever a new installation opened, experienced personnel were drained from the older facilities and soon the ranks of the veterans were spread thin. At the same time, the logistics command had to throw open its gates to thousands of new personnel, all of whom were inexperienced and many of whom were barely qualified for the complex clerical procedures of the

Statistical Control Unit at Fairfield in 1945. Across the command such units provided indispensable information on what and how much the supply depots should stock.

Supply units, such as this one at the Ogden depot, used a "menu board" to show aircraft grounded for parts.

The new headquarters of the Air Service Command at Patterson Field in 1943

supply world. The lack of experience was true not only of the line workers, but also of the new supply officers commissioned directly out of civilian life. Although some of these officers were familiar with commercial procedures, few had a background in the methods of military supply.

What finally saved the day for ASC—and for so much of American industry as well—was the employment of women. Hired in droves, they constituted 50 percent of the work force in the depots, and 40 to 80 percent in the subdepots; at both echelons their proportion was far greater in the supply fields than in maintenance. In both the depots and subdepots they performed not only most of the clerical work but also much of the physical labor of loading and unloading freight cars and trucks, stacking materials in the warehouses, and driving forklift trucks. Though skeptical at first, supervisors soon learned to value their new work force.

Meanwhile, the depot managers were having to deal with the equally serious and even more difficult problem of storage. In 1940 the storage facilities of the Army Air Corps were not much larger than those in 1918, and even two years later, when the number of depots had increased, ASC could not begin to accommodate the massive quantities of materiel that were then beginning to pour in from the factories. The command's only recourse was to seek more and more warehouse space, and slowly its efforts

began to pay off. Starting with only four million square feet at the beginning of the war, the command increased its warehouse space to over 7.5 million square feet by December 1942, and 17 million square feet by December 1943. But despite these efforts, ASC could not find enough space for thousands of tons of materiel, much of which was perishable. What the command really needed, according to a study at that time, was not 17 million but 52 million square feet of storage space.

In the spring of 1942, a solution to this problem began to take shape in the minds of several young supply officers at Headquarters ASC. They proposed that the command establish throughout the country a network of special supply depots for each of the more critical property classes. Each special depot would be a central storehouse for the items assigned to it, and each would have the capability to maintain a large reserve of stocks that could be distributed to the regular depots whenever necessary. Unlike the existing depots, the special depots would carry on no maintenance or repair activity and would confine their operations exclusively to the supply function.

This proposal struck General Frank as sound, and in the spring of 1943 he directed his command to carry out the plan. Since the government had neither the time nor the money to construct scores of new buildings, ASC had to make do with what was already available, which in many cases was far from desirable. As one supply officer of the time noted, even the worst facilities "served the immediate necessity of getting the materiel out of the weather." But if the project did not live up to the expectation of its designers, neither was it a failure. By the time it was completed in the summer of 1943, the Air Service Command had acquired 46 special depots handling 96 separate classes of materiel. Without question, the new depots had a significant impact on the efficiency and speed of the command's supply system.

THE WORKHORSE OF THE ARMY AIR FORCES

If a combat pilot of World War II had been asked to name the one support function on which he depended most, he would have replied: maintenance, for it was this service more than any other which determined the safety and efficiency of his aircraft. Because of its vital importance, maintenance was also—at least initially—a source of unremitting concern to the leaders of the AAF, and throughout the war a responsibility that claimed most of the manpower and the lion's share of attention within the Air Service Command. In this function, as in all others, the command's direct involvement in the overseas theaters was limited to training and issuing technical orders. But in the depots and subdepots in the United States, ASC was the workhorse of the Army Air Forces, inspecting, overhauling, and repairing thousands of aircraft of all types and models.

At the beginning of the war, the maintenance system of the Army Air Forces was hardly prepared for the enormous burden suddenly thrust upon it. As late as 1939, this system, employing a small but highly skilled work force and using the facilities of the four original depots, had been designed to keep some 2,000 planes in the air. But when U.S. forces entered the war, that same system was called upon to repair aircraft in desperately short supply and eventually to service the tens of thousands of aircraft that were just beginning to roll off the production lines. Leaving aside for the moment the question of how a prewar system could cope with those tens of thousands, it was clear enough in the early 1940s that the depots were under great strain just to repair the aircraft already in operation. The plight of the depots was further exacerbated in the early years of the war by the severe shortage of spare parts, since parts that could not be replaced had to be repaired.

What finally reduced some of the pressure was the tremendous surge in the production of aircraft and spare parts. But that did not solve the most serious problem facing depot maintenance—the lack of trained personnel. In fact, if anything the volume of production compounded that problem by increasing the overall work load. Repair was only one of the maintenance functions, albeit an extremely crucial one, and in the long run overhaul and modifications were just as important. All these were highly technical, complicated tasks demanding years of training and experience to produce the level of competence of the prewar work force. But during the war years, the Air Service Command had neither enough of the old-line maintenance crews nor the luxury of time to train the thousands upon thousands of new and inexperienced personnel who suddenly swelled their ranks. How then could these people be used to any purpose?

The answer was simple, ingenious, and entirely effective. Borrowing the techniques of the American automobile industry, the Air Service Command broke the work down to its smallest components, quickly trained each new employee in a narrow specialty, then assigned him to one or two repetitive tasks on an assembly line. To exploit the production line method to the fullest, ASC also introduced a program of specialized repair that became the forerunner of the Technology Repair Center concept

The fruits of labor on the home front: supplies piling up at the Guam Air Depot in the later stages of the war.

B-17s being repaired at Oklahoma City in 1943

adopted 30 years later. Under this program, each air depot, and in some cases two or three depots, were made responsible for the repair and overhaul of a particular type of airframe or engine. For example, ASC assigned all B-17s to the depots at Fairfield, Oklahoma City, and Warner Robins. The system of specialized maintenance was also applied to the repair of such aircraft accessories as propeller blades, generators, tires, and bombsights.

These measures were basically all the command needed to accomplish the wartime work load without sacrificing prewar quality. Although the maintenance operation was greatly expanded during the war, at no time did the Air Service Command or the Army Air Forces find it necessary to effect substantial changes in maintenance policies or procedures. Instead, the logistics managers introduced minor revisions and refinements of technique. For example, a standard tool of management in the prewar years was the annual "Depot Cost Report," which provided maintenance leaders with a wealth of information on the volume of operations and costs of labor and material. But as the name suggested, this report emphasized cost, and since that was not a consideration of the first importance in war, the report was discontinued soon after the outbreak of hostilities. In its place ASC substituted a new publication, the "Monthly Report of Depot Maintenance Activity," which primarily addressed the volume and type of work accomplished.

In sum, it could be said of the depot maintenance shops that theirs was an arduous job, technically complicated and filled with a variety of challenges which at the beginning must have seemed insurmountable. But for all their hard work, which was indisputable, just how well did they succeed in carrying out their mission? That is not only a question for historians, but also one asked during

Sacramento concentrated on such fighters as the P-38 and the P-39 (shown).

the war by those responsible for managing the maintenance work load. In 1944 they tried to find the answer by setting the depots in competition with each other. That effort failed, but the logistics leaders also had records at their disposal which were much more useful as management tools and which contained important information about their efforts. From these records they knew and we know that in just the two years between 1943 and 1945, the depot maintenance shops had performed the Herculean feat of servicing more than 230,000 engines and over 36,000 aircraft. Moreover, as the depots attained greater efficiency in the later stages of the war, the number of aircraft grounded for maintenance began to plummet. There were bound to be some flaws, of course, in any undertaking on the scale of World War II, but for a service organization the ultimate test was how it was viewed by those it served. In this regard, the using commands had begun to acknowledge their debt long before the end of the war.

THE POSTWAR INTERLUDE

DISMANTLING THE MACHINERY OF WAR

When World War II ended, it was the job of the Air Technical Service Command to preside over the vast holdings of the Army Air Forces accumulated during the war. Later, in March 1946, the name of the command was changed to the Air Materiel Command (AMC), but the mission was still the same—to serve as caretaker of the assets of the Army Air Forces, and later the United States Air Force. It was the job of ATSC and AMC not only to store or dispose of the huge quantities of aircraft and aeronautical equipment spread all over the globe, but also to reduce the greatly expanded support structure to the right size for the needs of the Army Air Forces. The fact that those needs had yet to be ascertained made the job all the harder, but the logistics leaders pressed on anyway, deactivating stations, closing down or consolidating warehouses, evacuating leased property, and terminating contracts. And all the while, their own manpower resources were melting away as rapidly as those of the rest of the armed forces. At the height of the war the Air Service Command and the Materiel Command had boasted a combined strength of more than 300,000 personnel. By the fall of 1946 that number had decreased to little more than 100,000 civilians, officers, and enlisted men.

The number one problem was to find a way to dispose of the staggering amount of materiel left over from the war. Thousands upon thousands of airplanes and many millions of dollars worth of equipment, engines, and other spare parts would either have to be stored or declared surplus and transferred to other government agencies. Most of the materiel would have to be screened and classified, a tedious business and one for which ATSC and AMC were undermanned. They were also hardpressed to do the job quickly, since many of the supplies were stored in leased warehouses which the government was anxious to vacate for reasons of economy.

What compounded this problem was not so much the lack of personnel as the lack of storage space, particularly space for the airplanes rolling in from the production lines and from the operating units. Sooner or later, some of these aircraft would be returned to the operational forces, others would go to the reserves or to training units, and still others would be sold to foreign countries. But many aircraft would remain in storage indefinitely, and each of these would have to be stripped down and protected against corrosion. In any case, it did not matter to the logisticians of the Army Air Forces whether storage was to be short-term or long-term; it was still storage, and that was something the logistics commands would have a hard time providing. Even before the defeat of Germany, the Army Air Forces had reported 28,000 aircraft as surplus, and by V-J Day that figure had risen to over 35,000. This was almost six times the number of aircraft that could be stored in the facilities of the Air Technical Service Command.

Some of the hundreds of aircraft stored at Oklahoma City after World War II

Fortunately, the experiences of the war had taught the Air Technical Service Command a great deal about the requirements and techniques of storage, and even though its search for storage sites was tentative and halting at first—a result of the constantly changing plans of the Army Air Forces—the command at least knew the limitations and capabilities of its installations. And it soon became evident that there were more limitations than capabilities. ATSC was in fact so dissatisfied with its existing facilities that in the spring of 1945 the command decided to acquire new ones that would more closely fit its needs. What ATSC was looking for were airfields in dry climates, convenient to staging areas, that could draw on a reasonably large work force to put the aircraft in storage. What the command found were very few facilities that met this ideal, but many that were adequate enough to help relieve the pressure. By 1946, when the storage program was at its peak, 30 facilities scattered across the country were housing approximately 16,000 aircraft of all types.

PT-13 trainers packed like sardines at Ogden in 1946

SUPPORTING THE PEACETIME AIR FORCE

For the most part, the mission of Air Force logistics did not change in the postwar years. There were, to be sure, shifts in emphasis and differences of degree, but the nature of the support itself did not change, with one significant exception: the logistics organizations at Wright-Patterson AFB were now engaged in aeronautical research and development (R & D). Throughout most of World War II this responsibility had belonged to the Materiel Command, forerunner of the future Air Force Systems Command, but when that command was merged with the Air Service Command, research and development became a function of logistics.

The impact of this new mission on the air logistics commands was slight at first, for in the final year of the war most of the research and development programs were already in the hands of the National Defense Research Council and private industry. After the war, however, the National Defense Research Council was disbanded, contracts with private industry were cancelled, and the logistics organizations began to shoulder more of the research and development burden. Some of the work load consisted of projects transferred from the Army Technical Services to the Army Air Forces—a not unwelcome opportunity for a service anxious to gain its independence. In many other cases, the logistics commands initiated their own research programs; these steadily increased to the point that research and development became a major part of the logistics mission. By 1947 the Air Materiel Command was actively engaged in more than 2,000 research projects.

The character as well as the extent of the R & D mission underwent considerable change in the early postwar period. As the Air Materiel Command became more deeply involved in R & D and greater attention was given to the experimental aspects of aeronautical research, the interests of the Air Force shifted from gadgets to complex, coordinated groups of weapons; from air defense aircraft to air defense systems; from conventional aircraft of the types used in World War II to supersonic jet aircraft. While AMC continued to use a portion of its R & D funds to improve conventional aircraft, by 1947 most of the research money was being spent on new areas of technology that were just beginning to be explored.

But for all its research efforts, the Air Materiel Command was still primarily a logistics support organization, not a research institution, which is to say that the command's basic interest was to make available and maintain the best possible equipment for the using organizations. This meant that research at AMC was inevitably oriented towards the fundamental mission of the command, towards the development of new and improved equipment, and hence towards service and production engineering. It also meant that more often than not, basic research took second place to applied research, and that over a period of time the technological base—so crucial to future military superiority—would necessarily suffer.

In 1949 a special committee of the USAF Scientific Advisory Board, under the chairmanship of Dr. Louis N. Ridenour, examined this dangerous trend and recommended that research and development be separated from production engineering and placed in an organization of its own. In full agreement, the leaders of the Air Force proceeded to organize a separate command for the research function. This was a tremendous task involving the reassignment of thousands of personnel, scores of facilities, and a substantial amount of equipment. But with the establishment of the Air Research and Development Command in April 1951, the transfer was completed and Air Force research and development had a new home.

THE ARSENAL OF THE AIR FORCE

When the armies of North Korea invaded the south and a new war broke out, the United States Air Force was better prepared than in 1940, but not by much. Although

Overhauling the B-29 at Sacramento

no longer "fifth rate," the Air Force was still not ready for a sustained war in the technologically advanced world of 1950. What the Air Force needed was thousands of aircraft reflecting the latest developments in technology, but in 1950 that was an impossible order to fill. In the five years following World War II, when Congress was intent on holding down expenses and storing aircraft was the order of the day, the acquisition of more airplanes was not high on the list of priorities. Once war did break out, there were of course the usual calls for more airplanes and a stronger Air Force. Although it seemed at first that the administration had no clear idea about the size of Air Force it wanted, the government finally settled on a program to double the size from 48 to 95 wings. Congress approved the necessary appropriations, and suddenly more than $10 billion was made available to buy new airplanes. That was almost 10 times the amount the Air Force was preparing to ask for when the Korean war started.

Procuring so many aircraft quickly and efficiently was an enormous responsibility that once had belonged to a separate organization for procurement, the old Materiel Command. But that responsibility had been passed on to another organization, the Air Materiel Command, and now that war was again upon us this command found itself with far more to do than servicing aircraft and distributing parts. AMC was the industrial heart of the Air Force, the command assigned to establish and utilize an industrial base capable of supporting whatever level of air power the nation deemed necessary. Setting goals for the industrial effort, scheduling industrial output, and evaluating the impact of aircraft programs on basic national resources—these were the challenges confronting AMC in the opening months of the new war.

To the Air Materiel Command also fell the task of removing aircraft from storage, overhauling and often modifying them, and then sending them off to Korea. The command's maintenance teams labored over all types of first-line aircraft, but their biggest assignment was to prepare the mighty B-29 for war—a project so large that AMC had to set up a special facility in Japan just to handle extra engine modifications. This vast increase in work load also caused the command to examine closely its facil-

ities in the United States, and it did not take long to find them wanting. Although AMC tried to utilize all existing facilities to the fullest, there was no getting around the fact that the command needed to expand and modernize. An even more serious problem, and one much like that at the outset of World War II, was the shortage of skilled maintenance personnel. Authorizing overtime and retaining temporary employees beyond their normal term of service brought some relief, and by November 1950 AMC was able to obtain 20,000 additional civilian positions.

The constraints and limitations under which the command operated should not obscure what AMC was able to accomplish in a remarkably short time: by November 1950, just a few months after the start of the war, the command had modified and reconditioned more than 400 aircraft destined for the Far East. In addition, AMC had staged and processed another 275 airplanes transferred from units in the United States to the Far East Air Forces (FEAF).

This was a splendid achievement, but it was only half the job, and the easier half at that. In this war, as in any war, it was also the responsibility of the air logistics organization to keep the supplies flowing to the front. When war broke out, the Far East Air Forces was caught unprepared, with enough spare parts for peacetime but not nearly enough for combat. These supplies were soon depleted and for a while the FEAF had to support itself from hand-to-mouth.

At that point the problems of supply were just beginning. Understandably, the Air Force was anxious to airlift supplies to Korea as fast as possible, but in the haste of the first few months there were too many high priority requests, resulting in confusion and an excessive backlog. The Air Force also found itself once again requisitioning common stock from Army depots, which meant not only that the Air Force depended too much on another supply system, but on one quite different from its own.

In the midst of all the frustrations and disappointments, the USAF's supply operations in Korea did achieve some notable successes. When, for example, the F-86 pilots were desperate for external fuel tanks, the supply managers came through. Furthermore, any verdict on supply support in Korea must take into account the fact that the United States and the USAF had many commitments all over the world. Towards the end of the war, the Air Materiel Command was shipping over four million tons of materiel to hundreds of bases and other military installations in the United States and abroad. At the same time, the command was also furnishing substantial logistics support to the countries in the North Atlantic Treaty Organization.

But with all that said, it is also true that the Air Materiel Command and the operational units in Korea were far from satisfied with the support provided. This war was one cause, but not the only cause, of a sweeping reexamination of the nation's military posture; the Cold War, the obvious predominance of air power, the emergence of the nuclear age—these too prompted a new look at the nation's preparedness for future conflicts. Though this investigation was carried on at the highest levels of government, no serious study could be pursued for long without reference to the role of AMC, purchaser for the Air Force and as such, the vital link between the nation's industrial potential and a combat-ready fleet. Conversely, the formulation of new national security objectives and policies had an enormous impact on AMC, obliging the command to reexamine its operations, revise its planning, and in some cases fundamentally alter its long-standing assumptions.

By far the most significant of the new doctrines was the one proclaiming that air power, combined with nuclear power, was potentially the primary military force of the future. That was hardly a surprising assumption in the aftermath of Hiroshima and Nagasaki, but when a group of senior officers from the Pentagon visited Headquarters AMC early in 1954, their message to the AMC commander and his staff was anything but commonplace: in the event of a nuclear war, the command could no longer count on a two- or three-year margin to build up industrial support for the Air Force; instead, the decisive phase of such a war would take place in the first 90 days, and it was within that time period that AMC would have to mobilize the full industrial strength of the nation.

This new policy quickly sent AMC's planning staff back to the drawing boards, but it did not catch them unaware. They too had been planning for future contingencies, and although they had been thinking primarily in terms of conventional warfare, they knew that AMC should be prepared to provide whatever support was needed, whether for a small war, full-scale war, or an extended Cold War. They also knew that even for a conventional war the command would have to revise its assumptions about industrial mobilization, for the Korean War had shown that a buildup of two or three years was too long to do any good in a war of short duration. During the conflict the armament industry had actually produced nothing that was used on the battlefield, and by the time weapons did begin to roll off the production lines, a truce had been declared.

It was plain enough, then, that one item high on the agenda was to find new and better ways of harnessing the power of industry. But there were also many other priorities conceived in the early 1950s to modernize the mechanisms of support. Improving the distribution system and the computation of requirements, simplifying maintenance techniques and contracting procedures, decentralizing management responsibilities to achieve more flexibility—these too were among the ambitions of a command that was no longer a postwar caretaker. In charge of $30 billion worth of assets, the Air Materiel Command had become the arsenal of the Air Force.

THE CHALLENGE OF THE COLD WAR
THE LOGISTICIANS' RESPONSE

The Air Materiel Command responded to the challenges of the 1950s by turning to a combination of technology and innovative management. Direction of this effort was in the hands of Gen. Edwin W. Rawlings, who served as the commander of AMC from August 21, 1951, through February 28, 1959, the longest tenure in the history of the command to date. General Rawlings brought to the Air Materiel Command the abilities and experience in procurement and financial management that had enabled him to rise rapidly through the ranks in World War II. He attained his fourth star in February 1954.

The fundamental logistical problem for the Air Materiel Command was to be able to support military forces at the same speed with which they could be employed tactically or strategically. During World War II it had become painfully apparent that the mobility of air power was too often shackled by the limitations of surface logistics, stodgy communications technology, and manual record-keeping. The Air Materiel Command attacked this sluggishness with the weapons of airlift in combination with automation in its various forms—electronic data processing, communications, inventory control, material handling, and manufacturing methods. Many of the policies and actions which the Air Materiel Command undertook

A new war breaks out, this time in Korea, and women return to the maintenance lines.

High priority cargo for the Korean front: a jet engine is loaded aboard a C-54 Skymaster. The engine will be landed at a base near the combat zone for immediate installation in one of the Fifth Air Force's jet fighters.

during the period following the Korean War had their origins in the concept known as "Logistics for 1956," which was generated by Air Force headquarters during the early 1950s and endorsed by the Chief of Staff in February 1953. This package of ideas called for ending the practice of prestocking supplies overseas, reducing the work load at overseas depots, and reducing the amount of materiel which was in the supply pipeline. The objective was to place as much of the peacetime stocks as possible in the hands of the operational commands, with the remainder located where they could be made available promptly.

Of all the elements in the logistics function, information flow was the slowest and most unwieldy. The information processing work load had multiplied, yet the work force handling it had shrunk by some 55 percent between 1945 and 1955. Delays and errors were the result. The size of the Air Force inventory for which the Air Materiel Command was responsible was almost beyond comprehension—in 1955, more than 41 million items, about four and one-half million tons of equipment composed of 1.2 million separately defined items. Actual expenditures for aircraft and related equipment were over $11 billion, and the total value of outstanding contracts was some $36 billion. In some cases, it was necessary to order items about five years before they actually would be needed. To anticipate Air Force needs, estimate the costs, and manage such a vast and fluid stockpile required a veritable mountain of data, the apex of which was some 350 recurring reports that poured steadily into the headquarters.

The means to bring this monster under control was a miracle of modern technology, the electronic computer. Electronic data processing could provide a massive boost to Air Materiel Command management and administrative operations with the ability to store data, manipulate it, and churn out products with incredible speed. Although a great deal of time was needed to prepare data and instructions to be entered into the machine, it still surpassed the speed of existing methods and was vastly superior in handling complex transactions. Moreover, the state of the art was constantly advancing. The greatest challenge was to use the full potential of the equipment and to anticipate future applications. In fact, due to the pace of technological progress, the federal government preferred to lease equipment with the option to buy, rather than to purchase it outright.

Although computers made possible things in the field of Air Force logistics that had not been feasible—or even imagined—there were still limitations. One was economic: regardless of the money computers might save, the machines were still very expensive, even when leased rather than purchased. Moreover, manpower costs to prepare programs and data for input meant that the Air Force could not afford to exploit all the applications of electronic data processing. Even more crucial were the restrictions imposed by the human factor. The computer could not compensate for human error in programs and data, and considerable time was spent verifying the accuracy of in-

put and preparing data in appropriate forms. This accentuated the need for trained personnel, who were relatively scarce. Although the highest possible grade structures were established to lure qualified people, personnel shortages soon developed, especially among programmers. And perhaps most vital of all was the need to educate managers to think in terms of what computers could do to enhance the Air Force logistics process—a matter of creativity and imagination.

To reap the full benefits of electronic data processing and to exercise control over activities at overseas depots, the Air Materiel Command also needed to modernize its communications. AMC needed a faster communications system, and one that could interface with the command's new electronic data processing system. In March 1955 AMC began to use a new communications system that was based on the transceiver, a device that could use leased telephone lines to electronically transmit coded punched card impressions to another location, where a second transceiver would punch an identical card. With no increase in costs, AMC could realize a threefold increase in information traffic, and attain one hundred percent accuracy at the same time. In 1956 this system was extended overseas, using radio waves, and by the end of that year the AMC transceiver network was worldwide. The command transferred its communications system, along with some 1,500 civilians and 300 military personnel, to the Air Force Communications Service on January 1, 1962.

THE NEW SHAPE OF LOGISTICS MANAGEMENT

One of the major innovations of the Air Materiel Command in the 1950s was the systems approach to weapons management. This approach entailed treating any process as an entity, an interlocking design; it emphasized coordinating the relationships and interactions among component parts (subsystems), rather than regarding them as basically separate and discrete units. The impetus for the adoption of weapon systems management came primarily from the realization that as aircraft and other weapons became more complex and less similar to one another, and as missiles entered the scene, the traditional approach of dividing the management of a weapon system into compartments or stages was no longer appropriate. Weapon systems management affected the Air Materiel Command on two fronts: in its participation in the production process leading up to the deployment of a weapon system, and in the way the command supported a system once it had become operational.

Adoption of the weapon systems concept and the establishment of project offices to implement that concept offered the advantages of speeding up the process of acquiring operational systems and of reducing the number of Air Force people needed to support a system. Each weapon system project office steered its weapon system through the major functions of development, procurement, and production and through the logistics support

The B-36 represented America's strategic deterrent during the mid-1950s. San Antonio workers ready an 8,200-pound power pack on the B-36 maintenance line.

planning phase. During this time, the project office not only managed the procurement and production, it also acted to coordinate and integrate the project, serving as a nexus where industry and the Air Force operational commands could present their problems and get answers to their questions. AMC contributed procurement, supply, and maintenance personnel to the project office. These personnel carried out the command's duties in the procurement field and monitored the production program; they also made certain that all maintenance and supply requirements for a system were considered throughout the development phase.

Another management initiative to enhance the effectiveness of AMC's logistical system was the decentralization of the operational work load. This process was begun in April 1952. The goal was to improve responsiveness, reduce the vulnerability of logistical processes to enemy attack, and allow the headquarters to focus on policy and planning functions. The change also would enable the command's air materiel areas and depots to be self-sufficient during the initial phase of war. The effort to transfer the operational elements of supply, maintenance, and procurement to the depots continued in phases into the mid-1950s. As Headquarters AMC's primary mission shifted from operations to program management, the field commanders became responsible for certain aspects of

procurement, worldwide depot support, and stock control.

Along with decentralization, each depot was made the specialist for certain commodities and became the exclusive agent for computing requirements, purchasing, receiving, storing, shipping, and maintaining those items. By 1957 the new arrangement was working well. Besides freeing the headquarters to concentrate on nonoperational matters, decentralization improved the command's support to the combat forces by bringing the logistical processes—as well as industry—closer to them. General Rawlings observed that, "The combined effect of decentralization and the weapon system concept has been a deep-rooted change in the molecular structure of our air logistics system."

LOGISTICS ON A TIGHT BUDGET

As the Cold War and the price of new technology drove the defense budget higher, considerable pressure developed to control costs in normal operations. The Air Materiel Command continually sought ways to reduce the expense of logistics through better management and applications of technology. The Hi-Valu, Inspect and Repair as Necessary (IRAN), and Bench Check programs exemplified this response.

The concept behind the Hi-Valu program, instituted in 1954, was that expensive items should be managed selectively and controlled closely, and that undue resources should not be lavished on low cost items. In other words, "diamonds' should be treated differently from "popcorn." The Hi-Valu approach to expensive items meant paying close attention to such matters as determining how many of an item to procure, improving the distribution of the items, and expediting their repair, so the Air Force could avoid buying more of them than necessary. Hi-Valu items received special attention "from cradle to grave" in provisioning, programming, supply, procurement, transportation, and maintenance.

AMC depot maintenance during the 1950s was based on the IRAN principle. Initiated by the Air Force on a limited basis in 1952, the policy went into effect across-the-board in July 1953. The goal was to enable an aircraft to perform safely and efficiently until its next reconditioning cycle without expending surplus time, effort, or money. Previously, the practice had been to disassemble an item, inspect it, and recondition it completely, replacing anything that was doubtful, and return it "like new"; this sometimes meant replacing items that did not affect operational capability, or replacing an entire component rather than only a part of it. This latter approach burdened the depots with work which was not essential to making an aircraft safe and serviceable, added to costs, and kept the aircraft out of service longer. Dual benefits of this change were faster turnaround of aircraft awaiting maintenance and reduced costs.

When the Atlas missile blasted off, it carried Air Force logistics into a new era.

The Air Materiel Command also benefited from a maintenance policy known as Operation Bench Check, which required the using organizations to screen items, instead of automatically sending them to AMC for repair. If an engine or some other piece of equipment could be repaired at a lower level, or if it were unrepairable, the using command handled the matter, rather than adding to AMC's large backlog. This also saved the cost of packaging and transportation. Beginning in July 1953 this procedure was adopted Air Force-wide, and the results were well worth the effort. By mid-1954 the air materiel areas had screened some 12 million items in their own backlogs and had found that only one-third needed depot overhaul, resulting in a savings of some $27 million. The same proportion showed up when the other major commands bench-checked their own items. The Air Materiel Command issued a technical order making Operation Bench Check a standard procedure, and the backlog disappeared. Prolonging the time between overhauls, as the IRAN and Bench Check programs did, made it more important than ever to forecast the service lives of parts and engines. AMC began in late 1953 to apply actuarial techniques to computing requirements for engines and other items.

THE CREATION OF THE AIR FORCE LOGISTICS COMMAND

On 1 April 1961, the Air Materiel Command was redesignated the Air Force Logistics Command. The rationale for the name change can be traced to adoption of the system management concept in response to the need to develop and support sophisticated and dependable weapon systems. The separation of the research and development function from the Air Materiel Command in 1951 had been the first step. That step had upgraded the research phase, but it left an organizational and management gap between the development phase and that of procurement, and it failed to shorten appreciably the time required to create a weapon system from research to deployment.

The Air Force continued to ponder the problem of compressing the weapon cycle throughout the 1950s, and in 1959 appointed a special study group, under the chairmanship of the AMC Commander, Gen. Samuel E. Anderson, to conduct a formal examination of the problem. The consensus of the Anderson committee was that a single focal point of authority should be established for each stage of a system's cycle, and that the system manager should be given the authority to integrate a program without usurping the responsibilities of the functional managers. The committee further indicated that AMC should retain its current procurement responsibilities. The Commander of the Air Research and Development Command (ARDC) disagreed, however, and he continued to seek the transfer of the procurement function to his command.

In 1961 the situation was resolved when the new Secretary of Defense, Robert S. McNamara, decided to assign responsibility for the military space program to the Air Force and directed that Service to adjust its organization to the new mission. After a series of conferences, the Air Force drew up a major reorganizational plan that met with the approval of Secretary McNamara and was put into effect on April 1, 1961. The plan called for AMC and ARDC to be redesignated as the Air Force Logistics Command and the Air Force Systems Command (AFSC) respectively. While AFLC would retain those materiel and procurement functions necessary to carry out the logistics mission, the contract management regions and 67 Air Force-owned industrial facilities and contractor test sites that had belonged to AMC would go to AFSC.

Under the new arrangement, the Air Force Systems Command was responsible for a new weapon system during the research and development stage, and through the initial procurement of the system, while AFLC was responsible for materiel acquired to support systems that were in being. The matter of initial spares, however, caused considerable discussion. Ultimately, AFLC was given the job of determining requirements, budgeting, funding, and carrying out all other actions related to the management of spare parts. Altogether, AFLC gave up a net total of 14,965 manpower spaces to AFSC, most of them connected to the contract management regions of the

The B-52 modification line at San Antonio in the early 1960s.
The principle of Inspect and Repair as Necessary (IRAN) saved time and money on F-86 repair at Sacramento.

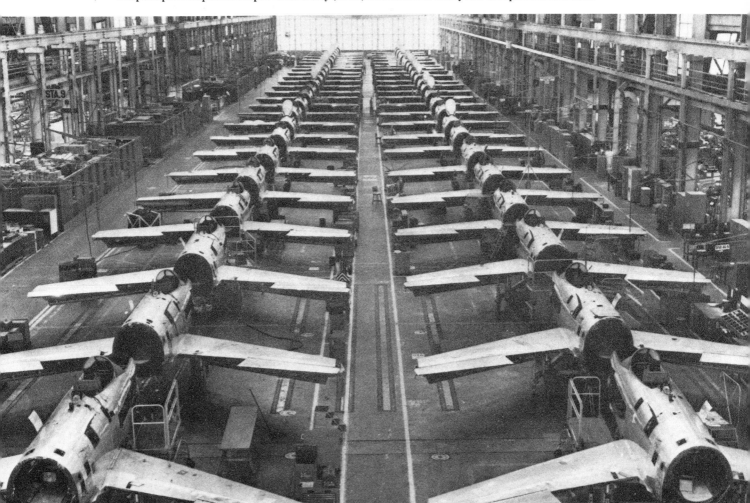

old AMC. AFLC also established detachments at AFSC's four major product divisions to ensure that logistics was considered along with research and development.

LOGISTICS IN THE 1960s

BASE BUILDUP IN SOUTHEAST ASIA

The Air Force sent only small units and small groups of individual aircraft to Southeast Asia in 1962 and 1963. The aircraft accompanying these units carried 30-day mission support kits, and AFLC resupplied the kits through its aerial resupply system. Two years later, however, the war in Southeast Asia had intensified and the Pacific Air Forces (PACAF) embarked on a major base expansion program in that area of the world. In the summer of 1965, Headquarters AFLC drew up a preliminary support plan for PACAF that was not fundamentally different from the command's normal support procedures. However, the plan did make the Sacramento Air Materiel Area responsible for developing a schedule for the shipment of all equipment and spares that would be initially required by new main operating bases. The plan also made PACAF responsible for identifying the materiel that would be needed by the bases.

In July 1965, Headquarters AFLC informed its field units that the name BITTERWINE would be used to identify all materiel that would be needed to establish the new main operating bases and expand some of the other bases. It advised the field units that the required materiel ranged from just a few spares to increase the capabilities of the existing bases to the "complete range of spares and equipment needed to transpose a bare strip at a jungle base into a full blown main operating base capable of providing full maintenance support to various high performance tactical fighter and troop carrier aircraft."

BITTERWINE developed into a project of such magnitude during the last half of 1965 that it almost defied accomplishment. Between July and December 1965, AFLC became responsible for supporting the deployment of some 32 tactical fighter and troop carrier squadrons, equipping eight main operating bases, supplying 12 bases with administrative and housekeeping items, and providing three bases with common shop equipment. In these six months, AFLC assembled more than 57,000 items at the Sacramento Air Materiel Area and shipped some 22,000 of these to Southeast Asia.

In January 1966 AFLC took a number of important steps to obtain needed materiel for Project BITTERWINE. For example, Headquarters AFLC gave its field units permission to redistribute materiel from Air Force units to Project BITTERWINE and to remove items from AFLC aircraft when materiel needed to improve PACAF's operational readiness could not be obtained from such sources as depot or reparable assets, stored aircraft, or other Air Force units. At the same time, Head-

quarters AFLC instructed its field units to remove items from AFLC aircraft only when absolutely necessary and to use the utmost discretion at all times. It also asked the field units to notify the headquarters when an Air Force unit refused to honor an AFLC request for materiel.

SPECIAL TEAMS IN SOUTHEAST ASIA

In the early stages of the base expansion program in Southeast Asia, huge quantities of materiel arriving from the United States often overwhelmed the base supply systems because none of the bases were equipped to handle such vast quantities of supplies. Inadequate storage facilities at the bases also led to the use of temporary shelters and outside storage. As a result, all marks were often obliterated by the weather and the identification of items became extremely difficult and time-consuming. To solve this problem, the AFLC Commander, Gen. Mark E. Bradley, Jr., instructed each air materiel area to select a minimum of 10 well-qualified and experienced personnel, military or civilian, to serve as the initial cadre for the command's Rapid Area Supply Support (RASS) teams.

The initial 10-man RASS teams consisted of eight materiel facility specialists and two logistics specialists. Three packaging specialists and a traffic supervisor were added to each team when its size was expanded to 14. The 30-man team contained 18 materiel facility specialists, five inventory management specialists, three packaging specialists, and one traffic supervisor. AFLC simply doubled the representation in each skill to get from the 30-man team to the 60-man team.

AFLC inaugurated its RASS team program in late May 1965 when a team of four people departed for Southeast Asia to help various bases in South Vietnam and Thailand refine their property accounting records. The next team, which consisted of 22 military personnel, departed for Clark Air Base in late June. AFLC dispatched 12 other RASS teams to Southeast Asia during the last six months of 1965. During that year a total of 333 AFLC personnel served on the RASS teams.

Despite many personal hardships, the AFLC RASS teams did an outstanding job. A team of 81 military personnel worked at Tan Son Nhut Air Base from the end of July to the middle of November 1965. During this time the team constructed enough storage bins to accommodate 54,000 items, placed almost 26,000 line items in storage, and processed a backlog of 80,000 documents. In December 1966, Headquarters PACAF asked Headquarters AFLC to send a RASS team to Tan Son Nhut to help base personnel conduct a complete materiel inventory. AFLC immediately dispatched a team of 56 civilian personnel to the base. During its four months there, the team inspected and identified 110,724 line items, condemned 448 items, inventoried 45,523 items, and packed 222,473 units for shipment and 34,253 units for on-base storage. Other RASS teams accomplished similar feats.

Meanwhile, the command had to deal with the equally serious problem of repairing crash and battle damaged aircraft, the number of which increased as the Air Force intensified its actions and expanded its operations in Southeast Asia. One way in which AFLC dealt with this problem was to dispatch Rapid Area Maintenance (RAM) teams to that theater. The purpose of these teams was to evaluate the damage to an aircraft, and then either make repairs on site, or accomplish enough repairs to permit the aircraft to make a one-time flight to a main base repair facility. Like the RASS teams, the RAM teams were composed of both military and civilian personnel and normally consisted of 18 highly skilled individuals—a group leader, an aeronautical engineer, an aircraft maintenance technician, and three advance teams. Each advance team consisted of an aircraft maintenance technician who was also the team chief, an electrical repair technician, a pneudraulic repair technician, and two airframe repair technicians.

For most RAM team members, service in Southeast Asia entailed all the risks and frustrations of war. The lack of housing was probably the greatest single problem faced by most of the AFLC personnel, because base accommodations were usually filled to capacity. Consequently, most AFLC personnel in South Vietnam lived in whatever accommodations they could find. Another problem was the long commuting distance between quarters and the job sites. For the most part, the RAM teams travelled in Navy buses which had some type of wire over the windows to deflect grenades that might be thrown by terrorists. In general, food was not a problem for the AFLC teams, for although they ate out of mess kits, the food was good. Sometimes, AFLC personnel ate in restaurants, but they did so at their own risk. On June 25, 1965, for example, two bombs exploded in a Saigon restaurant, killing four civilian members of a RAM team and seriously injuring another member of that team. The civilians killed were Leon Forcum, Leo D. Nelson, John M. Kilzer, and Floyd R. McKinney. The injured civilian was Alfred H. Charamza. On August 31, 1965, the AFLC Commander,

Gen. Kenneth B. Hobson, presented Purple Heart medals to the widows of the slain men and to Mr. Charamza.

Between April 1965 and the end of July 1969, AFLC's RAM teams processed a total of 1,077 aircraft; 845 were repaired at the site, 87 were prepared for a one-time flight to a repair facility, 120 were prepared for shipment to a repair facility, and 25 were so badly damaged that they could not be repaired. The acquisition value of the aircraft that were repaired or sent to a repair facility was more than $1.6 billion. The 845 aircraft repaired at the site consisted of 30 different models.

THE ELIMINATION OF FIELD UNITS

AFLC began the decade of the 1960s with nine air materiel areas. These were located at Warner Robins, Georgia; San Antonio, Texas; Sacramento, California; Ogden, Utah; Oklahoma City, Oklahoma; Rome, New York; Middletown, Pennsylvania; Mobile, Alabama; and San Bernardino, California. At the end of the decade, only the first five remained within the command; the last four had been eliminated, with their functions and some of their personnel transferred to the remaining AFLC organizations.

The blow fell first on the air materiel area at Rome, when late in 1963 Secretary of Defense Robert McNamara announced the closing of that organization by the end of June 1967. At the time of the announcement, Rome was authorized 4,037 manpower spaces. Of this total, 1,570 were to be transferred to other AFLC organizations, 1,276 were to be assigned to the organization that would assume the host responsibilities for Griffiss Air Force Base, and 1,190 were to be eliminated. Of those to be eliminated, almost all were civilian positions.

While AFLC was working on its program to inactivate the Rome Air Materiel Area, the Secretary of Defense announced that three more of the command's field units—Middletown, Mobile, and San Bernardino—would be closed and their functions transferred elsewhere by

A SEAIR shipment being loaded on a C-141 at Hill AFB

July 1969. As it turned out, only a relatively small percentage of the civilian personnel at Middletown, Mobile, and San Bernardino transferred with their positions to the remaining air materiel areas.

One other significant loss for the command occurred on April 1, 1970, when the Ground Electronics Engineering Installation Agency, with some 7,000 personnel, was transferred to the Air Force Communications Service. This agency had belonged to the logistics command since the day of its activation, in 1958.

DEVELOPMENT OF THE COMMAND'S DATA SYSTEMS

AFLC spent a large part of the 1960s searching for the best way to make greater use of the computer's potential for improving the command's management capabilities. But by 1967, new advances in the development of automatic data processing equipment had made many of AFLC's data systems and computers both cumbersome and inefficient. As a result, AFLC had to decide whether it should buy additional second generation computers or develop new and more sophisticated systems that would involve the use of more advanced computers. AFLC decided on the second alternative and in September 1967 established a new organization, the Advanced Logistics Systems Center (ALSC). The center was responsible for developing a single, closed loop, real-time, all-encompassing system for managing all of AFLC's logistics operations. This system eventually became known as the Advanced Logistics System (ALS).

In 1968 the new center prepared a plan that defined the objectives, concepts, and characteristics of the Advanced Logistics System. This plan became known as the ALS Master Plan. Later in the year, the Computer Science Corporation, an experienced software organization, worked with the ALSC in confirming various critical segments of the Advanced Logistics System. The corporation's final report, issued in December 1968, confirmed the feasibility of the design that had developed for the ALS. During the first half of 1969, various individuals from the ALSC reviewed the specifications that had been developed for the ALS with personnel from the Directorate of Data Automation, Headquarters USAF, and with representatives from various equipment manufacturers. As a result of these discussions, the ALSC revised the specifications and submitted them to Headquarters USAF in June 1969. Headquarters USAF approved the new specifications in early July, and the Assistant Secretary of the Air Force for financial management approved AFLC's equipment selection plan for the ALS three months later.

In September 1969, the ALSC initiated a number of organizational realignments to improve its operations. In the first realignment, the ALSC eliminated three of its staff offices and restructured three of its directorates. In the next realignment, the ALSC compressed all of its activities into three major units—a Directorate of Operating Systems, a Directorate of Advanced Systems and Control, and a Directorate of Technical Support. The Directorate of Operating Systems became responsible for all existing systems, including maintenance and modification; the Directorate of Advanced Systems for maintaining the ALS Master Plan, designing and implementing the ALS, and coordinating the activities of the ALS with the Headquarters AFLC staff and air materiel area; and the Directorate of Technical Support for all ALS hardware, software, communications, modeling, and simulation. A few days after this reorganization, the AFLC Commander, Gen. Jack G. Merrill, announced that the ALSC would be abolished and that its responsibilities would be transferred to Headquarters AFLC's DCS/Comptroller on February 1, 1970.

Upon completion of the transfer, the AFLC Comptroller became responsible for managing the ALS. This change marked the beginning of a new stage in the life of the ALS, since the system moved from the concept phase to the development phase.

MODERNIZING THE COMMAND

DETERRENCE AND AUSTERITY

Although the conflict in Southeast Asia continued into the early 1970s, the primary focus for the Air Force Logistics Command during most of that decade was on what one commander, General Jack J. Catton, called "the logistics of deterrence." Gen. Catton saw logistics as a prime deterrent: the enemy assesses not only the weaponry and the personnel, but also the adversary's ability to support and maintain its equipment and men once war begins. If AFLC could guarantee that the Air Force could continue to fight indefinitely, the effectiveness of the force would be multiplied, and this would work to dissuade a potential aggressor.

At the same time, however, economic and political pressures in the post Vietnam era combined to usher in a period of austerity for defense. The economy had entered a period of inflation, budget deficits swelled, and there were demands for government programs in areas other than defense. These circumstances were particularly injurious to logistics, since defense planners attempted to get the most out of limited funds by skimping on support in order to channel more money into the acquisition of weapon systems. The result was to place greater emphasis than ever before on AFLC's ability to find ways of cutting its requirements and improving cost effectiveness. As in the past, the command exploited new technologies, particularly the ever-expanding frontier of computers, and devised management initiatives to accomplish its ends more effectively and more cheaply. In one respect, at least, AFLC did enjoy stability: the command closed the decade with the same group of installations and the same organizational structure that had existed in 1970.

REHABILITATING THE DEPOTS

By 1970 it was clear that AFLC's depot facilities were becoming a choke point, largely because many of them were outmoded technologically or inadequate physically. The rapid expansion of maintenance and distribution facilities demanded by World War II actually had become a burden by 1970, because AFLC now had to function with many buildings and much equipment that had become old and obsolete. Almost 70 percent of the industrial plant dated from the World War II era, and some of it even predated 1920. Modernization plans had not fared well over the years in the competition for the defense dollars. A study concluded that some 70 percent of the facilities were substandard, and that 80 percent of the industrial equipment ought to be replaced. Crowded storage meant inefficient handling and wasted funds. Materials and equipment were exposed to the elements because of lack of space; about 40 percent of the storage space was outside, and it cost AFLC half a million dollars annually to repair weather damage to equipment stored outdoors at Warner Robins alone.

By the late 1970s, test equipment such as this central air data computer had been introduced to the flight line, enabling maintenance crews to make a rapid check of the complex avionic components.

All of these factors made it clear that it was time to remodel the physical plant of the depot system, and so AFLC decided that its best course was to embark on a five-year Depot Plant Modernization Program. Gradually, new buildings replaced old ones, with most of the money being spent on warehouses, materiel processing facilities, and hangar modifications. When the Depot Plant Modernization Program concluded, AFLC had received $206 million for 75 facility projects, with another $162 million for equipment. Despite the considerable scope of the Depot Plant Modernization Program, however, AFLC could not complete the renovation of the depots in such a relatively short span of time, and they continued to suffer

from a lack of adequate modern facilities. The result was a successor program, the Logistics Improvement of Facilities and Technology, launched in 1979.

Funding for equipment to go into the buildings was separate, and generally was granted more readily than money for construction. In fiscal year 1977 AFLC inaugurated the Depot Plant Equipment Program to promote its needs in that area. Over a three-year period the effort was rewarded with $52 million in equipment funding. One approach was to install mechanized materiel handling systems—basically machinery that could move items automatically within a warehouse, terminal, or maintenance facility. Besides doing the job faster than the human hands it replaced, the equipment was more economical than manual labor over a period of years. Automation also allowed more accurate control over the inventory. Toward the latter part of the 1970s, computerized control was possible and these systems promised to become ever more sophisticated.

THE TECHNOLOGY REPAIR CENTERS

While the modernization of the command's depot facilities centered on new buildings and machinery, the introduction of the technology repair centers was based on an innovative approach to maintenance management. The concept derived from a Department of Defense instruction in 1971 which required that no more than 70 percent of the maintenance essential to the Air Force mission should be done organically, and that the depots should use at least 85 percent of their capacities. This reflected a desire to allocate part of the military work load to private contractors, on the one hand, and to operate military facilities productively, on the other. AFLC's leaders, for their part, were concerned with sustaining the command's ability to provide support during a war situation, while adjusting to a shrinking work load and striving for efficiency. The Technology Repair Center program would have each air materiel area specialize in the maintenance of particular items with similar technological characteristics. Some 300 types of items were grouped into 18 technologies, such as weapons, airmunitions, airborne avionics, missile components, and landing gears. Each category was comprised of items with a degree of technological commonality that lent itself to servicing at a single depot. Major items such as airframes and missile frames, engines, and inertial guidance systems were excluded.

The AFLC Commander approved the concept in October 1972 and in March 1973 he accepted a two-year plan, to commence the following January, which reduced the number of work centers to 23. The realignment of the maintenance work loads involved considerable juggling and balancing to adjust each depot's burden to its capacity. More than 9,300 kinds of items and some 6.2 million manhours of work were shifted among the air logistics centers. Although the realignment went smoothly for the most part, there was one serious disappointment due to the fact that of the more than 3,300 employees whose jobs were transferred to another depot, only 460 agreed to move in order to follow the work load. Overall, the outcome was a more balanced distribution by the end of 1975, when the process neared its conclusion. Although it cost about $26 million to bring about, institution of the technology repair centers promised to repay the investment within two years through savings and cost avoidances. At the same time, it improved AFLC's ability to respond to the demands of war.

DATA PROCESSING

As AFLC's mission became increasingly complex and the pressures for virtually instantaneous responsiveness mounted, the command relied more and more on the "miracle" of electronic data processing to bridge the gap between what was demanded by the situation and what human beings could do by themselves. By 1970 both the capabilities of the technology and AFLC's use of it had progressed to the point where it was inconceivable that the Air Force logistics system could function adequately without automatic data processing.

During the early 1970s, AFLC continued to develop the Advanced Logistics System begun in the late 1960s. A far-reaching and highly ambitious project, it aimed to use automatic data processing to achieve a truly comprehensive control over logistics management. The master plan of the ALS envisioned a single computer at each of the five air materiel areas and the headquarters, replacing 89 of the 129 computers then being used for logistics support by AFLC. The Advanced Logistics System would function in real time, permitting data to be entered and used as soon as it was available. Each of the new computers would have immediate access to those at the other sites, greatly reducing the duplication of data in the various independent systems. This would allow extensive interfacing among heretofore discrete information systems that used a number of different types of computers.

As the Advanced Logistics System unfolded, it ran into many problems of various types and severity. This was not entirely unexpected, given the scope of the project and the fact that AFLC was pioneering in many respects. Delays occurred, which set the Advanced Logistics System behind schedule, and in September 1974 AFLC undertook an extensive assessment of the program. Fifteen months later, in December 1975, Congress instructed the Air Force to terminate the program.

During the remainder of the 1970s, AFLC was very thorough and cautious in developing its automatic data processing plans because of the close supervision from higher levels. As a result, progress was modest in developing new logistics management systems and upgrading existing ones. AFLC did proceed with work on a number of systems, including one that would manage the entire engine inventory and another that would handle stock control and distribution. By 1980 the command had revamped

its program and was preparing for an era in which automatic data processing would be more important than ever to its basic mission.

The computer era had reached the fourth generation by 1980, and the new models far surpassed the older ones in terms of capacity, speed, and capability. At one of the air logistics centers, for example, a unit hardly larger than a desk replaced another that had filled a good-sized room, and provided several times the capacity as well. In fact, as the size and cost fell simultaneously, AFLC could bring them into the work place instead of confining them to special computer rooms with controlled environments. Computers could manage the operations of lathes and other similar machines, a practice known as numerical control, and could function in the automatic test equipment used at the air logistics centers.

SPACE LOGISTICS

It was obvious that the military dimension of the space shuttle and space platforms would become progressively more important, and in 1979 AFLC began to explore the possibility of a role for itself. Initially, the command found that the support apparatus for the Space Transportation System, as the space shuttle was called, already was in place under the aegis of the National Aeronautics and Space Administration, so that there was little room for AFLC to enter that sphere. Accordingly, AFLC's planners decided that the command should be content with developing an interface with the National Aeronautics and Space Administration and the Air Force Systems Command's Space Division, the two organizations which thus far had dominated the program, so as to work within the existing framework. AFLC could seek management responsibility for the relatively small number of items for which it was the acknowledged expert, form a cadre of space logistics personnel, and study the matter of whether AFLC could provide a cost effective alternative to the existing approach of relying on contractor support of the shuttle and its ground support system. Behind this was the assumption that eventually AFLC would play a larger part in supporting the Air Force space mission.

THE VIEW FROM 1980

As AFLC entered the 1980s, it was clear that the commanders and logisticians of the future would have to deal with many of the same major problems and challenges that had engaged the command's attention for the past 10 years. If anything, the Air Force's logistics posture was more important than ever. The Warsaw Pact countries had been vigorously building up their forces while those of the United States grew at a significantly more modest rate, and relied on technological superiority to compensate for the Warsaw Pact's numerical advan-

Air Force Logistics Command Headquarters, Gillmore Hall, Building 262, Area A

tage. This policy placed a great deal of pressure on the support system to achieve constant and immediate readiness, and to be able to maintain a high rate of operational capability once fighting began.

Unfortunately, these goals collided with the rising cost of logistics support and the chronic underfunding of the mission. AFLC's costs for labor had risen 154 percent between 1968 and 1979, materiel costs 129 percent, and utility costs a staggering 499 percent. At the same time, because there had been a cutback in the procurement of new aircraft immediately after the close of the Vietnam conflict, the age of the inventory was rising, and so was the expense of maintaining it. The average age of the active inventory was nearly 12 years.

As the defense budget became tighter, funding for logistics was curtailed in order to allocate more money for additional weapon systems. AFLC was especially concerned about being able to provide the materiel that would be used to keep the combat units operational during the first stages of a conflict—materiel known as War Readiness Spares Kits and Base-Level Self-Sufficiency Spares. From 94 percent funding in fiscal year 1977, the level plummeted in succeeding years to 49 percent, 32 percent, and eventually to 15 percent in fiscal year 1980. Adding to this bleak picture was the fact that lead times for industrial production had become increasingly longer, so that it might take months, even years, to secure certain aircraft parts and components after orders were placed. At the

AIR FORCE LOGISTICS COMMAND COMMANDERS

Gen. Samuel E. Anderson	Apr 1961-Jul 1961
Gen. William F. McKee	Aug 1961-Jun 1962
Gen. Mark E. Bradley, Jr.	Jul 1962-Jul 1965
Gen. Kenneth B. Hobson	Aug 1965-Jul 1967
Gen. Thomas P. Gerrity	Aug 1967-Feb 1968
Gen. Jack G. Merrill	Mar 1968-Sep 1972
Gen. Jack J. Catton	Sep 1972-Aug 1974
Gen. William V. McBride	Sep 1974-Aug 1975
Gen. F. Michael Rogers	Sep 1975-Jan 1978
Gen. Bryce Poe II	Feb 1978-Jul 1981
Gen. James P. Mullins	Aug 1981-Sep 1984
Gen. Earl T. O'Loughlin	Sep 1984

same time that AFLC's traditional mission was becoming more difficult, new missions were emerging as well. The creation of the rapid deployment force in 1979 led HQ AFLC to commence planning in anticipation that this force would make new demands upon the command's resources, although the nature of these demands was not yet clearly formed. And logistics to support Air Force operations in space presented another arduous, if exciting frontier. Obviously, AFLC's ingenuity, determination, and capacity for hard work would be tested continually in the years ahead as they had been in the past.

X. THE AERONAUTICAL SYSTEMS DIVISION

By

Clarence J. Geiger, Ph.D.
Michael H. Levy, M.A.

The Aeronautical Systems Division manages the development and procurement of aeronautical systems, related components, and associated technology. This division is the product of a long search by the nation's military and civilian leaders for the most effective organization to acquire advanced weapon systems. The Aeronautical Systems Division has evolved over decades into a highly professional institution for the application of science and technology to the acquisition of air-breathing operational systems.

PRELUDE 1903-1947

Between 1897 and 1903, Orville and Wilbur Wright methodically advanced the science of aeronautics. They demonstrated glider designs, experimented with airfoil and propeller shapes, and tested components in a rudimentary wind tunnel. These efforts enabled them to achieve a technological breakthrough of great significance: the means for three-axis control of flight. They also designed and fabricated an airframe and developed and constructed a 12-hp, four-cylinder engine. By formulating fundamental research and development techniques, the Wright brothers were able to build an aircraft prototype. On December 17, 1903, they made the first controlled, powered flight.

By 1908, the Wright brothers had convinced the military of the usefulness of their aircraft. The Army Signal Corps wanted a two-place flying machine capable of a speed of 40 miles per hour, with a range of 125 miles. When the Army accepted the 1909 Military Flyer as a trainer, this marked the beginning of American military aviation and the key role of the contractor in aircraft engineering.

In December 1916, the government purchased land for an experimental aviation station near Hampton, Virginia. Because of delayed construction this complex, later designated Langley Field, was not available when the United States entered the First World War in April 1917. The Signal Corps was unprepared for war and had less than 200 aircraft, almost all of which were trainers. This lack of a combat air force pointed to the need for an aeronautical research, development, and procurement organization.

The Army formed the Airplane Engineering Department on October 13, 1917, and established McCook Field near Dayton, Ohio, on October 18 as an experimental aeronautical laboratory. On December 4, 1917, the Airplane Engineering Department transferred its operations from temporary headquarters in downtown Dayton to the newly-constructed experimental station at McCook Field. While Langley Field engaged in flight instruction and developed components for bombing, photography, and radio communication, McCook Field became the center for air-

craft and engine development. Soon after, the Army began a series of reorganizations that resulted in the formation on August 31, 1918, of the Airplane Engineering Division. The official designation of the division became Engineering Division, Air Service, which it retained until 1926.

During the European war, McCook Field engineers modified aircraft of British design. The most important was the DeHavilland DH-4, a biplane with an open cockpit and a fabric-covered airframe. The engineers installed an American Liberty engine in the British aircraft. The Dayton-Wright Company and other associated contractors produced over 4,500 of these DH-4s. Some 1,200 became operational in Europe. McCook engineers also worked on an American version of the DH-9 and the Standard Handley-Page bomber.

In 1918, the Airplane Engineering Division employed over 2,000 people. Its facilities included workshops, laboratories, and design and test departments. Until the mid-1920s, the engineers concentrated on such projects as the design and construction of pursuit, attack, and observation aircraft. They studied night attack, ground attack, and close air support aircraft; air-cooled and liquid-cooled engines; and improvements to other aircraft components.

DeHavilland DH-4

The end of the conflict in Europe resulted in a decrease in orders for military aircraft. Industrialists complained that McCook's engineers performed too much designing and testing. Consequently, in 1925, Maj. Gen. Mason M. Patrick, Chief of the Army Air Service, introduced a program in which government engineers would only establish specifications and review designs submitted by the contractors. Although this policy accelerated experimental aircraft contracts, it shifted the task of engineering from the Army to industry. Moreover, the Engineering Division was prohibited from building experimental aircraft.

The Engineering Division comprised all the personnel at McCook Field. The division had separate departments for airplane and production engineering. In October 1926, the newly-created Army Air Corps established the Materiel Division by combining the Engineering Division with the Supply Division (including the Field Service Section at the Fairfield Air Depot), the Industrial War Plans Section, and the Materiel Disposal Section of the Air Service. The Army hoped that this reorganization would increase component standardization and place more emphasis on procurement.

Martin B-10 bomber

Boeing B-17 bomber

374

Due to McCook Field's size and location, the Air Service was unable to expand its aeronautical activities. In 1924, the Dayton Air Service Committee donated 4,500 acres of land to the government for the creation of a new and expanded facility to be known as Wright Field. On October 12, 1927, the Air Corps dedicated Wright Field as the new location of the Materiel Division. Wright Field thus became the center for the acquisition of aeronautical weapon systems. (In July 1931, Wright Field was divided, and that portion of the field east of Huffman Dam, including the Fairfield Air Depot Reservation, was redesignated Patterson Field.)

By 1930, American military aircraft exhibited many design improvements. The streamlined monoplane of all-metal, lightweight, enclosed cockpit construction was replacing the fabric biplane with its open cockpit. Nevertheless, the Materiel Division had been slow in adapting technical advances from commercial aviation. (For example, the German Junkers F-13, an all-metal monoplane, began flying in 1919.)

The Materiel Division ordered the Douglas XB-7 bomber, a two-engine monoplane, in 1930. The Douglas Aircraft Company built the wings with fabric but used corrugated aluminum for the fuselage. Procurement of the first Martin XB-10 bomber in 1933 represented a more notable advance. This all-metal aircraft had a retractable landing gear, an enclosed cockpit, and a rotating, trans-

Republic P-47C Thunderbolt

North American P-51A Mustang

parent turret. The Materiel Division obtained more than 150 of the B-10 model and its modified versions.

The acquisition procedures established by General Patrick continued into the 1930s. An important example was the B-17 program. In 1933, Wright Field design engineers studied a concept for a long-range strategic bomber. The following year, The Boeing Company won a competition with the Martin Company for the XB-15. This large aircraft had a wingspan of 149 feet, a fuselage length of almost 88 feet, a speed of 197 miles per hour, a range of 3,400 miles, and a bomb capacity of up to 12,000 pounds.

In August 1934, the Materiel Division issued more stringent specifications for the bomber; Boeing independently, however, had been considering another model. Later designated the B-17 Flying Fortress, this aircraft had a speed of 236 miles per hour, a range of over 2,000 miles, and a bomb capacity of 6,000 pounds. The Army Air Corps ordered 13 B-17s, and the production engineers monitored the work.

By 1937, the Engineering Section of the Materiel Division began to reflect a project office concept. While the experimental engineering function remained part of the laboratory activities, the Engineering Procurement Branch had organized its project officers and engineers according to attack and observation, bombardment, pursuit, and training and transport aircraft. In 1939, the Experimental Engineering Section consisted of nine laboratories: Aircraft, Armament, Equipment, Materials, Photographic, Power Plant, Propeller, Aircraft Radio, and Engineering Shops. Significantly, some of the experimental engineering staff separately aligned their functions according to laboratory projects such as aircraft, armament, and engines. This rudimentary concept involving dual project offices became more clearly defined by 1951.

Wright Field officials considered America's air arm of 1939 inferior to that of other nations but were confident of their ultimate ability to provide a superior air force. The Second World War brought greatly increased investment in military aeronautics. The Materiel Division and its organizational successors completed development of such advanced fighters as the Republic P-47 Thunderbolt and the North American P-51 Mustang. Both attained speeds over 400 miles per hour and ranges between 550 and 750 miles. The United States produced over 15,000 of these aircraft.

Bomber advancement and production was also a major effort at Wright Field. While Boeing's B-17 attracted more publicity, the Consolidated B-24 Liberator had been more widely deployed. Both had speeds of 300 miles per hour, with ranges of more than 3,000 miles. An advanced version of the Liberator carried up to 12,800 pounds of bombs. American companies produced over 12,000·B-17s and 18,000 B-24s.

A series of wartime organizational changes at Wright and Patterson Fields led in 1946 to the formation of the Air Materiel Command (AMC). By 1947, this Command had three directorates: Research and Development, Procurement and Industrial Mobilization Planning, and Supply and Maintenance.

Boeing B-17G Flying Fortress

Consolidated B-24D Liberator

THE CASE OF THE B-29 SUPERFORTRESS

In 1939, Capt. Donald L. Putt, future Commander of the Air Research and Development Command, envisioned an advanced bomber. By September 1940, the Army Air Corps awarded Boeing a contract for two XB-29 aircraft. The Boeing design involved a large vehicle with a wing-span of 141 feet and a fuselage length of 99 feet. It would have a speed of 383 miles per hour and a ferry range of over 7,000 miles. In spite of such unique features as a pressurized cabin and a remote fire control system, Materiel Division officials considered the design technically feasible.

Boeing B-29 Superfortress

The B-29 program presented complexities which necessitated management procedures combining development and production. After the mockup inspection in November 1940, Boeing became aware of serious technical problems. These involved development of a more powerful engine and four-bladed propellers, proper wing-loading ratio, and the pressurization and fire control systems. Furthermore, a production program with Boeing and three other companies required close coordination. The Army Air Forces recognized the need for a central program authority.

By 1942, Brig. Gen. Kenneth B. Wolfe directed the development, production, and deployment aspects of the B-29 program. He was the first program official to have such extensive responsibility and authority. In June 1944, the aircraft became operational, and by the end of the war the Army Air Forces had acquired almost 4,000 B-29s.

FORMING THE WRIGHT AIR DEVELOPMENT CENTER 1944-1955

Gen. Henry H. Arnold, Chief of Staff of the Army Air Forces, became associated during the 1930s with Dr. Theodore von Karman, a noted aeronautical expert at the California Institute of Technology. From this relationship came Arnold's appreciation for the application of science and technology to the development of weapons for the Army Air Forces. In December 1944 he established the Scientific Advisory Group (later Board) to assure a continuing relationship between the scientific and military communities.

During the war, there was considerable progress in military aeronautics, but one development led to a revolution: jet propulsion. Although the British had demonstrated a jet engine as early as 1937, the Bell XP-59A aircraft did not make its first jet flight until October 1942. The Germans, however, had made a startling advance with an operational jet fighter in October 1944; America's P-80A Shooting Star by Lockheed did not reach operational status until the following April.

Bell XP-59

In 1945, von Karman and his associates on the Scientific Advisory Group completed several studies on American aerospace technology. He emphasized that scientific knowledge had allowed man to overcome the natural limitations against flight. Moreover, German advances in jet and rocket propulsion had occurred not because of superior scientific personnel but as the result of substantial government support for these endeavors. Von Karman believed that a closer relationship between the military officer and the scientist would enable the Army Air Forces to achieve supersonic flight, pilotless aircraft, all-weather flying, improvements in navigation and communication, and large transports. He thought that some of these advances were a decade or more away, and required more emphasis on research and development.

In September 1949, a special committee of the Scientific Advisory Board, chaired by Louis N. Ridenour of the University of Illinois, completed a major study of Air Force systems acquisition. The committee stated that only by separating the research and development function from procurement and production could the Air Force (created as an independent service in 1947) rapidly provide advanced weapons for its operational units. The committee, therefore, recommended the creation of a single research and development agency, staffed by technically-trained military and civilian personnel.

On January 23, 1950, Air Force Chief of Staff Gen. Hoyt S. Vandenberg announced the formation of the Research and Development Command in Washington, D.C. It was redesignated the Air Research and Development Command (ARDC) on September 16; the Air Force subsequently located the headquarters of the new command at Wright-Patterson Air Force Base, Ohio. Disagreement about ARDC's mission continued throughout the year. Finally, on March 22, 1951, the Air Materiel Command formed the Air Development Center, Provisional. This independent organization resulted from the separation of AMC's research and development directorate.

The new Development Center received the Air Materiel Command's Engineering, Flight Test, and All-Weather Flying Divisions. The Air Force also transferred the applied research function of the recently-created Office of Air Research. On April 2, 1951, ARDC became a major Air Force command, and in June moved its headquarters to Baltimore, Maryland. Also on April 2, 1951, the Air Force established the Air Development Force at Wright Field; on June 7, the Wright Air Development Center (WADC) became the official designation.

The Wright Air Development Center had seven divisions. The *Weapon Systems Division* consisted of the Aircraft, Guided Missiles, Special Weapons, and Climatic Projects sections. The old Engineering Division of the Air Materiel Command had 12 laboratories. WADC officials placed the development laboratories—aircraft radiation, armament, communication and navigation, components and systems, equipment, and photographic—under the *Weapons Components Division*. The *Research Division* contained the Aero-Medical, Materials, and Flight Research Laboratories. The Aircraft, Power Plant, and Propeller Laboratories went under the *Aeronautics Division*. In addition to an *All-Weather Flying Division*, the Center had a *Flight Test Division* with responsibility for missile and aircraft testing activities at Holloman Air Force Base, New Mexico, and Edwards Air Force Base, California. Finally, the *Materiel Division* provided logistical and engineering support and, despite Air Materiel Command objections, in-service engineering. (The Materiel Command, however, regained this function in 1959.)

During the Korean War, the Air Force fought its battles for the first time with jet aircraft. The performance of straight-wing jets, Lockheed's F-80C Shooting Stars and Republic's F-84E and G Thunderjets, was good in the bombing role but inferior to that of their Soviet counterparts in aerial combat. The North American F-86A Sabre, the first American swept-wing fighter, soon established itself as the premier air superiority weapon because of its ability to operate at high speeds and altitude. Lockheed's F-94 Starfire, the first operational all-weather jet, was useful as an interceptor.

When the Wright Air Development Center assumed control of Air Force research and development in 1951, the Air Materiel Command had completed most of the work on

North American F-86A Sabre

Lockheed F-80 Shooting Star

Republic F-84 Thunderjet

Lockheed F-94B Starfire

the propeller-driven Convair B-36 intercontinental bomber and the Fairchild C-119 Flying Boxcar. The Center initiated work on the Lockheed C-130 Hercules turboprop cargo aircraft. The Boeing B-47A Stratojet had already flown in 1950 and Wright Field engineers were directing Boeing's XB-52 and YB-52 Stratofortress projects. In addition, WADC had several missile programs in various stages of development: Martin's B-61A Matador air-to-ground tactical missile, Boeing's XF-99 Bomarc ground-to-air interceptor, Hughes' XF-98 Falcon air-to-air missile, and North American's XB-64 Navaho ground-to-ground intercontinental missile.

Demands of the Korean War and the Air Force need for more B-47s required new management procedures. Early in 1951, the Air Materiel Command had established closer coordination between the engineering and production organizations through the use of joint project offices. With the formation of WADC, the Materiel Command and Wright Center continued to coordinate development and production engineering within the joint project offices. Air Force Regulation 20-10 formalized this procedure. By the beginning of 1954, weapon system project office had become the official designation.

Convair B-36D Peacemaker

Boeing B-52E Stratofortress with AGM-28 Hound Dog Missile

Boeing B-47A Stratojet

Fairchild C-119 Flying Boxcar

Lockheed C-130 Hercules

Boeing IM-99B Bomarc

THE EXPERIENCE OF GENERAL DYNAMICS'
CONVAIR DIVISION

The Air Force implemented the weapon system concept under a prime contractor for the supersonic F-102 Delta Dagger interceptor and later the B-58 Hustler bomber. General Dynamics planned to build the F-102 and the B-58 at its San Diego, California, and Fort Worth, Texas, facilities, respectively. The objective of these programs was to accelerate development of advanced technology aircraft without a prototype phase, a major change since earlier programs had used experimental aircraft. The F-102 would meet the threat of new Soviet bombers beginning in 1956, and the B-58 would be a high-altitude supersonic bomber in operation by 1957. Both designs featured delta wings, a technology Convair adopted from the Germans.

Convair F-102A Delta Dagger

In December 1952, Major General Putt, then Vice Commander of the Air Research and Development Command, outlined the weapon system concept and the roles of the Air Force and the aerospace contractor. Under this concept, the Air Force would consider all aspects of an entire weapon system, including not only the airframe but the engine, weapon delivery subsystems, support and training equipment, manpower requirements, as well as the time needed for development and production. Consequently, the Air Force would plan, schedule, and control the weapon system from design through deployment.

General Putt described several prerequisites for this new approach. The operating commands would specify their requirements. Management procedures for the joint project offices required further refinement. Most significant was the idea of the prime contractor, to whom the Air Force delegated design and systems engineering authority for a total weapon system. The Air Force project engineer was responsible for monitoring this work. In spite of the Ridenour committee's recommendation to strengthen Air Force engineering resources, this approach meant a continued reliance on the contractor.

A supersonic interceptor required an automatic fire control system and in July 1950, the Hughes Aircraft Company received a contract for this work. After several studies, the Air Force gave Convair responsibility for F-102 development in September 1951. Originally designed for Mach 2, this aircraft would be capable of Mach 1.3 flight at altitudes of 60,000 feet, with a combat radius of 375 nautical miles. Its operation would be tied automatically to a ground control system.

The Air Force then introduced a production approach developed by Lieutenant Generals Orval R. Cook and Laurence C. Craigie, both of Air Force Headquarters. By proceeding with the use of production tooling to build the first flight article, a weapon system could be placed into operation in less time. All phases of the program—early flight test through production—would involve the same airframe. Generals Cook and Craigie argued that hand-built

Convair B-58 Hustler

experimental aircraft could not provide suitable test data. Program managers would set initial production at a minimum rate to provide a sufficient number of test aircraft. These would be equipped with available production components. After enough testing, Air Force Headquarters would authorize full production, and the test aircraft would be modified to the final configuration—both to finish the test program and to enter the operational inventory. The Cook-Craigie plan committed the Air Force to production early in the program, thus accelerating the acquisition process.

Development problems relegated the F-102 to the role of an interim interceptor. The Wright J67 engine could not be qualified and had to be replaced with the less powerful Pratt & Whitney J57 engine, which was already slated for the North American F-100 Super Sabre and B-52 aircraft. Hughes could not deliver its advanced MX-1179 fire control system, and the Air Force had to substitute the contractor's older E-9 system. Due to a redesign of the Hughes GAR-1 Falcon missile, Convair had to change the F-102 weapon bay, which increased the weight of the aircraft. Also, because of poor transonic performance in flight test, Convair had to significantly alter the fuselage configuration. All of these problems complicated the advanced production tooling concept of Generals Cook and Craigie. By 1957, the cost of the F-102 had more than doubled.

Convair delivered the first operational F-102 in May 1956. Even with these changes, the Air Defense Command was not satisfied with its performance or fire control system capability. The Air Force turned to a more advanced version, Convair's F-106 Delta Dart, which entered the inventory in 1959.

Convair F-106 Delta Dart

In February 1953, the Air Force and Convair completed contractual arrangements for development of a medium-range, high-altitude, high-speed bomber. This became the Mach 2 B-58 Hustler, the first supersonic bomber. Early in 1954, the Air Force questioned whether Convair could provide a suitable aircraft and, therefore, cut the program from 244 bombers to 30 test vehicles. This reduction was facilitated by lack of Strategic Air Command support for the B-58 because of its short range. Eventually, the Air Force initiated production, but with considerable increase in program cost. The Air Force acquired only 116, including test and operational aircraft. The first operational Hustler was delivered in November 1959; the fleet was retired in 1970.

The search for the proper management structure and procedures for such advanced programs as the supersonic F-102 and B-58 continued.

MARKING THE NEW DIRECTION 1954-1959

Brig. Gen. Bernard A. Schriever brought the SM-65 Atlas intercontinental ballistic missile into the operational inventory after a development effort of only five and a half years. His methods would profoundly influence the acquisition process. This new approach combined authority for research and development with production, utilized a complete program plan or package, and established a distinct engineering organization.

Late in 1953, the Department of the Air Force convened a Strategic Missiles Evaluation Committee. The committee stressed that an intercontinental ballistic missile could only be developed through exceptional management techniques. Accordingly, in July 1954, the Air Research and Development Command established the Western Development Division under the direction of General Schriever. While he reported to the Air Research and Development Commander, he also had access to the other major commands and Air Force Headquarters.

An important missile study of the time criticized the prime contractor concept, insisting upon an independent organization for engineering. The Western Development Division accepted this idea and awarded a contract to the Ramo-Wooldridge Corporation for technical direction and systems engineering on the SM-65 program. In 1959, the Command and Control Division at Hanscom Air Force Base, Massachusetts, contracted with the MITRE Corporation for support of new development programs.

At the same time, the ARDC Commander, Lt. Gen. Thomas S. Power, considered transferring his headquarters from Baltimore to Wright Field, the center of systems development. The ARDC command structure then included the Commander for the Western Development Division and the Deputy Commanders for Technical Operations and Support Operations, but a command study recommended transferring responsibility for program management to the headquarters by establishing a Deputy Commander for Weapon Systems. Some difficulties had previously arisen because the Wright Air Development Center had to exercise control over other centers in ARDC, such as for flight testing activities. Rather than moving, however, in July 1955 ARDC formed the Deputy Commander for Weapon Systems within the headquarters and assumed managerial control of WADC's Directorate of Weapon Systems Operations. In August, the Command created its Detachment One at Wright Field as the organization to possess the project offices. WADC now only consisted of the twelve laboratories and the Directorates of Flight and All-Weather Testing.

To some degree, the arrangements at Command headquarters and Wright Field approximated those of the Western Development Division. There was a Deputy Commander for Weapon Systems, and WADC responsibilities were similar to the functions of Ramo-Wooldridge. The Soviet Union's launching of the first artificial earth satellite in October 1957, however, placed renewed emphasis on research and development and organizational changes.

PLANNING FOR A NEW COMMAND

To many Americans, the Sputnik satellite indicated the superior state of Soviet technology, particularly military weaponry. In November 1957, the Air Staff directed the Scientific Advisory Board to examine Air Force research and development. Dr. H. Guyford Stever of the Massachusetts Institute of Technology chaired a committee for this assignment. Dr. Stever submitted his report to the Air Force in June 1958.

The Stever committee offered four major recommendations for the Air Research and Development Command. It favored creating four functional field divisions within ARDC: research, technical development, testing, and systems management. Opposing the headquarters deputy commanders structure, the committee favored delegating greater program authority to these field units. Furthermore, it concluded that ARDC required the procurement and production function from AMC to better fulfill its mission, and the project director for a weapon system needed overall authority for the program. These proposals contradicted the 1955 ARDC reorganization of Wright Field but were in agreement with General Schriever's experience on the Atlas program.

The Air Force reacted negatively to the Stever report. Both the Air Materiel Command and the Air Research and Development Command pointed to far-reaching implications for their responsibilities, organization, and operations. Air Force Headquarters described the report as too general, and said that any direction had to come from that level. Nevertheless, the Stever report foreshadowed changes in systems management.

The appointment of Lieutenant General Schriever as Commander of the Air Research and Development Command in April 1959 was indicative of renewed Air Force interest in the questions raised by the Stever committee. In May 1959, Gen. Curtis E. LeMay, Air Force Vice Chief of Staff, initiated a review of the formal procedure for acquiring weapon and support systems. He appointed Gen. Samuel E. Anderson, Commander of the Air Materiel Command, as Chairman of the Weapon System Management Group. The Group performed its assignment during 1959 and 1960. A key issue concerned combining research and development with procurement and production.

The study group formulated principles for a new approach. These included the idea of centralized program authority; specific program phases, with a separate management office for each phase; and a system package. There would be a single-program manager with supervisory authority for management, engineering, and procurement personnel. The program cycle would consist of three phases. The Air Staff would have authority for the conceptual phase. The system centers—ballistic, space, aeronautical, and electronic—would handle development, testing, and production for the acquisition (development and production) phase. The using command would have responsibility for the operational phase. The system package would represent a comprehensive planning and programming document encompassing all the milestones and events for developing and producing the system. Many of these ideas were subsequently incorporated into the Air Force 375-series of regulations.

The management group, however, could not agree on an appropriate division of authority in the acquisition cycle. One reason for having formed the Air Research and Development Command had been to elevate the role of research as opposed to procurement. There was concern that the example of the Western Development Division would only result in an organization similar to the Air Materiel Command prior to 1951. The process of reorganization, however, was taking new directions.

With a presidential election scheduled in November 1960, a compromise, not a major reorganization, seemed attractive. In June 1960, Gen. Thomas D. White, Chief of Staff of the Air Force, favored this approach. His decision involved the single-manager and a program package. As before, the mission of the Air Research and Development Command only involved research and development. The Air Materiel Command still had responsibility for procurement and production as well as operational support. To implement these changes, the Air Force published the 375-series of regulations in August 1960.

CREATING THE WRIGHT AIR DEVELOPMENT DIVISION

Before the Air Force could make any changes to the systems acquisition process, General Schriever knew that he had to reorganize his command, now located at Andrews Air Force Base, D.C. He certainly was aware of the importance of science and technology to military and political policy, and he wanted his command to be a major instrument for research and development. Therefore, he initiated a review of its mission and organization as the first step towards shortening the time for producing weapon systems.

A committee appointed by General Schriever maintained that the development process could be improved by separating the functions of engineering and management. Such an innovation would assure the proper emphasis for science and technology. This could be accomplished at Wright Field with new directorates for systems management, advanced technology, and engineering. The authority for Detachment One, the Directorate of Systems Management (the project offices), would be returned to Wright Field from the Command headquarters, and the laboratory engineers would be merged with their counterparts from the project offices. While systems planning would be the responsibility of the headquarters staff, Wright Field would manage its aeronautical programs.

Previously, in September 1958, the Air Materiel Command had realigned its Directorate of Procurement and Production to separate the staff and operational elements. This action resulted in the creation of the Aeronautical Systems Center to accomplish the operational procurement and production mission. Center personnel in the project offices had responsibility for procurement and production of aeronautical systems. A parallel Ballistic Missile Center had been established in California.

On December 15, 1959, General Schriever established the Wright Air Development Division (WADD) with responsibility for aeronautical and related systems. The Division had three components: the Directorates of Systems Management, Advanced Systems Technology, and Systems Engineering. The technology and engineering groups came from WADC's Directorate of Laboratories. The Technology Directorate included an Advanced Systems Planning Office that worked on new development concepts. At the headquarters level, General Schriever replaced the deputy commanders with deputy chiefs of staff. Now his Command and WADD were ready to receive the procurement function.

The creation of the Wright Air Development Division and the work of the Weapon System Management Group did not initially inject a great increase in efficiency into the acquisition process. At Wright Field, the authority of the project director was not clearly established. The director of the project office and some of his staff came from the Directorate of Systems Management. The Directorate of Systems Engineering furnished the engineers. The rest belonged to another Air Force command—procurement and production personnel from the Air Materiel Command's Aeronautical Systems Center. The program director, therefore, only had immediate supervision over the systems management people.

To make the project office operate more effectively, officials of the Wright Air Development Division and the Aeronautical Systems Center were preparing a manual, but by the end of August 1960 the Air Force published the 375-series. Now there would be a central program authority, and attention turned to implementing the new directives.

On December 12, the Commanders of the Wright Air Development Division and the Aeronautical Systems Center instructed their respective organizations to prepare for the establishment of system program offices for the XB-70 Valkyrie, GAM-87 Skybolt, X-20 Dyna-Soar, and F/RF-105 Thunderchief programs. The redesignation of the weapon system project offices to system program offices became effective on January 9, 1961.

THE AERONAUTICAL SYSTEMS DIVISION

On March 17, 1961, the Air Force announced a major change in its systems acquisition structure, effective April 1. This included a separate command for applied research, development, procurement, and production—the Air Force Systems Command (AFSC). The Air Force also recognized the importance of supporting its worldwide missions, and the new Air Force Logistics Command (AFLC) received the supply and maintenance function. Basic research was assigned to an independent Office of Aerospace Research.

The Air Force now had a more unified command structure for acquiring and maintaining its weapons. An Air Force Systems Command unit at Wright Field, the Aeronautical Systems Division (ASD), emerged from the combination of the Wright Air Development Division and the Aeronautical Systems Center. The new Division had three major deputates: the Deputies for Systems Management, Engineering, and Technology.

The system program office managed development and production of a weapon system. It was staffed with specialists for program control, financial management, systems engineering, test and evaluation, procurement, contract management and production. Unlike the previous directorate structure, the ASD Commander could immediately charge the new deputies with the systems acquisition mission. ASD also had a Deputy Commander for the B-70 program, considered part of the Command Section. All of the mission deputates received support from the staff elements, for example, Personnel, Comptroller, and Administrative Services.

With a command responsible for development and production, the Air Force turned to new programs. In March 1963, General LeMay, Air Force Chief of Staff, discussed with General Schriever the application of science and technology to the Air Force defense role. This led to a comprehensive study of new weapon systems for the 1960s and 1970s. In April 1963, Project FORECAST began under the direction of General Schriever, with participation by the Aeronautical Systems Division. The study had six main areas: technology; threat; policy and military considerations; military capabilities; cost; and analysis, evaluation, and synthesis.

FORECAST identified selected technologies for materials, propulsion, flight dynamics, nuclear weapons, guidance, and computers, along with their application. The report discussed new and improved capabilities for current and projected Air Force missions in the 1970s. Some of the projected systems included an advanced manned bomber aircraft; an extremely precise air-to-ground missile; and a large cargo aircraft. Areas that required an improved capability included the accuracy of intercontinental ballistic missiles and the mobility of air defense systems.

In October 1963, General Schriever instructed the Aeronautical Systems Division planning deputate to study several recommendations by Project FORECAST. These represented potential acquisition programs for the Air Force. Eventually, the work of the planning deputate culminated with the C-5 Galaxy, the B-1 bomber, AGM-65 Maverick, F-15 Eagle, and AGM-69 Short Range Attack Missile (SRAM).

THE CASE OF THE EXPERIMENTAL VEHICLES

Aside from weapons development, the Aeronautical Systems Division and its forerunner organizations have advanced the science of aeronautics. One example was the X-15 program. In 1954, the National Advisory Committee on Aeronautics, the Air Force, and the Navy agreed to a program for hypersonic and extreme high altitude flight. The Air Force would manage the vehicle and the engine

North American X-15

programs. In November 1955, it awarded the systems contract to North American Aviation and, in September 1956, the rocket engine contract to Reaction Motors, Incorporated. The planners envisioned an X-15 system launched from a B-52 aircraft. The 57,000-pound-thrust engine would operate for 90 seconds, boosting the vehicle to high speed and high altitude. With completion of its flight objectives, the X-15 would glide to its base for a conventional landing. In 1960, the Air Force accomplished its part of the program, and transferred the three vehicles to the National Aeronautics and Space Administration (formed in 1958). On November 19, 1961, the X-15 attained a speed of 4,093 miles per hour, and on August 22, 1963 it reached an altitude of 354,200 feet.

The B-70 program began not as an experimental airplane but as a replacement for the B-52. The Air Force wanted an aircraft that could achieve Mach 3 flight at 75,000 feet. The vehicle would have to withstand temperatures up to 600 degrees Fahrenheit. In 1957, the Air Force chose the North American design, having a welded-

North American XB-70 Valkyrie

steel and honeycomb airframe with titanium in the forward structure. Prominent features included a canard on the long-nose fuselage, a delta wing with fold-down tips, and twin rudders. The B-70 had six General Electric YF93-GE-3 engines with controllable induction systems, mounted underneath the rear fuselage. This design, based on research by the National Advisory Committee on Aeronautics, allowed supersonic shock waves to create a high compression area under the wing, providing greater lift for less drag penalty.

By 1959, however, the Air Force began to question whether a high altitude bomber could penetrate sophisticated air defenses. Technical difficulties, such as fuel-tank sealing, ultimately resulted in only a two-prototype program in 1963. On October 14, 1965, vehicle number one attained a speed of Mach 3. The technology from this program subsequently proved instrumental in the success of the British and French Concorde, which began supersonic passenger service in January 1976, and was useful in the design of several other aircraft.

In December 1957, Wright Field engineers began work on the X-20 Dyna-Soar, an orbital vehicle capable of maneuverable reentry and conventional landing. In November 1959, the Air Force chose a Boeing design for the glider. It had to withstand dynamic pressures up to 1,020 pounds per square foot and velocities up to 25,000 feet per second, with temperatures of 3,650 degrees Fahrenheit. Several advanced materials would be used: René 41 in the structure and zirconium insulated with graphite in the nose cap. Boeing had advanced the project to the point of fabricating the first vehicle when the Department of Defense terminated the program in December 1963 in favor of the Manned Orbiting Laboratory. The work of the Aeronautical Systems Division on the X-20 facilitated the development of the Space Shuttle. The *Columbia* made its historic first flight on April 21, 1981.

INTRODUCING TOTAL PACKAGE PROCUREMENT

The Department of Defense under Secretary Robert S. McNamara recognized that previous methods of acquiring weapon systems had not promoted cost efficiency. Companies had competed only for development contracts, which approximated about 20 percent of overall program cost. They had often submitted low cost estimates and exaggerated statements of technical performance. With a single contractor responsible for development work, such a company gained an advantageous position for the production contract. This had often been the case because the government could not afford the expense of having another company perform similar development to produce a design for competition.

The production phase usually comprised 80 percent of a program. Therefore, Air Force officials in the Kennedy Administration proposed a different approach to procurement—development and production together in one contract. They insisted on competitively-awarded contracts with cost and performance commitments for the complete program. The Air Force anticipated that this approach would offer more economical and timely acquisition programs, as well as minimize production changes and encourage purchases of material from cost-efficient suppliers.

THE C-5A EXPERIENCE

On December 9, 1963, the Aeronautical Systems Division established a project office for a new cargo aircraft. The concept of global air mobility required a transport capable of accommodating large weapons and equipment: big guns, helicopters, and tanks. This aircraft would enable the United States to send military forces and equipment to combat areas without intermediate stops. The new design became the C-5A Galaxy, the largest cargo airplane in the world.

The C-5A was the first system contracted as a total package. Air Force officials considered the design within the state of current technology, and one that would not present any serious difficulty in development. The Aeronautical Systems Division would award contracts to the airframe and propulsion companies whose technical, management, and cost proposals presented the best system cost over a 10-year period. Also, their designs had to meet the minimum standards established by the operational command.

The Boeing Company, the Douglas Aircraft Company, and the Lockheed-Georgia Company received study and definition contracts for the airframe. The General Electric Company and the Pratt & Whitney Aircraft Division of United Aircraft Corporation worked on the propulsion system. In September 1965, Secretary McNamara selected Lockheed and General Electric as the C-5A contractors; the cost for 120 aircraft would total $2 billion.

The total package approach on the C-5A program proved disappointing. Inadequate guidance from higher headquarters left program office personnel confused about the new management techniques. Often, they had to improvise their own solutions. Moreover, managing a total package program required a greater effort than expected. Finally, the C-5A program office was not adequately staffed throughout, and the schedule for the definition phase had been too ambitious.

Lockheed originally had conceived of the C-5A as a larger version of its successful C-141 Starlifter. The course of events indicated otherwise. The Galaxy required different manufacturing techniques, which increased cost. Government funding constraints necessitated an adjustment in the delivery schedule, with a further addition in the price to the Air Force. With program costs rising, members of Congress called for terminating the C-5A program. In November 1969, the Air Force decided to limit its purchase to 81 aircraft, but at a price more than two times the estimate for the original 120 aircraft.

Lockheed C-5A Galaxy

Lockheed C-141A Starlifter

The Air Force faced major service problems with the C-5A wing. Static and fatigue test failures between 1969 and 1973, along with wing cracks in operational aircraft, convinced officials that the service life of the wing was only 8,000 hours rather than the required 30,000. In order to meet a strict contractual aircraft weight requirement, Lockheed had reduced the strength of the wing too much. This necessitated a later modification program to provide a new wing structure for the Galaxy fleet.

The Military Airlift Command received its first Galaxy in December 1969 and the last in May 1973. The operational C-5As, the only Air Force aircraft capable of handling outsized military equipment, were essential for airlift missions.

The Aeronautical Systems Division had more success with its other total package programs, the AGM-65 and AGM-69 missiles. The AGM-65A and B Mavericks were highly accurate tactical air-to-surface missiles. In conjunction with the Navy and the Army, the Air Force in 1964 established the feasibility of a TV-guided seeker. Four years later, after the definition phase, the Aeronautical Systems Division awarded a total package contract to the Hughes Aircraft Company for the AGM-65A. The Air Force achieved operational capability with this missile in February 1973. In 1978, Hughes completed production of the A model and the optically-improved B version. Program officials had experienced only minor technical and cost problems. The Air Force accepted over 20,000 missiles for its F-4, A-7D, F-111, A-10, and F-16 aircraft.

In October 1966, The Boeing Company received a contract for the AGM-69A Short Range Attack Missile (SRAM). In spite of technical studies, Lockheed's two-pulse, solid-propellant rocket motor required an advance in technology. Missile integration problems with the FB-111A strategic bomber persisted. Nevertheless, both the B-52G and H models as well as the FB-111A reached operational status with the AGM-69A in 1972. By 1975, ASD completed production of the missile below cost.

Hughes AGM-65A Maverick

General Dynamics FB-111A with SRAM missiles

THE WRIGHT LABORATORIES AND THE SYSTEMS ENGINEERING GROUP

After the formation of the Wright Air Development Division in 1959, the Air Research and Development Command placed the 12 Wright Field laboratories under its new Deputy for Technology. The Directorates of Advanced Systems Planning, Aeromechanics, Avionics, and Materials and Processes composed the deputy. This organizational arrangement continued after the formation of the Aeronautical Systems Division in 1961.

As part of the Kennedy Administration's effort to strengthen national defense, the Scientific Advisory Board completed a study of the Air Force laboratory structure in April 1962. Pointing to the different approaches within Air Force Systems Command, the Board recommended placing the laboratories under a single division. The Aeronautical Systems Division had its own research and engineering deputates, but the Space Systems and Electronic Systems Divisions relied respectively upon the Aerospace and MITRE Corporations for engineering and technical support. The Advisory Board thought that AFSC should align ASD's engineering and laboratory resources in a manner similar to that of the Space and Electronic Systems Divisions.

On April 4, 1962, Air Force Systems Command announced the establishment of a provisional Research and Technology Division headquarters at Bolling Air Force Base, D.C. The new Division would be responsible for the engineering and laboratory functions at Wright Field. AFSC officially formed the Research and Technology Division on July 26, and completed managerial transfer of the Aeronautical Systems Division organizations by October 25, 1963. At Wright Field, the Deputy for Engineering became the Systems Engineering Group. Also, AFSC divided the Deputy for Technology into the Air Force Aero Propulsion, Avionics, Flight Dynamics, and Materials Laboratories.

Prior to this reorganization, first the Wright Air Development Division and then the Aeronautical Systems Division began to align the engineering functions according to subsystem specialties. The division commanders assigned engineers to the project office and tasked others to support laboratory functions. Under the new Systems Engineering Group, specialization continued to be refined, but more importantly, the Group collocated its engineers to the program offices. Now they could be more responsive to ASD projects.

By November 1966, the Air Force Systems Command believed that it would be more efficient to return control of the engineering function to the Aeronautical Systems Division. Consequently, Gen. James Ferguson, Commander of AFSC, authorized the transfer effective August 15, 1967. This meant a reunification of responsibilities and ultimately some savings of manpower. The Systems Engineering Group became the ASD Deputy for Engineering.

Air Force Systems Command deactivated the Research and Technology Division on March 10, 1967, and placed the independent laboratories under the authority of its Director of Laboratories. Early in 1974, the Department of Defense became concerned about this arrangement and initiated a study to improve the utility of the laboratories to the Air Force. Apparently rejecting the use of independent engineering organizations, such as the Aerospace and MITRE Corporations, the committee insisted that the Air Force continue a strong commitment to its laboratories. It further recommended combining the four laboratories at Wright Field and eventually establishing a closer association with the Aeronautical Systems Division. On July 1, 1975, AFSC created the Air Force Wright Aeronautical Laboratories, reporting directly to Headquarters AFSC. Finally, on November 1, 1982, AFSC transferred the laboratories back to ASD, making this complex more responsive to weapon systems development.

PROTOTYPES AND SYSTEMS ACQUISITION

When Richard M. Nixon became President in January 1969, the rising costs of military procurement presented a serious problem. As a result, in July President Nixon and Secretary of Defense Melvin R. Laird appointed a Blue Ribbon Defense Panel to examine the organization and operation of the Department of Defense. Their charter required the panel to propose ways to make the Department function more effectively. Gilbert W. Fitzhugh, of the Metropolitan Life Insurance Company, served as chairman for the one-year study. He submitted a report to the President on July 1, 1970.

The panel recommended a more flexible approach for Air Force systems acquisition. Prior to full-scale development, systems had to be tested and the technical risks defined. Greater use had to be made of competitive prototypes, with production decisions following thorough testing. Total package procurement had to be discontinued, as well as concurrent development and production. Also, the Air Force needed a broader base for advanced research, with application to components and subsystems as well as systems.

In 1971, the Department of Defense and Air Force Systems Command issued management regulations to supersede the 375-series. Now the acquisition cycle for a major system would consist of five distinct phases: conceptual, validation, development, production, and deployment. A newly-established Defense System Acquisition Review Council would advise the Secretary of Defense whether the system was ready to advance through each of these stages.

In the conceptual phase, the Air Force determined the need for the capability, decided which areas required further work, and received approval to commence the second phase. During system validation, the Air Force substantiated performance, cost, and schedule factors through hardware development or prototype testing. Design, fabrication, and testing of a pre-production system occurred during development, as well as the necessary support systems. The contractor built the system in the production phase, and delivery to the operating command constituted the deployment phase.

The F-15 program demonstrated that the Air Force was not rigid in implementing this new approach to systems acquisition. After a series of studies, without any aircraft prototype demonstration, the Aeronautical Systems Division conducted a competition and awarded the development contract to the McDonnell Aircraft Company for the F-15 in December 1969. In March 1970, after an 18-month engine prototype competition, ASD awarded Pratt & Whitney a contract to develop the F100 engine for both the Air Force and the Navy. ASD used a Joint Engine Project Office for this effort, located in the Deputy for F-15. This

acquisition provided the Air Force with an outstanding fighter. It was not without its problems, however, particularly in the development of the high performance F100 engine. Innovative acquisition measures, such as giving the program director reporting access to the Secretary of the Air Force, played a role in this success.

DEVELOPING THE A-10 THUNDERBOLT II

The Air Force needed an aircraft capable of destroying heavily armored and mechanized equipment threatening American and allied ground forces. Central Europe would be the principal area of operation. In December 1970, as the

McDonnell Douglas F-15B Eagle

Fairchild A-10A Thunderbolt II

result of a competition, the Aeronautical Systems Division awarded contracts for the construction and testing of prototype A-X aircraft to the Fairchild-Hiller Company and the Northrop Corporation. Fairchild and Northrop subcontracted with General Electric and the Avco Corporation for their respective engines.

The Air Force planned a competitive fly-off between the two companies. This evaluation would emphasize handling and maneuvering, the accuracy and capability for delivering weapons, and integration and operation of the engine with the airframe. In June 1971, the Aeronautical Systems Division also provided contracts to General Electric and the Philco-Ford Corporation to develop a 30-millimeter gun system, designated the GAU-8/A. Additional armament for the A-X included an external load of 16,000 pounds of conventional rockets and bombs.

The competitive prototype flight phase extended from May through December 1972; it consisted of both development and operational testing of Fairchild's A-10 and Northrop's A-9. In January 1973, the Secretary of the Air Force selected the A-10. The Defense System Acquisition Review Council approved development, and Fairchild and General Electric received their contracts in March. The Air Force evaluated the prototype GAU-8/A guns between January and April 1973, and the Aeronautical Systems Division awarded a development contract to General Electric in June. In July 1974, the Department of Defense approved initial production of the A-10 system.

The Tactical Air Command accepted its first A-10 in March 1976. In October 1977, the 356th Tactical Fighter Squadron at Myrtle Beach Air Force Base, South Carolina, became the first combat-ready A-10 squadron. The Air Force sent a squadron of 18 A-10s to Europe in January 1979, becoming part of the 81st Tactical Fighter Wing at the Royal Air Force facility at Bentwaters-Woodbridge, United Kingdom. Subsequently, the Air Force began modernization of its reserve forces with deliveries of A-10s to Air National Guard and Air Force Reserve units. For the first time, these units received new aircraft simultaneously with operational squadrons.

THE CASE OF THE F-16 FIGHTING FALCON

In contrast to the A-X competitive prototypes, the Aeronautical Systems Division used prototypes to demonstrate advanced lightweight fighter technology. In May 1971, the

Lockheed F-104A Starfighter

General Dynamics F-16A Fighting Falcon

Air Force formed a Prototype Study Group. By the end of the summer, this Group recommended several prototype programs. Soon after the study, Lt. Gen. James T. Stewart, ASD Commander, set up a prototype office. In April 1972, the General Dynamics Corporation and the Northrop Corporation won a competition and received contracts to demonstrate their respective YF-16 and YF-17 aircraft. Because the Air Force had no plans to develop or produce either aircraft, there would be no competitive fly-off; however, each had to fulfill identical test requirements.

In 1974, Belgium, Denmark, the Netherlands, and Norway expressed interest in acquiring a replacement for their Lockheed F-104Gs. (The American candidates, the YF-16 and YF-17, competed against the French Mirage F-1 and Swedish AJ-37 Viggen.) At the same time, an Air Force tactical modernization fighter group recommended development of a lightweight fighter to complement the F-15 fleet. With the incorporation of these two ideas into Air Force planning, there was a possibility for a 1,000-aircraft program. On January 13, 1975, the Aeronautical Systems

Division selected the YF-16 and awarded the development contract to General Dynamics.

For the Department of Defense, the F-16 would be an austere fighter and the program would have stringent cost controls. The Defense System Acquisition Review Council approved full-scale engineering development on April 21, 1975. Finally, on June 10, the United States and the four European nations concluded a memorandum of understanding, establishing a co-production program of equal partners. For the first time, European manufacturers would make major airframe and engine components for the United States Air Force. In December 1977, the Department of Defense approved production.

The F100 engine presented a significant challenge as more experience was gained with it and as it was converted for use in the single-engine F-16. Both Pratt & Whitney and the Air Force worked hard to insure that it achieved the required reliability while maintaining its excellent performance. Five years after beginning development, the F-16 became operational in October 1980.

FORECAST AND FULFILLMENT

The aircraft which the Air Force deployed during its early involvement in Vietnam were the supersonic Century-series fighters. The first Air Force combat unit to arrive in Vietnam in 1961 flew McDonnell RF-101C Voodoos. The most widely used in the air war in North Vietnam and South Vietnam were, respectively, the Republic F-105D Thunderchief fighter-bomber and the venerable North American F-100 Super Sabre. In 1962, the Air Force directed the Aeronautical Systems Division to have McDonnell modify the Navy's F-4B design into a configuration for the Air Force. The F-4C Phantom II became operational in Vietnam in 1965. Beginning in June 1965, the Air Force deployed B-52s for missions in Vietnam. Three years later, it began using the General Dynamics swing-wing F-111A as a night tactical bomber. Throughout the Vietnam era, ASD conducted hundreds of rapid-response programs, ranging from modification of cargo aircraft into side-firing gunships to the development of tactical electronic warfare systems and guided bombs.

The Air Force had already anticipated advances in Soviet military forces. To offset these developments, American strategists had prepared a formidable tactical and strategic force for the 1970s and 1980s. Both the F-15 and F-16 aircraft were capable of fulfilling air superiority missions. For ground-attack, Grumman's EF-111A electronic jammer would assist the F-4s, multi-role F-16s, and the A-10s, each armed with Maverick missiles.

Equipped with advanced avionics and the AGM-69A Short Range Attack Missile, the B-52G and H models, along with the FB-111As, would suppress ground-to-air sites and attack enemy targets. The Air Force began development, with the Rockwell International Corporation, of the B-1B swing-wing bomber, which would be capable of low-level flight in order to complete its strategic missions. Although President Carter stopped B-1 production in 1977 and replaced it with cruise missiles launched by B-52s, the B-1B program was started in 1981 to provide a strengthened nuclear deterrent force. Both the B-52 and the B-1B could attack targets with a range of weapons, including nuclear air-launched cruise missiles. These air-breathing systems and future ones would compose America's air arm through the remainder of this century.

Republic F-105 Thunderchief

North American F-100F Super Sabre

General Dynamics F-111A fighter

McDonnell Douglas F-4E Phantom II

Boeing B-52H Stratofortress

THE AERONAUTICAL SYSTEMS DIVISION COMES OF AGE

General Schriever knew that efficiency in weapon system management depended upon the effective use of resources, particularly people. To respond as professionals, the men and women of a modern, technically-oriented air force required the best training and weapons. In the 1970s, the Commanders of the Aeronautical Systems Division initiated a series of management innovations which enabled the technical staff to more efficiently acquire Air Force weapon systems.

As early as 1964, the Aeronautical Systems Division began the process of collocating engineering manpower in the system program offices while retaining control of them in a central engineering office. This enabled the Systems Engineering Group to give specialized help to more organizations simultaneously; fewer engineers had to be located in each program office. When engineers with specific skills were needed, they could be obtained temporarily from the Systems Engineering Group. This provided flexibility in extending assistance and enabled the Engineering Group to give immediate support. In 1976, ASD began the matrices of the procurement, manufacturing, and program control functions.

In the same time frame, the Air Force Logistics Command (AFLC) recognized that the requirements for supporting an operational system had to be established early in the acquisition cycle. However, the Air Force lacked an organization responsible for acquisition logistics. In July 1976, AFLC established an Acquisition Logistics Division to provide necessary logisticians collocated to the Aeronautical Systems Division and other AFSC product divisions. The Air Force hoped that this would lower lifetime costs for weapon systems and related equipment. In addition, the new Logistics Division jointly managed the KC-10A Extender (refueling tanker) and TR-1 (tactical reconnaissance) programs with ASD.

By the beginning of 1980, the Aeronautical Systems Division had several acquisition deputates responsible for a number of programs of similar technology: Propulsion, Simulators, and Aeronautical Equipment. This enabled the Division to improve its management services by gathering these programs into one office. Now ASD was more responsive to the needs of the using commands. In April 1980, Lt. Gen. Lawrence A. Skantze, ASD Commander, established a mission-area structure by creating Deputies for Reconnaissance and Electronic Warfare Systems, Tactical Systems, and Airlift and Trainer Systems in addition to the existing Deputy for Strategic Systems. The F-16 office remained a separate deputate because of the magnitude of foreign sales for the Fighting Falcon.

In August 1982, when Lt. Gen. Thomas H. McMullen became Commander of the Aeronautical Systems Division, he directed the activities of more than 7,500 civilian and military people, increasing to 10,600 as a result of the November 1982 merger with the Wright Aeronautical Laboratories. The Division was more than an organization of civil service and military men and women; it employed professionals—dedicated people, many possessing advanced degrees, and with expertise in science, engineering, contracting, and manufacturing.

The mission and product deputies performed the central functions of the Division. In November 1981, the Aeronautical Systems Division created a separate Deputy for B-1B. The Deputy for Development Planning worked on concepts for new systems. The Deputies for Engineering, Contracting and Manufacturing, and Comptroller assisted through the method of matrices. The Wright Aeronautical Laboratories added their applied research expertise and facilities. The 4950th Test Wing managed flight and test support programs and also modified aircraft for test purposes.

The Aeronautical Systems Division in 1982 represented the culmination of a 65-year search for the proper methods and organization for acquiring weapon systems. The program deputies, usually general officers, were trained in science, engineering, and management. They followed directly in the tradition of Brigadier Generals Wolfe and Schriever. What had once been the extraordinary measures of the past became the normal procedure for developing and obtaining the most advanced aeronautical weapon systems in the world.

ASD COMMANDERS

Maj. Gen. Frederick R. Dent, Jr.	Apr 1951
Maj. Gen. Donald L. Putt	Feb 1952
Maj. Gen. Albert Boyd	Jun 1952
Maj. Gen. Thomas L. Bryan	Jul 1955
Maj. Gen. Stanley T. Wray	Sep 1957
Maj. Gen. Joseph R. Holzapple	Jul 1960
Maj. Gen. Waymon A. Davis	Apr 1961
Maj. Gen. Robert G. Ruegg	Jul 1962
Maj. Gen. Charles H. Terhune	Jul 1964
Maj. Gen. Harry E. Goldsworthy	Jun 1967
Maj. Gen. Lee V. Gossick	Aug 1969
Lt. Gen. James T. Stewart	Jun 1970
Lt. Gen. George H. Sylvester	Sep 1976
Lt. Gen. Lawrence A. Skantze	Mar 1979
Lt. Gen. Thomas H. McMullen	Aug 1982

Rockwell B-1 bomber

XI. THE AIR FORCE INSTITUTE OF TECHNOLOGY

By

Capt. Sanders A. Laubenthal

Wright-Patterson and its people have long played a key role in the forefront of aviation. One vital facet of that role has been in educating those who will continue to forge the future of aviation. The Air Force Institute of Technology and its predecessor organizations have fulfilled that role for over 60 years.

In 1919, the Air School of Application was established at McCook Field —one of the many innovations of Col. Thurman H. Bane, Commander of McCook Field and Chief of the Army Air Service Engineering Division from 1919 to 1922. Bane initiated action establishing the technical school in November 1918, just three weeks after cessation of hostilities in "the war to end all wars." His was not an easy battle to win: people who questioned the need for air power were not easily persuaded to support a military school teaching air power technology.

In a letter to the Director of Military Aeronautics in Washington, Bane wrote:

> Authority is respectfully requested to inaugurate at McCook Field an Air Service School of Application similar to the Ordnance School of Application at Sandy Hook Proving Ground, N.J.
>
> The object of this school would be to give the proper technical training to the permanent officers of the Air Service. . . .
>
> Our old flyers are familiar with conditions at San Diego before the war—such conditions do not spell progress.* We worked until noon only. If the entire afternoons had been devoted to good sound technical training, we would have been in much better shape to have handled the war expansion. . . . The Air Service will never be a complete success until all officers in command of air stations and in staff positions understand the game from its very foundation. . . . No man can efficiently direct work about which he knows nothing.

McCook Field, founded in the fall of 1917, had officially replaced San Diego as the site of the Signal Corps' aviation engineering and experimental activities. In May 1918, when President Woodrow Wilson relieved the Signal Corps of responsibility for aviation development and created an Air Service within the War Department, the organization at McCook was known as the Airplane Engineering Department. After the war, it became known as the Engineering Division, and reported directly to the Chief of the Army Air Service.

McCook Field functioned as a huge experimental laboratory, with scientists, engineers, and technicians engaged in a large number of research and development projects. Bane decided that the best plan in managing such a diverse organization was to adopt some of the methods of private industry. He had the value of each project carefully weighed, its results appraised, and devices set up to measure the progress of each undertaking. In the face of postwar cutbacks and a growing demand for scientists and technicians in industry, Bane had to battle to keep the appropriations and staff necessary to continue all of his essential projects.

Bane resolved part of the problem by turning over some of the research projects to private firms. But it seemed clear that the only way to insure a continuing body of technical experts for the Air Service was to train some. He pursued the idea of an Air Service School of Application and finally, almost a year after his original request for authorization, received a letter from the Director of the Air Service ordering him to begin the course of instruction on November 10, 1919.

As Commanding Officer of McCook, Colonel Bane was the official Commandant of the school. His executive officer served as Assistant Commandant. But both had heavy responsibilities, so most of the work actually fell on the shoulders of Lt. Edwin E. Aldrin, who had graduated earlier from the Massachusetts Institute of Technology (MIT) with a masters degree in aeronautical engineering. Aldrin ran the school for the first few years, first as Secretary and later as Assistant Commandant.

The group that assembled in a hangar for the first official class on November 10, 1919, was small: four lieutenant colonels, two majors, Aldrin, and another lieutenant. Al-

Col. Thurman H. Bane (seated), Commanding Officer of McCook Field and Commandant of the Air School of Application, 1919

---

*In January 1913, the Signal Corps flying school at College Park, Maryland, was relocated to North Island, San Diego. The new site marked the Army's "first permanent aviation school."

McCook Field, about 1922

The first class to complete its studies at the Air Service Engineering School (Class of 1920). Standing (l to r): Mr. LaBaie (Instructor), Lt. Wilcox, Col. Dargue, Maj. Frank, Col. McIntosh, Pvt. Perkins. Seated (l to r): Lt. Aldrin, Col. Benedict, Col. Rader, Maj. Sneed.

drin read them an introduction to the course and gave a copy of it to each officer. In the months that followed, the course envisioned by Colonel Bane became a reality. The class-rooms were small frame buildings and hangars clustered near McCook's macadam-and-cinder runway, and the main educational tools were the blackboard and practical experience. On some evenings, prominent men from colleges and commercial plants delivered lectures illustrated by lantern slides.

AIR SERVICE ENGINEERING SCHOOL

Meanwhile, the battle of postwar reorganization of the War Department had been fought to completion in Washington. On June 4, 1920, Congress passed the National Defense Act which established the Air Service as a combatant arm of the Army. The school at McCook was officially renamed the Air Service Engineering School; the first official class graduated in September 1920.

The second class was more junior in make-up: four majors, three captains, and two lieutenants—among them a Capt. George C. Kenney, who would one day achieve considerable fame. The trend toward lower entering ranks continued throughout the Twenties: fewer majors, more lieutenants and captains.

McCook Field in those years was an ideal place for participation in the development of new knowledge. Aldrin saw that as the distinguishing characteristic of the school. From 1919 through 1921, McCook Field's progress reports to Washington were devoted almost entirely to experimental development and testing: the design (and sometimes the construction) of experimental, pursuit, attack, and observation airplanes; studies and layouts of other airplanes for bombing, night attack, and infantry liaison; work on air-cooled engines, cooling systems, and superchargers; and testing (and sometimes independent designing) of parachutes, leak-proof tanks, photographic equipment, radios, aerial torpedoes, armament, and bombing equipment. Students of the Engineering School participated in many of these efforts.

Lieutenant Aldrin left for the Philippines in early 1922; Colonel Bane retired at the end of the year. But the Engineering School was firmly established by that time, and its graduates were beginning to show their worth. The technological advances of the Twenties made new aerial achievements possible, and many Engineering School graduates pioneered significantly both in technology and in flight. Maj. Follett Bradley of the 1922 class was credited with having sent the first radio message from an airplane; he had also participated in the first airplane-directed artillery firing in the U.S. (in 1912), and in the 1922 Pulitzer Air Races. Lt. Harold R. Harris of the same class was the first American to save his life by means of a parachute in jumping from a disabled airplane.

Another member of the 1922 class, Lt. Burton F. Lewis, later served as project engineer for experimentation with aerial torpedoes and new aircraft types at McCook Field. It

1922 students conduct a test in the McCook Field wind tunnel.

Brig. Gen. George C. Kenney ('21)

was an era when practically every flight was an experiment, and when world records were continually made and then broken.

Many of the Air Service test pilots—among them Capt. George C. Kenney, Lt. John A. Macready, Lt. James H. Doolittle, Capt. Wendell H. Brookley—went through the Engineering School at one time or another. Both Macready and Doolittle were in the class of 1923. Macready won the Mackay Trophy three times: once for the altitude flight, once for the transcontinental flight, and once for an endurance flight of 36 hours, 4 minutes, and 32 seconds. He was the only person ever to receive it three times.

Lt. John A. Macready ('23) in gear used for early high-altitude flights

Lt. James "Jimmie" Doolittle ('23) at the 1924 International Air Races
(Darlene Gerhardt)

Lt. James "Jimmy" Doolittle had also won fame as a pilot before he entered the Engineering School. On September 5, 1922, he made the first one-day flight from coast to coast, spanning the continent in 21 hours and 19 minutes.

A third member of the class of 1923, Donald L. Bruner, made night flying possible through a series of experimental flights undertaken during his service at McCook Field. He invented the first revolving aircraft beacon, flew the first airplane with electric lights, and developed the airplane landing light. In 1922, he established the first night airway in the United States, from McCook Field to Columbus, Ohio. He won the Distinguished Flying Cross for his pioneer work in night flying and was in charge of night flying at the National Air Races in 1926.

Similar pioneering work by Engineering School graduates went on through the Twenties and for many years after. Richard C. Coupland ('24) eventually held patents covering radio control of dynamic bodies, aircraft gun synchronizers, feed mechanisms for aircraft weapons, computing gun sights, aerial mechanisms, and various types of ammunition. Hugh Downey ('25) was active in the development of retractable landing gear and pioneered in air service maintenance. Edwin R. Page ('25) worked in aircraft engine development and was active in the development of self-sealing fuel tanks. Lewis R. P. Reese ('25) was later active in bombsight development. A member of the 1926 class, Carl F. Greene, eventually developed pressure cabin airplanes.* He won the Collier Trophy for pioneering stratosphere flights. In addition, Greene worked on the design and development of metal wing structural configurations to overcome high-speed flutter, as well as tricycle undercarriages and cowlings for radial air-cooled engines. David G. Lingle ('26) did important work in the development of petroleum and fuels.

Capt. Donald L. Bruner ('23) receives the Distinguished Flying Cross for pioneer work in night flying.

*In June 1921, Lt. Harold R. Harris ('22) made the first flight in a pressurized cabin. He flew a specially-configured USD-9A biplane (American version of the DeHavilland DH-9) at McCook Field.

Maj. Carl Greene (left) with an early pressure cabin airplane

The 1924 class in aerial navigation receives training with state-of-the-art equipment.

Marathon distance and endurance flights were important throughout the Twenties. Capt. Elmer E. Adler ('25) was a member of the Round-the-World Flight Committee. When five Air Corps airplanes flew on a goodwill tour of Central and South America, from December 1926 to May 1927, they were led by Maj. Herbert A. Dargue ('20); other Engineering School graduates were also on the tour. They flew in all kinds of weather and climate, braving uncharted mountains, jungles, lakes, and swamps. The flight was hailed as a diplomatic success. Burnie R. Dallas of the 1924 class was in charge of ground operations for the *Question Mark* endurance flight in 1929, when Maj. Carl Spaatz and Capt. Ira Eaker stayed aloft for almost 151 hours by refueling in mid-air.

By 1923, the Air Service School of Engineering had four courses, three for Air Service officers and one for civilian employees of the Engineering Division. The one-year course in General Aeronautical Engineering, primarily airplane design and aircraft engine design, was the most substantial. The school also had a five-month course in Maintenance Engineering—a practical course "for the purpose of training officers in the proper maintenance of aeronautical equipment"; a three-month course in Maintenance Engineering for reserve officers; and a group of six evening courses in aerodynamics, metals, and the like open to all civilian employees as well as officers of McCook Field.

Air Service Engineering School staff and students, 1924-1925. Assistant Commandant Lt. Edwin Aldrin is seated second from left. Lt. Edwin R. Page stands second from left, followed by Lt. Lewis R. P. Reese. Capt. Elmer E. Adler stands second from right, third row.

THE EARLY YEARS AT WRIGHT FIELD

In 1926, the Engineering Division at McCook Field merged with other Air Corps elements to become the Materiel Division. In 1927, the new Division moved to more spacious facilities at the newly-constructed Wright Field. When the class of 1927 graduated from the Air Corps Engineering School (as it was now called), McCook Field was already being dismantled. No class entered that summer. On October 12, 1927, the new facilities were dedicated at Wright Field. A new class entered the Air Corps Engineering School in 1928; classes were held in the Materiel Division headquarters building (now Building 11, Area B).

The physical setting for the school was not the only thing that had changed. During the Twenties there had been a change in philosophy regarding the government's role in aeronautical research. Between 1919 and 1922, Air Service engineers had designed and built 27 airplanes of 11 types at McCook Field. But after 1923, experimental activities began to decline. Money was scarce; and the infant aircraft industry, starving for contracts, became vocal about its desire for a greater role in aircraft development. Maj. Gen. Mason M. Patrick, Chief of the Air Service at the time, had a problem on his hands. As he, himself, later recalled: "Furthermore, at this same Engineering Division, aircraft were actually being built, not in numbers, but a few of an

Maj. Gen. Mason M. Patrick, Chief of Air Service, 1924

Students at the Air Corps Engineering School, 1929. Front row (l to r): Lt. George Tourtellot, Lt. Clements McMullen, Maj. Adelai M. Gilkeson, Capt. Hubert V. Hopkins, Lt. Harold N. Carr, Lt. Muir S. Fairchild. Back row (l to r): Lts. Charles W. Caldwell, Alfred A. Kessler, Jr., George F. Schulgen, James G. Taylor, and John W. Bowman.

experimental character, and again the manufacturers complained that this was undue interference with their enterprises."

After studying the situation, General Patrick became convinced that the manufacturers had a valid point and that the Engineering Division should play a different role. Commented Patrick:

I decided that we would build no more airplanes at the Division and, further, that no more aircraft designs would be created there. We would still maintain a designing staff, but its function would be to pass upon the designs submitted to the Air Service, while it would be available for consultation with outside designers, manufacturers, and those who had ideas to propose.

With the greater role given to aircraft manufacturers, Air Service funds for research and development slowly dried up in the mid-Twenties. The civilian complement of the work force at McCook Field and later at Wright Field grew smaller. This reduction in research had far-reaching effects. For one, the Air Service and later the Air Corps had to depend primarily on private aviation firms for aircraft designs. Since these firms were primarily interested in developing large, long-range aircraft which could also serve as commercial airliners, attack and pursuit aircraft got relatively little attention; the major effort went into the development of bombers.

These changes in philosophy, doctrine, and technology had their impact on the Air Corps Engineering School. Because of the increasing importance of science and the need for specialization, the mission of the school broadened: after 1926 the object of the school was "to train Air Corps officers in the higher phases of aeronautical engineering," providing "a general technical training from the standpoint of possibilities and limitations of Air Corps materiel and equipment, in addition to instruction in the fundamental principles and practices."

1930s student studies the effects of propeller vibration. Line of dust across blade indicates area of weakness.

Class of 1931

Changes in philosophy notwithstanding, the structure of the school in the mid-Thirties was not greatly different from what it had been ten years earlier. The Chief of the Materiel Division was still the official Commandant; the Assistant Commandant was the one directly in charge of instruction and supervision of the activities of the school. He was also an instructor. By 1935, he had a staff consisting of two civilians: an acting Senior Instructor and an acting Secretary.

The Senior Instructor for some years was Ezra Kotcher, who had arrived at Wright Field in July 1928 as a junior aeronautical engineer. His potential as an instructor was quickly recognized, and within months he was assigned to the Engineering School as Instructor in Higher Mathematics. Laurence C. Craigie, a lieutenant in the class of 1935, remembered Kotcher clearly:

> A full-time instructor and a fine engineer. . . . Everybody who went through Wright Field, and this includes people by the dozens who had a three- and four-star rank, all look back on their relationship with Ezra Kotcher as being a very significant element in their career. He was that impressive as an individual.

Kotcher stayed on at the school until the outbreak of World War II.

Some things, however, had changed at the school. The school term had expanded to run from the beginning of

Capt. George V. Holloman ('35) with his Q-2 radar-controlled target drone

Building 12, home of the Army Aeronautical Museum, used by the Engineering School from 1935 to 1939, and from August to December 1941

August to the end of July. The curriculum had been revised to appeal to a younger group of students, most of whom were graduates either of the U.S. Military or U.S. Naval Academies or of civilian technical institutions. The Engineering School had four departments: fabrication, materials and structures, testing, and design.

The school had acquired its own insignia in 1931: a coat-of-arms, azure with a sprinkling of gold stars and a border of clouds; the central design was a Wright Flyer in gold. With this went a motto, *Animis opibusque parati,* "Prepared in mind and resources." But heraldry did not necessarily guarantee elbow room, and by 1935 the school had outgrown its assigned space. In the summer of 1935, the Engineering School moved out of the Materiel Division headquarters into the building next door, an impressive yellow brick structure with a concrete facade featuring square pillars and a frieze of eagles: the home of the Army Aeronautical Museum. There the school remained until the outbreak of World War II.

PRELUDE TO WAR

In September 1938, after British Prime Minister Neville Chamberlain's final trip to Munich to seek peace with Hitler, President Franklin D. Roosevelt called a meeting of his top military advisors. The growing power of Hitler's Germany made clear to Roosevelt the need to build American air power, fast. "I want airplanes—now—and lots of them," he announced. He envisioned an American air arm of 10,000 airplanes of which 3,750 would be combat airplanes, in production in 1940.

The Materiel Division went into high gear. In the past, the Air Corps had acquired about 200 airplanes a year; suddenly it was expected to expand at an unheard-of speed. The responsibility of providing for the increased engineering, procurement, inspection, and testing—with a goal of 5,500 Air Corps aircraft in the inventory by July 1, 1941—was no small task.

With personnel at a premium, the Division could not spare resources for the Air Corps Engineering School. By order of the Secretary of War in March 1939, its courses were suspended for the academic year 1939-1940. It stayed closed for almost seventeen months while the Materiel Division labored to meet the demands of the expansion program.

The Engineering School was able to resume operations on August 1, 1940, for the regular 12-month course. During this period, the Air Corps organization was taking the shape it would carry into war. Air Corps leaders had long been struggling for greater autonomy, and at last they got it. On June 20, 1941, the Army Chief of Staff, Gen. George C. Marshall, directed the establishment of the Army Air Forces, to give the air arm more unity of command and authority to manage its own affairs. When a new class arrived at the Museum building at Wright Field in August 1941, it entered what was technically the Army Air Forces Engineering School.

The Engineering School class of 1942 had been told to expect assignments, after graduation, to work in the engineering and production phases of the Materiel Division. But the march of events outpaced the measured process of technical education. The graduation of the Class of 1942 did not occur.

After Roosevelt asked Congress on December 7, 1941—the "day of infamy"—to declare war between the United States and Japan, Wright Field moved immediately to a wartime schedule, with three shifts operating 24 hours a day. On December 9, 1941, the Engineering School closed its doors. The Army Air Forces was short of technically trained officers; school personnel and students were assigned to vital functions in Production Engineering, Experimental Engineering, and other areas of critical need.

REOPENING OF THE ENGINEERING SCHOOL

While its graduates were proving their worth in so many capacities to the war effort, the Engineering School itself was in abeyance. In June 1942, the regulations pertaining to the school were suspended pending further orders.

Even before the war, there had been a shortage of engineering officers. The shutting off of the pipeline did not help. This was obvious to the Materiel Command, which inherited the engineering and procurement responsibilities of the Materiel Division early in 1942. The Materiel Division had depended heavily on Engineering School graduates to monitor programs, solve problems, and otherwise make the system work. Without them, the Materiel Command had many more jobs than it had qualified men to do them.

By 1943, it became clear to people like Maj. Gen. Oliver P. Echols ('27), Assistant Chief of Air Staff, Materiel, Maintenance, and Distribution that the pipeline must be started again, to produce a flow of younger officers to the Materiel Command in order to insure continuity of effort. Otherwise, who would do the job when one of the handful of existing engineering officers was not available?

The first attempt at a solution was a civilian institutions program. In 1943, sixteen officers from the Engineering Division of the Materiel Command were sent to the California Institute of Technology for specialized training. Other officers were sent to the Massachusetts Institute of Technology, Purdue University, and similar centers. But these programs could not produce technically-trained personnel in the numbers the AAF needed, nor in the specialties—engineering, maintenance, and procurement—that were most critical.

On December 1, 1943, less than two years after the closing of the school, Echols sent a memorandum to the Chief of Air Staff, requesting reactivation of the AAF Engineering School. On March 17, 1944, an Army Air Forces regulation formally reestablished the school, assigning it to the Materiel Command.

Students of the Air Corps Engineering School applied their training in all theaters of World War II. Here three students study an electrical model of an engine similar to those used in World War II airplanes.

Class 44B, Engineering School, in front of frame barrack classroom located across the road from Wright Field proper, bordering the main highway into Dayton (now Springfield Street)

"A SOURCE OF STIMULATION TO THE IMAGINATION OF OFFICERS"

Meanwhile, at higher levels, planners were already outlining the future of the Army Air Forces in the postwar world. Research and development, it was clear, would be part of the picture.

In June 1945, Maj. Gen. Hugh Knerr was placed in command of the Air Technical Service Command (ATSC). Knerr was vitally interested in aeronautical research and development. In the 1930s, he and Clinton W. Howard ('21) had evolved a 10-year plan for the development of successively larger bombers that resulted in the famous B-17, B-17B, B-19, and B-29 aircraft. More recently, he had served as Deputy Commanding General, U.S. Strategic Air Forces in Europe, where he had helped plan a program for exploiting German scientific and aeronautical research. He had, in fact, suggested that the key German scientists and their families be brought to Wright Field, where they could work in an atmosphere conducive to creative thought, with the aid of all the laboratory equipment available at Wright Field.

General Knerr was also concerned with the development of the Engineering School. Early in July 1945, Knerr drafted a memo to Lt. Col. William R. Weems, Assistant Commandant of the AAF Engineering School:

Experience gained in the current war has clearly demonstrated the desirability of expanding the activities of the AAF Engineering School to include a Department of Maintenance Engineering and a Department of Air Logistics, co-equal with the present Aeronautical Engineering activities of the school.

It has been my observation during the past 25 years of the development of aeronautics that the aeronautical engineer has a tendency to seek laboratory perfection at the expense of the hard realities of field utilization. This is not the fault of the engineer. The responsibility rests upon those charged with his training.

We are at the threshold of a new era in aeronautics, both military and civil. That nation will prosper most and survive the longest that has the most realistic appreciation of the time and space factors involved in its aeronautical resources. It will not be sufficient that these resources be perfection itself unless they are available in sufficient quantities at the right place at the proper time. Hence, maintenance and logistics. It is our duty to be *fully* prepared.

Please prepare for my consideration an organization and curriculum for the AAF Engineering School that will accomplish these objectives.

On November 21, the Office of the Chief of Air Staff gave the go-ahead, and on December 5, the AAF Institute of Technology was officially authorized, with an effective date of December 15, 1945. On Air Staff instructions, Lt. Gen. Nathan F. Twining, who in early December had succeeded Knerr as Commander, ATSC, appointed a resident committee of ATSC officers to prepare an operating plan for the proposed institute. Col. Donald J. Keirn ('37) was chairman.

The committee went into session on January 24, 1946, to review the existing plans and decide on such questions as organization and key personnel. In the meantime, the current Engineering School classes were to continue under existing policies until they graduated in April 1946. The Commandant—as soon as one was appointed—was to "assemble a faculty composed of civilian and military specialists with outstanding ability and vision and institute policies designed to assure the faculty continuity, tenure and freedom of thought and expression." The instruction offered was to be designed to "avoid routine job training and . . . stimulate constructive critical scrutiny of present and past practices and equipment." It was to consist of a basic course for all students, focusing on "the development, procurement, supply, and maintenance of AAF equipment" plus specialized courses giving each student specific instruction in one of those areas. Classes were to begin on July 1, 1946, for 200 students; subsequent classes would be even larger, up to 350 students.

While the committee worked out detailed plans for the Institute, the AAF was being reorganized for the postwar world. The Air Technical Service Command became the Air Materiel Command (AMC) on March 9, 1946. The

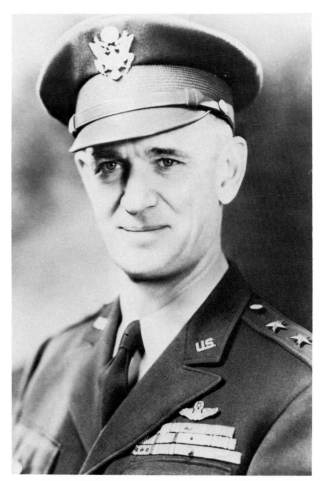

Maj. Gen. Hugh Knerr, Commander, Air Technical Service Command

Army Air Forces University was being organized at Maxwell, under the leadership of Maj. Gen. Muir S. Fairchild ('29). The AAF itself was working slowly towards autonomy as a separate service within a unified Department of Defense.

In May 1946, a Commandant arrived at the Institute, Brig. Gen. Mervin E. Gross, a graduate of the old Engineering School ('33). During the war he had been Chief of Staff for the U.S. Forces in China and later Deputy Assistant Chief of Staff, Personnel, Headquarters AAF. In Washington, he had been one of Echols' most important assistants. He was an extremely dynamic man who liked to fly airplanes, especially the still very new F-80. Ezra Kotcher, who had served as a major during the war, returned in the spring of 1946 as Director of the Institute.

Before long, however, it was clear that classes would not start on July 1. It was taking too long to get the faculty recruited and organized.

Plans, at that point, called for the organization of the Institute into two Colleges—the College of Engineering and Maintenance, and the College of Logistics and Procurement—each of which was to have a dean. Deans, department heads, and at least half of the faculty were to be civilians, so that the program would have continuity. To get good people, the planners hoped to develop within the Institute a "university atmosphere," with security of tenure, dignified surroundings, a reasonable teaching load, and opportunities for research, including a non-teaching quarter each year for each faculty member, to allow time for such research. But in the early summer of 1946, all this was in the future, and the Institute was still trying to recruit enough instructors to start classes.

Finally everything was ready. Eight civilians and five officers—including at least one from the old Engineering School faculty, Albert F. Carson—had been brought on board. Almost 250 students had been enrolled. Two of them—Col. Dan Coupland and Lt. Col. Roy W. Gustafson—had been members of the Class of 1942 that had scattered abruptly after Pearl Harbor.

On September 3, 1946, Lt. Gen. Nathan F. Twining, Commanding General of Air Materiel Command, formally dedicated the Army Air Forces Institute of Technology (AAFIT), in the Institute auditorium. Gen. Benjamin Chidlaw and General Gross were present, as well as other guests, including Col. Donald Putt. The Institute—still part of the Engineering Division, but one of a system of schools under the educational coordination of Air University—was officially in operation.

As fall moved towards winter, the Institute settled into its new format. Each of the two colleges had a one-year graduate level refresher course, and a two-year program of undergraduate studies. AAFIT supervised the education of graduate students at such institutions as Stanford, Princeton, and Cal Tech, and administered all undergraduate education purchased from over a hundred civilian universities. The Institute also monitored the training of officers assigned to civilian industries and administered a graduate program for civilian employees conducted on base by The Ohio State University.

1947 students in front of the Wright Field 5-foot wind tunnel. Their course in Wind Tunnel Testing included study of this early swept-wing model.

YEARS OF DEVELOPMENT

By the end of the Forties, several other important developments had occurred. On July 26, 1947, on board his plane, the "Sacred Cow," President Harry S. Truman signed the National Security Act of 1947, which established the Department of Defense and provided for a separate Air Force. A few months later, on December 5, 1947, the Army Air Forces Institute of Technology became the Air Force Institute of Technology (AFIT) for the first, but not the last time. (This first period as AFIT was brief; on July 16, 1948, the Institute became the USAF Institute of Technology, or USAFIT.)

At the time of the first name change, the Institute had recently completed a significant change in its organization. Prior to 1947, it had been under Headquarters Air Force for policies and the assignment of missions; but organizationally it was part of the Engineering Division. Brig. Gen. Edgar P. Sorensen ('23), who succeeded General Gross as Commandant on January 3, 1947, felt that the Institute belonged at a higher organizational level.* Sorensen sent General Twining a memorandum pointing out that the broad scope of AAFIT curricula took in the interests of all four of AMC's major divisions, not just Engineering, and that there was no real logic in submerging AAFIT within any particular division. He urged that AAFIT be placed directly under AMC.

General Twining thought this made sense. On July 1, 1947, AAFIT was placed directly under the Commanding General, AMC, and a few weeks later was formally given the mission of conducting "educational courses primarily in the field of engineering sciences and industrial administration, at undergraduate and graduate level, for AAF officers, to improve and maintain at a high level the technical competence of the AAF." Shortly after, on September 2, 1947, the Institute transferred most of its Civilian Institutions Program to Air University, in compliance with instructions from Headquarters AAF.

By the end of the decade, the Institute had acquired such a reputation for excellence that it was being given some important projects for student research. One typical project involved the F-86. At the end of the Forties, the Air Force was having problems with the F-86—problems severe enough to ground all F-86s more than once. Gen. Malin Craig suggested that aeronautical engineering students of the Institute investigate the problem and gave Capt. Harold Larsen ('45)—who was to head the investigation—and his students a "blank check" to go anywhere necessary.

The project yielded important results. Larsen introduced into the procurement system the concept of the "learning curve": in-process production changes cause everything to slip back. The remedy: test experimental airplanes 24 hours a day to accumulate flying hours fast and identify problems early enough to correct them in the experimental phase. Backed by Generals Orval R. Cook ('30) and Laurence Craigie ('35), the Cook-Craigie Pro-

Gen. Orval R. Cook

Maj. Gen. Laurence C. Craigie

*The Institute had been stunned by General Gross' death on October 18, 1946, in the crash of his F-80.

curement System kept airplanes from getting into service before they were properly tested. This had been the overall problem with the F-86, and with other Air Force jets of the same period.

The character of the Institute had changed somewhat by the end of the decade. Schools of engineering, logistics, and civil engineering were present, though under different names. The Civilian Institutions Program had returned to USAFIT late in 1948 so that all college-level Air Force education was logically combined in one organization. Graduate level courses expanded, partly through Civilian Institutions, partly through the one-year refresher programs in the two resident schools. In the summer of 1949, USAFIT had also acquired responsibility for supervising the education of Air Force medical personnel, including senior dental students and medical interns. A Plans Division established in 1949 had the feasibility of a nuclear engineering program under study, as well as other projects, including raising the general educational level of the Air Force.

The USAFIT mission was under serious discussion, as was the question of accreditation. The mission was clarified in May 1949, to "provide such education and training as will meet the technical, professional, and scientific training requirements of the Air Force." The accreditation issue rose again with the inauguration of the first real graduate program in the fall of 1949.

In January 1950 a board of general officers recommended that emphasis shift over a five-year period from undergraduate to graduate level instruction, noted that the planned creation of an Air Research and Development Command (ARDC) at Wright-Patterson would attract the faculty to support such a change, and recommended that USAFIT become part of Air University as of April 1, 1950.

On June 19, 1950, Maj. Gen. Grandison Gardner ('27) assumed command of USAFIT. Gardner was a veteran of the old Aviation Section of the Signal Corps, which he had joined in 1917. He was no stranger to the school. Not only had he graduated from it; he had been Assistant Commandant of the small-scale Engineering School in 1930. Since then he had held a series of positions mostly related to engineering or research; he had been one of the principal figures in the early development of radar in the U.S. Most recently he had been president of the Air Force Base Development Board.

Less than a week after he arrived, hostilities broke out in Korea.

"PRESIDENT SIGNS DEGREE GRANTING BILL"

This time there was no abrupt scattering, as there had been after Pearl Harbor.

However, some rapid re-planning was going on behind the scenes. On July 22, 1950, the Chief of Staff, Gen. Hoyt S. Vandenberg, announced that Air Force higher education was to be cut back, so that additional officers would be available to meet "present operational requirements"—

meaning the Korean emergency. Training programs with civilian universities were to be cut back, and the number of officers attending the Colleges of Engineering Sciences and Industrial Administration would be reduced to "a minimum consistent with Air Force requirements in critical technical fields." Part of the reduction was taken as the beginning of the planned phase-out of the undergraduate programs, and affected only nontechnical areas. Part was temporary in nature and was relieved by fall.

USAFIT was reorganized that fall, in preparation for the coming year when it was to begin the active period of transition from undergraduate to primarily graduate education. Instead of two colleges, there was a single Resident College oriented mostly to Engineering Sciences, though Industrial Administration formed a department. The Air Installations School became the Installations Engineering School.

Civilian Institutions was recognized as a Division of USAFIT, with some new programs such as bioradiology and the management of research and development. Through this program, the Institute increased its influence on the content and character of courses taught in civilian schools, helping civilian educators build tailored curricula to meet Air Force requirements. It developed an education-with-industry program, which included plans for training officers on the subject of guided missiles at the plants of several leading missile producers.

As USAFIT moved toward graduate education, it also moved into the age of rapid developments in electrical engineering. Computer technology appeared on campus in 1950, when a seminar on large-scale automatic calculating machines was held to acquaint Wright-Patterson engineers with the principles and uses of the "Mechanical Brain," of which ENIAC was the best-known example. Computer technology was already being applied to weapon systems. In fact, Brig. Gen. Leighton I. Davis, who took over as Commandant on January 22, 1951, had developed the automatic computing gun sights then being used on high-speed jet fighters in Korea.

Five new graduate programs started in September 1951, mostly to fill the needs of the Air Research and Development Command (ARDC)—industrial administration, elec-

Students in the Electronics Lab, 1950

tronics, armament, automatic control, and aeronautical engineering.

One ongoing graduate program achieved new recognition. The Wright-Patterson Professional Graduate Office was a program established through The Ohio State University, as mentioned earlier, to bring graduate education on an after-hours basis to AMC and ARDC engineers and specialists. In the fall of 1951, it awarded the first doctorate ever granted through a USAFIT program: a Ph.D. in Chemical Engineering to Capt. James Bierlein of the Wright Air Development Center.

On October 1, 1951, Brig. Gen. Ralph P. Swofford, Jr. ('36)—the man who had been the first Air Force project officer on the F-80, and most recently Chief of Staff, ARDC—became Commandant of USAFIT. One of General Swofford's primary objectives was to achieve formal accreditation for the school, and the authority to grant its own degrees.

Over the next two years the Institute completed its transition to predominantly graduate-level education in terms of curricula. In September 1953, USAFIT enrolled students in three new graduate programs—nuclear engineering, air ordnance, and servomechanisms and computers—in addition to the earlier engineering graduate programs in aeronautical engineering, electronics, automatic control and armament engineering, and the two logistics-oriented graduate programs, industrial administration and engineering administration.

The accreditation effort was pursued with the North Central Association of Colleges and Schools (NCACS). NCACS had only recently initiated a program for developing criteria for the accreditation of technical and scientific institutions. The draft legislation for degree-granting authority, however, was still under study by the Department of Health, Education, and Welfare (HEW).

On October 30, 1953, HEW called a meeting to discuss the USAFIT legislation in the context of the whole question of federal participation in education, and the special problems faced by the Services in offering high-quality graduate work. USAFIT and Air University representatives outlined the Institute's programs and described the status of the accreditation effort and the need for degree-granting authority. HEW formed an ad hoc committee of educators to study the whole situation and act as an advisory body to the Commissioner of Education.

In December 1953, the committee submitted its recommendations to HEW. As 1954 opened, the Institute waited anxiously for some sort of news. Informal reports indicated that though the Office of Education felt that degree-granting was primarily a function of civilian institutions, they would not close the door on outstanding federally-supported schools which had specific and unique education responsibilities. The Institute hoped to see a degree-granting Bill presented to the 83rd Congress before it adjourned in mid-summer 1954.

Finally, on July 7, 1954, a New Jersey senator introduced Senate Bill 3712, to authorize the Commander, Air University, to confer appropriate degrees. The bill read, in part:

> Be it enacted by the Senate and House of Representatives of the United States of America in Congress assembled, that under regulations prescribed by the Secretary of the Air Force, the Commander, Air University, may, upon accreditation of the United States Air Force Institute of Technology by a nationally recognized accreditation association or authority, confer appropriate degrees upon persons who meet all requirements for those degrees in the Resident College of the United States Air Force Institute of Technology.

The bill passed both houses and reached President Dwight D. Eisenhower by August 31, 1954. He signed it.

The news flashed immediately to the Institute. "The right to grant degrees will give our graduates the recognition they deserve and help in building the school to make its contribution to scientific and technological development in the Air Force," Swofford told local papers that night. The next day, a handbill given to all the students proclaimed the news in bold headlines: "PRESIDENT SIGNS DEGREE GRANTING BILL FOR USAF INSTITUTE OF TECHNOLOGY."

Only one obstacle remained: accreditation. After the passage of the bill as Public Law 733, the Institute contacted the Engineers Council for Professional Development (ECPD)—which gave accreditation only to degree-granting schools—and arranged a meeting with their representatives in November. ECPD told USAFIT that since it could legally grant degrees, the Institute could move forward to accreditation by them.

Meanwhile, at the suggestion of Dr. Floyd H. Marvin, Secretary-Treasurer of the National Commission on Accreditation, a Commission representative visited the Institute from October 19-22, 1954. From this visit emerged an objective study of the status of USAFIT, as recommended by the North Central Association. It recommended that the Resident College make formal inquiry to both ECPD and the North Central Association for accreditation.

The battle for accreditation was about to be won at last. On April 18-19, 1955, an ECPD Inspection Committee visited the Institute to make a careful study of the undergraduate curricula in electrical engineering and aeronautical engineering. On October 14, 1955, the ECPD granted accreditation for both these curricula.

General Swofford was able to announce on October 26:

> Since the ECPD is the only nationally recognized accrediting authority in engineering, this accreditation of the Resident College curricula by them fully meets the requirement of Public Law 733, 83rd Congress for conferral of appropriate graduate and undergraduate degrees in engineering to graduates of the resident programs.

Another name change had also occurred. On September 1, 1955, USAFIT was redesignated Institute of Technology, USAF (ITUSAF).* The Institute gave its first degrees at last. Twenty-two master of science degrees were awarded to electrical engineering and nuclear engineering students on March 13, 1956.

---

*At this period of the Institute's history, names came and went rather rapidly. ITUSAF lasted less than a year. The Institute became Air Force Institute of Technology (AFIT), for the second time, on April 16, 1956, and kept this name for just over three years.

BUILDING A "SPACE AGE CAMPUS"

The same month, the Board of Visitors at the Institute set a major change in motion. The Board recommended that separate schools for engineering and business be established—a plan the Institute had been considering for some time. In July 1956, the Resident Instruction Division (as the Resident College had come to be called) was reorganized into the School of Engineering and the School of Business, each headed by a dean.

The problem of classroom space was becoming critical, especially since the Installations Engineering School was about to extend its 21-week course to nine months to provide more time for management subjects. Air Force Chief of Staff, Gen. Nathan F. Twining, established a special board headed by Gen. Edwin W. Rawlings of AMC, to study aspects of Air Force educational programs. One of the recommendations of this board was that better facilities be provided. Brig. Gen. Cecil E. Combs, the Air Force Deputy Director for Personnel Procurement and Training, stressed the importance of the board's findings because of the shortage of engineers in the United States and the progress of scientific training in the Soviet Union.

The same serious note was sounded by Maj. Gen. Mark E. Bradley, Jr. ('38), Assistant Deputy Chief of Staff for Materiel, when he addressed graduates of the Advanced Logistics Course and the Advanced Installations Engineering Course in 1957. General Bradley reminded the graduates how much had happened since his own days as a student at the Engineering School. At that time, the Army had considered the Air Corps little more than a tool for aerial observation—not even a complete substitute for cavalry reconnaissance—now air power was the first line of defense for the free world. He mentioned the introduction of the B-52 into active units, the development of whole families of missiles, the growing sophistication of electronic devices and controls. "But we must still push the state-of-the-art across the board," he told them, "toward the development and production of still higher performing air vehicles. Directly associated with this is the concurrent demand for accurate programming of both installations and logistics support."

He also made a curiously prophetic comment: "I do not truly believe we are any farther, in a relative way, from space travel today than the world was from world-wide travel in 1457 when Columbus was a boy."

No one guessed on that day in 1957 how soon it would start to happen. None of the group sitting in front of Bradley was to travel in space; but the previous year, a young officer named Virgil "Gus" Grissom had received a diploma in aero-mechanics from the School of Engineering.

On October 4, 1957—less than a month after Brig. Gen. Cecil E. Combs had taken command of AFIT—the world learned that Russian scientists had just orbited a small satellite. Sputnik 1—a metal sphere with four aerials and a radio transmitter—swung around the earth every 96 minutes, its bleeps advertising the fact that, somehow, a country most people considered technologically backward had launched into the space age ahead of the United States.

Gen. Mark E. Bradley ('38), Commander, Air Force Logistics Command

In 1958, Hq Air Force gave AFIT approval to initiate a full-fledged astronautics program at the School of Engineering and in the Civilian Institutions Division. The Institute embarked on a period of frenzied activity aimed at achieving U.S. space power. A masters-level astronautics program was developed, with courses scheduled to begin in July at MIT and in September at the School of Engineering. Its aim was to provide officers with a basic knowledge essential for the analysis and synthesis of vehicles functioning in the extreme limits of the earth's atmosphere and levels of space beyond. Courses in scientific Russian were introduced. The Civilian Institutions Division arranged for training-with-industry courses in Management of Air Force Aeronautics and Space Vehicles. Maj. Alexander P. de Seversky, internationally known authority on air power, came to the Institute to deliver a lecture titled "Air Power is Space Power." Maj. Gen. Bernard A. Schriever ('41), Commander of the Air Force Ballistic Missile Division, spoke at the Institute's graduation on March 18, 1958. "The military must take the lead in developing the space age," Schriever told them. "We must have qualitative superiority. . . . Our response has been too slow to the state-of-the-art advances."

In an interview afterward, Schriever told the press that the Air Force had had a military satellite program in progress for some time and that he knew when the first Air Force satellite was to be launched. He had to know: the space program was very closely integrated with the ballistic missile program. Schriever stated that though the Soviets

Gen. Bernard A. Schriever ('41), Commander, Air Force Systems Command

dominated the space scene for the present, he did not expect that to continue. The first American satellite, Explorer 1, had already gone up, on January 31, 1958. He further alluded to a recent statement of the Secretary of Defense, suggesting that the Air Force might be given the job of putting a man into space.

Schriever's missile program was going full-steam in 1958. The intermediate-range Thor was being delivered to bases in England. The Atlas program was ahead of schedule, as was the Titan; and yet another missile, the solid-fueled Minuteman, was under accelerated development.

All this affected not just engineering research and development, but management, logistics, and installations engineering. AMC had pointed out its special needs in this area, and AFIT had not been neglecting these other phases of its mission. The School of Business finally received its accreditation from the American Association of Collegiate Schools of Business in the spring of 1958, thus allowing the Institute to grant the degree of Master of Business Administration. The Logistics Education and Research Project (LERP) was in the process of becoming a centralized and integrated logistics education program. In August 1958, it was redesignated the School of Logistics. It was relocated to Building 288, Area A.

AFIT had run out of space, and had not been able to initiate any new construction. Consequently, in the fall of 1958, the School of Business also moved away from the

headquarters and School of Engineering, to Building 1455, Area A, a "blockhouse" building just vacated by an Air Defense Command division.

The astronautics program, however, started on schedule—in July at MIT, in September at the School of Engineering. One of the students who entered in September was Capt. Donn F. Eisele, who ten years later would take part in the first Apollo test flight. He and his classmates graduated on August 31, 1960, with some of the first Master of Science degrees in Astronautics ever awarded.

DRAMATIC CHANGES

On October 23, 1958, the Air Force Vice Chief of Staff, Gen. Curtis LeMay, sent a letter to all major commanders encouraging maximum support for AFIT. He asked commanders to interview all officers who qualified for AFIT programs and encourage them to apply. LeMay's letter was given wide publicity; the Air Force hoped to get at least 5,000 applications, from which it would select about 1,500 officers for AFIT programs. The letter was effective; applications went up. But not nearly to the desired level of 1,500.

AFIT certainly made an attractive offer, academically. AFIT—or IT, as it was redesignated as of July 1, 1959, in an Air University effort to streamline school names—had five major elements: the School of Engineering, the School of Logistics, the School of Business, the Civil Engineering Center (as the Installations Engineering School had come to be called), and the Civilian Institutions Program. It was no longer all-male; it had "gone co-ed," as the local papers termed it, in September 1958, with the enrollment of Lt. Col. Mary J. Strong in the School of Business (though actually there had been women in the Civilian Institutions Program for years). But the Institute was scattered all over a large base, in buildings that were grossly inadequate. The reaction of Congress to the Institute's latest appeal for new buildings had been to suggest that maybe it should move to some installation where there was more room, like Moffett Field, California. The Institute had gone through a lengthy study of alternative sites and had been left with the same conclusion: the research facilities it had to have were at Wright-Patterson.

General Combs, the AFIT commander, wanted his new buildings. Even the last Board of Visitors had taken exception to the dispersal of buildings, which in some cases were miles apart, and called for the construction of permanent quarters. So in 1959, another attempt was launched to get adequate facilities for the Institute.

This time the Institute tried a different approach: an effort to mobilize popular opinion. On February 8, 1959, the *Dayton Daily News* carried a full-page display headed "Space Age Campus," publicizing the Institute's mission and accomplishments. The stories also dramatized the Institute's need for facilities, in both pictures and words: "It's like Studying in a Factory—Noisy, Crowded, Too Hot or Cold;" "Library Overflows into Hallway;" "Small Offices

Make Private Counseling Difficult." One article also gave recognition to the efforts of Representative Paul Schenck, of Dayton, who for years had been trying to help the Institute get funding for modernization, and who planned to try again. The publicity effort continued all year, but again the Institute's request for construction funds was turned down.

The situation remained basically the same through 1960 and 1961, though the school itself expanded in scope, and new voices were added to the bid for new facilities. In May 1961, for example, the Institute announced plans to extend the Advanced Logistics Courses from nine to twelve months. The Institute ran all phases of the Logistics School, though some of the teaching was still done under contract by Ohio State University faculty. In July the School was given responsibility for all Department of Defense training in contract administration.

Gen. Bernard A. Schriever ('41), Commander, Air Force Systems Command, visited Dayton in September 1961, making a strong pitch for community support of the Institute's effort to get modern buildings. He mentioned a large figure: $15 million, which would cover not only a proposed classroom building for the School of Engineering, but a full-scale campus complex suitable for 1,500 students, with library, auditorium, and administration building. He characterized the Institute as "a major factor in national survival."

In December 1961, the Institute learned that its request had again been deleted from the 1963 military construction program. But as a result of Schriever's efforts, the Ohio Congressional delegation took a more active role in seeking appropriations for the Institute. Early in January 1962, Senator Frank Lausche of Ohio announced that he would seek an amendment to the general military authorization bill, to provide $4 million for new facilities for the Institute, even though the Office of the Secretary of Defense had not included the item in its budget request. On February 26, Senator Lausche took the problem to the floor of the Senate in an attempt to get the expenditure authorized—the old authorization had expired—and the money appropriated. He read to the Senate portions of an article just written by retired Air Force Maj. Gen. Edward P. Mechling, which alluded to the "run-down, barnlike building" which served as the main facility for the school which provided "the background of the Air Force technical manpower program."

It was an uphill fight. The Department of Defense did not have to spend the money even if it was appropriated; they had killed the project once before. In March, Congressman Schenck added his efforts to Lausche's by urging the House Armed Services Committee to include Institute funds in the budget. On March 15, the House Armed Services Committee approved almost $4.5 million for the modernization of the Institute.

The next step was the Senate. On March 30, the Senate Armed Services Committee heard testimony from Maj. Gen. Augustus M. Minton, director of Air Force Civil Engineering, in support of the new education facility. On April 2, Senator Lausche and General Combs both appeared before the Committee. Lausche made an urgent plea for the inclusion of the funds in the 1963 military construction bill. Combs described Institute programs, telling the Committee that AFIT was helping to close the scientific and engineering gap in the Air Force.

By this time the House had passed the bill authorizing funds for military construction, with the AFIT amendment in it; Schenck and his Ohio colleague, Representative Clarence J. Brown, had succeeded there. They were now working to get a similar amendment to the military construction appropriations bill, which would actually provide the money.

On June 14, 1962, the Senate Armed Services Committee included a $4 million authorization for AFIT construction in the authorization bill—less than Lausche wanted and the House had allowed, but a sum that could still build a suitable classroom building for the School of Engineering. On June 21, in a voice vote, the Senate passed the authorization bill. After it had been reviewed by both houses, President John F. Kennedy signed it on July 28, 1962. The appropriations bill passed the House on August 14, with $4 million for AFIT construction included. The Senate passed it on September 25, and President Kennedy signed it before the end of the month.

AFIT lost no time in getting underway. Bids were opened in early November, and a contract was awarded at the end of the month. On December 18, 1962, ground was broken for the new School of Engineering building, with Gen. Curtis LeMay, Chief of Staff, as guest of honor. Some eighty distinguished guests, including Congressman Schenck, were present; Schenck himself took shovel in hand for the actual groundbreaking, as did Combs and LeMay.

Gen. Curtis LeMay, Chief of Staff, breaks ground for the new School of Engineering building, December 18, 1962.

THE AIR FORCE ENTERS SPACE

While the fight was on to get the Institute a decent roof over its head, some of its earlier graduates had been closely involved with U.S. efforts in space. The X-15 research plane had made its first powered flight in September 1959 at Edwards AFB, California. Maj. Robert A. Rushworth, Class of '54, the man destined to fly the X-15 on more flights than anyone else, flew it for the first time on November 4, 1960. In the course of his thirty-four X-15 flights, he achieved several "firsts" and set several records. On June 27, 1963, he piloted the aircraft to a peak altitude of 285,000 feet, thereby qualifying as an astronaut. On December 5, 1963, he set the unofficial speed record for the unmodified X-15 at Mach 6.06.

The X-15 program went on through most of the Sixties. Another alumnus of AFIT, Maj. William J. Knight ('58), flew the X-15 to an unofficial world speed record of 4,520 miles per hour in August 1966. He, too, earned an astronaut rating in the X-15 by attaining altitudes above 50 miles.

But the eyes of the world were not on test flights at Edwards AFB, but on what was happening elsewhere in the space program. Manned spaceflight was already in the plans. On April 9, 1959, the government announced the names of the men who came to be called the Original Seven: the first Americans selected to attempt spaceflight. Three were Air Force pilots; of these, two—Capt. Leroy G. "Gordon" Cooper ('56), and Capt. Virgil I. "Gus" Grissom ('56)—were graduates of the Institute.

There was much local excitement, especially over Grissom, who was a fighter test pilot at the Wright Air Development Center (WADC). A native of Mitchell, Indiana, he had begun flying as a World War II air cadet, but the war ended before he could complete the program. He had flown one hundred F-86 combat missions in Korea. After studying aeronautical engineering at AFIT, he had begun his test pilot career.

The Original Seven went off to Langley AFB, Virginia, to start training. The space gap was beginning to close. By the spring of 1961, three of the Original Seven—Grissom was one—had been chosen to complete the rigorous final phases of training for the first Project Mercury space shot. On July 21, 1961, Virgil Grissom became the second American in space, making a suborbital flight in the capsule Liberty Bell.*

In September 1962, NASA released the names of a second group of astronauts, nine this time, for the Gemini program. Three of the four Air Force members had studied in AFIT Civilian Institutions programs: Frank Borman ('57), James "Jim" McDivitt ('59), and Edward White ('59).

Neil Armstrong, one of the two civilians among the nine, came from another advanced project in which AFIT was well represented: Dyna-Soar. In September 1961, Maj.

Capt. L. Gordon Cooper, Jr. ('56), member of the Original Seven, holds a model of the Mercury spacecraft in which he orbited the earth for 34 hours May 15-16, 1963, the longest American orbital flight to that date.

Astronaut Ed White ('59) made the first American space walk during the four-day Gemini 4 mission, June 1965.

*The first American in space was Cmdr. Alan B. Shepard, Jr., USN, who made a 15-minute suborbital flight on May 5, 1961. Lt. Col. John H. Glenn, Jr., USMC, made a three-orbital flight on February 20, 1962.

AFIT graduates piloted the X-15 to record speeds and altitudes.

Gen. Bernard Schriever had described the Dyna-Soar program as the most advanced manned aerospace research system the Air Force possessed: a manned space glider intended to re-enter the earth's atmosphere under control of a pilot who would land it at a conventional air base. "The Dyna-Soar will look and act like an airplane," Schriever had told a Dayton group, "in contrast to the ballistic re-entry of the Discoverer and Mercury capsules. Furthermore, it will be re-usable after normal servicing." It would be boosted into orbital flight by a Titan rocket.

Boeing was the system contractor for the manned orbital space glider. But Ezra Kotcher was working on the solution of Dyna-Soar programs at Wright-Patterson; and two former AFIT students—Capt. William J. Knight ('58) and Maj. James W. Wood ('56)—were assigned to the program as pilot-engineer consultants. Wood was chief of the Manned Spacecraft Center at Edwards Air Force Base, where much of the Dyna-Soar work was being done.

Project Gemini—a series of flights by two-man spacecraft launched by Schriever's Titan II—got off to a good start on March 23, 1965. Maj. Virgil Grissom ('56) had been named as pilot of Gemini 3, with Navy Lt. Cmdr. John Young as copilot. Grissom thus became the first American to make two flights into space, though this one was to be something very different from his fifteen-minute suborbital flight in 1961.

The Gemini 4 crew, Jim McDivitt and Ed White, were both AFIT graduates —the first, but not the last, all-AFIT team. On June 3, 1965, they lifted off for a four-day flight. Four hours after lift-off, Ed White became the first American to walk in space. He found the experience so enthralling that McDivitt and Mission Control had to urge him to get back into the spacecraft on schedule.

Gordon Cooper ('56) teamed up with Navy Lt. Cmdr. Pete Conrad for Gemini 5, August 21-29, 1965. This was the longest flight yet attempted—eight days in a tiny cockpit, mostly devoted to medical and technical experiments. At the end of it, Cooper had more space time than any other man—over 226 hours.

This flight paved the way for Gemini 6 and Gemini 7, which were to rendezvous with each other in space. Gemini 7 took off first, on December 4, 1965, with Frank Borman ('57) and Jim Lovell as crew. It was to be a fourteen-day flight, with two main purposes: to prove that weightlessness was endurable for the length of a lunar voyage (eight days) and to conduct the rendezvous.

On December 15, eight days after the Gemini 7 takeoff, Gemini 6 was launched with Wally Schirra and Tom Stafford as crew. After a four-orbit chase, they pulled up alongside Gemini 7 and flew in formation with it for five hours. Then Gemini 6 pulled away, returning to earth on December 16. Borman and Lovell stayed up for two more days. No docking had taken place during this rendezvous flight. That was scheduled for Gemini 8.

NASA had meanwhile selected yet another group of astronauts, fourteen this time. Seven were Air Force. Of these, six were graduates of AFIT programs, either in residence or in civilian institutions: Capt. William A. Anders ('62), Capt. Charles A. Bassett ('60), Capt. Michael Collins ('64), Capt. Donn F. Eisele ('60), Capt. David R. Scott ('62), and Maj. Edwin E. "Buzz" Aldrin, Jr. ('63). This younger Aldrin, in fact, was the son of the Lt. Edwin Aldrin who had helped organize the Air School of Application back in 1919, and had graduated in its first class. Besides the Air Force group, there was Navy Lt. Roger E. Chaffee, who was working on a master's degree in Reliability Engineering at AFIT's School of Engineering when he was notified of his selection. He had to leave in January 1964 for the astronaut training center in Houston, and continue his studies correspondence-style.

Dave Scott ('62) was the first of the fourteen to fly, selected to accompany Neil Armstrong on Gemini 8. Their main task was to dock in orbit with an unmanned Agena target satellite. They launched on March 16, 1966, found the Agena, and docked. But half an hour after the two spacecraft had come together, the crew noticed unplanned yaw and roll movements developing. Something was wrong. Armstrong undocked from the Agena, and suddenly the Gemini began to spin and then tumble: apparently a thruster was stuck open. They shut down the maneuvering system; but they were already drifting much too near the Agena. The only thing to do was return to earth. They came down safely, though in the Pacific rather than in the Atlantic area as planned.

Gemini 9 flew June 3-6, 1966, crewed by Tom Stafford and Navy Lt. Eugene A. Cernan. It featured rendezvous with Agena—no docking, because of an Agena malfunction—and a space walk by Cernan.

Mike Collins ('64) and John Young flew Gemini 10 on July 18-21, 1966. On this flight they docked smoothly with their Agena and used, for the first time, the extra power the Agena was intended to provide. They also rendezvoused with the Gemini 8 Agena; and Mike Collins, in a space walk, went over to the older Agena and retrieved an experimental package.

Gemini 11 on September 12-15 and Gemini 12 on November 11-15, 1966, also involved rendezvous, docking, and space walks. Lovell piloted the final Gemini, with Aldrin ('63) as copilot. During this flight, Aldrin spent five and a half hours outside the spacecraft, testing various devices designed to make space walking easier.

Projects Mercury and Gemini were tremendous successes. Credit belonged, of course, not only to the astronauts themselves, but to vast numbers of people on the ground—people like Lt. Col. Charles J. Gandy, Jr. ('62), who was launch vehicle operations officer for Mercury; Capt. Ernest P. Hanavan, Jr. ('64), who, in the Aerospace Medical Research Laboratories at Wright-Patterson, worked to develop space maneuvering units and other devices for weightless flight. Because of the work of people like these, NASA was already preparing for Project Apollo, in which the objective was the moon.

YEARS OF EXPANSION 1962-1965

Meanwhile, the Institute was moving steadily ahead. On January 1, 1962, it had become AFIT once more—apparently because people had steadfastly refused to call it IT, except with humorous intent. (A favorite journalistic ploy of the IT era had been to play games with the acronym; as one Air Force Times journalist put it, "It—IT, that is—made for some weird reading regs.")

In September 1962, AFIT began providing managerial as well as technical education. A 12-week System Program Office (SPO) Management Course was established to provide advanced management training for AFSC System Program Office personnel. To give formal recognition to this expanded mission, the name of the Logistics School was changed (effective February 1963) to the School of Systems and Logistics.

The learning process

Another major AFIT program got underway in 1962—the Minuteman On-Site Program. Late in 1961, the Strategic Air Command (SAC) had been considering how it could maintain the morale of Minuteman ICBM missile crews who would have to sit at control consoles forty feet underground in the wilderness of central Montana, where the first Minuteman complex was nearing completion. How could SAC get alert, responsible officers to stand by in the Minuteman control stations, with nothing to do but wait for the firing signal everyone hoped would never come? One answer was to offer them incentive: the chance to study for a graduate degree. This solution would also help the Air Force increase its educational level without taking people away from active duty.

SAC approached AFIT about the idea. General Combs, a former SAC officer himself, was enthusiastic. By April 1962, the idea had become a decision: AFIT would start the first SAC program, leading to a masters degree in aerospace engineering, at Malmstrom Air Force Base near Great Falls, Montana. On July 30, 1962, AFIT's Detachment No. 5 came into existence at Malmstrom. Minuteman education programs soon followed at Whiteman Air Force Base, Missouri; Minot Air Force Base, North Dakota; and Francis E. Warren Air Force Base, Wyoming.

The School of Engineering was given initial responsibility for monitoring the Malmstrom program. It had other new programs too, some of them directly related to what was going on in NASA. The Graduate Space Facilities program had grown out of Civil Engineering Center research on the engineering problems of sustained operations in free space and on the lunar surface. The researcher concluded that AFIT needed a graduate program aimed at these problems. AFSC and NASA agreed, and the curriculum in Space Facilities Engineering began in September 1962. Simultaneously, a Graduate Space Physics program got underway, designed to develop competence in dealing with engineering physics problems peculiar to space.

Since the School of Systems and Logistics was still seeking accreditation, the School of Engineering also took responsibility in early 1963 for developing and implementing a full-scale Graduate Systems Management program. Designed to provide a broad background in management, economics, and allied disciplines for technically-oriented officers, the program got underway in September 1963.

A few months earlier, on March 16, 1963, the North Central Association of Colleges and Schools had voted to grant accreditation to the graduate logistics program of the School of Systems and Logistics. On June 3, 1963, AFIT granted its first Master of Science in Logistics Management degrees to the students whose curriculum had been accredited. The first official Graduate Logistics class began a few days later with 19 students—a diversified group, as was typical of the School: mostly Air Force, but with two Army officers, one Navy officer, and one Department of the Air Force civilian.

At the beginning of 1964, AFIT's situation was very promising. The new School of Engineering building was almost completed (Building 640). The School of Systems

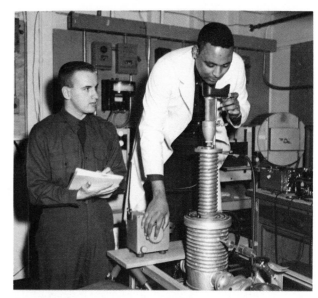

Students experiment with thermodynamics, 1964.

and Logistics was accredited. A study begun the preceding year, on the feasibility of extending the resident academic program through the doctoral level, had concluded that a doctoral program in aerospace engineering was not only possible but highly desirable. A faculty committee was already preparing a plan for such a program. And the new Air University commander—as of January 1, 1964, Lt. Gen. Ralph P. Swofford, Jr. ('36)—seemed likely to approve it.

On the afternoon of August 28, 1964, a distinguished company gathered for the dedication of the Engineering building. The Secretary of the Air Force, Eugene M. Zuckert, was speaker for the occasion. There were some 200 other distinguished guests, including Congressional representatives, educational leaders, senior military officers, and local dignitaries.

Zuckert began by reading a congratulatory letter from President Lyndon B. Johnson. In it Johnson alluded to the doctoral program, which had been approved at Headquarters USAF on August 13: "The establishment of a doctoral level program in the aerospace sciences, announced today by Secretary Zuckert, will expand and strengthen the important role of the Air Force Institute of Technology in our nation's defense program."

Zuckert then spoke of the significance of this new building:

It is a symbol of the coming of age of the Air Force Institute of Technology, as the first permanent structure that the Institute has had since its beginning as the Air School of Application in 1919. It can also be regarded as a vote of confidence in the mission and future of the Air Force Institute of Technology, and it certainly embodies in a very real sense the spirit of mutual esteem and cooperation that has always existed between the Air Force and the people of Dayton . . . the birthplace of man's wings. . . . Finally, this building is a tangible recognition of the place of education in the defense of our country, and the significance of the Air Force Institute of Technology to the future of the Air Force and to the nation.

Building 640, dedicated August 28, 1964, as the new School of Engineering.

By the end of 1964, AFIT had acquired a new element: the Defense Weapon System Management Center (DWSMC). Transferred to AFIT control in July, the DWSMC was to provide education for managers of major weapon programs and to perform research and development of weapon systems management concepts, doctrines, and techniques. The DWSMC began its first twelve-week Senior Managers Course in late September.

VIETNAM ERA 1965-1969

In 1965, President Lyndon Johnson came to the painful conclusion to send U.S. troops to South Vietnam. After Communist attacks on an American stronghold in South Vietnam that spring, he had invoked a policy of sustained reprisal against North Vietnam. Air strikes by U.S. airplanes rose to levels comparable to those of World War II. By the end of 1965, the U.S. had 184,000 troops in Vietnam; another 200,000 went in 1966.

These events had an enormous impact on the whole concept of logistics. As an AFIT historian wrote in mid-1966:

> The waging of widespread counterguerrilla warfare in Southeast Asia under the most difficult circumstances has made for a host of logistical problems that do not lend themselves to conventional solutions. Response to this current challenge has resulted in the development of unusual procedures for the determination of logistical requirements, the replenishment of fighting forces in remote areas, and the maintenance of complex weapon systems far removed from supporting depots. Climate, terrain, and the nature of the conflict have compounded these problems. The human need is not only for competence in the ordinary sense, but also for a corps of logisticians who are imaginative and creative in devising new procedures, who are practical in their approach to emergencies, and who are able to apply scientific methods in the practice of their profession.

The School of Systems and Logistics responded with an ongoing adjustment of its curricula to meet the demands of change. The other schools responded similarly. But the war was affecting the Institute in wider ways: suddenly there were far more people who needed to be educated, not only

beginners but experienced people whose earlier education had been outpaced by the rate of change. At the same time, AFIT operations expanded to an international scale.

International students had been coming to AFIT for decades, and every now and then an AFIT course had been presented somewhere else. The first major overseas expedition had taken place in the spring of 1965, when three members of the Logistics faculty had presented five weeks of logistics courses in Korea to key members of the Republic of Korea Air Force (ROKAF). The instruction was extremely successful—the AFIT team was credited with greatly improving the entire ROKAF logistical system—and inaugurated a series of similar ventures, known as the School of Systems and Logistics International Program.

Faced with a wartime workload, the Logistics school reorganized itself to improve operational efficiency: a directorate for graduate education, another for continuing education, and a third for curriculum review. Continuing education was the fastest-growing area; the increasing complexity of logistics and the growing sophistication of logistical methods had led to greater demands from the field for job-oriented short courses. The school taught some of these courses in residence, but the size of the resident program was limited by available living quarters and teaching space. And there were literally thousands of military logisticians who, for one reason or another, were unable to attend a resident course, anyway. In early 1965, the Logistics school had created a Department of Non-resident Studies to provide courses of two types: on-site courses in the continental U.S. and at American bases overseas; and job-oriented presentations and seminars offered at foreign installations as part of the Military Assistance Program. By mid-1966, the School had greatly expanded its overseas operations; Logistics faculty had taken courses to Hawaii, Japan, France, Germany, Taiwan, the Philippines, Turkey, and Australia.

The Civil Engineering Center was also dramatically affected by wartime demands. The RED HORSE squadrons (Rapid Engineer Deployment, Heavy Operational Repair Squadron, Engineering) had been created to meet operational civil engineering needs in the combat zone. At the request of Headquarters Tactical Air Command (TAC),

Building 125, which houses the School of Civil Engineering, served for many years as the Wright Field Headquarters building.

the Center devised special courses to familiarize RED HORSE squadron members with such things as the kinds of soils they were likely to encounter during construction in Southeast Asia. The Civil Engineering faculty was also caught up in the need to carry instruction to civil engineers overseas. In 1964, at the request of U.S. Air Forces in Europe (USAFE), they had offered the Center's first overseas course in Europe. The following year they expanded the program, offering courses in Germany, England, Turkey, Crete, Hawaii, and Thailand.

The School of Engineering was not immediately drawn into this rapid expansion. Since it was primarily a graduate school, its operations were less ruffled by what was happening in the field. Its major concerns revolved around the new doctoral program which had received preliminary accreditation by the North Central Association in August 1965, and new research facilities, especially the Nuclear Engineering Test Facility. All the preliminary testing of the nuclear facility, located in its own building in Area B, was complete; AFIT had accepted operational control and safety responsibility in November 1965, and a two-year development program was underway. Not only AFIT, but the entire Department of Defense research and development community was making use of the facility for research in everything from biomedical studies to solid-state electronics.

But the School of Engineering, too, was soon drawn into the business of continuing education. A faculty committee was formed in August 1966 to design a short course for the purpose of updating Air Force scientists and engineers. The course was first offered in April 1967 to participants from five Wright-Patterson laboratories and the Los Angeles-based Space Systems Division; it was a great success and the beginning of a regular continuing education program.

The resident programs in all schools were thus going strong, despite the war. The Air Force needed people with advanced degrees, especially in engineering, so badly that instead of cutting back on AFIT programs, it was making a concerted effort to keep the classrooms full. Even people who had not asked for AFIT education, but seemed eligible, were being offered the chance to study at AFIT and urged to accept.

On November 1, 1967, Maj. Gen. Ernest A. Pinson assumed command of the Institute. By the time of Pinson's arrival, the Institute was even more heavily committed to support of the U.S. effort in Southeast Asia.

In the summer of 1966, the School of Systems and Logistics had extended its overseas operations to Vietnam, offering Military Assistance Program courses at Tan Son Nhut, Bien Hoa, Nha Trang, and Da Nang—the first courses of their kind ever presented by the Air Force under combat conditions. In early 1967, one of its faculty had made a two-week survey of South Vietnam to study Vietnamese Air Force supply and maintenance procedures and to develop a program for further logistics education courses. The Civil Engineering Center concentrated on preparing young officers, mostly second lieutenants, for

The AFIT Nuclear Engineering Test Facility, Area B, the only Air Force research reactor

assignment to RED HORSE units in Southeast Asia; it had started taking such classes on field trips to Eglin Air Force Base, Florida, where RED HORSE enlisted personnel were being trained. Members of the Civil Engineering faculty served temporary duty tours in Southeast Asia, solving problems in such areas as construction and the modification of electrical distribution systems. Both schools were involved in Project CORONA HARVEST, an Air Force project designed to evaluate the effectiveness of air power in Southeast Asia. The Logistics school's role was to identify logistics lessons learned in Vietnam, while the Civil Engineering Center documented the role of civil engineering in the logistics support of air power in Southeast Asia.

The School of Engineering was also deeply committed to support of the war effort; but it managed to maintain its research mission, as well. The school's current Assistant Dean for Research, Dr. Janusz S. Przemieniecki, was well known in research and development circles for his theoretical and design work on the Concorde supersonic transport. Beginning in April 1966, he managed the school's broad research program. There was, of course, the Nuclear Engineering Center, but there was also a lot more. Some of the projects were futuristic, like laser research and studies related to the exploration of space; but some had immediate applicability, like a design for a counterinsurgency aircraft.

The Civilian Institutions Division was also involved. In addition to its usual programs in subjects ranging from engineering to medicine, it developed a new program for foreign area specialists—essential to the intelligence field, among others—and unraveled the administrative problems involved in arranging area clearances for students planning field studies in South Vietnam and Thailand.

Many Institute graduates had now been to Southeast Asia, seen combat service, and returned to research and development assignments. Capt. James L. Klaus, for instance, earned a master's degree at AFIT, then went to Southeast Asia as a forward air controller. After earning a

Silver Star, a Distinguished Flying Cross, and numerous other decorations, he returned to Wright-Patterson for an assignment in the Aeronautical Systems Division (ASD). Maj. John M. Clark had similar experience; after earning a master's degree at AFIT and serving in two research and development assignments, he went to Southeast Asia as an A-1E pilot with the First Air Commando Squadron, then came back for an assignment in ASD. Klaus and Clark were among the first representatives of a new generation which combined scientific and technical education with combat experience.

By this time, much of AFIT's resident population consisted of officers recently returned from Southeast Asia. It was not unusual for the Commandant to present well over one hundred military decorations to faculty and students at a single awards ceremony—including the Distinguished Flying Cross, Bronze Star, and Air Medal.

Meanwhile, because of the pace of development in scientific fields, the number of people to be educated seemed to be getting larger instead of smaller. To keep up with the demands for both graduate and continuing education, AFIT turned more and more to advanced educational techniques. The School of Systems and Logistics had been exploring the use of simulation since 1966, to allow its students to study automated logistics management systems and see, in the safety of the classroom, what would happen if certain policy changes were made. The School also developed extensive plans for the use of computer-assisted instruction and other management science techniques in the classroom. The Defense Weapon Systems Management Center (DWSMC) also used computer-supported exercises in its curricula, including a simulation of the entire life-cycle of a fictitious weapon system, from concept through deployment. All the schools were involved in Project IN-NOVATE, an advanced development program concerned with new educational methods and techniques, and Project CREATE, a joint AFIT/AFLC effort to obtain, install, operate, and manage state-of-the-art computer support for educational use.

TO THE MOON

Meanwhile, the space program moved forward. Project Apollo, which aimed at placing a man on the moon before the end of the Sixties, was scheduled to make its first test flight in February 1967. Three former AFIT students—Virgil Grissom, Ed White, and Roger Chaffee—were selected to make an earth-orbital journey of fourteen days, a shakedown test of the Apollo moon ship.

Instead, there was tragedy. On January 27, 1967, just weeks before the scheduled launch, a flash fire swept through the command module where the three astronauts were making a final systems test. All three were killed.

Twenty extremely busy months of investigation and redesign followed. All combustible material in the command modules was replaced with nonflammables—even personal gear like pressure suits and food bags. The side

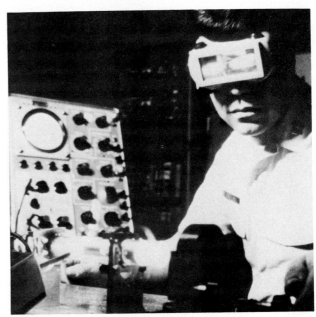

AFIT engineering student performs an experiment in the laser laboratory.

hatch was redesigned to allow swift egress. Numerous other changes were made. Finally, on October 11, 1968, Apollo 7 was ready for the first test flight of the new system.

Even the launch vehicle was new—a vast three-stage Saturn developed by Wernher von Braun and his team. The whole system was longer than a football field and involved over nine million parts. But everything worked, and the three astronauts—Wally Schirra, Donn Eisele, and Walt Cunningham—piloted Apollo 7 into a perfect earth orbit. They stayed up eleven days, giving the new space hardware a thorough test. The splashdown on October 22 occurred within a mile of the predicted landing point.

Two months later, the second manned flight, Apollo 8, was ready to go. This was a major undertaking for NASA and for the crew—Frank Borman, William A. Anders, and Jim Lovell. Not only was it the first mission for the biggest Saturn of them all, Saturn V; it was to be the first time that men ventured beyond earth's gravity. They were going to circle the moon.

On December 21, 1968, Apollo 8 lifted off. After orbiting the earth for almost three hours while the crew made one final check of vital equipment, the astronauts reignited the third-stage Saturn V engine for translunar injection, the burst of power that would propel them beyond the earth's gravitational field. Mike Collins ('64) as capsule communicator—the astronauts' spokesman within Mission Control—was waiting for that moment. He wrote later, "As we counted down to . . . ignition, a hush fell over Mission Control. . . . For the first time in history, man was going to propel himself past escape velocity. . . . This the people in Mission Control knew; yet there were no immortal words on the wall proclaiming the fact, only a thin green line, representing Apollo 8 climbing, speeding, vanishing—leaving us stranded behind on this planet, awed by the fact that we humans had finally had an option to stay or to leave—and had chosen to leave."

On the fourth day, Christmas Eve, Apollo 8 entered lunar orbit. The crew took hundreds of photographs, made scientific observations—and celebrated Christmas, while a hushed world listened, by reading from Genesis the first verses of the story of creation.

After ten revolutions of the moon they started for home. They had seen the most incredible sights mankind had ever seen: the black sky; the grey, crater-scarred lunar surface; and the fragile-looking blue sphere that was earth, rising over the horizon of the moon. Borman was later to say, "When we first were able to look toward home across the moon's horizon from Apollo 8 on Christmas Eve, the good earth appeared very small and very beautiful—an oasis of life in the desolate loneliness of space."

Apollo 8 splashed down safely on December 27. Apollo 9, a second earth orbital mission, flew March 3-31, 1969, with Jim McDivitt, Dave Scott, and Rusty Schweikart as crew. Its mission was to test all the equipment for the manned lunar landing, including the spider-like lunar module never before tested in flight.

Apollo 10—May 18-26, 1969—was the final dress rehearsal for the lunar landing. Its crew—Tom Stafford, John Young, and Gene Cernan—went to lunar orbit and maneuvered the lunar module down to 50,000 feet above the moon's surface for final checkout before returning to earth.

The crew of Apollo 11—Neil Armstrong, Buzz Aldrin, and Mike Collins—were now down to the final preparations for their mission, in which they hoped to actually land on the lunar surface.

On the morning of July 16, 1969, a Saturn V rocket lifted Apollo 11 into earth orbit. An orbit and a half later, the crew reignited the third-stage engine for translunar injection. Soon afterwards, the command and service module, called Columbia, separated from the Saturn third stage, turned around, and connected nose-to-nose with the lunar module, Eagle, which had nestled in a protective container of its own behind the Columbia. (Mike Collins, who maneuvered the Columbia's probe to connect the two modules, later said it was rather like aerial refueling of aircraft.) With the Eagle attached, the Columbia drew away from the third stage and began the flight to the moon.

The earth grew noticeably smaller behind them—white clouds, blue water, four times brighter than the moon against a sky of absolute black. Within a few hours it was so far behind that it hardly filled a single window of the command module.

On July 19, they approached the moon—a huge, cratered sphere, haloed by the sun's corona, partly dark, partly lit by white earthshine. They entered lunar orbit and studied the surface below. The next morning—July 20, 1969—Neil Armstrong and Buzz Aldrin entered the lunar module. Mike Collins threw the switch which released the Eagle from the Columbia. Armstrong and Aldrin began their descent to the lunar surface.

They approached a landing site on the Sea of Tranquility—a crater the size of a football field covered with large boulders. Armstrong took over manual control to avoid the rocks, while Aldrin gave him altitude readings.

When the probes beneath the Eagle's footpads touched the surface, Armstrong shut down the engine. The Eagle settled to the surface like a jet landing on a runway. Armstrong radioed back to Mission Control: "Tranquility Base here—the Eagle has landed."

Later, Armstrong opened the hatch and climbed down the ladder, then halted on the last step. With a sense of the historical importance of the moment, he placed one foot on the surface of the moon: "That's one small step for a man, one giant leap for mankind."

Aldrin joined him on the lunar surface, and they tried walking in the light gravity. They took out an American flag, its top edge braced by a wire to keep it extended, and erected it on a staff pressed into the lunar surface.

Mike Collins, orbiting in the Columbia, kept track of their situation by radio. The public had expected him to feel lonely; instead, he felt very much a part of what was happening on the surface. This venture had been structured for three men, he reflected, "and I consider my third to be as necessary as either of the other two."

The Eagle spent that night on the surface of the moon. The next day, the ascent stage of the Eagle made its critical maneuver up to the Columbia and docked with it. The three astronauts began their return to earth. The command module splashed down in the Pacific Ocean on July 24, 1969, concluding what President Nixon later described as "the greatest week in the history of the world since the Creation."

Apollo 8 astronaut Edwin E. Aldrin, Jr. ('63) was the first military man to walk on the moon.

THE EXPLORATION OF SPACE

Project Apollo continued. On November 14-24, 1969, just months after the trail-blazing Apollo 11 flight, Apollo 12 went to the moon, making a pinpoint landing on the Ocean of Storms. Apollo 13—April 11-17, 1970—went less smoothly: on the way to the moon, the command service module was disabled by an explosion. The crew took refuge in the lunar module, using its oxygen and electricity while Apollo 13 swung around behind the moon and back toward earth. After three days that tested the endurance of man and machine in the hostile environment of space as never before, they made the most accurate splashdown in the history of manned spaceflight.

Apollo 14—January 31-February 9, 1971—was successful. While command module pilot Stewart Roosa ('60) stayed aloft in the command ship Kitty Hawk, Alan Shepard and Ed Mitchell descended to the lunar surface and made the longest moonwalk yet, in the foothills of the Fra Mauro region.

Apollo 15, the most spectacular of the manned spaceflights, took place July 26-August 7, 1971. All three crew members were AFIT graduates: Dave Scott ('62), Al Worden ('63), and Jim Irwin ('58). Instead of landing on one of the smoother areas of the lunar surface, they made the first landing in the mountains of the moon, in a crater in the rugged Hadley-Apennine region. Worden orbited in the command ship Endeavor; Scott and Irwin descended in the Falcon. On this trip they had a Lunar Roving Vehicle to aid their exploration; after setting it up, Scott and Irwin began history's first drive on the moon. They observed the canyon depths of the Hadley Rille, the crater-scarred Marsh of Decay, the towering Apennine Mountains, recorded the spectacular lunar landscape on color television, and gathered geological samples. When they launched the Falcon back toward the command ship, Scott switched on a taped recording of "Off We Go into the Wild Blue Yonder"—surely the wildest yonder ever to have been background for the Air Force tune. Before leaving lunar orbit, the crew of the Endeavor launched a scientific satellite to provide further details on lunar gravity. On the way back, some 197,000 miles from earth, Worden made mankind's first walk in deep space, to retrieve some film from the instrument bay of the command module.

On Apollo 16—April 16-27, 1972—astronauts John Young and Charlie Duke ('64) explored another mountainous area of the moon, the Descartes region. During three sorties in their lunar rover, they gathered lunar material and climbed down into a deep crater to get samples of rock believed to be four billion years old.

Apollo 17, the last mission of the series, took place December 7-19, 1972. For the first time, a professional scientist came along as crewmember and made geological observations in the Taurus-Littow region.

The emphasis was changing: where the first explorers had gone, the professional scientists were beginning to follow. The next major phase of the space program, Project Skylab, was already in the final stage of preparation. Sky-

lab—a Saturn IV-B rocket stage converted into an orbiting workshop, with docking facilities for Apollo spacecraft—was launched May 14, 1973.

One of its solar "wings" was torn away as it left the atmosphere along with its meteoroid shield, and the other wing failed to deploy. When the Skylab 2 mission—May 25-June 22, 1973—took the first boarding party of astronauts up to the orbiting laboratory, they installed an improved sun shield and released the stuck solar panel. They spent 28 days in the orbiting laboratory. The Skylab 3 mission—July 28-September 25, 1973—bettered that record, as the crew spent 59 days in Skylab, continuing important earth and sun studies. The crew of the final mission, Skylab 4—November 16-February 8, 1974—included AFIT's William Pogue. They set a record of 84 days in space, completing the program of experiments and proving that man had the physical endurance to go to Mars.

Meanwhile, the plans for a manned space glider had advanced far beyond the Dyna-Soar program of the early Sixties. The Space Transportation System—better known as the Space Shuttle—was already under serious investigation in the summer of 1969. It was to be essentially an aerospace plane, capable of being boosted into orbit and reentering the earth's atmosphere for winged return flight to earth. Designed as an all-purpose space freighter, it would be used to fly scientists into orbit for research purposes,

AFIT students in front of the School of Engineering building

Astronaut Maj. Guion S. Bluford, Jr. (M.S. '74, Ph.D. '78), with Space Shuttle model

launch satellites and space probes, retrieve or repair satellites, and take sections of space stations or space ships into orbit for assembly.

In early 1977, a series of captive inert flight tests with the unmanned Shuttle orbiter mounted atop a Boeing 747 were fully completed. Captive active tests, with two-man astronaut crews riding in the orbiter during flights on the 747, began that spring. Astronauts like Lt. Col. Karol Bobko ('70) were already training in Shuttle simulators and making tests for the free flight missions which were to follow. The manned captive flights were completed in July 1977. Free-flight tests began in August.

AFIT people were assigned to the Space Shuttle program in increasing numbers—as pilot astronauts; as mission specialists (the scientist-astronauts who would work in the Spacelab the Shuttle would carry into space and back); as detailees to the simulation section at Johnson Space Center, to train the astronauts for their missions; and elsewhere within the vast project.

In April 1981, the Space Shuttle Orbiter *Columbia* was launched on its maiden voyage from the Kennedy Space Center. Fifty-four and a half hours after launch, the *Columbia* re-entered the earth's atmosphere and made a perfect landing on Rogers Dry Lake at Edwards AFB, California. This marked an end of a perfect mission and the beginning of a new era in space travel.

Space Shuttle orbiter *Columbia*, Rogers Dry Lake, Edwards AFB, California, 1981

YEARS OF CONSOLIDATION 1969-1982

As AFIT graduates participated in the space program, AFIT itself was taking steps to consolidate its mission and to address the most pressing educational needs of the Air Force.

The Fiftieth Anniversary celebration of AFIT, in 1970, marked the end of an era of unprecedented activity, expansion, and achievement. AFIT had not only its resident schools and Civilian Institutions Directorate; it also had the Defense Weapon Systems Management Center and the only Air Force research reactor. Its quota of students for officer programs for fiscal year 1969 was 1,720—1,473 of these spaces being for graduate education—and the quota for fiscal year 1970 was for 1,843 officer students, with 1,510 in graduate programs. Additionally there were the Airman Education and Commissioning Program, which involved over 400 students, mostly in technical areas; and the Minuteman Education Program, funded by SAC but managed by AFIT through six detachments at SAC missile bases. The Institute's prestige was high, and its graduates were doing spectacular things like going to the moon.

An era of austerity lay ahead, however. In May 1970, Air University asked AFIT to develop a list of potential programs for reduction, enough to approximate ten percent of the Institute's funding outlay and five percent of its manpower.

The first move toward consolidation involved closing the Nuclear Engineering Center, which was already slated to be decommissioned. On June 12, 1970, the nuclear reactor was operated for the last time, thus ending the facility's brief operational history and its contribution to nuclear technology. This final experiment was the end of a long series of experiments in such areas as activation analysis, radio-chemistry, neutron radiography, radiation effects studies, and bio-medicine. Useable equipment was transferred to other agencies and safely disposed of over the following year.

The Defense Weapon Systems Management Center underwent Department of Defense review beginning in the summer of 1969. In July 1970 the review group rendered its report, recommending that the existing 10-week course for senior project management personnel be replaced with a longer graduate-level course for lower level personnel, and that the entire DWSMC program be moved to the Washington area. On January 14, 1971, the Department of Defense announced that the DWSMC would move to Fort Belvoir, Virginia, as the Defense Systems Management School.

In another consolidation effort, the contract program with The Ohio State University was phased out during 1971 and 1972. Contract faculty members were converted to civil service instructors, so that Continuing Education operated with the same mixture of military and civil service faculty as the rest of AFIT.

Thus, within little more than a year, AFIT had trimmed three of its major elements. It was left with its core, however: the three resident schools and the Civilian Institutions Directorate. After a flurry of reorganizing, the Institute got down to the business of strengthening that core and trying to do more with less.

Continuing education programs of all sorts, from Military Assistance Program short courses to School of Engineering update courses for Air Force scientists and engineers, continued to expand throughout the 1970s. New methods of instruction were also tried: Air War College-type seminars, correspondence courses, closed circuit television, and videotapes for use in classrooms and in a small Systems and Logistics learning center. Among the innovative methods used for continuing education, the most prominent was a format developed by the Civil Engineering School and the School of Systems and Logistics, known as "Telelecture" or "Teleteach." In the beginning it consisted simply of using a speaker phone and a telephone circuit to reach on-site seminar programs; this allowed professors with full teaching schedules at Wright-Patterson to deliver occasional lectures to students elsewhere without the need of travel funds. AFIT was beginning to think in terms of a worldwide classroom.

Special emphasis was also placed on strengthening AFIT's ties with the civilian academic community, and on receiving formal accreditation for all AFIT programs. The Institute's doctoral program was granted full accreditation in 1972.

In 1973, AFIT became involved in the transition to peacetime status as Air Force personnel returned from Southeast Asia. Many former prisoners of war had expressed a desire to enter Civilian Institutions programs. In late January 1973, AFIT learned that they could be entered in any program they wanted, regardless of quotas. Admissions and the Civilian Institutions Directorate moved quickly to make arrangements; a few officers were placed in school as early as June 1973, many more in September.

Overall, AFIT educational programs were still consolidating, however. The undergraduate engineering program at the School of Engineering was quietly phased out, since officers no longer came into the Air Force without degrees. The last undergraduate Electrical Engineering class graduated in June 1975. The quotas for fully-funded graduate education were steadily lowered each year. In the fall of 1974, Congress halted all entries into the Airman Education and Commissioning Program.

Late in 1976, AFIT was given a new school to look after: the Defense Institute of Security Assistance Management (DISAM), which was established to provide education in security assistance management (defense assistance, foreign military sales, and the like). It was not to be part of AFIT, however; DISAM was to remain a joint organization, with the Air Force acting as executive agent. The AFIT Commandant was also to serve as Commandant of DISAM. Beginning in January 1977, DISAM presented a series of short courses aimed primarily at middle managers in the security assistance field.*

Also beginning in 1976, plans were laid for a new graduate program in Strategic and Tactical Sciences. The objective was to prepare officers with operational background for strategic and tactical operations, evaluation,

Building 641, dedicated October 4, 1977, as the School of Systems and Logistics.

analysis, and planning roles in the 1980s and beyond. Under the guidance of Dr. Janusz Przemieniecki, Dean of the School of Engineering, the first class of 15 students—senior captains and junior majors, with degrees in science or engineering and experience as pilots or navigators or missile crew members—entered the Strategic and Tactical Sciences program in August 1977.

In October 1977, Building 641 was dedicated as the new facility of the School of Systems and Logistics. The issue of a new building for the School of Systems and Logistics had first been raised in 1970, but had not received Congressional approval until 1975. The framework for the new building was completed in early January 1976, and the construction crew held the traditional topping-off ceremony. Because it was the Bicentennial year, they placed a Bennington flag and a Bicentennial flag on the final beam along with the traditional evergreen.

The new Systems and Logistics building was completed in early summer of 1977. A monumental three-story structure of light reddish-brown brick, it held classrooms, office space, a branch library, and a computer center. Students, faculty, and staff moved into it in July. At the official dedication on October 4, 1977, the Under Secretary of the Air Force, the Honorable Hans M. Mark, delivered the dedication address. The dedication of Building 641 marked the reintegration of all elements of the Institute at one location, after approximately two decades of separation.

On April 21, 1978, Maj. Gen. Gerald E. Cooke assumed command of AFIT upon the retirement of Maj. Gen. Frank J. Simokaitis. The Institute itself was in a time of transition. As part of Air University, AFIT was brought under Air Training Command (ATC) on May 15, 1978, as the Air Force consolidated its management of both education and training.

General Cooke realized how unique AFIT was—and that it had the potential for even greater things. He formulated three priorities to guide his actions as Commandant: to

*See Chapter IX, Associate Organizations, for further information on DISAM's mission and activities.

integrate the long-separated elements of AFIT into a single, modern Institute; to halt the downward trend in Air Force graduate education; and to lead the Institute into new areas of usefulness to the Air Force.

In the spring and summer of 1978, he began several initiatives to attain these ends. General Cooke first introduced the concept of a single, closely-integrated Institute with four "centers of excellence"—the three schools and the Civilian Institutions Program. During the fall of 1978, a concept study was conducted centering on a realignment of the Institute along functional lines. Among other things, this study called for the movement of certain subject areas—humanities and organizational sciences—from the School of Engineering to the School of Systems and Logistics; the elimination of separate divisions for Graduate Education and Continuing Education within the Logistics school; the elevation of the Associate Dean for Research to the Institute level; the establishment of a centralized scheduling system; and the creation of an Institute-level faculty senate. General Cooke approved the study, and implementation began early in 1979.

Along with this concept of a single Institute went the concept of an AFIT campus—a possibility now that the schools were no longer miles apart. This involved an enhancement of AFIT facilities, in several ways. First, since nothing had been heard for years about the possibility of a third new building, something had to be done about Building 125, the World War II-vintage structure that housed the headquarters and the School of Civil Engineering. Extensive renovation began in 1979. Second, work began on two projects designed to give the Institute capabilities it had not had before: an enhanced library and an updated computer support system. The new computer capability was needed to serve not only the educational mission, but the centralized scheduling envisioned in the realignment, and a considerable expansion of AFIT capability to keep academic records.

General Cooke's second goal was to reverse the downward trend in graduate education and deal with the educational needs of the Air Force. He intended to maximize the potential AFIT offered in the solution of real problems confronting the Air Force.

The problems were unquestionably there. AFIT quickly became involved in finding solutions for three of the most outstanding: the engineer shortfall which was making itself felt in AFSC; the educational needs of Air Force civilians, especially within AFLC; and the almost unrecognized needs for scientific and technical education with the operational commands.

The engineer shortfall problem surfaced first. Gen. Alton H. Slay, Commander of the Air Force Systems Command (AFSC), was particularly aware of a continuing shortage of qualified engineers in AFSC. On June 27, 1978, General Slay wrote to ATC about AFSC's "absolutely critical effort" to get more engineers. "One further means of possible relief, which perhaps has not yet been fully explored, is the manner and degree in which AFIT could contribute to solution of our engineer shortfall problem."

In the Education with Industry Program at the Boeing Company, Seattle, Washington, AFIT student Capt. Gregory W. McKillop confers with the Boeing Industrial Engineering Manager for the 747, Mr. Darrell Cotten.

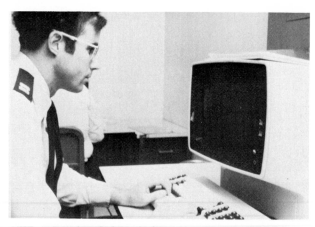

AFIT students benefit from the latest in computer technology.

Lt. Col. James Mayers lectures on Environmental/Sanitary Engineering in the School of Civil Engineering, an AFIT resident program.

SSgt. Russell D. Eslich, student in the Airman Education and Commissioning Program at the University of California

General Cooke assigned members of his staff to develop reasonable alternatives by which AFIT could help alleviate the shortfall. By late summer, AFIT had proposals for near, middle, and long-term solutions.

A near-term solution was implemented in the spring of 1979 in the form of a pilot program known as Crossflow. The goal of the program was to bring officers with quantitative backgrounds to the School of Systems and Logistics and, with School of Engineering support, cross-educate them for positions in systems acquisition management. The first Crossflow class graduated in June 1979.

The middle and long-term solutions, developed in 1978 and 1979, attacked the problem from three directions. One plan was to attract young engineers into the Air Force by offering them graduate education as an incentive: they could go to Officer Training School, then come to AFIT immediately after commissioning. A second approach was to re-establish a program analogous to the former undergraduate program for officers. This time, however, the concept was to select people who already had a bachelor's degree in a scientific field and provide them the education required for a second baccalaureate, in electrical engineering. A third approach was to establish a resident Airman Education and Commissioning Program, to produce graduates with bachelors degrees in computer systems, mechanics, and aeronautics and astronautics.

Another major AFIT initiative in the 1970s addressed the educational problems of Air Force civilians. The Air Force Logistics Command (AFLC) was especially concerned with the educational needs of its civilian force. In August 1978, AFIT presented several proposals to AFLC, two of which were chosen for implementation: graduate

education in the Logistics school for some AFLC civilians, and a special arrangement to provide education through local universities, Minuteman Education style, to civilians at its Air Logistics Centers (ALCs). Twenty-eight people from AFLC and six more from the Defense Logistics Agency entered the Logistics school in 1979, and a program for providing both bachelors and masters degrees at the San Antonio ALC was arranged through the University of Texas. These programs became part of an ongoing effort to provide continuing education for Air Force civilians.

In the closing years of the 1970s, AFIT made a concerted effort to publicize the benefits of its Strategic and Tactical Sciences program to potential students in Strategic Air Command, Tactical Air Command, and Military Airlift Command. In addition, AFIT developed new programs to meet the specific educational needs of these operational commands. Toward this end, a Maintenance Management option within the masters program in Logistics Management was approved in the summer of 1979.

At the same time, the Institute increased its effort to reach out: to the local community; to the vast, hitherto unreachable pool of Department of Defense people who needed the education AFIT could provide; and to the Air Force of the future.

AFIT had always had close ties with the people of Dayton and surrounding communities. Now it sought to strengthen those ties. In cooperation with the University of Dayton's Student Science Training program, high school students were brought to the Institute for special lectures on topics like computers, to introduce them to the technical disciplines. Through a Community Outreach program, Institute representatives participated in high school Career Days and job fairs, provided talks on the Engineering and Logistics programs to high schools, offered guidance and counseling to minority students, operated a worker opportunity program through which it hired students part-time, and supported a cooperative education program which went to graduate level.

As AFIT entered its seventh decade, the challenges of the 1980s and the space age lay ahead. The Institute's motto, "Prepared in Mind," remained the spirit with which AFIT faculty and students prepared to meet those challenges.

AFIT CHRONOLOGY

Air School of Application	1919-1920
Air Service Engineering School	1920-1926
Air Corps Engineering School	1926-1941
Army Air Forces Engineering School	1944-1945
Army Air Forces Institute of Technology	1945-1947
Air Force Institute of Technology	1947-1948
United States Air Force Institute of Technology	1948-1955
Institute of Technology, USAF	1955-1956
Air Force Institute of Technology	1956-1959
Institute of Technology	1959-1962
Air Force Institute of Technology	1962-pres.

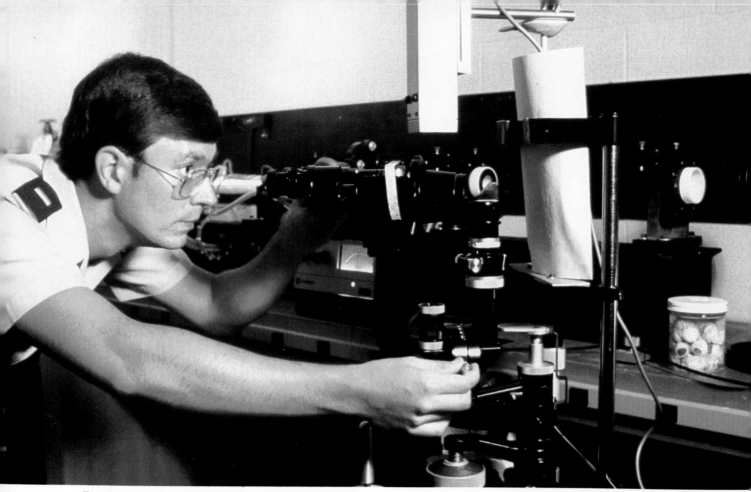

Experimental laser lab project in the School of Engineering

1982 RETROSPECTIVE

In September 1982, Maj. Gen. Herbert L. Emanuel became the thirteenth Commandant of AFIT since the U.S. Air Force became an independent service. Prior to coming to AFIT, he was Assistant Deputy Chief of Staff for Manpower and Personnel, Hq USAF. Col. William J. Schaff, a command pilot with more than 3,900 flying hours, was assigned as Vice Commandant.

Since 1955, when AFIT was first authorized to grant academic degrees, more than 246,000 military members and civilians have attended the Institute, and by the end of 1982, AFIT awarded 772 baccalaureate, 7,301 masters, and 109 doctoral degrees. Many AFIT graduates have gone on to pursue illustrious careers. An AFIT graduate was project officer for the Space Ground Link subsystem, the Air Force's prime system for tracking military satellites. An AFIT graduate was chosen as the only American member of a British expedition to make the first polar circumnavigation of the earth. An AFIT graduate, as chairman of a permanent committee of NATO, was one of the key people behind the NATO decision to buy the E-3A—the unprecedented purchase by NATO of a major weapon system. An AFIT graduate was the first woman military attaché in American history. An AFIT graduate—the first Venezuelan Air Force exchange officer—designed a logistics system for the Venezuelan Air Force and saw it through implementation. An AFIT graduate was responsible for the activation

AIR FORCE INSTITUTE OF TECHNOLOGY COMMANDERS

Col. Thurman H. Bane	1919-1922
Col. Lawrence W. McIntosh	1922-1924
Lt. Col. John F. Curry	1924-1927
Brig. Gen. William E. Gillmore	1927-1929
Maj. Gen. Benjamin D. Foulois	1929-1930
Brig. Gen. Henry C. Pratt	1930-1935
Brig. Gen. Augustine W. Robins	1935-1939
Brig. Gen. Mervin E. Gross	Jan 1946-Oct 1946
Maj. Gen. B. W. Chidlaw (Acting)	Oct 1946-Jan 1947
Brig. Gen. Edgar P. Sorensen	Jan 1947-Aug 1948
Maj. Gen. Laurence C. Craigie	Sep 1948-Jun 1950
Maj. Gen. Grandison Gardner	Jul 1950-Jan 1951
Brig. Gen. Leighton I. Davis	Jan 1951-Oct 1951
Brig. Gen. Ralph P. Swofford	Oct 1951-Nov 1955
Maj. Gen. J. K. Lacey	Nov 1955-Aug 1957
Col. John Tyler (Temporary)	Aug 1957-Sep 1957
Maj. Gen. Cecil E. Combs	Sep 1957-Apr 1964
Col. John A. McCann (Temporary)	Apr 1964-Nov 1964
Maj. Gen. Cecil E. Combs	Nov 1964-Aug 1965
Maj. Gen. Victor R. Haugen	Sep 1965-Oct 1967
Maj. Gen. Ernest A. Pinson	Nov 1967-Jan 1973
Maj. Gen. Frank J. Simokaitis	Feb 1973-Apr 1978
Maj. Gen. Gerald E. Cooke	Apr 1978-Aug 1980
Maj. Gen. Stuart H. Sherman, Jr.	Aug 1980-Aug 1982
Maj. Gen. Herbert L. Emanuel	Sep 1982-Jul 1983
Brig. Gen. James T. Callaghan	Jul 1983

of all F-15 units, worldwide, as the aircraft came into the inventory. An AFIT graduate was a pioneer in hyperbaric medicine, helping to set up a prototype hyperbaric medicine facility and serving as Chief of Diving Operations.

The range and diversity of achievements by graduates of the Air Force Institute of Technology is extraordinary. AFIT graduates have designed a whole spectrum of aerospace equipment, from the world's most accurate inertial navigation system to blast-resistant missile facilities. They have been pioneers in the development of satellite laser communication, magnetically torqued spacecraft, reliable and inexpensive space boosters, flight resolution meteorological satellites, and a host of other innovations. They have researched an array of subjects ranging from high-energy electric lasers, to the effects of ultraviolet radiation on the human eye. They have written books on everything from the integration of the Air Force to their experiences walking on the moon.

The achievements of countless others have never made front-page headlines, but are real and valuable, nonetheless. As one graduate has summed up his experience: "In no small way, AFIT was responsible for preparing me to make my small contributions to the Air Force mission. They may not have been spectacular; but for thousands of graduates over the years, I suspect this is the real story of AFIT."

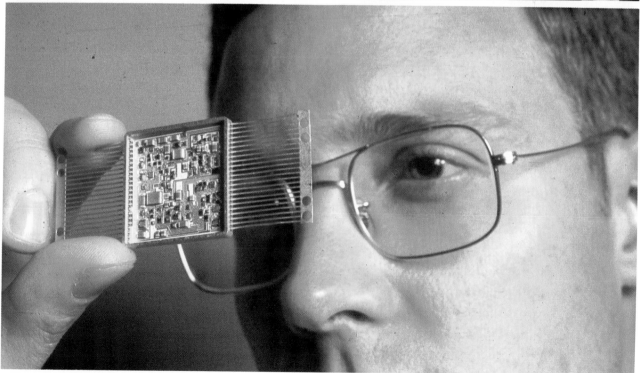

XII. ASSOCIATE ORGANIZATIONS

THE UNITED STATES AIR FORCE MUSEUM

The United States Air Force Museum is internationally recognized as the world's oldest and largest museum of military aviation.

The museum originated in 1923 at McCook Field. In the early days, the museum collection was composed of an informal exhibition of World War I airplanes and equipment. Today, the collection has grown to more than 200 aircraft and missiles, plus over 20,000 miscellaneous aviation items of historical interest.

With the establishment of Wright Field in 1927, the museum was relocated to the new installation along with the laboratories of the Materiel Division, and between 1927 and 1935 occupied 1,500 square feet of space in a laboratory building. In 1935, the museum received more formal recognition when it was moved into a new $235,000 structure (now Building 12, Area B) especially designed to house and display artifacts, which was funded by a government Works Progress Administration (WPA) project. By this time, the museum collection had increased to about 2,000 items. The new home was all too soon destined for other uses, however. The building was closed to the public in 1940, prior to its conversion to wartime use, and the collection was placed in storage.

After the war, the museum program was directed towards collection of items for eventual re-opening of the museum. Mr. Mark Sloan, as Curator from 1946 to 1972, was responsible for locating items for the National Air Museum of the Smithsonian Institution and, additionally, for an Air Force "technical museum" to be located at Wright-Patterson Air Force Base. As a result of his collection efforts, in April 1954 the USAF Museum again opened to the public, this time in a temporary World War II struc-

ture (Building 89, Area C). The 1954 attendance figures totalled 10,000 visitors.

The museum started changing in the late 1950s from a huge open-storage display format to one which featured a unique "maze" floor plan. This more modern display plan directed visitors along a controlled walkway and presented the unfolding story of military aviation in chronological sequence.

Building 12, Area B, 1930s home of the Army Aeronautical Museum

Building 89, Area C, home of the Air Force Museum from 1954 to 1971

The museum had outgrown Building 89 by the early 1960s. It was neither fireproof nor air-conditioned, and was restrictive because of the number of supporting posts throughout the structure, all of which made it unsuitable for properly protecting and displaying the growing priceless collection.

Thanks to the Air Force Museum Foundation, a philanthropic, nationally-recognized non-profit organization established in 1960, the long-standing need for a new structure was finally met with the donation of a $6 million museum building to USAF in August 1971. Formal dedication ceremonies were held in September 1971, attended by President Richard M. Nixon. The museum building, located on a 400-acre site in Area B, was paid for entirely with money donated by the public to the Museum Foundation. A $1 million visitor center was added in 1976 as a gift to the Air Force.

Designed especially to display aircraft, the building provides environmentally-controlled indoor protection for about 100 aircraft. Two large exhibit galleries are connected by a central core which houses a 500-seat theater, administrative offices, a gift shop, a book store, and reception services. Not only does the museum house an extensive collection of aircraft dating from the early 1900s to the space age, but it also includes an art gallery, Medal of Honor gallery, and extensive historical artifacts such as uniforms, diaries, armament, models, prisoner of war items, aircraft engines, an observation balloon, wind tunnels, instruments, and a host of personal memorabilia. In effect, the United States Air Force Museum is the story of people, with the hardware on display to support the historical storyline. Since 1954, annual attendance at the museum has spiraled to over one million visitors.

In recent years, the role of the U.S. Air Force Museum has been expanded to include operation of what is called the "Museum Program." This program includes support of over 24 Air Force base museums and 75 other museums operated by the Department of Defense and numerous civilian organizations here and abroad. Over 3,500 items are now on loan to these museums, including 800-plus aircraft.[4]

Aircraft on static display at the U.S. Air Force Museum

Headquarters complex, Foreign Technology Division (AFSC), Buildings 856, 828, and 829, Area A

FOREIGN TECHNOLOGY DIVISION (FTD)

The Foreign Technology Division of the Air Force Systems Command (AFSC) is headquartered in Buildings 856, 828, and 829 in Area A. The mission of the Foreign Technology Division is to acquire, collect, analyze, produce, and disseminate foreign aerospace scientific and technical (S & T) intelligence to meet the requirements of AFSC, the USAF Assistant Chief of Staff, Intelligence, and the Defense Intelligence Agency. It is the only S & T intelligence organization in the Air Force. Basically, FTD collects all possible knowledge about the strengths and weaknesses of foreign aerospace technology and attempts to provide accurate predictions as to what technologies other nations might develop, in order to prevent technological surprises to the United States.

Under various titles, the Foreign Technology Division traces its lineage directly from the establishment of the Technical Data Laboratory at Wright Field in December 1942. FTD served most of World War II in this capacity, and its operations included the evaluation of foreign documents, aircraft, and related equipment. Part of the related equipment included the dreaded German V-2 rocket.

During the war years, the impact of the radical and advanced design concepts of new enemy weapons forced the Allies to a new appreciation of technical intelligence. The V-2 intelligence analysis was a good example. Several months before the Germans launched the V-2 missiles against London, the Soviets noticed a number of large blast craters on the Polish front. An Army Air Forces intelligence team operating out of the Technical Data Laboratory went to

Poland, retrieved all the fragments in and around the craters, and returned to England. By assembling these fragments, a joint British-American intelligence team was able to identify the weapon as a ballistic missile.

As the war reached its climax in Europe and the intelligence needs of air operations declined, the technical exploitation mission expanded. After the Allied landing on D-Day, Air Forces officers and civilian scientists closely followed the ground armies to exploit captured German research and development (R & D) centers. Wright Field provided the majority of the officers and civilian scientists detailed to this operation.

Meanwhile, important organizational changes were taking place at Wright Field. With the merging of the Materiel Command and the Air Service Command in 1944, T-2 Intelligence was created and replaced the Technical Data Laboratory. This organization continued its major role in exploiting captured materiel, documents, and manpower. On April 27, 1945, Gen. Carl Spaatz gave top priority orders to T-2 Intelligence to complete the collection and transfer of enemy materiel and documents to the United States as quickly as possible.

Late model German aircraft and engines were spotted all over the Reich, but their removal to the United States presented a major logistical problem. Furthermore, a war was still being fought, and although most of the airplanes were either flyable or reparable, they did not have sufficient range to cross the Atlantic Ocean. If these advanced design aircraft were to be saved from destruction, either by friendly or enemy troops, someone had to act quickly.

Col. Harold E. Watson of Wright Field masterminded a bold plan to organize and train pilots to fly out captured German aircraft, including the new jets.* Much of this "acquisition" occurred under enemy fire, and required both bravery and resourcefulness. Scarcity of jet fuel was another major hurdle. On several occasions, German tractors were drained of their diesel fuel so that captured aircraft could be evacuated.

Naturally, the priority items were jet airplanes. In one instance, Colonel Watson located an ME-262 jet fighter, received a quick cockpit check from Willi Messerschmitt, the famed aircraft designer, circled the field, refueled, and delivered the prize to Melun, France. He returned in a war-weary C-47 and checked out other American pilots.

Transportation problems became a prime concern when the British told Watson that a small aircraft carrier, the *H.M.S. Reaper,* would be leaving Liverpool, England, for New York in July 1945. This gave the colonel less than three weeks to get the remaining captured aircraft to Cherbourg, France, to meet the sailing date.

Forty German airplanes were delivered to Cherbourg in 20 days, although some had to be flown in from Denmark and Norway. When deliveries stopped on July 8, 1945, nine jet airplanes, including six different versions of the ME-262, and 30 unorthodox propeller types, had been flown to Cherbourg without a single pilot injury. The operation provided the United States with a flyable model of every German combat airplane.

One of the more interesting stories to come out of the operation occurred in May, immediately following General Spaatz's directive. Colonel Watson had learned that a German defector might deliver a Junkers 290 in Munich, and was on hand to take possession. Within minutes after the plane landed, Watson and his copilot took off for Nuremberg and later Orly, France. The plane was fitted with American radio equipment and flown by Colonel Watson to Wright Field in July. A thorough inspection upon his arrival revealed explosive charges under the main fuel tanks. For some inexplicable reason, they had not exploded.

This exploitation, however, was not limited to aircraft. T-2 Intelligence at Wright Field also concentrated on the capture of German technical libraries and document re-positories. As the captured documents began to flow into Wright Field in December 1945, the evaluation, classification, cataloging, indexing, and microfilming of Nazi Germany's aeronautical R & D literature from 1933 to 1945 became one of the outstanding accomplishments in the history of documentation. At the completion of this project in November 1947, 1,500 tons of documents had been processed.

Meanwhile, top United States military leaders became convinced that the abilities of captured German scientists were needed in this country's R & D programs. While the Army concentrated on the Peenemunde rocket experts, the Air Force chose gifted individuals whose talents matched R & D requirements in a large number of fields. Beginning in July 1945, contacts were made with these scientists during which time their capabilities, willingness to work, Nazi affiliations, and other necessary information were determined. The first scientists arrived at Wright Field in the fall of 1945.

Maj. Gen. Harold E. Watson

FOREIGN TECHNOLOGY DIVISION LINEAGE

FTD Predecessor	Command	Date
Technical Data Laboratory	Materiel Command	December 1942
	AAF Air Technical Service Command	August 31, 1944
T-2 Intelligence	Air Technical Service Command	July 1, 1945
	Air Materiel Command	March 9, 1946
Technical Intelligence Department	Air Materiel Command	August 1947
Air Technical Intelligence Center	Dir/IN, Hq USAF	May 1951
Aerospace Technical Intelligence Center	Dir/IN, Hq USAF	September 21, 1959
Foreign Technology Division	Air Force Systems Command	July 1, 1961

---

*Colonel Watson later served as commander of FTD predecessor organizations at Wright-Patterson AFB.

FOREIGN TECHNOLOGY DIVISION COMMANDERS

Col. Donald L. Putt	Jul 1945-Dec 1946
Col. Howard M. McCoy	Dec 1946-Jul 1949
Col. Harold E. Watson	Jul 1949-Sep 1951
Col. Frank L. Dunn	Sep 1951-Aug 1952
Col. John A. O'Mara	Aug 1952-Sep 1952
Brig. Gen. William M. Garland	Sep 1952-Oct 1953
Col. George L. Wertenbaker	Oct 1953-Jul 1954
Maj. Gen. Harold E. Watson	Jul 1954-Jul 1958
Col. John G. Eriksen	Jul 1958-Nov 1958
Maj. Gen. Charles B. Dougher	Nov 1958-Feb 1961
Brig. Gen. Arthur J. Pierce	Feb 1961-Jul 1964
Brig. Gen. Arthur W. Cruikshank, Jr.	Jul 1964-Aug 1966
Col. Raymond S. Sleeper	Aug 1966-Nov 1968
Col. George R. Weinbrenner	Nov 1968-Jul 1974
Col. James W. Rawers	Jul 1974-Jul 1975
Col. John B. Marks, Jr.	Jul 1975-Jan 1977
Col. Howard E. Wright	Jan 1977-Jun 1981
Col. David S. Watrous	Jun 1981-Feb 1983
Col. Earl A. Pontius	Feb 1983

Air Technical Intelligence operations also progressed in the Pacific. As the Japanese abandoned aircraft and other materiel, analyses of these items pinpointed many of their production problems and shortages of resources.

In the late 1940s, the Foreign Technology Division began to develop its scientific and technical (S & T) data base with the exploitation of published foreign literature. By the mid-1950s, this emphasis on documentation produced an impressive file of retrievable S & T information. With the addition of raw intelligence gained from the Korean conflict, including a MiG-15 Russian-made jet fighter delivered by a North Korean defector, more modern methods and techniques were needed to reduce this vast amount of documentation to useable data. As a result, FTD became a pioneer in the use of computers for intelligence analysis. It was also during this period that radar intelligence, electronic intelligence, and machine translation capabilities were established.

By 1961, the division's photo analysis process had become automated, with a capability added in 1963 which provided invaluable information on foreign aerodynamic, ballistic missile, and space vehicle systems. That same year, the data base was automated as a computerized library of scientific and technical information from many sources, available for instant recall.

Capabilities acquired by FTD during the 1970s included Human Intelligence Targeting and Laser Signal Analysis, and the consolidation of all scientific and technical data bases into a single, comprehensive scientific and technical data base. The use of automated microfilm storage, retrieval, and display equipment gave improved accessibility of parent documents, and thus improved overall processing, as well as information dissemination and retrieval.

With the completion of Building 856 in 1976, the FTD headquarters complex included Buildings 856, 828, and 829 and totalled over 460,000 square feet of modern office and laboratory facilities. A project of special significance was completed in 1982 with the modernization of FTD's Photo Laboratory.[5]

AIR FORCE AEROSPACE MEDICAL RESEARCH LABORATORY (AFAMRL)

The Air Force Aerospace Medical Research Laboratory is a component of the Aerospace Medical Division of the Air Force Systems Command (AFSC). The mission of the laboratory is to conduct behavioral and biomedical research to define the limits of human tolerance and the degradation of human performance under the conditions of environmental stress associated with aerospace operations. The laboratory is also responsible for establishing design criteria and developing new biotechnology techniques for future aerospace systems to protect and sustain personnel in any conceivable operational situation.

The laboratory was established at Wright Field on May 18, 1935, as the Physiological Research Unit, under the guidance of then Capt. Harry G. Armstrong, MC [Medical Corps], the laboratory's first Commander. Early work conducted at the unit was pioneering aeromedical research on flight stresses and equipment concepts to protect the aviator.

During the 1940s, the laboratory began to study the physiologic effects of abrupt deceleration, curvilinear flight, and the problems associated with high altitude operations, including requirements for G-suits, oxygen systems, and pressure breathing. During the latter part of 1941, Capt. A. Pharo Gagge investigated the benefits of administering pure oxygen at pressures of 15 to 25 mmHg above the ambient pressure during high altitude chamber flights. The first of his experiments was carried out in the chamber up to 43,000 feet, using himself as the first subject. In November 1942, Lt. Col. William R. Lovelace, II, MC, with Boeing pilot A. C. Reed and copilot J. A. Fraser, made the first aircraft flight using pressure breathing equipment in a B-17E to an indicated altitude of 42,900 feet. The problem of high altitude bail-out was a major concern of the Army Air Forces in 1943. In June of that year, Colonel Lovelace jumped from a height of 40,000 feet at Ephrata, Washington, the highest altitude jump attempted up to that time. The magnitude of parachute opening shock was found to be far greater at altitudes above 30,000 feet than when the parachute was opened closer to the ground. In 1945, the laboratory began biodynamics research on upward ejection seats for safer escape from high-speed aircraft. Much of the activity was based on earlier work done by the German Air Force.

On April 2, 1951, the laboratory transferred from the Air Materiel Command to the Wright Air Development Center of the Air Research and Development Command (ARDC), and during the 1950s, the laboratory efforts moved into the space era. Some of the laboratory's signifi-

Headquarters AF Aerospace Medical Research Laboratory, Building 29, Area B

Maj. Gen. Harry G. Armstrong

cant work included the study of effects of zero G on monkeys and mice in the Aerobee rocket, large-scale anthropometry studies of USAF flying personnel, development of an operational partial pressure suit in 1951, the full-pressure X-15 suit in 1957, downward ejection studies with the B-47, the weightlessness program using a C-131 aircraft, and the 120-hour aircrew habitability studies for nuclear powered aircraft in 1958. Early in 1959, the laboratory began a series of physiological, psychological, and biomechanical tests on the candidates for NASA's Project Mercury. To better reflect its expanded mission, the laboratory was renamed the Aerospace Medical Research Laboratory in August 1959.

On January 1, 1962, AFAMRL was reassigned to the Aerospace Medical Division. During the 1960s, the laboratory acquired a number of major new facilities, including the computer-based Human Engineering System Simulator and the Dynamic Environmental Simulator (a three-axis centrifuge) to conduct advanced biomedical research on the effects of aerospace flight on crew performance and safety. Consequently, during the latter part of the 1960s and early 1970s, a great expansion in research activity occurred.

The research efforts of the laboratory led to establishment of national and international standards on aircraft noise hazards, human engineering design procedures, and toxic exposure limits. Much of this work supported the System Program Offices responsible for development of the highly sophisticated F-15, F-16, and F-111 aircraft. In addition, many joint efforts were conducted with NASA, the Department of Transportation, Environmental Protection Agency, and the Army and Navy.

Dynamic Environmental Simulator (Multimode Human Centrifuge)

In the 1980s, AFAMRL continues to contribute to advances in aerospace medicine in the areas of human engineering, biodynamics, and toxicology. The multidisciplinary staff is composed of approximately 300 scientists, engineers, and support personnel. Additionally, approximately 200 on-site contractors provide invaluable mission support.

AFAMRL is currently organized into five divisions. The three research divisions—Biodynamics and Bioengineering, Human Engineering, and Toxic Hazards—make major contributions to the biotechnology program of the Aerospace Medical Division. The other two divisions—Veterinary Sciences and Technical Services—perform diverse support activities in the care, proper use, and handling of animals and in administration, maintenance and materiel, resource management, and plans and programs.[6]

AIR FORCE AEROSPACE MEDICAL RESEARCH LABORATORY COMMANDERS

Maj. Harry G. Armstrong	May 1935-May 1940
Dr. J. William Heim (Acting)	May 1940-Sep 1940
Capt. Otis O. Benson	Sep 1940-Jun 1943
Col. W. Randolph Lovelace	Jun 1943-Oct 1945
Col. Lloyd Griffis	Oct 1945-May 1946
Col. Edward J. Kendricks	May 1946-Jun 1946
Lt. Col. A. Pharo Gagge	Jun 1946-Dec 1949
Col. Walter A. Carlson	Dec 1949-Jul 1951
Col. Robert H. Blount	Jul 1951-Jan 1954
Col. Jack Bollerud	Jan 1954-Apr 1958
Col. John P. Stapp	Apr 1958-Aug 1960
Col. Andres I. Karstens	Aug 1960-Jan 1964
Col. Joseph M. Quashnoch	Jan 1964-Jun 1966
Col. Raymond A. Yerg	Jun 1966-Aug 1968
Col. Clyde H. Kratochvil	Aug 1968-Oct 1970
Col. Clinton L. Holt	Oct 1970-Aug 1973
Col. Frederick F. Doppelt	Aug 1973-Jul 1976
Col. Roy L. DeHart	Jul 1976-Jun 1980
Col. George C. Mohr	Jun 1980

AIR FORCE HUMAN RESOURCES LABORATORY (AFHRL)

The Air Force Human Resources Laboratory, with headquarters at Brooks AFB, Texas, is a component of the Aerospace Medical Division of the Air Force Systems Command (AFSC). It is the principal organization for planning and executing USAF exploratory and advanced development programs in the areas of manpower and personnel, education and training, simulation and training devices, and logistics and group aspects of human factors.

AFHRL research and development is carried out by four research divisions, including the Logistics and Human Factors Division located at Wright-Patterson AFB. AFHRL also maintains a liaison office at WPAFB with the Deputy for Simulators, Aeronautical Systems Division.

The Logistics and Human Factors Division conducts research and development efforts in support of three basic objectives. The Division's major programs are aimed at integrating human resource and logistics considerations into weapon systems design, designing computer-based maintenance diagnostic and assessment systems in order to improve the performance of logistics and maintenance organizations, and developing methods to enhance the performance of Air Force mission teams.

In the area of technological development, the Logistics and Human Factors Division is concerned with the logistics aspects of Air Force weapon systems. Its mission is to develop the technology needed to improve maintenance diagnostics for these systems, as well as the technology for automating logistics elements such as technical data. The Division also develops improved techniques for planning maintenance and logistics for combat environments.

In the area of performance enhancement, the Division deals with technical training, with special attention to training maintenance personnel. A new system is being developed for job-site training and proficiency certification. The Division also works with the technology necessary for the extensive application of computer-based instruction in the Air Force.

AFHRL GEOGRAPHICAL LOCATIONS

Team training systems developed by the Logistics and Human Factors Division are aimed at improving the performance of non-flying crews, groups, teams, and units. Special attention is given to teams involved in command, control, and communications systems because of the pressing current needs for improvements in those systems.

The Logistics and Human Factors Division makes a significant contribution to the work of the Air Force Human Resources Laboratory as a whole. The AFHRL mission is related to all functional areas of the Air Force since there is no area that escapes the requirement for trained and qualified personnel. The work accomplished by AFHRL, in general, promises unusually high payoff as new technological developments in microcomputer systems and new theoretical developments in cognitive psychology open possibilities previously unimagined.[7]

USAF MEDICAL CENTER WRIGHT-PATTERSON

The first Medical Department personnel, one officer and three enlisted men, arrived at Wilbur Wright Field on July 8, 1917. A converted barrack was set up as a temporary infirmary. By August 21, 1917, the first hospital building was completed. Despite unsanitary conditions, good health prevailed among post personnel during that first brutal winter at Wilbur Wright Field. On May 1, 1918, the medical staff consisted of 14 physicians and dentists, 63 enlisted men, and 11 commissioned nurses.*

For the period from 1918 to 1942, few details are available on hospital personnel or the valuable services they performed. Two permanent hospital facilities, however, were put in service in 1942. A fifty-bed hospital was activated June 17, 1942 in what is now Building 219, Area C. It was followed on December 21, 1942, by the activation of a cantonment-type hospital facility in Wood City. This cantonment-type hospital remained the main Base Hospital for many years, its bed capacity varying according to the needs of the command.

In 1952, planning for the current hospital began. This Area A facility was designed as a 348-bed general hospital, and incorporated all of the latest hospital improvements. It was also designed to allow for a 200-bed expansion, should the need arise, without taxing the ancillary sections. The new hospital was dedicated on September 21, 1956, with Col. Edgar L. Olson as Commander.

The USAF Hospital Wright-Patterson was redesignated as the USAF Medical Center Wright-Patterson effective July 1, 1969. It was also designated as the main Department of Defense medical institution within DOD Region 6, which encompasses a 10-state area with more than 450,000 eligible beneficiaries. As a result, it became a major referral and consultant center for the region. Locally, the Medical Center provides care for approximately 10,000 active-duty military personnel and their dependents, as well as approx-

Wilbur Wright Field hospital, 1918

Patterson Field hospital, constructed 1942 (Building 219, Area C)

Cantonment-type hospital in Wood City, 1942

imately 43,000 retired military personnel from all U.S. services, and their dependents. Over 8,000 patients are hospitalized annually, and 400,000 outpatient visits are accommodated per year.

Besides its support of the base military population and its DOD Region 6 responsibilities, the Medical Center is the only Air Force center which offers hyperbaric compression therapy. Patients, both military and civilian, are referred to the center from the entire Midwest. Also unusual is the Occupational Medicine Service which provides medical support to the base civilian population of approximately 16,000. Support is also provided in aerospace medicine, dental care, environmental health, and veterinary service.

*See Chapter II, Wilbur Wright Field, for further details of this period.

USAF Medical Center, Wright-Patterson

The Medical Center has a staff of over 1,200, including physicians, dentists, nurses, and technical and administrative specialists. In addition, there are approximately 140 assigned officer and enlisted personnel engaged in training programs in the following areas:

Medical Residencies:
   Internal Medicine
   Obstetrics/Gynecology
   Pediatrics
   Psychiatry
   General Surgery
Dental General Practice Residency
Hospital Administration Residency
Specialty Training:
   Medical Lab Specialist - Phase II
   Radiology Specialist - Phase II
   Cardiopulmonary Specialist - Phase II
Internships:
   Nursing
   Medical Materiel Management
   Clinical Psychology

The medical residencies in Obstetrics/Gynecology, Pediatrics, General Surgery, and Psychiatry are unique within the Department of Defense. They are fully integrated with the Wright State University School of Medicine, thus allowing Air Force physician trainees and their civilian colleagues to share clinical experiences and faculties. Clinical rotations are shared using the Medical Center and five major teaching hospitals in Dayton. Additionally, many of the Medical Center's clinical staff hold appointments as Wright State University faculty members, and actively share teaching responsibilities with civilian clinical faculty members in the private health sector. This program is an excellent example of cooperation between the federal and private health and education sectors.

Groundbreaking for $115.3 million expansion of the Medical Center, September 14, 1982

The Medical Center hosted a service-wide medical training exercise, entitled Medical Red Flag No. 6, May 19-26, 1982. This annual event is specifically designed to provide training in battlefield medicine for medical professionals. More than 600 physicians, dentists, veterinarians, physicians' assistants, and nurse practitioners from the Air Force, Army, Navy, and Marines participated in the 1982 exercise. Classroom instruction was combined with training under simulated combat conditions. A complete air transportable hospital (ATH) was airlifted to WPAFB from the First Tactical Hospital at Langley AFB, Virginia, and provided training in a realistic environment. A UH-1 Huey helicopter used in air rescue missions was also on-site. Lt. Gen. Paul W. Myers, the Air Force Surgeon General and the originator of Medical Red Flag, participated in the exercise and commended this 6th annual event as being the best conducted so far.

The Medical Center uses in excess of 400,000 square feet of space to accommodate 356 beds and a 28-chair dental clinic, as well as outpatient, ancillary, and support facilities. The present facility has been recognized as being overcrowded, and additional mission requirements have forced the conversion of certain space to other than intended usage. To facilitate the use of space within the Medical Center, several departments and clinics have been relocated to other areas on base, far removed from the main complex, complicating the effective management of all Medical Center activities and inconveniencing patients.

The above deficiencies were originally identified in the early 1970s. In 1976, the Air Force started planning for a modernized and expanded physical plant to accommodate the increased workload and implementation of new residency programs. In 1981, the expansion and modernization of the USAF Medical Center was finally approved. On August 12, 1982, the contract for a $115.3 million construction project was awarded to Blount Brothers Corporation of Montgomery, Alabama. Formal groundbreaking was held on September 14, 1982, with completion scheduled for October 1987. This project is designed to increase the size of the Medical Center from 297,000 square feet to 657,000 square feet, making it the second largest in the Air Force Medical Service.

Major aspects of the hospital expansion include two additions for expanded outpatient facilities (bringing in functions from four outlying buildings), and construction of the largest and most comprehensive hyperbaric medicine chamber in the Air Force. Provision has also been made for additional ambulatory care services, specialized operating rooms, a dedicated ICU/CCU area, major dental services, professional training facilities including an auditorium, and a complete renovation of the interior of the existing structure to ensure compliance with appropriate building codes and accreditation standards.[8]

2046TH COMMUNICATIONS GROUP (2046TH CG)

The 2046th Communications Group provides communications-electronics (C-E) and air traffic control services and facilities to all organizations on Wright-Patterson AFB. It also provides selected services to a number of off-base facilities, including the Automatic Digital Network (AUTODIN) Switching Center at Gentile Air Force Station, Ohio; Springfield Municipal Airport, Ohio (air traffic control services); Fort Knox, Kentucky (weather maintenance support); Youngstown Municipal Airport, Ohio, and Newark Air Force Station, Ohio (base C-E services for both).

The Commander of the 2046th CG wears two hats, as do all communications managers: he commands the 2046th CG under the direction of Continental Communications Division (CCD) and the Air Force Communications Command (AFCC), and he serves as the C-E Staff Officer for the 2750th Air Base Wing Commander. Other members of the 2046th CG serve in similar capacities as C-E staff officers for ASD, FTD, and the TR-1 System Program Office (SPO). While mainly concerned with the C-E needs of Wright-Patterson AFB, the 2046th CG is often called upon by higher echelons and other units to provide technical assistance, emergency maintenance, and augmentation throughout the world.

The 2046th CG provides record communications to both on and off-base customers through five separate telecommunications centers (TCCs). The main TCC for the base is in Area A. Aside from message routing and distribution, this TCC also operates the common-user TELEFAX machine for the base, the International Logistics Support System for AFLC's Foreign Military Sales program, and the Bulk Data Network. Collocated with the TCC functions, the Automated Telecommunications Center uses the UNIVAC 418III computer system to route message and data traffic to and from some 21 Air National Guard and remote stations, three Department of Defense civilian contractor terminals, seven on-base tributaries (including the Consolidated Command Post, the AFLC Transportation Control Center, and the TCCs in Areas A and B), and the magnetic tape terminal.

WPAFB telephone switchboard, Building 1455, Area A

The remaining four TCCs at Wright-Patterson are the Area B TCC, serving ASD and other organizations in Area B; the Logistics Airlift TCC, serving AFLC's LOGAIR transport network; the Advanced Range Instrumentation Aircraft (ARIA) Air Operations Control Center TCC, providing teletype communications to the 4950th Test Wing in support of manned and unmanned space launches; and the Air Force Special Security Office TCC, which handles both sensitive and general message traffic for FTD, and manages and operates the Automatic Secure Voice Communications switchboard for the base.

Voice communications services are provided by the Defense Metropolitan Area Telephone System - Dayton (DMATS-D). The office of the DMATS-D manager was activated in February 1982. The DMATS-D function is responsible for providing communications services to authorized customers, including switched telephone services and cable support for private line communications service. The DMATS-D functions include three branches: the requirements branch, telephone plant branch, and telephone operations. With these branches the division acts as a government telephone company providing service not only to Wright-Patterson AFB, but also to Gentile Air Force Station and other DOD users that have requirements for services from the DMATS-D electronic telephone switches. The DMATS-D hardware consists of three electronic telephone switches having a complement of approximately 18,500 lines serving approximately 36,000 telephone users.

In providing these and other services, the 2046th CG maintains a myriad of C-E equipment and systems, including teletypewriter units, navigational aids facilities, ground radio and closed-circuit television equipment, meteorological forecasting and monitoring equipment, cryptographic devices, digital subscriber terminal equipment, and of course, all components of the government-owned base telephone system. The 2046th CG also manages and operates two centralized repair activities (CRAs). The Digital Subscriber Terminal Equipment (DSTE) CRA provides intermediate-level maintenance for DSTE end items throughout the continental United States (CONUS), and is the only DSTE facility in the CONUS involved in electronic installation work. The Meteorological CRA performs intermediate-level maintenance of weather equipment supporting over 64 units of the USAF, Air Force Reserve, Air National Guard, and U.S. Army located in a 25-state area and in Greenland, Labrador, and the Azores.

The 2046th CG is one of the oldest organizations at Wright-Patterson AFB. The first communications unit activated at Wright Field was a detachment of the 2nd Communications Region, established on November 15, 1938, with headquarters at Langley Field, Virginia. This detachment was deactivated on May 15, 1944, following the activation of the 103rd Airways and Air Communications Service (AACS) Squadron. The 103rd AACS Squadron was redesignated as the 1914th AACS Squadron by Hq Military Air Transport Service (MATS) on October 1, 1948. On January 1, 1951, the 1062nd USAF Communications Squadron was organized, as part of the USAF Special Activities Wing, Hq Command USAF, to operate the Wright-Patterson AFB message traffic relay center on the Air Communications Network. This unit was redesignated as the 2046th AACS Squadron and transferred to MATS on January 1, 1953. The 1914th AACS Squadron was absorbed by the 2046th AACS Squadron on November 1, 1954. The Squadron was redesignated as the 2046th Communications Squadron (CS) on July 1, 1961, under the newly-established Air Force Communications Service (which became Air Force Communications Command on November 15, 1979). On January 1, 1965, the 2046th CS became the 2046th Communications Group (CG).

The 2046th CG today serves Hq AFLC and other organizations on Wright-Patterson AFB in a highly proficient manner, utilizing state-of-the-art equipment and innovative management techniques to meet the growing communications needs of the DOD community on the base. These accomplishments were recognized by the group's receipt of the Air Force Outstanding Unit Award for the period February 1, 1972 through January 31, 1974, and again for the period February 1, 1974 through January 31, 1975.[9]

2046TH COMMUNICATIONS GROUP COMMANDERS

Lt. Col. Richard F. Amann	Jan 1951-Dec 1952
Maj. Alexander R. Bonner	Dec 1952-May 1954
Maj. Willard L. Money	May 1954-Oct 1955
Maj. George E. Slouka	Oct 1955-Jul 1956
Lt. Col. Jack Laubscher	Jul 1956-Mar 1959
Maj. Bruno Peters	May 1959-Jul 1959
Lt. Col. Leon H. Golinsky	Jul 1959-Nov 1962
Lt. Col. Milton Y. Veynar	Nov 1962-Jun 1964
Lt. Col. Alfred Iannoccone	Jun 1964-Dec 1965
Lt. Col. John Smith	Dec 1965-Jun 1966
Lt. Col. Harvey Curran	Jun 1966-May 1968
Lt. Col. Robert D. Reckner	May 1968-May 1969
Col. Joseph A. Novak	May 1969-Mar 1971
Maj. Victor E. Jaclo	Mar 1971-May 1971
Col. Alexander Disanto	May 1971-May 1973
Lt. Col. Arthur Yarrington	Jun 1973-Aug 1973
Col. Thomas J. Cavanaugh	Aug 1973-Aug 1975
Col. William M. Rainwater	Aug 1975-Jun 1977
Col. Clyde F. Bunch	Jul 1977-Aug 1980
Col. Clarence R. Smith	Aug 1980-Jul 1982
Col. Nicholas W. Raffaele	Jul 1982-Apr 1984
Col. Bernhard R. Pett, Jr.	Apr 1984-Jul 1984
Col. Raymond L. French	Aug 1984

DEFENSE INSTITUTE OF SECURITY ASSISTANCE MANAGEMENT (DISAM)

The Defense Institute of Security Assistance Management, headquartered in Building 125, Area B, provides consolidated professional education to all selected personnel involved in security assistance and Military Assistance Advisory Group (MAAG) functions. DISAM is a Department of Defense activity. The Institute's Commandant also serves as the Commandant of the Air Force Institute of Technology. The Deputy Commandant is selected alternately from the Army and the Navy.

DISAM conducts courses of study that prepare military (U.S. and foreign) and civilian (U.S. Government, foreign and U.S. contractor) personnel for assignment in security assistance/MAAG positions, and assignments in security assistance, including both defense grant assistance and foreign military sales positions. DISAM is also responsible for conducting research in defense assistance/MAAG concepts and methods; for assembling and disseminating information concerning new policies, methods, and practices in security assistance/MAAG; and for providing consulting services to the Office of the Secretary of Defense (OSD) and the military departments on security assistance/MAAG managerial matters.

DISAM EMBLEM

The DISAM emblem represents the security assistance goals of the United States and the mission of DISAM. The globe is emblematic of the worldwide nature of security assistance. The strength and peace enhanced by security assistance programs are depicted by the sword and olive branches. The Pentagon-shaped interior border characterizes DISAM as a Department of Defense institution. Central to the emblem is the Lamp of Knowledge, depicting the educational mission of DISAM. The large shield in the background is symbolic of a sovereign nation's commitment to self-preservation which security assistance is designed to promote. The essence of DISAM's spirit is embodied in its motto: "Strength and Peace through Knowledge."

DISAM was established in January 1977 to provide education and research and consultation services to managers at all levels within the security assistance community throughout the U.S. and overseas. Its students come from all branches of the military service, from other government agencies and civilian contractor agencies, from embassies and consulates, and from foreign friendly nations. The DISAM faculty is composed of civilians and Army, Navy, and Air Force officers selected for their academic background, technical expertise, and experience in security assistance management subject areas. Staff and support personnel are Air Force military and civilian personnel.

The DISAM curriculum is structured to be flexible and current, and to address the specific needs of the security assistance manager. In addition to on-site instruction, DISAM also provides a continuing program of field visits, publishes and distributes a quarterly journal, and actively participates in study groups, workshops, and high-level government policy seminars. DISAM publishes its own series of textbooks, handbooks, and guides to accomplish its specialized education programs. The Institute also offers a major management exercise program through which students can become deeply involved in the security assistance process in a simulated management environment.

In order to make its unique curriculum more broadly available, DISAM sends Mobile Training Teams (MTT) on a faculty-available basis to interested foreign countries. During 1982, DISAM conducted overseas programs of instruction in Lisbon, Portugal, and Amsterdam, the Netherlands.[10]

ORIENTATION GROUP, UNITED STATES AIR FORCE (AFOG)

Creating and displaying exhibits that inform the American public about Air Force people, equipment, and contributions to the nation are the key objectives of the Orientation Group, United States Air Force. These efforts play a major role in Air Force public affairs and recruiting efforts.

Orientation Group members travel worldwide. Their exhibits show advances in air power as well as the significance of the Air Force to the security of the United States. Millions of people view the displays every year.

The Orientation Group was established shortly after the 1945 Army Air Forces Fair held at Wright Field, which featured Allied and enemy airplanes and equipment from World War II. Public response to the event was so favorable that Gen. Henry H. Arnold, Commanding General of the AAF, ordered a traveling show developed. What was ultimately called the 4140th Army Air Forces Base Unit was formed, and toured most of the northeastern United States during 1946. That year the unit also presented aerial demonstrations of the P-51 Mustang. In 1956, the traveling exhibit unit received its present name: Orientation Group, United States Air Force. (The Group is more commonly referred to as the Air Force Orientation Group—AFOG.)

In 1974, the Group was responsible for the Armed Forces Bicentennial Caravan Project. Vans were prepared with displays from each military service, and traveled throughout the United States during 1975 and 1976. This project was one of the largest efforts by the Department of Defense in celebration of the nation's 200th anniversary.

For its Bicentennial Caravan Project, the unit received the Air Force Organizational Excellence Award in 1977. The Group received the award again in 1979 and 1981 for "increasing public understanding and awareness concerning the Air Force."

Today, the Orientation Group produces both outdoor and indoor exhibits. Outdoor exhibits include display vans and full-sized aircraft. Among the display vans are theater vans, which feature audiovisual programs on the history of aviation and the Air Force's technological contributions to the nation. Full-sized aircraft exhibits include an F-15 Eagle, an F-16 Fighting Falcon, an A-10 Thunderbolt II, and three T-38 Talons.

Indoor exhibits depict a variety of Air Force stories. The displays feature large color transparencies, graphics, models, artwork, and multi-image productions, and can be used alone or in groups to emphasize particular themes.

Overall, the indoor exhibits are of several types. Space rings are circular floor exhibits featuring revolving aircraft models. At the base, lighted transparencies show the aircraft performing various missions. Push buttons activate sound recordings on an outer ring around the exhibit.

Hex Table Units are free-standing pedestals that support scale models of first-line Air Force aircraft. These units can travel as packages in order to emphasize aircraft of the Strategic Air Command and the Tactical Air Command.

Heritage Panel Exhibits feature milestones in American aviation, Medal of Honor recipients from all services, and pioneers in American aviation. These exhibits occupy about 200 square feet and are designed to be the center of attraction in a large room.

Theme Graphics Panel Displays consist of six plexiglas panels mounted on three frames radiating from a central core. They feature transparencies and messages relating to various themes, such as Air Force people in action and new aircraft.

Portions of the Air Force Art Collection are also used for displays. Two art shows, each with about 35 paintings from the collection, are mounted on self-supporting exhibit forms.

The AFOG High Technology Exhibit was built as the only U.S. government display of military technology for the Farnborough, England, 1980 International Air Show. Various models of hardware and a multi-screened audiovisual presentation were used to show the Air Force's current and future research and development plans. The exhibit was updated to represent the U.S. Air Force at the Farnborough 1982 International Air Show and other appropriate technology-oriented events.

Recruiting requirements normally are given top priority for use of exhibits. Displays are typically shown at high schools, conventions, fairs, community events, and other civilian and military functions. Most exhibits are scheduled six months in advance along a planned route. The displays generally travel for months, but the crews with them are changed every 35 to 45 days. There are permanent displays at the Pentagon and at the Chicago Museum of Science and Industry.[11]

906TH TACTICAL FIGHTER GROUP (906TH TFG)

The 906th Tactical Fighter Group is a component of the Air Force Reserve and is the largest Reserve element at Wright-Patterson AFB. The 906th was officially activated at Wright-Patterson on July 1, 1982, and is subject to worldwide deployment. Col. Duane L. Foster was the Group's first Commander.

The 906th TFG is authorized 103 officers, 719 airmen, and 21 non-reserve civilians. Assigned units include the 906th Consolidated Maintenance Squadron, the 906th Combat Support Squadron, the 906th Tactical Air Command Clinic, the 906th Mobility Support Flight, and the 906th Weapons System Security Flight.

F-4D Phantom II assigned to the 906th Tactical Fighter Group

The 89th Tactical Fighter Squadron (Buckeye Phantoms) is the flying squadron assigned to the group and is the only operational tactical flying organization on WPAFB. The 89th is authorized 18 F-4D Phantom II aircraft. The F-4D is a two-seat tactical fighter capable of speeds in excess of 1,600 miles per hour. Equipped with dual controls, long-range air intercept radar, an inertial navigation system, and inflight refueling capability, the combat-tested aircraft is versatile in performing a wide variety of missions.

The 906th is assigned to the 482nd Tactical Fighter Wing at Homestead AFB, Florida, and comes under the direction of 10th Air Force, headquartered at Bergstrom AFB, Texas. In the event that the unit is called to active duty through Presidential order, the 906th would be transferred to 9th Air Force (Shaw AFB, South Carolina) and become a member of the Tactical Air Command.

Monthly weekend training helps reservists maintain job proficiency. During their first full quarter at WPAFB, the 89th TFS flew 369 sorties for 532.4 total flying hours. Training was received in such areas as air-to-air, air-to-ground, DACT (dissimilar air combat tactics), and other tactical weapons delivery techniques.[12]

Lt. Col. William H. Lawson assumed command of the 906th TFG on August 21, 1983.

OTHER ASSOCIATE ORGANIZATIONS

The following list reflects additional associate organizations located on Wright-Patterson AFB effective October 1, 1982, by Air Force Command or management agency.[13]

HQ UNITED STATES AIR FORCE

Air Force Audit Agency
Dayton Patent Prosecution Office
Air Force Maintenance, Supply, and Munitions
    Management Engineering Team

HQ AIR FORCE LOGISTICS COMMAND

2762nd Logistics Squadron
661st Air Force Band
3025th Management Engineering Squadron

HQ AIR FORCE COMMUNICATIONS COMMAND

1815th Test and Evaluation Squadron

HQ AIR FORCE SYSTEMS COMMAND

Joint Aeronautical Materials Activity
Det. 30, 6592nd Management Engineering Squadron
Acquisition Management Information Systems
    Program Office

HQ AEROSPACE DEFENSE CENTER

Hq SPACECOM/NORAD/ADCOM Liaison Affairs
    Office

HQ AIR TRAINING COMMAND

ATC Resident Office
3552nd USAF Recruiting Squadron
Air Force Business Research Management Center
Det. 3, USAF Civil Air Patrol, Great Lakes Region
Air Force Coordinating Office for Logistics Research

HQ MILITARY AIRLIFT COMMAND

Det. 4, MAC
Det. 15, 15th Weather Squadron
Det. 1, 2nd Weather Squadron
Det. 2, 1361st Audiovisual Squadron
Det. 2, 1401st Military Airlift Squadron

HQ STRATEGIC AIR COMMAND

Det. 1, Hq SAC/XPH
SAC Liaison Officer

HQ TACTICAL AIR COMMAND

Tactical Air Command Systems Office
TAC Liaison Officer

HQ AIR FORCE COMMISSARY SERVICE

Air Force Commissary

ARMY AND AIR FORCE EXCHANGE SERVICE

WPAFB Exchange

HQ AIR FORCE INTELLIGENCE SERVICE

AFIS Detachment Training Site #2
Det. 22, Air Force Special Activities Center

HQ AIR FORCE OFFICE OF SPECIAL INVESTIGATIONS

Air Force Office of Special Investigations,
    District 5

HQ AIR FORCE RESERVE

    401st Combat Logistics Support Squadron
    35th Medical Service Squadron
    87th Aerial Port Squadron

HQ ARMED FORCES COURIER SERVICE

    Armed Forces Courier Station, WPAFB

DEFENSE LOGISTICS AGENCY

    Defense Property Disposal Office

U.S. ARMY

    U.S. Army Corps of Engineers
    Department of Defense Wage Fixing Authority,
      Central Region
    71st Ordnance Detachment

HQ U.S. COAST GUARD

    U.S. Coast Guard Liaison Office

U.S. NAVY

    Naval Medical Research Institute, Toxicology
      Detachment

NON-DEPARTMENT OF DEFENSE/FEDERAL

    U.S. General Accounting Office
    Library of Congress Motion Picture Broadcasting
      and Recorded Sound Division
    Small Business Administration
    U.S. Postal Service
    Supporting Council of Preventive Effort (SCOPE)

CIVILIAN ORGANIZATIONS

    Winters National Bank and Trust Company
    Wright-Patt Credit Union, Inc.
    Scheduled Airline Traffic Office
    American Red Cross

FOREIGN ORGANIZATIONS

    Canadian Department of Industry, Trade, and
      Commerce
    1st Canadian Forces Logistics Liaison Unit

APPENDICES

2750th AIR BASE WING

APPENDIX 1

2750TH AIR BASE WING AND
WRIGHT-PATTERSON AIR FORCE BASE
COMMANDERS

BRIG. GEN. JOSEPH T. MORRIS
August 28, 1948 - March 28, 1952

BRIG. GEN. C. PRATT BROWN
March 29, 1952 - September 30, 1953

BRIG. GEN. PAUL L. BARTON
October 2, 1953 - August 9, 1957

BRIG. GEN. DONALD L. HARDY
August 10, 1957 - June 30, 1958

BRIG. GEN. JOHN D. HOWE
July 1, 1958 - May 19, 1960

BRIG. GEN. ELBERT HELTON
August 10, 1960 - August 2, 1962

BRIG. GEN. GLEN J. McCLERNON
August 3, 1962 - July 31, 1964

BRIG. GEN. ARTHUR E. EXON
August 1, 1964 - December 20, 1965

BRIG. GEN. JOWELL C. WISE
December 21, 1965 - July 8, 1968

BRIG. GEN. C. O. WILLIAMS
July 9, 1968 - September 2, 1970

BRIG. GEN. EDMUND A. RAFALKO
September 3, 1970 - June 14, 1972

BRIG. GEN. IRBY B. JARVIS, JR.
June 15, 1972 - January 30, 1975

BRIG. GEN. ROBERT W. CLEMENT
January 31, 1975 - January 12, 1976

COL. TITUS C. HALL
January 13, 1976 - January 13, 1977

COL. RANO E. LUEKER
January 14, 1977 - April 22, 1979

COL. JAMES H. RIGNEY, JR.
April 23, 1979 - June 25, 1981

COL. LEONARD R. PETERSON
June 26, 1981 - June 28, 1984

COL. CHARLES E. FOX, JR.
June 29, 1984

APPENDIX 2

PERSONNEL STRENGTHS

Comprehensive population figures are not available for the period prior to World War II.

Sources indicate that at the end of World War I, McCook Field had a strength of 58 officers, 267 enlisted, and 1,915 civilians. Wilbur Wright Field, at the height of World War I operations, functioned with approximately 1,700 men, all military with the exception of several civilian instructors. The Fairfield Aviation General Supply Depot had a combined population of approximately 1,000 during World War I, again mostly military. Following the war, the depot staff was converted almost entirely to civilian workers.

In the years between World War I and World War II, only approximate figures are available for each of the major installations then functioning. From 1920 to 1926, the Engineering Division at McCook Field had a personnel force of about 50 officers and from 1,100 to 1,500 civilians. The Materiel Division at Wright Field in the period from 1927 to 1937 had a steady strength of approximately 3,100, with a slight dip during the Great Depression. Assigned military at Wright Field numbered about 150 with slight variations. Employment at the Fairfield Air Intermediate Depot and later Patterson Field also remained steady, at approximately 500.

The following are combined strength figures for Wright and Patterson Fields, and subsequently for Wright-Patterson Air Force Base, for the years since 1937.

Date	Civilian	Military	Total
Dec. 30, 1938	2,222	212	2,434
Dec. 31, 1939	3,059	652	3,711
Dec. 31, 1940	7,455	708	8,163
Dec. 31, 1941	15,398	2,125	17,523
Dec. 31, 1942	36,908	9,592	46,500
Dec. 31, 1943	30,926	14,821	45,747
Dec. 31, 1944	29,356	16,119	45,475
Jun. 30, 1945	30,116	18,892	49,008
Dec. 31, 1945	20,180	11,100	31,280
Jan. 31, 1946	19,358	8,261	27,619
Dec. 31, 1947	17,588	3,192	20,780
Dec. 31, 1948	20,108	5,082	25,190
Dec. 31, 1949	20,443	4,434	24,877
Dec. 28, 1950	23,781	4,745	28,526
Dec. 28, 1951	25,738	8,946	34,684
Dec. 25, 1952	22,144	8,284	30,428
Dec. 31, 1953	20,478	6,805	27,283
Dec. 26, 1954	20,264	7,098	27,362
Dec. 25, 1955	20,627	7,248	27,875
Dec. 23, 1956	21,701	6,762	28,463
Dec. 22, 1957	19,557	6,313	25,870

Date	Civilian	Military	Total
Dec. 15, 1958	18,893	6,284	25,177
Dec. 20, 1959	18,331	6,471	24,802
Dec. 20, 1960	20,966	6,948	27,914
Dec. 20, 1961	20,714	7,364	28,078
Dec. 20, 1962	20,301	7,301	27,602
Dec. 31, 1963	19,273	12,185	31,458
Dec. 31, 1964	19,112	11,431	30,543
Dec. 31, 1965	19,170	7,082	26,252
Dec. 30, 1966	19,234	7,531	26,765
Dec. 29, 1967	19,299	7,290	26,589
Dec. 30, 1968	19,163	7,207	26,370
Dec. 31, 1969	18,568	7,557	26,125
Dec. 31, 1970	17,761	7,596	25,357
Oct. 1, 1971	17,744	7,875	25,619
Jul. 1, 1972	17,520	8,167	25,687
Jul. 1, 1973	16,920	8,323	25,243
Jul. 1, 1974	17,037	8,694	25,731
Jul. 1, 1975	15,975	7,548	23,523
Oct. 1, 1976	15,812	7,182	22,994
Sep. 30, 1977	15,523	7,607	23,130
Sep. 30, 1978	15,879	7,686	23,565
Sep. 30, 1979	15,832	7,636	23,468
Oct. 1, 1980	17,031	7,992	25,023
Oct. 1, 1981	15,662	7,608	23,270
Oct. 1, 1982	17,549	8,919	26,468

APPENDIX 3

SIGNIFICANT RECORDS SET BY McCOOK FIELD PILOTS

Date	Pilot/Crew	Locale	Type Aircraft	Record/Notes
Sep. 6, 1919	Maj. R. W. Schroeder Lt. G. A. Elfrey	McCook Field	LePere biplane with Liberty 400-hp engine	World two-man altitude record of 28,250 ft
Sep. 24, 1919	Maj. R. W. Schroeder	McCook Field	LePere biplane with Liberty 400-hp engine	World altitude record of 30,900 ft for an airplane with passenger
Feb. 27, 1920	Maj. R. W. Schroeder	McCook Field	LePere biplane with Liberty 400-hp engine	World altitude record 33,114 ft
Sep. 28, 1921	Lt. John A. Macready	McCook Field	LePere biplane with Liberty 400-hp engine	World altitude record 34,509.5 ft
Apr. 6, 1922	Lt. John A. Macready	McCook Field	LePere biplane with Liberty 400-hp engine	World altitude record 34,563 ft
Jun. 12, 1922	Lt. A. W. Stevens	McCook Field		High altitude parachute test jump from 24,200 ft
Aug. 2, 1922	Lt. Leigh Wade Capt. A. W. Stevens Sgt. Roy Langham	McCook Field	Martin MB-2 super-charged bomber	Three-man altitude record of 23,350 ft
Sep. 4, 1922	Lt. James H. Doolittle	Pablo Beach, FL to Rockwell Fld, San Diego, CA	DeHavilland DH-4B Liberty 400-hp engine	First transcontinental crossing in single day: 2,163 miles in 21 hours, 20 minutes actual flying time. Awarded Distinguished Flying Cross.
Oct. 5, 1922	Lt. John A. Macready Lt. Oakley G. Kelly	Rockwell Fld, San Diego, CA	Fokker Transport T-2 Liberty 375-hp engine	Endurance record of 35 hours, 18 minutes, 30 seconds
Oct. 20, 1922	Lt. Harold R. Harris	McCook Field		Jumped from disabled airplane at 2,500 ft; first time parachute used in emergency situation
Nov. 4, 1922	Lt. John A. Macready Lt. Oakley G. Kelly	Rockwell Field, CA, to Indianapolis	Fokker T-2 transport	Greatest distance traveled non-stop to that date
Mar. 29, 1923	Lt. Harold R. Harris Lt. Ralph Lockwood	McCook Field	DeHavilland DH-4L Liberty 400-hp engine	World speed record for 1,000 kilometers of 127.42 mph
Mar. 29, 1923	Lt. R. L. Maitland	McCook Field	Curtiss 465	World speed record of 236.587 mph over one kilometer
Mar. 29, 1923	Lt. Alexander Pearson	McCook Field	Verville-Sperry R-3 Racer	World speed record of 167.807 mph for 500 kilometers
Apr. 16–17, 1923	Lt. John A. Macready Lt. Oakley G. Kelly	McCook Field	Fokker T-2 transport	World speed record of 71.83 mph for 2,500 kilometers

Date	Pilot/Crew	Locale	Type Aircraft	Record/Notes
Apr. 16–17, 1923	Lt. John A. Macready Lt. Oakley G. Kelly	McCook Field	Fokker T-2 transport	World speed record of 71.62 mph for 3,000 kilometers
Apr. 16–17, 1923	Lt. John A. Macready Lt. Oakley G. Kelly	McCook Field	Fokker T-2 transport	World speed record of 71.34 mph for 3,500 kilometers
Apr. 16–17, 1923	Lt. John A. Macready Lt. Oakley G. Kelly	McCook Field	Fokker T-2 transport	World speed record of 70.77 mph for 4,000 kilometers
Apr. 16–17, 1923	Lt. John A. Macready Lt. Oakley G. Kelly	McCook Field	Fokker T-2 transport	World endurance record of 36 hours, 4 minutes and distance record of 2,516.55 miles set over triangular course
Apr. 17, 1923	Lt. Harold R. Harris	McCook Field	DeHavilland DH-4L Liberty 375-hp engine	World speed record of 114.35 mph for 1,500 kilometers
Apr. 17, 1923	Lt. Harold R. Harris	McCook Field	DeHavilland DH-4L Liberty 375-hp engine	World speed record of 114.22 mph for 2,000 kilometers
May 2–3, 1923	Lt. John A. Macready Lt. Oakley G. Kelly	Roosevelt Fld, NY, to Rockwell Fld, CA	Fokker T-2 transport Liberty 375-hp engine	First transcontinental nonstop flight in 26 hours, 50 minutes. Pilots awarded Distinguished Flying Cross and Mackay Trophy
Oct. 25, 1923	Lt. Harold R. Harris	Wilbur Wright Field	XNBL-1 Barling bomber	World altitude record of 6,722 ft with a 4,409.2-lb payload
Mar. 7, 1924	Lt. Eugene H. Barksdale Lt. B. Q. Jones	McCook Field to Mitchel Fld, NY	DeHavilland DH-4B Liberty 400-hp engine	Navigated on instruments only for a distance of 575 miles
May 2, 1924	Lt. John A. Macready Lt. A. W. Stevens	McCook Field		Unofficial two-man altitude record of 31,540 ft. Also on same flight, records set for highest altitude photograph taken and greatest area ever included in one photo.
Jan. 24, 1925	Lt. John A. Macready	McCook Field		American altitude record of 37,569 ft
Oct. 27, 1925	Lt. James H. Doolittle	Bay Shore, MD	Curtiss R3C floatplane	Won prestigious Schneider Cup Race with average speed of 232.573 mph.

Sources: *A Chronology of American Aerospace Events from 1903 through 1964,* Air Force Pamphlet 190-2-2, September 1, 1965; Pamphlet *Wright Field* (Wright Field, Materiel Division, July 29, 1938); "American Airmen Credited with 11 Records in 20 Days," *Aerial Age* 16 (June 1923), p 285.

GLOSSARY

A	Attack airplane; Ambulance airplane		B	Bomber airplane
AAC	Army Air Corps		BLR	Bomber, Long Range
AACS	Airways & Air Communications Service		BOQ	Bachelor Officers' Quarters
AAF	Army Air Forces		Brig. Gen.	Brigadier General
AAFIT	Army Air Forces Institute of Technology		BT	Basic Trainer airplane
AAFTB	Army Air Forces Technical Base			
AAHS	American Aviation Historical Society		C	Cargo airplane
AAS	Army Air Service		CAA	Civil Aeronautics Administration
ABW	Air Base Wing		CAP	Civil Air Patrol
ADD	Air Documents Division		CCC	Civilian Conservation Corps
AEF	American Expeditionary Forces		CCD	Continental Communications Division
AF	Air Force		C-E	Communications-Electronics
AFALD	Air Force Acquisition Logistics Division		CG	Communications Group
AFAMRL	Air Force Aerospace Medical Research Laboratory		CIAPS	Customer Integrated Automatic Procurement System
AFB	Air Force Base		CO	Two-seat Corps Observation airplane; Commanding Officer
AFCC	Air Force Communications Command			
AFCMC	Air Force Contract Maintenance Center		Co.	Company
AFCS	Air Force Communications Service		Col.	Colonel
AFHRL	Air Force Human Resources Laboratory		CONUS	Continental United States
AFIS	Air Force Intelligence Service		CRA	Centralized Repair Activity
AFIT	Air Force Institute of Technology		CS	Communications Squadron
AFLC	Air Force Logistics Command		CWA	Civil Works Administration
AFOG	Air Force Orientation Group (Orientation Group, United States Air Force)			
			DACT	Dissimilar Air Combat Tactics
AFPEA	Air Force Packaging Evaluation Agency		DAWG	Dynamic Air War Game
AFRES	Air Force Reserve		DB	Two-seat Day Bomber
AFROTC	Air Force Reserve Officer Training Corps		DC	Douglas Company commercial airplane
AFSC	Air Force Systems Command		DCSC	Defense Construction Supply Center
AFTB	Air Force Technical Base		DELCO	Dayton Engineering Laboratories Company
AFWAL	Air Force Wright Aeronautical Laboratories		DESC	Defense Electronics Supply Center
AGM	Air-to-Ground Missile		Det.	Detachment
AGMC	Aerospace Guidance and Metrology Center		DH	DeHavilland airplane
AICUZ	Air Installation Compatible Use Zone		DISAM	Defense Institute of Security Assistance Management
AID	Air Intermediate Depot			
ALC	Air Logistics Center		DSAME	Defense Security Assistance Management Education
ALCM	Air Launched Cruise Missile			
AMC	Air Materiel Command		DMATS-D	Defense Metropolitan Area Telephone System—Dayton
AO	Two-seat Army/Coast Guard Artillery Observation airplane			
			DoD	Department of Defense
ARDC	Air Research and Development Command		DSTE	Digital Subscriber Terminal Equipment
ARIA	Advanced Range Instrumentation Aircraft		D-WC	Douglas World Cruiser
AS	Air Service		DWSMC	Defense Weapon System Management Center
ASC	Air Service Command			
ASD	Aeronautical Systems Division			
AT	Advanced Trainer airplane		e-1	Electronic-luminescent lighting
ATC	Air Training Command		ECPD	Engineers Council for Professional Development
ATH	Air Transportable Hospital			
ATIC	Aerospace Technical Intelligence Center		EODS	Explosive Ordnance Disposal Squadron
ATSC	Air Technical Service Command		ERC	Enlisted Reserve Corps
AUTODIN	Automatic Digital Network			
Avn	Aviation			
AWACS	Airborne Warning and Control System			

F	Fighter airplane; Photographic airplane	MIT	Massachusetts Institute of Technology
FAA	Federal Aviation Administration	MOD/PDM	Modification/Programmed Maintenance
FAD	Fairfield Air Depot	MRC	Medical Reserve Corps
FADCAC	Fairfield Air Depot Control Area Command	MSE	Master Signal Electrician (corresponded to Master Sergeant, E-7)
FADO	Fairfield Air Depot—Operations	MTT	Mobile Training Team
FADR	Fairfield Air Depot Reservation		
FAGSD	Fairfield Aviation General Supply Depot	NAA	National Aeronautic Association
FAID	Fairfield Air Intermediate Depot	NACA	National Advisory Committee for Aeronautics
FASC	Fairfield Air Service Command	NASA	National Aeronautics and Space Administration
FATSC	Fairfield Air Technical Service Command		
FDAT	Federal Disaster Assistance Team	NATO	North Atlantic Treaty Organization
FEAF	Far East Air Forces	NBL	Multi-seat Night Bomber—Long distance
FIS	Fighter-Interceptor Squadron	NBS	Two-seat Night Bomber—Short distance
Ft.	Fort	NCACS	North Central Association of Colleges and Schools
G	Autogiro airplane	NCO	Non-commissioned Officer
GA	Two-seat Ground Attack airplane	NCR	National Cash Register
GAM	Ground-to-Air Missile	n.d.	No date
GAR	Ground-to-Air Rocket	NDRC	National Defense Research Council
GAX	Ground Attack experimental airplane	NO	Two-seat Night Observation airplane
GCA	Ground Controlled Approach		
GEEIA	Ground Electronics Engineering Installations Agency	O	Observation, Corps and Army airplane
		OA	Observation, Amphibian airplane
Gen.	General (four stars)	OCAS	Office, Chief of Air Service
GHQAF	General Headquarters Air Force	OD	Olive drab (color)
GO	General Orders	OLR	Observation, Long Range airplane
		OSD	Office, Secretary of Defense
HB	Heavy bomber		
HEW	Department of Health, Education and Welfare	P	Pursuit, monoplane airplane
Hq	Headquarters	PA	Single-seat Pursuit Airplane with air-cooled engine
Hq Sq	Headquarters Squadron		
		PB	Pursuit, Biplane airplane
ICBM	Intercontinental Ballistic Missile	PG	Single-engine Pursuit, Ground attack
ICU/CCU	Intensive Care Unit/Coronary Care Unit	PMCCS	Property, Maintenance and Cost Compilation Section
IL	Two-seat Infantry Liaison airplane		
ILC	International Logistics Center	PMEL	Precision Measurement Equipment Laboratory
IT	Institute of Technology (USAF)		
ITUSAF	Institute of Technology, USAF	PMGA	Provisional Maintenance Group Area
		PN	Single-seat Pursuit, Night attack
JPO	Joint Project Officer	POL	Petroleum/Oil/Lubricants
		POW	Prisoner of War
KB	Bomber modified as aerial tanker	PRAM	Productivity, Reliability, Availability and Maintainability
		Prime BEEF	Base Engineering Emergency Force
L	Liaison airplane	PT	Primary Trainer airplane
LB	Light Bomber	PW	Single-engine Pursuit airplane with Water-cooled engine
LERP	Logistics Education and Research Project		
LOGAIR	Logistics Airlift	PWA	Public Works Administration
Lt.	Lieutenant	PX	Post exchange
Lt. Col.	Lieutenant Colonel		
		QMC	Quartermaster Corps
MAAG	Military Assistance Advisory Group		
MAC	Military Airlift Command	R & D	Research and Development
Maj.	Major (military rank)	RED HORSE	Rapid Engineer Deployment, Heavy Operational Repair Squadron, Engineering
Maj. Gen.	Major General		
MARS	Military Amateur Radio System; Military Affiliate Radio System	Ret.	Retired
		RF	Reconnaissance-Fighter airplane
MAS	Military Airlift Squadron	RMA	Reserve Military Aviator
MASDC	Military Aircraft Storage and Disposition Center	ROKAF	Republic of Korea Air Force
MATS	Military Air Transport Service		
MB	Martin Bomber		
MC	Medical Corps		
MES	Management Engineering Squadron		

S & T	Scientific and Technical (intelligence)
SAC	Strategic Air Command
SCAS	Signal Corps Aviation School
SEA	Southeast Asia
SERC	Signal Enlisted Reserve Corps
SIA	Societe Italiano Aviazione
SM	Strategic Missile
SO	Special Orders
SPACECOM/ NORAD/ADCOM	Space Command/North American Air Defense Command/Air Defense Command
SPO	System Program Office
SRAM	Short-Range Attack Missile
SVA	Societa Verduzio Ansaldo
T	Trainer airplane; Transport airplane
TA	Trainer, Air-cooled engine
TAC	Tactical Air Command
TCC	Telecommunications Centers
Telefax	Telecommunications Facsimile
TFG	Tactical Fighter Group
TFS	Tactical Fighter Squadron
TP	Two-seat Pursuit airplane
TW	Trainer, Water-cooled engine
U	Utility airplane
UC	Utility/Cargo airplane
UNIVAC	Universal Automatic Computer
USA	United States Army
USAF	United States Air Force
USAFE	United States Air Forces in Europe
USAFIT	USAF Institute of Technology
USMA	United States Military Academy
USMC	United States Marine Corps
USN	United States Navy
USNA	United States Naval Academy
V-E Day	Victory in Europe
V-J Day	Victory in Japan
VHB	Very Heavy Bomber
VLR	Very Long Range
VOQ	Visiting Officers' Quarters
VVHB	Very, Very Heavy Bomber
WADC	Wright Air Development Center
WADD	Wright Air Development Division
WASP	Women Airforce Service Pilots
WPA	Works Progress Administration
WPAFB	Wright-Patterson Air Force Base
WWASD	Wilbur Wright Air Service Depot
X	Experimental airplane
Y	Service test airplane
YMCA	Young Men's Christian Association
Z	Obsolete type airplane

NOTES

I. HUFFMAN PRAIRIE 1904-1916

1. Fred C. Kelly, *The Wright Brothers* (New York, 1950), p 72.
2. *Ibid.*
3. Arthur G. Renstrom, *Wilbur & Orville Wright: A Chronology Commemorating the Hundredth Anniversary of the Birth of Orville Wright, August 19, 1871* (Washington, 1975), p 13. The acreage is variously described by other writers as 68, 80, or 90 acres.
4. Gilbert Guinn, "A Different Frontier: Aviation, the Army Air Forces, and the Evolution of the Sunshine Belt," *Aerospace Historian* 29 (Mar 1982), 34-35.
5. Marvin W. McFarland, ed., *The Papers of Wilbur and Orville Wright, Including the Chanute-Wright Letters and Other Papers of Octave Chanute,* Vol One: *1899-1905* (New York, 1972 ed), p 441.
6. Renstrom, p 141.
7. Kelly, p 77.
8. Renstrom, p 142.
9. *Ibid.,* pp 140-45.
10. Charles H. Gibbs-Smith, "The World's First Practical Airplane," *NCR World* (Dayton, 1978), p 6.
11. Renstrom, p 17.
12. Kelly, p 131.
13. Charles deF. Chandler and Frank P. Lahm, *How Our Army Grew Wings: Airmen and Aircraft Before 1914* (New York, 1943), p 150.
14. Kelly, p 131.
15. Chandler and Lahm, p 153.
16. *Ibid.,* p 152.
17. *Ibid.,* p 153; Renstrom, pp 165-66.
18. Renstrom, p 166; Kelly, p 141.
19. Renstrom, p 176.
20. *Ibid.,* pp 42, 177.
21. Chandler and Lahm, pp 158-59.
22. Renstrom, pp 42, 178.
23. Chandler and Lahm, pp 295-98, citing Signal Corps Specification No. 486, Dec 23, 1907, "Advertisement and Specification for a Heavier-than-Air Flying Machine."
24. Brochure, *Wright Flyers,* published by Wright Aircraft Corporation, Dayton, Ohio, about 1915.
25. Henry H. Arnold, *Global Mission* (New York, 1949), p 17.
26. *Ibid.,* p 26.
27. Renstrom, p 204. Captain deF. Chandler had previously been qualified as a balloon pilot in 1907 and as a dirigible pilot in 1909.
28. *Ibid.,* p 206.

II. WILBUR WRIGHT FIELD 1917-1925

1. Charles deF. Chandler and Frank P. Lahm, *How Our Army Grew Wings: Airmen and Aircraft Before 1914* (New York, 1943), p 113. Signal Corps Specification Number 483, Jan 21, 1908, contained the data for the "Dirigible Balloon."

2. *Ibid.,* p 193.
3. Arthur Sweetser, *The American Air Service* (New York, 1919), p 11.
4. Chandler and Lahm, pp 277-78.
5. War Dept. GO 75, Dec 4, 1913, as published in Chandler and Lahm, pp 314-15.
6. *The United States Army Air Arm, April 1861 to April 1917* (USAF Historical Study 98, 1958), pp 236-37.
7. *Organization of Military Aeronautics 1907-1935* (AAF Historical Study 25, 1944), pp 26-27.
8. Robert Casari, "Number of U.S. Aircraft WWI," AAHS *Journal* 20 (Spring 1977), 36-38. The three squadrons were based, respectively, at Columbus, N.M., Manila, Philippine Islands, and Fort Sam Houston, Tx.
9. Alfred Goldberg, ed., *A History of the United States Air Force 1907-1957* (Princeton, 1957), p 14.
10. Sweetser, p 79.
11. *Ibid.,* p 81.
12. *Ibid.,* p 104.
13. *Ibid.,* pp 109-11.
14. *Ibid.,* pp 114-17.
15. *Ibid.,* p 98.
16. *Ibid.,* p 101.
17. "Aircraft Production in Dayton," *NCR World* (Sep-Oct 1970), pp 21-24.
18. Charlotte Reeve Conover, *Dayton, Ohio—An Intimate History* (Dayton, n.d.), p 299.
19. *Story of the Miami Conservancy District* (Dayton, n.d), pp 8-10.
20. Isaac F. Marcosson, *Colonel Deeds, Industrial Builder* (New York, 1947), p 215.
21. Sweetser, p 106.
22. History of the Air Depot at Fairfield, Ohio 1917-1943 (FASC, Patterson Field, 1944), p 4. Hereafter cited as Hist, FAD, 1917-1943.
23. Copy of Lease, Purchase Request A-6951, Order No. 50214, between the Miami Conservancy District and Lt Col C. G. Edgar, Signal Corps, Jul 1, 1917.
24. Memo, Office of the Chief Signal Officer, to all Divisions, no subj., Jun 6, 1917; *The Army's Order of Battle of United States Land Forces in the World War (1917-1919),* Vol 3, Part 1 (Washington, 1949), p 897.
25. Annual Report, Signal Corps Aviation School, Wilbur Wright Field, Fairfield, Ohio, May 31, 1918, signed by Maj Arthur E. Wilbourn, Commanding Officer. Hereafter cited as Wilbourn Report.
26. *Ibid.,* p 3.
27. *Ibid.,* p 22.
28. Sweetser, pp 347-48; Gilbert S. Guinn, "A Different Frontier: Aviation, The Army Air Forces and the Evolution of the Sunshine Belt," *Aerospace Historian* 29 (Mar 1982), 34-35.
29. R. K. McMaster, ed., "The Adventures of a Junior Military Aviator: Extracts from the Diary of Leo G. Heffernan," *Aerospace Historian* 25 (Jun 1978), 92-102.
30. Wilbourn Report, p 25.
31. *Ibid.,* pp 25-27.
32. Sweetser, pp 140-41.
33. *Ibid.,* p 144.

34. Wilbourn Report, pp 23-24
35. Sweetser, p 126.
36. Maurer Maurer, ed., *The U.S. Air Service in World War I*, Vol I: *The Final Report and a Tactical History* (Washington, 1978), 68-69; 70-72; 102-3; 105-6.
37. *Ibid.*, pp 234-35.
38. *The World Almanac and Book of Facts, 1980* (New York, 1979), p 333. Total U.S. armed forces were 4,743,826: Army (including Air Service) 4,057,101; Navy 599,051; Marines 78,839; and Coast Guard 8,835.
39. Ltr, U.S. Army General Supply Depot Zone Seven, Chicago, Ill., to CO, Aviation School, Wilbur Wright Field, Fairfield, Ohio, subj: Stations, Feb 28, 1919, First Indorsement, Hq Wilbur Wright Air Service Depot, Fairfield, Ohio, to Zone Supply Officer, Zone 7, Chicago, Mar 4, 1919 (Hist, FAD, 1917-1943, Exhibit 11). An important adjunct to the former Fairfield Aviation General Supply Depot had been the Airplane Acceptance Park at Moraine City, four miles southwest of Dayton. This military organization was responsible for accepting or rejecting airplanes (mainly DeHavilland DH-4s) produced by the Dayton-Wright Airplane Co.
40. Hist, FAD, 1917-1943, p 17.
41. Hq Aviation General Supply Depot, Fairfield, Ohio (Wilbur Wright Field), SO 178, Nov 1, 1920 (Hist, FAD, 1917-1943, Exhibit 26).

III. FAIRFIELD AIR DEPOT 1917-1931

1. History of the Air Depot at Fairfield, Ohio, 1917-1943 (FASC, Patterson Field, 1944), pp 1-16. Hereafter cited as Hist, FAD, 1917-1943.
2. Telegram, Hq Air Service, to Maj C. T. Waring, Jan 10, 1919 (Hist, FAD, 1917-1943, Exhibit 10).
3. Hist, FAD, 1917-1943, p 16. About 40 squadrons resided at Wilbur Wright Field and the Fairfield Aviation General Supply Depot for varying lengths of time between Jul 8, 1917, and Feb 20, 1919. Many of the squadrons came from Kelly Field, Texas, stayed about 90 days, then transferred to the Air Service Depot, Garden City, Long Island, New York, for probable reassignment to Europe.
4. Ltr, Chief of Air Service, to Commanding Officer, Aviation General Supply Depot, Fairfield, Ohio, citing "Orders 49, O.D.A.S., Nov. 3, 1919," Jul 31, 1920 (Hist, FAD, 1917-1943, Exhibit 16).
5. Hist, FAD, 1917-1943, pp 16-17.
6. *Ibid.*, pp 35-36.
7. Edward O. Purtee, *History of the Army Air Service, 1907-1926* (AMC, WPAFB, 1948), p 111.
8. *Ibid.*, Alfred Goldberg, ed., *A History of the United States Air Force 1907-1957* (New York, 1957), p 29.
9. Ltr, Office, Director of Air Service, to Commanding Officer, Aviation General Supply Depot, Fairfield, Ohio, subj: Removal of Aviation Repair Depot, Indianapolis, to Fairfield, Jul 16, 1920 (Hist, FAD, 1917-1943, Exhibit 22).
10. Rprt, Historical Data, Maintenance Div, Fairfield Air Service Command, Patterson Field, May 1, 1944.
11. Ltr, CO, Aviation Repair Depot, Speedway, Indianapolis, Indiana, to CO, Aviation General Supply Depot, Fairfield, Ohio, subj: Re Move to Fairfield, Ohio, Aug 9, 1920; ltr, CO, Avn Gen Supply Depot, Fairfield, Ohio, to CO, Avn Repair Depot, Speedway, Indianapolis, Ind., subj: Moving of Aviation Repair Depot to Fairfield, Ohio, Aug 12, 1920 (Hist, FAD, 1917-1943, Exhibits 23, 24).
12. Rprt, Historical Data, Maintenance Div, FASC, May 1, 1944.
13. *Ibid.*
14. Rprt, Chief of the Air Service to the Secretary of War for Fiscal Year 1920, Oct 4, 1921; rprt, Aircraft Condition in the Air Service, June 1924 (Hist, FAD, 1917-1943, Exhibit 37).
15. Hq Aviation General Supply Depot, Fairfield, Ohio, SO 178, Nov 1, 1920 (Hist, FAD, 1917-1943, Exhibit 26).
16. War Dept GO 2, Jan 14, 1921 (Hist, FAD, 1917-1943, Exhibit 28).
17. War Dept SO 179, Aug 4, 1921 (Hist, FAD, 1917-1943, Exhibit 30).
18. War Dept SO 71, Mar 26, 1923 (Hist, FAD, 1917-1943, Exhibit 36).
19. Hq Materiel Division SO 101, May 19, 1927 (Hist, FAD, 1917-1943, Exhibit 32). The Materiel Division, commanded by Brig. Gen. William E. Gillmore, succeeded the Army Air Service Engineering Division when the Army Air Corps was established. At the time of its establishment, Oct 15, 1926, the Materiel Division was located at McCook Field.
20. War Dept Circular 76, Oct 25, 1921 (Hist, FAD, 1917-1943, Exhibit 29).
21. Memo, Depot Supply Officer, to CO, FAID, no subj, May 2, 1922 (Hist, FAD, 1917-1943, Exhibit 34).
22. *Ibid.*
23. Hq FAID GO 3, Feb 12, 1924 (Hist, FAD, 1917-1943, Exhibit 31).
24. Lowell J. Thomas, *The First World Flight* (Boston, 1925), introduction by Maj Gen Mason M. Patrick, Chief of Air Service, p xxi.
25. Air Service *News Letter* VII (Nov 22, 1923), 6-8.
26. *Aircraft Year Book for 1924* (New York, 1925), p 237.
27. Lowell J. Thomas and Lowell Thomas, Jr., *Famous First Flights That Changed History* (Garden City, New York, 1968), pp 19-20; AF Pamphlet 190-2-2, *A Chronology of American Aerospace Events from 1903 through 1964* (Sep 1965), p 20.
28. Thomas and Thomas, *Famous First Flights*, pp 18-31.
29. Thomas, *First World Flight*, p 4.
30. Joe Christy, "That First Round-the-World Flight," *AIR FORCE* Magazine 57 (Mar 1974), 53-59. For a continuation of the story, see Alva Harvey's article, "Seattle Has Crashed in Alsaska," *AIR FORCE* Magazine 57 (Sep 1974), 103-7.
31. Thomas, p 4.
32. Christy, p 53.
33. Lloyd Morris and Kendall Smith, *Ceiling Unlimited: The Story of American Aviation from Kitty Hawk to Supersonics* (New York, 1953), pp 236-37.
34. Morris and Smith, p 237.
35. Air Service *News Letter* VII (Jul 19, 1923), 4; Air Service *News Letter* VII (Nov 22, 1923), 6-8.
36. Thomas, p 5; Air Service *News Letter* VIII (Feb 1, 1924), 12-13; booklet, *First Around the World* (Douglas Aircraft Corp., Santa Monica, Ca., ca 1974), p 2.
37. *Aircraft Yearbook for 1924*, p 239.
38. *Ibid.*
39. Thomas, pp 17-18.
40. *Aircraft Yearbook for 1924*, pp 72-73.
41. *Ibid.*
42. Thomas, p 7.
43. *Ibid.*, p 8.
44. *Ibid.*, p 9.
45. Thomas and Thomas, p 63.
46. Harvey, pp 103-7. Sergeant Harvey graduated from pilot primary school in 1925, advanced through commissioned grades to the rank of colonel, and retired in that grade after World War II.
47. Thomas, pp 293-94.
48. *Ibid.*, pp 304-5.
49. *Ibid.*, p 315.
50. *Ibid.*, p 325.
51. Thomas and Thomas, p 87.
52. National Aeronautic Association *Review* 2 (Special Dayton Air Race Edition, Sep 18, 1924), 1.
53. Air Service *News Letter* VIII (Oct 31, 1924).
54. Air Service *News Letter* VIII (Jul 31, 1924); NAA *Review* 2 (Sep 18, 1924), 4.
55. Air Service *News Letter* VIII (Oct 31, 1924).
56. NAA *Review* 2 (Sep 18, 1924), 1.
57. Arthur G. Renstrom, *Wilbur & Orville Wright: A Chronology Commemorating the Hundredth Anniversary of the Birth of Orville Wright, August 19, 1871* (Washington, 1975), p 78; Hist, FAD, 1917-1943, pp 42-43.

58. Hist, FAD, 1917-1943, p 32.
59. *Ibid.*
60. *Ibid.*, p 48.
61. *AMC and Its Antecedents (1917-1960)* (AMC Historical Study 329, 1960), pp 3-4.
62. Hist, FAD, 1917-1943, p 131.
63. *Ibid.*, p 57.
64. *Ibid.*, p 61.
65. *Ibid.*, pp 62-63.
66. Hist, 2750 ABW, Jul 1974-Dec 1975, Vol II: WPAFB and 2750 ABW Heritage and Lineage 1917-1975, pp 45-46; Hist, FAD, 1917-1943, pp 66-67; "When Pilots Flew on Two Wings," *Skywrighter*, May 15, 1981, pp 16, 19.

IV. McCOOK FIELD 1917-1927

1. Robert I. Curtis, John Mitchell, and Martin Copp, *Langley Field, the Early Years 1916-1946* (Langley AFB, Va., 1977), p 11.
2. *Organization of Military Aeronautics 1907-1935* (AAF Historical Study 25, 1944), p 26.
3. Arthur Sweetser, *The American Air Service* (New York, 1919), p 66.
4. *Organization of Military Aeronautics*, p 28.
5. Sweetser, p 68.
6. *Ibid.*, p xxvii.
7. Curtis et al., p 14.
8. Isaac F. Marcosson, *Colonel Deeds: Industrial Builder* (New York, 1947), pp 216-17.
9. *Ibid.*, p 221.
10. Sweetser, p 94.
11. Curtis et al., p 22.
12. Marcosson, p 215.
13. *Ibid.*
14. *Ibid.*
15. George B. Smith, "History of North Dayton Property, Temporarily Called Wright Field, Now McCook Field" (unpublished recollections, n.d.).
16. Terence M. Dean, "The History of McCook Field, Dayton, Ohio, 1917-1927" (unpublished thesis, University of Dayton, 1969); Maurer Maurer, "McCook Field, 1917-1927," *The Ohio Historical Quarterly* 67 (Jan 1958), 23.
17. Memo, Brig Gen George O. Squier, Chief Signal Officer of the Army, to Adjutant General of the Army, subj: Approval of Buildings for Experimental Purposes, Dayton, Ohio, Sep 28, 1917.
18. Telegram, J. K. Grannis, A.M.E.S.C., Superintendent of Construction, to Lt Col C. G. Edgar, Signal Corps, Sep 28, 1917.
19. See Note 17.
20. Dean, p 13.
21. Ltr, J. K. Grannis, A.M.E.S.C., Supt. of Construction, to Lt Col C. G. Edgar, S.C., U.S.R., subj: Experimental Field, Sep 28, 1917.
22. Memo, Col E. A. Deeds, Signal Corps, to Lt Col Edgar (Construction Division), no subj., Oct 1, 1917.
23. Resolution Passed at Meeting of the Aircraft Production Board, Oct 1, 1917, submitted to Lt Col C. G. Edgar, Construction Division, Signal Corps.
24. Capt H. H. Blee, *History of Organization and Activities of Airplane Engineering Division, Bureau of Aircraft Production* (Misc. Report No. 220, McCook Field, 1919), p 82; Maurer, "McCook Field," p 23.
25. Dean, p 14.
26. R. M. McFarland, ed., *History of the Bureau of Aircraft Production*, Vol II (AMC, WPAFB, 1951), p 278.
27. Blee, p 82.
28. "Survey and History of McCook Field, Dayton, Ohio," *History of McCook Field (Miscellaneous Correspondence) 1918-1926.*
29. *Ibid.*
30. Blee, p 83.
31. *Ibid.*
32. *Ibid.*
33. Dean, p 10.
34. Marguerite Jacobs, "Flying Fields and Fashions Change" (unpublished recollections, 1928).
35. Dean, p 12.
36. McFarland, Vol II, p 279.
37. Dean, p 18.
38. McFarland, Vol II, p 280.
39. "History of the Air Corps Materiel Division," (unpublished history), p 17.
40. Ltr, C. W. Nash, Assistant Director of Aircraft Production, to Col J. G. Vincent, Chief Engineer, Aircraft Production, subj: McCook Field, Nov 7, 1918.
41. Dean, p 16.
42. *Ibid.*, p 19.
43. Walt Boyne, "The Treasures of McCook Field," *Wings* 5 (Aug 1975), 8.
44. Walt Boyne, "The Treasure Trove of McCook Field," *Airpower* 5 (Jul 1975), 10.
45. Dean, p 47; ltr, Director of Air Service to Chief, Engineering Division, Air Service, Dayton, Ohio, subj: Administration Matters Regarding Civilian Personnel and Telegraph Service, May 14, 1919.
46. Dean, p 15.
47. Rprt, C. F. Simmons, Factory Manager, Airplane Engineering Division, Organization and Activities of the Factory Department including Construction and Maintenance, November 1917-November 1918, Serial No. 376.
48. Edward O. Purtee, *History of the Army Air Service, 1907-1926* (AMC, WPAFB, 1948), pp 42-44.
49. J. F. Curry, "What McCook Field Means to Aviation" (unpublished recollections, n.d.).
50. McCook Field, Engineering Division, Weekly Progress Reports No. 27 (Oct 22, 1918) and No. 29 (Nov 5, 1918). D0012M/468 and D0012M/497.
51. Blee, p 84.
52. Maurer, "McCook Field," p 24.
53. See Note 28.
54. Record of Military Administration, Airplane Engineering Division, McCook Field, Ohio, Dec 16, 1918; *The Army's Order of Battle of the United States Land Forces in the World War (1917-1919)*, Vol 3, Part 1 (Washington, 1949), p 881.
55. Dean, p 20.
56. Alfred Goldberg, ed., *A History of the United States Air Force* (New York, 1957), p 15.
57. Purtee, pp 101-2.
58. Dean, p 32.
59. Sweetser, pp 237-38.
60. McFarland, p 300.
61. Dean, p 45.
62. Purtee, p 107.
63. Telegram, War Department, McCook Field, Dayton, Ohio, to Division of Military Aeronautics, Washington, D.C., Executive Section, Dec 20, 1918.
64. Curtis et al., p 16.
65. "Remembering the Forgotten Field," *Skywrighter*, Oct 19, 1979. pp 17, 22.
66. Boyne, "Treasures," p 20.
67. Dean, p 98.
68. Purtee, p 128; Charles Worman, "McCook Field: A Decade of Progress," *Aerospace Historian* 17 (Spring 1970), 15.
69. Dean, p 110.
70. *Ibid.*, pp 72-76.
71. Maurer, "McCook Field," p 25.
72. Dean, pp 74-75.
73. *Ibid.*, p 73.
74. See Note 49.

75. T. C. McMahon, "Something About McCook Field" (unpublished recollections, n.d.).
76. Air Force Institute of Technology, *Yesterday, Today and Tomorrow* (AFIT, WPAFB, 1979), pp 2, 4.
77. *Ibid.*, p 4.
78. *Ibid.*
79. *Ibid.*, p 7.
80. *Ibid.*, p 9.
81. Brig Gen William E. Gillmore, Chief, Materiel Division, "McCook Field Review - 1926," Dec 20, 1926, Doc. X in papers of George A. Biehn: *Indexed Documents Concerning McCook Field, Wright Field, 1929, and Air Service Progress through 1929*.
82. "Wright Field Today," Doc. XII, in *Indexed Documents,* p 4.
83. *Ibid.*
84. Dean, p 64.
85. "Valuation of Assets of Engineering Division Air Service, McCook Field, Dayton, Ohio" (unpublished financial report, Oct 31, 1923).
86. Maurer, "McCook Field," p 33.
87. *Ibid.*
88. See Note 49.
89. Maurer, "McCook Field," p 33.
90. Curtis et al., p 16.
91. *Ibid.*, pp 44-45.
92. Memorandum for Chief of Staff, from Maj Gen Charles T. Menoher, Director of Air Service, subj: Purchase of Dayton-Wright Airplane Plant for Use as Air Service Engineering Experimental Station and Testing Field, Apr 11, 1919.
93. "Report of the Director of Air Service to the Secretary of War, 1920," War Department Annual Reports, Fiscal Year Ended Jun 30, 1920 (Washington, 1920), pp 1493-94.
94. Charlotte Reeve Conover, ed., *Dayton and Montgomery County,* Vol I (New York, 1932), p 303.
95. *NCR Progress* (May 13, 1922), p 1.
96. Samuel Crowther, *John H. Patterson, Pioneer in Industrial Welfare* (New York, 1924), pp 363-64.
97. Conover, p 304.
98. Shelby E. Wickam, "Wright Field: Looking Back Over 50 Years of Aviation History," *The Skywrighter,* Oct 7, 1977, pp 6, 20.
99. *NCR Progress* (Nov 23, 1922), p 1.
100. *Ibid.*
101. *The Dayton Journal,* Oct 26, 1922, p 1.
102. *Ibid.*
103. *The Dayton News,* Oct 27, 1922, p 1.
104. See Note 99.
105. Conover, p 304.
106. See Note 99.
107. *Ibid.*
108. Ltr, 2750 ABW/DEIC (Real Estate, Cost Accounting Section), to 2750 ABW/HO, subj: History of Acquiring Fee Land, WPAFB (Your letter 16 Jul 1980), Jul 25, 1980, with attachment: Listing of Fee Land.
109. Warranty Deed, Dayton Air Service Incorporated Committee, to United States of America, Aug 9, 1924.
110. Deed, The Dayton Air Service Incorporated Committee, to The United States of America, Dec 18, 1924.
111. *Ibid.*
112. Photocopies of subject warranty deeds in 2750 ABW/HO Archives.
113. *The Dayton Evening Herald,* Jan 5, 1923.
114. "Wright Field Today," Doc. XII in *Indexed Documents.*
115. Completion Report, "Wright Field, Dayton, Ohio," Vol I, Office Constructing Quartermaster, Dayton, Ohio, about Jul 1927, p 1.
116. War Department General Order 20, Aug 21, 1925.

V.   WRIGHT FIELD 1927-1948

1. "Dedication of Wright Field," *U.S. Air Services 12* (Nov 1927), 32.
2. The most extensive contemporary account of the Wright Field dedication ceremonies is given in A. M. Jacobs, "The Dedication of Wright Field," *Air Corps News* XI (Nov 10, 1927).
3. First Annual Report of the Chief, Materiel Division, Air Corps, Fiscal Year 1927, pp 176-79. Also, A. M. Jacobs, general press release for publicity purposes and for the Air Corps newsletter, 1927.
4. First Annual Report, Chief, Materiel Division, FY 1927, p 179.
5. Third Annual Report, Chief, Materiel Division, FY 1929, p 274.
6. James J. Niehaus, *Five Decades of Materials Progress, 1917-1967* (Materials Lab, WPAFB, 1967), p 40.
7. First Annual Report, p 180.
8. Niehaus, p 40.
9. First Annual Report, p 23.
10. Second Annual Report, Chief, Materiel Division, FY 1928, p 227.
11. Third Annual Report, p 274.
12. First Annual Report, pp 4-5; *U.S Air Services* 11 (Oct 1926), 24.
13. First Annual Report, p 26.
14. "Program, Dedication of Wright Field in Honor of Wilbur Wright, Orville Wright, and The Citizens of Dayton Who Presented the Wright Field Site to the Government," Dayton, Ohio, Oct 12, 1927, p 15. (Hereafter cited as Wright Field Dedication Program.)
15. Annual Reports, Chief, Materiel Division: FY 1929, p 9; FY 1930, p 9; FY 1931, p 183; FY 1932, pp 10-11; FY 1933, p 10.
16. *Air Corps News Letter XX* (Special Materiel Division Number) (Jan 1, 1937), 4, 25.
17. First Annual Report, pp 183-84.
18. Eighth Annual Report, Chief, Materiel Division, FY 1934, pp 12-13.
19. Sixth Annual Report, Chief, Materiel Division, FY 1932, p 10.
20. Pamphlet, "Wright Field," Materiel Division, U.S. Army Air Corps, Dayton, Ohio, 1938, p 9.
21. *Air Corps News Letter, XX* (Jan 1, 1937), 8.
22. Pamphlet, "Wright Field," p 12.
23. *Ibid.*, p 10.
24. *Ibid.*, p 14.
25. *Air Corps News Letter XX* (Jan 1, 1937), 12.
26. *Ibid.*, p 12.
27. Pamphlet, "Wright Field," p 17.
28. *Ibid.*, p 18.
29. Seventh Annual Report, Chief, Materiel Division, FY 1933, p 7; *Air Corps News Letter XX* (Jan 1, 1937), 18.
30. *Air Corps News Letter XX* (Jan 1, 1937), 18-19.
31. David Gold, "The Parachute in Perspective: Looking Backward to 1931, circa A.I.A.A. Origin," paper presented to the A.I.A.A. 7th Aerodynamic Decelerator and Balloon Technology Conference, San Diego, California, Oct 21-23, 1981, pp 2-5, 8; David Gold, "Milestones in the History of Parachute Development," *SAFE* 9 (Spring 1979), 15.
32. Eleventh Annual Report, Chief, Materiel Division, FY 1937, p 24.
33. *Air Corps News Letter XX* (Jan 1, 1937), 17.
34. Eleventh Annual Report, p 25.
35. Pamphlet, "Wright Field," pp 24-25.
36. *Air Corps News Letter XX* (Jan 1, 1937), 17.
37. Pamphlet, "Wright Field," p 26.
38. Niehaus, p 62.
39. *Ibid.*, pp 62, 65.
40. *Ibid.*, p 61; *Air Corps News Letter XX* (Jan 1, 1937), 13.
41. Niehaus, p 61.
42. *Ibid.*, pp 59-60.
43. *Ibid.*, p 64.

44. Pamphlet, "Wright Field," p 16.

45. *Ibid.*, p 25.

46. Eleventh Annual Report, p 20.

47. "The Materiel Center and You," Wright Field, Dayton, Jan 1943, p 39.

48. Eleventh Annual Report, p 1.

49. First Annual Report, pp 198-99; 26.

50. Annual Reports, Chief, Materiel Division, Fiscal Years 1927 through 1940.

51. *History of the Army Air Forces Materiel Command 1926-1941* (AMC Historical Study 281, 1943), p 39.

52. Niehaus, p 57.

53. Ninth Annual Report, Chief, Materiel Division, FY 1935, p 5.

54. Thirteenth Annual Report, Chief, Materiel Division, FY 1939, p 9.

55. Brig Gen W. E. Gillmore, "Industrial War Planning in the Army Air Corps," *U.S. Air Services* 14 (Mar 1929), 30-32.

56. Maj J. A. Mars, "Government Must Encourage Commercial Aviation," *U.S. Air Services* 10 (Jun 1925), 29.

57. Ninth Annual Report, p 15; Thirteenth Annual Report, p 55.

58. Eighth Annual Report, p 14; Ninth Annual Report, p 16.

59. Eleventh Annual Report, p 39.

60. *Ibid.*, p 40.

61. Fourteenth Annual Report, Chief, Materiel Division, FY 1940, pp 30-31.

62. Alfred Goldberg, ed., *A History of the United States Air Force 1907-1957* (New York, 1957), pp 43-49.

63. "WPAFB Population Data 1927-1971," 2750 ABW/HO Archives.

64. *History of the Army Air Forces Materiel Command 1926-1941*, pp 6-8.

65. *Ibid.*, p 9.

66. Niehaus, p 67.

67. Hist, 2750 Air Base Wing, July 1974-December 1975, Vol II: WPAFB and 2750 ABW Heritage and Lineage 1917-1975, p 28.

68. *History of the Army Air Forces Materiel Command 1926-1941*, pp 58-59.

69. Ibid.

70. Interview with Mr. Harry S. Price Jr., Price Brothers Company, Dayton, Jan 3, 1984.

71. *History of the Army Air Forces Materiel Command (Materiel Center) 1942* (AMC Historical Study 282, 1946), p 167.

72. Fourteenth Annual Report, p 3.

73. *History of the Army Air Forces Materiel Command (Materiel Center)*, pp 167-71.

74. *Ibid.*, p 8.

75. *History of the Army Air Forces Materiel Command 1926-1941*, pp 39-40.

76. *Ibid.*, p 40.

77. "The Materiel Center and You," p 10.

78. *History of the Army Air Forces Materiel Command 1943* (AMC Historical Study 283, 1946), p 86.

79. "History of McCook and Wright Field," ASD History Office, p 5.

80. Annual Report, Hq Wright Field, Part II: Wright Field Under the Materiel Command, Jan-Jun 1944, pp 6-7.

81. *History of the Army Air Forces Materiel Command 1943*, p 13; "The Materiel Center and You," p 20.

82. *Flying and Popular Aviation* XXIX (Special U.S. Army Air Forces Issue) (Sep 1941), 84-85.

83. *Administrative History of the Air Technical Service Command 1944* (AMC Historical Study 284, 1946), p 8.

84. "The Materiel Center and You," pp 40-41.

85. *Flying and Popular Aviation* XXIX, p 119.

86. *Ibid.*, p 200.

87. *History of the Army Air Forces Materiel Command 1926 through 1941*, pp 86-89.

88. *Flying and Popular Aviation* XXIX, p 86.

89. *Ibid.*, p 200.

90. *Administrative History of the Air Technical Service Command 1944*, pp 39-40.

91. *History of the Army Air Forces Materiel Command 1943*, p 12.

92. *Ibid.*, pp 10-11.

93. Hist, 2750 Air Base Wing, Jul 1974-Dec 1975, Vol II, pp 31-33.

94. *Ibid.*, pp 33-34.

95. *History of the Army Air Forces Materiel Command 1943*, p 85.

96. *Ibid.*, p 86.

97. *Air Force Logistics Command 1917-1976* (AFLC Historical Study 329, Dec 1977), p 7.

98. *Administrative History of the Air Technical Service Command 1944*, pp 103-4.

99. *The Post Script*, May 12, 1945, p 1.

100. "Thanks for the Memories," *The Skywrighter*, Jan 9, 1981, p 8.

101. *The Post Script*, 1945.

102. *The Post Script*, Aug 4, 1945, pp 1, 3.

103. *Ibid.*, Aug 18, 1945, pp 1, 3.

104. Frederic C. Lynch, "The 1945 Army Air Forces Fair—Forerunner of Today's Air Force Orientation Group," *Aerospace Historian* 28 (June 1981), 104-5.

105. Press release, "All in Readiness for Big Air Fair at Wright Field," 16 Oct 1945, Public Information Office files, *History of the Air Technical Service Command 1945* (AMC Historical Study 285, 1951), p 89.

106. Lynch, p 107.

107. From information provided by the Foreign Technology Division Office of History.

108. *History of the Air Technical Service Command 1945*, p 19.

109. Herbert A. Shaw, "German Air Force Secrets Are Bared," *Dayton Daily News*, Nov 2, 1947.

110. *History of the Air Materiel Command 1946* (AMC Historical Study 286, 1951), p 84.

111. *The Wright Flyer*, Aug 18, 1945, p 1.

112. *A Pictorial Review, Wright-Patterson Air Force Base, 1917-1967* (2750 ABW, WPAFB, 1967), p 36; Goldberg, p 105.

113. *History of the Air Technical Service Command 1945*.

114. *History of the Air Materiel Command 1946*, p 92.

115. Chronology, 35th Anniversary, Milestones.

116. *The Post Script*, Aug 30, 1946, p 1.

117. *History of the Air Materiel Command 1946*, p 93.

118. *Ibid.*, p 94.

119. *History of the Air Technical Service Command 1945*.

120. *A Pictorial Review, Wright-Patterson Air Force Base, 1917-1967*, p 37.

121. "Air Force Technical Achievements at Dayton," prepared by Richard D. Thomas, Historical Division, ASD, Jul 20, 1961, p 8.

VI. DEVELOPING AIR POWER 1917-1951

1. Walt Boyne, "The Treasures of McCook Field," *Wings* 5 (Jul 1975), 8.

2. R. M. McFarland, ed., *The History of the Bureau of Aircraft Production*, Vol II, pp 280-81; Terence M. Dean, *History of McCook Field, 1917-1927* (Dayton, 1969), pp 18-19.

3. Capt H. H. Blee, *History of Organization and Activities of Airplane Engineering Division, Bureau of Aircraft Production*, Aug 15, 1919, pp 5-14.

4. *Ibid.*, p 51.

5. *Ibid.*, pp 56-57.

6. Lt Harold H. Emmons, "U.S. Airplane Production, The Official History of Air Progress," *Motor Age*, Dec 5, 1918, pp 18-19, 30.

7. Air Force Pamphlet 70-7, *U.S. Air Force Historical Aircraft, Background Information*, Jun 1970, p 2. Hereafter cited as AFP 70-7.

8. Gordon Swanborough and Peter M. Bowers, *United States Military Aircraft Since 1908* (London, 1971), p 215.

9. *Ibid.*

10. *Ibid.*, pp 220-21.

11. Walt Boyne, "The Treasure Trove of McCook Field," *Airpower* 5 (Jul 1975), 18; Royal Frey, *Evolution of Maintenance Engineering 1907-1920*, Vol. I: *Narrative* (AMC, WPAFB, 1960), p 126.

12. Boyne, "Treasure Trove," p 18.
13. *Ibid.*, pp 220-22; Frey, p 127; Blee, pp 42-44.
14. Blee, pp 42-44.
15. *Ibid.*, pp 43-44.
16. Ltr, C. W. Nash, Asst. Director, Aircraft Production, Airplane Engineering Dept., to Col J. G. Vincent, Chief Engineer, Bureau of Aircraft Production, subj: McCook Field, Nov 7, 1918.
17. Blee, p 44.
18. Peter Bowers, "Forgotten Fighters," *Air Progress* (Fall 1962), p 42.
19. Walt Boyne, "Martin's Marvel," *Airpower* 2 (Jun 1972), 51.
20. According to Glenn L. Martin's biographer, the original contract called for 20 bombers to be constructed. See Henry Still, *To Ride the Wind: A Biography of Glenn L. Martin* (New York, 1964), p 133.
21. Still, p 139; Boyne, "Martin's Marvel," p 68.
22. Maurer Maurer, ed., *The U.S. Air Service in World War I*, Vol I: *The Final Report and A Tactical History* (Washington, 1978), pp 358-71.
23. Richard P. Hallion, *Test Pilots: The Frontiersmen of Flight* (New York, 1981), pp 62-63.
24. Maurer Maurer, "McCook Field, 1917-1927," *The Ohio Historical Quarterly* 57 (Jan 1958), 24.
25. Boyne, "Treasure Trove," p 13.
26. Edward O. Purtee, *History of the Army Air Service 1907-1926* (AMC, WPAFB, 1948), pp 128-29.
27. Dean, p 79.
28. *Ibid.*, p 80.
29. Frey, p 190.
30. *Ibid.*, p 191.
31. Gardner W. Carr, "Organization and Activities of Engineering Division of the Air Service," *U.S. Air Services* 7 (Feb 1922), 22-25.
32. Boyne, "Treasures," p 10; Charles G. Worman, "McCook Field, A Decade of Progress," *Aerospace Historian* 17 (Spring 1970), p 14.
33. Carr, p 23.
34. *Ibid.*
35. Worman, p 15.
36. Carr, p 25.
37. Marshall Lincoln, "The Barling," *Air Classics* 2 (Feb 1965), 29.
38. Earl H. Tilford, Jr., "The Barling Bomber," *Aerospace Historian* 26 (Jun 1979), p 94.
39. Henry H. Arnold, *Global Mission* (New York, 1949), p 110.
40. *Ibid.*, p 120.
41. C. H. Hildreth and Bernard C. Nalty, *1001 Questions Answered About Aviation History* (New York, 1969), p 182; Joseph A. Ventolo, Jr., "Col. John A. Macready," *AIR FORCE* Magazine (Feb 1980), pp 76-78; Air Force Pamphlet 190-2-2, *A Chronology of American Aerospace Events from 1903 through 1964*, Sep 1965, p 22. Hereafter cited as AFP 190-2-2.
42. Dr. Robert F. Futrell, "The Development of Aeromedical Evacuation in the USAF 1909-1939," AAHS *Journal* 23 (Fall 1978), 216-18.
43. Paul Lambermont and Anthony Pirie, *Helicopters and Autogyros of the World* (New York, 1959), p 164.
44. Hallion, *Test Pilots*, p 147.
45. Carr, p 26.
46. Booklet, *A Little Journey to the Home of the Engineering Division, Army Air Service* (Hq Engineering Division, McCook Field, ca 1926), p 15.
47. Wright Field Dedication Program, Oct 12, 1927, p 12.
48. Brig Gen Ross G. Hoyt, "The Curtiss Hawks," *AIR FORCE* Magazine (Oct 1976), pp 68-69.
49. C. G. Grey, ed., *(Jane's) All The World's Aircraft*, 1926, p 240b.
50. Andrew W. Waters, *All the U.S. Air Force Airplanes, 1907-1983* (New York, 1983), p 285; James C. Fahey (ed.), *U.S. Army Aircraft 1908-1946* (New York, 1946), p 21.
51. Hoyt, "The Curtiss Hawks," p 68.
52. *Ibid.*, pp 68-69; AFP 70-7, p 6.
53. Waters, p 215; Fahey, p 30.
54. *Ibid.*, p 63; Fahey, p 20.
55. *(Jane's) All The World's Aircraft*, 1928, p 212c; Waters, p 15.
56. *(Jane's) All The World's Aircraft*, 1927, pp 249b-250b.
57. Frederick P. Neely, "Army Makes Longest Overwater Flight," *U.S. Air Services* 12 (Aug 1927), 21-22; William B. Murphy, "The Flying *Bird of Paradise*," *Aerospace Historian* 26 (Mar 1979), pp 30-33.
58. John Goldstrom, *A Narrative History of Aviation* (New York, 1942), pp 235-36; Lloyd Morris and Kendall Smith, *Ceiling Unlimited: The Story of American Aviation from Kitty Hawk to Supersonics* (New York, 1953), pp 267-68.
59. Neely, p 20.
60. Murphy, p 33; AFP 190-2-2, p 25.
61. Third Annual Report, Chief, Materiel Division, FY 1929, p 21.
62. Fourth Annual Report, Chief, Materiel Division, FY 1930, pp 15-16.
63. Fifth Annual Report, Chief, Materiel Division, FY 1931, pp 23-24.
64. Sixth Annual Report, Chief, Materiel Division, FY 1932, Part II: Engineering Activities, pp 19-20; Fahey, p 20.
65. Seventh Annual Report, Chief, Materiel Division, FY 1933, Part II: Engineering Activities, pp 13-14; Fahey, p 20; Waters, p 12.
66. Fifth Annual Report, pp 27-28.
67. AFP 70-7, p 6.
68. Sixth Annual Report, p 21; Waters, p 16; Fahey, p 22.
69. Seventh Annual Report, p 14.
70. Still, p 181.
71. AFP 70-7, p 7; Waters, p 16.
72. Waters, p 16.
73. AFP 190-2-2, p 30.
74. Third Annual Report, p 29.
75. *Ibid.*, p 30; Waters, p 378.
76. Fifth Annual Report, p 37.
77. Sixth Annual Report, p 25.
78. *Ibid.*
79. *Ibid.*, p 25; Seventh Annual Report, p 18.
80. Sixth Annual Report, p 26; Waters, p 379.
81. Waters, p 218.
82. Fahey, pp 30-31.
83. Sixth Annual Report, p 22.
84. AFP 70-7, p 5; Fahey, p 32.
85. Secretary of the Air Force, Office of Information, Photo Package No. 2, 1971, p 5.
86. Sixth Annual Report, p 23; Fahey, p 32.
87. Seventh Annual Report, p 16; Photo Package No. 2, p 5.
88. Seventh Annual Report, p 16.
89. Fourth Annual Report, pp 35-36.
90. Fahey, p 28.
91. Waters, p 284.
92. Sixth Annual Report, p 24.
93. Wesley F. Craven and James L. Cate, eds., *The Army Air Forces in World War II*, Vol. I: *Plans and Early Operations* (Chicago, 1950), pp 54-71.
94. Ninth Annual Report, Chief, Materiel Division, FY 1935, Part II: Engineering, p 13.
95. Douglas J. Ingells, *They Tamed the Sky* (New York, 1947), p 20.
96. Waters, p 68; AFP 70-7, p 11; Fahey, p 20.
97. Ninth Annual Report, p 14.
98. Lambermont and Pirie, pp 194-95; Fahey, p 28.
99. Waters, p 203-4.
100. Craven and Cate, Vol. I, pp 65-66.
101. Edward Jablonski, *Flying Fortress* (New York, 1949), p 155.
102. DeWitt S. Copp, *A Few Great Captains* (New York, 1980), p 328.
103. *Ibid.*
104. *Ibid.*, p 329.
105. Herbert Molloy Mason, Jr., *The United States Air Force: A Turbulent History* (New York, 1976), pp 120-21.
106. Jablonski, p 6; Copp, p 330.
107. Hallion, *Test Pilots*, pp 140-41; Jablonski, pp 12-13.
108. Tenth Annual Report, Chief, Materiel Division, FY 1936, p 7.
109. Waters, p 16; AFP 70-7, p 8; USAF Photo Package No. 2, p 6.
110. Tenth Annual Report, p 7; Hallion, *Test Pilots*, p 141; Jablonski, p 11.

111. Eleventh Annual Report, Chief, Materiel Division, FY 1937, p 8.
112. Arnold, p 155.
113. Fahey, p 22.
114. Jablonski, pp 19-20; AFP 190-2-2, p 32.
115. Jablonski, p 128; AFP 190-2-2, p 33.
116. Craven and Cate, Vol. VI: *Men and Planes*, pp 206-7.
117. *Ibid.*, pp 207-8; *U.S. Air Force Museum Photo Album*, p 44. (Hereafter cited as AFM Album.)
118. Fahey, p 23; AFP 170-7, pp 12-13.
119. AFM Album, pp 40, 47.
120. Craven and Cate, Vol. VI, pp 202-3.
121. *Ibid.*, pp 208-10; Steve Birdsall, *Saga of the Superfortress* (New York, 1980), p 323.
122. Craven and Cate, Vol. VI, pp 210-11.
123. Waters, p 129.
124. Hist., 2750 Air Base Wing, July 1974-December 1975, Vol. II, Wright-Patterson AFB and 2750 ABW Heritage and Lineage (2750 ABW, WPAFB, 1976), pp 66-69.
125. Twelfth Annual Report, Chief, Materiel Division, FY 1938, p 8.
126. Richard C. Hubler, *Big Eight: Biography of an Airplane* (New York, 1960), p 8.
127. Craven and Cate, Vol. VI, p 224.
128. Waters, p 134.
129. Craven and Cate, Vol. VI, p 224; Hubler, p 54.
130. Ninth Annual Report, p 15; AFM Album, p 31.
131. Twelfth Annual Report, pp 9-10.
132. Fahey, p 31.
133. Thirteenth Annual Report, Chief, Materiel Division, FY 1939, pp 40-42; Fahey, p 31.
134. Waters, p 220.
135. Tenth Annual Report, p 6; Fahey, p 32; Waters, p 251.
136. AFP 70-7, p 10; AFM Album, p 27.
137. Craven and Cate, Vol. VI, pp 212-14; Waters, pp 256-57.
138. Craven and Cate, Vol. VI, pp 214-15; AFP 70-7, p 16; AFM Album, p 42.
139. Craven and Cate, Vol. VI, pp 215-17; AFP 70-7, p 13; USAF Photo Package No. 2, p 10; AFM Album, p 48.
140. Craven and Cate, Vol. VI, pp 218-20; AFP 70-7, p 15; AFM Album, p 51.
141. Craven and Cate, Vol. VI, pp 220-21; AFP 70-7, pp 15-16; AFM Album, p 60.
142. Waters, p 289; Fahey, pp 35-36.
143. Ninth Annual Report, p 17.
144. *Ibid.*; Waters, p 52.
145. Waters, p 289.
146. Thirteenth Annual Report, pp 41-42; AFP 70-7, pp 10-11; AFM Album, p 38.
147. Waters, p 291; Fahey, pp 21-22.
148. USAF Photo Package No. 2, p 10; AFM Album, p 36.
149. Fahey, p 27; Waters, p 26.
150. Waters, p 28.
151. AFP 70-7, pp 17-19; Birdsall, p 233; AFP 190-2-2, p 48.
152. Alfred Goldberg, ed., *A History of the United States Air Force 1907-1957* (New York, 1957), p 124.
153. Craven and Cate, Vol. VI, pp 243-45; AFP 70-7, p 18; Waters, pp 111-12; Lloyd S. Jones, *U.S. Bombers 1928 to 1980s*, 3rd ed. (Fallbrook, Ca., 1980), pp 121-23, 166-68.
154. Waters, p 176.
155. Grover Heiman, *Jet Pioneers* (New York, 1963), pp 52-67, 127-29; Hallion, *Test Pilots*, pp 168-72; Hildreth, p 310.
156. Craven and Cate, Vol. VI, pp 250-51; AFM Album, p 68.

VII. PATTERSON FIELD 1931-1948

1. Ltr, Registrar Yale College [University], New Haven, Conn., to Frank S. Patterson, no subj., Apr 27, 1918; Certificate of Enlistment, ERC (AGO Form 422-1).
2. War Department Special Order 110, paragraph 83, May 10, 1918.
3. Hq Signal Corps Aviation School, Wilbur Wright Field, SO 124, para 7, May 9, 1918.
4. History of the Air Depot at Fairfield, Ohio 1917-1943 (FASC, Patterson Field, 1944), Exhibit 4. Hereafter cited as Hist, FAD, 1917-1943.
5. Ltr, Wilbur Wright Field Armorers School Commanding Officer (Maj H. C. K. Muhlenberg) to Director of Military Aeronautics, Technical Section, Washington, D.C., subj: Report on Accident to DeHavilland Four Plane No. 32098, Jun 26, 1918.
6. LeRoy Amos Swan Collection, U.S. Air Force Museum Archives.
7. Air Force Pamphlet 190-2-2, *A Chronology of American Aerospace Events from 1903 through 1964*, Sep 1965, p 18.
8. Tom D. Crouch, *The Giant Leap: A Chronology of Ohio Aerospace Events and Personalities 1815-1969* (Columbus, 1971), p 32.
9. Hist, FAD, 1917-1943, p 69.
10. *Ibid.*, p 68.
11. *Ibid.*, p 22.
12. *Ibid*, pp 65-66.
13. "Historical Sketch, Supply Division, FASC, 1917-1938," no author, n.d.
14. *Ibid.*, pp 6-8.
15. Hist, FAD, 1917-1943, pp 73-74.
16. *Ibid.*, p 10.
17. *Ibid.*, p 78.
18. *Ibid.*, p 81.
19. *Ibid.*, p 83.
20. *Ibid.*, pp 83-84.
21. *A Pictorial Review, Wright-Patterson Air Force Base 1917-1967* (2750 ABW, WPAFB, 1967), p 26.
22. Hist, FAD, 1917-1943, p 89.
23. *Ibid.*, pp 78-79.
24. *Ibid.*, p 92.
25. *Ibid.*, p 94.
26. *Ibid.*
27. History of Fairfield Air Depot Control Area Command (FADCAC) and Fairfield Air Service Command (FASC), 1 Feb 1943-1 October 1944, p 35. (Hereafter cited as Hist, FADCAC and FASC, 1943-1944.)
28. "New Post Hospital Open," *Patterson Field Postings,* May 20, 1942, p 1.
29. Hist, FAD, 1917-1943, pp 95, 97.
30. Hist, FADCAC and FASC, 1943-1944, p 44.
31. "Photograph of Wright-Patterson Air Force Base and its Master Plan," 1948, p 5.
32. Hist, FAD, 1917-1943, pp 95-96.
33. "Service Awards to Civilian Employees Authorized by WD," *Patterson Field Postings,* Nov 5, 1943, p 2.
34. Hist, FAD, 1917-1943, p 141.
35. *Ibid.*, p 144.
36. Hist, FADCAC and FASC, 1943-1944, p 57.
37. Maurer Maurer, ed., *Air Force Combat Units of World War II* (Maxwell AFB, Al, 1960), pp 52-53.
38. Maurer Maurer, ed., *Combat Squadrons of the Air Force During World War II* (Maxwell AFB, Al, 1969), pp 9-10.
39. Maurer, *Combat Units*, pp 129-39.
40. *Ibid.*, pp 193-94.
41. Maurer, *Combat Squadrons*, pp 63-64, 75, 261-62, 160.
42. Hist, FADCAC and FASC, 1943-1944, p 125.
43. *Ibid.*, pp 187-88.
44. *Ibid.*, p 383.
45. Hist, FAD, 1917-1943, pp 109, 104.
46. Notes on Joint Meeting of Air Service Command and Fairfield Air Depot Planning Board, p 5, Feb 17, 1943, as cited in "Comprehensive History of Patterson and Wright Field Planning, Nov 1942-Feb 1945."
47. Hist, FAD, 1917-1943, p 99.
48. *Ibid.*, p 101.
49. *Ibid.*, p 111.

50. Hist, FADCAC and FASC, 1943-1944, p 135.
51. Hist, FAD, 1917-1943, pp 113-14.
52. *Ibid.,* p 102.
53. Hist, FADCAC and FASC, 1943-1944, pp 137-38.
54. *Ibid.,* pp 141-45.
55. *Ibid.,* pp 145-46.
56. Hist, FAD, 1917-1943, pp 118-25.
57. *Ibid.,* p 121.
58. Doris A. Baker, *History of AMC Field Organization 1917-1955* (AMC, WPAFB, 1956).
59. Hist, FADCAC and FASC, 1943-1944, p 4.
60. *Ibid.,* p 112.
61. War Dept GO 68, August 18, 1944.
62. *The Post Script,* Sep 21, 1945; *The Post Script,* Sep 28, 1945; *The Post Script,* Nov 16, 1945; *Wright-Patterson Post Script,* Nov 21, 1945; *Wright-Patterson Post Script,* Dec 14, 1945; *Wright-Patterson Post Script,* Dec 28, 1945.
63. "Integration of Wright and Patterson Fields Into a Single Unit."
64. Army Air Forces Technical Base Planning Board, Preliminary Master Plan Report, Approved Mar 18, 1947, pp 15-16.

VIII.   WRIGHT-PATTERSON AFB 1948-1982

1. Authority for the merger was General Orders No. 2, Hq USAF, Jan 13, 1948.
2. Hist, 2750 ABW, Jul-Dec 1948, p 3.
3. *Logistics: An Illustrated History of AFLC and Its Antecedents 1921-1981* (AFLC, WPAFB, 1983), pp 97-99; Alfred Goldberg, ed., *A History of the United States Air Force* (New York, 1957), p 241.
4. Hq WPAFB GO 32, Aug 27, 1948.
5. Hist, 2750 ABW, Jan-Jun 1951, pp 1-2, 4, 33.
6. *A Pictorial Review, Wright-Patterson Air Force Base, 1917-1967* (2750 ABW, WPAFB, 1967), pp 41-42.
7. Hist, 2750 ABW, Jan-Jun 1952, pp 63-64.
8. *Engineering History, 1917-1978, McCook Field to the Aeronautical Systems Division,* 4th ed. (ASD, WPAFB, 1979), p 16.
9. *Logistics: An Illustrated History of AFLC,* pp 128-29.
10. Hist, 2750 ABW, Jan-Jun 1952, p 33, 51; Hist, 2750 ABW, Jul-Dec 1952, p 77.
11. Hist, 2750 ABW, Jul-Dec 1953, pp 91-92.
12. *History of the AMC Contract Airlift System (LOGAIR) 1954-1955* (AMC, WPAFB, 1956), pp 17-18.
13. *Ibid.,* p 35; *Logistics: An Illustrated History of AFLC,* pp 114-17.
14. Hist, 2750 ABW, Jan-Dec 1957, pp 22-23.
15. Hq SAC GO 6, Feb 6, 1959.
16. Hist, 2750 ABW, Jan-Jun 1951, pp 2-3.
17. Hist, 2750 ABW, Jan-Jun 1954, p 46.
18. James J. Niehaus, *Five Decades of Materials Progress 1917-1967* (Materials Lab, WPAFB, 1967), p 96.
19. Base Guide, 1956 (2750 ABW, WPAFB, 1956), p 11.
20. Hist, 2750 ABW, Jul 1960-Jul 1961, pp 18, 41.
21. *Ibid.,* p 156.
22. Hist, 2750 ABW, Jul 1967-Jun 1969, p 36.
23. *Ibid.,* p 12.
24. *Skywrighter,* Aug 18, 1967, p 1.
25. *Skywrighter,* Jun 9, 1967, p 1.
26. *Skywrighter,* Sep 26, 1969, p 1.
27. *Skywrighter,* Jun 17, 1960, p 1.
28. *Skywrighter,* Jun 9, 1961, p 1.
29. *Ibid.*
30. Hist, 2750 ABW, Jul 1974-Dec 1975, p 34.
31. *Ibid.,* p 32.
32. Hist, 2750 ABW, Jan-Dec 1976, p 48.

XII.   ASSOCIATE ORGANIZATIONS

1. "Facts Pack, Air Force Logistics Command," pamphlet published by the AFLC Office of Public Affiars, 1982; "Air Force Logistics Command," *AIR FORCE Magazine,* May 1983, pp 78-79; *Air Force Logistics Command FY 82 Annual Report,* Feb 1, 1983.
2. *Ibid.*
3. Information provided by Ms Barbara Cooper, Historian, Air Force Contract Maintenance Center.
4. Information provided by the Office of Public Affairs, U.S. Air Force Museum.
5. Information provided by Mr. Bill B. Stacy, Historian, Foreign Technology Division.
6. Information excerpted from an article by Col George C. Mohr, MC, Commander of the Air Force Aerospace Medical Research Laboratory, entitled "AMRL Biotechnology Research and Development Activities," appearing in the Summer 1983 edition of *Medical Service Digest,* pp 1-3.
7. Air Force Human Resources Laboratory Annual Report FY 82 (AFHRL Technical Paper 83-15), p 132; "AFHRL," Pamphlet published by the AFHRL Office of Public Affairs, 1982.
8. Information provided by the USAF Medical Center Wright-Patterson, Office of the Commander.
9. Information provided by 1Lt Michael R. Barry, Group Historian, 2046th Communications Group.
10. DISAM Catalog 1984; *DISAM Annual Report 1982,* Feb 25, 1983.
11. Information provided by Maj. Temple H. Black, Chief, Public Affairs Division, Orientation Group, USAF.
12. Information provided by the Office of Public Affairs, 906th Tactical Fighter Group.
13. Base and Tenant Strength Report, 2750 ABW Base Plans Division, Oct 1, 1982.

BIBLIOGRAPHY

BOOKS

Aircraft Year Book for 1924. New York: Aeronautical Chamber of Commerce, 1925.

Chandler, Charles deF. and Lahm, Frank P. *How Our Army Grew Wings: Airmen and Aircraft Before 1914*. New York: Ronald Press, 1943.

Conover, Charlotte Reeve, ed. *Dayton and Montgomery County*. Vol. I. New York: Lewis Historical Publishing Co., 1932.

——— . *Dayton, Ohio—An Intimate History*. Dayton: Landfall Press, n.d.

Copp, DeWitt S. *A Few Great Captains*. Garden City, New York: Doubleday, 1980.

Craven, Wesley F. and Cate, James L., eds. *The Army Air Forces in World War II*, Vol. I: *Plans and Early Operations;* Vol. VI: *Men and Planes*. Chicago: University of Chicago Press, 1950.

Crouch, Tom D. *The Giant Leap: A Chronology of Ohio Aerospace Events and Personalities 1815-1969*. Columbus: Ohio Historical Society, 1971.

Crowther, Samuel. *John H. Patterson, Pioneer in Industrial Welfare*. New York: Doubleday, Page & Co., 1924.

Delury, George E., ed. *The World Almanac and Book of Facts, 1980*. New York: Newspaper Enterprise Association, Inc., 1979.

Fahey, James C., ed. *U.S. Army Aircraft 1908-1946*. New York: Ships and Aircraft, 1946.

Goldberg, Alfred, ed. *A History of the United States Air Force 1907-1957*. Princeton: D. Van Nostrand Co., 1957.

Goldstrom, John. *A Narrative History of Aviation*. New York: Macmillan Co., 1942.

Grey, C. G., ed. *(Jane's) All The World's Aircraft*. London: Sampson Low, 1926.

Hallion, Richard P. *Test Pilots: The Frontiersmen of Flight*. New York: Doubleday & Co., 1981.

Heiman, Grover. *Jet Pioneers*. New York: Duell, Sloan and Pearce, 1963.

Hildreth, C. H. and Nalty, Bernard C. *1001 Questions Answered About Aviation History*. New York: Dodd, Mead & Co., 1969.

Hubler, Richard C. *Big Eight: Biography of an Airplane*. New York: Duell, Sloan & Pearce, 1960.

Ingells, Douglas J. *They Tamed the Sky*. New York: D. Appleton-Century, 1947.

Jablonski, Edward. *Flying Fortress*. Garden City, New York: Doubleday, 1949.

Jones, Lloyd S. *U.S. Bombers 1928 to 1980s*, 3rd ed. Fallbrook, Ca.: Aero Publishers, 1980.

Kelly, Fred C. *The Wright Brothers*. New York: Farrar, Straus and Young, Inc., 1950.

Lambermont, Paul and Pirie, Anthony. *Helicopters and Autogyros of the World*. New York: Philosophical Library, 1959.

Marcosson, Isaac F. *Colonel Deeds, Industrial Builder*. New York: Dodd, Mead & Co., 1947.

Mason, Herbert Molloy, Jr. *The United States Air Force: A Turbulent History*. New York: Mason/Charter, 1976.

Morris, Lloyd and Smith, Kendall. *Ceiling Unlimited: The Story of American Aviation from Kitty Hawk to Supersonics*. New York: Macmillan Co., 1953.

A Pictorial Review, Wright-Patterson Air Force Base, 1917-1967. WPAFB: 2750th Air Base Wing, 1967.

Renstrom, Arthur G. *Wilbur & Orville Wright: A Chronology Commemorating the Hundredth Anniversary of the Birth of Orville Wright, August 19, 1871*.Washington: Library of Congress, 1975.

Still, Henry. *To Ride the Wind: A Biography of Glenn L. Martin*. New York: Julian Messner, 1964.

Swanborough, Gordon and Bowers, Peter M. *United States Military Aircraft Since 1908*. London: Putnam, 1971.

Sweetser, Arthur. *The American Air Service*. New York: D. Appleton and Co., 1919.

Thomas, Lowell J. *The First World Flight*. Boston: Houghton, Mifflin Co., 1925.

Thomas, Lowell J. and Thomas, Lowell, Jr. *Famous First Flights That Changed History*. Garden City, New York: Doubleday & Co., 1968.

U.S. Air Force Museum Photo Album.

Waters, Andrew W. *All the U.S. Air Force Airplanes, 1907-1983*. New York: Hippocrene Books, 1983.

PUBLISHED MEMOIRS AND PAPERS

Arnold, Henry H. *Global Mission*. New York: Harper and Bros., 1949.

McFarland, Marvin W., ed. *The Papers of Wilbur and Orville Wright, Including the Chanute-Wright Letters and Other Papers of Octave Chanute*. Vol. I: 1899-1905. New York: Arno Press, 1972.

ARTICLES

"Air Force Logistics Command." *AIR FORCE Magazine* (May 1983), 78-79.

Bowers, Peter. "Forgotten Fighters." *Air Progress* (Fall 1962), 38-61.

Boyne, Walt. "Martin's Marvel." Airpower II (June 1972), 51-67.

——— . "The Treasure Trove of McCook Field." *Airpower* 5 (Jul 1975), 6-25.

——— . "The Treasures of McCook Field." *Wings* 5 (Aug 1975), 8-25.

Carr, Gardner W. "Organization and Activities of Engineering Division of the Air Service." *U.S. Air Services* 6,7 (Jan, Feb 1922), 9-12; 22-27.

Casari, Robert. "Number of U.S. Aircraft WWI." American Aviation Historical Society *Journal* 20 (Spring 1977), 36-38.

Christy, Joe. "The First Round-the-World Flight." *AIR FORCE Magazine* 57 (Mar 1974), 53-59.

"Dedication of Wright Field." *U.S. Air Services* 12 (Nov 1927), 32.

Emmons, Lt Harold H. "U.S. Airplane Production, The Official History of Air Progress." *Motor Age* (Dec 5, 1918), 18-19, 30.

Futrell, Dr. Robert F. "The Development of Aeromedical Evacuation in the USAF 1909-1939." American Aviation Historical Society *Journal* 23 (Fall 1978), 212-25.

Gibbs-Smith, Charles H. "The World's First Practical Airplane." *NCR World* (4th Qtr, 1978), 5-6.

Gillmore, Brig Gen W. E. "Industrial War Planning in the Army Air Corps." *U.S. Air Services* 14 (Mar 1929), 30-32.

Gold, David. "Milestones in the History of Parachute Development." *SAFE* 9 (Spring 1979), 10-17.

Guinn, Gilbert S. "A Different Frontier: Aviation, the Army Air Forces, and the Evolution of the Sunshine Belt." *Aerospace Historian* 29 (Mar 1982), 34-35.

Hoyt, Brig Gen Ross G., Ret. "The Curtiss Hawks." *AIR FORCE Magazine* (Oct 1976), 68-69.

Jacobs, A. M. "The Dedication of Wright Field." *Air Corps News* XI (Nov 10, 1927), 1.

Justus, Graham, ed. "Aircraft Production in Dayton." *NCR World* (Sep-Oct 1970), 20-25.

Lincoln, Marshall. "The Barling." *Air Classics* II (Feb 1965), 28-32.

Lynch, Frederic C. "The 1945 Army Air Forces Fair—Forerunner of Today's Air Force Orientation Group." *Aerospace Historian* 28 (Jun 1981), 104-5.

McMaster, R. K., ed. "The Adventures of a Junior Military Aviator: Extracts from the Diary of Leo G. Heffernan." *Aerospace Historian* 25 (Jun 1978), 92-102.

Mars, Maj J. A. "Government Must Encourage Commercial Aviation." *U.S. Air Services* 10 (Jun 1925), 29.

Maurer, Maurer. "McCook Field, 1917-1927." *The Ohio Historical Quarterly* 67 (Jan 1958), 21-34.

Mohr, Col George C. "AMRL Biotechnology Research and Development Activities." *Medical Service Digest* (Summer 1983), 1-3.

Murphy, William B. "The Flying *Bird of Paradise*." *Aerospace Historian* 26 (Mar 1979), 30-33.

National Aeronautic Association *Review* 2, Special Air Race Edition (Sep 18, 1924).

Neely, Frederick P. "Army Makes Longest Overwater Flight." *U.S. Air Services* 12 (Aug 1927), 18-22.

Tilford, Earl H., Jr. "The Barling Bomber." *Aerospace Historian* 26 (Jun 1979), 91-97.

Ventolo, Joseph A., Jr. "Col. John A. Macready." *AIR FORCE Magazine* (Feb 1980), 76-78.

Worman, Charles G. "McCook Field, A Decade of Progress." *Aerospace Historian* 17 (Spring 1970), 12-16, 35-36.

HISTORIES, HISTORICAL STUDIES

ARMY AIR FORCES HISTORICAL STUDIES

Army Air Forces Historical Study No. 25, *Organization of Military Aeronautics 1907-1935*, 1944.

USAF HISTORICAL STUDIES

USAF Historical Study No. 98, *The United States Army Air Arm, April 1861 to April 1917*, 1958.

USAF HISTORIES

Maurer, Maurer, ed. *The U.S. Air Service in World War I*. Vol. I: *The Final Report and a Tactical History*. Washington: AF Historical Office, 1978.
———. *Air Force Combat Units of World War II*. Maxwell AFB, Al.: Albert F. Simpson Historical Research Center, 1960.
———. *Combat Squadrons of the Air Force During World War II*. Maxwell AFB, Al.: Albert F. Simpson Historical Research Center, 1969.

COMMAND HISTORICAL STUDIES

AMC Historical Study No. 281, *History of the Army Air Forces Materiel Command 1926-1941*, 1943.

AMC Historical Study No. 282, *History of the Army Air Forces Materiel Command (Materiel Center) 1942*, 1946.

AMC Historical Study No. 283, *History of the Army Air Forces Materiel Command 1943*, 1946.

AMC Historical Study No. 284, *Administrative History of the Air Technical Service Command 1944*, 1946.

AMC Historical Study No. 285, *History of the Air Technical Service Command 1945*, 1951.

AMC Historical Study No. 286, *History of the Air Materiel Command 1946*, 1951.

AMC Historical Study No. 329, *AMC and Its Antecedents 1917-1960*, 1960.

AFLC Historical Study No. 329, *Air Force Logistics Command 1917-1976*, 1977.

COMMAND HISTORIES

Frey, Royal. *Evolution of Maintenance Engineering 1907-1920*. Historical Office, Air Materiel Command, 1960.

Baker, Doris A. *History of AMC Field Organization 1917-1955*. Historical Office, Air Materiel Command, 1956.

History of the AMC Contract Airlift System (LOGAIR) 1954-1955. Historical Office, Air Materiel Command, 1956.

History of Fairfield Air Depot Control Area Command (FADCAC) and Fairfield Air Service Command (FASC), 1 Feb 1943-1 Oct 1944. Historical Office, Air Materiel Command, n.d.

Logistics: An Illustrated History of AFLC and Its Antecedents 1921-1981. WPAFB: Air Force Logistics Command, 1983.

McFarland, R. M. *History of the Bureau of Aircraft Production*. Historical Office, Air Materiel Command, 1951.

Pendergast, 1st Lt Frank J. History of the Air Depot at Fairfield, Ohio 1917-1943. Historical Office, Fairfield Air Service Command, 1944.

Purtee, Dr. Edward O. *History of the Army Air Service 1907-1926*. Historical Office, Air Materiel Command, 1948.

WING HISTORIES

Histories of the 2750th Air Base Wing
Jan-Jun 1948; Jul-Dec 1948; Jan-Jun 1949; Jul-Dec 1949; Jan-Jun 1950; Jul-Dec 1950; Jan-Jun 1951; Jul-Dec 1951; Jan-Jun 1952; Jul-Dec 1952; Jan-Jun 1953; Jul-Dec 1953; Jan-Jun 1954; Jul-Dec 1954; Jan-Dec 1955; Jan-Jun 1956; Jul-Dec 1956; Jan-Dec 1957; Jan-Jun 1958; Jul-Dec 1958; Jan-Jun 1959; Jul 1959-Jun 1960; Jul 1960-Jun 1961; Jul 1961-Jun 1962; Jul 1962-Jun 1967; Jul 1967-Jun 1969; Jul 1969-Jun 1971; Jul 1971-Jun 1972; Jul 1972-Jun 1974; Jul 1974-Dec 1975; Jan-Dec 1976; Jan-Dec 1977; Jan-Dec 1978; Oct 1978-Sep 1979; Oct 1979-Sep 1980.

OFFICIAL PUBLICATIONS

A Little Journey to the Home of the Engineering Division, Army Air Service. McCook Field, Hq Engineering Division, about 1926.

Air Force Pamphlet 70-7, U.S. Air Force Historical Aircraft, Background Information, Jun 1970.

Air Force Pamphlet 190-2-2, A Chronology of American Aerospace Events from 1903 through 1964, Sep 1965.

"AFHRL." Pamphlet published by the Air Force Human Resources Laboratory Office of Public Affairs, 1982.

The Army's Order of Battle of United States Land Forces in the World War (1917-1919). Vol. 3, Part 1. Washington: Government Printing Office, 1949.

Base Guide, 1956. WPAFB: 2750th Air Base Wing, 1956.

"Comprehensive History of Patterson and Wright Field Planning, Nov 1942-Feb 1945."

Curtis, Robert I., Mitchell, John, and Copp, Martin. *Langley Field, the Early Years 1916-1946*. Langley AFB, Va.: Historical Office, 4500th ABW, 1977.

Engineering History, 1917-1978, McCook Field to the Aeronautical Systems Division, 4th ed. WPAFB: Aeronautical Systems Division, 1979.

Laubenthal, Capt Sanders A. *Yesterday, Today, and Tomorrow*. WPAFB: Air Force Institute of Technology, Office of Public Affairs, 1979.

"The Materiel Center and You." Wright Field, Jan 1943.

Niehaus, James J. *Five Decades of Materials Progress, 1917-1967*. WPAFB: Materials Lab, 1967.

"Photograph of Wright-Patterson Air Force Base and its Master Plan," 1948.

Secretary of the Air Force, Office of Information, Photo Package No. 2, 1971.

"WPAFB Population Data 1927-1971." 2750th ABW History Office Archives.

"Wright Field." Pamphlet published by the Materiel Division, U.S. Army Air Corps, 1938.

REPORTS

Annual Report, Signal Corps Aviation School, Wilbur Wright Field, Fairfield, Ohio, May 31, 1918, Maj Arthur E. Wilbourn, Commanding Officer.

Report, C. F. Simmons, Factory Manager, Airplane Engineering Division, Organization and Activities of the Factory Department Including Construction and Maintenance, November 1917-November 1918. Serial No. 376.

Blee, Capt. H. H. History of Organization and Activities of Airplane Engineering Division, Bureau of Aircraft Production. Miscellaneous Report 220, McCook Field, 1919.

McCook Field, Engineering Division, Weekly Progress Reports, Numbers 27 (Oct 22, 1918) and 29 (Nov 5, 1918).

"Report of the Director of Air Service to the Secretary of War, 1920." War Department Annual Reports, Fiscal Year Ended Jun 30, 1920.

Completion Report, "Wright Field, Dayton, Ohio." Vol. I. Office Constructing Quartermaster, Dayton, Ohio, about Jul 1927.

Annual Reports, Chief, Materiel Division, Fiscal Years 1927 through 1940.

Report, Historical Data, Maintenance Division, Fairfield Air Service Command, Patterson Field, May 1, 1944.

Annual Report, Hq Wright Field, Part II: Wright Field Under the Materiel Command, Jan-Jun 1944.

Army Air Forces Technical Base Planning Board, Preliminary Master Plan Report, Approved Mar 18, 1947.

Annual Report, Air Force Logistics Command, FY 1982, Feb 1, 1983.

Annual Report, Air Force Human Resources Laboratory, FY 1982 (AFHRL Technical Paper 83-15).

Annual Report, Defense Institute of Security Assistance Management, 1982, Feb 25, 1983.

Base and Tenant Strength Report, 2750 ABW Base Plans Division, Oct 1, 1982.

UNPUBLISHED MATERIALS

Curry, J. F. "What McCook Field Means to Aviation." Unpublished recollections, n.d.

Dean, Terence M. "The History of McCook Field, Dayton, Ohio, 1917-1927." Masters thesis, University of Dayton, 1969.

Gold, David. "The Parachute in Perspective: Looking Backward to 1931, circa A.I.A.A. Origin." Paper presented to the A.I.A.A. 7th Aerodynamic Decelerator and Balloon Technology Conference, San Diego, California, Oct 21-23, 1981.

"Historical Sketch, Supply Division, FASC, 1917-1938," no author, n.d.

"History of McCook and Wright Field." ASD History Office, n.d.

"History of the Air Corps Materiel Division." Unpublished history.

Jacobs, Marguerite. "Flying Fields and Fashions Change." Unpublished recollections, 1928.

McMahon, T. C. "Something About McCook Field." Unpublished recollections, n.d.

Smith, George B. "History of North Dayton Property, Temporarily Called Wright Field, Now McCook Field." Unpublished recollections, n.d.

Thomas, Richard D. "Air Force Technical Achievements at Dayton." Historical Division, Aeronautical Systems Division, Jul 20, 1961.

DOCUMENTS

C. W. Nash, Asst. Director, Aircraft Production, Airplane Engineering Dept. Letter to Col J. G. Vincent, Chief Engineer, Bureau of Aircraft Production, subj: McCook Field, Nov 7, 1918.

Copy of Lease, Purchase Request A-6951, Order No. 50214, between the Miami Conservancy District and Lt Col C. G. Edgar, Signal Corps, Jul 1, 1917.

The Dayton Air Service Incorporated Committee. Deed to The United States of America, Aug 9, 1924.

The Dayton Air Service Incorporated Committee. Deed to The United States of America, Dec 18, 1924.

Deeds, Col E. A., Signal Corps. Memo to Lt Col Edgar (Construction Division), no subj., Oct 1, 1917.

Director of Air Service. Letter to Chief, Engineering Division, Air Service, Dayton, Ohio, subj: Administration Matters Regarding Civilian Personnel and Telegraph Service, May 14, 1919.

Grannis, J. K., A.M.E.S.C., Superintendent of Construction. Letter to Lt Col C. G. Edgar, S.C., U.S.R., subj: Experimental Field, Sep 28, 1917.

History of McCook Field (Miscellaneous Correspondence) 1918-1926.

Indexed Documents Concerning McCook Field, Wright Field, 1929, and Air Service Progress through 1929.

LeRoy Amos Swan Collection, U.S. Air Force Museum Archives.

Menoher, Maj Gen Charles T., Director of Air Service. Memorandum for Chief of Staff, subj: Purchase of Dayton-Wright Airplane Plant for Use as Air Service Engineering Experimental Station and Testing Field, Apr 11, 1919.

Nash, C. W., Assistant Director of Aircraft Production. Letter to Col J. G. Vincent, Chief Engineer, Aircraft Production, subj: McCook Field, Nov 7, 1918.

Registrar Yale College [University], New Haven, Conn. Letter to Frank S. Patterson, no subj., Apr 27, 1918; Certificate of Enlistment, ERC (AGO Form 422-1).

Resolution Passed at Meeting of the Aircraft Production Board, Oct 1, 1917, submitted to Lt Col C. G. Edgar, Construction Division, Signal Corps.

Squier, Brig Gen George O., Chief Signal Officer of the Army. Memo to Adjutant General of the Army, subj: Approval of Buildings for Experimental Purposes, Dayton, Ohio, Sep 28, 1917.

Wilbur Wright Field Armorers School Commanding Officer (Maj H. C. K. Muhlenberg). Letter to Director of Military Aeronautics, Technical Section, Washington, D.C., subj: Report on Accident to DeHavilland Four Plane No. 32098, Jun 26, 1918.

2750th ABW/DEIC (Real Estate, Cost Accounting Section). Letter to 2750th ABW/HO, subj: History of Acquiring Fee Land, WPAFB (Your ltr 16 Jul 1980), Jul 25, 1980, with attachment: Listing of Fee Land.

"Valuation of Assets of Engineering Division Air Service, McCook Field, Dayton." Financial report, Oct 31, 1923.

War Department, McCook Field, Dayton, Ohio. Telegram to Division of Military Aeronautics, Washington, D.C., Executive Section, Dec 20, 1918.

NEWSPAPERS AND PERIODICALS

Air Service News Letter
Jul 19, 1923, Vol VII
Nov 22, 1923, Vol VII
Feb 1, 1924, Vol VIII
Jul 31, 1924, Vol VIII
Oct 31, 1924, Vol VIII

Air Corps News Letter
Jan 1, 1937, Vol XX (Special Materiel Division Number)

The Dayton Evening Herald, Jan 5, 1923.

The Dayton Journal, Oct 26, 1922.

The Dayton News, Oct 27, 1922.

Flying and Popular Aviation, Sep 1941, Vol XXIX (Special U.S. Army Air Forces Issue).

NCR Progress, May 13, 1922, Vol 3, No 3; Nov 23, 1922, Vol 3, No 8.

"New Post Hospital Open." *Patterson Field Postings,* May 20, 1942, p 1.

The Post Script
Aug 4, 1945
Sep 21, 1945
Sep 28, 1945
Nov 16, 1945
Aug 30, 1946

"Remembering the Forgotten Field." *Skywrighter,* Oct 19, 1979, pp 17, 22.

"Service Awards to Civilian Employees Authorized by WD," *Patterson Field Postings,* Nov 5, 1943, p 2.

Shaw, Herbert A. "German Air Force Secrets Are Bared." *Dayton Daily News,* Nov 2, 1947.

Skywrighter
Jun 17, 1960
Jun 9, 1961
Jun 9, 1967
Aug 18, 1967
Sep 26, 1969

"When Pilots Flew on Two Wings." *Skywrighter,* May 15, 1981, pp 16, 19.

Wickam, Shelby E. "Wright Field: Looking Back Over 50 years of Aviation History." *Skywrighter,* Oct 7, 1977, pp 6, 20.

The Wright Flyer, Aug 18, 1945.

Wright-Patterson Post Script
Nov 21, 1945
Dec 14, 1945
Dec 28, 1945

INTERVIEWS

Interviews, Mr. Harry S. Price, Jr., Price Brothers Company, Dayton, Jan 3. 1984; Jun 22, 1984.

Interviews, Mr. D. Adam Dickey, Dayton, Ohio, Sep 2, 1983; Sep 16, 1983.

Interviews, Mrs. Darlene Gerhardt, Dayton, Ohio, 1983-1984.

OTHER

First Around the World. Santa Monica, Ca.: Douglas Aircraft Corp., 1974.

Program, Dedication of Wright Field in Honor of Wilbur Wright, Orville Wright, and The Citizens of Dayton Who Presented the Wright Field Site to the Government. Dayton, Ohio, Oct 12, 1927.

Story of the Miami Conservancy District. Brochure, Dayton, Ohio, n.d.

Wright Flyers. Brochure published by the Wright Aircraft Corporation, Dayton, Ohio, about 1915.

INDEX

Allyn Hall, Wright State University, 322
Altus AFB, Oklahoma, 306
Aluminum Company of America, 137
Amann, Lt. Col. Richard F., 444
America, Fokker T-2, 207
American Association of Collegiate Schools of Business, 414
American Bicentennial, 333-35, 427, 445-46
American Export and Import Company, 304
American Model Aircraft Association, 334
American Red Cross, 259, 282, 313, 339, 449
Ames, Dr. James S., 22
Ames, Dr. Joseph, 119
Anaconda Copper Company, 97
Anders, Capt. William A., 417, 422
Anderson, Robert, 191
Anderson, Gen. Samuel E., 364, 371, 384
Andrews AFB, D.C., 301, 311, 313, 385
Anger, Frank G., 318
Antioch College, 185
ARC LIGHT operations, 317
Area A, Wright Field, 149, 163-64, 272
Area A, WPAFB, 82, 109, 121, 147, 163-64, 257, 263, 293, 305, 322, 331, 334, 335, 336, 341, 440, 442
Area B, Wright Field, 164
Area B, WPAFB, 14, 48, 63, 79, 80, 82, 103, 121, 148, 161, 163, 169, 195, 293-94, 301, 302-3, 307, 308, 310, 312, 313, 319, 320, 322, 327, 329, 330, 331, 336, 442, 443
Area C, WPAFB, 5, 30, 51, 52, 63, 75, 77, 109, 121, 153, 164, 257, 262, 283, 293, 298, 299, 302-3, 305, 307, 308, 310, 311, 313, 318, 321, 327, 440
Area D, WPAFB, 272
Argentina, 64, 215, 229
Arlington National Cemetery, 7, 296
Armament Branch [Laboratory], Wright Field/WPAFB, 118, 130, 138-39, 150, 172, 310, 375
Armament training, World War I, 42
Armed Forces Courier Station, WPAFB, 449
Armed Forces Day celebrations, 321, 333
Armstrong, Maj. Gen. Harry G., 437-38, 439
Armstrong, Neil, 336, 416, 418, 423
Army Aeronautical Museum (see also Building 12, Area B), 100, 122, 127, 142, 153, 169, 406, 433
Army Air Forces Air Technical Service Command, 148
Army Air Forces Engineering School, 170, 406-8, 429
Army Air Forces Fair, Wright Field, 1945, 165-68, 445
Army Air Forces Institute of Technology, 170-71, 408, 409-10
Army Air Forces Technical Base, 149, 161, 170, 171, 285, 291, 296
Army Air Forces Technical Service Command, 287, 436
Army Air Forces University, 408
Army Industrial College, 275
Army Reorganization Act of 1920, 55
Army-Air Force Exchange Service, 332, 448
Arnold, Gen. Henry H. "Hap," 12, 14, 15, 59, 61, 79, 80, 145, 199, 215, 229, 231, 251, 265, 267, 377, 445
Arnold, Lt. Leslie P., 69, 70, 71
Ashburn Field, Chicago, Illinois, 21, 28, 30, 31
Associate organizations, Wright-Patterson AFB, 432-49
Astronautics program, AFIT, 414, 429
Atlantic Aircraft Corporation, 206-7
Atlantic Ocean, 63, 65, 70, 174, 418, 435
Atomic weapons, 173, 235
Augusta, Georgia, 11, 19
Australia, 231, 420
Austria-Hungary, 20
Autogiro School, Patterson Field, 265-66
Autogiros, 117, 224-25, 265-66
    KD-1, 224
    XR-2, 225
    XR-3, 225
    XR-25, 225
    YG-1, 224, 225, 265-66
    YG-2, 224
    YO-60, 225
Automated Telecommunications Center, 442
Automatic Digital Network (AUTODIN), 442
Automatic landing, Patterson Field, 266

Automatic stabilizer, 13
Avco Corporation, 392
Aviation Armorers' School, Wilbur Wright Field, 28, 42, 46, 53, 59
Aviation General Supply Depot, Fairfield, Ohio (see also Fairfield Aviation General Supply Depot and Fairfield Air Depot), 46, 54, 56, 59
Aviation Hall of Fame, 334
Aviation Mechanics' School, Wilbur Wright Field, 40-41, 42, 53
Aviation Progress, 114
Aviation Repair Depot, Indianapolis, Indiana, 37, 56-57
Aviation Section, U.S. Army Signal Corps, 20-25, 27, 35, 40, 42, 85-87, 168, 258, 411
Avionics Laboratory, 315, 319-20, 329, 333, 390
Azores, 63, 443
Baer Field, Indiana, 280
Bakelite Micarta, 180
Baker, Newton D., 23, 26, 87
Baldwin, Thomas Scott, 17
Ball, Guy M., 194
Balloons, 17, 18, 19, 34, 55, 58, 75, 120, 132, 137-38, 202-3, 224, 344-45, 434
Bands:
    FADR Band, 80
    Wilbur Wright Air Service Depot Band, 55
    361st Army Air Forces Band, 288, 311
    661st Air Force Band, 288, 305, 311, 315, 317, 345, 448
    752nd Army Air Forces Band, 162-63
Bane, Col. Thurman H., 92, 95, 96, 97, 98, 101-3, 105-6, 108, 174, 188, 201, 335, 352, 399, 401, 430
Banks, Lt. Frank, 191
Barker, Lt. John DeF., 104
Barksdale, Lt. Eugene H. "Hoy," 191, 461
Barksdale Field, Louisiana, 260
Barling, Walter J., Jr., 197, 199
Barling bomber (see Aircraft types [U.S.], XNBL-1)
Barnes, Maj. Gen. Frank G., 335
Barrett, P1C Joseph E., 17
Barron Field, Texas, 35
Barton, Brig. Gen. Paul L., 454
Bartron, Brig. Gen. H. A., 73, 285, 287
Base Commissary Store, WPAFB, 332
Base Exchange, WPAFB, 310, 332, 448
Base Heritage Center, 347
Base Memorialization Committee, 334
Baseball team, Fairfield Air Depot, 263
Baseball team, McCook Field, 125
Baseball team, Wright Field, 125
Bass, Col. Bernard, 319
Bassett, Capt. Charles A., 417
Bath Township, Greene County, 33, 51, 112
Bath Township Herald and Mad River Valley Journal, 34
Baumgartner, Ann, 117, 254
Beale AFB, California, 327, 329
Beau, Lt. L. V. 73
Becher, Maj. Eugene M., 275
Beckel, Charles and Susan, 109
Belgium, 145, 393
Bell, Dr. Alexander Graham, 7, 13
Bell Aircraft Company, 235, 254
Belmont Park, New York, 11
Benedict, Lt. Col. C. C., 102, 400
Bennett, Floyd, 207
Benson, Capt. Otis O., 439
Benton, C. B., 227
Bentwaters-Woodbridge, United Kingdom, 392
Berger, Adolf L., 174
Bergstrom AFB, Texas, 447
Berlin Airlift, 293-95, 303
Berliner-Joyce Aircraft Corporation, 220
Berry, E. C., 114
Bettis, Lt. Cyrus, 74, 77
Bicentennial observance (see American Bicentennial)
Bierlein, Capt. James, 412
Big Four Railroad Company, 52
Bill, H. L., 95
Biodynamics, 360

McCook Field, 23, 38, 43-44, 46, 47, 53, 58-59, 63, 64, 65-71,
72, 73, 74, 75, 77, 78-79, 80, 82, 85-115, 118, 121-22,
124-25, 127, 130, 132, 135, 136, 168, 169, 177-203, 255,
299, 334, 335, 349, 352, 373-75, 399-405, 433, 458, 460-61
McCook Field Aeronautical Reference Library, 122, 195
McCook Field Experimental Factory, 178
McCoy, Col. Howard M., 437
McDivitt, James, 416, 417, 423
McDonnell Aircraft Company, 391
McGuire AFB, New Jersey, 330
McIntosh, Lt. Col. Lawrence W., 98, 102, 400, 430
McKee, Gen. William F., 371
McKenny, Joseph, 114
McKillop, Capt. Gregory W., 428
McKinley, Ray, 345
McKinney, Floyd R., 367
McMahon, T. C., 114
McMullen, Lt. Clements, 404
McMullen, Lt. Gen. Thomas H., 396
McNamara, Robert S., 364, 367, 388
McNarney, Col. Joseph T., 129
McPike, Lt. George V., 62
Mead, George, 23
Mechling, Maj. Gen. Edward P., 415
Medal of Honor, 334, 434, 446
Medical Department, Wilbur Wright Field, 38-39, 440
Medical Detachment, Wright Field, 163
Medical Red Flag No. 6, 441
Medical Reserve Corps, 30
Mediterranean theater, World War II, 231, 244, 245
Meister, Louis G., 121, 191
Memphis, Tennessee, 21
Menoher, Maj. Gen. Charles T., 55, 56, 100, 188
Mercury Service (see also LOGAIR), 303-4
Merrill, Gen. Jack G., 368, 371
Merrill, Lt. William G., 30
Messerschmitt, Willi, 436
Meteorological School, Patterson Field (see Air Corps Weather
School)
Meteorology, 22, 78, 265, 431, 443
Metzger, Lt. William E., 334
Mexico, 20
Meyers, Maj. Gen. Bennett E., 129, 149, 163, 164
Miami, Florida, 229, 304
Miami Conservancy District, 25-27, 33-34, 51, 87, 106, 109,
270, 322, 336
Miami County, Ohio, 328
Miami Hotel, Dayton, 92, 111
Miami River, 26, 313
Miami University, 322
Miami Valley, 23, 25
Microwave Building, 310
Middle East theater, World War II, 224
Middletown, Pennsylvania, 59
Middletown Air Depot, 60, 62, 104, 143, 213, 262
Middletown Air Materiel Area, 316, 367-68
Military Affiliate Radio System (MARS), 312, 337
Military Air Transport Service, 249, 444
Military Aircraft Storage and Disposition Center, 326-27
Military Airlift Command, 327, 389, 429, 448
Military Amateur Radio System (MARS), 312
Military Assistance Advisory Group, 444
Military training programs, Patterson Field, World War II,
279-81
Miller, Glenn, 164, 345
Miller, Harold, 319
Miller, Col. Henry J. F., 147
Miller, Mrs. Ivonette Wright, 27, 319, 333, 336
Miller, Col. Lester T., 146, 149
Millett, Dr. John W., 322
Milling, Lt. Thomas DeWitt, 12, 14
Mills, Lt. H. H., 74, 77
Mineola, Long Island, New York, 21, 88, 207, 258, 296
Minot AFB, North Dakota, 419
Minton, Maj. Gen. Augustus M., 415
Minuteman Education Program, AFIT, 419, 426
Miscellaneous Equipment Laboratory, 136

Missiles:
AGM-28 North American Hound Dog, 380
AGM-65 Hughes Maverick, 386, 389
AGM-69 Boeing SRAM, 386, 389, 394
B-61A Martin Matador, 380
GAM-87 Douglas Skybolt, 385
GAR-1 Hughes Falcon, 383
IM-99B Boeing Bomarc, 382
SM-65 Convair Atlas, 364, 384, 414
SM-68 Martin Titan, 414
SM-75 Douglas Thor, 414
SM-80 Boeing Minuteman, 414, 419
XB-64 North American Navaho, 380
XF-98 Hughes Falcon, 380
XF-99 Boeing Bomarc, 380
Mississippi River, 60, 62, 88, 198
Mitchel Field, Long Island, New York, 62, 68, 78, 80, 197, 279
Mitchell, Ed, 424
Mitchell, Brig. Gen. William B., 64, 97, 106, 107-8, 197, 202
MITRE Corporation, 384, 390
Mitscher, Rear Admiral Marc A., 232
Mobile, Alabama, 147
Mobile Air Materiel Area, 314, 317, 367-68
Model Airway, 78-79, 260
Moffat, Capt. Reuben C., 74, 120, 140, 191
Moffett Field, California, 414
Mohr, Col. George C., 439
Money, Maj. Williard L., 444
Monocoque construction, 130, 210-11, 219, 220
Montgomery, Robert L., 95
Montgomery, Alabama, 11, 62, 442
Montgomery County, Ohio, 109, 112, 328, 340, 342
Moody AFB, Georgia, 311
Moon, Lt. Odas, 104, 128
Moore, William, 120
Moorman, Tom, 342
Moraine, Ohio, 14, 23-24, 89, 106
Moraine Farm, 88
Morale, Welfare, and Recreation programs, WPAFB, 340, 342
Moriarty, Lt. L. P., 191
Morris, Brig. Gen. Joseph T., 129, 149, 171, 285, 291, 295-96,
335, 453
Mullins, Gen. James P., 371
Muroc Army Air Base (see also Rogers Lake, Muroc, California),
160, 163
Muroc Flight Test Base (see also Materiel Command Flight Test
Base), 172
Mutual Home Building, Dayton, 94, 110
My Oklahoma Gal, 229
Myers, Lt. Devereaux Maitland, 73, 77
Myers, Gen. Paul W., 441
Myers, R. J., 95
Myrtle Beach AFB, South Carolina, 392
Nagasaki, Japan, 235, 361
National Advisory Committee for Aeronautics, 85-87, 105, 173,
386, 387
National Aeronautic Association, 72, 75, 76, 108
National Aeronautics and Space Administration, 370, 386, 416-
18, 419, 422-25, 438
National Air and Space Museum, Smithsonian Institution, 4, 71
National Cash Register Company [Corporation], 72, 75, 87, 106-
12, 258, 315
National Defense Act of June 3, 1916, 21
National Defense Act of June 4, 1920, 401
National Defense Research Council, 173, 359
National Homes Construction Corporation, 331
National Housing Act, 307
National Housing Agency, 272
National Military Home, Dayton, 257
National Register of Historic Places, 5, 15
National Road, 310
National Security Act, 1947, 410
Naval Expansion Act, May 1938, 145
Naval Medical Research Institute, Toxicology Detachment, 449
Navigation School, Wright Field, 128
NCO Academy, WPAFB, 311
NCO Club, Patterson Field, 165, 266, 268

☆ U.S. GOVERNMENT PRINTING OFFICE: 1986 — 761-595

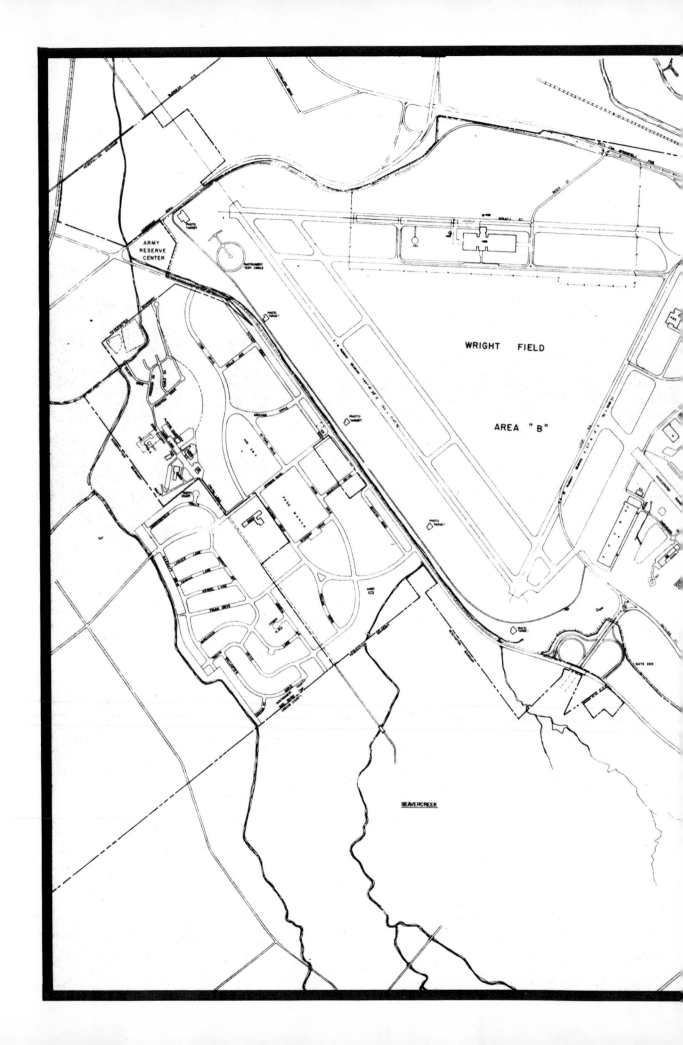

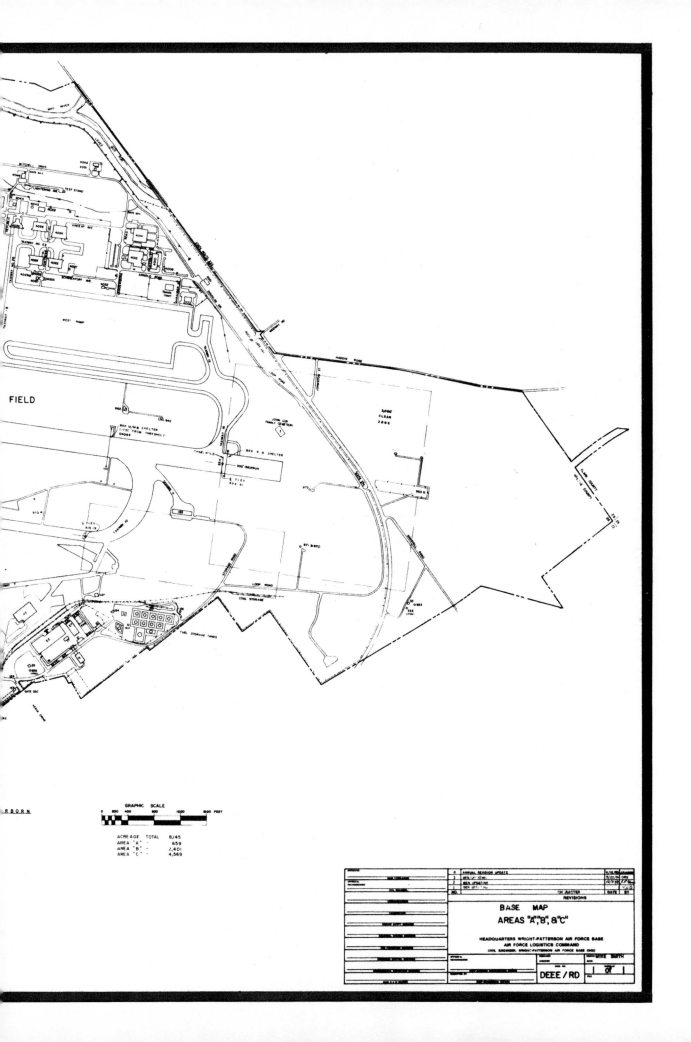

FIELD

GRAPHIC SCALE
0   200 400   800   1600   1800 FEET

ACREAGE TOTAL   8,145
AREA "A" -   659
AREA "B" -   2,401
AREA "C" -   4,569

BASE MAP
AREAS "A","B", & "C"

HEADQUARTERS WRIGHT-PATTERSON AIR FORCE BASE
AIR FORCE LOGISTICS COMMAND
CIVIL ENGINEER, WRIGHT-PATTERSON AIR FORCE BASE OHIO

DEEE / RD